DATE DUE

MR 0 '98			
NV 4 '98			
JA 31 02			
JE 9 03			
SE 24 09			

DEMCO 38-296

The Book of
Great
Hors d'Oeuvre

The Book of
Great
Hors d'Oeuvre

Updated and Expanded

Terence Janericco

VAN NOSTRAND REINHOLD
New York

Copyright © 1990 by Van Nostrand Reinhold

I(T)P™ Van Nostrand Reinhold is a division of International Thomson Publishing, Inc.
The ITP logo is a trademark under license

Printed in the United States of America

For more information, contact:

Van Nostrand Reinhold
115 Fifth Avenue
New York, NY 10003

Chapman & Hall GmbH
Pappelallee 3
69469 Weinheim
Germany

Chapman & Hall
2-6 Boundary Row
London
SE1 8HN
United Kingdom

International Thomson Publishing Asia
221 Henderson Road #05-10
Henderson Building
Singapore 0315

Thomas Nelson Australia
102 Dodds Street
South Melbourne, 3205
Victoria, Australia

International Thomson Publishing Japan
Hirakawacho Kyowa Building, 3F
2-2-1 Hirakawacho
Chiyoda-ku, 102 Tokyo
Japan

Nelson Canada
1120 Birchmount Road
Scarborough, Ontario
Canada M1K 5G4

International Thomson Editores
Campos Eliseos 385, Piso 7
Col. Polanco
11560 Mexico D.F. Mexico

97 98 99 00 01 MVB MP 15 14 13 12 11 10 9 8

Library of Congress Cataloging-in-Publication Data
Janericco, Terence.
   The book of great hors d'oeuvre / Terence Janericco.—Updated and
expanded.
        p. cm.
   ISBN 0-442-00183-5
   1. Appetizers. I. Title.
TX740.J36 1990
641.8'12—dc20   89-70426
                                                      CIP

To
Barbara Clemence
with everlasting thanks, not only for unstinting support and faith, but
also for joyous refuge and a place to create this and many other books,
and
to
Philip G. Clemence
for also providing a space and an atmosphere conducive to writing.

Contents

Preface

One of the most basic instincts of social behavior is to offer a drink and something to eat. It can be a cup of coffee and a doughnut, a cup of tea and toast, or most popularly, perhaps, a cocktail and an hors d'oeuvre. To many it is unthinkable to offer a drink without a nibble, a nosh, a little something. Drinking without food suggests alcoholism or, worse, a lack of caring. Even those people who prefer nonalcoholic beverages will preface a meal with a glass of juice or mineral water, often accompanied by various spreads, dips, or even more elaborate hors d'oeuvre. We desire to entertain others, and we want them to remember our efforts.

For many, the easiest form of all entertaining is the cocktail party. It covers a multitude of sins within a few hours, with possibly the least amount of effort. The hostess who hates to entertain will often have a cocktail party. The corporation that needs to promote a new product most often provides drinks and some food along with the publicity. The university that wishes to honor an esteemed professor does it with wine and cheese. The visiting dignitary is feted with a cocktail party. The clever campaigning politician takes advantage of such parties to hit three or four a night while letting each host feel he has been given his due. Many hostesses choose to replace a meal with a substantial offering of hors d'oeuvre. This allows her to entertain many people at one time, in a small space, and for less money.

The cocktail party has a finite time limit in most instances. It is called for one, two, three, or perhaps four hours. The guests arrive, immediately get a drink, and are off on their own. Usually there are lots of people to meet, and the hostess can be as visible or invisible as her personality allows. She does not have to worry about setting a table or even owning the finest china, silver, or damask. She can have a party that is formal, with crystal and silver trays, or funky, with colored plastic glasses and "found" objects as the serving platters. She can express herself with elaborate centerpieces made from food and flowers, or she can have a small party for six around the coffee table with just one or two simple and simply presented hors d'oeuvre. She can invite far too many people for the space or limit it to a choice few. She can serve almost anything, and she can afford some rather expensive foods, because the other items on the menu can be inexpensive.

The most important part of this form of entertaining is the food. Hors d'oeuvre hold an appeal that is extraordinary. It is the first food the guests receive, whether for the cocktail party or as a prelude to dinner. People often approach it tired and hungry. The food should be abundant, varied, flavorful, and intriguing. The same old hors d'oeuvre at every party quickly pall. Fortunately, that need never happen as the selections are almost limitless.

Virtually every culture indulges in small bits of foods to accompany a drink or to demonstrate the beginning of their hospitality. In France, the hors d'oeuvre is often a salad or a selection of salads, perhaps accompanied by a slice of pâté or sausage. *Hors d'oeuvre* literally means "outside the work," or the main course. The French term for the appetizers we call hors d'oeuvre is *amuse-gueule* or *amuse bouche,* "amusements for the mouth." These range from the tiny tidbits served with a glass of wine before dinner to a lavish spread for a cocktail party. In Russia, both Imperial Russia and the upper echelons of current Soviet society, *zakuski* are a thing to behold. Tables are laden with an enormous variety of foods. The Chinese indulge in *dim sum* as an appetizer, and more often as a full meal called "tea lunch." In Greece and the Middle East, the word is *metza*. In Spain, *tapas* reign supreme — so much so that in the last few years tapas restaurants have become the rage in other countries. Americans have never created a single word to describe this sort of food other than appetizer, but rather take the names from other countries and add a few phrases to cover the area, such as "cocktail food" or "finger food." We Americans adopt, adapt, and frankly steal food and food ideas from all over the world. Foods intended for one use are redesigned to suit our menus.

In the United States we eat anything and everything with a drink. The preference is for finger food — food to be eaten, without a plate or fork, held with one hand while the other is holding a glass. Regrettably, in the process we have devised some foods that present serious difficulties. Barbecued chicken wings, while delicious and popular, are a mess to eat. Canapés, when made properly, can be delicious and beautiful, but are a chore to prepare. For example, canapé à la Danoise consists of a rectangular slice of dark rye bread spread with horseradish butter and garnished alternately with thin strips of smoked salmon and herring fillets separated by strips of caviar and bordered by minced chives — all this on a slice of bread 1 by 2 inches. But imagine making these for 200 people. (There are, of course, less complicated canapés.) You can easily see that the time involved makes them less than practical for large numbers unless you have the staff available to do nothing but prepare canapés just before serving to prevent them from becoming soggy and limp.

Canapés, fortunately, are only one version of countless hors d'oeuvre. Since the first edition of this book, the attitudes about hors d'oeuvre have changed. We are less restricted as to what is suitable for an hors d'oeuvre at the cocktail hour and more willing to look at hors d'oeuvre as the meal itself. In fact, some people, in their desire to hit every hot spot in town, have made a habit of ordering only hors d'oeuvre. Restaurants have found that a fruit cup or tomato juice no longer sells. However, a cheese spread set up to welcome guests relaxes them so that they give greater consideration to their meal. It sets the mood that makes them feel they are dining rather than just grabbing a bite. The barkeeper who offers specially seasoned nuts rather than the usual peanuts or perhaps a selection of low-cost hot hors d'oeuvre will find sales and profits increasing. Distinctive hors d'oeuvre can set your establishment apart.

The hostess who wishes to impress her friends and make a statement about her style sets the theme with hors d'oeuvre. Some hostesses present lavish platters piled with cheeses, pâtés, and sausages and carry it off with panache — as much for the presentation as for the quality and variety of the offerings. Others are only comfortable preparing exquisite tastes — a small bowl of caviar, a few slices of smoked salmon, and vintage champagne — for the limited few. Others love an international mix. These are the hostesses who let us know that there will be something new and delightful; they choose the unusual not simply because it is unusual, but rather because it is wonderful.

Needless to say, the importance of distinctiveness applies to the professional as well as to the amateur. The chef who wishes to make a name must set a style that reflects his or her good taste, and that includes a dash of the unusual. You must give your clients a reason to select you. If you are creating a look for a restaurant, then serving specially seasoned nuts and olives at the bar or offering a delicious spread to accompany the cocktails while guests are deciding on their dinner will immediately define your image. If you cater an event, whether in a hotel or in someone's home, you must present exciting menus to display your skills, to provide a reason for selecting you, and to reflect the attitudes of your client, his or her style, and the occasion. Of course, all this work also must fit the budget.

To accomplish all this is no small task, but it is one that can be greatly helped by this book. The goal of this book is to present numerous ideas for hors d'oeuvre that you can prepare in advance with relative ease. It will not only provide you with hundreds of recipes, but also will give you countless ideas on presentation. The objective of any cookery book should be to make food that not only tastes good, but also looks beautiful. Perhaps nowhere is this more important than in the field of hors d'oeuvre, where different foods designed to entice both eye and palate are repeatedly presented to the guest.

The recipes are written in quantities that serve 8 to 12 for a small party and about 50 or more persons for larger occasions. (Note that when ingredient amounts are specified within the recipe instructions, the amount for the larger yield is set in parentheses in italics, following the smaller quantity.) However, the number any recipe will serve almost always depends on what else is on the menu. In some instances, this is easy because you can plan on so many pieces of a particular hors d'oeuvre per person, but that number changes with the number of other items on the menu, the length of the party, and the appetite of the guests. Allowing four or five hors d'oeuvre per person per hour is a rough guide, but if it is new, unusual, awfully good, or just a standard popular item, this guide can easily be put aside. For instance, allowing four sushi per person may seem fine until you find that half the group does not eat meat. In other instances the proper quantity depends on how much dip guests use to anoint a vegetable or spread on a cracker. Experience alone is your best teacher. Any professional chef will be able to increase the quantities. The nonprofessional should not be concerned if quantities are greater than needed, as all recipes have instructions for keeping. In most instances, this means the cook may store a treasure trove of delights to be served on another occasion.

Introduction: *Planning the Party*

Whether you are a professional chef or a private host or hostess, first consider the type of party you wish to prepare. The number of guests and the location can influence the menu as much as the party theme. For instance, a corporation may want to entertain several hundreds or thousands of people with wine and something to eat to show off a new product. Management decides on an exciting location, such as a local museum, and looks to you to plan a party that reflects all the company's best qualities. The problem is that there is no kitchen. You will have to work out of a small anteroom with limited counter space, and you may not even have a sink. Unless you are a caterer with all sorts of equipment built into your trucks, you will be in a difficult situation. Help your client select a menu that is possible for you to do well, showing off their attributes as well as yours. In this situation, hot hors d'oeuvre may be impossible because of a lack of electricity. However, huge displays of fruit, cheeses, pâtés, cold fish, and so on can let you and your client shine.

If you are doing a party in an elegant apartment decorated with antiques and silk brocades, do not choose a menu that includes messy finger food such as broiled baby lamb chops. At the same time, although this party may seem to be the setting for exquisite canapés and a bowl of caviar — and it is — there is no reason why you cannot try some of the more exotic offerings in this book to demonstrate the originality of the host or hostess. Beware of being mundane. Instead of a bowl of caviar, serve the caviar on corn cakes; instead of canapés, serve broiled tuna with wasabi sauce or an assortment of perfectly prepared cheese pastries. If the hostess announces she is going to use her linen napkins, do not select food that is apt to stain them beyond cleaning. On the other hand, if you have been asked to prepare a backyard barbecue, Chinese spareribs are a wonderful variation.

Consider the look of the party. Some foods require plates and forks. I recommend avoiding plates; they get in the way and cause people to waste food. Guests cannot manage a fork, a plate, and a drink while standing. Also, there is a tendency for people to fill a plate and then return to a group, only to find that the group has disbanded. Guests eat what they wish and put the plate down. The uneaten food gets discarded. So many foods can be eaten out of hand easily that eliminating plates is not a problem.

Consider the setup of the rooms to determine how you can best display your food. Some homes are not designed to allow for a large buffet but require that everything be passed to guests on serving trays. Other homes and most public spaces allow for buffets. The advantage of the buffet is that it gives the party a focal point other than the bar, and if the buffet is placed properly, it will give the party flow. Consider how the foods will look on the buffet and how they will be consumed. It is pointless to prepare an elaborate pâté en croûte only to have to cut it in small cubes so the guests can eat it without plates and forks.

— *Staffing* —

Obviously, the professional chef must always have help to prepare and serve. He or she cannot expect to assemble the hors d'oeuvre as well as make drinks, take coats, pass the canapés, pick up used napkins and cocktail skewers, and empty ashtrays. Oddly, hostesses and hosts often try to do all this and still greet guests and be gracious. If the group is small, the private host can take over these chores. Six persons for cocktails entails preparing a few hors d'oeuvre before they arrive and serving the drinks as the guests enter. On informal occasions with somewhat larger groups you can suggest that guests make their own refills.

Large cocktail parties can become difficult, if not impossible, if the hostess does not make staffing arrangements beforehand. In the over 40 years I have been catering, I have found staffing to be an area of particular difficulty for the host or hostess. They want the food prepared and served beautifully, but they seem to be afraid of appearing too lavish if there are many servers. Obviously, too much help can be as bad as too little, but it is necessary to have sufficient help to take care of the guests' needs. To handle a large party with a minimum of help, plan on a buffet of cold foods that need little attention. Hot foods need not only to be heated often, but also to be passed frequently while still appetizingly warm. Equipment designed to keep foods warm can often do more harm than good. Chafing dishes can make some foods dry and others soggy, with a steam-table quality. Hot trays often dry out or scorch the bottom of the food while the top stays unappealingly cool. Guests will forgive this in a home cook, but a professional can find that no one is asking for his or her card. Use such equipment only with small quantities of food for short periods of time. It is far better to have a small chafing dish that must be replenished regularly than a large chafing dish piled with food that becomes less and less appealing as time advances. Some professional chefs seem to think that putting out all the food at once shows lavishness. However, to the guest at the end of the line, the fare no longer looks desirable.

My suggestions for staffing are based on years of experience. If there are more than 15 guests, a host or hostess should seriously consider at least one server (the host or hostess serves the drinks). For more than 20 persons, a bartender is necessary as well. Beyond this number, staff is required. I recommend a bartender for every 50 persons; they can serve up to 60. However, at a large reception where only wine is served, the bartender can easily handle 100 to 150 persons. Have the bartender start to fill glasses just before the guests enter the room, and shortly, he or she will only have to refill the glasses. For a cocktail buffet with only one or two hors d'oeuvre being passed (the other dishes will be on the buffet), one server for every 20 to 30 guests plus one kitchen worker to prepare the food and set up the trays are necessary. However, if there are six different hors d'oeuvre to be passed, there should be a server for every 20 guests to provide full coverage. Again, if the reception is large with one or more major buffets of cold food that need little attention once arranged, each server can handle 50 persons or more. I am often surprised at large functions to see staff lined around the walls of the room (unfortunately, sometimes clearly gossiping about the guests) because there is nothing more for them to do until the guests leave. Fewer staff, perhaps paid a premium, make far more sense. Guests dislike staff hanging around, and if they are just standing about, their use is certainly questionable.

There are, however, occasions when a lot of help may be in order. Certain parties when all the food is passed can require as many as one server for every 12 guests. Interestingly enough, this happens in smaller locations where there is not enough space for a buffet. The servers pass the food and perhaps the drinks through the crowd and return to the serving area without standing around in front of the guests. All my staff are trained so that no job is outside their job description. Bartenders are taught that when they are not making drinks, they should clear glasses, empty ashtrays, and so on. They are also taught to wash glasses. In addition, if I have appointed several bartenders at the beginning of a party, I may switch them to passing hors d'oeuvre if needed. Waiters are also taught to do other jobs besides serving. The only area they are not involved in is the actual cooking, but they can set up trays, and certainly help clean up as a necessary part of the team effort.

I recommend that the caterer arrive at least two hours prior to the party to learn where everything is located and what is expected. (Pity the poor bartender who arrives only a half hour before the guests and then has to find and arrange the glasses, ice, lemons and limes, liquors, and mixers.) Some clients seem to think that they can have the server arrive shortly before the guests, point to the kitchen, and then go take a shower. You must make it clear that there must be time to get organized and to find out exactly how they want things presented. Yes, the client must pay for this time; it is part of the cost of the party, just as is travel time if it is an hour or more in one direction. After you have worked with certain hostesses and hosts for a number of parties, you will know exactly what they want and their presence may not be required, but you will still need the time to get prepared. The caterer who arrives two hours ahead should be in full command of the kitchen when the guests arrive and ready to serve without delay. In that time, he or she should see that the staff has set up the bar, arranged the buffet table, assigned each server his or her duties, and prepared all the garnishes for the trays. You will have decided with the host or hostess prior to the party what look is required and will have correlated your garnishes with the colors as well as the look and feel of the party.

Both caterers and clients should understand that the kitchen is off limits to guests. Unless it is impossible to do otherwise, no guest should be allowed in the kitchen. The staff is handling hot, possibly greasy food that can burn people or stain their clothing. Guests are there to enjoy a party, but the staff is there to work. For some reason, certain people think it is fun to be in the kitchen when the staff is working. This is rather like going into the bank and sitting at the loan officer's desk while he or she writes a loan for someone else and saying, "I wanted just to watch how you do things." If the kitchen is open to the party area, provide screens to create a divider. Over the years, I have found that large plants or floral arrangements can act as a reasonably friendly barrier. You should explain to the hostess when you book a party that once you arrive, no one is allowed in the kitchen. Not her, the kids, the baby-sitter, or anyone else. If the children are to be fed, they should be taken out to the local pizza parlor or fed before you arrive.

Incidentally, a firm attitude here will save you much anguish but will be met with a certain hostility from some guests, especially if they have had a few drinks. This is the principal reason to enlist the aid of the host and hostess prior to the party.

—— *Selecting the Foods* ——

Whatever the size of the party, the food must be delicious and fresh. Cold foods should be chilled, but not served straight out of the refrigerator. Serving them close to room temperature provides a better flavor. Hot foods must be served hot and therefore must be passed frequently. Once they cool, many foods are truly unappealing, and some foods cannot be reheated.

Remember that the food is intended to complement the other aspects of the party. People come to have a good time, have a drink, meet friends, and have something to eat. Your job is to make that something to eat memorable.

It is important to have sufficient food for the number of guests and their lifestyle and the time of day. For example, a two-hour midafternoon business reception may require only a few hors d'oeuvre per person, but a four-hour reception held from 5 to 9 P.M. could require much more. An evening party starting at 7 or 7:30 P.M. will require even more food. Some people will dally over a raw vegetable and a dot of sauce, while others will find whole fillets of beef barely substantial.

One error that many clients and chefs make is to think that more is better. Although it is important to have enough food for the number of guests, it is a mistake to have too great a variety. Although many people feel that it is necessary to have 10 or more different hors d'oeuvre, a large variety of hors d'oeuvre is unfair to your guests. The many different flavors and textures can cause a "confusion of the stomach" the next day. To ensure enough food, plan on plenty of a reasonable variety and not a few of an overwhelming variety.

Before dinner or another event, when the cocktail hour is brief, three or four hors d'oeuvre at most are suitable. They should be light and tantalizing to lead into the meal or at least not to leave the guests too full to go on to the next event, whether it is another party, the theater, or a concert.

When the cocktail party is three to four hours long, plan on six to eight varieties of hors d'oeuvre, with perhaps three or four additional items with the same ingredients, prepared differently, to serve after the second hour. The additional hors d'oeuvre should be chosen to complement those already served. If you began with a curried chicken-filled puff, you could serve chicken fingers or minced chicken in phyllo leaves to create a variation on the theme. You may choose not to count nuts and olives as hors d'oeuvre, or you may offer a variety of cheese pastries and count them as one item.

Of course, the menu must have balance. It is possible to create exciting menus with varying types of foods from various cultures that offer contrasts in flavor, color, shape, and texture, but beware of trying to be so different that you overwhelm one hors d'oeuvre with another. For example, serving fresh beluga caviar on the same menu as Szechuan chicken fingers can obliterate both.

—— *Cocktails* ——

If you believe some of the food writers, what to serve to drink at a cocktail party changes every year. They emphatically announce that everyone is drinking white wine and no one is drinking hard liquor, or only low-calorie sodas, or only the latest island fantasy. When you are working with the public, you soon realize that such statements may sell magazines, but they do not satisfy guests. People drink. They drink what appeals to them, and although the consumption of wine has increased and that of hard liquor has diminished, you must plan for all tastes. Unless the hostess or host demands that you serve only white wine, I strongly recommend that you provide not only some red wine, but also a soft drink such as mineral water. Some clients think that serving only champagne, any champagne, is the height of elegance. This is not true. First, the champagne should be first rate, and second, a still wine should be offered for those people who do not care for the efferves-cence. In fact, many people do not care for champagne and consider those who only serve it as show-offs or uncaring hosts. If the host or hostess can afford champagne, then he or she can afford to provide for all the guests' tastes. Have an open bar with the champagne prominently displayed so the guests will feel free to indulge if they choose. However, if it is not going to be a wine reception, you should be prepared to make most of the standard cocktails. If a new drink is all the rage it may be offered, but there is no need, except for the fully set up hotel or restaurant bar, to provide for every possibility. Certainly in home entertaining it is not necessary to offer every exotic drink in memory. A dietetic drink, however, is de rigueur. Mineral water usually fills the bill.

Arrange beforehand with the hostess or host who will provide the lemons, limes, olives, and other garnishes for the drinks. Also determine who is providing the ice and ensure that there are suitable containers to store it for the drinks as well as for chilling the wine.

It is vital to place the food table and the bar as far apart as reasonable to prevent people from filling one area of the room to the exclusion of the rest of the space, as well as to prevent one small group from eating and drinking their fill while the other guests look on in envy. Separating these functions also allows for the guests to walk easily back and forth. It gives the party life and allows people to socialize with more than just one small group.

The glasses for drinks are important in making a party a party. Ordinary barware is suitable for a quick function, but the hostess or host who wants to make a statement or the caterer who wishes to stand apart from the crowd will provide glasses with a little more style. I have long used oversized wine glasses for all drinks. Whether the guests want mineral water, a martini, white wine, or champagne, I use the same glass. My bartenders have been taught to prepare suitably sized drinks in these glasses without overfilling them. In other words, we do not fill the glass to the brim with a martini. In fact, most drinks fill only half the glass. You can be more generous with mineral water, as people appreciate not having to return to the bar every other minute. The glass gives the immediate look of a party. The first item that a guest receives helps to set the mood and elevate his or her spirits. Many establishments use small glasses in order to encourage larger sales, and although this may work in some instances, people are more likely to remember the "stingy" drinks than anything else.

—— *Presentation* ——

Nothing sets the tone of a party like presentation. In the last 10 years, this feature has become even more important. Some restaurants spend so much effort on designing fascinating looking plates that the food becomes secondary. Some restaurants have not served a hot meal in years because of the lilies drawn in the sauces, the precise arrangement of the vegetables, and so on.

Hors d'oeuvre should be fun and amusing, and these qualities should be reflected, in good taste, in their presentation. You can be expensive and frivolous or serious and studied. Cut vegetables into flowers or other shapes, but avoid dying them other colors. Combine real flowers and fruits for a pretty platter. Arrange the foods in rigid geometric patterns, or use farm baskets lined with herbs set atilt on a table with the food spilling out onto the surface.

Almost 20 years ago I started garnishing platters with fresh flowers and greens. Since then I have seen these ideas repeated across the country. My preference is to use small blocks of floral foam to create miniature flower arrangements that complement the flowers selected by the client. On rare occasions, I lay a singular spectacular flower, such as a ginger flower or proteus, across the tray with no further embellishment. However, this idea has been abused. Handfuls of wild flowers tied with a ribbon and dropped on a tray can droop in minutes. Uninteresting flowers scattered among the food confuse the guest. Carved vegetables dyed inappropriate colors, such as white radishes dyed kelly green for St. Patrick's Day, are unappealing.

The garnishes for trays should be placed so the guests can get at the food. It should not be a challenge. Lovely napkin-lined woven baskets holding pastries can be beautiful, unless the food is buried so deep that it is like digging for treasure while everyone stands around waiting for their turn. Place the garnishes off center and to the rear of the tray so that they provide a backdrop for the food and make it easy for guests to reach. Use large rather than small skewers so people can see them and pick them up without getting stabbed or inadvertently chewing on one. Some things, such as cheese puffs, can look wonderful if piled on a platter, but food usually looks best if it is well-spaced so that it stands out and looks inviting. Use 10- to 12-inch trays rather than larger ones for passing so people constantly see a fresh display. Larger trays of food quickly become messy and unattractive. Use fresh floral or vegetable leaves in place of lace doilies for variety. It is usually best to present one food on a platter unless you have two or more related foods. Assorted cheese pastries might be arranged on the same platter, and certain dim sum, where the dipping sauces are shared, would be fine on the same tray. But sardine canapés, cheese balls, and stuffed vegetables should all be on separate platters for two reasons: the guest can quickly make up his or her mind and the server need describe only one item. This makes passing more efficient.

On occasion, I arrange fruits on skewers inserted in halved grapefruits, but always with the stick end covered by the food so no one gets hurt. Bread dough cornucopias are a delightful way to display fresh fruits to accompany a cheese platter, but I have also used them for stacks of small sandwiches, raw vegetables, or assorted cheese pastries. One of my signature presentations is a vegetable construction. A wire form is covered with kale and mustard greens and surrounded with

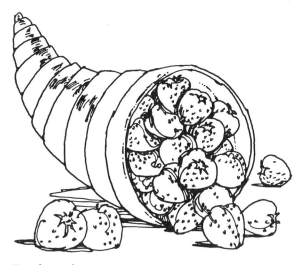

Bread Dough Cornucopia

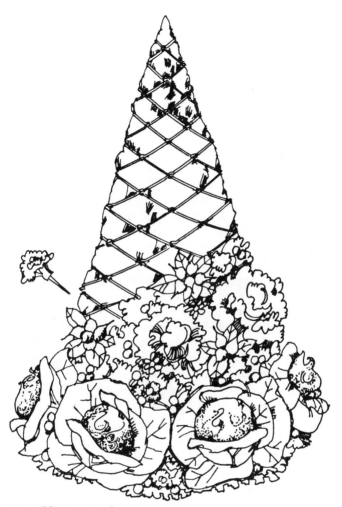

Vegetable Construction

hollowed-out cabbages to be filled with a dip or spread. Other vegetables and flowers are inserted over the greens. Styrofoam cones make bases for almost architectural displays of vegetables such as eggplants. Use baskets to display fruits and vegetables, letting them flow across the table. Over the years for various occasions I have created extremely elaborate settings with ice sculptures and with "peacocks" made from sliced turkeys arranged on wire forms. However, some of the most exciting and interesting settings were made from everyday objects. A spring party for a local university was made with long tables decorated with an antique wooden wagon filled with potted plants and galvanized watering cans, all set on a pavement of brick arranged on the table; spaces between the bricks were planted with crocus bulbs and tulips set in soil.

Creating a look and feel can be costly, but with imagination, you can design settings that are both exotic and inexpensive. Use your imagination and what you have on hand to create the look you want, or buy what you need. There are a lot of low-cost trays, baskets, and so on that can be used to start your collection of objects to create your own look and style. It is costly initially to buy a full silver service. However, diligent shopping at thrift stores and antique shops can soon provide much of what you need. An advantage is that the look is far less commercial. For a caterer, the advantage to silver is that it does not break easily. Beautiful platters of porcelain or pottery are wonderful, but transporting them can be a problem because they are so easily chipped or broken. Chipped plates and platters are never allowed.

Generally, food looks better on bolder, more vibrant colors. Pallid floral designs get lost and seem to draw the color from the food. Use sleek black lacquer in a contemporary setting for a stunning look. On the other hand, clear glass presents a crisp, clean look. White platters can be used in every setting, no matter what the color scheme. Copper works well in a country setting, as does brass, but remember that metal platters must always be perfectly polished. Tarnished silver or heavily fingerprinted brass brings no honor. Wooden ware can work in many settings.

Use flowers for the platters not only as a decoration, but also in place of doilies. Plan to work with the florist if possible so that the flowers and food complement each other. If you work well with a particular florist, it is possible that he or she can make the platter decorations, if this is not your forte. Beware, however, of the florist who makes arrangements that overwhelm the food rather than set it off.

The Book of
Great
Hors d'Oeuvre

= 1 =

The Great Hors d'Oeuvre

Certain hors d'oeuvre stand above others. Truly magnificent foods— some so special they justify almost any expense—stand alone. These foods often are correctly served in their original containers, no matter how elaborate the party, because of their fragility or to show their quality. This chapter details how to serve these foods on their own and with accompaniments. In later chapters these foods are used as ingredients in combination with others, so if the suggestions here do not meet your needs, check the index for other possibilities.

—— *Caviar* ——

Caviar, genuine beluga malassol caviar, is the undisputed emperor of hors d'oeuvre. The other grades, osetra and sevruga, rank almost as highly and are well worth the cost—provided they are fresh. Vacuum-packed or pasteurized caviars are not the same. Salmon caviar is a wonderful addition to this grouping, but it is not as special. In recent years, American caviars have gained an appreciative audience, but they still have a way to go to compete with fresh caviar from the Caspian Sea. Other fish roe sold as caviar are no substitute. Lumpfish roe, for instance, is often sold as a caviar and, depending on the need, is dyed black or red. Regrettably, the dye often runs if the roe is mixed with another ingredient. The eggs are small, hard, and sort of gritty, whereas the sturgeon caviars are relatively soft, bursting like tiny grapes when bitten, giving a rush of flavor.

1

The best caviar needs only the simplest of treatments. Serve it in its original container packed into a dish of crushed ice. Use a bone or wooden spoon for a scoop. The ice keeps the caviar properly chilled at 32°F, and the spoon allows you to scoop the eggs without damaging them or imparting an off-flavor, as will a silver spoon. If the hostess or host insists, the caviar can be transferred to a "caviar bowl" (a crystal bowl set inside another bowl filled with crushed ice). Accompany the caviar with butter curls, hot toast, and lemon wedges. The lemon wedges can be wrapped in squares of cheesecloth wrung out in cold water. Some people prefer to serve caviar with other traditional garnishes, such as sieved egg yolk, minced egg white, minced onion, and/or sour cream. The aficionado will only want the toast and perhaps a squeeze of lemon. In place of the toast, buckwheat blinis are a standard accompaniment. More elaborate presentations are listed among the recipes.

Later in this chapter there are a number of recipes calling for caviar to be served with other flavorful ingredients. For these recipes, I recommend that you consider osetra or the even less expensive sevruga instead of beluga caviar. The price is half as much, and the difference is the size of the eggs. The largest eggs are the most expensive. The flavor remains in the smaller eggs.

Whitefish and lumpfish caviar can be used when a salt flavor is desired and the caviar is truly secondary to the rest of the recipe. These caviars are also acceptable as a filling for cherry tomatoes or as a tiny garnish on a canapé.

—— *Foie Gras* ——

If caviar is the emperor, foie gras is certainly the king. The fresh liver of a force-fed goose is studded with truffles and poached until just done to provide a particularly luscious buttery pale, rose-colored liver with a definite but subtle flavor. There are American goose livers that are quite good, but they are not as fine as the best of French foie gras. If fresh is not available, it is possible to buy prepared livers in pottery crocks or in roughly triangular-shaped tins, called *blocs*. Serve foie gras cold with warm toast, or to increase the flavor, heat it in a 300°F oven for about 10 minutes, until warmed through but not melted. Serve the pottery crock with a spoon, and let guests scoop their portions. If the foie gras is in a *bloc*, open both ends and push it through so that it can be cut into thin slices. Foie gras is expensive. Do not confuse it with cheaper tins of pâté de foie or other liver pâté mixtures, which can be very good but are definitely not the same.

—— *Smoked Salmon* ——

Smoked salmon is certainly next on the list of great hors d'oeuvre. It comes in numerous versions, including Irish, Scottish, Norwegian, and Nova Scotian. Many firms produce their own special smoked salmon, and a local product may well be worth featuring. Before you place a large order, try a sample first. Some versions are so heavily smoked the flavor of the salmon is hidden, and others are so lightly smoked the smoke flavor is barely noticeable. Some salmon is hot-smoked, while others are cold-smoked. The techniques can produce a salmon that is quite firm, almost chewy in texture, or soft to the point of mushiness. The salmon you need varies according to its use. If you wish to use it on bagels spread with cream cheese, Nova Scotia lox will serve nicely, but for a slice of buttered pumpernickel with a paper-thin slice of smoked salmon and a grind of black pepper, Irish or Scottish salmon may be the answer. For a grand display, use whole sides of salmon, and if it is not precut, have a carver slice it at the buffet. Serve the salmon with buttered pumpernickel or rye bread, black pepper, and lemon wedges. What is most important is that the salmon be of top quality. The presliced smoked salmon or lox found in many supermarkets is appropriate for mixing with other ingredients, but it is not suitable for serving on its own.

—— *Gravlax* ——

It is possible to buy smoked salmon locally or by mail order with ease, but you must make gravlax unless there is a take-out store in your area that provides it. The traditional recipe is made with sugar, salt, and dill, and other versions are made with different herbs. Serve the gravlax as you would smoked salmon, in paper-thin slices on buttered rye or pumpernickel.

—— *Raw Bars* ——

A favorite feature of many large and some small parties is the raw bar: a display, the more magnificent the better, of selected raw and cooked shellfish. The traditional contents are oysters, clams, shrimp, and crab claws. Scallops, raw or cooked, or cooked mussels may also be a part of the display. Sometimes sides of smoked salmon are included or placed near the other seafood. A large tray or entire table is covered with crushed ice and the shellfish are placed on top, and often decorated with seaweed. Ice sculptures can hold the seafood to keep it cold. Shuckers stand by to open the shellfish as needed. Arranged at convenient locations are the traditional sauces and other accompaniments. The most common sauces are the American "cocktail" sauce made with a tomato base and the less intrusive mignonette sauce. Other accompaniments include bottles of horseradish, bowls of oyster crackers, and, of course, lemon wedges.

It is imperative that the shellfish be the freshest possible and that it come from nonpolluted waters. Most purveyors know the source of their fish and should be willing to tell you. If there is any question, change the menu. Many suppliers on both coasts will ship shellfish from safe waters air express. Oysters and clams should be tightly closed, and any shells that are partially opened and do not close if tapped gently should be discarded.

Oysters and Clams

Oysters are a true delicacy when served raw and so fresh that they quiver when squirted with lemon juice. Traditionally, guests slurp the oyster or clam off the shell after spooning on the desired sauce. Since guests may not be decorous as they slurp the fish and juices from the shell halves, serve the shellfish on the half shell with plates and forks for those who prefer neatness to tradition.

Shrimp

Bowls of fresh shrimp are one of the most popular hors d'oeuvre you can present. Choose shrimp that can be eaten discreetly in one or two bites. Medium and large shrimp known as 26 to 30's or 21 to 25's are preferred for both size and price. Larger shrimp are too big to consume without "double dipping," and smaller shrimp look as if you are being cheap. Also, smaller shrimp take longer to peel. Peel the shrimp, leaving the tail attached, devein if needed, and cook until just done. Allow to cool to just below room temperature for the best flavor. Do not overcook the shrimp or they will be tough. If budget is a concern, pass the shrimp on platters. This controls the consumption to a certain extent. Otherwise, bowls placed on the buffet table or around the rooms work well. Of course, for a grand party, mounding the shrimp in an ice sculpture is appealing. Shrimp are somewhat expensive, but not as much as their image. Clients seem to feel that they will go bankrupt if they order shrimp, but over the years I have found that passing cold shrimp or using shrimp as an ingredient in other dishes allows the hostess or host to serve shrimp without mortgaging the house. Plain shrimp can be served with countless sauces besides the standard "cocktail sauce." Try remoulade sauce, tartar sauce, aïoli, aillade, Vietnamese mint sauce, or horcher sauce, for example.

Crab Claws

Sometimes called "cocktail claws" or "crab fingers," these are the forward pincer claws of the Alaskan king crab. They come frozen and prepared with the shell cut away to expose half the meat. The guests bite the visible part of the meat off the cartilage and then separate the pincers, using the smaller one to scoop out the remaining morsels of flesh. Serve with various dipping sauces. Stone crab claws from Florida are similar, but the shell completely covers the meat and, unless you have time for the staff to cut off half the shell, are impractical for an hors d'oeuvre.

—— *Other Fish* ——

Although sardines, smoked mussels, smoked oysters, and smoked clams do not rate as highly as fresh shellfish, they are still considered special. They are often served from their original containers, drained of any oil, and accompanied by small wedges of lemon and plain crackers.

Herring

Herring comes in many forms and can usually be eaten without further preparation. Many delicatessens and markets carry varieties of herring in wine sauce or sour cream or as a salad. Serve herring with dark bread, on skewers, or as a stuffing for vegetables, small puffs, or tart shells.

Whitefish

A presentation that works well is to remove the meat and bones from the skin of a large whitefish, and refill the skin with the flaked flesh mixed with whitefish salad. Serve it accompanied with thinly sliced bagels, bagel chips, or other crackers and an assortment of dark breads.

—— *Cheese* ——

Although not necessarily costly, fine cheese can be among the most select of hors d'oeuvre. Avoid packaged and processed cheeses, and strive to obtain a variety of the world's more interesting cheeses. True Vermont or New York Cheddar, Liederkranz, or Monterey Jack from the United States; Caerphilly, Stilton, or Cheshire from England; Gouda or

Edam from Holland—these are superior to the domestic copies. You might also serve Gjetost from Norway for a unique flavor, Esrom from Denmark, or any of the hundreds of cheeses from France. Some of these have become so popular that they are a cliché: politicians refer to fund-raising parties as the Brie-and-white-wine circuit. Other cheeses are rare and wonderful. Try Bleu de Bresse in place of Roquefort, or any of the dozens of chèvres. Italy not only has wonderful old standards such as Taleggio and *mozzarella di bufalo,* but also *torta* or cakes of cheese with layers of provolone sandwiched with layers of herbed mascarpone. Or try some of the spread recipes in Chapter 5.

Serve the cheeses on a board, marble slab, or straw or reed mat lined with grape, chestnut, or other pretty leaves. Accompany the cheeses with rye, pumpernickel, French bread, Swedish flat bread, or other interesting crackers or breads. Hard cheeses can be cut into cubes to be eaten alone. Try to avoid putting out huge rounds of hard cheeses such as wheels of Cheddar or Stilton. These cheeses are difficult for guests to cut neatly, and the display soon looks like a disaster. Also avoid the Cheddar and Swiss standbys that so many hosts substitute for imagination and taste. Be creative in your offerings. A few years ago, Brie-in-pastry was a new and exciting idea; now it is hackneyed. However, using flavored Bries or substituting other semisoft cheeses such as St. André gives the idea a new twist. (Do test a small quantity first because some cheeses turn rubbery when heated.) Better yet, try making one of your own cheeses (see Chapter 5), or serve cheeses in combination with other foods. Many of the recipes in this book use cheese as an ingredient, so you need never be limited merely to putting a chunk of cheese on a plate with some crackers.

Poultry and Meats

Smoked Turkey or Capon

These can be found in specialty markets. Mail-order smokehouses offer a wide variety of smoked meats and poultry to serve as delectable hors d'oeuvre. Usually they are shipped frozen and can be kept in the freezer for months. When you are ready to use them, thaw and cut into paper-thin slices. Serve with breads, hot toast, a mayonnaise-based sauce, and black pepper.

Beef

One of the finest hors d'oeuvre for providing substance, elegance, and flavor is roasted tenderloin. The meat is roasted at 450°F for 10 minutes per pound, allowed to cool for 15 minutes, and served in thin slices with assorted breads, horseradish cream sauce, and various mustards. Guests can make small sandwiches or simply eat the meat with no more than a sprinkling of salt. The secret to perfect tenderloin is to remove every bit of fat and membrane before roasting.

Cook rump or sirloin roasts to medium rare, chill, and slice as thinly as possible with an electric meat slicer. To serve, fluff the slices with your fingers onto a platter and serve with buttered bread, salt, and various mustards. Take care to do this shortly before serving, and keep the piles small or the weight of the meat will compact the beef into one large lump.

For the host or hostess who wishes to serve substantial hors d'oeuvre, broiled steaks that are allowed to cool almost to room temperature and then are cut into cubes or thin slices make a lavish display. These can be served on skewers to be dipped into sauces such as béarnaise, Chinese soy and ginger, or garlic mayonnaise, or they can be thinly sliced and served with sliced breads to make small sandwiches. Make sure that the bread slices are small, about 2 to 3 inches square. My experience is that tiny rolls are too much bread for the amount of meat.

Bundnerfleisch from Switzerland is an air-dried beef that is available in some delicacy stores. Like prosciutto, it is cut in the thinnest possible slices. Serve it with thin slices of bread or wrapped around fresh fruits such as pears.

Lamb

Broiled baby lamb chops have become a costly specialty item over the last several years. Racks of lamb, trimmed of all fat, are cooked to the medium-rare stage, allowed to cool for 5 minutes, and cut into individual chops. The chops are correctly served with paper frills wrapped around the bone. Although these are delicious, they are awkward for guests, who stand gnawing on a bone and then must find a place to put it and still appear civilized. Butterflied legs of lamb, marinated and broiled until medium, are a better choice. Let the lamb rest after cooking, and cut it into thin slices. Serve with breads and perhaps some of the marinade, briefly simmered and strained, or a yogurt garlic mint sauce. Guests can make small sandwiches that can be eaten in a civilized manner.

Ham

One of the most suitable and useful foods for the cocktail hour is ham. It can be boiled, baked, or dry-cured and served alone, in combination with other ingredients, or mixed into a filling.

The finest hams for the cocktail hour are the dry-cured hams from Italy, Germany, and America: prosciutto, Westphalian, or Smithfield. These hams are cut into paper-thin slices and are served with a grating of black pepper on thin slices of bread or baking powder biscuits. Alternatively, the slices can be wrapped around pieces of fruit or seafood. Prosciutto and Westphalian hams are ready to be thinly sliced and served, but read the packaging on Smithfield hams carefully. Often they require that you soak and cook them. A whole ham will serve 50 to 75 people.

Wet-cured hams also work particularly well for hors d'oeuvre. These, like smoked salmon, can be smoked a lot or a little, and you should choose a brand that you prefer. The hams are baked and served whole, with a carver to slice portions as required. In the past it was common to cover these hams with a thick coating of brown sugar, mustard, and assorted fruits. With the current interest in lighter, simpler foods, it is best to score the ham fat in a diamond pattern, pour on a bottle of fruity wine such as a Moselle, and bake the ham at 300°F for about 3 hours or until it is heated through, basting every 15 minutes. (The hams are sold fully cooked and need only be heated.) This allows the flavor of the ham to predominate. Arrange the ham on a platter and surround it with grapes, possibly frosted, and/or other fruits or flowers.

Sausage and Salami

There are numerous sausages, salamis, and other cold cuts that can be served on their own. Simply cut them into cubes and serve with a variety of mustards, or skewer them with cheeses and fruits (see Chapter 9). Uncooked sausages such as Italian sausage or kielbasa must be cooked. Grill or poach them, cut them into slices, and serve while warm with mustards.

≡ *Caviar*

How much caviar to provide depends on your budget and the number of guests. Although this superb food is loved by many, there are probably as many who detest it. As a rough estimate, I recommend ½ ounce per person.

fresh beluga caviar	toast fingers
lemon wedges wrapped in	unsalted butter curls
squares of cheesecloth	

Open the container of caviar and set it firmly into a bowl of crushed ice. Serve the lemon wedges, toast, and butter on the side.

NOTE: The toast is best made by baking it in a 350°F oven until golden and dry and crisp. Keep the toast warm.

☰ Caviare Garniture (Garnished Caviar)

═ Yield: 8 servings

4 ounces fresh beluga caviar
8 lemon wedges wrapped in
  squares of cheesecloth
2 hard-cooked eggs

½ cup minced onion or chives
½ cup sour cream
24 toast fingers, buttered, or
  buckwheat blinis (page 628)

═ Yield: 14 servings

7 ounces fresh beluga caviar
24 lemon wedges wrapped in
  squares of cheesecloth
4 hard-cooked eggs

1 cup minced onion or chives
1 cup sour cream
42 toast fingers, buttered, or
  buckwheat blinis (page 628)

1. Open the container of caviar, and set it firmly in a bowl of crushed ice. Surround with lemon wedges.

2. Separate the egg yolks and whites and force them through a sieve separately. Place in small bowls. Place the minced onion or chives and sour cream in separate bowls. Serve the toast in a napkin-lined basket. Do not cover it or it will become soggy.

NOTE: Sieve the yolks and whites separately to keep their colors separate. If you sieve them together, the color will not be yellow and white, but pale yellow.

☰ Caviar with Hot Potatoes

In this and the following recipes, osetra or sevruga caviar is more than suitable. Often I use various caviars—sevruga, salmon, and golden caviars—to provide variety. The less expensive salmon and golden caviars also help to keep the food cost in line.

═ Yield: 8 servings

8 tiny new potatoes
½ cup sour cream

1 ounce fresh caviar

═ Yield: 24 servings

24 tiny new potatoes
1 cup sour cream

4 ounces fresh caviar

1. Cut a small slice from one side of each potato, and with a melon baller, scoop out a small indentation in the center of the potato on the other side. Steam the potatoes until just tender.

2. Fill the hollow of each potato with a scoop of sour cream and top with a dollop of caviar.

3. Serve warm.

NOTE: The potatoes can be baked until tender and then cut and filled.

≡ Corn Cakes with Caviar

These corn cakes are also delicious on their own or with a salsa topping. You may use fresh, canned, or frozen corn.

═ Yield: 32 servings

2 cups kernel corn	1 egg yolk
⅓ cup milk	7 tablespoons minced chives
⅓ cup flour	salt and pepper, to taste
½ cup melted butter	1 cup sour cream
⅓ cup cornmeal	6 tablespoons golden caviar
2 eggs	6 teaspoons black caviar

═ Yield: 96 servings

1½ quarts kernel corn	3 egg yolks
1 cup milk	1 cup minced chives
1 cup flour	salt and pepper, to taste
1½ cups melted butter	2 cups sour cream
1 cup cornmeal	2 cups golden caviar
6 eggs	4 ounces black caviar

1. In a food processor, mix the corn, milk, flour, half the butter, and cornmeal and process for 30 seconds. Add the eggs, egg yolk(s), a third of the chives, salt, and pepper.

2. In a skillet, heat some of the remaining butter and drop the mixture by the tablespoon to make 2- to 3-inch pancakes, turning once. They should be golden on both sides.

3. Top each pancake with a dollop of sour cream, caviar, and a sprinkle of the remaining chives.

≡ *Carrot Blinis with Sour Cream and Caviar*

These blinis are delicious served on their own or topped with tiny steak tartare balls.

≡ **Yield: 12 servings**

½ pound carrots, grated
4 scallions, minced
salt and pepper, to taste
2 eggs
2 to 4 tablespoons butter

½ cup sour cream
4 to 8 tablespoons caviar
1 tablespoon minced chives, optional

≡ **Yield: 24 servings**

1½ pounds carrots, grated
12 scallions, minced
salt and pepper, to taste
6 eggs
⅓ to ½ cup butter

1½ cups sour cream
2 to 3 ounces caviar
3 tablespoons minced chives, optional

1. In a bowl, mix the carrots, scallions, salt, pepper, and eggs.

2. Heat enough butter in a skillet or on a griddle to just moisten the surface.

3. Drop tablespoons of the carrot mixture on the griddle and flatten slightly. Brown on both sides and drain on paper towels.

4. Put a dollop of sour cream on each blini and top with a small spoonful of caviar and a sprinkling of chives, if desired.

≡ *Hot Foie Gras with Warm Toast*

An allowance of about 1 ounce foie gras per person is in order. The simplest of preparations accents the special quality of this exquisite hors d'oeuvre.

1 *bloc* foie gras
warm toast

1. Preheat the oven to 350°F.

2. Open the *bloc* at both ends and push the foie gras onto an ovenproof serving dish. Bake until the fat is melted and the foie gras is heated. (Insert a metal skewer into the center and let it stay 30 seconds. Remove it and feel the skewer to determine if the foie gras is warm.)

3. Serve with toast.

≡ *Smoked Salmon*

You will find many recipes using smoked salmon throughout this book.

═ **Yield: 10 to 20 servings per side**

1 side smoked salmon
fingers of pumpernickel bread
lemon wedges

black pepper, preferably in a
mill
olive oil

1. Place the salmon on a board, silver platter, or marble slab. With a very sharp, thin-bladed knife, cut the thinnest possible slices starting about 1½ inches from the tail and cutting on a diagonal, almost horizontally toward the tail.

2. Lay the slices in front of the salmon, and let your guests top the bread with the salmon and season with lemon, pepper, and oil as desired. Capers and thinly sliced onions may be served on the side.

An alternative presentation is to slice the salmon, roll each slice, and arrange the rolls on platters. Of course, the salmon can be sliced and arranged on bread as canapés to be passed, but a side of salmon looks more impressive.

If the salmon has been presliced with cellophane inserts, it is best to roll the slices, toward the tail, leaving them on the skin. Remove and discard the cellophane.

≡ *Loaf of Smoked Salmon Sandwiches*

═ **Yield: 8 to 10 servings**

1 large loaf Russian
    pumpernickel, about 15
    inches long, 8 inches wide,
    and 6 inches high
½ cup unsalted butter, softened

2 large white onions, thinly sliced
½ cup capers
1 pound smoked salmon, thinly
    sliced
parsley sprigs, optional

1. With a bread knife, cut off the top of the bread and set aside. With a sharp, thin knife, cut along each side, ½ inch in from the outer edge, almost to the bottom of the loaf, as if cutting around the sides of a box. Insert the knife into the end of the bread, ½ inch from the bottom of the loaf, and cut toward one side. Remove the knife, turn it over, and reinsert into the same hole and repeat. Do the same at the opposite end. You can remove the center of the loaf in one piece. (This is the same method as removing the center of a pineapple; see illustration, page 534.)

2. Cut the center block of bread into thin lengthwise slices. Butter the slices and top half of them with a layer of onions, a sprinkle of capers, and slices of salmon. Cover with the remaining bread slices, buttered side down.

3. Cut into small sandwiches, and place the sandwiches into the hollowed loaf. Place on a platter and decorate with the parsley sprigs. Set the top of the loaf askew.

NOTE: Plan on one loaf for every 8 to 10 persons. If there are many other hors d'oeuvre, a loaf could serve up to 15 persons. For economy's sake, make one loaf for presentation and refill it with sandwiches made from additional loaves.

≡ *Gravlax (Scandinavian Cured Salmon)*

For the proper texture, this must be started at least 48 hours in advance; 3 days is better. It will keep for a week in the refrigerator.

═ Yield: 10 to 20 servings

2 salmon fillets, all bones and skin removed
1 large bunch dill, chopped
¼ cup coarse (kosher) salt
¼ cup sugar
2 tablespoons peppercorns, crushed

1. Place salmon, skin side down, in a noncorrosible baking dish. Sprinkle the fillet with half the dill.

2. In a bowl, mix the salt, sugar, and peppercorns and sprinkle over the dill. Cover with remaining dill. Place the second fillet on top, skin side up, and cover first with parchment or waxed paper and then with foil. Set a 4- to 5-pound weight on the fish. Refrigerate for 48 to 72 hours, turning the fillets every 12 hours and basting with the liquid in the baking dish. Separate the fillets to baste, then reassemble.

3. When ready to serve, remove the fish from the marinade, scrape away the dill and seasonings, and pat the fillets dry. Slice the fish on the diagonal toward the tail, as described under smoked salmon, page 12.

4. Serve with toast or pumpernickel and mustard dill sauce.

▶ The fish can be frozen after curing, but it is best if it is cured and served within one to two days.

≡ Mustard Dill Sauce for Gravlax

This sauce will keep for several days in the refrigerator, but it needs to be beaten before serving to reemulsify it. The sauce is delicious with other fish, such as poached shrimp or fish balls.

═ Yield: ¾ cup

4 tablespoons Dijon mustard
1 teaspoon dry mustard
3 tablespoons sugar
2 tablespoons white wine
   vinegar

⅓ cup vegetable oil
3 tablespoons minced dill

═ Yield: 1½ cups

12 tablespoons Dijon mustard
1 tablespoon dry mustard
½ cup sugar

⅓ cup white wine vinegar
1 cup vegetable oil
⅓ cup minced dill

1. In a bowl or food processor, mix the mustards, sugar, and vinegar to a paste.
2. Slowly beat in the oil until it becomes as thick as mayonnaise.
3. Stir in the dill.

≡ Gravlax aux Herbes (Cured Salmon with Herbs)

This version uses the same techniques but carries the flavors of Provence.

═ Yield: 10 to 20 servings

2 salmon fillets, all bones and
   skin removed
¼ cup lemon juice
4 teaspoons salt
1 teaspoon crushed fennel seeds
¼ teaspoon ground cloves
½ teaspoon ground pepper

1 teaspoon Pernod
2 teaspoons Cognac
1 teaspoon white wine vinegar
1 tablespoon minced thyme
1 tablespoon minced sage
1 teaspoon minced rosemary
buttered toast or dark bread

1. Place one fillet in a noncorrosible baking pan.
2. In a bowl, mix the salt, lemon juice, fennel, cloves, pepper, Pernod, Cognac, vinegar, lemon juice, thyme, sage, and rosemary. Spread this over the fillet and cover with the second fillet. Cover first with parchment or waxed paper and then with foil, and place a 5-pound weight on top. Refrigerate for 48 to 72 hours, turning the fillets every 12

hours, and basting with the accumulated juices. Separate the fillets to baste, then reassemble.

3. When ready to serve, drain the juices, scrape off the herbs, and cut on the diagonal, as described under smoked salmon, page 12.

4. Serve with toast or bread on the side.

5. If desired, the accumulated juices can be used as a sauce for the fish, but strain and discard the herbs and spices.

▶ Can be frozen after curing.

≡ *Gravlax with Peppercorns*

This version is enhanced with a drizzle of hazelnut or walnut oil over the slices. Present the oil in a pretty cruet, and let your guests add their own.

═ Yield: 10 to 20 servings

2 salmon fillets, all bones removed
⅓ cup coarse (kosher) salt
1 tablespoon sugar
½ cup green peppercorns, in brine, drained and crushed

¼ cup each minced tarragon, chervil, chives, and parsley
buttered toast or dark bread

1. Place one fillet, skin side down, in a noncorrosible baking pan and sprinkle with the salt and sugar.

2. Using a mortar and pestle, crush the peppercorns and herbs to a paste and spread over the fillet. Place the second fillet on top, skin side up. Cover first with parchment or waxed paper and then with foil, and top with a 5-pound weight. Refrigerate for 48 to 72 hours, turning the fillets every 12 hours and basting with the accumulated juices. Separate the fillets to baste, then reassemble.

3. When ready to serve, drain the juices, scrape off the herbs, and cut on the diagonal, as described under smoked salmon, page 12.

4. Serve with toast or dark bread.

▶ Can be frozen.

2

Nuts and Olives

*N*uts and olives are among the oldest snack foods. These delicacies fall from the tree for quick and easy consumption. The bitterness of unripe olives probably took a little getting used to, but people soon learned to cure olives to improve the taste. Today, nuts are readily available by just opening the container and olives by dipping into the jar, but they can be embellished, if not actually improved. The recipes here contain suggestions for flavoring so that you may never again just open a can.

If you choose to serve nuts plain, warm them in a 350°F oven for about 10 minutes to bring out their flavor. Nuts mixed with diced dried fruits are great. Cashews with golden raisins and walnuts with diced figs are two of many possibilities. If you are running a bed and breakfast, offer these as a snack before guests retire, along with a glass of fruity or fortified wine such as Rhine wine, sherry, Madeira, or port.

You can vary the flavor of nuts if you sauté, deep fry, or bake them. Or, you can flavor nuts with herbs and spices. There are some traditional combinations — curry and cashews, for instance — but the rules exist to be broken. Use your imagination — with discretion — to create your specialty. Some of the combinations presented here are sweet and can be used as part of a dessert course or can be served after dinner with coffee, as well as an accompaniment to hors d'oeuvre. Although recipes often specify a particular type of nut, you can use almost any nut of your choice in almost any recipe. Experiment.

A pound of nuts will feed 6 to 7 people if there is little else offered, but with a variety of hors d'oeuvre, a pound will serve more. Plan on about 1 pound for up to 20 people, 2 pounds for up to 60 people, and 3 pounds for up to 100 people if you are supplying a full complement of hors d'oeuvre. Interestingly, there is seldom a complaint if you run out of nuts halfway through an event, unless you run out of everything else. It is as if people expect the nuts to be eaten.

Nuts are relatively expensive and can turn rancid. Be sure to buy them with care from a reliable supplier and immediately return any that are not up to standard. Shelled nuts keep well in a cool area for several weeks. If the weather is hot or you need to keep them longer, store them in the freezer. They will thaw in a matter of minutes if spread out on a baking sheet.

Around the Mediterranean, a bowl of olives has long served as an appetizer indicating welcome. Olives are readily available in most areas and come in great variety. Imported olives bought in bulk are far superior to canned olives from anywhere. Frankly, canned olives have little or no flavor. (If you flavor such olives, you will taste the seasoning, but the olive flavor will be almost nonexistent.) Good imported olives can be served as is. However, they can be enhanced by marinating, stuffing, and wrapping them with other ingredients. Of course, they can also be mixed with other foods.

Marinating olives consists of draining off the brine, adding the seasonings, and letting them marinate, shaking fairly often, for 12 hours to 2 months. Once they have been marinated, they can be kept for up to 4 months in the refrigerator. However, if you have used crushed garlic in the marinade, discard it before storing the olives. Although most recipes specify green or black olives, one can be substituted for the other.

It is impossible to say how many olives to prepare. A pound of olives, about 2 cups, will serve 6 or 7 persons if they are sitting on a deck overlooking a harbor, eating olives, feta cheese, and fresh tomatoes for an afternoon, and about 30 persons at a cocktail party when served with six other hors d'oeuvre. The recipes that follow are for 1 pound but can be easily increased. Since most of the preparations keep for long periods, leftovers can be used for another occasion. If you end up with several different preparations, serve small bowls of all types and let guests pick and choose.

—— *Nuts* ——

Certain nuts, especially almonds, hazelnuts, and Brazil nuts, are better if blanched first. It is possible to blanch walnuts, but frankly it is not worth the trouble. Purchasing blanched nuts saves time and effort, but if this is not possible, here are instructions for how to do it.

≡ Blanched Almonds

In a saucepan, cover almonds with water and bring to a boil. Drain. When the nuts are cool enough to handle, squeeze each nut with your thumb and forefinger until it pops from the skin.

≡ Blanched Hazelnuts, Brazil Nuts, and Walnuts

1. Preheat the oven to 350°F.

2. On a baking sheet, bake the nuts in a single layer for 20 minutes or until the skins have darkened and split.

3. Transfer the nuts to a coarse towel, wrap, and let cool for 5 minutes.

4. Rub the nuts briskly in the towel to remove most of the skins. Pick out the nuts, discarding the skins.

NOTE: The nuts can be shaken in a spaetzle maker or chestnut roaster. The skins will fall through the large holes. Do not use a colander or sieve—the holes are too small.

≡ Deep-Fried Nuts

═ Yield: 1 pound

4 cups oil for deep frying   salt
1 pound blanched nuts

1. Heat the oil to 325°F.

2. In a frying basket, fry the nuts until golden, about 30 to 50 seconds. Drain on paper towels and sprinkle with salt.

3. Serve warm.

▶ Keeps 3 to 4 weeks. Reheat on paper towel–lined baking sheets before serving.

≡ Sautéed Nuts

═ Yield: 1 pound

olive oil   salt
1 pound blanched nuts

1. In a large skillet, heat the olive oil until hot but not smoking.
2. Add the nuts and sauté until golden, stirring often. Drain on paper towels, reserving any leftover oil for use in salads.
3. Season the nuts with salt and serve warm, if possible.

▶ Keeps 1 week; can be frozen. Reheat before serving.

≡ Baked Nuts

= Yield: 1 pound

1 pound blanched nuts   1 teaspoon salt

1. Preheat the oven to 350°F.
2. Butter a baking sheet, add the nuts, and bake for about 10 minutes, stirring often. The nuts should smell nutty and darken in color. Take care not to burn them.
3. Drain the nuts on paper towels.
4. Place in a bowl and season with the salt.

▶ Keeps 2 to 3 weeks; can be frozen. Reheat before serving, if possible.

≡ Salt and Pepper Almonds

The egg white gives a crispy coating to these nuts.

= Yield: 1 pound

1 egg white, lightly beaten   1 pound blanched almonds
¼ teaspoon Tabasco sauce, or   1 tablespoon coarse (kosher)
   to taste   salt

1. Preheat the oven to 350°F.
2. In a bowl, beat the egg white and Tabasco sauce until frothy. Add the almonds and stir to coat evenly. Drain in a sieve. Sprinkle the almonds with salt and mix.
3. Butter a baking sheet, spread the nuts in a single layer, and bake until dry and golden, stirring often, about 20 minutes. Cool.

▶ Keeps 2 to 3 weeks; can be frozen.

≡ *Garlic Almonds*

== **Yield: 1 pound**

1 tablespoon butter
2 tablespoons soy sauce
2 teaspoons Tabasco sauce
3 garlic cloves, crushed

1 pound blanched almonds
3 teaspoons pepper
¼ teaspoon red pepper flakes
salt

1. Preheat the oven to 350°F.

2. Butter a baking sheet. Sprinkle with soy sauce, Tabasco sauce, and garlic. Scatter almonds over the sheet and mix well. Sprinkle with 1½ teaspoons pepper, dried pepper flakes, and salt. Bake 10 minutes. Sprinkle with remaining pepper and salt, and stir to mix. Bake 15 minutes longer. Cool before serving.

▶ Keeps 2 to 3 weeks; can be frozen.

≡ *Gingered Almonds*

== **Yield: 1 pound**

1 pound almonds or other nuts
¼ cup butter

2 teaspoons salt
2 teaspoons ground ginger

1. Preheat the oven to 350°F.

2. On a baking sheet, bake the nuts and butter for 20 minutes, stirring occasionally until golden.

3. Drain on paper towels. Season with salt and ginger, and serve warm.

▶ Keeps 2 to 3 weeks; can be frozen.

≡ *Brazil Nut Chips*

== **Yield: 1 pound**

1 pound blanched Brazil nuts
2 tablespoons melted butter

salt, to taste

1. Preheat the oven to 350°F.

2. In a saucepan, add enough water to cover the nuts and simmer 5 minutes. Drain. Cut the nuts into thin slices with a sharp knife or the finest blade of a food processor.

3. Spread on a baking sheet and toss with the butter and salt.
4. Bake, stirring often, until light brown and crisp. Watch carefully.

▶ Keeps 2 to 3 weeks; can be frozen.

≡ Deviled Cashew Nuts

≡ **Yield: 1 pound**

1 pound cashews or walnuts	¼ teaspoon cayenne pepper
2 tablespoons butter	½ teaspoon ground cumin
1 teaspoon salt	½ teaspoon ground coriander

1. In a large skillet, sauté the nuts in the butter over moderate heat, stirring constantly, until golden. Drain on paper towels.
2. In a large bowl, mix the salt, cayenne, cumin, and coriander. Add the nuts and stir to coat evenly.

▶ Keeps 2 to 3 weeks; can be frozen.

≡ Curried Nuts

The flavor of curry, like that of paprika, is greatly enhanced by sautéing in a fat. Since commercial curry powder varies greatly from one producer to another, test several to find the flavor that pleases you.

≡ **Yield: 1 pound**

1 pound unsalted cashews or other nuts	3 tablespoons butter
1 tablespoon curry powder	salt, to taste

1. In a skillet, sauté the nuts and curry in the butter over moderate heat, stirring often, until lightly browned and very fragrant.
2. Drain on paper towels and season with salt.

▶ Keeps 2 to 3 weeks; can be frozen.

≡ Mexican Peanuts

≡ **Yield: 1 pound**

1 pound blanched raw peanuts	1 tablespoon salt
1½ tablespoons chili powder	pinch of cayenne pepper
¼ teaspoon ground coriander	

1. Preheat the oven to 350°F.
2. On a baking sheet, bake the nuts in a single layer until golden, stirring occasionally.
3. In a large bowl, mix the chili powder, coriander, salt, and cayenne. Stir in the nuts, and toss to coat evenly.

▶ Keeps 2 to 3 weeks; can be frozen.

≡ *Roasted Walnuts*

≡ **Yield: 1 pound**

1 pound walnuts	1 teaspoon salt
2 tablespoons sugar	½ teaspoon cumin
1 tablespoon oil	½ teaspoon red pepper flakes

1. Preheat the oven to 350°F.
2. In a bowl, mix the nuts, sugar, oil, salt, cumin, and pepper flakes.
3. Transfer to a baking sheet and bake until brown, about 8 minutes, stirring occasionally.

▶ Keeps 2 to 3 weeks; can be frozen.

≡ *Anise Roasted Nuts*

≡ **Yield: 1 pound**

1 pound raw peanuts	⅛ teaspoon curry powder
⅓ cup anise-flavored liqueur	salt, to taste
½ teaspoon crushed garlic	

1. Preheat the oven to 350°F.
2. In a bowl, mix the peanuts, liqueur, garlic, curry powder, and salt.
3. Transfer to a baking sheet and bake for 10 to 20 minutes, stirring often, until golden.

▶ Keeps 2 to 3 weeks; can be frozen.

≡ *Peppered Pecans*

≡ Yield: 1 pound

1 tablespoon olive oil
½ teaspoon black pepper
½ teaspoon white pepper
½ teaspoon cayenne pepper
¼ teaspoon dried thyme
1 egg white

2 teaspoons Worcestershire
   sauce
½ teaspoon Tabasco sauce
½ teaspoon salt
1 pound pecans

1. Preheat the oven to 375°F.

2. Brush a large baking sheet with the oil.

3. In a bowl, mix the black pepper, white pepper, cayenne, and thyme. In another bowl, whisk the egg white until frothy. Whisk in the Worcestershire sauce, Tabasco sauce, and salt. Add the nuts and toss to coat. Sift the pepper mixture over all, tossing quickly.

4. Spread the nuts evenly on the baking sheet and bake for 5 minutes. Stir the nuts and bake until crisp and deep golden brown. Cool.

≡ *Soy Garlic Nuts*

These nuts, although not crisp, are delicious and a pleasant change from the expected.

≡ Yield: 1 pound

1 pound assorted nuts
3 tablespoons tamari (see
   Glossary)

2 tablespoons water
2 garlic cloves, minced
⅛ teaspoon cayenne pepper

1. In a large skillet, marinate the nuts in the tamari, water, garlic, and cayenne for 1 hour.

2. Simmer the mixture until the liquid has evaporated. Spread the nuts on a baking sheet in a single layer and dry for 2 hours.

▶ Keeps 1 week; can be frozen.

≡ *Chili Walnuts*

== **Yield: 1 pound**

1 pound walnuts	1 teaspoon coarse (kosher) salt
¼ cup walnut oil	½ teaspoon ground cumin
2 teaspoons chili powder	½ teaspoon turmeric

1. Preheat the oven to 325°F.

2. On a baking sheet, bake the nuts, stirring occasionally, until golden, about 20 minutes.

3. In a large bowl, mix the oil, chili powder, salt, cumin, turmeric, and roasted nuts.

4. Return to the baking sheet and roast 20 minutes longer, stirring often. Drain on paper towels.

▶ Keeps 2 to 3 weeks; can be frozen.

≡ *Orange Glazed Nuts*

== **Yield: 1 pound**

1 pound hazelnuts or walnuts	½ cup orange juice
1⅔ cups sugar	½ cup water

1. Preheat the oven to 350°F.

2. On a baking sheet, bake nuts for 10 minutes or until golden. Place in a kitchen towel and let rest, covered, for 5 minutes. Rub off and discard the skins.

3. In a 1-quart saucepan, mix the sugar, orange juice, and water. Bring to a boil, stirring gently, and cook to the soft-ball stage (238°F). Remove from the heat and stir in the nuts until the mixture turns creamy and dull. (This will take several minutes.)

4. Pour onto a buttered baking sheet and separate the nuts with two forks. Remove the nuts to a cake rack to dry.

▶ Keeps 1 week; can be frozen.

≡ Candied Orange Nuts

== **Yield: 1 pound**

1 pound pecans	½ cup milk
¾ cup shredded orange peel	1 tablespoon white vinegar
1½ cups firmly packed light brown sugar	

1. On a buttered baking sheet, spread the nuts and orange peel.

2. In a 2-quart saucepan, bring the sugar and milk to a boil, stirring. Add the vinegar, stop stirring, and boil until the mixture registers 238°F.

3. Pour over the nuts and orange peel and stir to coat. Cool and separate the nuts.

▶ Keeps 1 week; can be frozen.

≡ Sugar Spiced Nuts

== **Yield: 1 pound**

½ cup milk	½ teaspoon ground allspice
1 cup firmly packed dark brown sugar	¼ teaspoon white pepper
	1 teaspoon vanilla
1 teaspoon salt	1 pound almonds or pecans,
¾ teaspoon cinnamon	toasted

1. In a covered saucepan, boil the milk, brown sugar, salt, cinnamon, allspice, and white pepper over high heat until the mixture reaches the soft-ball stage (238°F).

2. Remove from the heat, stir in the vanilla and nuts, and stir until coated.

3. Turn onto lightly oiled baking sheets and separate the nuts.

▶ Keeps 1 week; can be frozen.

≡ Sweet Spiced Nuts I

== **Yield: 2 pounds**

1 pound blanched almonds	1 teaspoon cinnamon
2 cups blanched hazelnuts	½ teaspoon grated nutmeg
1 egg white, lightly beaten	⅛ teaspoon ground allspice
1 cup sugar	

1. Preheat the oven to 325°F.

2. Line a baking sheet with parchment paper or brush with oil.

3. In a bowl, mix the nuts and egg white to coat evenly. Drain.

4. In another bowl, mix the sugar, cinnamon, nutmeg, and allspice. Add the nuts and toss to coat.

5. Arrange in a single layer on the baking sheet and roast for 25 minutes, stirring occasionally.

▶ Keeps 1 week; can be frozen.

≡ *Sweet Spiced Nuts II*

═ Yield: 1 pound

1 pound walnuts or pecans	1 tablespoon cinnamon
½ cup butter	2 tablespoons ground cloves
1½ cups confectioners' sugar	2 tablespoons ground nutmeg

1. In a large skillet, over low heat, cook the nuts and butter, stirring often, for 20 minutes or until the nuts are lightly browned.

2. Drain on paper towels.

3. In a bowl, mix the nuts, sugar, cinnamon, cloves, and nutmeg until well coated, put into a sieve, and shake off the excess.

▶ Keeps 1 week; can be frozen.

≡ *Sweet Spiced Nuts III*

═ Yield: 1 pound

1 egg white	3 tablespoons cinnamon
2 tablespoons cold water	1 tablespoon ground cloves
1 pound nuts, all one kind or mixed	2 teaspoons salt
	2 teaspoons ground ginger
2 cups sifted confectioners' sugar	1 teaspoon ground nutmeg

1. Preheat the oven to 250°F.

2. In a bowl, beat the egg white until frothy. Add the water and nuts, mix well, and drain in a sieve.

3. In another bowl, mix the sugar, cinnamon, cloves, salt, ginger, and nutmeg. Toss the nuts in ½ cup of the sugar mixture.

4. Spread a ¼-inch layer of sugar on a baking sheet, arrange nuts in a single layer on top, and cover with remaining sugar.
5. Bake for 2 hours. Shake the nuts in a sieve to remove the excess sugar. The sugar can be used again.

▶ Keeps 1 week; can be frozen.

≡ Savory Spiced Nuts

= **Yield: 1 pound**

2 tablespoons olive oil
½ teaspoon ground cumin
½ teaspoon chili powder
½ teaspoon curry powder
½ teaspoon minced garlic
½ teaspoon cayenne pepper

¼ teaspoon ground ginger
¼ teaspoon cinnamon
1 pound almonds, cashews, pecans, or walnuts
1 tablespoon salt, preferably coarse (kosher)

1. Preheat the oven to 325°F.
2. In a saucepan, cook the olive oil, cumin, chili powder, curry powder, garlic, pepper, ginger, and cinnamon for 3 minutes.
3. Add the nuts and toss to coat.
4. Turn the nut mixture onto a baking sheet and spread in a single layer. Bake 15 minutes, shaking the pan occasionally.
5. Remove from the oven, turn into a bowl, and toss with the salt. Cool.

▶ Keeps 1 week; can be frozen.

≡ Sugared Nuts

= **Yield: 1 pound**

1½ cups sugar
½ cup water
½ cup corn syrup

½ teaspoon salt
½ teaspoon vanilla
1 pound nuts

1. Butter a baking sheet.
2. In a saucepan, boil the sugar, water, and corn syrup, washing down the sides of the pan with a pastry brush dipped in cold water, until the mixture reaches 238°F.
3. Stir in the salt and vanilla and remove from the heat. Add the nuts, stirring until the mixture is creamy. Pour the nuts onto a baking sheet

and separate with two forks. If the mixture gets too thick, place in a 200°F oven for a few minutes or until the nuts can be separated.

4. Let stand for 2 to 8 hours or until the coating dries.

▶ Keeps 2 to 3 weeks; best not frozen.

Variations

Spiced Nuts Add 1½ teaspoons cinnamon and ½ teaspoon ground allspice to the syrup with the salt and vanilla.

Orange Caramel Nuts Substitute 2 cups dark brown sugar for the 1½ cups sugar, and add 4 tablespoons grated orange rind with the nuts.

Candied Ginger Nuts Add ¼ cup minced candied ginger with the nuts.

≡ *Cocoa Pecans*

≡ **Yield: 1 pound**

1 tablespoon vegetable oil	⅓ cup sugar
1 pound pecan halves	½ teaspoon salt
1 egg white, beaten to a froth	½ teaspoon cinnamon
3 tablespoons cocoa	¼ teaspoon ground cloves

1. Preheat the oven to 350°F.

2. Brush two baking sheets with oil.

3. In a bowl, toss the pecans with the egg white. Drain.

4. In another bowl, mix the nuts, cocoa, sugar, salt, cinnamon, and cloves, and spread on the baking sheets in a single layer.

5. Bake 15 minutes or until dry and crisp.

▶ Keeps 1 week; can be frozen.

≡ *Sugared Almonds*

≡ **Yield: 1 pound**

1 pound unblanched almonds	1½ teaspoons cinnamon
2 cups sugar	1½ teaspoons vanilla
½ cup water	¾ teaspoon salt

1. Preheat the oven to 350°F.

2. On a baking sheet, bake the nuts in a single layer for 20 minutes, stirring occasionally. Cool.

3. In a saucepan, boil the sugar and water until it registers 250°F. Stir in the nuts, cinnamon, vanilla, and salt. Remove from the heat and stir briskly until the nuts are separated and the coating is dry, about 2 to 3 minutes.

4. Spread on a baking sheet to cool.

▶ Keeps 2 to 3 weeks; best not frozen.

≡ *Nut Clusters*

═ Yield: 1 pound

1 pound unblanched almonds	1 teaspoon vanilla
½ cup sugar	¾ teaspoon salt
2 tablespoons butter	

1. In a large skillet, cook the almonds, sugar, and butter over medium heat, stirring constantly, until golden. Remove from the heat and stir in the vanilla.

2. Spread the mixture on a buttered baking sheet and sprinkle with the salt.

3. Cool and break into clusters.

▶ Keeps 1 week; best not frozen.

≡ *Apricots and Almonds*

═ Yield: 1 pound

1 pound blanched almonds, toasted	1 cup dried apricots

1. Place the almonds in a bowl.

2. Julienne the apricots and toss with the almonds.

▶ Keeps 2 weeks.

≡ *Cashews and Raisins*

═ Yield: 1 pound

1 pound salted cashews   1 cup golden raisins

In a bowl, mix the cashews and raisins.

▶ Keeps 2 weeks.

≡ *Walnuts and Figs*

═ Yield: 1 pound

1 pound walnuts   1 cup dried figs

1. Place the walnuts in a bowl.

2. With sharp knife dipped into hot water, remove the hard stems from the figs and dice the figs into ¼-inch pieces.

3. Mix the figs with the nuts.

▶ Keeps 2 weeks.

—— *Olives* ——

≡ *Green Olives with Garlic*

═ Yield: 1 pound

1 pound green olives   3 garlic cloves, peeled and
1 cup olive oil   crushed
5 to 6 tablespoons peppercorns,
   crushed

1. Drain the olives of their brine and place in a bowl or plastic container.

2. Add the oil, peppercorns, and garlic.

3. Refrigerate for 3 days, turning twice a day.

▶ Keeps 1 month, refrigerated.

NOTE: This recipe will give some flavor to tinned black olives as well.

≡ Olives with Rosemary and Garlic

= Yield: 1 pound

1 pound green olives, rinsed
 and drained
1 lemon, thinly sliced
1 tablespoon minced rosemary

2 garlic cloves, crushed
1 teaspoon peppercorns,
 crushed
fruity olive oil

1. With a mallet, gently crack each olive to split open one side.
2. In a container, alternate the olives, lemon slices, rosemary, garlic, and peppercorns, packing tightly.
3. Cover with oil and marinate for 2 to 3 days, shaking occasionally.

▶ Store in the refrigerator for up to 2 months. It is best to remove and discard the lemon and garlic after a week.

≡ Spanish Olives

= Yield: 1 pound

1 pound pitted green olives
shredded rind of 6 lemons
1 cup water

1 cup dry sherry
1 tablespoon olive oil
¼ teaspoon dried thyme

1. Drain the olives and stuff the cavities with the lemon rind.
2. Place in a large jar and add the water, sherry, olive oil, and thyme.
3. Marinate for 2 days in the refrigerator, shaking occasionally.

▶ Store in the refrigerator for up to 2 months.

≡ Sicilian Olives

= Yield: 1 pound

1 pound green olives
½ cup diced celery
¼ cup olive oil
¼ cup wine vinegar

1 onion, thinly sliced
1 tablespoon minced basil
1 teaspoon minced oregano

1. With a mallet, crack each olive to split open one side.
2. In a bowl, mix the olives, celery, oil, vinegar, onion, basil, and oregano.
3. Marinate for 24 hours.

▶ Store in the refrigerator, covered, for up to 2 months.

≡ *Anchovy-Cured Green Olives*

= **Yield: 1 pound**

1 pound green olives
1½ teaspoons salt
red wine vinegar
4 garlic cloves, thinly sliced
8 anchovy fillets

½ teaspoon minced rosemary
¼ teaspoon crushed fennel
  seeds
olive oil

1. Drain the olives and place in a container.
2. In a saucepan, bring the salt and 2 cups of water to a boil. Pour over the olives and let stand at room temperature for 12 hours. Drain and discard any soft or bruised olives.
3. Cover the olives with a mixture of half water and half red wine vinegar. Marinate for 24 hours. Drain and discard the marinade.
4. In the bottom of a 1-pint jar, make a layer of one-quarter of the olives, 1 garlic clove, and 2 anchovies. Repeat until the jar is filled. Add the rosemary and fennel, cover with oil, and marinate for 1 month.

▶ Store in refrigerator for up to 6 months.

≡ *Brandied Olives*

= **Yield: 1 pound**

1 pound green olives

½ cup Cognac

In a container, mix the olives and Cognac and let stand for 3 days.

▶ Keeps 2 months.

≡ *Black Olives with Rosemary*

= **Yield: 1 pound**

1 pound black olives
½ cup fruity olive oil

1 tablespoon minced rosemary

In a container, mix the olives, olive oil, and rosemary and marinate for 2 days, turning often.

▶ Keeps up to 2 months; remove and discard the herb before storing.

Variation
Substitute 3 tablespoons minced fresh basil, oregano, or marjoram for the rosemary.

≡ *Herbed Olives*

═ **Yield: 1 pound**

1 pound black olives
¼ cup olive oil
1 small dried chili pepper,
    crushed

1 tablespoon minced dill

In a container, mix the olives, olive oil, chili pepper, and dill, and marinate for 2 days.

▶ Keeps 2 months.

≡ *Spiced Ripe Olives*

═ **Yield: 1 pound**

2 cups pitted ripe olives
1 garlic clove, halved
2 small dried chili peppers,
    crushed

1 tablespoon peppercorns,
    crushed
1 jalapeño pepper, minced
1 cup olive oil, or to cover

1. Rub each olive with the garlic clove and place in a jar.
2. Mix the chili peppers, peppercorns, and jalapeño pepper, and add to the jar with enough olive oil to cover.
3. Seal tightly and marinate for 2 to 3 weeks.

▶ Keeps 2 months.

≡ *Aegean Olives*

═ **Yield: 1 pound**

1 pound mixed green and black
    olives
1 garlic clove, lightly crushed

1 tablespoon mustard seeds,
    lightly crushed
olive oil

1. Choose olives of different sizes as well as color.
2. In a container, mix the olives, garlic, mustard seeds, and enough olive oil to cover.
3. Let stand for 5 days.

▶ Keeps 2 months.

≡ Oregano Olives

≡ **Yield: 1 pound**

1 pound black olives
¼ cup olive oil
3 tablespoons red wine vinegar

1 teaspoon minced oregano
1 garlic clove, sliced

1. In a jar, mix the olives, olive oil, vinegar, oregano, and garlic.
2. Shake well, and marinate at least 2 days.

▶ Keeps 2 months.

≡ Spiced Tinned Olives

There are occasions when only tinned olives are available, or perhaps it is the wish of the client. This recipe gives them some flavor.

≡ **Yield: 1 pound**

2 8-ounce cans black olives
8 small dried chili peppers
8 teaspoons pickling spices

4 large garlic cloves, sliced
¼ cup red wine vinegar
olive oil

1. Drain the olives and place a layer of 2 chili peppers, 2 teaspoons of spices, and 1 garlic clove in the bottom of a quart container.
2. Add a layer of one-quarter of the olives, then repeat the layers with the remaining ingredients.
3. Add the vinegar and enough olive oil to cover.
4. Let marinate for 3 days, shaking every 12 hours.
5. Remove and discard the spices, reserving the marinade and the olives.

▶ Store in the marinade for up to 2 months.

≡ *Cheese Stick Olives*

= Yield: 1¼ pounds

¼ pound imported Gruyère cheese	1 pound pitted green olives

1. Cut the cheese into sticks ¼ inch thick and 1½ inches long.
2. Stuff each olive with a cheese stick.

▶ Keeps 1 day.

≡ *Ham-Stuffed Olives*

= Yield: 1½ pounds

½ pound ham, cut ¼-inch thick	1 pound pitted green olives

1. Cut the ham into sticks ¼ inch thick and 1½ inches long.
2. Stuff the olives with the ham sticks.

▶ Keeps 1 day.

Variations
Stuff the olives with smaller sticks of both cheese and ham, or use a hard salami.

≡ *Almond-Stuffed Olives*

= Yield: 1¼ pounds

1 cup blanched almonds	1 pound pitted olives

Insert a whole blanched almond into each olive.

▶ Keeps 1 week or longer.
NOTE: These are also available ready-made; however, the nuts lose their crunch and are better if freshly prepared.

≡ *Horseradish Cream–Stuffed Olives*

This is particularly attractive if made with black olives and presented on a nest of parsley sprigs like miniature Easter eggs in the grass. Otherwise they should be very carefully arranged in a bowl so the centers stand upright. They also make an eye-catching canapé (see Chapter 7).

═ **Yield: 1 pound**

3 ounces cream cheese

2 tablespoons heavy cream

1 tablespoon drained
  horseradish

salt, to taste

1 pound pitted black or green
  olives

1. In a bowl, cream the cheese with the heavy cream, horseradish, and salt to a smooth paste.

2. Insert a no. 30 star tip into a 10-inch pastry bag and fill with the cheese mixture.

3. Pipe the mixture into the olives and chill before serving.

▶ Keeps 1 day.

═ *Anchovy Cheese–Stuffed Olives*

═ **Yield: 1¼ pounds**

6 anchovy fillets, drained

3 ounces cream cheese

pinch of cayenne pepper

1 pound pitted black or green
  olives

1. In a bowl, mash the anchovy fillets to a paste, then beat in the cheese and cayenne until smooth.

2. Put a no. 30 star tip into a 10-inch pastry bag and fill with the cheese mixture.

3. Pipe the filling into each olive and chill before serving.

▶ Keeps 1 day.

≡ *Blue Cheese–Stuffed Olives*

═ **Yield: 1¼ pounds**

1 ounce blue cheese

3 ounces cream cheese

1 tablespoon Cognac

1 pound pitted black or green
  olives

1. In a bowl, mash the blue cheese until smooth. Beat in the cream cheese and Cognac until smooth.

2. Put a no. 30 star tip into a 10-inch pastry bag and fill with the cheese mixture.

3. Pipe the mixture into each olive.

▶ Keeps 1 day.

=== 3 ===

Basic Sauces

Sauces should enhance the foods they accompany, not overwhelm them. Some chefs use sauces as the goal rather than the means to reach the goal. Choose sauces with care so that they complement the food and bring out its special quality. Do not be limited by tradition. Shrimp served with cocktail sauce is an old standby and wonderful in its own right, but boring. If your client insists on the tomato-based cocktail sauce, suggest an additional sauce such as per bacco or aillade. If a recipe suggests serving a sauce with a particular food—vegetables, for instance, consider whether it will work with other foods as well.

Certain hors d'oeuvre, such as croquettes, require a base sauce. The sauces in this chapter include these bases and variations.

Sauces are simpler to prepare than many writers would have us believe. If a sauce "breaks," the repair is usually simple and quick. Have confidence in yourself and the recipes, and proceed apace. If you have a problem, try the suggested corrections.

Mustard

It is not necessary to prepare your own mustards. However, it can be fun. Considering the cost of some specialty mustards, making your own can amount to a considerable savings. You will quickly see the possibility of making versions to suit your particular needs. You can flavor mustards by steeping them with herbs, using flavored vinegars, or adding additional ingredients.

Vinaigrette

Vinaigrette is made with oil, vinegar, salt, and pepper whisked together rapidly to form an emulsion. It may include dry or prepared mustard, garlic, herbs, or other ingredients. Vinaigrette is used alone or in combination with other ingredients to marinate vegetables, fish, or meat. It is never the thick, creamy-red mixture sold as "French dressing." Use of such a product will change the recipe drastically.

Mayonnaise

Make your own mayonnaise! With the machinery available in every kitchen today there is no reason why everyone cannot prepare their own mayonnaise. It takes but a few minutes, the cost is similar to, if not less than, the cost of prepared mayonnaise, and you have control over the quality. You can select quality oil, preferably an equal mix of a good, not superexpensive olive oil and a pleasant unflavored vegetable oil such as cottonseed, soybean, or corn oil. Fresh eggs are always available. You can control the acidity by the type and amount of vinegar and, of course, the salt. Sugar never belongs in mayonnaise.

Hollandaise Sauce

In the last few years the accent for main courses has been on beurre blanc — hollandaise without the eggs — but for hors d'oeuvre, the somewhat more substantial hollandaise seems more appropriate. Béarnaise, a child of hollandaise, is still one of the most popular accompaniments to roasted or broiled meat.

Béchamel Sauce

The French béchamel starts with more liquid and is cooked longer than its American counterpart, cream sauce. The French method of reducing the sauce slowly creates a silkier sauce that is worth the extra few minutes of cooking. Do not use prepared cream sauces or substitute some form of cream soup.

Velouté Sauce

Velouté is another version of cream sauce made with stock rather than milk and enriched with cream. This sauce, although not as popular as it used to be, is the base for croquettes and certain sauces served with hors d'oeuvre. Take the time to let it simmer gently, and sieve it properly for the right effect. Hastily made, it will be floury and heavy.

Tomato Sauce

There are many versions of tomato sauce, ranging from a simple uncooked, puréed fresh tomato with seasonings to a long-simmered, multi-ingredient ragù Bolognese. Select a light, freshly made sauce for most hors d'oeuvre. If a recipe calls for 1 to 2 tablespoons of tomato sauce, feel free to use a good, subtly flavored canned sauce. If the tomato sauce is the main ingredient, making your own is better.

Other Sauces
In addition to the basic sauces listed above, this chapter includes a selection of sauces that are suitable for serving with a variety of hors d'oeuvre.

Asian Dipping Sauces
Many people consider hot mustard and duck or plum sauce as the appropriate accompaniments to Chinese food—any Chinese food. The Chinese do use hot mustard to add spark to some dishes, and they also serve plum sauce; however, these are far less common than other dipping sauces. Try some of the sauces listed below instead of, or at least along with, hot mustard and plum sauce.

Serve the sauces in small dishes and keep replenishing them so they always look appealing. Large bowls often begin to look "used" and unappetizing. The sauces are quite simple and should be made shortly before serving. The recipes are for small portions, but they can be doubled or tripled without any problem.

—— *Mustard Sauces* ——

≡ *Mustard*

═ Yield: 3½ cups

4 ounces dry mustard	¾ cup sugar
1 cup tarragon vinegar	½ cup butter or vegetable oil
6 eggs	1 teaspoon salt

1. In a covered bowl, soak the mustard in the vinegar overnight.

2. In the top of a double boiler, over simmering water, whisk the eggs into the mustard mixture, one at a time.

3. Add the sugar, butter, and salt, and cook, whisking until thickened, about 5 minutes. Do not let it boil.

4. Store in jars.

▶ Keeps 2 weeks, refrigerated.

≡ Spiced Mustard

≡ **Yield: 3 cups**

2 large onions, sliced	2 teaspoons salt
2 garlic cloves, minced	pinch of cayenne pepper
2 cups wine vinegar	2 tablespoons corn syrup
1 cup dry mustard	vegetable oil

1. In a bowl, marinate the onions and garlic in the vinegar overnight. Strain the marinade and reserve.

2. In another bowl, mix the mustard, salt, and cayenne with ½ cup reserved marinade to make a smooth paste.

3. In a saucepan, bring the remaining marinade to a boil and stir in the mustard paste. Simmer stirring about 5 minutes.

4. Cool and stir in the corn syrup and just enough oil (about 1 cup) to make a smooth mixture.

5. Store in jars.

▶ Keeps 1 month, refrigerated.

≡ Coarse-Ground Mustard with Red Wine and Garlic

≡ **Yield: 1 quart**

1 cup mustard seeds	1 teaspoon pepper
1 cup red wine	2 teaspoons crushed garlic
1⅓ cups red wine vinegar	1½ tablespoons salt
1 cup water	2 bay leaves, very finely
1 teaspoon ground allspice	crumbled
2 teaspoons honey	

1. In a bowl, marinate the mustard seeds, red wine, and vinegar for 6 hours.

2. Pour into a food processor with the water, allspice, honey, pepper, garlic, salt, and bay leaves, and process until the mustard seed is fairly coarse.

3. Turn into a saucepan and cook over medium heat, stirring until the mustard is thickened.

4. Pour into jars and let cool.

▶ Keeps 1 month, refrigerated.

≡ French Mustard

≡ **Yield: 1 quart**

2 large onions, sliced	1 tablespoon salt
4 garlic cloves, sliced	¼ teaspoon cayenne pepper
3 cups red wine vinegar	3 tablespoons olive oil
1½ cups dry mustard	1½ tablespoons dry tarragon,
3 tablespoons sugar	crumbled

1. In a bowl, marinate the onions, garlic, and vinegar overnight. Strain the vinegar and reserve.

2. In a bowl, mix the mustard with ½ cup vinegar, sugar, salt, and cayenne to a paste.

3. In a saucepan, bring the remaining vinegar to a boil, add the mustard mixture, stirring constantly, and cook over medium heat until the mixture thickens.

4. Cool 5 minutes and stir in the oil and tarragon.

5. Store in jars.

▶ Keeps 1 month, refrigerated.

≡ Crème du Moutarde (Mustard Cream)

≡ **Yield: 1 cup**

½ cup heavy cream	lemon juice, to taste
1 teaspoon or more of Dijon	salt and pepper, to taste
mustard	

≡ **Yield: 1 quart**

2 cups heavy cream	1 tablespoon lemon juice
2 tablespoons Dijon mustard	salt and pepper, to taste

1. In a bowl, beat the cream to the soft peak stage and fold in the mustard, lemon juice, salt, and pepper.

2. Taste for seasoning, and add additional mustard and pepper if desired.

3. Store in jars.

▶ Keeps 2 days, refrigerated.

≡ Hot Mustard Sauce

This is a very spicy mustard sauce to accompany cold meats. Chinese mustard, which is similar, is listed with the Asian dipping sauces at the end of this chapter.

═ Yield: ⅓ cup

2 tablespoons dry mustard	½ teaspoon vinegar
4 tablespoons water	pinch of salt

═ Yield: 1 quart

1½ cups dry mustard	2 tablespoons vinegar
3 cups water	2 teaspoons salt

1. In a bowl, mix the mustard and 1½ tablespoons water to a smooth paste.
2. Stir in the remaining water gradually to prevent lumps.
3. Add the vinegar and salt.
4. Cover and refrigerate for 1 hour.

▶ Keeps 2 days.

≡ Mild Mustard Sauce

═ Yield: 1 cup

2 tablespoons flour	pinch of salt
2 teaspoons Dijon mustard	¾ cup wine vinegar
1 teaspoon sugar	2 egg yolks, lightly beaten

═ Yield: 1 quart

½ cup flour	1 teaspoon salt
3 tablespoons Dijon mustard	3 cups wine vinegar
1 tablespoon sugar	8 egg yolks, lightly beaten

1. In a saucepan over medium heat, whisk together the flour, mustard, sugar, and salt.
2. Slowly add the vinegar and cook, stirring, until thickened and smooth.
3. Remove from the heat and whisk in the egg yolks.
4. Return to the heat and cook, stirring, until thickened. Do not boil. Serve hot or cold.

▶ Keeps 1 week, refrigerated.

≡ *Horseradish Mustard Sauce*

≡ **Yield: 1 cup**

1 cup sour cream	1 teaspoon dry mustard
2 tablespoons horseradish	salt, to taste

In a saucepan, mix the sour cream, horseradish, and mustard. Correct seasoning with the salt. Heat until warm.

▶ Keeps 2 days, refrigerated.

≡ *Orange Honey Mustard Sauce*

≡ **Yield: 1½ cups**

½ cup honey	1 tablespoon turmeric
½ cup orange juice	1 teaspoon ground ginger
⅓ cup cider vinegar	1 teaspoon arrowroot
1 tablespoon dry mustard	2 tablespoons cold water

≡ **Yield: 1 quart**

1½ cups honey	2 tablespoons turmeric
1½ cups orange juice	1 tablespoon ground ginger
1 cup cider vinegar	1 tablespoon arrowroot
¼ cup dry mustard	⅓ cup cold water

1. In a saucepan, simmer the honey and orange juice for 5 minutes. Add the vinegar, mustard, turmeric, and ginger.
2. In a bowl, mix the arrowroot and water to a slurry and stir into the hot mustard mixture.
3. Cook, stirring, until thickened and smooth.
4. Store in jars.

▶ Keeps 1 month, refrigerated.

≡ *Fruit Mustard Sauce*

≡ **Yield: 2 cups**

1½ cups apricot purée	2 tablespoons Dijon mustard
2 teaspoons curry powder	1 tablespoon ground ginger
3 tablespoons honey	2 tablespoons dry sherry
1 teaspoon almond extract	

= **Yield: 1 quart**

3 cups apricot purée
1½ tablespoons curry powder
⅓ cup honey
1½ teaspoons almond extract

¼ cup Dijon mustard
2 tablespoons ground ginger
¼ cup dry sherry

1. In a bowl, mix together the apricot purée, curry powder, honey, almond extract, mustard, ginger, and sherry.
2. Store in jars.

▶ Keeps 1 month, refrigerated.

≡ *Mustard Sauce for Fish Balls*

= **Yield: 2 cups**

¾ cup mayonnaise
juice of ½ lemon
1½ tablespoons Dijon mustard

½ cup heavy cream, whipped
salt, to taste

= **Yield: 4 cups**

1½ cups mayonnaise
juice of 1 lemon
3 tablespoons Dijon mustard

1 cup heavy cream, whipped
salt, to taste

1. In a bowl, mix the mayonnaise, lemon juice, and mustard.
2. Fold in the cream, and correct the seasoning with salt.
3. Store in jars.

▶ Keeps 12 to 24 hours.

—— *Vinaigrettes* ——

≡ *Vinaigrette*

= **Yield: ½ cup**

2 tablespoons vinegar or lemon
  juice
2 teaspoons Dijon mustard

¼ teaspoon salt
pinch of pepper
6 tablespoons olive oil

= **Yield: 1 quart**

1 cup vinegar or lemon juice
⅓ cup Dijon mustard
2 teaspoons salt

1 teaspoon pepper
3 cups olive oil

1. In a bowl, mix the vinegar, mustard, salt, and pepper.
2. Gradually whisk in the oil until the mixture thickens and emulsifies.
3. Taste for seasoning.

▶ Keeps 1 week, refrigerated.

NOTE: Depending on the acidity of the vinegar, you may need to add more or less oil. Also, vinaigrette can be made in a food processor. If the vinaigrette separates, beat it before using to reemulsify.

≡ *Herbed Vinaigrette*

= **Yield: ½ cup**

2 tablespoons wine vinegar
¼ teaspoon salt
pinch of pepper
¼ teaspoon dry mustard

6 tablespoons olive oil
1 tablespoon minced parsley,
    chervil, basil, tarragon,
    and/or chives

= **Yield: 1 quart**

1 cup wine vinegar
2 teaspoons salt
1 teaspoon pepper
2 teaspoons dry mustard

3 cups olive oil
½ cup minced parsley, chervil,
    basil, tarragon, and/or chives

1. In a bowl, mix together the vinegar, salt, pepper, and mustard.
2. Gradually beat in the oil to create an emulsion, then fold in the herbs.
3. Store in jars.

▶ Keeps 1 week, refrigerated.

≡ *Sauce Ravigote*

= **Yield: ¾ cup**

½ cup vinaigrette
1 tablespoon minced onion
1 tablespoon Dijon mustard
1 hard-cooked egg, minced

2 tablespoons mixed minced
    parsley, tarragon, chives, and
    chervil

═ **Yield: 3¾ cups**

2½ cups vinaigrette
⅓ cup minced onion
⅓ cup Dijon mustard

5 hard-cooked eggs, minced
⅓ cup mixed minced parsley,
  tarragon, chives, and chervil

1. In a bowl, mix the vinaigrette, onion, mustard, eggs, and herbs.
2. Store in jars.

▶ Keeps 1 week, refrigerated.

—— *Mayonnaise-based Sauces* ——

≡ *Mayonnaise*

═ **Yield: 1 cup**

2 egg yolks
½ teaspoon salt
pinch of white pepper

½ teaspoon dry mustard
2 tablespoons vinegar
1 cup oil

═ **Yield: 1 quart**

8 egg yolks
2 teaspoons salt
½ teaspoon white pepper

2 teaspoons dry mustard
½ cup vinegar
1 quart oil

1. In a bowl, whisk the egg yolks, salt, pepper, mustard, and one-quarter of the vinegar until the mixture starts to thicken.
2. Slowly beat in the oil drop by drop until one-quarter of the oil has been incorporated.
3. Add another one-quarter of the remaining vinegar and continue to beat in the oil in a thin, steady stream.
4. When half the oil has been added, add another one-quarter of the vinegar and continue beating in the remaining oil.
5. Taste for seasoning, and beat in as much additional vinegar as needed.
6. Store in jars.

▶ Keeps 2 weeks or longer, refrigerated.
NOTE: When making the sauce by hand, it will help to have the ingredients at room temperature and to use a warm bowl. However, with electric mixers, this precaution is not necessary. Use half olive oil and half vegetable oil for the best flavor. The acidity of vinegar varies greatly, so add it sparingly to achieve a properly tart mayonnaise. You can substitute lemon juice or lime juice if desired.

If the mayonnaise does not emulsify or it curdles, you probably added the oil too quickly. To correct the problem, put a fresh egg yolk in a clean, warm bowl and beat in the broken sauce, a teaspoon at a time, until it begins to look like mayonnaise. Continue adding the broken sauce in a slow, steady stream until it is fully incorporated.

If you wish to make the sauce in a blender or food processor, use 1 whole egg for every 2 egg yolks. Place the eggs, salt, pepper, and mustard in the bowl with a small amount of vinegar and turn on the machine. Add the oil in a slow, steady stream. Continue adding the vinegar and oil as outlined above. Taste, and correct the seasoning.

≡ Anchovy Mayonnaise

═ Yield: 1 cup

1 cup mayonnaise   2 to 4 anchovy fillets, minced

In a bowl, mix the mayonnaise with the anchovies.

▶ Can be prepared several days ahead.

≡ Red Pepper and Watercress Sauce

═ Yield: ¾ cup

3 sweet red peppers   salt and pepper, to taste
½ bunch watercress   dash of Tabasco sauce
¼ cup mayonnaise

1. Preheat the broiler.

2. Broil the peppers until the skin is darkened and blistered. Put into a paper bag and let stand for about 10 minutes. Peel the peppers, cut in half, and remove and discard the seeds.

3. In a food processor, purée the peeled peppers with the watercress. If the mixture is too wet, let drain in a fine sieve or coffee filter.

4. Fold in the mayonnaise, salt, pepper, and Tabasco sauce.

▶ Can be prepared several days ahead.

≡ Jalapeño Sauce

== Yield: 1 cup

¼ cup packed parsley leaves
1 garlic clove
1 shallot
½ small jalapeño pepper, seeded
1 egg yolk
½ cup olive oil

1 teaspoon creole mustard (see Glossary)
2 tablespoons horseradish
⅓ teaspoon salt
⅛ teaspoon sugar
⅛ teaspoon Worcestershire sauce

== Yield: 4 cups

1 cup packed parsley leaves
4 garlic cloves
4 shallots
2 small jalapeño peppers, seeded
4 egg yolks
2 cups olive oil

4 teaspoons creole mustard (see Glossary)
½ cup horseradish
1⅓ teaspoons salt
½ teaspoon sugar
½ teaspoon Worcestershire sauce

1. In a food processor, finely chop the parsley, garlic, shallot(s), and jalapeño.

2. Add the egg yolk(s), one-quarter of the olive oil, and the mustard, and process until thickened. Slowly drizzle in the remaining oil.

3. Add the horseradish, salt, sugar, and Worcestershire sauce.

▶ Keeps 1 week, refrigerated.

≡ Sauce Crème Marie Rose

== Yield: 1 cup

½ cup mayonnaise
½ cup whipped cream

dash of Tabasco sauce
1 tablespoon ketchup

== Yield: 1 quart

2 cups mayonnaise
2 cups whipped cream

⅛ teaspoon Tabasco sauce
¼ cup ketchup

1. In a bowl, fold the mayonnaise and cream together with the Tabasco sauce and ketchup.

2. Chill for 30 minutes. Serve with poached seafood.

▶ Keeps about 24 hours; best freshly made and served.

≡ *Sauce Andalouse*

═ **Yield: 1½ cups**

½ cup tomato purée
2 pimientos, minced

1 cup mayonnaise
½ teaspoon paprika

═ **Yield: 1 quart**

1½ cups tomato purée
6 pimientos, minced

3 cups mayonnaise
1½ teaspoons paprika

1. In a bowl, mix the tomato purée, pimientos, mayonnaise, and paprika.
2. Store in jars.

▶ Keeps 1 week, refrigerated.

≡ *Sauce Tartare (Tartar Sauce)*

This sauce has a less-than-wonderful reputation. Too many preparers assume that it is mayonnaise mixed with a not-very-good pickle relish. Properly made with all the ingredients, it is a wonderful sauce worth serving with pride.

═ **Yield: 2 cups**

1½ cups mayonnaise
¼ cup minced cornichons
2 scallions, minced
1 anchovy fillet, minced
1 teaspoon minced parsley

1 tablespoon capers, minced
2 teaspoons Dijon mustard
1 tablespoon heavy cream
½ teaspoon lemon juice
salt and pepper, to taste

═ **Yield: 1 quart**

3 cups mayonnaise
½ cup minced cornichons
4 scallions, minced
2 anchovy fillets, minced
2 teaspoons minced parsley

2 tablespoons capers, minced
1½ tablespoons Dijon mustard
2 tablespoons heavy cream
1 teaspoon lemon juice
salt and pepper, to taste

1. In a bowl, mix the mayonnaise, cornichons, scallions, anchovies, parsley, capers, mustard, cream, lemon juice, salt, and pepper.
2. Let the flavors meld for 2 hours before serving. Serve with fried foods, especially fish, seafood, mushrooms, and zucchini.

▶ Keeps 2 weeks, refrigerated.

≡ *Sauce Verte (Green Sauce)*

═ **Yield: 1¼ cups**

1 cup mayonnaise
1 tablespoon minced parsley
1 tablespoon minced
   watercress
1 tablespoon minced chervil

1 tablespoon minced tarragon
½ tablespoon cooked, sieved
   spinach
lemon juice, to taste
salt and pepper, to taste

═ **Yield: 1¼ quarts**

1 quart mayonnaise
¼ cup minced parsley
¼ cup minced watercress
¼ cup minced chervil
¼ cup minced tarragon

2 tablespoons cooked, sieved
   spinach
lemon juice, to taste
salt and pepper, to taste

1. In a bowl, mix the mayonnaise with the parsley, watercress, chervil, tarragon, and spinach.

2. Mix well and correct the seasoning with lemon juice, salt, and pepper. Serve with cold poached fish and vegetables.

▶ Keeps 3 to 5 days, refrigerated.

≡ *Sauce Rémoulade*

This sauce is similar to tartar sauce but is not as tart.

═ **Yield: 2 cups**

2 teaspoons dry mustard
2 teaspoons lemon juice
1 teaspoon capers, minced
2 tablespoons minced dill
1 tablespoon minced parsley

½ teaspoon minced garlic
1 hard-cooked egg, minced
2 cups mayonnaise
salt and cayenne pepper, to
   taste

═ **Yield: 1 quart**

4 teaspoons dry mustard
4 teaspoons lemon juice
2 teaspoons capers, minced
¼ cup minced dill
2 tablespoons minced parsley

1 teaspoon minced garlic
2 hard-cooked eggs, minced
1 quart mayonnaise
salt and cayenne pepper, to
   taste

1. In a bowl, mix the mustard and lemon juice to a paste, and stir in the capers, dill, parsley, garlic, and egg.

2. Fold in the mayonnaise and correct the seasoning with salt and cayenne pepper. Serve with cold seafood, fritters, and croquettes.

▶ Keeps 3 to 5 days, refrigerated.

≡ *Dill Mayonnaise*

═ Yield: 1½ cups

1 cup mayonnaise	½ cup minced dill

═ Yield: 1½ quarts

1 quart mayonnaise	2 cups minced dill

1. In a bowl, mix the mayonnaise and dill.

2. Let the flavors meld for at least 30 minutes before serving.

▶ Keeps 1 week, refrigerated.

≡ *Sauce Horcher*

This delicious sauce from a famous Madrid restaurant is also very good with cold beef.

═ Yield: 2 cups

1 cup mayonnaise	2 tablespoons grated
2 tablespoons Cognac	horseradish
2 tablespoons chili sauce	2 tablespoons minced shallots
2 tablespoons lemon juice	1 tablespoon minced chives
2 tablespoons minced celery	1 tablespoon minced parsley

═ Yield: 1 quart

2 cups mayonnaise	¼ cup grated horseradish
¼ cup Cognac	¼ cup minced shallots
¼ cup chili sauce	2 tablespoons minced chives
¼ cup lemon juice	2 tablespoons minced parsley
¼ cup minced celery	

1. In a bowl, mix the mayonnaise, Cognac, chili sauce, lemon juice, celery, horseradish, shallots, chives, and parsley.
2. Let stand at least 30 minutes. Serve with cold shellfish.

▶ Keeps 4 days, refrigerated.

≡ Sauce Corail (Coral Sauce)

═ Yield: 1 cup

2 egg yolks
2 teaspoons Armagnac
2 teaspoons paprika
½ teaspoon Worcestershire
  sauce

½ teaspoon salt
pinch of pepper
¾ cup vegetable oil
⅓ cup heavy cream, whipped

═ Yield: 1 quart

8 egg yolks
3 tablespoons Armagnac
3 tablespoons paprika
1 teaspoon Worcestershire
  sauce

1 teaspoon salt
¼ teaspoon pepper
3 cups vegetable oil
1 cup heavy cream, whipped

1. In a food processor, process the egg yolks, Armagnac, paprika, Worcestershire sauce, salt, and pepper until mixed.
2. Add the oil in a slow, steady stream until thickened.
3. Remove the sauce to a bowl and fold in the cream.
4. Correct the seasoning with salt and pepper. Serve with cold shellfish.

▶ Keeps 2 days, refrigerated.

—— Hollandaise Sauces ——

≡ Sauce Hollandaise

═ Yield: 1 cup

3 egg yolks
1 tablespoon water
½ cup butter, softened

salt, to taste
lemon juice, to taste

═ Yield: 1 quart

12 egg yolks

¼ cup water

2 cups butter, softened

salt, to taste

lemon, juice to taste

1. In a heavy saucepan, whisk the egg yolks and water over medium heat until light and fluffy.

2. Beat in the butter in bits, whisking constantly until the butter is fully incorporated. If the sauce gets too hot and starts to look as if it is going to turn into scrambled eggs, remove from the heat and whisk in a bit of cold butter.

3. When all the butter has been incorporated, strain into a clean container and correct the seasoning with salt and lemon juice.

▶ Keeps 2 to 3 hours over warm water.

NOTE: The sauce can be kept over warm water. Use unsalted butter in the sauce so you can control the amount of salt. If the sauce starts to break, whisk in 1 tablespoon of boiling water. If this does not work, whisk in 1 ice cube. If the sauce does break, place 1 egg yolk in a warm bowl and whisk in the separated sauce, a teaspoon at a time, until the mixture emulsifies. Continue adding the separated sauce until it is all incorporated.

═ *Processor or Blender Hollandaise*

═ Yield: 1 cup

4 egg yolks

2 tablespoons lemon juice

dash of Tabasco sauce, optional

½ cup hot melted butter

salt and pepper, to taste

═ Yield: 1 quart

16 egg yolks

½ cup lemon juice

Tabasco sauce, optional

2 cups hot melted butter

salt and pepper, to taste

1. In a food processor, place the egg yolks, lemon juice, and Tabasco sauce. With the machine running, add the butter in a slow, steady stream.

2. When the butter is incorporated, season to taste with salt and pepper.

3. Remove the sauce to a double boiler and keep warm.

▶ Keeps 2 to 3 hours over warm water.

☰ Sauce Maltaise
(Orange-Flavored Hollandaise Sauce)

The pinkish juice of blood oranges colors this sauce a rosy shade. If blood oranges are not available, adding food coloring gives the color, if not the flavor, of these oranges.

═ Yield: 1 cup

1 cup hollandaise sauce
  (page 54)
3 tablespoons orange juice

½ teaspoon grated orange rind
red food coloring, optional

═ Yield: 1¼ quarts

1 quart hollandaise sauce
  (page 54)
¾ cup orange juice

2 teaspoons grated orange rind
red food coloring, optional

1. Prepare the hollandaise sauce.

2. Fold in the orange juice, orange rind, and just enough food coloring to tint the sauce a delicate pink. Serve with steamed asparagus, shrimp, or scallops.

▶ Keeps 2 to 3 hours over warm water.

NOTE: If the sauce is to be held for any length of time, add the food coloring shortly before serving. Food coloring intensifies in the air, so beware, or a very delicate pink could turn into a rather bright orange.

☰ Mustard Hollandaise

═ Yield: 1 cup

1 tablespoon Dijon mustard, or
  to taste

1 cup hollandaise sauce
  (page 54)

═ Yield: 1¼ quarts

¼ cup Dijon mustard, or to
  taste

1 quart hollandaise sauce
  (page 54)

Fold the mustard into the hollandaise sauce. Serve with seafood, beef, or lamb.

≡ *Sauce Paloise (Minted Hollandaise Sauce)*

═ **Yield: 1 cup**

1 cup hollandaise sauce
(page 54)
1 tablespoon mint infusion
(recipe follows)

1½ teaspoons minced mint, or
to taste

═ **Yield: 1 quart**

1 quart hollandaise sauce
(page 54)
¼ cup mint infusion (recipe
follows)

2 tablespoons minced mint, or
to taste

1. In a bowl, mix the hollandaise and mint infusion and let steep for
10 minutes.
2. Fold in the fresh mint just before serving. Serve with lamb.

▶ Keeps 2 to 3 hours over warm water.

≡ *Mint Infusion*

═ **Yield: 1 tablespoon**

4 tablespoons water
2 tablespoons vinegar

2 tablespoons minced mint

═ **Yield: ¼ cup**

1 cup water
½ cup vinegar

½ cup minced mint

In a saucepan, simmer the water, vinegar, and mint until the liquid
is reduced. Strain.

▶ Keeps 2 days.

≡ *Sauce Béarnaise*

═ **Yield: 1 cup**

2 tablespoons minced tarragon
2 tablespoons minced chervil
2 shallots, minced
¼ cup tarragon vinegar
¼ cup white wine

3 egg yolks
1 tablespoon water
½ cup butter
salt, to taste
cayenne pepper, to taste

=== **Yield: 1 quart**

½ cup minced tarragon	12 egg yolks
½ cup minced chervil	¼ cup water
1 cup minced shallots	2 cups butter
1 cup tarragon vinegar	salt, to taste
1 cup white wine	cayenne pepper, to taste

1. In a small saucepan, simmer half the tarragon, half the chervil, shallots, vinegar, and wine until reduced to a thick paste. Let cool slightly.

2. Place the tarragon paste in a saucepan and add the egg yolks and water. Over medium heat, whisking constantly, beat the mixture until it starts to thicken.

3. Whisk in the butter bit by bit until fully incorporated.

4. Strain the sauce through a fine sieve.

5. Correct the seasoning with the salt and cayenne, and fold in the remaining tarragon and chervil.

▶ Keeps 2 to 3 hours over warm water.

≡ *Sauce Choron (Tomato-Flavored Béarnaise Sauce)*

=== **Yield: 1¼ cups**
¼ cup hot tomato purée
1 cup béarnaise sauce
(page 57)

=== **Yield: 1¼ quarts**
1 cup hot tomato purée
1 quart béarnaise sauce
(page 57)

Stir the hot, but not boiling, tomato purée into the béarnaise sauce.

▶ Keeps 2 to 3 hours over warm water.

—— *Béchamel Sauces* ——

≡ *Sauce Béchamel*

= Yield: 2 cups

2 tablespoons butter	¼ teaspoon salt
1 tablespoon minced onion	3 white peppercorns
4 tablespoons flour	sprig of parsley
3 cups milk, scalded	pinch of grated nutmeg

= Yield: 1 quart

4 tablespoons butter	½ teaspoon salt
2 tablespoons minced onion	6 white peppercorns
½ cup flour	2 sprigs of parsley
6 cups milk, scalded	⅛ teaspoon grated nutmeg

1. In a saucepan, melt the butter and sweat the onion until soft.

2. Stir in the flour, and cook the roux until it just starts to turn golden and is foamy.

3. Add the milk, whisking constantly, until the mixture is thick and smooth.

4. Stir in the salt, peppercorns, parsley, and nutmeg, and simmer the sauce over low heat for about 30 minutes or until reduced to two-thirds of the original quantity.

5. Strain through a very fine sieve.

▶ Keeps 4 days, refrigerated; can be frozen.

≡ *Sauce Mornay (Cheese Sauce)*

This is the most common use of béchamel sauce.

= Yield: 2 cups

3 egg yolks	2 tablespoons butter
½ cup heavy cream	2 tablespoons grated Gruyère
2 cups hot béchamel sauce	cheese
(preceding recipe)	

= Yield: 1 quart

6 egg yolks	4 tablespoons butter
1 cup heavy cream	4 tablespoons grated Gruyère
4 cups hot béchamel sauce	cheese
(preceding recipe)	

1. In a bowl, mix the egg yolks and cream.

2. Add one-quarter of the béchamel sauce, whisking constantly, to warm the mixture, then turn the egg yolk mixture into the remaining béchamel sauce.

3. Set over medium heat and cook, stirring, until the sauce just reaches the boiling point.

4. Remove from heat and stir in the butter and cheese.

▶ Can be reheated; do not freeze.

≡ *Béchamel Sauce for Croquettes*

═ **Yield: 1 cup**

2 tablespoons butter	salt and white pepper, to taste
3 tablespoons flour	2 eggs, lightly beaten
1 cup hot milk	

═ **Yield: 1 quart**

½ cup butter	salt and white pepper, to taste
¾ cup flour	8 eggs, lightly beaten
1 quart hot milk	

1. In a saucepan, melt the butter, stir in the flour, and cook until the roux is foamy and just starts to turn golden.

2. Add the milk and cook, stirring, until thickened and smooth.

3. Simmer, stirring often, for 12 to 15 minutes or until very thick.

4. Correct seasoning with salt and pepper.

5. Stir about one-quarter of the hot sauce into the eggs to warm them.

6. Return the egg mixture to the béchamel and cook, stirring, until it just reaches the boiling point. Do not boil.

▶ Keeps 2 to 3 days, refrigerated; can be frozen.

≡ *Curried Béchamel Sauce I*

═ **Yield: 2 cups**

1 teaspoon butter	⅛ teaspoon turmeric
1 garlic clove, crushed	⅛ teaspoon ground cloves
1 teaspoon minced shallot	⅛ teaspoon cinnamon
1 teaspoon minced green pepper	2 cups béchamel sauce (page 59)
1 teaspoon curry powder, or to taste	

= **Yield: 1 quart**

2 teaspoons butter
2 garlic cloves, crushed
2 teaspoons minced shallots
2 teaspoons minced green
 pepper
2 teaspoons curry powder, or to
 taste

¼ teaspoon turmeric
¼ teaspoon ground cloves
¼ teaspoon cinnamon
1 quart béchamel sauce
 (page 59)

1. In a skillet, melt the butter and sauté the garlic, shallots, green pepper, curry powder, turmeric, cloves, and cinnamon for 2 to 3 minutes or until the vegetables are soft and the spices fragrant.

2. Stir spice mixture into the béchamel.

▶ Keeps 2 to 3 days, refrigerated; can be frozen.

≡ *Curried Béchamel Sauce II*

= **Yield: 1 cup**

1 large onion, minced
3 tablespoons olive oil
2 tablespoons curry powder
pinch of saffron

salt and pepper, to taste
1 cup béchamel sauce
 (page 59)

= **Yield: 1¼ quarts**

4 large onions, minced
¾ cup olive oil
¼ cup curry powder
½ teaspoon crushed saffron
 threads

salt and pepper, to taste
1 quart béchamel sauce
 (page 59)

1. In a saucepan, cook the onion in the olive oil over low heat for 20 minutes or until very soft.

2. Stir in the curry powder, saffron, salt, and pepper, and cook 5 minutes longer until very fragrant.

3. Stir in the béchamel sauce and strain through a food mill.

4. Return to the heat and correct the seasoning.

▶ Keeps 3 days, refrigerated; can be frozen.

—— *Velouté Sauces* ——

≡ *Sauce Velouté*

= **Yield: 2 cups**

2 tablespoons butter	3 white peppercorns
¼ cup flour	salt, to taste
3 cups hot chicken, veal, or fish	sprig of parsley
stock	½ cup chopped mushrooms

= **Yield: 1 quart**

¼ cup butter	1 teaspoon white peppercorns
½ cup flour	salt, to taste
6 cups hot chicken, veal, or fish	2 sprigs of parsley
stock	1 cup chopped mushrooms

1. In a saucepan, melt the butter, stir in the flour, and cook until the roux is foamy and just starts to turn golden.

2. Gradually add the stock and cook, stirring, until it comes to a boil.

3. Add the peppercorns, salt, parsley, and mushrooms; simmer, stirring often, until reduced by one-third to two-thirds of the original quantity.

4. Strain through a fine sieve.

▶ Keeps 5 days, refrigerated; can be frozen.

≡ *Sauce Villeroi*

This sauce is used as a base for croquettes.

= **Yield: 1 cup**

1½ cups velouté sauce (preceding recipe)	1 egg yolk, lightly beaten

= **Yield: 1 quart**

6 cups velouté sauce (preceding recipe)	4 egg yolks, lightly beaten

1. In a saucepan, reduce the velouté by one-third.

2. Add one-quarter of the mixture to the egg yolk(s) and mix well.

3. Return the egg yolk mixture to the body of the sauce, and cook over medium heat, stirring, until it just reaches the boiling point.

4. Strain through a fine sieve immediately. Cool before using.

▶ Keeps 4 days, refrigerated.

——— *Tomato Sauces* ———

≡ *Simple Tomato Sauce*

= Yield: 2 to 3 cups

1 tablespoon minced onion	¼ teaspoon dried oregano
¼ teaspoon crushed garlic	1 teaspoon minced basil
2 cups tomato purée	1 cup heavy cream, optional

= Yield: 4 to 6 cups

2 tablespoons minced onion	½ teaspoon dried oregano
½ teaspoon crushed garlic	2 teaspoons minced basil
4 cups tomato purée	2 cups heavy cream, optional

1. In a saucepan, sauté the onion and garlic in the butter until soft but not brown.

2. Add the tomato purée, oregano, and basil and simmer 15 minutes.

3. Strain and add the cream, if desired.

► Keeps 3 days, refrigerated; can be frozen.

≡ *Uncooked Tomato Sauce*

= Yield: 2 cups

1¼ pounds tomatoes, peeled and seeded	½ teaspoon salt
	½ teaspoon pepper
1 teaspoon tomato paste	1 tablespoon minced tarragon
4 teaspoons red wine vinegar	1 tablespoon minced parsley
¼ cup olive oil	

= Yield: 1 quart

2½ pounds tomatoes, peeled and seeded	1 teaspoon salt
	1 teaspoon pepper
2 teaspoons tomato paste	2 tablespoons minced tarragon
3 tablespoons red wine vinegar	2 tablespoons minced parsley
½ cup olive oil	

1. Force the tomato pulp through a sieve.

2. Just before serving, whisk in the tomato paste and vinegar, beat in the oil a little at a time, and season with salt, pepper, tarragon, and parsley.

► Keeps 2 days, refrigerated.

NOTE: Substitute fresh basil for the tarragon, if desired.

≡ *Tomato Sauce*

=== Yield: 2 cups
2 pounds ripe tomatoes
¼ pound butter
1 onion, peeled and cut in half

salt and pepper, to taste
¼ teaspoon sugar

=== Yield: 1 quart
4 pounds ripe tomatoes
½ pound butter
2 onions, peeled and cut in half

salt and pepper, to taste
½ teaspoon sugar

1. Cut the tomatoes in half and cook, covered, for 10 minutes over medium heat.

2. Purée the tomatoes through a food mill into a saucepan. Add the butter, onion, salt, pepper, and sugar and simmer slowly, uncovered, for 45 minutes.

3. Correct the seasoning and discard the onion.

▶ Keeps 3 days, refrigerated; can be frozen.

≡ *Fresh Tomato Sauce*

=== Yield: 3 cups
3 tablespoons butter
1 cup minced onion
1 garlic clove, crushed
1½ pounds tomatoes, peeled, seeded, and chopped

½ bay leaf
½ teaspoon dried thyme
1 dried chili pepper
salt and pepper, to taste

=== Yield: 6 cups
6 tablespoons butter
2 cups minced onion
2 garlic cloves, crushed
3 pounds tomatoes, peeled, seeded, and chopped

1 bay leaf
1 teaspoon dried thyme
1 dried chili pepper
salt and pepper, to taste

1. In a saucepan, melt a third of the butter and sauté the onions until soft but not brown.

2. Add the garlic, tomatoes, bay leaf, thyme, chili, salt, and pepper and simmer, stirring occasionally, for about 15 minutes.

3. Stir in the remaining butter and cook until the tomatoes are soft but still have some shape.

▶ Keeps 2 to 3 days, refrigerated; can be frozen. For a smoother sauce, strain through a food mill.

≡ *Creole Sauce*

═ **Yield: 2 cups**

½ cup diced green pepper
½ cup diced onion
1 tablespoon butter
¾ cup chicken stock
¾ cup peeled, seeded, and
  diced tomatoes
½ cup tomato juice
1 bay leaf
1 teaspoon dried thyme leaves
¼ teaspoon paprika

1 teaspoon cornstarch,
  dissolved in 1½ tablespoons
  water
¼ teaspoon hot green pepper
  sauce
¼ teaspoon creole seasoning
  (see note)
salt, to taste
red pepper flakes, to taste

═ **Yield: 6 cups**

2 cups diced green pepper
2 cups diced onion
¼ cup butter
3 cups chicken stock
3 cups peeled, seeded, and
  diced tomatoes
2 cups tomato juice
2 bay leaves
1 tablespoon dried thyme leaves

1 teaspoon paprika
4 teaspoons cornstarch,
  dissolved in ⅓ cup water
1 teaspoon hot green pepper
  sauce
1 teaspoon creole seasoning
  (see note)
salt, to taste
red pepper flakes, to taste

1. In a saucepan, melt the butter over low heat and cook the pepper and onion until soft, but not brown.

2. Add the stock, tomatoes, tomato juice, bay leaf, thyme, and paprika. Simmer 45 minutes, stirring often.

3. Add the cornstarch, hot green pepper sauce, creole seasoning, salt, and red pepper flakes. Simmer 10 minutes and purée in a blender.

▶ Keeps 1 week, refrigerated; can be frozen.

NOTE: To make creole seasoning, combine ¼ cup salt, 1 tablespoon granulated garlic, 1 tablespoon pepper, 1 tablespoon paprika, ¾ teaspoon granulated onion, ¼ teaspoon cayenne pepper, ¼ teaspoon dried thyme, and ¼ teaspoon dried oregano. Mix well.

—— *Other Sauces* ——

≡ *Creamy Tartar Sauce*

This is not a true tartar sauce, since the whipped cream base gives a slightly different finish.

= Yield: 1 cup

2 tablespoons minced cornichons	½ teaspoon paprika
2 tablespoons capers, minced	½ cup minced parsley
1 teaspoon Dijon mustard	½ cup heavy cream
	salt and pepper, to taste

In a bowl, mix the cornichons, capers, mustard, paprika, and parsley. Whip the cream until stiff and fold into the cornichon mixture. Adjust seasoning with salt and pepper, if required.

▶ Keeps 24 hours, refrigerated.

≡ *Curry Sauce*

= Yield: 1 cup

2 tablespoons butter	½ cup chicken stock
2 tablespoons minced onion	½ cup heavy cream
2 tablespoons minced tart apple	1 tablespoon sherry, or to taste
1½ teaspoons curry powder, or to taste	¼ teaspoon salt
4 teaspoons flour	¼ teaspoon pepper

= Yield: 1 quart

½ cup butter	2 cups chicken stock
½ cup minced onion	2 cups heavy cream
½ cup minced tart apple	2 tablespoons sherry, or to taste
2 teaspoons curry powder, or to taste	1¼ teaspoons salt
⅓ cup flour	1 teaspoon pepper

1. In a saucepan, melt the butter and sauté the onion and apple with the curry powder until the apple is soft.

2. Stir in the flour and cook, stirring, for 5 minutes without browning.

3. Stir in the chicken stock and cook until thickened.

4. Strain, pressing on the vegetables to extract as much flavor as possible.

5. Stir in the cream and sherry and simmer 5 minutes.
6. Correct the seasoning with the salt and pepper.

▶ Keeps 4 days, refrigerated; can be frozen.

≡ Sauce Mona Lisa

= **Yield: 1¼ cups**

1 teaspoon paprika	2 tablespoons heavy cream,
1 teaspoon grated horseradish	whipped
1 teaspoon dry mustard	salt and pepper, to taste
1 cup sour cream	

= **Yield: 1¼ quarts**

1 tablespoon paprika	1 quart sour cream
1½ tablespoons grated	½ cup heavy cream, whipped
horseradish	salt and pepper, to taste
1 tablespoon dry mustard	

1. In a bowl, stir the paprika, horseradish, and mustard into the sour cream until well mixed.
2. Fold in the heavy cream and correct the seasoning with salt and pepper.

▶ Keeps 24 hours, refrigerated.

≡ Mignonette (Vinegar Pepper Sauce for Shellfish)

= **Yield: ½ cup**

½ cup mild vinegar	¼ teaspoon salt
1½ tablespoons minced shallots	pinch of white pepper

= **Yield: 1 quart**

1 quart mild vinegar	2 teaspoons salt
¾ cup minced shallots	½ teaspoon white pepper

1. In a bowl, mix the vinegar, shallots, salt, and pepper.
2. Let the flavors meld for at least 30 minutes. Serve with raw oysters and clams.

▶ Keeps 3 days, refrigerated.

≡ *Pesto Sauce*

In recent years, this sauce has become abused by overuse. It has been put on or into every sort of dish. It was designed to complement pasta and can be used successfully with vegetables, but do use it sparingly. It has a strong flavor that often overwhelms the main ingredient.

≡ Yield: 1 cup
1 cup firmly packed basil leaves
1 large garlic clove, chopped
½ cup pine nuts

½ cup grated Parmesan cheese
¼ cup olive oil, approximately
salt, to taste

≡ Yield: 1 quart
1 quart firmly packed basil
  leaves
4 large garlic cloves, chopped
1½ cups pine nuts

2 cups grated Parmesan cheese
1 cup olive oil, approximately
salt, to taste

1. In a food processor, purée the basil and garlic, stopping to push the mixture down several times.
2. Add the pine nuts and cheese, and continue blending until almost smooth.
3. With the motor running, add the oil in a steady stream until the pesto is the consistency of mayonnaise. Add salt to taste. Serve as a dip, as a stuffing for vegetables, or as a flavoring ingredient.

▶ Keeps 2 days, refrigerated; can be frozen, but is best fresh.
NOTE: A blender makes a smoother sauce than a processor.

≡ *Salsa (Mexican Tomato Chili Sauce)*

In the last few years, the interest in Southwestern cooking has made this a standard at many parties. There are many variations, but this is the simplest in preparation and flavoring.

≡ Yield: 1 cup
2 large ripe tomatoes, diced
1 jalapeño pepper, seeded and
  minced
1 tablespoon minced fresh
  coriander (cilantro)

salt and pepper, to taste
2 ice cubes

＝ Yield: 1 quart

8 large ripe tomatoes, diced

2 jalapeño peppers, seeded and minced

¼ cup minced fresh coriander (cilantro)

salt and pepper, to taste

6 ice cubes

1. In a bowl, mix the tomatoes, jalapeños, coriander, salt, pepper, and ice cubes.

2. Stir until the ice cubes melt. Serve very cold with tortilla chips, broiled meats, or shellfish.

▶ Keeps 2 days, refrigerated.

Noᴛᴇ: People's tolerance for spicy foods varies greatly. A spicy dish to one can seem mild to another. Take care when adding chilies to this dish. There should be no question that the food is hot, but do not make it too hot.

＝ *Sauce Vierge (Cold Tomato-Herb Sauce)*

This is a French version of salsa. Use it to top broiled fish or as a dip for vegetables or toasted pita bread.

＝ Yield: 1¼ cups

1 cup tomatoes, peeled, seeded, and chopped

1 garlic clove, crushed

1 teaspoon minced chervil

1 teaspoon minced parsley

1 teaspoon minced tarragon

1 teaspoon coriander seeds, crushed

3 tablespoons extra virgin olive oil

salt and pepper, to taste

＝ Yield: 1¼ quarts

1 quart tomatoes, peeled, seeded, and chopped

4 garlic cloves, crushed

1½ tablespoons minced chervil

1½ tablespoons minced parsley

1½ tablespoons minced tarragon

1 tablespoon coriander seeds, crushed

¾ cup extra virgin olive oil

salt and pepper, to taste

In a bowl, mix the tomatoes, garlic, chervil, parsley, tarragon, coriander, oil, salt, and pepper. Serve at room temperature.

▶ Keeps 2 days, refrigerated.

NOTE: This sauce is best if freshly made and allowed to sit for 30 minutes. If you must refrigerate it, let it come to room temperature before serving.

≡ *Pungent Fruit Sauce*

This sauce is wonderful with deep-fried seafood and can be served with Chinese appetizers in place of sweet and sour sauce or duck sauce.

=== **Yield: 1¼ cups**

¾ cup orange marmalade
¼ cup lemon juice
2 tablespoons orange juice
2 teaspoons grated horseradish

1 teaspoon minced gingerroot
½ teaspoon salt
½ teaspoon dry mustard

=== **Yield: 1¼ quarts**

3 cups orange marmalade
1 cup lemon juice
½ cup orange juice
3 tablespoons grated
  horseradish

1½ tablespoons minced
  gingerroot
1½ teaspoons salt
2 teaspoons dry mustard

1. In a food processor, blend the marmalade, lemon juice, and orange juice until smooth.

2. Remove to a bowl and stir in the horseradish, ginger, salt, and mustard.

3. Let flavors meld for at least 30 minutes before serving.

▶ Keeps 2 days, refrigerated.

≡ *Yogurt Garlic Mint Sauce*

=== **Yield: 1 cup**

1 cup plain yogurt
2 tablespoons minced mint

2 tablespoons lemon juice
1 teaspoon minced garlic

=== **Yield: 1 quart**

1 quart plain yogurt
⅓ cup minced mint

¼ cup lemon juice
1½ tablespoons minced garlic

1. In a bowl, mix the yogurt, mint, lemon juice, and garlic.
2. Let mature in the refrigerator overnight. Serve with broiled lamb, beef, or lamb or beef meatballs.

▶ Keeps 3 days, refrigerated.

Variation: Yogurt Cucumber Sauce
Omit the garlic from the preceding recipe and add ½ cup (2 *cups*) finely chopped cucumber.

≡ *Lemon Dill Sauce*

══ **Yield: 1½ cups**

3 egg yolks	1 cup chicken stock
1 tablespoon arrowroot	1 tablespoon lemon juice, or
1 teaspoon salt	to taste
pinch of cayenne pepper	2 tablespoons minced dill

══ **Yield: 1½ quarts**

12 egg yolks	1 quart chicken stock
¼ cup arrowroot	¼ cup lemon juice, or to taste
1 tablespoon salt	½ cup minced dill
¼ teaspoon cayenne pepper	

1. In a saucepan, mix the egg yolks, arrowroot, salt, and cayenne.
2. Stir in the stock and cook over moderate heat, stirring until the mixture reaches 185°F and is thick enough to coat the back of a spoon. Do not let it boil.
3. Stir in the lemon juice and dill. Correct the seasoning with lemon juice, salt, and pepper. It should have a tart lemon flavor.
4. Serve with chicken or fish croquettes or fish balls.

▶ Keeps 4 to 6 hours. Can be reheated.

≡ *Avgolemonou (Egg Lemon Sauce)*

This sauce is the Greek version of hollandaise sauce. It requires care to make, but is so delicious that it is worth the effort.

══ **Yield: 1 cup**

2 eggs	½ cup hot chicken or fish stock
3 tablespoons lemon juice	1 tablespoon melted butter

═ **Yield: 1 quart**

8 eggs

¾ cup lemon juice

2 cups hot chicken or fish stock

¼ cup melted butter

1. In a saucepan, beat the eggs until light and foamy. Beat in the lemon juice and stock.

2. Place the pan over medium heat and cook, beating constantly, adding the butter gradually until the sauce is thick enough to coat the back of a spoon.

3. Serve warm with lamb meatballs or fish balls. Sauce may be kept warm over hot, not simmering, water.

▶ Keeps 4 to 6 hours over warm water.

═ *Garlic Butter*

═ **Yield: 1 cup**

1 cup butter

1 tablespoon minced shallots

2 garlic cloves, crushed

1 tablespoon minced parsley

salt and pepper, to taste

═ **Yield: 1 quart**

2 pounds butter

¼ cup minced shallots

8 garlic cloves, crushed

¼ cup minced parsley

salt and pepper, to taste

In a food processor, cream the butter. Add the shallots, garlic, parsley, salt, and pepper and process until combined. Chill until ready to use.

▶ Keeps 3 days, refrigerated.

—— *Asian Dipping Sauces* ——

For more information on the Asian ingredients specified in many of these recipes, refer to the Glossary of Ingredients following Chapter 18.

═ *Cantonese Salt or Chinese Pepper-Salt*

═ **Yield: 1 cup**

1 cup salt

1 teaspoon ground Szechuan
   pepper (see Glossary)

1. In an ungreased skillet, heat the salt until it turns brown. Add the pepper, mix well, and let cool.

2. Serve as a dip for shrimp balls, pearl balls, and other dim sum.

▶ Keeps indefinitely.

☰ *Chinese Mustard*

There is no mystery to Chinese mustard. It is just mustard powder mixed with a cold liquid until the desired consistency is reached. (For dipping, make this mustard the consistency of heavy cream.) I prefer to use beer as the liquid, but cold water or white wine will also work well. Make it fresh for each occasion, mixing what you need as you need it.

☰ **Yield: ¼ cup**

3 tablespoons dry mustard powder	1 to 2 tablespoons cold beer, white wine, or water

In a small bowl, mix the mustard with enough liquid to make a fluid mixture. Let it stand for 10 minutes to develop flavor.

▶ Keeps 1 day, refrigerated.

☰ *Wasabi*

wasabi powder	water

In a bowl, mix the wasabi with enough water to make a mixture about as fluid as Chinese mustard (above).

▶ Keeps 1 day, refrigerated.

☰ *Chekiang Vinegar Sauce*

☰ **Yield: ¼ cup**

⅓ cup malt vinegar	1 tablespoon soy sauce

In a bowl, mix the vineger and soy sauce.

▶ Keeps indefinitely.

≡ *Ginger Soy Dip*

═ Yield: ¼ cup

¼ cup light or dark soy sauce   2 teaspoons minced gingerroot

In a bowl, mix the soy sauce and ginger and let stand for 20 minutes.

▶ Keeps 2 days.

≡ *Garlic Soy Dip*

═ Yield: ¼ cup

2 garlic cloves, crushed   ¼ cup soy sauce

In a bowl, mix the garlic and soy sauce and let stand for 30 minutes.

▶ Keeps 2 days.

≡ *Sesame Soy Dip*

═ Yield: ¼ cup

1 tablespoon peanut oil   ¼ cup soy sauce
1 teaspoon Asian sesame oil

In a bowl, mix the peanut oil, sesame oil, and soy sauce.

▶ Keeps indefinitely.

≡ *Vinegar Garlic Dipping Sauce*

═ Yield: ¾ cup

½ cup soy sauce   1½ teaspoons Asian sesame oil
2 tablespoons Chinese black   1 tablespoon minced garlic
  vinegar

In a bowl, mix the soy sauce, vinegar, sesame oil, and garlic. Let stand for 30 minutes.

▶ Keeps 2 days.

≡ Spicy Chinese Dipping Sauce

═ Yield: ¾ cup

½ cup soy sauce
2 tablespoons Chinese black
vinegar

1 tablespoon chili oil
1 tablespoon minced garlic
1 tablespoon minced gingerroot

In a bowl, mix the soy sauce, vinegar, chili oil, garlic, and gingerroot. Let stand for 20 minutes.

▶ Keeps 2 days.

≡ Dipping Sauce for Fried Foods

═ Yield: ½ cup

¼ cup soy sauce
2 tablespoons honey
2 tablespoons dry sherry

½ teaspoon salt
pinch of pepper
1 garlic clove, minced

═ Yield: 3 cups

2 cups soy sauce
½ cup honey
½ cup dry sherry

2 teaspoons salt
¼ teaspoon pepper
4 garlic cloves, minced

1. In a saucepan, mix the soy sauce, honey, sherry, salt, pepper, and garlic. Bring just to a boil.

2. Serve warm as a dip for deep-fried dim sum and other deep-fried foods.

▶ Keeps 2 days, refrigerated. Can be reheated.

≡ Sesame Dipping Sauce

This is the original of the many versions of peanut sauces. The sesame paste tastes remarkably like peanut butter. This sauce is not very spicy.

═ Yield: 1 cup

¼ cup sesame paste (see
Glossary)
3 tablespoons cold water
2 tablespoons chili oil
3 tablespoons light soy sauce
3 tablespoons rice vinegar

2 teaspoons sugar
salt, to taste
¼ cup vegetable oil
2 tablespoons minced garlic
1 tablespoon Asian sesame oil

= **Yield: 1 quart**

1 cup sesame paste	2 tablespoons sugar
(see Glossary)	salt, to taste
¾ cup cold water	1 cup vegetable oil
½ cup chili oil	½ cup minced garlic
¾ cup light soy sauce	¼ cup Asian sesame oil
¾ cup rice vinegar	

* **1.** In a bowl, mix the sesame paste with the water. Stir in the chili oil, soy sauce, vinegar, sugar, salt, vegetable oil, garlic, and sesame oil. Mix well.
2. Use as a dip for broiled meats.

▶ Keeps 3 to 4 days, refrigerated.

≡ *Thai Spring Roll Dipping Sauce*

The sugar helps to offset some of the fire in this sauce.

= **Yield: 1½ cups**

1 cup sugar	1 teaspoon salt
½ cup water	2 teaspoons chili paste with
½ cup white vinegar	garlic
1 tablespoon minced garlic	

= **Yield: 6 cups**

4 cups sugar	4 teaspoons salt
2 cups water	3 tablespoons chili paste with
2 cups white vinegar	garlic
¼ cup minced garlic	

In a saucepan, simmer the sugar, water, vinegar, garlic, and salt for 20 minutes. Remove from the heat and add the chili paste.

▶ Keeps 1 week, refrigerated. Serve at room temperature.

≡ *Sate Sauce*

= **Yield: ¾ cup**

¼ cup butter	1 teaspoon sambal oelek (see
½ cup ketjap manis	Glossary) or ½ teaspoon
(see Glossary)	Tabasco sauce
1 tablespoon lemon juice	salt and pepper, to taste
grated rind of 1 lemon	

═ **Yield: 2¼ cups**

¾ cup butter

1½ cups ketjap manis
(see Glossary)

3 tablespoons lemon juice

grated rind of 3 lemons

1 tablespoon sambal oelek (see
Glossary) or 1½ tablespoons
Tabasco sauce

salt and pepper, to taste

In a saucepan, simmer the butter, ketjap, lemon juice, lemon rind, sambal oelek, salt, and pepper for 3 minutes.

▶ Can be prepared a week in advance and reheated.

═ *Sweet and Sour Sauce I*
_____

═ **Yield: 2½ cups**

1 cup sugar

¾ cup white vinegar

½ cup water

¾ cup pineapple juice

1½ tablespoons cornstarch mixed
with 3 tablespoons water

½ teaspoon red food coloring,
optional

═ **Yield: 1¼ quarts**

4 cups sugar

3 cups white vinegar

2 cups water

3 cups pineapple juice

4 tablespoons cornstarch mixed
with ¾ cup water

2 teaspoons red food coloring,
optional

1. In a saucepan, simmer the sugar, vinegar, water, and pineapple juice, stirring until the sugar dissolves.

2. In a bowl, mix the cornstarch and remaining water and stir into the sauce. Stir in the food coloring. Simmer until thickened and clear.

3. Serve with broiled meat and deep-fried fish.

▶ Keeps 3 days, refrigerated. Can be reheated.

NOTE: Taste this sauce and adjust the seasoning for sweet and sour. If you are using the red food coloring, add it judiciously to bring about a rosy-colored sauce rather than a bright red one. In much of Asia, red is the color of luck and happiness, but you can omit it if you prefer.

≡ *Sweet and Sour Sauce II*

═ Yield: 1½ cups

6 tablespoons ketchup
6 tablespoons water
6 tablespoons sugar
2 tablespoons rice vinegar

2 teaspoons soy sauce
2 teaspoons salt
1 teaspoon Asian sesame oil
2 teaspoons cornstarch

═ Yield: 1½ quarts

3 cups ketchup
3 cups water
3 cups sugar
½ cup rice vinegar

3 tablespoons soy sauce
2 tablespoons salt
1 tablespoon Asian sesame oil
2½ tablespoons cornstarch

1. In a saucepan, bring the ketchup, water, sugar, vinegar, soy sauce, salt, and sesame oil to a boil.

2. In a small bowl, mix the cornstarch and enough water to make a thin slurry. Add to the simmering liquid and cook, stirring until thickened and clear.

3. Serve with broiled meats and deep-fried fish.

▶ Keeps 3 to 4 days, refrigerated. Can be frozen.

≡ *Nuoc Cham (Vietnamese Dipping Sauce)*

Serve with Vietnamese spring rolls and other fried Asian hors d'oeuvre.

═ Yield: ¾ cup

¼ cup nuoc mam or nam pla
  (see Glossary)
¼ cup water
3 tablespoons lime juice

2 tablespoons white vinegar
2 tablespoons sugar
1 garlic clove, crushed
⅛ teaspoon cayenne pepper

═ Yield: 3 cups

1 cup nuoc mam or nam pla
  (see Glossary)
1 cup water
¾ cup lime juice

½ cup white vinegar
½ cup sugar
4 garlic cloves, crushed
½ teaspoon cayenne pepper

In a bowl, mix the nuoc mam, water, lime juice, vinegar, sugar, garlic, and cayenne pepper until the sugar dissolves.

▶ Keeps 1 week, refrigerated.

≡ *Hoisin-Peanut Sauce*

═ Yield: 1½ cups

¾ cup dry-roasted peanuts
⅔ cup chicken stock
½ cup hoisin sauce

4 garlic cloves
1½ tablespoons white vinegar
1 tablespoon sugar

═ Yield: 6 cups

3 cups dry-roasted peanuts
2⅔ cups chicken stock
2 cups hoisin sauce

½ cup garlic cloves
⅓ cup white vinegar
¼ cup sugar

1. In a food processor, chop the nuts to a fine meal.

2. With the motor running, add the chicken stock, hoisin sauce, garlic, vinegar, and sugar, and process to a paste.

▶ Keeps 1 week, refrigerated.

NOTE: The peanuts should retain some of their texture.

≡ *Vietnamese Mint Dipping Sauce*

═ Yield: ¾ cup

⅓ cup mint leaves, lightly
 packed
½ serrano chili, seeded
2 garlic cloves
3½ tablespoons lemon juice
2 tablespoons water

2 tablespoons white vinegar
2 tablespoons light corn syrup
1½ tablespoons nuoc mam or
 nam pla (see Glossary)
1 tablespoon sugar

═ Yield: 3 cups

1⅓ cups mint leaves, lightly
 packed
2 serrano chilies, seeded
8 garlic cloves
1 cup lemon juice
½ cup water

½ cup white vinegar
½ cup light corn syrup
⅓ cup nuoc mam or nam pla
 (see Glossary)
¼ cup sugar

1. In a food processor, mince the mint, chili, and garlic.

2. Add the lemon juice, water, vinegar, corn syrup, nuoc mam, and sugar, and process until the sugar dissolves.

▶ Keeps 2 days, refrigerated.

≡ *Sweet Hot Dipping Sauce for Mu Sarong*

This wonderful sauce can be served with a number of Asian recipes besides Mu Sarong.

═ Yield: 1 quart

½ pound fresh chili peppers (see note)	2 cups rice vinegar
4 garlic cloves	1 pound sugar
	1 teaspoon salt

═ Yield: 5 quarts

2½ pounds fresh chili peppers (see note)	10 cups rice vinegar
20 garlic cloves	5 pounds sugar
	2 tablespoons salt

1. Cut the peppers into ½-inch pieces. Remove and discard the seeds.
2. In a food processor, purée the peppers and garlic, adding just enough vinegar to make a paste.
3. In a noncorrosible pan, simmer the pepper paste, vinegar, sugar, and salt, stirring occasionally for 30 minutes.

▶ Keeps 1 month, refrigerated.

NOTE: Red or green chilies can be used. Chilies can be very hot. Take care not to touch your face while working with them, especially around the eyes. This sauce may seem excessively strong as the chilies are being puréed, but the sugar softens the fire greatly.

≡ *Sambal Ketjap*

This sauce is used most often with Indonesian sates. It is a blessed relief from the overused peanut-based sauces.

═ Yield: 1¼ cups

1 cup ketjap manis (see Glossary)	2 jalapeño peppers, seeded and cut in julienne
⅓ cup lime juice	

═ Yield: 1¼ quarts

1 quart ketjap manis (see Glossary)	6 jalapeño peppers, seeded and cut in julienne
1⅓ cups lime juice	

1. In a bowl, mix the ketjap manis, lime juice, and jalapeños.
2. Serve with broiled fish or meats.

▶ Keeps 1 week, refrigerated.

≡ *Hot Pepper Relish*

== **Yield: 1¼ cups**

1 cup freshly grated coconut	2 red chili peppers, seeded
½ cup chopped onion	⅓ cup lemon juice

== **Yield: 1¼ quarts**

1 quart freshly grated coconut	8 red chili peppers, seeded
2 cups chopped onion	1⅓ cups lemon juice

1. In a food processor, blend the coconut, onions, chilies, and lemon juice until smooth. Let stand 1 hour.
2. Serve with deep-fried fish or broiled or roasted meats.

▶ Keeps 2 days, refrigerated.

≡ *Hot Peanut Sauce*

This is one version of a sauce that has become common at many parties. This version is less spicy than some. For a truly hot sauce, see the recipe for hacked chicken in Chapter 7.

== **Yield: 1½ cups**

¾ cup thinly sliced onion	1 tablespoon soy sauce
2 garlic cloves, chopped	½ teaspoon salt
1 tablespoon vegetable oil	1 teaspoon sugar
1 cup roasted peanuts	2 tablespoons lime juice
½ teaspoon minced gingerroot	boiling water
1 red chili pepper, seeded	

== **Yield: 1½ quarts**

3 cups thinly sliced onion	¼ cup soy sauce
8 garlic cloves, chopped	2 teaspoons salt
¼ cup vegetable oil	1½ tablespoons sugar
1 quart roasted peanuts	½ cup lime juice
2 teaspoons minced gingerroot	boiling water
4 red chili peppers, seeded	

1. In a skillet, sauté the onion and garlic in the oil until soft and just turning golden.

2. Place in a food processor with the peanuts, gingerroot, chili pepper, soy sauce, salt, sugar, and lime juice. Process until smooth, adding just enough water to make a thick paste.

3. Serve with broiled meat or chicken.

▶ Keeps 1 week, refrigerated.

4

Dips

*F*or no clear reason, people love dips, perhaps because they like to work for their food. Dips are equally popular with the professional cook who soon realizes that a dip or two on a menu means an easily prepared dish that, depending on its accompaniment, can be visually spectacular. A vegetable construction, for instance, can be the centerpiece for the entire party. Dips save preparation time, most often can be made ahead, and need little or no attention except to be replenished. Because they can be changed for every event, clients do not feel a sense of déjà vu.

When you prepare dips, remember that they must be suitable for the food being dipped. The sauce for a potato chip has to be soft enough to be scooped easily without breaking the chip or dripping off of it, while the sauce for a vegetable can be much firmer. In this book you will find many other recipes suitable for dipping. Many of the spreads can serve as dips with the addition of a softening ingredient such as sour cream, yogurt, or mayonnaise. Conversely, many dips can be served as a spread or as the filling for vegetables or pastries by using less of those ingredients. Let your imagination soar using the recipes as a launching point.

There is no clear method for determining how many guests a dip will serve, because it depends on the amount of other foods on the menu. Experience has shown that for a small menu, 1 cup will serve 10 persons; however, 2 cups will serve up to 50, because the menu will generally be larger and the guests consume less of any one item. In other words, 10 people for cocktails means 3 to 4 hors d'oeuvre including the dip. But for 50 or more, the menu will have 6 hors d'oeuvre on the menu, with possibly another 1 or 2 to be introduced as the party progresses. With this in mind, I have provided a single quantity unless it is apparent that increasing or decreasing the quantity would be a problem.

Besides potato chips, there are dozens of foods that can be used to dip, whether store-bought or freshly made crackers (see Chapter 17), taco chips, vegetables, meats, or fish. This chapter contains many suggestions. Just make sure that the dipping material is a reasonable size. Large pieces of bread, vegetables, meat, and fish should be cut into bite-size pieces. What is bite-size? A morsel of food that a lady can consume in two bites, without filling out her cheeks. If it is much larger, the guest will have to chomp away on a log of raw carrot forever or, more likely, decide to dip again. Apart from the sanitary problems of double-dipping, it is repulsive. This rule applies to virtually all cocktail food: make it small enough to be consumed with two polite bites.

Please note that because some commercially prepared chips and crackers are often heavily salted, you may need to adjust the salt in a particular recipe.

Chips

There are dozens of varieties of products made for dipping. Whether you select potato chips, corn chips, or pork rinds, choose a type that suits the food to be dipped and a brand that is of high quality. Try also to find more unusual products, such as blue tortilla chips rather than plain corn, so that you can present food that is out of the ordinary. Of course, the choice is sometimes determined by the occasion. A dip for a casual Superbowl party would be perfect with potato chips, but an elegant cocktail buffet before the symphony requires something more sophisticated.

Crackers and Breads

In many instances it is wise to serve a relatively bland cracker without a great deal of flavor so that it does not detract from the dip. At other times, however, a flavored cracker or bread, such as Swedish flat bread, can enhance the flavor of the dip. Choose crackers of a reasonable size, and if they are too large, cut them into smaller pieces. Some crackers are perforated so they can be easily broken into smaller segments; avoid large crackers that cannot be broken neatly.

Many breads are suitable: apart from French bread, try Westphalian pumpernickel, *bauernbrot*, or an assortment of whole grain breads. Possibly the most popular bread for dipping is pita (also called Syrian, Lebanese, Armenian, and pocket bread). Unfortunately, too often this bread is used incorrectly. Loaves should be cut into strips or triangles and separated into two pieces—they are too thick if they are not separated. Toasting the pieces not only brings out the flavor, but also makes them more rigid. Italian bread sticks are also fun.

Fish and Meat
We seldom think of serving fish and meats with a dip, but that of course is what shrimp cocktail is. Do not limit yourself to shrimp, however. Lobster chunks, scallops, crab claws, or firm-fleshed fish such as swordfish work beautifully. Fish cakes and fish balls are usually served with a dipping sauce. Skewered meats such as sausages, steak, or broiled lamb can all be served with dipping sauces.

Now that you consider these foods as dipping foods, consider the recipes that follow as ways to add excitement to your menus. For example, serve shrimp with horseradish sauce or lamb cubes with Saint Pierre relish.

Crudités, or Raw Vegetables
Perhaps the most common food to dip is a raw vegetable. People feel virtuous because they eat just a few vegetables, while forgetting that the dip is what made them so wonderful. Vegetables are colorful and can be presented beautifully. Serve vegetables whole if they are baby size or partially sliced, letting the guests break off the sections, if they are larger. For large groups it is best to cut the vegetables into bite-size pieces about 1½ to 2 inches long, so the guests can dip politely without a need to dip again. Do not cut the vegetables in all the same shape, but provide some visual interest by cutting them in slices, florets, sticks, diagonals, and brushes. If you have the time, you can shape the vegetables into flowers, although for a large group this is time consuming. Sometimes using a few carved vegetables will enhance a platter and give the impression that they are all carved.

Carrot Pansy
1. *Soak slices of carrot in cold water until they curl.*
2. *Skewer slices and top with small knob of carrot to form center.*

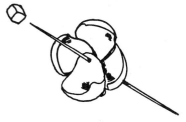

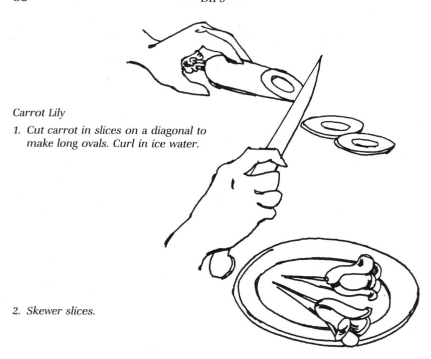

Carrot Lily

1. *Cut carrot in slices on a diagonal to make long ovals. Curl in ice water.*

2. *Skewer slices.*

Plan interesting combinations of shapes, colors, flavors, and textures. Use less familiar vegetables such as turnip, daikon, or jicama rather than the common carrots, celery, and cucumbers. Combine vegetables on the basis of flavor, color, or texture. Make an arrangement of a single vegetable such as cauliflower; or a single color using cauliflower, mushrooms, and white turnips; or a single texture, using broccoli and cauliflower, or white turnips, carrots (you need not always avoid carrots), and white radishes.

Arrange the vegetables with flair on platters, group them in bowls, or use a variety of baskets. Construct a pyramid using whole and cut vegetables. Use flowerpots, mushroom baskets, market baskets, cachepots, wooden boxes, oriental lacquer trays, large wine glasses, or napkins folded like flowers. Arrange them very formally or heap them casually in an antique kitchen mixing bowl. Use vegetables as the focal point of the table because of their color and low cost. With a certain amount of skill you can turn vegetables into the centerpiece of the table instead of purchasing floral arrangements. Use flowers to complement the vegetable arrangement to create your own, unique signature.

Serve the dipping sauces in any bowl-shaped object you wish. Carve out the inside of loaves of bread or of vegetables like peppers, cabbage, and squashes. If you are an overzealous gardener or know one, get a huge zucchini and hollow it into sections to hold the dips and the vegetables.

Certain vegetables taste better if parboiled in salted water for 2 to 3 minutes to remove the raw taste, but most vegetables are wonderful served raw. To blanch or parboil vegetables, bring 2 quarts of water and 2 tablespoons salt to a full, rolling boil. Add 2 or more cups vegetables and cook, uncovered, until tender-crisp or fully cooked, depending on the vegetable. Drain vegetables and immediately run under cold water to stop the cooking, refresh the vegetable, and set the color. Vegetables can also be steamed. Either method is suitable.

Vegetables for Crudités

Artichokes, globe Trim leaves and stems. Rub cut areas with half a lemon. Cook until tender in boiling salted water with 2 teaspoons lemon juice for each artichoke (an outside leaf will pull off easily). Separate leaves from base and arrange attractively on a platter; save the base for another use or feast on it.

Artichokes, jerusalem Serve raw or blanched until tender crisp. When serving raw, cut and serve immediately (they darken when exposed to the air and tossing them in lemon juice makes them too acid).

Asparagus Serve raw or blanched. The flavor is better if blanched. Serve the top 2 to 3 inches and save the stems for soup.

Beans: wax, green, or snap Serve raw or blanched. Trim ends and cut to size if long.

Beans, lima: Too small for dipping. They must be cooked. Toss them with a little olive oil, minced garlic, salt, and pepper, and use to stuff tomatoes or cucumber cups.

Beets Boil or bake before serving. Cut into sticks or serve whole with plenty of napkins as they are messy. Tiny beets can be hollowed and stuffed with sour cream, caviar, or herring salad. You can also use them in a mixed vegetable salad to stuff pastry cups or other vegetables.

Broccoli Serve raw or blanched. Cut into florets. Peel and slice the stems into disks or sticks.

Brussels sprouts Serve raw or blanched. To blanch, cut a deep cross into the base with the point of a sharp knife before cooking.

Cabbage: green, red, or savoy Not suitable for dipping. Use to garnish a platter or hollow the center and use as a container for the sauce. Buy untrimmed heads and gently fold back the outer leaves to make a giant flower.

Cabbage: Chinese, celery, napa, or bok choy Napa and bok choy are not usually used for dipping. Celery cabbage stalks can be cut into strips and served raw.

Cardoon Cut cardoons into sticks and blanch. They taste like globe artichokes.

Carrots Serve raw or blanched. If small, use whole or halved. Cut into sticks or slices, roll cut, or use to make flowers.

Cauliflower Serve raw or blanched. Cut into florets.

Celery Serve raw. Cut into sticks, on the diagonal, or as brushes. To make celery brushes, cut into 2 to 3 inch lengths. Cut the lengths in fine strips, toward the ends, leaving ½ inch in the center of the strip uncut. Soak in ice water until the edges curl.

Celery root, celeriac, celery knob Serve raw or blanched. Peel and cut into sticks or slices, or carve into vegetable flowers. Dip in acidulated water (1 teaspoon lemon juice to 1 cup water) to prevent darkening.

Chard Not used for dips.

Corn Not usually served with dips. However, tiny ears can be used. For a very casual affair, cut fresh cobs into 1-inch sections, cook, and serve hot.

Cucumber Serve raw. Unwaxed cucumbers are preferable. Use seedless or pickling cucumbers for fewer seeds. If large, split in half lengthwise and scrape out the seeds with a teaspoon. Cut into strips or slices, or carve into vegetable flowers.

Eggplant Not popular, but can be served raw. Leave skin on or peel, according to taste. Cut into sticks or slices.

Endive, Belgian Serve raw. Separate the leaves.

Greens: escarole, chicory, and Boston or Bibb lettuces are unsuitable. **Romaine** can be served raw. Cut sections from the stem and save the leafy parts for salads.

Kale Unsuitable for dipping.

Kohlrabi Serve raw or blanched. Cut into slices or sticks.

Leeks Serve raw if very small.

Mushrooms Serve raw. Use whole, halved, or quartered depending on the size.

Okra Whole okra can be served raw, but it is not recommended.

Onions Blanch tiny white onions whole, or serve spring onions with part of green still attached.

Parsnip Serve raw or blanched. Cut into sticks, slices, or vegetable flowers.

Peas Unsuitable for dipping. Some people serve fresh garden peas, tossed with salt, rather like peanuts.

Peas, snow (sugar peas or edible pea pods) Serve raw or barely blanched (about 30 seconds). Remove strings before serving.

Peppers: sweet and chili Serve the sweet varieties raw. Cut into strips or squares. Hollow out to serve as containers for dips. Cut chili peppers into flowers by slitting several times from the tips almost to the stem and soaking in ice water. Raw chili strips can be served to the forewarned.

Potatoes Unsuitable when raw. The taste is good, but they turn dark too quickly. They can be steamed or baked and stuffed (if tiny).

Pumpkin Serve raw. Cut into slices or sticks.

Rutabaga See Turnip.

Salsify Blanch in salted acidulated water. Cut into sticks or rounds.

Scallions Serve raw. Trim roots and excess green. To make brushes, split both ends toward the middle and soak in ice water.

Spinach Unsuitable for dipping.

Squash: summer or zucchini Serve raw. Trim and cut into strips or slices. If tiny, they can be roll cut.

Squash: winter, acorn, blue hubbard, or butternut Serve raw. Peel and cut into slices or sticks.

Tomatoes: green or red Serve raw. Cut into wedges.

Tomatoes: cherry Serve raw. Buy tiny—one bite—cherry tomatoes, as some tomatoes sold as cherry are too large.

Turnip Common types are white (purple-top), yellow (rutabagas or Swede turnips), and green-top (Cape Cod). Serve raw or blanched. Peel and cut into sticks, slices, or vegetable flowers.

≡ *Mantequilla de Pobre (Poor Man's Butter)*

≡ **Yield: about 2 cups**

2 ripe avocados	2 to 3 tablespoons lime juice
2 tomatoes, peeled, seeded, and chopped	1 tablespoon olive oil
	salt and pepper, to taste

1. In a bowl, coarsely mash the avocados with a fork and stir in the tomatoes, lime juice, oil, salt, and pepper.

2. Serve with vegetables, fried pork rinds, Carnitas (page 394), and meatballs. Or, use to stuff tomatoes, mushroom caps, or small puffs.

▶ Keep tightly covered until serving time. Use within 2 hours.

NOTE: Use a fork to mash the avocado so that the mixture is chunky.

≡ *Guacamole*

≡ **Yield: about 2 cups**

2 ripe avocados	1½ teaspoons salt
1 to 2 jalapeño peppers, seeded and minced	2 tomatoes, peeled, seeded, and chopped
2 tablespoons lime juice	

1. In a bowl, mash the avocados and add the jalapeños, lime juice, and salt. Fold in the tomatoes.

2. Serve with corn chips or vegetables.

▶ Keep tightly covered until serving time. Use within 2 hours.

≡ Avocado Cream

═ Yield: about 2 cups

2 ripe avocados
⅔ cup sour cream
2 tablespoons mayonnaise
2 tablespoons lime juice

2 teaspoons grated onion
¼ teaspoon minced garlic
salt and pepper, to taste

1. In a food processor, purée the avocado, sour cream, mayonnaise, lime juice, onion, garlic, salt, and pepper.
2. Serve with raw vegetables or seafood.

▶ Keep tightly covered until serving time. Use within 2 hours.

≡ Avocado Horseradish Dip

═ Yield: about 2 cups

2 large, ripe avocados
1 cup sour cream
2 tablespoons grated
  horseradish
2 teaspoons minced onion

2 teaspoons salt
dash of Tabasco sauce, or to
  taste
paprika

1. In a food processor, purée the avocado, sour cream, horseradish, onion, salt, and Tabasco sauce.
2. Pour into a bowl and sprinkle with paprika. Cover tightly and chill.
3. Serve with vegetables or seafood.

▶ Use within 3 hours.

≡ Pistou

═ Yield: about 2 cups

3 cups packed, chopped fresh
  basil leaves
4 to 6 garlic cloves, crushed
¾ cup grated Gruyère or
  Parmesan cheese

½ cup olive oil
salt, to taste

1. In a food processor, purée the basil, garlic, cheese, olive oil, and salt.
2. Serve with vegetables, roasted meats, or seafood.

▶ Keeps 4 days, refrigerated.

≡ Caper Sauce

≡ Yield: 2 cups

2 cups sour cream
2 tablespoons capers

juice of 1 lime

1. In a bowl, mix the sour cream, capers, and lime juice.
2. Serve with vegetables, meat, or fish.

▶ Keeps 1 week, refrigerated.

NOTE: Capers come in different sizes. Use the smallest, called nonpareils, which come packed in brine and must be drained before using. If you must use larger capers, rinse them and chop finely, but not to a paste.

≡ Chili Dipping Sauce

This version calls for mild chilies, but you can substitute hotter chilies, depending on your guests. Or, serve a bowl of each, labeled hot and mild, and let guests sample as they like.

≡ Yield: 2 cups

3 medium tomatoes, chopped
3 mild green chilies, minced
1 garlic clove, minced

1 teaspoon lime juice
1 teaspoon salt

1. In a bowl, mix the tomatoes, chilies, garlic, lime juice, and salt.
2. Chill for at least 2 hours before serving.
3. Serve as a dip for crackers or corn chips, or serve as a sauce with broiled meat or chicken.

▶ Keeps 2 days, refrigerated.

≡ Curried Yogurt Sauce

The curry paste sold in Asian or Indian markets will give a stronger, but not necessarily hotter, curry flavor than many curry powders.

≡ Yield: 2 cups

1⅓ cups yogurt
⅔ cup sour cream
2 tablespoons curry powder or
    paste, or to taste

2 teaspoons lemon juice
salt and pepper, to taste

1. In a bowl, mix the yogurt, sour cream, curry powder, lemon juice, salt, and pepper.
2. Let stand, covered, for at least 1 hour.
3. Serve with vegetables, meats, or seafood.

▶ Keeps 1 week, refrigerated.

≡ *Curry Dipping Sauce*

== **Yield: 2 cups**

1 cup mayonnaise
1 cup sour cream
1 tablespoon curry powder or
    paste, or to taste

½ teaspoon soy sauce
salt and pepper, to taste

1. In a bowl, mix the mayonnaise, sour cream, curry powder, and soy sauce. Correct seasoning with salt and pepper.
2. Chill, covered, for 2 hours.
3. Serve with vegetables, chicken, or fish.

▶ Keeps 1 week, refrigerated.

≡ *Curry Mayonnaise*

== **Yield: 2 cups**

2 eggs
2 teaspoons curry powder, or to
    taste
1 teaspoon dry mustard

¼ cup white vinegar
2 cups oil
salt and pepper, to taste

1. In a food processor, mix the eggs, curry powder, and mustard.
2. Add 2 tablespoons of vinegar and, with the machine running, add the oil in a slow, steady stream until the mixture has thickened. Add the remaining vinegar to taste. Season with salt and pepper. Let stand 10 minutes and add more curry if desired.
3. Serve with vegetables.

▶ Keeps 2 weeks, refrigerated.

≡ *Curried Honey Dipping Sauce*

== **Yield: 1½ cups**

1 cup mayonnaise
1½ tablespoons tomato purée
1½ tablespoons honey
1½ tablespoons minced onion

1½ tablespoons curry powder
1½ teaspoons lemon juice
Tabasco sauce, to taste

1. In a bowl, mix the mayonnaise, tomato purée, honey, onion, curry powder, lemon juice, and Tabasco sauce. Cover and chill overnight.

2. Serve with vegetables.

▶ Keeps 1 week, refrigerated.

≡ *Dill Dip*

== **Yield: 2½ cups**

11 ounces cream cheese, softened
1 cup sour cream
3 ounces Spanish olives, chopped
¼ cup minced dill
1 teaspoon minced shallots
½ teaspoon Dijon mustard

⅛ teaspoon crushed garlic
dash of Worcestershire sauce
white pepper, to taste
2 dashes of Tabasco sauce
juice of 1 lemon
¼ teaspoon paprika
salt, to taste

1. In a food processor, blend the cream cheese, sour cream, olives, dill, shallots, mustard, garlic, Worcestershire sauce, pepper, Tabasco, lemon juice, paprika, and salt until smooth. Taste for seasoning.

2. Cover and refrigerate for at least 2 hours before serving. Serve with vegetables.

▶ Keeps 4 days, refrigerated.

☰ *Sour Cream Dill Sauce*

═ Yield: 2 cups

2 cups sour cream
1 cup minced dill

salt and pepper, to taste

1. In a bowl, mix the sour cream and dill. Correct seasoning with salt and pepper.
2. Serve chilled with vegetables, or warm in a double boiler and serve with poached fish balls or other seafood.

▶ Keeps 4 days, refrigerated.

☰ *Herbed Mayonnaise*

═ Yield: 1½ cups

2 cups mayonnaise
2 tablespoons each minced
   chives, parsley, and chervil

1. In a bowl, mix the mayonnaise, chives, parsley, and chervil. Chill for 3 hours before serving.
2. Serve with vegetables or seafood.

▶ Keeps 3 days, refrigerated.

☰ *Garlic Caper Dip*

═ Yield: 2½ cups

2 cups cottage cheese
½ cup buttermilk
¼ cup minced scallions
3 tablespoons capers, drained
3 garlic cloves, minced

2 tablespoons lime or lemon
   juice
cayenne pepper, to taste
salt, to taste

1. In a food processor, purée the cottage cheese and buttermilk. Stir in the scallions, capers, garlic, and lime or lemon juice. Correct the seasoning with cayenne and salt.
2. Serve with vegetables.

▶ Keeps 2 days, refrigerated.

≡ Aïoli I

═ **Yield: about 2 cups**

3 egg yolks
6 garlic cloves, or more
2 tablespoons lemon juice

1 teaspoon salt
1½ cups olive oil

1. In a food processor, process the egg yolks, garlic, lemon juice, and salt for 30 seconds. With the machine running, add the oil slowly until it forms a mayonnaise.

2. Serve with vegetables, fish, or broiled meats.

▶ Keeps 3 days, refrigerated.

≡ Aïoli II

═ Yield: about 2 cups

1 tablespoon dry bread crumbs
1 tablespoon wine vinegar
4 to 6 large garlic cloves
3 egg yolks

1½ cups olive oil
1 to 2 tablespoons lemon juice
pinch of cayenne pepper
salt, to taste

1. In a food processor, soften the bread crumbs in the vinegar for 2 to 3 minutes.

2. Add the garlic and process until smooth, stopping to scrape the sides down as needed. Add the egg yolks and blend. With the machine running, add the oil slowly until thick and smooth. Add the lemon juice, cayenne, and salt.

3. Serve with vegetables and seafood.

▶ Keeps 3 days, refrigerated.

≡ Skordalia with Almonds

This Greek garlic mayonnaise is made with almonds for a different flavor and texture.

═ Yield: 2½ cups

2 cups aïoli I (recipe above)
¼ cup fresh bread crumbs
¼ cup ground blanched
  almonds

3 tablespoons minced parsley
lemon juice, to taste
salt and cayenne pepper, to
  taste

1. In a bowl, mix the aïoli, bread crumbs, almonds, parsley, lemon juice, salt, and cayenne.
2. Serve with raw vegetables or lamb meatballs.

▶ Keeps 2 days, refrigerated.

≡ *Frozen Horseradish Dip*

This is not really frozen, just well chilled. Placing it in the freezer gives the sauce body. Ideally, it is made from freshly grated horseradish to give it real zing; however, the same amount of drained, prepared horseradish can be substituted.

═ Yield: 3 cups

1 cup heavy cream	½ cup grated horseradish
1 cup cottage cheese, sieved	2 tablespoons tarragon vinegar
3 tablespoons minced chives	2 teaspoons sugar
pinch of cayenne pepper	1 teaspoon Dijon mustard
salt, to taste	

1. Whip the cream until almost stiff. Fold in the cottage cheese, chives, cayenne, and salt.
2. In a bowl, mix the horseradish, vinegar, sugar, and mustard. Fold into the cream mixture, place in a serving bowl, and freeze for 2 hours. Do not freeze longer.
3. Serve as a dip for crackers, toast, or Melba toast.

▶ Keeps 1 day, refrigerated.

≡ *Horseradish Mayonnaise*

═ Yield: 2½ cups

1½ cups mayonnaise	2 teaspoons tarragon vinegar
⅔ cup ketchup	lemon juice, to taste
1½ tablespoons grated horseradish	black pepper, to taste

In a bowl, mix the mayonnaise, ketchup, horseradish, vinegar, lemon juice and pepper. Chill for 2 hours before serving.

▶ Keeps 5 days, refrigerated.

≡ *Warm Horseradish Mustard Sauce*

═ Yield: 2¼ cups

2 cups sour cream
¼ cup grated horseradish

2 teaspoons dry mustard
salt, to taste

1. In a saucepan, mix the sour cream, horseradish, and mustard. Season with salt and cook over medium heat until warm. Do not bring to a boil or it will curdle.

2. Serve with vegetables, fingers of black bread, meat, or shellfish.

▶ Keeps 3 days, refrigerated.

≡ *Creamy Mustard Sauce*

═ Yield: 2 cups

¼ cup Dijon mustard
2 tablespoons lemon juice

1 cup heavy cream, whipped
salt and pepper, to taste

1. In a bowl, mix the mustard and lemon juice. Fold in the cream, and correct the seasoning with salt and pepper.

2. Serve with vegetables, ham, or corned beef.

▶ Keeps 1 day, refrigerated.

≡ *Mustard Sauce*

═ Yield: 2 cups

½ cup dry mustard
½ cup cold water
⅓ cup heavy cream
1 cup light soy sauce

2 tablespoons sesame seeds,
   toasted and crushed
2 teaspoons grated lemon rind

1. In a bowl, mix the mustard and water to a paste. Whisk in the cream, soy sauce, sesame seeds, and lemon rind. Refrigerate for 2 hours.

2. Serve with vegetables or broiled meats.

▶ Keeps 4 days, refrigerated.

≡ Mustard Vegetable Sauce

═ Yield: 2 generous cups

1 stalk celery, chopped
1 scallion, chopped
1 tablespoon minced parsley
2 hard-cooked eggs, chopped
2 tablespoons Dijon mustard
2 tablespoons white wine
   vinegar

2 tablespoons white wine
½ teaspoon salt
1 cup olive oil
Tabasco sauce, to taste
cayenne and black pepper, to
   taste

1. In a food processor, process the celery, scallion, parsley, eggs, mustard, vinegar, wine, and salt with a few quick on-off turns. With the machine on, add the oil in a steady stream. Correct the seasoning with the Tabasco, cayenne, and black pepper. Chill for 1 hour.

2. Serve with vegetables.

▶ Keeps 3 days, refrigerated.

≡ Pink Mayonnaise

═ Yield: 2½ cups

2 cups mayonnaise
¼ cup tomato paste
salt and pepper, to taste

1 tablespoon lemon juice
6 tablespoons minced green
   pepper

1. In a bowl, mix the mayonnaise, tomato paste, salt, and pepper. Stir in the lemon juice and green pepper. Chill.

2. Serve with vegetables or cold seafood.

▶ Keeps 3 days, refrigerated.

≡ Sauce Niçoise

═ Yield: 2½ cups

2 cups mayonnaise
1½ tablespoons tomato paste
1 red or green pepper, minced

½ tablespoon minced tarragon
½ tablespoon minced chives

1. In a bowl, mix the mayonnaise, tomato paste, pepper, tarragon, and chives. Let stand, covered, in the refrigerator for 1 hour.

2. Serve with vegetables.

▶ Keeps 4 days, refrigerated.

≡ *Mayonnaise Tyrolienne*

═ Yield: 2 cups

2 cups mayonnaise
2 tablespoons tomato paste

1 teaspoon Dijon mustard
1 teaspoon white wine vinegar

1. In a bowl, mix the mayonnaise, tomato paste, and mustard. If too thick, thin with vinegar.
2. Serve with vegetables or seafood.

▶ Keeps 4 days, refrigerated.

≡ *per Bacco Sauce (Orange Fish Sauce)*

═ Yield: 2 cups

1 cup heavy cream
½ cup ketchup
2 tablespoons tomato purée

2 tablespoons Scotch whiskey
1 orange, peeled

1. In a bowl, mix the cream, ketchup, tomato purée and Scotch. Whip the mixture until it thickens.
2. Cut the orange into segments and cut the segments into ¼-inch pieces. Fold into the sauce.
3. Serve with fish or seafood.

▶ Keeps 2 days, refrigerated.

≡ *Pecan Dip*

═ Yield: 2 cups

½ cup pecans
½ cup milk
1 teaspoon salt

1 cup cottage cheese
pepper, to taste

1. In a food processor, process the pecans, milk, and salt to a paste. Add the cottage cheese and process until combined. Correct the seasoning with pepper.
2. Serve with vegetables or crackers.

▶ Keeps 4 days, refrigerated.

≡ *Pecan Parsley Sauce*

═ **Yield: 2 cups**

1 cup sour cream
½ cup peeled, seeded, and
  minced cucumber
½ cup chopped pecans
¼ cup minced parsley

1 garlic clove, crushed
¼ teaspoon paprika
salt and cayenne pepper, to
  taste

1. In a bowl, mix the sour cream, cucumber, pecans, parsley, garlic, paprika, salt, and cayenne. Chill for about 2 hours.
2. Serve with vegetables or crackers.

▶ Keeps 3 days, refrigerated.

≡ *Salsa Colorado (Spanish Pepper and Almond Sauce)*

═ **Yield: 2½ cups**

3 garlic cloves
1 teaspoon salt
½ cup blanched almonds,
  lightly toasted
2 tomatoes, peeled and seeded

2 red peppers, peeled
2 hard-cooked egg yolks
1 cup olive oil
¼ cup sherry vinegar
¼ teaspoon cayenne pepper

1. In a food processor, chop the garlic, salt, and almonds with on-off turns until it forms a coarse meal.
2. Add the tomatoes and peppers and process until smooth. Blend in the egg yolks, and with the machine running, add the olive oil in a slow, steady stream. Add the vinegar and cayenne with on-off turns.
3. Serve with vegetables, thin slices of garlic toast, or toasted pita bread.

▶ Keeps 4 days, refrigerated.

≡ *Ritz Sauce*

═ **Yield: 2 cups**

1 cup mayonnaise
1 large tomato, peeled, seeded,
  and chopped
1 tablespoon chili sauce

1 teaspoon each minced chives,
  chervil, and parsley
¼ teaspoon Worcestershire
  sauce

1. In a bowl, mix the mayonnaise, tomato, chili sauce, chives, chervil, parsley, and Worcestershire sauce.

2. Serve with vegetables or shellfish.

▶ Keeps 3 days, refrigerated.

≡ Ribes (Sesame Dip)

Prepare this in more generous quantities, because people tend to scoop up large amounts with the pita bread.

═ Yield: 3 cups

2 cups tahini (see Glossary; recipe, page 103)	⅛ teaspoon cayenne pepper
1 cup olive oil	pinch of allspice
juice of 2 lemons	salt and pepper, to taste
2 teaspoons ground cumin	additional lemon juice, to taste
	paprika or minced parsley

1. In a bowl, cream the sesame paste with the olive oil and lemon juice. Add enough water, gradually, until the mixture is the consistency of a dip. Blend in the cumin, cayenne, allspice, salt, and pepper, adding more lemon juice if desired.

2. Place in a serving bowl and sprinkle with paprika or parsley.

3. Serve with pita bread, preferably toasted.

▶ Keeps 4 days, refrigerated.

≡ Sour Cream and Green Peppercorn Dip

Although not the rage they were a few years ago, green peppercorns still add a delightful pungency to many recipes.

═ Yield: 2 cups

2 cups sour cream	2 teaspoons Cognac
¼ cup green peppercorns, crushed	salt, to taste

1. In a bowl, mix the sour cream, peppercorns, and Cognac. Correct seasoning with the salt.

2. Serve with vegetables, broiled meats, or fish.

▶ Keeps 5 days, refrigerated.

≡ Spinach Vegetable Dip

═ Yield: 2 cups

½ cup minced, cooked spinach
3 ounces cream cheese,
  softened
⅔ cup yogurt or sour cream

⅔ cup minced scallions
grated nutmeg, to taste
salt and pepper, to taste

1. Squeeze any excess moisture from the spinach. In a bowl, mix the spinach, cream cheese, yogurt, scallions, nutmeg, salt, and pepper. Let rest 1 hour.

2. Serve with vegetables or toasted pita bread.

▶ Keeps 4 days, refrigerated.

≡ Spinach Dip

═ Yield: 2 cups

1 cup sour cream
½ cup mayonnaise
½ cup minced parsley
½ cup minced onion
10 ounces fresh spinach, stems
  stripped, cooked, pressed
  dry, and minced

1 teaspoon salt
½ teaspoon celery salt
¼ teaspoon pepper
pinch of nutmeg
dash of lemon juice

1. In a bowl, mix the sour cream, mayonnaise, parsley, onion, spinach, salt, celery salt, pepper, nutmeg, and lemon juice. Chill for several hours for the flavors to meld.

2. Serve with vegetables.

▶ Keeps 4 days, refrigerated.

≡ Tahini (Sesame Seed Paste)

═ Yield: 2 cups

1 cup sesame seeds
1 cup water
2 garlic cloves, chopped
juice of 2 lemons

1 teaspoon salt
dash of cayenne pepper
few drops of vinegar

1. In a food processor or blender, purée the sesame seeds, water, garlic, and lemon juice. Add a little more water, if needed, to reach the consistency of mayonnaise. Season with salt, cayenne, and vinegar.
2. Serve with toasted pita bread, vegetables, or broiled meats.

▶ Keeps 3 weeks, refrigerated.
NOTE: A blender seems to do a better job than a food processor. If the oil separates, whisk it back into the paste.

≡ *Tomato Cheese Sauce*

= Yield: 2 cups

6 ounces cream cheese, softened
1 cup buttermilk
¼ cup tomato paste

1 tablespoon lemon juice
salt and pepper, to taste
Tabasco sauce, to taste

1. In a food processor, cream the cheese and buttermilk. Add the tomato paste and lemon juice. Season with salt, pepper, and Tabasco sauce.
2. Serve with vegetables.

▶ Keeps 4 days, refrigerated.

≡ *Sauce Tunisienne*

This is the Tunisian version of salsa.

= Yield: 2 to 3 cups

1½ cups peeled, seeded, and chopped tomatoes
⅓ cup olive oil
¼ cup minced parsley
1½ tablespoons minced scallions

2 garlic cloves, minced
½ teaspoon red pepper flakes
½ teaspoon ground coriander
¼ teaspoon sugar
salt and pepper, to taste
1 cup sour cream, optional

1. In a bowl, mix the tomatoes, olive oil, parsley, scallions, garlic, red pepper, coriander, sugar, salt, and pepper.
2. Serve with broiled shrimp, scallops, or flank steak, or add the sour cream and serve with vegetables.

▶ Keeps 5 days, refrigerated.

≡ *Spiced Vegetable Dip*

== **Yield: 2¼ cups**

2 cups sour cream	1 tablespoon minced celery
1 tablespoon lemon juice	1 teaspoon salt
1 tablespoon Worcestershire	¼ teaspoon crushed garlic
sauce	¼ teaspoon Tabasco sauce
2 teaspoons minced onion	

In a bowl, mix the sour cream, lemon juice, Worcestershire sauce, onion, celery, salt, garlic, and Tabasco sauce.

▶ Keeps 5 days, refrigerated.

≡ *Vegetable Dip*

== **Yield: 2½ cups**

1 cup sour cream	2 tablespoons minced celery
½ cup peeled, seeded, and	1 tablespoon minced green
minced tomatoes	pepper
2 tablespoons minced scallions	salt and pepper, to taste
2 tablespoons minced parsley	Tabasco sauce, to taste

1. In a bowl, mix the sour cream, tomatoes, scallions, parsley, celery, green pepper, salt, pepper, and Tabasco sauce.

2. Serve with tortilla chips, sesame crackers, or vegetables.

▶ Keeps 4 days, refrigerated.

≡ *Watercress Sour Cream Dip*

== **Yield: 2 cups**

1½ cups sour cream	juice of 2 lemons
½ cup chopped watercress	salt, to taste

1. In a bowl, mix the sour cream, watercress, lemon juice, and salt.

2. Serve with seafood or vegetables.

▶ Keeps 2 days, refrigerated.

☰ *Yogurt Dipping Sauce*

═ Yield: 2 cups

2 cups yogurt
2 shallots, minced
1 tablespoon minced basil
1 teaspoon dried chervil

pinch of dried marjoram
dash of Worcestershire sauce
salt and pepper, to taste

1. In a bowl, mix the yogurt, shallots, basil, chervil, marjoram, Worcestershire sauce, salt, and pepper. Let flavors meld for 2 hours.
2. Serve with vegetables or seafood.

▶ Keeps 5 days, refrigerated.

☰ *Camembert Cheese Dip*

═ Yield: 2 cups

8 ounces Camembert cheese
1 cup dry sherry
⅓ cup butter

¼ cup blanched almonds,
   ground

1. Remove the white crust from the cheese. In a bowl, marinate the cheese in the sherry overnight in the refrigerator. Drain and reserve the sherry.
2. In a food processor, cream the butter and almonds. Add the cheese and process until smooth, adding as much sherry as needed to make a dip. Pour into a bowl and chill for 1 hour.
3. Serve with crackers.

▶ Keeps 1 week, refrigerated.

☰ *Fondue Dipping Sauce*

═ Yield: 2 cups

¼ pound Italian Fontina
   cheese, diced
1 tablespoon potato starch

¾ cup milk
1 egg yolk
2 tablespoons kirsch

1. In a saucepan over low heat, cook the milk and potato starch, stirring until blended and smooth. Add the cheese, stirring until melted. Remove from the heat and beat in the egg yolk and kirsch. Serve in a chafing dish or fondue pot.

2. Serve with vegetables or bread cubes.

3. Once made, must be served immediately.

NOTE: Italian Fontina is very different from the domestic and other imitations. Be sure to use the original.

≡ *Fundido (Hot Mexican Cheese Dip)*

This very hearty dip is suitable for the next barbecue.

═ Yield: 2½ cups

1 teaspoon lard
⅔ cup drained canned
  tomatoes
1 cup minced onion
2 mild green chilies, seeded
  and minced
1 tablespoon minced coriander
  (cilantro)

2 garlic cloves, minced
pinch of sugar
pinch of salt
2 cups grated Monterey Jack
  cheese
¼ pound chorizo sausage,
  finely diced

1. In a skillet, melt the lard and cook the tomatoes, onion, chili, coriander, and garlic until tender. Stir in the sugar and salt. Lower the heat and sprinkle on the cheese. Cook, stirring until melted and combined.

2. In a skillet, sauté the chorizo until cooked. Add to the fundido.

3. Serve immediately with tortilla chips.

▶ Best if made and served immediately.

≡ *Cream Cheese and Roasted Pepper Dip*

═ Yield: 2½ cups

½ pound cream cheese,
  softened
1 cup sour cream
½ cup thinly sliced onion
8 dashes Tabasco sauce
½ teaspoon Worcestershire
  sauce

salt, to taste
2 tablespoons minced chives
1 large green pepper, roasted,
  peeled, and chopped

1. In a food processor, cream the cheese, sour cream, onion, Tabasco sauce, Worcestershire sauce, and salt. Scrape into a bowl and mix in the chives and green pepper.

2. Serve with vegetables.

▶ Keeps 4 days, refrigerated.

≡ *Gorgonzola Dip with Walnuts*

═ **Yield: 2½ cups**

½ cup crumbled Gorgonzola cheese
½ pound cream cheese, softened

⅓ cup chopped walnuts
2 teaspoons Cognac

1. In a processor, cream the Gorgonzola and cream cheese until smooth. Fold in the walnuts and Cognac. Chill.
2. Serve with vegetables or crackers.

▶ Keeps 4 days, refrigerated.

≡ *Salsa al Gorgonzola (Gorgonzola Sauce)*

═ **Yield: 2 cups**

½ pound Gorgonzola cheese
⅔ cup milk
⅓ cup butter

½ cup heavy cream
½ cup grated Parmesan cheese
salt, to taste

1. In a saucepan, mix the Gorgonzola, milk, and butter, and cook over low heat, stirring, until the cheese is melted and blended. Stir in the cream, Parmesan, and salt.
2. Serve warm with vegetables.

▶ Best if made and served immediately.

≡ *Blue Cheese Sauce*

═ **Yield: 2 cups**

6 ounces cream cheese, softened
2 ounces blue cheese
2 tablespoons heavy cream

1 tablespoon minced onion
2 tablespoons minced chives
2 teaspoons Cognac

1. In a food processor, cream the cream cheese, blue cheese, cream, onion, chives, and Cognac until smooth.
2. Serve with vegetables, crackers, or broiled steak.

▶ Keeps 5 days, refrigerated.

≡ *Mexican Sauce*

You can use mild or very hot chilies, depending on the mood of the party.

══ Yield: 2½ cups

1 onion, minced	salt, to taste
3 tablespoons butter	Tabasco sauce, to taste
2 cups drained canned	1 tablespoon softened butter
tomatoes	1 tablespoon flour
¼ cup peeled, minced green	½ cup heavy cream
chilies	¾ cup diced Cheddar cheese

1. In a saucepan, sauté the onion in 3 tablespoons of butter until golden. Add the tomatoes and simmer until the liquid evaporates. Add the chilies, salt, and Tabasco sauce.

2. In a bowl, mix the tablespoon of softened butter and flour to a smooth paste. Stir the butter-flour mixture into the simmering tomato mixture, bit by bit, until the sauce thickens. Stir in the cream.

3. When ready to serve, reheat the sauce and stir in the cheese until it melts.

4. Serve warm with tortilla chips, roasted pork cubes, meatballs, or vegetables.

▶ The tomato mixture can be made several days ahead, but do not add the cheese until just before serving.

≡ *Tapenade I*

There are many versions of this Provençal anchovy dip. Here are a few favorites.

══ Yield: 2½ cups

2 eggs	⅓ cup capers
3 tablespoons lemon juice	4 garlic cloves, minced
2 teaspoons Dijon mustard	12 anchovy fillets, minced
3 tablespoons white wine	⅓ cup minced parsley
vinegar	2 teaspoons grated lemon rind
2 cups olive oil	

1. In a food processor, mix the eggs, lemon juice, mustard, and vinegar. With the machine running, add the oil in a steady stream and process until thickened.

2. Stir in the capers, garlic, anchovies, parsley, and lemon rind.

▶ Keeps 1 week, refrigerated.

≡ Tapenade II

═ **Yield: 2¼ cups**

3 tablespoons salted capers	½ cup olive oil
24 anchovy fillets	juice of 1 lemon
18 imported black olives, pitted	

1. Rinse the capers and dry on paper towels. Purée in a food processor with the anchovies, olives, olive oil, and lemon juice.

2. Serve with vegetables.

▶ Keeps 3 days, refrigerated. Bring to room temperature before serving.

≡ Tapenade III

═ **Yield: 2 cups**

4 ounces anchovy fillets	¼ cup capers
⅓ pound black olives, pitted	2 tablespoons Dijon mustard
6 garlic cloves	⅓ cup Cognac
½ cup olive oil	lemon juice and pepper, to
8 ounces tuna, packed in olive oil	taste

1. In a food processor, purée the anchovies, olives, and garlic, adding oil if needed. Add the tuna, capers, mustard, Cognac, lemon juice, and pepper, using on-off turns to combine.

2. Serve with vegetables or toasted French or pita bread, or use to stuff vegetables.

▶ Keeps 8 days, refrigerated.

≡ *Bagna Cauda I (Warm Anchovy Sauce I)*

Bagna cauda is the classic dip for vegetables in Italy. As with many old recipes, there are several variations on a theme.

== **Yield: 2½ cups**

1 quart heavy cream	2 teaspoons minced garlic
¼ pound butter	2 small white truffles, minced,
16 anchovy fillets, minced	optional

1. In a saucepan, simmer the cream until reduced by half.

2. In another saucepan over low heat, melt the butter and stir in the anchovies and garlic. Cook, stirring over low heat until the anchovies dissolve. If using the truffles add them to the anchovy butter, bring to a simmer, stirring, and whisk into the cream.

3. Serve with vegetables.

▶ Can be reheated, but best if made and served immediately.

NOTE: Truffles are expensive, but if there is room in the budget, they will add immeasurably to this recipe. Fortunately, the sauce is delicious even if the truffles must be omitted.

≡ *Bagna Cauda II (Warm Anchovy Sauce II)*

== **Yield: 2½ cups**

2 cups butter	12 anchovy fillets, chopped
½ cup olive oil	1 white truffle, minced, optional
6 garlic cloves, minced	salt, to taste

1. In a shallow heavy pan, heat the butter and oil and sauté the garlic until tender, without letting it brown. Remove from the heat and stir in the anchovies until they dissolve. Add the truffles, if desired. Season with salt.

2. Serve warm with vegetables.

▶ Can be reheated, but best if made and served immediately.

☰ *Bagna Cauda III (Warm Anchovy Sauce III)*

═ Yield: 2½ cups

2 cups olive oil	½ tablespoon minced parsley
4 garlic cloves, crushed	2 tablespoons capers
16 anchovy fillets, mashed	¼ cup minced black olives
1 tablespoon minced mint	
leaves	

1. In a saucepan, cook the oil and garlic until the garlic turns golden, without burning. Discard the garlic. Add the anchovies and cook until they dissolve. Remove from the heat and stir in the mint, parsley, capers, and olives.

2. Serve warm with vegetables.

▶ Can be reheated, but best if made and served immediately.

☰ *Cream Cheese and Anchovy Dip*

═ Yield: about 2 cups

½ pound cream cheese,	1 cup minced onion
softened	2 garlic cloves, minced
8 anchovy fillets	½ to 1 cup sour cream
¼ cup capers	2 tablespoons minced chives

1. In a food processor, purée the cream cheese, anchovies, capers, onion, and garlic. Add enough sour cream to make a proper dipping consistency. Stir in the chives and chill.

2. Serve with vegetables.

▶ Keeps 4 days, refrigerated.

NOTE: If the sour cream is omitted, the mixture can be used to fill small cocktail puffs or served as a spread.

☰ *Saint Pierre Relish*

═ Yield: 3½ to 4 cups

8 ounces anchovy fillets	2 tablespoons Dijon mustard
2 cups mayonnaise	1 tablespoon ground white
⅓ cup lemon juice	pepper
¼ cup wine vinegar	1 cup sour cream, approximately
¼ cup Worcestershire sauce	

1. In a bowl, mash the anchovies and blend in the mayonnaise, lemon juice, vinegar, Worcestershire sauce, mustard, and pepper. Mix in enough sour cream to thin it for dipping.

2. Serve with vegetables or broiled meats.

▶ Keeps 4 days, refrigerated.

≡ *Le Sassoun or Sauce aux Amandes de Var* (*Almond Sauce from the Var*)

═ **Yield: about 2 cups**

2 tablespoons minced mint leaves
8 anchovy fillets
¼ pound almonds, ground

½ cup olive oil
½ cup water
salt, to taste
lemon juice, to taste

1. In a blender, purée the mint and anchovies until smooth. Alternately add the almonds, olive oil, and water. The mixture should resemble a firm mayonnaise. Season with salt and lemon juice.

2. Serve as a dip for vegetables.

▶ Keeps 4 days, refrigerated. Bring to room temperature before serving.

≡ *Hot Clam Curry Sauce*

═ **Yield: 2½ cups**

2 scallions, minced
1 garlic clove, crushed
2 tablespoons butter
1 teaspoon curry powder, or to taste
3 tablespoons white wine

1 pound minced clams, drained
1 cup heavy cream
salt, to taste
lemon juice, to taste
cayenne pepper, to taste

1. In a saucepan, sauté the scallions and garlic in the butter until soft. Stir in the curry powder and cook 2 minutes. Add the wine and reduce by one-third. Add the clams to the sauce, stir in the cream and correct the seasoning with salt, lemon juice, and cayenne.

2. Serve warm with vegetables, fish balls, or seafood.

▶ Can be made 1 day in advance and reheated.

☰ *Crabmeat Dipping Sauce*

══ Yield: 2 cups

8 ounces cream cheese
3 tablespoons white wine
1 teaspoon Dijon mustard
1 teaspoon grated onion
1 garlic clove, crushed

salt and pepper, to taste
cayenne pepper, to taste
½ pound cooked crabmeat,
   flaked

1. In a saucepan over low heat, combine the cheese, wine, mustard, onion, garlic, salt, pepper, and cayenne. When heated, stir in the crabmeat.

2. Serve warm with raw vegetables, crackers, or toast or use to fill cream puffs or bouchées.

▶ Can be made 2 days in advance and reheated.

☰ *Spuma Fredda di Salmone (Salmon Foam)*

══ Yield: 3 cups

1 pound salmon steak, poached
¼ cup olive oil
2 tablespoons lemon juice

salt and pepper, to taste
1½ cups heavy cream

1. Discard the skin and bones from the salmon, and flake the meat into a food processor. Purée the salmon with the olive oil and lemon juice and season with salt and pepper.

2. Whip the cream until stiff. Fold the cream into the salmon mixture and refrigerate for 2 hours.

3. Serve with raw vegetables or as a filling for puffs.

▶ Keeps 24 hours, refrigerated.

NOTE: A 15½-ounce can of salmon can be substituted for the fresh salmon.

☰ *Smoked Salmon Dip*

══ Yield: 2 cups

½ pound smoked salmon,
   shredded
⅔ cup heavy cream

black pepper, to taste
2 teaspoons capers

1. In a food processor, purée the salmon, cream, pepper, and capers. Transfer to a bowl and sprinkle with black pepper.

2. Serve with crackers, black bread, or vegetables.

▶ Keeps 2 days, refrigerated.

≡ *Smoked Salmon Avocado Dip*

= **Yield: 2 cups**

½ pound smoked salmon
3 ounces cream cheese,
   softened
⅓ cup mashed avocado
2 tablespoons heavy cream
¼ teaspoon crushed green
   peppercorns

2 teaspoons lemon juice
salt and white pepper, to taste
whole green peppercorns, for
   garnish

1. In a food processor, purée the salmon and cheese. Add the avocado, cream, crushed peppercorns, lemon juice, and pepper; mix well. Correct seasoning with salt. Chill.

2. Place in a serving bowl and garnish with whole green peppercorns. Serve with apple or pear slices, crackers, or vegetables. Can also be used to fill small puffs or cucumber cups.

▶ Keeps 3 days, tightly sealed and refrigerated.

≡ *Shrimp Dip*

= **Yield: 3 cups**

½ pound shrimp, cooked and
   peeled
1 cup sour cream
¼ cup bourbon
1 teaspoon minced parsley

1 teaspoon minced dill
¾ teaspoon salt
½ teaspoon black pepper
½ teaspoon paprika
1 tablespoon minced chives

1. In a food processor, purée the shrimp, sour cream, bourbon, parsley, dill, salt, pepper, and paprika. Stir in the chives. Chill.

2. Serve with raw vegetables or pita toast.

▶ Keeps 3 days, tightly sealed and refrigerated.

≡ *Taramasalata (Carp Roe Dip)*

This dip is very difficult to describe to a client, but the taste is worth the effort.

═ **Yield: 2½ cups**

3 ounces tarama, or carp roe
   (see Glossary)
½ cup minced onion
1½ cups olive oil

4 to 5 slices white bread, crusts
   removed
¼ to ½ cup lemon juice

1. In a food processor, purée the tarama and onion. With the machine running, add 3 tablespoons olive oil and process until smooth.

2. Soak the bread slices in ½ cup water until soft. Drain, squeezing out the excess moisture. With the machine running, alternately add the bread, remaining olive oil, and lemon juice. The taramasalata should be pale pink, the consistency of mayonnaise, and with a slightly tart finish.

3. Serve with pita toast or vegetables, or use to stuff vegetables or cocktail puffs.

▶ Keeps 4 to 5 days, refrigerated.

≡ *Tonno Alla Veneziana (Tuna Fish Venetian-Style)*

═ **Yield: 2½ cups**

2 cups mayonnaise
7 ounces tuna, packed in
   olive oil
juice of 1 lemon

2 garlic cloves, crushed
2 tablespoons minced onion
salt and pepper, to taste

1. In a food processor, purée the mayonnaise, tuna, lemon juice, garlic, onion, salt, and pepper.

2. Serve with vegetables, toasted breads, or crackers.

▶ Keeps 5 days, refrigerated.

5

Spreads

*T*he only difference between dips and spreads is the thickness of the mixture. Therefore, it is possible to turn one into another with little effort. The choice is yours. Remember that a dip must be thin enough to dip without breaking the cracker or chip, and a spread must be thick enough to spread easily while adhering to the bread. Often, this only requires that the spread be served at room temperature, but it can also mean keeping it cold enough so that it does not melt. Although pâtés and terrines can be considered spreads, they are discussed in a separate chapter because of their special qualities.

Spreads, like dips, vary greatly in the number of people they can serve. As a general rule, 1 cup of spread serves 8, and 1 quart serves 36, unless specified otherwise.

Serve spreads with toast, crackers, cocktail breads, or slices of vegetables, much like dips. For variety and interest, serve a variety of breads—dark, light, soft, crisp, bland, and strongly flavored. Check your market and various small bakeries to find interesting and unusual breads and crackers. Select breads and spreads that complement each other, rather than letting one overwhelm the other. They should also enhance the other foods on the menu. Beware of using an herbed bread with an herbed spread, or the flavors may cancel each other out.

Slice the breads just before serving. Too often zealous employees will slice the French bread as soon as they arrive on the job. However, two hours later when it is time to serve it, the bread will be dry and stale. If you must slice the bread early, cover it first with waxed paper and then with a towel wrung out in cold water. This method works well for most breads, but not for those with a crisp crust such as French bread. Crackers usually can be set out well ahead without any loss of quality

117

unless it is extraordinarily humid. Ideally, toast is made continuously and served hot, or baked in a 325°F oven until crisp and dry and served at room temperature. Oven-toasting is better because toasters tend to brown the outside of the slice while leaving the inside moist. Such toast quickly becomes soggy and chewy.

For the cheese spreads, follow the directions or create the flavors you want. Feel free to substitute a cheese of a similar type if the kind specified is not available. Processed or imitation cheeses or "cheese foods" are not acceptable in fine cooking. They have a different consistency as well as flavor. For the best flavor, serve cheese at, or just below, room temperature; this applies to most other "cold" foods as well. Refrigerator temperatures deaden the flavors of the food.

—— Shaping Cheese Spreads ——

Cheese mixtures can be made into decorative shapes such as balls, trees, or logs once they have been chilled. Recipes that call for tiny balls are in Chapter 10.

Large Cheese Balls
Chill the cheese mixture until it is firm enough to mold. Rinse your hands in cold water, and, working quickly, shape the cheese into a large ball. Roll the ball in chopped nuts, minced parsley, paprika, or minced onions to give it color. Chill until ready to serve.

Small Cheese Balls
Shape teaspoons of the cheese mixture into small balls and roll them in minced olives, parsley, or paprika. Chill. Do not make the balls too large—no more than two modest bites. To serve, arrange them on a platter to resemble a bunch of grapes, or skewer them and push the skewers into a styrofoam form. For smaller presentations, insert the skewers into half an orange, grapefruit, or cabbage.

Cheese Trees
A cheese tree can be a very impressive presentation if you have at least a quart of cheese. It will also work with smaller amounts. Use a cheese mixture that has the consistency of butter. Shape the cheese into a tall cone with your hands and chill until semifirm. Dip a butter curler into hot water and, starting near the base of the cone, shave downward on the tree to form curls. Continue around the base. Move up 1 inch and repeat another row of curls. Continue until you reach the top. Chill. If some of the curls break or are not perfect, fill those spaces with sprigs

Cheese or Butter Tree

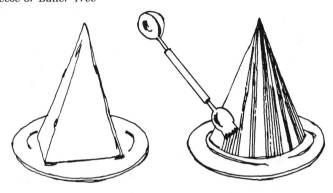

1. *Shape mixture into a cone.*   2. *Score sides with butter curler.*

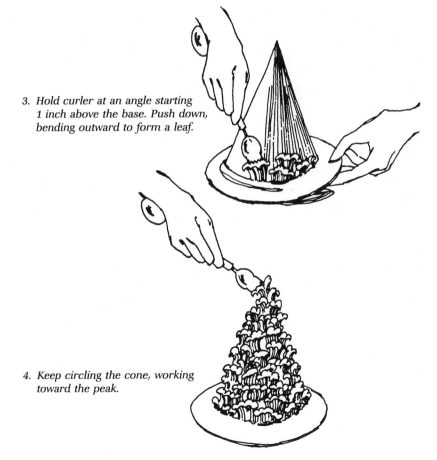

3. *Hold curler at an angle starting 1 inch above the base. Push down, bending outward to form a leaf.*

4. *Keep circling the cone, working toward the peak.*

of parsley or a small flower. For added texture before you begin to shave the curls, score the sides of the cone with a butter curler.

Another method is to make the cone with part of the cheese and put the remainder into a pastry bag fitted with a grooved tip, either a round star tip or a flat ribbon tip. Starting at the base, pipe around the base and continue up the cone to the top.

Cheese Pineapples

This presentation is also impressive. It requires at least a quart of cheese. Form the chilled cheese into the shape of a pineapple. Roll it in paprika or ground nuts. With the back of a knife, score the sides to simulate the design of a pineapple. Set the pineapple on a platter, upright. Place the frond of a real pineapple on the top and chill. For a truly dramatic presentation for a large group, make a gallon of the cheese and shape it as described above, but instead of using a pineapple frond, which would be too small for this size, use palm fronds from the florist to create your own plume. In the center of the plume insert an exotic flower, such as a ginger flower or proteus.

Cheese Log

Chill the cheese and shape it into a log with the help of a sheet of waxed paper. The diameter can be anywhere from 1 to 3 inches. Present it as is or roll it in nuts, parsley, minced ham, or paprika.

—— *Vegetable Spreads* ——

≡ *Hummus (Chickpea Spread)*

═ Yield: 1¼ cups

1 cup canned, drained
  chickpeas (garbanzos)
2 tablespoons lemon juice
2 garlic cloves
½ teaspoon salt

pepper, to taste
¼ to ½ cup olive oil
minced mint or parsley
olive oil
paprika

═ Yield: 5 cups

4 cups canned, drained
  chickpeas (garbanzos)
½ cup lemon juice
6 garlic cloves
2 teaspoons salt

½ teaspoon black pepper
1 to 2 cups olive oil
minced mint or parsley
olive oil
paprika

1. Rinse the chickpeas in cold water and drain again. Dry on paper towels.

2. In a food processor, purée the chickpeas, lemon juice, garlic, salt, pepper, and half the olive oil, adding more oil if necessary, until the consistency is slightly thicker than mayonnaise. Correct the seasoning with additional salt and lemon juice.

3. Place in a bowl and sprinkle mint or parsley around the edge, drizzle oil over the top, and dust with paprika if desired.

▶ Keeps 2 weeks, refrigerated.

≡ *Hummus bi Tahini* (*Chickpea Spread with Sesame Paste*)

Stir ¾ cup tahini into the smaller quantity of hummus, or 1½ cups into the larger. Be sure to use the tahini sold in Middle Eastern markets or make your own (see page 103). Do not substitute Asian sesame seed paste for this product.

≡ *Cucumber Spread*

≡ Yield: 1 cup

2 cucumbers, peeled, seeded, and minced
salt, to taste
½ cup minced chives
pepper, to taste
¼ to ½ cup sour cream

≡ Yield: 1 quart

8 cucumbers, peeled, seeded, and minced
salt, to taste
2 cups minced chives
pepper, to taste
1 to 2 cups sour cream

1. Sprinkle the cucumbers with salt, place in a colander, and let drain for 1 hour. Rinse under cold water, drain, and pat dry.

2. In a bowl, mix the cucumbers and chives and season with black pepper. Stir in just enough sour cream to bind.

3. Serve with bread rounds or crackers.

▶ Keeps 8 hours, refrigerated.

≡ *Caponata*

═ Yield: 3 cups
¼ cup olive oil
1 eggplant, cut into 1-inch
  cubes
1 onion, chopped
1 pound tomatoes, peeled,
  seeded, and diced
¾ cup sliced celery
1 carrot, thinly sliced
1 medium zucchini, diced
1 pepper, cut into 1-inch
  squares
⅓ cup sliced stuffed olives

¼ cup minced parsley
3 tablespoons red wine
2 tablespoons minced basil
2 tablespoons capers
1½ tablespoons tomato paste
1 garlic clove, crushed
1 tablespoon salt, or to taste
1 tablespoon sugar
½ teaspoon pepper
¼ cup pine nuts, lightly
  browned in olive oil

═ Yield: 6 cups
½ cup olive oil
2 eggplants, cut into
  1-inch cubes
2 onions, chopped
3 pounds tomatoes, peeled,
  seeded, and diced
1½ cups sliced celery
2 carrots, thinly sliced
2 to 3 zucchini, diced
2 peppers, cut into 1-inch
  squares
¾ cup sliced stuffed olives

½ cup minced parsley
⅓ cup red wine
¼ cup minced basil
¼ cup capers
3 tablespoons tomato paste
2 garlic cloves, crushed
2 tablespoons salt, or to taste
2 tablespoons sugar
1 teaspoon pepper
½ cup pine nuts, lightly
  browned in olive oil

1. In a large casserole, heat the oil and sauté the eggplant and onion until golden. Add the tomatoes, celery, carrots, zucchini, peppers, olives, parsley, red wine, basil, capers, tomato paste, garlic, salt, sugar, and pepper. Cook, stirring, until it reaches a simmer. Cover and simmer 30 minutes, stirring occasionally. Remove the cover and cook until thickened.

2. Sprinkle with pine nuts and serve at room temperature with slices of Italian white and whole wheat breads.

▶ Keeps 3 weeks, refrigerated.

≡ Eggplant and Hazelnut Spread

== **Yield: 1 cup**

½ pound eggplant
½ cup toasted hazelnuts,
  ground
1½ tablespoons mayonnaise

1 tablespoon lemon juice
1 garlic clove, crushed
⅛ teaspoon ground ginger
salt and pepper, to taste

== **Yield: 1 quart**

2 pounds eggplant
1½ cups toasted hazelnuts,
  ground
⅓ cup mayonnaise

2 tablespoons lemon juice
4 garlic cloves, crushed
½ teaspoon ground ginger
salt and pepper, to taste

1. Preheat the oven to 400°F.

2. Remove and discard the eggplant stems. Place the eggplants in a shallow baking pan and bake 40 minutes or until soft. Cool.

3. Peel the eggplant and discard the skin. Purée the pulp in a food processor. Add the nuts, mayonnaise, lemon juice, garlic, ginger, salt, and pepper and mix well. Chill at least 2 hours. Correct the seasoning.

4. Serve with crackers or pita bread.

► Keeps 1 week, refrigerated.

≡ Eggplant Spread I

== **Yield: about 1 cup**

1 eggplant
1 tablespoon peanut oil
1 tablespoon wine vinegar

1 tablespoon mayonnaise
1 garlic clove, crushed
salt and pepper, to taste

== **Yield: about 1 quart**

3 eggplants
3 tablespoons peanut oil
3 tablespoons wine vinegar

3 tablespoons mayonnaise
3 garlic cloves, crushed
salt and pepper, to taste

1. Preheat the oven to 400°F.

2. Remove and discard the eggplant stems. Place the eggplant in a shallow baking pan and bake 40 minutes or until soft.

3. Peel the eggplant and discard the skin. Place the pulp in a bowl and mash with a fork. When cool, mix in the oil, vinegar, mayonnaise, and garlic, and season with salt and pepper. Chill at least 2 hours.
4. Serve with crackers or melba toast.

▶ Keeps 1 week, refrigerated.

≡ *Eggplant Spread II*

═ Yield: 1 cup

½ pound eggplant, cut in half	1 garlic clove, minced
salt	salt and pepper, to taste
¼ cup olive oil	2 tablespoons heavy cream
¼ cup minced green pepper	1 egg yolk
¼ cup minced onion	2 tablespoons peeled, seeded,
¼ cup minced parsley	and chopped tomato
2 teaspoons lemon juice	2 tablespoons peeled, seeded,
2 teaspoons vinegar	and minced cucumber
1 teaspoon minced dill	minced dill, to taste
pinch of sugar	

═ Yield: 1 quart

2 pounds eggplant, cut in half	4 garlic cloves, minced
salt	salt and pepper, to taste
1 cup olive oil	½ cup heavy cream
1 green pepper, minced	2 egg yolks
½ cup minced onion	½ cup peeled, seeded, and
½ cup minced parsley	chopped tomato
2 tablespoons lemon juice	½ cup peeled, seeded, and
2 tablespoons vinegar	minced cucumber
1 tablespoon minced dill	minced dill, to taste
½ teaspoon sugar	

1. Sprinkle the cut sides of the eggplant with salt and drain, cut side down, for 30 minutes. Dry with paper towels.
2. In a large skillet, heat half the oil, and cook the eggplant, turning often, for 30 minutes or until very tender and golden. Cool, cut side down, on a rack.
3. Scoop out the pulp and place in a food processor. Purée with the pepper, remaining olive oil, onion, parsley, lemon juice, vinegar, dill, sugar, garlic, salt, and pepper. While the machine is running, add the

cream and egg yolk. Transfer to a bowl and fold in the tomato, cucumber, and dill. Chill.

4. Serve with crackers and pita bread.

▶ Keeps 3 days, refrigerated.

≡ *Eggplant Caviar*

== **Yield: 1 cup**

1 small eggplant	1½ tablespoons minced parsley
½ cup minced onion	or dill
1 tomato, peeled, seeded, and	1 garlic clove, crushed
chopped	½ teaspoon sugar
2 tablespoons olive oil	salt and pepper, to taste
1 tablespoon lemon juice	

== **Yield: 1 quart**

2 large eggplants	¼ cup lemon juice
1 cup minced onion	¼ cup minced parsley or dill
4 tomatoes, peeled, seeded, and	2 garlic cloves, crushed
chopped	2 teaspoons sugar
½ cup olive oil	salt and pepper, to taste

1. Preheat the oven to 400°F.

2. Remove the eggplant stem. Place the eggplant in a shallow baking pan and bake for 40 minutes or until soft.

3. Peel the eggplant and discard the skin. Drain as much liquid as possible from the eggplant. Purée the pulp in a food processor. Add the onion, tomatoes, olive oil, lemon juice, parsley, garlic, and sugar, and process until smooth. Correct seasoning with salt and pepper. Chill.

4. Serve with buttered toast.

▶ Keeps 1 week, refrigerated.

≡ *Aubergine Purée à la Turque*
(Eggplant Purée Turkish Style)

== **Yield: 1 cup**

1 small eggplant	2 tablespoons lemon juice, or to
½ cup minced onion	taste
salt and pepper, to taste	1 tablespoon minced parsley
1 to 2 tablespoons olive oil	

═ **Yield: 1 quart**

2 large eggplants
1½ cups minced onion
salt and pepper, to taste

⅓ to ½ cup olive oil
¼ cup lemon juice, or to taste
¼ cup minced parsley

1. Preheat the broiler.

2. Remove and discard the eggplant stems and broil the eggplant until the skin blisters on all sides. Remove to a work surface and let cool. Peel.

3. In a bowl, mash the pulp and beat in the onion, salt, and pepper. Add enough oil to reach the consistency of mayonnaise and enough lemon juice to give a tart flavor. Correct seasoning with salt and pepper.

4. Sprinkle with parsley and serve with dark rye or pita bread. This spread can also be used to stuff vegetables or pastries.

▶ Keeps 1 week, refrigerated.

≡ *Baba Ghanouj*

═ **Yield: 1 cup**

1 small eggplant
3 tablespoons tahini (page 103;
  also see Glossary)

3 tablespoons lemon juice
1 large garlic clove, minced
salt and pepper, to taste

═ **Yield: 1 quart**

2 large eggplants
⅔ cup tahini (page 103; also see
  Glossary)

⅔ cup lemon juice
4 large garlic cloves, minced
salt and pepper, to taste

1. Preheat the oven to 400°F.

2. Remove and discard the eggplant stems. Bake the eggplant in a shallow baking pan for 40 minutes or until soft. Peel.

3. In a food processor, purée the pulp with the tahini, lemon juice, garlic, salt, and pepper.

4. Serve with sesame crackers, toast, or toasted pita bread.

▶ Keeps 4 days, refrigerated.

≡ Mushroom Caviar

═ Yield: 1 cup

3 tablespoons butter
½ pound mushrooms, minced
4 shallots, minced
1 tablespoon white wine

1 garlic clove, minced
2 tablespoons toasted pine nuts
1 to 2 tablespoons sour cream
salt and pepper, to taste

═ Yield: 1 quart

½ cup butter
2 pounds mushrooms, minced
1 cup minced shallots
¼ cup white wine

2 garlic cloves, minced
¼ cup toasted pine nuts
¼ to ½ cup sour cream
salt and pepper, to taste

1. In a skillet, melt the butter and sauté the mushrooms and shallots, stirring often until the mushrooms give up their liquid. Add the wine and garlic and cook until the liquid evaporates. Remove from the heat and let cool.

2. Fold in the pine nuts and sour cream and season with salt and pepper. Chill, covered.

3. Serve with sesame crackers.

▶ Keeps 4 days, refrigerated.

≡ Serbian Vegetable Caviar

═ Yield: 1 cup

4 to 5 green or red peppers
1 to 2 tablespoons lemon juice
½ cup minced onion

⅓ cup olive oil
salt and pepper, to taste

═ Yield: 1 quart

16 to 20 green or red peppers
¼ to ½ cup lemon juice
2 cups minced onion

1⅓ cups olive oil
salt and pepper, to taste

1. Preheat the oven to 400°F.

2. In a shallow baking pan, roast the peppers for 30 to 45 minutes or until tender. Remove and cool.

3. Discard the stems, seeds, and peel. Chop the peppers coarsely. Mix with the lemon juice, onion, olive oil, salt, and pepper. Cool completely and serve with crackers.

▶ Keeps 3 days, refrigerated.

—— *Cheese Spreads* ——

≡ *Schmierkäse (Spreading Cheese)*

═ **Yield: 1 cup**

2 cups thick sour milk	1 tablespoon heavy cream
⅓ cup heavy cream	paprika
salt and pepper, to taste	minced parsley or chives

═ **Yield: 1 quart**

8 cups thick sour milk	2 tablespoons heavy cream
1⅓ cups heavy cream	paprika
salt and pepper, to taste	minced parsley or chives

1. Heat the milk to 100°F. Remove from heat and let rest. When the curds and whey (liquid) have separated, pour off the whey and discard. Place the curds in a cheesecloth-lined sieve and suspend over a bowl. Set in a warm place until the curds have drained, about 6 hours.

2. Mix in the larger amount of cream and the salt and pepper. Arrange on a platter and pour the remaining cream over the top. Sprinkle with paprika, parsley, or chives.

▶ Keeps 4 days, refrigerated. If drained longer, it will keep for up to 2 weeks.

NOTE: The cheese can be returned to the cheesecloth-lined sieve after adding the cream, salt, and pepper and allowed to drain for 12 to 48 hours longer. The longer the cheese drains, the drier it becomes.

To sour milk, purchase pasteurized, unhomogenized milk and let stand at room temperature until soured, two to three days.

≡ *Yogurt Cheese*

═ **Yield: 1 cup**

2 cups yogurt	salt, to taste

═ **Yield: 1 quart**

2 quarts yogurt   salt, to taste

1. Pour the yogurt into a large sieve lined with a double thickness of dampened cheesecloth. Set over a bowl and let drain for 8 to 12 hours in the refrigerator. Discard the liquid. Remove the cheese from the sieve and beat in the salt.

2. Serve with crackers or use in making cheese hors d'oeuvre.

▶ Keeps 2 weeks, refrigerated.

NOTE: For a richer cheese, substitute half heavy cream for half the yogurt.

≡ *Homemade Creamy Cheese*

═ **Yield: about 1 cup**

2 cups medium cream   2 tablespoons buttermilk
½ cup heavy cream   salt, to taste

═ **Yield: 1 quart**

2 quarts medium cream   ½ cup buttermilk
2 cups heavy cream   salt, to taste

1. In a saucepan, heat the medium and heavy creams to 90°F. Stir in the buttermilk, pour into a large bowl, and cover with plastic wrap. Place in a draft-free place and wrap in a blanket. Let stand until it reaches the consistency of soft yogurt. This can take up to 48 hours.

2. Rinse a sheet of fine cheesecloth in cold water and wring it out. Line a colander with the cheesecloth and place the colander in a sink. Gently pour the thickened cream into the colander and let drain for 15 minutes. Fold the ends of the cheesecloth over the cheese and place the colander in a deep bowl. Refrigerate for 12 to 18 hours or until well drained. Drain for up to 48 hours for a drier cheese. Season the cheese with salt.

▶ Keeps 1 week, refrigerated.

NOTE: The cheese can be flavored with port or Madeira, caraway seeds, garlic, or herbs. To firm the cheese and give it shape, place it in unvarnished straw baskets lined with cheesecloth, sieves, or coeur à la crème molds. Chill overnight and turn out to serve.

≡ *Port and Walnut Cheese*

═ Yield: 1 cup

1 cup homemade creamy
cheese (page 129)
2 tablespoons confectioners'
sugar

2 tablespoons port, or to taste
chopped walnuts

═ Yield: 1 quart

1 quart homemade creamy
cheese (page 129)
½ cup confectioners' sugar

¼ cup port, or to taste
chopped walnuts

1. In a bowl, mix the cheese and sugar. With a table knife, swirl the port through the cheese, making streaks. Chill at least 4 hours.

2. Before serving, press walnuts into the top and sides.

▶ Keeps 1 week, refrigerated.

≡ *Rumanian Cheese*

═ Yield: 1¼ cups

½ cup crumbled feta cheese
½ cup unsalted butter

¼ cup homemade creamy
cheese (page 129)

═ Yield: 5 cups

2 cups crumbled feta cheese
2 cups unsalted butter

1 cup homemade creamy
cheese (page 129)

1. In a mixer or food processor, mix the feta cheese, butter, and creamy cheese until smooth. Wrap in a double thickness of cheesecloth and chill at least 4 hours.

2. Serve with crackers or breads.

▶ Keeps 5 days, refrigerated.

≡ *Calvados Cheese Spread*

This cheese is allowed to drain and ripen in a cheese mold. If you do not have a cheese basket, any unvarnished straw basket will do, as will a coeur à la crème mold or even a sieve or colander. Be sure to suspend the mold above the pan so the liquid can drain. The longer it drains, the firmer the cheese will become.

= **Yield: 1¼ cups**

½ cup cream cheese, softened,   2 tablespoons heavy cream
  or ½ cup homemade creamy   1 tablespoon Calvados or
  cheese (page 129)   applejack
½ cup ricotta cheese   pinch of salt

= **Yield: 1¼ quarts**

1 pound cream cheese,   1 pound ricotta cheese
  softened, or 1 pound   ½ cup heavy cream
  homemade creamy cheese   ¼ cup Calvados or applejack
  (page 129)   ½ teaspoon salt

1. In a mixer or food processor, beat the cream cheese until smooth. Beat in the ricotta, heavy cream, Calvados, and salt.

2. Line a cheese mold with cheesecloth wrung out in cold water. Scrape in the cheese, cover with the ends of the cheesecloth, and weight with a plate and a 2 to 4 pound weight. Place in a shallow pan and let ripen in the refrigerator for 24 hours.

3. Unmold, remove the cloth, and serve with crackers or fruit.

▶ Keeps 1 week, refrigerated.

≡ *Cervelle de Canut (Silkworker's Brains, or Fresh Cheese Seasoned with Shallots and Herbs)*

This cheese was considered the poor man's substitute for a dinner of veal brains.

= **Yield: 1½ cups**

6 ounces cream cheese   1 garlic clove, minced
½ cup heavy cream   1 tablespoon minced parsley
1 tablespoon white wine   1 tablespoon minced chives
2 teaspoons olive oil   salt and pepper, to taste
1 shallot, minced

= **Yield: 1½ quarts**

1½ pounds cream cheese   4 garlic cloves, minced
2 cups heavy cream   ¼ cup minced parsley
¼ cup white wine   ¼ cup minced chives
2½ tablespoons olive oil   salt and pepper, to taste
¼ cup minced shallots

In a processor, cream the cheese, cream, wine, oil, shallot, and garlic. Transfer to a bowl and stir in the parsley, chives, salt, and pepper. Chill for 2 hours before serving.

▶ Keeps 1 week, refrigerated.

☰ Coeur à la Crème au Caviar (Heart-Shaped Cheese with Caviar)

☰ Yield: 1½ cups

½ cup cottage cheese, sieved	½ cup heavy cream
½ cup cream cheese, softened, or ½ cup homemade creamy cheese (page 129)	salmon or sturgeon caviar (see note)
	lemon wedges

☰ Yield: 6 cups

1 pound cottage cheese, sieved	2 cups heavy cream
1 pound cream cheese, softened, or 2 cups homemade creamy cheese (page 129)	salmon or sturgeon caviar (see note)
	lemon wedges

1. In a mixer or food processor, beat the cottage cheese until blended, then gradually beat in the cream cheese and heavy cream until smooth.

2. Line a 6-cup coeur à la crème basket or a sieve with cheesecloth wrung out in cold water. Fill with the cheese mixture and place in a bowl in the refrigerator to drain overnight. Unmold onto a platter and remove the cheesecloth. Surround with caviar and lemon wedges.

3. Serve with hot toast, crackers, or blinis.

▶ Keeps 5 days, refrigerated.

NOTE: This spread can also be served with fruits instead of caviar at the end of a meal or at a fruit-and-cheese party. Because the cheese is the feature of this recipe, not the caviar, it is acceptable to use a less expensive caviar. For an attractive presentation, make ribbons of salmon, golden, and sevruga caviars across the top of the cheese, rather than around the edges. The cheese can also be mixed with minced smoked salmon and onion before draining.

≡ *Herbed Garlic Cheese*

═ Yield: 1 cup

½ pound cream cheese,
softened, or 1 cup
homemade creamy cheese
(page 129)
1 tablespoon heavy cream, if
required

2 tablespoons minced parsley
2 garlic cloves, minced
2 teaspoons minced marjoram
2 teaspoons minced oregano
2 teaspoons minced savory
salt, to taste

═ Yield: 4 cups

2 pounds cream cheese,
softened, or 4 cups
homemade creamy cheese
(page 129)
2 to 4 tablespoons heavy cream,
if required
½ cup minced parsley

4 garlic cloves, minced
2 tablespoons minced
marjoram
2 tablespoons minced oregano
2 tablespoons minced savory
salt, to taste

1. In a bowl, mix the cream cheese until soft and smooth, adding the cream, if required. Beat in the parsley, garlic, marjoram, oregano, savory, and salt. Chill at least 2 hours.
2. Serve with crackers.

▶ Keeps 1 week, refrigerated.

≡ *Bibelkäse (Bible Cheese)*

This old German specialty is a wonderful inexpensive spread with universal appeal.

═ Yield: 1 cup

1 cup small curd cottage
cheese
¼ cup heavy cream

2 garlic cloves, minced
1 tablespoon minced parsley
salt and pepper, to taste

═ Yield: 1 quart

2 pounds small curd cottage
cheese
1 cup heavy cream

6 garlic cloves, minced
2 tablespoons minced parsley
salt and pepper, to taste

1. Force the cottage cheese through a sieve into a bowl. Beat in the cream, garlic, parsley, salt, and pepper. Chill, covered, for at least 4 hours.

2. Serve with crackers.

▶ Keeps 1 week, refrigerated.

≡ *Coconut Cheese Spread*

== **Yield: 1 cup**

½ cup cream cheese, softened, or homemade creamy cheese (page 129)

¼ cup grated coconut

2 tablespoons minced chutney
½ teaspoon curry powder
½ teaspoon ground ginger

== **Yield: 1 quart**

3 cups cream cheese, softened, or homemade creamy cheese (page 129)

1½ cups grated coconut

¾ cup minced chutney
1½ tablespoons curry powder
1½ tablespoons ground ginger

1. In a bowl, mix the cheese, coconut, chutney, curry powder, and ginger. Chill for at least 2 hours before serving.

2. Serve with buttered toast fingers.

▶ Keeps 1 week, refrigerated.

≡ *Walnut-Orange Cheese Spread*

== **Yield: 1½ cups**

1 cup cream cheese (see note)
¼ cup heavy cream
¼ cup chopped walnuts

salt and paprika, to taste
¼ cup bitter orange marmalade
1 teaspoon dry mustard

== **Yield: 6 cups**

2 pounds cream cheese (see note)
1 cup heavy cream
1 cup chopped walnuts

salt and paprika, to taste
1 cup bitter orange marmalade
1 tablespoon dry mustard

1. In a bowl, blend the cream cheese, cream, walnuts, salt, and paprika together. Shape into a flat cake on a serving dish. In a bowl, mix the marmalade and mustard and spoon over the cheese.

2. Serve with bread or crackers.

▶ Keeps 2 days, refrigerated.

NOTE: If you have made homemade creamy cheese (page 129), substitute an equivalent amount of it for the cream cheese and eliminate the heavy cream.

≡ Sacher Cheese

═ Yield: 1½ cups

1 cup cottage cheese, sieved
2 hard-cooked egg yolks, sieved

3 anchovy fillets, minced
¼ cup butter, softened

═ Yield: 6 cups

1 quart cottage cheese, sieved
8 hard-cooked egg yolks, sieved

12 anchovy fillets, minced
1 cup butter, softened

1. In a bowl, beat the cottage cheese, egg yolks, anchovies, and butter. Chill.

2. Serve with crackers or dark bread.

▶ Keeps 1 week, refrigerated.

≡ Blue Cheese and Olive Roll

═ Yield: 1¼ cups

¼ pound blue cheese
¼ pound cream cheese
2 tablespoons butter
½ cup ripe olives, chopped

2 tablespoons minced chives
2 tablespoons Cognac
½ cup chopped toasted
almonds

═ Yield: 1½ quarts

1 pound blue cheese
1 pound cream cheese
½ cup butter
1½ cups ripe olives, chopped

2 tablespoons minced chives
2 tablespoons Cognac
2 cups chopped toasted
almonds

1. In a food processor, purée the blue cheese, cream cheese, and butter. Turn into a bowl and fold in the olives, chives, and Cognac. On a sheet of waxed paper, shape the cheese into a log and roll it in the almonds. Wrap in plastic wrap and chill.

2. Serve with crackers or breads.

▶ Keeps 3 weeks, refrigerated.

≡ *Blue Cheese–Port Walnut Spread*

The sharpness of this spread can be controlled by the blue cheese you select. Roquefort gives it a sharp flavor; Bleu de Bresse or Saga blue make it much softer, more buttery.

= **Yield: 1½ cups**

½ pound blue cheese, crumbled
¼ cup butter, softened

3 to 4 tablespoons tawny port
¾ cup chopped walnuts

= **Yield: 6 cups**

2 pounds blue cheese, crumbled
1 cup butter, softened

⅔ to 1 cup tawny port
3 cups chopped walnuts

1. In a food processor, purée the cheese and butter and gradually add enough port to make a smooth, creamy mixture. Fold in the almonds and pack into crocks. Chill at least 3 hours.

2. Serve with crackers or breads, or use to fill vegetables or pastries.

▶ Keeps 2 weeks, refrigerated.

≡ *Malexe (Roquefort Calvados Spread)*

= **Yield: 1 cup**

½ cup Roquefort cheese
½ cup butter, softened

2 tablespoons Calvados, approximately

= **Yield: 1 quart**

2 cups Roquefort cheese
2 cups butter, softened

½ cup Calvados, approximately

1. In a food processor, purée the cheese and butter, adding enough Calvados to make it smooth and creamy. Pack into crocks.

2. Serve with crackers or use to fill pastries.

▶ Keeps 1 week, refrigerated.

≡ *Roquefort Cheese Mold*

== **Yield: 3 cups**

¾ pound Roquefort cheese
8 ounces cream cheese
½ cup minced celery leaves
½ green pepper, minced
1 tablespoon minced onion

1 tablespoon melted butter
1 tablespoon Worcestershire
    sauce
salt and pepper, to taste
¾ pound pecans, chopped

== **Yield: 6 cups**

1½ pounds Roquefort cheese
1 pound cream cheese
1 cup minced celery leaves
1 green pepper, minced
2 tablespoons minced onion

2 tablespoons melted butter
2 tablespoons Worcestershire
    sauce
salt and pepper, to taste
1½ pounds pecans, chopped

1. In a bowl, mix the Roquefort, cream cheese, celery, pepper, onion, butter, Worcestershire sauce, salt, and pepper. Shape into a ball, log, or pineapple (see pages 118–120 for directions). If too soft, chill first. Roll in pecans and chill before serving.

2. Serve with bread and crackers.

▶ Keeps 4 days, refrigerated.

≡ *Roquefort–Sesame Seed Cheese Spread*

== **Yield: 1 cup**

¼ pound cream cheese
¼ pound Roquefort cheese,
    crumbled

2 tablespoons sesame seeds,
    toasted
¼ cup Armagnac or Cognac

== **Yield: 1 quart**

1 pound cream cheese
1 pound Roquefort cheese,
    crumbled

½ cup sesame seeds, toasted
¾ to 1 cup Armagnac or
    Cognac

1. In a food processor, purée the cream cheese and Roquefort. Add the sesame seeds and enough Armagnac to make a smooth mixture.

2. Serve with thin crisp bread.

▶ Keeps 1 week, refrigerated.

≡ Stilton Spread

═ Yield: 1 cup

¼ pound Stilton cheese
¼ pound cream cheese
2 tablespoons butter, softened

1 tablespoon port
1 tablespoon heavy cream

═ Yield: 1 quart

1 pound Stilton cheese
1 pound cream cheese
½ pound butter, softened

¼ cup port
¼ cup heavy cream

1. In a food processor, purée the Stilton, cream cheese, and butter. Add the wine and cream and blend until smooth.
2. Store in a crock for at least 24 hours.
3. Serve with crackers.

▶ Keeps 1 week, refrigerated.

≡ Brie with Roasted Garlic

═ Yield: 8 servings

2 large heads garlic, whole and
    unpeeled
2 tablespoons olive oil

1 small Brie cheese,
    approximately 8 ounces

═ Yield: 24 servings

6 large heads garlic, whole and
    unpeeled
6 tablespoons olive oil

1 large Brie cheese,
    approximately 2 pounds

1. Preheat the oven to 400°F.
2. In a small ovenproof dish, bake the garlic in the oil, uncovered, for about 1 hour or until very tender. Remove from the oven and cool.
3. Lower the oven to 350°F.
4. Cut off the tops of the garlic heads and squeeze out the softened pulp. Mix the pulp with the oil in the baking dish and spread smoothly over the Brie.
5. Place the Brie on a buttered heatproof platter and bake for 20 minutes or until puffy and softened. Serve with bread and crackers.

▶ Garlic can be prepared the day before, but serve cheese immediately after heating.

≡ Gefüllter Camembert Käse
(Camembert Farci, or Stuffed Camembert)

This cheese makes a stunning presentation. For a small party it lends just the right note of care, and for a large party it can easily be the centerpiece.

≡ **Yield: 8 servings**

1 small Camembert cheese,
  approximately 8 ounces
½ cup butter, softened
½ cup heavy cream
salt, to taste

paprika, to taste
¼ cup seedless grapes
½ cup slivered almonds,
  toasted

≡ **Yield: 24 or more servings**

1 large Camembert cheese,
  approximately 2 pounds
¾ pound butter, softened
2 cups heavy cream
salt, to taste

paprika, to taste
1 cup seedless grapes
1½ cups slivered almonds,
  toasted

1. Carefully cut the center out of the Camembert, leaving the bottom and sides about ¼ inch thick.

2. In a food processor, purée the removed cheese, including the rind. Add the butter and gradually add the cream. Then beat in the salt and paprika. Add enough paprika to give the cheese a delicate coral color.

3. Fit a pastry bag with a no. 4 large open star tip and fill the shell by piping little mounds of cheese evenly over the surface. When the bottom is covered, starting one row in from the edge, pipe another layer and continue in this fashion until you have a tall cone of cheese in the shell. Garnish the base of the shell with the grapes and sprinkle the almonds over the top.

4. Serve with buttered pumpernickel bread.

▶ Keeps 2 days, refrigerated.

≡ *Camembert Angemacht*

This spread should have a chunky texture.

== **Yield: about 2 cups**

1 small Camembert cheese, approximately 8 ounces, chilled

½ pound butter, chilled
¼ cup minced onion
paprika, to taste

== **Yield: about 4 cups**

1 large Camembert cheese, approximately 1 pound, chilled

1 pound butter, chilled
½ cup minced onion
paprika, to taste

1. Dice the cheese and butter into ¼- to ½-inch cubes, and toss in a bowl with the onion and paprika until they just hold together. Do not mash.

2. Shape into a mound on a platter.

3. Serve with rye bread or use to fill pastries.

▶ Keeps 3 days, refrigerated.

≡ *Camembert Roti aux Lardons (Broiled Camembert with Bacon)*

== **Yield: 8 servings**

⅓ pound slab bacon, cut into ¼-inch cubes
1 loaf French bread

1 garlic clove, peeled
butter, as needed
1 small Camembert cheese

1. Preheat the broiler.

2. In a skillet, sauté the bacon in its own fat until crisp. Drain and set aside.

3. Rub the crust of the bread with the garlic and slice the bread. Heat the butter in a skillet and sauté the bread slices until golden on both sides.

4. On a heatproof platter, broil the cheese until golden. Place on a warm serving platter and sprinkle the bacon over the top.

5. Serve with the sautéed bread on the side.

▶ Serve the cheese at once. For large parties, broil cheese as needed. Do not let it stand or it will become rubbery.

≡ Beer Cheese Spread

═ Yield: 1 cup

1 cup grated Cheddar cheese
2 tablespoons butter
1 teaspoon Dijon mustard
1 teaspoon minced shallots

¼ teaspoon anchovy paste
¼ teaspoon caraway seeds
pinch of cayenne pepper
2 tablespoons beer

═ Yield: 1 quart

1 quart grated Cheddar cheese
½ cup butter
1½ tablespoons Dijon mustard
1½ tablespoons minced shallots

1 teaspoon anchovy paste
1 teaspoon caraway seeds
⅛ teaspoon cayenne pepper
½ cup beer

1. In a bowl, mix the cheese, butter, mustard, shallots, anchovy paste, caraway seeds, and cayenne. Gradually beat in the beer until fluffy. Store in the refrigerator.
2. Serve with crackers or breads, or use to fill pastries.

▶ Keeps 1 week, refrigerated.

≡ Cheddar and Beer Spread

═ Yield: 1 cup

1 cup grated Cheddar cheese
½ garlic clove, crushed
2 teaspoons Worcestershire sauce

¼ teaspoon dry mustard
cayenne pepper, to taste
¼ cup beer

═ Yield: 1 quart

1 pound Cheddar cheese, grated
2 garlic cloves, crushed
2 tablespoons Worcestershire sauce

1 teaspoon dry mustard
cayenne pepper, to taste
2 cups beer

1. In a bowl, mix the cheese, garlic, Worcestershire sauce, mustard, and cayenne. Gradually beat in the beer. Pack into crocks and chill 12 hours.
2. Serve with crackers or use to fill pastries.

▶ Keeps 1 week, refrigerated.

≡ Cheddar Cheese Log

═ Yield: 1½ cups

4 ounces cream cheese, softened
4 ounces sharp Cheddar cheese, grated
¼ cup minced onion
1 garlic clove, crushed
⅓ cup ground walnuts

2 tablespoons chopped walnuts
2 tablespoons minced parsley
1½ teaspoons paprika
1½ teaspoons chili powder
1½ teaspoons curry powder
1 teaspoon minced dill

═ Yield: 6 cups

1 pound cream cheese, softened
1 pound sharp Cheddar cheese, grated
1 cup minced onion
3 garlic cloves, crushed
1⅓ cups ground walnuts

½ cup chopped walnuts
½ cup minced parsley
2 tablespoons paprika
2 tablespoons chili powder
2 tablespoons curry powder
4 teaspoons minced dill

1. In a bowl, mix the cream cheese, Cheddar, onion, garlic, and ground walnuts until smooth. Chill until firm enough to mold.

2. With the aid of a sheet of waxed paper, shape the cheese into one or more logs.

3. In a bowl, mix the chopped walnuts, parsley, paprika, chili powder, curry powder, and dill. Spread on a sheet of waxed paper, and firmly roll the log of cheese over the mixture to coat evenly. Chill.

4. Serve with crackers or breads.

▶ Keeps 4 days, refrigerated.

≡ Cheddar Pistachio Spread

═ Yield: 1½ cups

1½ cups grated sharp Cheddar cheese
3 tablespoons butter
2 tablespoons Cognac

⅛ teaspoon cayenne pepper
⅓ cup blanched pistachios, chopped

═══ **Yield: 1½ quarts**

6 cups grated sharp Cheddar
cheese
¾ cup butter
½ cup Cognac

½ teaspoon cayenne pepper
1⅓ cups blanched pistachios,
chopped

1. In a food processor, purée the cheese, butter, Cognac, and cayenne. Transfer to a bowl and fold in the nuts. Pack into crocks and cover.
2. Serve with crackers or breads.

▶ Keeps 3 weeks, refrigerated.

═══ *Cheddar Cheese with Sauternes*

True French Sauternes (from the Sauternes district of Bordeaux) is a sweet dessert wine and quite different from many sauternes sold in the United States. Fortunately, it is a wine that is often sold in half-bottles, because it is somewhat expensive. An inexpensive selection will do for this recipe.

═══ **Yield: 1½ cups**

½ pound Cheddar cheese,
grated
3 tablespoons sour cream
3 tablespoons butter, softened

¼ teaspoon Dijon mustard
pinch of ground mace
salt and pepper, to taste
3 tablespoons Sauternes

═══ **Yield: 1½ quarts**

1½ pounds Cheddar cheese,
grated
⅔ cup sour cream
½ cup butter, softened

1 tablespoon Dijon mustard
½ teaspoon ground mace
salt and pepper, to taste
½ cup Sauternes

1. In a food processor, purée the cheese, sour cream, and butter. Add the mustard, mace, salt, and pepper. With the machine running, incorporate the Sauternes. Pack into crocks and chill for several hours.
2. Serve with crackers.

▶ Keeps 2 weeks, refrigerated.

≡ *Cheddar and Walnut Spread*

═ Yield: 1½ cups

½ pound sharp Cheddar
cheese, grated
2 tablespoons butter, softened
2 tablespoons sour cream

pinch of ground mace
1 tablespoon Madeira or port
pinch of cayenne pepper
½ cup chopped walnuts

═ Yield: 6 cups

2 pounds sharp Cheddar
cheese, grated
½ cup butter, softened
½ cup sour cream

¼ teaspoon ground mace
¼ cup Madeira or port
¼ teaspoon cayenne pepper
2 cups chopped walnuts

1. In a food processor, purée the cheese, butter, sour cream, mace, Madeira, and cayenne. Stir in the nuts.

2. Serve with crackers or breads.

▶ Keeps 2 weeks, refrigerated.

≡ *Cheese and Walnuts*

═ Yield: 1 cup

½ pound Cheddar cheese,
grated
6 tablespoons butter
1 tablespoon white wine
vinegar

¼ teaspoon Dijon mustard
cayenne pepper, to taste
½ cup finely ground walnuts

═ Yield: 1 quart

2 pounds Cheddar cheese,
grated
1¼ cups butter
¼ cup white wine vinegar

1 tablespoon Dijon mustard
cayenne pepper, to taste
2 cups finely ground walnuts

1. In a food processor, purée the cheese, butter, vinegar, mustard, and cayenne. Add the nuts and incorporate with on-off turns.

2. Serve with dark bread or crackers.

▶ Keeps 2 weeks, refrigerated.

≡ *Chutney Cheese Log*

═ Yield: 1½ cups

6 ounces cream cheese,
  softened
4 ounces Cheddar cheese,
  grated
3 tablespoons sherry

¾ teaspoon curry powder
¼ teaspoon salt, or to taste
½ cup mango chutney, minced
¼ cup minced scallions

═ Yield: 6 cups

1½ pounds cream cheese,
  softened
1 pound Cheddar cheese,
  grated
½ cup sherry

1 tablespoon curry powder
1 teaspoon salt, or to taste
2 cups mango chutney, minced
1 cup minced scallions

    1. In a bowl, mix the cream cheese, Cheddar cheese, sherry, curry powder, and salt together. Shape into a mound on a platter, or roll into a log. Chill.
    2. Just before serving, spoon the chutney over the top and sprinkle with the scallions.
    3. Serve with crackers.

▶ Keeps 3 days, refrigerated.

≡ *Potted Cheese Spread*

═ Yield: about 1 cup

½ pound Cheddar cheese,
  grated
1 tablespoon minced parsley
1 tablespoon minced onion
2 teaspoons butter
¼ teaspoon dry mustard

¼ teaspoon Worcestershire
  sauce
⅛ teaspoon salt
Tabasco sauce, to taste
1 tablespoon sherry
2 teaspoons ketchup

═ Yield: 6 cups

3 pounds Cheddar cheese,
  grated
½ cup minced parsley
½ cup minced onion
¼ cup butter
1½ teaspoons dry mustard

1 teaspoon Worcestershire
  sauce
½ teaspoon salt
Tabasco sauce, to taste
½ cup sherry
½ cup ketchup

1. In a bowl, mix the cheese, parsley, onion, butter, mustard, Worcestershire sauce, salt, and Tabasco sauce. Mix well and beat in enough sherry and ketchup to make the mixture creamy. Chill overnight.

2. Serve with crackers and breads.

▶ Keeps 1 week, refrigerated.

≡ *Spiced Cheddar Cheese Spread*

≡ **Yield: 1 cup**

¼ pound sharp Cheddar cheese, grated	½ teaspoon Dijon mustard
¼ cup mayonnaise	½ teaspoon Worcestershire sauce
¼ cup minced onion	½ teaspoon paprika
2 tablespoons ketchup	salt, to taste

≡ **Yield: 1 quart**

1 pound sharp Cheddar cheese, grated	2 teaspoons Dijon mustard
1 cup mayonnaise	2 teaspoons Worcestershire sauce
1 cup minced onion	2 teaspoons paprika
½ cup ketchup	salt, to taste

1. In a bowl, mix the cheese, mayonnaise, onion, ketchup, mustard, Worcestershire sauce, paprika, and salt.

2. Serve with crackers, or spread on toast fingers and heat under the broiler.

▶ Keeps 4 days, refrigerated.

≡ *Stuffed Edam Cheese*

For a slightly different flavor, substitute brandy for the ale.

≡ **Yield: 1½ cups**

1 small Edam cheese, approximately 1 pound	½ teaspoon sesame seeds, toasted
½ cup butter, softened	¼ teaspoon celery seeds
¾ cup ale	¼ teaspoon dry mustard
½ teaspoon poppy seeds	

1 large Edam cheese,
approximately 3 pounds
(see note)
1½ cups butter, softened
2¼ cups ale

1½ teaspoons poppy seeds
1½ teaspoons sesame seeds,
toasted
¾ teaspoon celery seeds
¾ teaspoon dry mustard

1. With a sharp knife, cut a lid from the top of the cheese. Carefully scoop out the inside, leaving the sides and bottom ¼ inch thick.

2. In a food processor, purée the cheese and butter. Add the ale in a slow stream; then add the poppy seeds, sesame seeds, celery seeds, and mustard. Process just to combine.

3. Pack the mixture into the cheese shell.

4. Serve with rye or pumpernickel bread.

▶ Keeps 1 week, refrigerated.

NOTE: If you cannot buy a large Edam, use several smaller ones, or prepare just one shell and refill it as needed. With a large Edam, you can carefully score the wax rind in a decorative pattern, if desired.

≡ *Edam Cheese Spread Pineapples*

This is most effective made in large quantities.

══ **Yield: 8 cups**

4 pounds Edam or Mimolette
cheese, grated
2 large onions, minced
½ cup sweet Bavarian mustard
½ cup mango chutney
¼ cup brandy
6 scallions, minced

2 tablespoons Worcestershire
sauce
salt and pepper, to taste
paprika, optional
pineapple frond or fern or
palm leaves

1. In a large bowl, mix the cheese, onions, mustard, chutney, brandy, scallions, Worcestershire sauce, salt, and pepper.

2. In a food processor, purée the cheese mixture in batches. Pack into a bowl, cover, and let the flavor develop for 2 days in the refrigerator.

3. Using your hands, form the cheese into a pineapple shape and roll it in paprika if desired. With the edge of a teaspoon or the back of a knife blade, score the surface to resemble a pineapple. Place the pineapple frond on top, or insert fern or palm leaves to simulate a pineapple frond.

4. Serve with crackers.

▶ Keeps 1 week, refrigerated.

☰ *Feta Cheese Ball*

═ **Yield: 1½ cups**

1 small garlic clove, minced	1 teaspoon dried dill
2 scallions, minced	½ teaspoon dried oregano
½ pound cream cheese, softened	¼ teaspoon pepper salt, to taste
¼ pound feta cheese	2 tablespoons minced parsley
1 tablespoon sour cream	½ cup shredded radishes

═ **Yield: 6 cups**

4 garlic cloves, minced	1 tablespoon dried dill
8 scallions, minced	2 teaspoons dried oregano
2 pounds cream cheese, softened	1 teaspoon pepper salt, to taste
1 pound feta cheese	½ cup minced parsley
¼ cup sour cream	1½ cups shredded radishes

1. Line a bowl with plastic wrap.

2. In a food processor, purée the garlic, scallions, cream cheese, feta cheese, sour cream, dill, oregano, and pepper. Taste for seasoning and add salt, if needed. Turn into the bowl and pack firmly. Chill.

3. Using the plastic, shape the cheese into a ball, remove the plastic, and arrange on a serving platter. Garnish with the parsley and radishes.

4. Serve with wheat crackers or toasted pita bread.

▶ Keeps 5 days, refrigerated.

☰ *Herbed Goat Cheese*

═ **Yield: 1 cup**

½ pound chèvre, softened	¼ teaspoon dried tarragon
2 teaspoons minced chives	coarsely ground pepper
¼ teaspoon crushed garlic	

== **Yield: 1 quart**

2 pounds chèvre, softened
2 tablespoons minced chives
1 teaspoon crushed garlic

½ teaspoon dried tarragon
coarsely ground pepper

1. In a food processor, purée the cheese, chives, garlic, and tarragon. Mound on a serving dish and dust heavily with pepper.
2. Serve with crackers or toast.

▶ Keeps 2 weeks, refrigerated.

≡ *Horseradish Cream Cheese Spread*

== **Yield: ¾ cup**

3 ounces cream cheese
3 tablespoons sour cream

½ cup minced watercress
1 teaspoon grated horseradish

== **Yield: 4⅔ cups**

18 ounces cream cheese
1 cup sour cream
2 cups minced watercress

2 tablespoons grated
horseradish

In a bowl, beat the cream cheese with the sour cream, watercress, and horseradish until combined.

▶ Keeps 3 days, refrigerated.

≡ *Fromage Berrichon (Liederkranz Cheese Spread)*

== **Yield: 1 cup**

3 ounces cream cheese
1 package Liederkranz cheese
3 tablespoons heavy cream

½ teaspoon celery seeds
4 teaspoons Madeira
1 garlic clove, cut in half

== **Yield: 4 cups**

12 ounces cream cheese
4 packages Liederkranz cheese
¾ cup heavy cream

2 teaspoons celery seeds
3 tablespoons Madeira
1 garlic clove, cut in half

1. In a food processor, purée the cream cheese, Liederkranz, cream, celery seeds, and Madeira. Rub the inside of a crock with the garlic and discard the garlic. Pack the cheese in the crock and refrigerate for 24 hours.

2. Serve with crackers.

▶ Keeps 1 week, refrigerated.

≡ *Körözött Júhtúró (Hungarian Cheese Spread)*

═ Yield: 1½ cups

⅓ pound cottage cheese
3 tablespoons butter
⅓ cup Gorgonzola cheese
1 tablespoon beer
1 anchovy fillet, mashed
½ tablespoon caraway seeds
½ tablespoon minced chives

1 teaspoon paprika
½ teaspoon Dijon mustard
salt and pepper, to taste
3 tablespoons minced scallions
3 tablespoons minced radishes
3 tablespoons minced green
 pepper

═ Yield: 6 cups

2 pounds cottage cheese
1 cup butter, softened
4 ounces Gorgonzola cheese
⅓ cup beer
4 anchovy fillets, mashed
3 tablespoons caraway seeds
3 tablespoons minced chives

2 tablespoons paprika
1 tablespoon Dijon mustard
salt and pepper, to taste
1 cup minced scallions
1 cup minced radishes
1 cup minced green pepper

1. In a bowl, mix the cottage cheese, butter, Gorgonzola cheese, beer, and anchovies. Stir in the caraway seeds, chives, paprika, mustard, salt, and pepper.

2. Mound the cheese on a platter and just before serving garnish with the scallions, radishes, and green pepper. Serve with rye or pumpernickel bread or crackers.

▶ Keeps 2 weeks, refrigerated, without the garnish.

≡ *Liptauer Cheese I*

It has been said that there are as many versions of liptauer cheese as there are Hungarians. Here is the first of several favorites.

== **Yield: 1½ cups**

8 ounces cream cheese
½ green pepper, minced
¼ cup minced onion
1 garlic clove, minced
¼ teaspoon dry mustard

2 tablespoons caraway seeds
2 tablespoons paprika
1 can anchovy fillets, undrained
1 tablespoon olive oil

== **Yield: 6 cups**

2 pounds cream cheese
1 cup minced green pepper
1 cup minced onion
3 garlic cloves, minced
1 teaspoon dry mustard

6 tablespoons caraway seeds
4 tablespoons paprika
3 cans anchovy fillets,
   undrained
3 tablespoons olive oil

1. In a bowl, mix the cream cheese, green pepper, onion, garlic, mustard, caraway, paprika, anchovies, and olive oil. Pack into crocks and refrigerate overnight.

2. Serve with breads or crackers, or use to stuff pastries.

▶ Keeps 2 weeks, refrigerated.

≡ *Liptauer Cheese II*

== **Yield: 1¼ cups**

½ pound cream cheese
⅓ cup butter, softened
⅓ cup sour cream
2 teaspoons minced chives

2 teaspoons paprika
1 teaspoon minced capers
salt and pepper, to taste

== **Yield: 4 cups**

1½ pounds cream cheese
1 cup butter, softened
1 cup sour cream
2 tablespoons minced chives

2 tablespoons paprika
1 tablespoon minced capers
salt and pepper, to taste

1. In a food processor, purée the cream cheese, butter, sour cream, chives, and paprika. Turn into a bowl and fold in the capers, salt, and pepper.

2. Serve with crackers or pumpernickel bread.

▶ Keeps 2 weeks, refrigerated.

≡ Liptauer Cheese III

═ Yield: 1 cup
½ pound cream cheese
2 tablespoons butter, softened
⅛ teaspoon paprika
¼ cup minced scallions

¼ cup chopped radishes
¼ cup minced cucumber
¼ cup minced anchovies
¼ cup capers

═ Yield: 4 cups
2 pounds cream cheese
½ cup butter, softened
½ teaspoon paprika
1 cup minced scallions

1 cup chopped radishes
1 cup minced cucumber
½ cup minced anchovies
1 cup capers

1. In a food processor, purée the cream cheese, butter, and paprika. Serve in a bowl surrounded with smaller bowls of scallions, radishes, cucumbers, anchovies, and capers.

2. Serve with dark bread.

▶ Keeps 2 weeks, refrigerated. The garnishes should be freshly prepared.

≡ Liptauer Cheese IV

═ Yield: 1 cup
6 ounces cream cheese
2 ounces sharp Cheddar
  cheese, grated
2 tablespoons butter, softened
1 teaspoon Dijon mustard
2 teaspoons minced onion
1 tablespoon paprika

1 small round pumpernickel loaf
1 can anchovy fillets, rinsed
  and chopped
⅓ cup minced scallions
⅓ cup minced cucumber
⅓ cup minced radishes
3 tablespoons capers

═ Yield: 6 cups
2½ pounds cream cheese
12 ounces sharp Cheddar
  cheese, grated
⅔ cup butter, softened
2 tablespoons Dijon mustard
¼ cup minced onion
¼ cup paprika

1 large round pumpernickel loaf
4 cans anchovy fillets, rinsed
  and chopped
1 cup minced scallions
1 cup minced cucumbers
1 cup minced radishes
¾ cup capers

1. In a food processor, purée the cream cheese, Cheddar cheese, butter, mustard, onion, and paprika in batches, if necessary. Refrigerate for 24 hours.

2. To serve, hollow out the bread and pack the cheese inside.

3. Surround with bowls of anchovies, scallions, cucumbers, radishes, and capers.

▶ Keeps 2 weeks, refrigerated. The garnishes should be freshly prepared. **NOTE:** To carry the bread theme further, hollow out pumpernickel rolls to hold the garnishes.

≡ Parmesan-Romano Cheese Spread

Be sure to use freshly ground pepper and plenty of it to give this spread the right zing.

═ Yield: 1 cup

½ cup grated Parmesan cheese
½ cup grated Romano cheese

½ cup cottage cheese
pepper, to taste

═ Yield: 1 quart

2 cups grated Parmesan cheese
2 cups grated Romano cheese

2 cups cottage cheese
pepper, to taste

1. In a bowl, mix the Parmesan and Romano cheese together.

2. In a food processor, purée the cottage cheese. Add the grated cheeses and pepper and blend until smooth.

3. Serve with toast or dark bread.

▶ Keeps 2 weeks, refrigerated.

≡ Rüssischer Käse (Russian Cheese)

═ Yield: 3 cups

1 Camembert cheese, rind removed
¼ pound Roquefort cheese
3 ounces cream cheese
1 cup grated sharp Cheddar cheese

1 cup grated Gruyère cheese
¼ pound butter, softened
salt and pepper, to taste
butter balls
1 cup minced radishes

== **Yield: 6 cups**

2 Camembert cheeses, rinds
  removed
½ pound Roquefort cheese
6 ounces cream cheese
2 cups grated sharp Cheddar
  cheese

1 cup grated Gruyère cheese
½ pound butter, softened
salt and pepper, to taste
butter balls
2 cups minced radishes

1. In a food processor, purée the Camembert, Roquefort, and cream cheese. Add the Cheddar and Gruyère and process until smooth. Add the butter and process again. (It may be necessary to do this in batches.) Add the salt and pepper.

2. Place in a mold and chill until firm.

3. Unmold and surround with butter balls and radishes. Serve with pumpernickel bread, rye rounds, or whole-grain dark breads.

▶ Keeps 1 week, refrigerated.

NOTE: The cheese can be shaped into a log or ball and rolled in softened butter and radishes, or it can be shaped into a cheese tree (see page 119 for directions) and sprinkled with radishes. Serve the butter balls around the base.

== *Hot Scandinavian Cheese Spread*

This is an unusual spread not only because it is served hot, but also because it uses toasted goat cheese (Gjetost) to flavor it.

== **Yield: 1 quart**

1 egg yolk
¼ cup milk
¼ cup heavy cream
1 teaspoon salt
1 teaspoon sugar
¼ pound Gruyère cheese,
  grated

¼ pound Cheddar cheese,
  grated
¼ pound Gjetost cheese, grated
1 egg white
bread crumbs

1. Preheat the oven to 350°F.

2. In a bowl, mix the egg yolk, milk, cream, salt, and sugar. Stir in the Gruyère, Cheddar, and Gjetost cheeses. Beat the egg white until stiff but not dry and fold into the cheese mixture.

3. Butter a 1-quart mold and dust with bread crumbs. Pour the mixture into the dish and bake for 30 minutes. Serve immediately with Scandinavian flat bread or dark breads.

▶ Can be prepared for baking 1 day in advance.

≡ *Walnut Cheese Bowl*

═ **Yield: 1½ cups**

3 ounces Brie cheese	3 ounces cream cheese
3 ounces Liederkranz cheese	2 tablespoons kirsch, or to taste
3 ounces chèvre	½ cup chopped walnuts,
3 ounces Camembert cheese	toasted

═ **Yield: 6 cups**

12 ounces Brie cheese	12 ounces cream cheese
12 ounces Liederkranz cheese	¼ cup kirsch, or to taste
12 ounces chèvre	2 cups chopped walnuts,
12 ounces Camembert cheese	toasted

1. In a food processor, purée the Brie, Liederkranz, chèvre, Camembert, and cream cheese. With the machine running, add the kirsch. Pack into a crock and refrigerate for 24 hours.

2. Sprinkle with walnuts before serving or fold into the cheese before molding. Serve with crackers or black bread or use to fill pastries.

▶ Keeps 1 week, refrigerated.

NOTE: The flavor of imported kirsch is far superior to that of domestic versions. It is worth the difference in price. However, the real thing is potent and usually requires only a very small amount to flavor a large quantity of food. Flavor the cheese to taste with the kirsch, and, if needed, thin the cheese with heavy cream rather than adding more kirsch.

—— *Cheese Loaves* ——

Several years ago I discovered an Italian cheese preparation, *torta mascarpone*, in a local market. This wonderful cheese contains thin slices of provolone layered with mascarpone that has been mixed with fresh basil and pine nuts. The flavors were sensational and the idea led to many variations.

Because of the number of ingredients involved, the smallest size to make is a 7-inch loaf, which yields 25 to 45 servings. The recipes can be increased, however, to whatever size you may need. Several small loaves are more attractive than one large loaf since they can be replaced more quickly. A large loaf serving a hundred people or more can look impressive initially, but it soon looks awful unless you have someone cutting it into neat serving pieces. Small loaves can also be made in different varieties. If you choose to make larger loaves, however, be sure to keep each layer very thin for a contrast of textures and flavors.

I have also found that using thin slices of provolone or other firm cheeses make the loaf very difficult to serve. When cut, the filling gets pressed out from between the layers of the cheese slices and the loaf soon looks a mess. Grating the cheese, however, gives the appearance of layers and allows for easy serving. Use the large holes of a four-sided grater or the coarse grater blade of a food processor. (Do not grate the cheese to a powder as you would Parmesan.)

Because these cheese loaves are so rich, they serve many people. For a small party where this is *the* attraction, a 7-inch loaf will easily serve 12 or more. For a larger party with a correspondingly larger menu, the same loaf can serve at least 50.

Serve the cheese loaves on beds of large shiny leaves such as magnolia leaves or, if necessary, smaller flat leaves. Lemon leaves can be arranged around the edge of each loaf and brushed with oil to make the leaves shine. The loaves can also be made in round cakes or any other shape you select by using different pans. The top and sides of the loaves can be decorated with minced parsley, olives, or nuts.

≡ *Torta Mascarpone with Basil and Pine Nuts*

The original version of this loaf is made with ¼-inch layers of the mascarpone/basil/pine nut mixture spread on ⅛-inch slices of provolone. The look is lovely but difficult to serve unless the torta is precut into ½-inch slices and then cut again to fit on pieces of bread. If you choose to prepare the cheese this way, arrange the slices on a platter to serve.

This version uses grated provolone with fewer layers and allows the guests to spread the torta themselves. The presentation is prettier.

≡ Yield: 25 to 45 servings

vegetable oil
2 pounds mascarpone cheese
1 tablespoon minced garlic
3 tablespoons minced basil

salt and pepper, to taste
1 cup toasted pine nuts
½ pound provolone cheese, grated

1. Brush a 7-inch loaf pan with oil and press plastic wrap over the bottom and up the sides, letting the excess hang over the edge.

2. In a bowl, cream the mascarpone and fold in the garlic, basil, salt, and pepper, and ½ cup toasted pine nuts.

3. Spread one-third of the basil cheese over the bottom of the pan. Sprinkle on half the provolone and press lightly.

4. Spread another third of the basil cheese. Sprinkle on the remaining provolone and press lightly.

5. Spread the remaining basil cheese and cover with plastic wrap. Place a 1- to 2-pound weight on top and chill overnight.

6. Unmold onto a serving platter and sprinkle the top with the remaining pine nuts. If you have the time and the patience, the pine nuts can be arranged by hand in a decorative pattern, or in a circle or diamond by setting a template over the top.

7. Serve with crackers.

▶ Keeps 4 days, refrigerated.

NOTE: The mascarpone mixture must be very soft. It is easiest to drop the cheese into the mold by the spoonful and then spread it lightly together.

If mascarpone is not available, cream cheese can be substituted. Thin it with enough heavy cream to make it almost as soft as whipped cream.

≡ *Blue Cheese and Green Peppercorn Loaf*

≡ **Yield: 25 to 45 servings**

vegetable oil
1 pound mascarpone cheese
  (see note above)
¼ cup green peppercorns
1 tablespoon Cognac

salt, to taste
1 pound Bleu de Bresse or
  other creamy blue cheese
1 pound Gruyère cheese, grated
½ cup ground pecans

1. Brush a 7-inch loaf pan with oil and press plastic wrap over the bottom and up the sides, letting the excess hang over the edge.

2. In a bowl, cream the mascarpone and fold in the peppercorns, Cognac, and salt.

3. In another bowl, cream the Bleu de Bresse.

4. Spread half the mascarpone in the bottom of the loaf pan and sprinkle with one-third of the Gruyère. Press lightly.

5. Spread half the blue cheese over the Gruyère and sprinkle with another third of the Gruyère. Press lightly.

6. Spread the remaining mascarpone on top and sprinkle with the remaining Gruyère. Press lightly.

7. Spread with remaining blue cheese. Cover with plastic wrap. Place a 1- to 2-pound weight on top and chill overnight.

8. Unmold onto a platter and press the pecans into the sides.

▶ Keeps 4 days, refrigerated.

≡ *Olive Cheese and Scallion Loaf*

═ **Yield: 25 to 45 servings**

vegetable oil
1 pound mascarpone cheese
(see note, page 157)
¼ pound pitted Calamata olives
2 cups coarsely grated Gruyère
cheese

1 pound St. André or other
triple crème cheese
1 cup minced scallions
½ cup poppy seeds
3 to 4 roasted red peppers, cut
into ½-inch strips

1. Brush a 7-inch loaf pan with oil, and press plastic wrap over the bottom and up the sides, letting the excess hang over the edge.

2. In a bowl, cream the mascarpone and fold in the olives.

3. Spread half the olive-mascarpone mixture over the bottom of the pan. Sprinkle half the Gruyère, pressing it gently into the olive-mascarpone mixture.

4. In a bowl, beat the St. André until very soft and smooth. Spoon half the St. André over the Gruyère and spread it as evenly as possible. Sprinkle with scallions and spoon the remaining St. André over the top. Sprinkle with the remaining Gruyère. Gently press down.

5. Spread the remaining olive-mascarpone mixture over the top. Cover with plastic wrap, and place a 1- to 2-pound weight on top. Chill overnight.

6. Unmold and remove the plastic wrap. Press poppy seeds into the sides and over the top. Arrange the red pepper strips diagonally over the top, ½ inch apart.

7. Serve with crackers.

▶ Keeps 4 days, refrigerated.

☰ Mustard Cheese and Ham Loaf

☰ Yield: 25 to 45 servings

1 teaspoon olive oil
2 pounds mascarpone cheese
(see note, page 157)
¼ cup tomato paste
salt, to taste
½ teaspoon cracked black
pepper

2 tablespoons dry mustard
4 teaspoons Dijon mustard
2 cups grated Gruyère cheese
1 pound ham, chopped
½ cup minced parsley

1. Brush a 7-inch loaf pan with oil and press plastic wrap over the bottom and up the sides, letting the excess hang over the edge.

2. In a bowl, cream 1 pound of the mascarpone with the tomato paste, salt, and pepper.

3. In another bowl, cream the remaining mascarpone with the dry mustard, Dijon mustard, and salt.

4. Spread half the tomato cheese over the bottom of the pan. Sprinkle half the grated Gruyère and press the top gently.

5. Spoon on half the mustard-cheese mixture, smoothing as much as possible. Sprinkle half the ham over the top and press gently.

6. Spoon the remaining mustard-cheese mixture over the ham and smooth. Sprinkle with the remaining Gruyère and press gently.

7. Spread the remaining tomato cheese over the Gruyère. Cover with plastic wrap and place a 1- to 2-pound weight on top. Chill overnight.

8. Unmold onto a serving platter. Arrange 3 rows of the remaining ham down the length of the loaf, and sprinkle parsley between the rows. Serve with crackers.

▶ Keeps 4 days, refrigerated.

☰ Smoked Salmon and Dill Cheese Loaf

☰ Yield: 25 to 45 servings

vegetable oil
2 pounds mascarpone cheese
(see note, page 157)
½ pound smoked salmon,
minced

¼ cup minced onion
salt and pepper, to taste
¼ cup minced dill
1 pound Gruyère cheese, grated
minced dill

1. Brush a 7-inch loaf pan with oil and press plastic wrap over the bottom and up the sides, letting the excess hang over the edge.

2. In a bowl, cream 1 pound of the mascarpone with the smoked salmon, onion, salt, and pepper.

3. In another bowl, cream the remaining mascarpone with the dill, salt, and pepper.

4. Spread half the salmon mixture over the bottom of the pan. Sprinkle on one-third of the Gruyère and press the top lightly.

5. Spread with half the dill mixture and sprinkle on another third of the Gruyère. Press gently.

6. Spread with the remaining salmon mixture and sprinkle on the remaining Gruyère. Press gently.

7. Spread with the remaining dill and cover with plastic wrap. Place a 1- to 2-pound weight on top and chill overnight.

8. Unmold onto a platter and sprinkle with the minced dill. Serve with crackers.

▶ Keeps 4 days, refrigerated.

—— *Cheesecakes* ——

Cheesecakes are usually thought of as desserts, not hors d'oeuvre; however, they can be made as a savory as well as a sweet. They are delicious, different, and have great appeal for cheesecake lovers. Several appealing features for the busy chef are that they are easily assembled, can be prepared ahead, and require little last-minute work in terms of presentation. One note of caution though: Do not overcook cheesecake or it will be dry. As with cheese loaves, one cheesecake will serve many—about 50 people or more, depending on the other items on the menu.

≡ *Chèvre Cheesecake*

═ Yield: 50 servings

1 tablespoon butter
6 ounces sesame bread sticks,
  crushed
½ cup melted butter
2 pounds chèvre

1 pound cream cheese
3 eggs
2 tablespoons minced summer
  savory or rosemary

1. Preheat the oven to 350°F.
2. Butter a 9-inch springform pan.

3. In a bowl, mix the bread stick crumbs with the melted butter. Press the crumb mixture in the bottom and up about ½ inch on the sides of the pan. Chill for 20 minutes.

4. In an electric mixer, beat the chèvre, cream cheese, eggs, and savory until light and fluffy. Pour into the crust.

5. Bake 5 minutes, lower the heat to 325°F, and bake 50 minutes or until lightly browned and puffed.

6. Turn off the oven and let the cake cool in the oven for 1 hour longer. Remove to a rack and cool completely.

7. Unmold and serve on a platter with crackers or cocktail breads.

▶ Can be prepared 2 days before serving.

≡ *Roquefort Cheesecake*

≡ **Yield: 50 servings**

1 tablespoon butter	1½ pounds Roquefort cheese
6 ounces sesame bread sticks, crushed	1½ pounds cream cheese
½ cup melted butter	4 eggs

1. Preheat the oven to 350°F.

2. Butter a 9-inch springform pan.

3. In a bowl, mix the bread stick crumbs with the melted butter.

4. Press the crumb mixture in the bottom and up about ½ inch on the sides of the pan. Chill for 20 minutes.

5. In an electric mixer, beat the Roquefort and cream cheese with the eggs until light and fluffy. Pour into the crust.

6. Bake 5 minutes, lower the heat to 325°F, and bake 50 minutes or until lightly browned and puffed. Turn off the oven and let the cake cool in the oven for 1 hour longer. Remove to a rack and cool completely.

7. Unmold on a platter and serve with crackers or cocktail breads.

▶ Can be prepared 2 days before serving.

≡ *Smoked Salmon Cheesecake*

≡ **Yield: 50 servings**

1 tablespoon butter	½ pound smoked salmon, chopped
6 ounces sesame bread sticks, crushed	½ cup minced scallions
½ cup melted butter	¼ cup minced dill
2½ pounds cream cheese	4 eggs

1. Preheat the oven to 350°F.

2. Butter a 9-inch springform pan.

3. In a bowl, mix the bread stick crumbs with the melted butter.

4. Press the crumb mixture in the bottom and up about ½ inch on the sides of the pan. Chill for 20 minutes.

5. In an electric mixer, beat the cream cheese, smoked salmon, scallions, dill, and eggs until light and fluffy. Pour into the crust.

6. Bake 5 minutes, lower the heat to 325°F, and bake 50 minutes or until lightly browned and puffed. Turn off the oven and let the cake cool in the oven for 1 hour longer. Remove to a rack and cool completely.

7. Unmold on a platter and serve with crackers or cocktail breads.

▶ Can be prepared 2 days before serving.

≡ *Cirak (Egg and Horseradish Spread)*

This Middle European specialty at first seems strange, but is interesting to eat and different.

═ Yield: 3 cups

1 quart milk	½ teaspoon salt
12 eggs	prepared horseradish
1 tablespoon sugar	2 cups minced pickled beets
dash of cayenne pepper	

═ Yield: 1½ quarts

2 quarts milk	1 teaspoon salt
24 eggs	prepared horseradish
2 tablespoons sugar	1 quart minced pickled beets
¼ teaspoon cayenne pepper, or to taste	

1. In a double boiler, heat the milk until scalded.

2. Break the eggs into the milk, one at a time, stirring constantly, making sure each yolk is broken. Stir in the sugar, cayenne, and salt.

3. Cook over simmering water, stirring constantly until the mixture resembles dry scrambled eggs. Remove from the heat.

4. Line a sieve or colander with two layers of cheesecloth wrung out in cold water. Pour the egg mixture into the sieve. Gather the corners of the cloth and tie tightly. Hang the cheesecloth "bag" over a pot and drain for 1 hour. When cold, remove the cheesecloth and refrigerate until ready to serve.

5. To serve, arrange on a platter with the horseradish and beets on the side. Serve with crackers.

▶ Keeps 2 days, refrigerated.

—— *Seafood Spreads* ——

☰ *L'Anchoïade I (Anchovy Spread I)*

=== **Yield: 1 cup**

1 small can anchovy fillets
olive oil
1 tomato, peeled, seeded, and
  chopped
⅓ cup ground almonds
1 red pepper, peeled and
  minced

3 garlic cloves, crushed
2 tablespoons minced shallots
1 tablespoon red wine vinegar
½ teaspoon dried marjoram,
  thyme, and rosemary, mixed

=== **Yield: 1 quart**

4 small cans anchovy fillets
olive oil
4 tomatoes, peeled, seeded, and
  chopped
1⅓ cups ground almonds
4 red peppers, peeled and
  minced

12 garlic cloves, crushed
8 shallots, minced
¼ cup red wine vinegar
2 teaspoons dried marjoram,
  thyme, and rosemary, mixed

1. Drain the anchovies, discarding the oil. Place in a measuring cup and add just enough olive oil to equal ¼ cup for the smaller quantity or 1 cup for the larger quantity. Purée in a food processor.

2. In a bowl, mix the purée with the tomatoes, almonds, peppers, garlic, shallots, vinegar, and herbs.

3. Serve as a spread with French bread.

▶ Keeps 2 days, refrigerated.

NOTE: L'anchoïade can be spread on French bread slices and broiled as a toast. Serve with lemon wedges.

≡ *L'Anchoïade II (Anchovy Spread II)*

The butter gives this version a softer flavor.

═ Yield: ½ cup

1 can anchovy fillets, undrained	1½ tablespoons butter
1 large garlic clove, crushed	lemon juice or Cognac, to taste
1 tablespoon olive oil	pepper, to taste

═ Yield: 3 cups

8 cans anchovy fillets, undrained	¾ cup butter
8 large garlic cloves, crushed	lemon juice or Cognac, to taste
½ cup olive oil	pepper, to taste

1. In a food processor, purée the anchovies, their oil, garlic, olive oil, and butter. Season with lemon juice or Cognac and pepper.

2. Serve with French bread slices that have been toasted on one side.

▶ Keeps 1 week, refrigerated.

NOTE: This spread can also be used as a dip for vegetables.

≡ *Brazil Nut Clam Spread*

═ Yield: ¾ cup

3 ounces cream cheese	¼ cup lightly toasted minced Brazil nuts
pinch of curry powder	
1 10-ounce can minced clams, drained	

═ Yield: 1 quart

1 pound cream cheese	3 pounds minced clams, drained
1 teaspoon curry powder, or to taste	1¼ cups lightly toasted minced Brazil nuts

1. In a bowl, cream the cheese and curry powder. Stir the clams into the cheese and fold in the nuts.

2. Let ripen in the refrigerator for 4 hours.

▶ Keeps 4 days, refrigerated.

≡ *Brandade de Morue I (Salt Cod Spread I)*

This mainstay of Provençal cuisine is perfect as a spread for a party. It is different, but intriguingly flavorful.

═ Yield: about 5 cups

1 pound salt cod, skinned and boned
1 pound baking potatoes
⅓ cup heavy cream
½ cup milk

1½ cups extra virgin olive oil
3 to 4 large garlic cloves, crushed
cayenne pepper, to taste
black pepper, to taste

═ Yield: about 2½ quarts

2 pounds salt cod, skinned and boned
2 pounds baking potatoes
⅔ cup heavy cream
1 cup milk

3 cups extra virgin olive oil
6 to 8 large garlic cloves, crushed
cayenne pepper, to taste
black pepper, to taste

1. In a bowl, soak the salt cod in cold water to cover for 12 hours, changing the water every 2 hours.

2. Preheat the oven to 400°F.

3. Bake the potatoes until tender, about 50 minutes.

4. In separate saucepans, heat the cream, milk, and oil until very hot but not boiling.

5. Drain the cod and put it in a saucepan with cold water to cover. Bring to a boil and simmer 1 minute. Drain the cod and flake.

6. Crush the garlic to a paste. In an electric mixer, beat the garlic and cod on low speed. Scoop the potato pulp into the mixer and while the machine continues to run, alternately add the oil, cream, and milk in a slow stream.

7. Correct the seasoning with cayenne and black pepper, and beat the mixture until light and fluffy.

8. Serve warm with French bread slices and imported black olives.

▶ Best served immediately, but can be reheated over low heat, if stirred constantly.

NOTE: Food processors tend to make the potatoes pasty, so beating by hand or electric mixer is preferred.

≡ *Brandade de Morue II (Salt Cod Spread II)*

Of the two recipes, this is a lighter version.

== **Yield: about 3 cups**

1 pound salt cod, skinned and
boned
½ cup extra virgin olive oil

½ cup heavy cream
2 to 4 large garlic cloves
ripe imported olives, pitted

== **Yield: about 6 cups**

2 pounds salt cod, skinned and
boned
1 cup extra virgin olive oil
1 cup heavy cream

4 to 8 large garlic cloves
1 cup ripe imported olives,
pitted

    1. Soak the salt cod in cold water for 12 hours, changing the water every 2 hours. Drain the cod and put it in a saucepan with cold water to cover. Bring to a boil and simmer 1 minute. Drain the cod and flake.

    2. In separate saucepans, heat the oil and cream until hot but not boiling.

    3. In a food processor, purée the hot fish and garlic cloves. With the machine running, alternately add the oil and the cream in a steady stream. The mixture should be the consistency of a thick mayonnaise.

    4. Serve warm garnished with French bread slices sautéed in oil, with crackers, or warm French bread and the olives.

▶ Best served immediately.

≡ *Smoked Cod Pâté*

== **Yield: 2 cups**

1 cup fish stock
½ cup white wine
1 tablespoon butter
¼ pound halibut or haddock
steaks, skinned
¼ pound smoked cod, skinned
and boned
10 ounces cream cheese

2 tablespoons lemon juice
1 tablespoon Dijon mustard
½ tablespoon minced chives or
onion
½ teaspoon Worcestershire
sauce
Tabasco sauce, to taste

═ **Yield: 1 quart**

1 cup fish stock
½ cup white wine
1 tablespoon butter
½ pound halibut or haddock
   steaks, skinned
½ pound smoked cod, skinned
   and boned
1¼ pounds cream cheese

¼ cup lemon juice
2 tablespoons Dijon mustard
1 tablespoon minced chives or
   onion
1 teaspoon Worcestershire
   sauce
Tabasco sauce, to taste

1. In a saucepan, bring the stock, wine, and butter to a boil. Add the halibut and simmer, covered, until cooked through. Drain and let cool.

2. Bone the halibut and place it in a food processor with the cod. Chop with on-off turns. Add the cream cheese, lemon juice, mustard, chives, Worcestershire sauce, and Tabasco sauce and process until smooth.

3. Put into crocks and serve with crackers.

▶ Keeps 4 days, refrigerated.

≡ *Rummed Crab Spread*

═ **Yield: 1½ cups**

1 cup crabmeat, flaked
1 tablespoon capers
2 hard-cooked eggs, quartered
2 tablespoons lime juice

2 tablespoons Dijon mustard
1 tablespoon dark rum
salt and pepper, to taste

═ **Yield: 6 cups**

2 pounds crabmeat, flaked
¼ cup capers
8 hard-cooked eggs, quartered
⅓ to ½ cup lime juice, or to
   taste

½ cup Dijon mustard
2–4 tablespoons dark rum
salt and pepper, to taste

1. In a food processor, purée the crabmeat, capers, eggs, lime juice, mustard, rum, salt, and pepper.

2. Serve with crackers or toast, or use to fill pastries or vegetables.

▶ Keeps 2 days, refrigerated.

☰ Potted Crab

═ Yield: 1½ cups

1 cup crabmeat, flaked
¼ cup butter
2 egg yolks
½ cup heavy cream

salt and pepper, to taste
2 tablespoons melted clarified
   butter, optional

═ Yield: 6 cups

2 pounds crabmeat, flaked
1 cup butter
8 egg yolks
2 cups heavy cream

salt and pepper, to taste
½ cup melted clarified butter,
   optional

1. In a skillet, sauté the crabmeat in the butter for several minutes to bring out the flavor; do not brown. Transfer to a bowl.

2. In a saucepan, beat the egg yolks until light and beat in the cream. Cook over low heat, stirring until thickened. Do not boil. Fold in the crabmeat and season with salt and pepper.

3. Pack into small crocks and chill for 1 hour.

4. Pour the clarified butter over the top of the crocks to seal.

▶ Keeps 1 week, sealed and refrigerated.

Note: The clarified butter can be omitted. It is only used to preserve the crab mixture.

☰ Crabmeat and Water Chestnut Spread

═ Yield: 1¼ cups

1 cup crabmeat, flaked
¼ cup minced water chestnuts
1 tablespoon thin soy sauce

¼ cup mayonnaise
1 tablespoon minced scallions

═ Yield: 5 cups

2 pounds crabmeat, flaked
1 cup minced water chestnuts
¼ cup thin soy sauce

1 cup mayonnaise
¼ cup minced scallions

1. In a bowl, mix the crabmeat with the water chestnuts, soy sauce, mayonnaise, and scallions.

2. Serve with crackers, or use to fill pastries or vegetables.

▶ Keeps 4 days, refrigerated.

≡ Curried Crabmeat Pâté

═ Yield: 1 cup

2 tablespoons minced onion	2 tablespoons minced scallions
1 teaspoon curry powder	1 tablespoon sour cream
¼ cup butter	salt, to taste
1 cup crabmeat, flaked	melted clarified butter, optional

═ Yield: 1 quart

⅔ cup minced onion	½ cup minced scallions
4 teaspoons curry powder	¼ cup sour cream
1 cup butter	salt, to taste
2 pounds crabmeat, flaked	melted clarified butter, optional

1. In a skillet, sauté the onion and curry powder in the butter until the onion is soft but not brown.

2. Stir in the crabmeat, scallions, sour cream, and salt. Mix well and firmly pack into crocks. Cool and chill for 2 hours.

3. Pour a layer of clarified butter about ¼ inch thick over the top to seal. Chill.

4. Serve with crackers or toast.

▶ Keeps 1 week, refrigerated.

NOTE: The clarified butter may be omitted if serving within 2 days.

≡ Crabmeat Paste

═ Yield: 1½ cups

1 cup crabmeat	¼ teaspoon salt
¼ cup chopped almonds	2 tablespoons white wine
¼ cup olive oil	2 tablespoons minced parsley

═ Yield: 6 cups

2 pounds crabmeat	1 teaspoon salt
1 cup chopped almonds	¼ cup white wine
1 cup olive oil	¼ cup minced parsley

1. Reserve several large pieces of crab for a garnish. Flake the rest.

2. Sauté the almonds in half the oil until golden but not burned. Drain on paper towels.

3. In a food processor, purée the crabmeat, almonds, remaining oil, and salt. With the machine running, slowly add the wine. Spoon into a serving dish and sprinkle the top with parsley.

4. Serve with warm toast points or use to fill pastries.

▶ Keeps 4 days, refrigerated.

≡ *Smoked Bluefish Spread*

═ Yield: 2 cups

1½ pounds smoked bluefish
½ cup sour cream
1 tablespoon lemon juice

¼ cup minced scallions
black pepper, to taste

═ Yield: 2 quarts

6 pounds smoked bluefish
2 cups sour cream
¼ cup lemon juice

1 cup minced scallions
black pepper, to taste

1. Skin and bone the fish and mash it in a bowl.

2. Stir in the sour cream, lemon juice, and scallions to make a smooth paste. Season with black pepper and pack into a crock.

3. Serve with crackers or use to fill puffs.

▶ Keeps 4 days, refrigerated.

≡ *Bird's Nest*

This Swedish specialty makes a pretty presentation. The egg can be omitted, however, or everything can be mixed before serving. Although it is not as pretty to mix it ahead, for larger groups it is the only practical solution.

═ Yield: 2 cups

1 tablespoon capers
1 onion, minced
1¼ cups minced pickled
  herring or anchovy fillets

3 tablespoons minced parsley
½ cup minced cooked beets
1 egg yolk, shell reserved,
  optional

═ **Yield: 8 cups**

¼ cup capers
2 cups minced onion
5 cups minced pickled herring
  or anchovy fillets

¾ cup minced parsley
2 cups minced cooked beets
4 egg yolks, shells reserved,
  optional

1. On a platter arrange the ingredients as follows: mound the capers in the center, surround with a ring of onion, a ring of herring, a ring of parsley, and finally a ring of beets.

2. Just before serving, place the egg yolk(s) in an egg shell half at the side of the platter. When ready to serve, the guest of honor pours the egg yolk into the center and then mixes everything together.

3. Serve with Swedish flat bread.

▶ Can be prepared 6 hours in advance.

═ *Potted Kippers*

═ **Yield: 1½ cups**

1 pound kippered herring
½ cup butter
2 tablespoons lemon juice
black pepper, to taste

cayenne pepper, to taste
2 tablespoons melted clarified
  butter, optional

═ **Yield: 6 cups**

4 pounds kippered herring
2 cups butter
½ cup lemon juice
black pepper, to taste

cayenne pepper, to taste
½ cup melted clarified butter,
  optional

1. In a bowl, cover the herring with boiling water and soak for 10 minutes. Drain and pat dry. Remove and discard the skin and bones.

2. In a food processor, purée the fish, ½ cup (2 *cups*) butter, lemon juice, black pepper, and cayenne.

3. Pack into a crock and cover with melted butter if desired. Serve with toast points.

▶ Keeps 1 week or longer, refrigerated.

≡ Salmon Spread

≡ Yield: 1½ cups

1 cup flaked cooked salmon	¼ teaspoon pepper
3 tablespoons mayonnaise	2 teaspoons thin soy sauce, or
2 tablespoons minced onion	to taste
1 tablespoon sherry	2 teaspoons lime juice, or to
1 tablespoon minced parsley	taste
1 teaspoon Dijon mustard	salt, to taste
¼ teaspoon minced garlic	

≡ Yield: 6 cups

4 cups flaked cooked salmon	1 teaspoon pepper
⅔ cup mayonnaise	3 tablespoons thin soy sauce, or
½ cup minced onion	to taste
¼ cup sherry	3 tablespoons lime juice, or to
¼ cup minced parsley	taste
1 tablespoon Dijon mustard	salt, to taste
2 teaspoons minced garlic	

1. In a bowl, mix the salmon, mayonnaise, onion, sherry, parsley, mustard, garlic, and pepper. Add the soy sauce and lime juice to taste, and correct the seasoning with the salt.

2. Serve with melba toast, pita toast, pumpernickel rounds, or vegetables. Can be used to fill pastries.

▶ Keeps 4 days, refrigerated.

≡ Salmon Brandade

≡ Yield: 1 cup

1 cup flaked cooked salmon	⅓ cup olive oil
1 garlic clove, chopped	salt, to taste
⅓ cup heavy cream	

≡ Yield: 1 quart

2 pounds cooked salmon,	1¼ cups heavy cream
flaked	1¼ cups olive oil
4 garlic cloves, chopped	salt, to taste

1. In a food processor, purée the salmon and garlic.

2. In separate saucepans, heat the cream and olive oil until hot but not boiling.

3. With the machine running, alternately pour the oil and cream in a thin stream. Process until smooth. The mixture should resemble a thick mayonnaise.

4. Serve warm with toast triangles or use to fill pastries.

▶ Best if served immediately.

≡ *Salmon Rillettes with Salmon Caviar*

= **Yield: 1½ cups**

6 ounces salmon fillet
1 cup white wine
6 ounces butter
6 ounces smoked salmon, diced

few drops of lemon juice
black pepper, to taste
2 tablespoons salmon caviar

= **Yield: 1½ quarts**

1½ pounds salmon fillet
3 cups white wine
1½ pounds butter
1½ pounds smoked salmon,
  diced

2 teaspoons lemon juice
black pepper, to taste
½ cup salmon caviar

1. In a skillet, simmer the salmon in the wine for 8 minutes, or until just cooked. Drain and cool.

2. Flake the salmon, discarding any bones. In a food processor, purée the salmon and butter. Turn into a bowl and fold in the smoked salmon, lemon juice, and pepper. Chill until ready to serve.

3. Top with caviar and serve with pumpernickel rounds. Can also be used to fill small puffs.

▶ Keeps 4 days, refrigerated.

≡ *Salmon Tartare*

The raw fish will remind you of sushi. Do not let it marinate too long, or the lime juice will "cook" the fish. It is best served within an hour or two.

= **Yield: 2 cups**

1 pound salmon fillets
4 teaspoons minced dill
2 tablespoons olive oil
3 tablespoons lime juice

salt and pepper, to taste
¼ cup minced red onion
mustard dill sauce (page 14)

═ **Yield: 1½ quarts**

2 pounds salmon fillets
2 tablespoons minced dill
¼ cup olive oil
⅓ cup lime juice

salt and pepper, to taste
½ cup minced red onion
mustard dill sauce (page 14)

1. Remove any bones from the salmon. With a large knife, cut the salmon into ¼-inch dice.
2. In a bowl, mix the salmon, dill, oil, lime juice, salt, pepper, and onion. Stir to blend.
3. Serve with the dill sauce and hot toast.

▶ Keeps up to 8 hours.

═ *Salmon Chive Pâté*

═ **Yield: 1 cup**

¼ cup butter
¾ cup flaked cooked salmon
1 teaspoon minced onion
1½ teaspoons lemon juice

½ teaspoon salt
pinch of cayenne pepper
1½ tablespoons minced chives

═ **Yield: 1 quart**

½ pound butter
3 cups flaked cooked salmon
1 tablespoon minced onion
2 tablespoons lemon juice

2 teaspoons salt
⅛ teaspoon cayenne pepper
⅓ cup minced chives

1. In a food processor, purée the butter and salmon. With the machine running, add the onion, lemon juice, salt, and cayenne. Mix in the chives with a few on-off turns.
2. Pack into crocks and let ripen overnight. Serve with French, Italian, or pumpernickel bread, or vegetables.

▶ Keeps 5 days, refrigerated.

≡ Rillettes of Fresh and Smoked Salmon

═ **Yield: 2 cups**

10 ounces salmon fillet	1 tablespoon olive oil
1 egg yolk	3 ounces smoked salmon,
3 tablespoons yogurt	minced
2 tablespoons lemon juice	2 tablespoons minced chives
3½ tablespoons butter	salt and pepper, to taste

═ **Yield: 1½ quarts**

20 ounces salmon fillet	2 tablespoons olive oil
2 egg yolks	6 ounces smoked salmon,
⅓ cup yogurt	minced
¼ cup lemon juice	¼ cup minced chives
¼ pound butter	salt and pepper, to taste

1. On a rack over boiling water, steam salmon for 5 to 6 minutes or until just done. Cool. Remove and discard the bones and skin. Flake the salmon.

2. In a food processor, purée the egg yolk(s), yogurt, lemon juice, butter, oil, salt, and pepper until smooth. Turn into a bowl and fold in the fresh salmon, smoked salmon, and chives. Correct seasoning with salt and pepper.

3. Serve on thin slices of pumpernickel or French bread.

▶ Keeps 4 days, refrigerated.

≡ Smoked Salmon Spread

═ **Yield: 1 cup**

4 ounces cream cheese	2 ounces smoked salmon,
1 egg	minced
2½ teaspoons Pernod	2 ounces fresh salmon, cooked
1 teaspoon Dijon mustard	and minced
½ teaspoon lemon juice	1 tablespoon capers
dash of Worcestershire sauce	lemon wedges and minced
¼ cup minced red onion	parsley

=== **Yield: 1 quart**

1 pound cream cheese
2 eggs
2 tablespoons Pernod
1 tablespoon Dijon mustard
2 teaspoons lemon juice
½ teaspoon Worcestershire
    sauce
1 cup minced red onion

½ pound smoked salmon,
    minced
½ pound fresh salmon, cooked
    and minced
¼ cup capers
lemon wedges and minced
    parsley

1. In a food processor, blend the cream cheese, egg(s), Pernod, Dijon mustard, lemon juice, and Worcestershire sauce until smooth.

2. Transfer to a bowl and fold in the onion, smoked and fresh salmon, and capers. Garnish with lemon wedges and minced parsley.

3. Serve with rye toast points.

▶ Keeps 4 days, refrigerated.

=== *Smoked Salmon–Dill Paste*

Mince the ingredients so the spread has a definite texture.

=== **Yield: 1½ cups**

½ pound smoked salmon,
    minced
½ cup minced onion
1 tablespoon minced dill

¼ cup mayonnaise
2 tablespoons sour cream
minced dill

=== **Yield: 6 cups**

2 pounds smoked salmon,
    minced
1 cup minced onion
¼ cup minced dill

1 cup mayonnaise
½ cup sour cream
minced dill

1. In a bowl, mix the salmon, onion, dill, and mayonnaise. Add just enough sour cream to bind.

2. Spoon into a serving bowl and sprinkle with the minced dill.

▶ Keeps 5 days, refrigerated.

≡ *Salmon Caviar Butter*

= **Yield: 1 cup**

½ cup butter, softened   1 teaspoon lemon juice
½ cup salmon caviar   ½ teaspoon grated lemon rind

= **Yield: 1 quart**

2 cups butter, softened   1 tablespoon lemon juice
2 cups salmon caviar   2 teaspoons grated lemon rind

1. In a bowl, mix the butter, caviar, lemon juice, and lemon rind.
2. Serve with dark breads.

▶ Keeps 4 days, refrigerated.

≡ *Rillettes of Salmon*

= **Yield: 1¼ cups**

6 ounces fresh salmon, cooked   1 teaspoon mixed minced
1 shallot, minced   parsley, chervil, chives, and
9 tablespoons butter, softened   tarragon
5 ounces smoked salmon   salt and pepper, to taste
2 teaspoons Armagnac

= **Yield: 5 cups**

18 ounces fresh salmon, cooked   1½ tablespoons mixed minced
3 shallots, minced   parsley, chervil, chives, and
1 pound butter, softened   tarragon
1 pound smoked salmon   salt and pepper, to taste
2 tablespoons Armagnac

1. Remove the skin and bones from the salmon and flake.
2. In a food processor, purée the salmon, shallots, butter, smoked salmon, Armagnac, herbs, salt, and pepper.
3. Pack into a crock and let ripen overnight, refrigerated.

▶ Keeps 4 days, refrigerated.

≡ Smoked Salmon, Sour Cream, and Horseradish Spread

═ Yield: 1¼ cups

¼ pound smoked salmon, minced
¼ cup minced shallots
1 teaspoon minced dill
⅓ cup sour cream

1 tablespoon prepared horseradish
1½ teaspoons mayonnaise
salt and pepper, to taste

═ Yield: 5 cups

1 pound smoked salmon, minced
1 cup minced shallots
2 teaspoons minced dill

1½ cups sour cream
¼ cup prepared horseradish
2 tablespoons mayonnaise
salt and pepper, to taste

1. In a bowl, mix the salmon, shallots, dill, sour cream, horseradish, mayonnaise, salt, and pepper. Let ripen 4 hours in the refrigerator.

2. Serve with thinly sliced buttered pumpernickel or rye bread.

▶ Keeps 2 days, refrigerated.

≡ Smoked Salmon Mousse

═ Yield: 1 cup

6 ounces smoked salmon
2 tablespoons lemon juice
6 tablespoons melted butter
½ cup crème fraîche or heavy cream

lemon juice, to taste
salt and pepper, to taste
minced dill
capers

═ Yield: 1 quart

1½ pounds smoked salmon
½ cup lemon juice
1½ cups melted butter
2 cups crème fraîche or heavy cream

lemon juice, to taste
salt and pepper, to taste
minced dill
capers

1. In a food processor, purée the salmon and lemon juice. With the motor running, add the butter in a thin stream.

2. Scrape into a bowl and fold in the crème fraîche. (If using heavy cream, beat until soft peaks form before folding into the salmon.)

3. Fold in the lemon juice, salt, and pepper. Pack into small ramekins and garnish with dill and capers.

4. Serve with warm, buttered toast.

▶ Keeps 2 days, refrigerated.

≡ *Smoked Salmon Spread*

This recipe is for a dry-smoked, strongly flavored smoked salmon such as prepared in the Northwest.

═ Yield: 1 cup

½ pound smoked salmon	½ cup minced scallions
½ cup peeled, seeded, and chopped tomatoes	pepper, to taste
	ice water, if necessary

═ Yield: 1 quart

2 pounds smoked salmon	2 cups minced scallions
2 cups peeled, seeded, and chopped tomatoes	pepper, to taste
	ice water, if necessary

1. Soak the salmon in cold water for 2 hours, changing the water twice. Drain and chop.

2. In a food processor, purée the salmon, tomatoes, scallions, and pepper. Add a little ice water if needed to make a spreadable mixture.

3. Serve with crackers or raw vegetables.

▶ Keeps 2 days, refrigerated.

NOTE: To make a chunky spread, mix the ingredients by hand; do not purée.

≡ *Sardine Spread I*

═ Yield: 1 cup

2 cans Norwegian sardines, drained	2 teaspoons lemon juice
⅓ pound cream cheese, softened	¼ teaspoon grated onion
3 tablespoons minced parsley	¼ teaspoon paprika
	salt, to taste

= **Yield: 1 quart**

8 cans Norwegian sardines,
  drained
1⅓ pounds cream cheese,
  softened
¾ cup minced parsley

2½ tablespoons lemon juice
1 tablespoon grated onion
1 tablespoon paprika
salt, to taste

1. In a food processor, purée the sardines, cream cheese, parsley, lemon juice, onion, paprika, and salt.

2. Correct the seasoning with additional salt and lemon juice. Pack into crocks and chill.

3. Serve with crackers.

▶ Keeps 5 days, refrigerated.

NOTE: If desired, pack into lightly oiled decorative molds, chill until firm, and unmold.

≡ *Sardine Spread II*

= **Yield: 1½ cups**

8 ounces cream cheese
1 can Norwegian sardines
1 tablespoon anchovy paste

1 teaspoon lemon juice
1 teaspoon Worcestershire
  sauce

= **Yield: 6 cups**

2 pounds cream cheese
4 cans Norwegian sardines
¼ cup anchovy paste

4 teaspoons lemon juice
4 teaspoons Worcestershire
  sauce

1. In a food processor, purée the cream cheese, sardines, anchovy paste, lemon juice, and Worcestershire sauce.

2. Serve with crackers.

▶ Keeps 1 week, refrigerated.

≡ *Sardine Pâté I*

= **Yield: 1 cup**

2 cans Norwegian sardines
4 hard-cooked eggs
½ cup minced onion
2 teaspoons minced parsley

2 teaspoons mayonnaise
½ teaspoon brandy
lemon juice, to taste
salt and pepper, to taste

=== **Yield: 1 quart**

6 cans Norwegian sardines
12 hard-cooked eggs
1 cup minced onion
2 tablespoons minced parsley

¼ cup mayonnaise
2 teaspoons brandy
lemon juice, to taste
salt and pepper, to taste

1. In a food processor, purée the sardines, eggs, onion, parsley, mayonnaise, brandy, lemon juice, salt, and pepper.
2. Serve with crackers.

▶ Keeps 4 days, refrigerated.

≡ *Sardine Pâté II*

=== **Yield: 1 cup**

¼ pound cream cheese
1 can Norwegian sardines
2 teaspoons lemon juice

2 teaspoons grated onion
2 teaspoons minced parsley
minced parsley

=== **Yield: 1 quart**

1 pound cream cheese
4 cans Norwegian sardines
3 tablespoons lemon juice

2 tablespoons grated onion
2 tablespoons minced parsley
minced parsley

1. In a food processor, purée the cream cheese, sardines, lemon juice, onion, and parsley. Shape into a mound on a platter and sprinkle with minced parsley.
2. Serve with crackers.

▶ Keeps 4 days, refrigerated.

≡ *Fresh Shrimp Pâté I*

=== **Yield: 1 cup**

½ pound shrimp, cooked and
   peeled
½ cup olive oil

1 to 2 tablespoons lemon juice
salt and pepper, to taste
paprika, to taste

=== **Yield: 1 quart**

2 pounds shrimp, cooked and
   peeled
2 cups olive oil

2 to 4 tablespoons lemon juice
salt and pepper, to taste
paprika, to taste

1. In a food processor, purée the shrimp with half the olive oil and half the lemon juice.

2. With the machine running, add the remaining olive oil. Correct the seasoning with salt, pepper, paprika, and the remaining lemon juice. Chill for several hours.

3. Serve with toast or crackers.

▶ Keeps 1 week, refrigerated.

NOTE: Add minced fresh dill for a variation.

≡ *Fresh Shrimp Pâté II*

═ **Yield: 1½ cups**

1 pound shrimp, peeled and deveined	¼ teaspoon chili powder
½ teaspoon peppercorns	1 tablespoon minced parsley
1 teaspoon salt	1 tablespoon minced tarragon
1 cup butter, softened	½ tablespoon Pernod
pinch of mace	½ tablespoon lemon juice

═ **Yield: 6 cups**

4 pounds shrimp, peeled and deveined	1 teaspoon chili powder
2 teaspoons peppercorns	¼ cup minced parsley
2 teaspoons salt	¼ cup minced tarragon
2 pounds butter, softened	2 tablespoons Pernod
½ teaspoon mace	2 tablespoons lemon juice

1. In a saucepan, cover shrimp with cold water and add the peppercorns and salt. Bring to a boil and remove from the heat. The shrimp should be just cooked. (If very large, they may need to simmer 1 minute— no longer.) Let cool in the liquid and drain. Chop the shrimp finely.

2. In a mixer, cream the butter and beat in the chopped shrimp, 1 tablespoon at a time. Season with mace, chili powder, parsley, tarragon, Pernod, lemon juice, and salt, to taste. Pack into crocks and chill overnight.

3. Serve with toast or use to fill pastries.

▶ Keeps 1 week, refrigerated.

☰ *Potted Shrimp I*

═ Yield: 1½ cups

½ pound shrimp, cooked,
  peeled, and deveined
½ cup butter

1 small garlic clove, crushed
1 teaspoon minced tarragon
salt and pepper, to taste

═ Yield: 6 cups

2 pounds shrimp, cooked,
  peeled, and deveined
1 pound butter

2 garlic cloves, crushed
1 tablespoon minced tarragon
salt and pepper, to taste

1. In a food processor, purée the shrimp, butter, garlic, tarragon, salt, and pepper. Pack into crocks and chill for 24 hours.

2. Serve at room temperature with crackers or warm toast.

▶ Keeps 1 week, refrigerated.

☰ *Potted Shrimp II*

═ Yield: 1½ cups

½ pound tiny shrimp, peeled
½ cup clarified butter
½ to 1 tablespoon lemon juice
⅛ teaspoon nutmeg

salt, to taste
Tabasco sauce, to taste
melted clarified butter, optional

═ Yield: 6 cups

2½ pounds tiny shrimp, peeled
1 pound clarified butter
2 to 4 tablespoons lemon juice
½ teaspoon nutmeg

salt, to taste
Tabasco sauce, to taste
melted clarified butter, optional

1. In a skillet, sauté the shrimp in the butter, stirring until just done. Remove from the heat and mash the shrimp slightly with the back of a spoon. Stir in the lemon juice, nutmeg, salt, and Tabasco.

2. Transfer to crocks and chill until firm. If desired, seal the crocks with clarified butter.

3. Serve with hot toast points.

▶ Keeps 5 days, refrigerated; can be frozen.

☰ *Potted Shrimp III*

═ Yield: 1 cup

¼ cup butter
¼ teaspoon curry powder
⅛ teaspoon ground mace
⅛ teaspoon grated nutmeg
pinch of cayenne pepper

½ pound shrimp, cooked and
chopped
1 teaspoon lemon juice
½ teaspoon onion juice
melted clarified butter, optional

═ Yield: 1 quart

½ pound butter
1 teaspoon curry powder
½ teaspoon ground mace
½ teaspoon grated nutmeg
pinch of cayenne pepper
2 pounds shrimp, cooked and
chopped

4 teaspoons lemon juice, or to
taste
2 teaspoons onion juice
melted clarified butter, optional

1. In a saucepan over low heat, melt the butter and cook the curry powder, mace, nutmeg, and cayenne for 5 minutes. Stir in the shrimp, lemon juice, and onion juice and stir to coat the shrimp.

2. Pack into crocks and cool. When cold, pour on clarified butter to seal, if desired.

3. Serve as a spread for crackers or brown bread.

▶ Keeps one week, refrigerated and sealed or 4 days without the seal.
NOTE: To make onion juice, cut an onion in half and ream out the juice using a citrus juice reamer.

☰ *Purée of Smoked Trout*

═ Yield: 2 cups

3 smoked trout, skinned and
boned
⅓ cup heavy cream

1 to 2 tablespoons lemon juice
2 tablespoons olive oil
minced radishes

═ Yield: 1 quart

6 smoked trout, skinned and
boned
⅔ cup heavy cream

2 to 4 tablespoons lemon juice
¼ cup olive oil
minced radishes

In a food processor, purée the trout, cream, lemon juice, and olive oil. Garnish with the radishes, and serve melba toast on the side.

▶ Keeps 4 days, refrigerated.

☰ *Brandade of Smoked Trout*

═ Yield: 1 cup
8 ounces smoked trout, skinned
  and boned
1½ teaspoons olive oil
1½ teaspoons lemon juice

½ cup heavy cream
cayenne pepper, to taste
salt, to taste
minced parsley

═ Yield: 1 quart
2 pounds smoked trout,
  skinned and boned
2 tablespoons olive oil
2 tablespoons lemon juice

2 cups heavy cream
cayenne pepper, to taste
salt, to taste
minced parsley

1. In a food processor, purée the trout, olive oil, and lemon juice. Add the cream in a slow, steady stream. Correct the seasoning with cayenne pepper and salt.

2. Pack into a crock and sprinkle with parsley. Chill.

3. Serve with toast points.

▶ Keeps 4 days, refrigerated.

☰ *Tuna and Green Peppercorn Spread*

═ Yield: 1 cup
1 7-ounce can chunk light tuna,
  drained
3 tablespoons mayonnaise
½ teaspoon lemon juice, or to
  taste

salt, to taste
2 teaspoons green peppercorns

═ Yield: 1 quart
4 7-ounce cans chunk light
  tuna, drained
¾ cup mayonnaise
2 teaspoons lemon juice, or to
  taste

salt, to taste
2 tablespoons green
  peppercorns

1. In a food processor, purée the tuna, mayonnaise, lemon juice, and salt. With on-off turns, mix in the peppercorns.

2. Serve with crackers, or use to stuff vegetables or pastries.

▶ Keeps 1 week, refrigerated.

≡ *Tuna Pâté I*

═ Yield: 1 cup

1 3½-ounce can Italian tuna packed in olive oil, drained	¼ teaspoon dry mustard pinch of cayenne pepper
¼ cup butter	2 tablespoons Madeira
2 tablespoons heavy cream	salt and pepper, to taste

═ Yield: 1 quart

2 7-ounce cans Italian tuna packed in olive oil, drained	1 teaspoon dry mustard ½ teaspoon cayenne pepper
1 cup butter	¼ cup Madeira
½ cup heavy cream	salt and pepper, to taste

1. In a food processor, purée the tuna, butter, cream, mustard, cayenne, Madeira, salt, and pepper. Pack in crocks and smooth the top.

2. Serve with bread or crackers.

▶ Keeps 1 week, refrigerated.

≡ *Tuna Pâté II*

═ Yield: ¾ cup

1 7-ounce can Italian tuna packed in olive oil, drained	pepper, to taste 1 tablespoon capers
½ cup butter	minced parsley and chives
lemon juice, to taste	

═ Yield: 3 cups

4 7-ounce cans Italian tuna packed in olive oil, drained	pepper, to taste ¼ cup capers
2 cups butter	minced parsley and chives
¼ cup lemon juice, or to taste	

1. In a bowl, mash the tuna to a paste and work in the butter, lemon juice, and pepper. Stir in the capers and spoon into a serving bowl. Sprinkle with the parsley and chives.

2. Serve with hot toast.

▶ Keeps 1 week, refrigerated.

NOTE: For a smoother texture, prepare in a food processor.

≡ *Tuna Shrimp Pâté*

≡ **Yield: 2½ cups**

oil for mold
1 7-ounce can Italian tuna
   packed in oil, drained
½ cup butter
1 teaspoon onion juice (see
   note, page 184)
Tabasco sauce, to taste
salt and pepper, to taste

½ pound shrimp, cooked and
   peeled
3 tablespoons minced
   pimientos
2 tablespoons capers
lemon juice, to taste
parsley sprigs

≡ **Yield: 5 cups**

oil for mold
2 7-ounce cans Italian tuna
   packed in oil, drained
1 cup butter
2 teaspoons onion juice (see
   note, page 184)
Tabasco sauce, to taste

salt and pepper, to taste
1 pound shrimp, cooked and
   peeled
⅓ cup minced pimientos
¼ cup capers
lemon juice, to taste
parsley sprigs

1. Lightly oil a 3 or 6 cup mold (for the small or large quantity, respectively).

2. In a food processor, purée the tuna, butter, onion juice, Tabasco sauce, salt, and pepper. Transfer to a bowl.

3. Chop the shrimp finely and mix into the tuna with the pimientos and capers. Correct seasoning with salt, pepper, lemon juice, and Tabasco sauce.

4. Pack into a mold and chill for 24 hours.

5. Unmold and garnish with parsley sprigs. Serve with toast points or use to fill pastries or vegetables.

▶ Keeps 1 week, refrigerated.

≡ Tuna and Red Pepper Spread

=== Yield: 1 cup

1 large red pepper
1 6½-ounce can tuna packed in
  oil, drained
6 tablespoons butter, softened

1 tablespoon lemon juice
½ teaspoon salt
½ teaspoon ground pepper

=== Yield: 1 quart

4 large red peppers
1 26-ounce can tuna packed in
  oil, drained
1½ cups butter, softened

¼ cup lemon juice
2 teaspoons salt
2 teaspoons ground pepper

1. Roast the red peppers over a gas flame or under the broiler. Remove and discard the charred skin. Core, seed, and chop coarsely.

2. In a food processor, purée the tuna, butter, lemon juice, salt, ground pepper, and half the roasted pepper until smooth. Add remaining roasted pepper and process until just finely chopped.

3. Pack into a crock and refrigerate, covered, overnight. Let soften slightly before serving.

4. Serve with toast or crackers.

▶ Keeps 4 days, refrigerated.

≡ Taïba (Tuna, Chili, and Tomato Spread)

=== Yield: 2½ cups

4 tomatoes
2 fresh red chili peppers,
  4 inches long
3 garlic cloves, minced
3 tablespoons olive oil
1 tablespoon tomato paste

2 7-ounce cans Italian tuna
  packed in oil, drained
1 chili pepper, 4 inches long,
  seeded and minced
¼ teaspoon ground coriander
salt and pepper, to taste

=== Yield: 5 cups

8 tomatoes
4 fresh red chili peppers,
  4 inches long
6 garlic cloves, minced
⅓ cup olive oil
2 tablespoons tomato paste

4 7-ounce cans Italian tuna
  packed in oil, drained
2 chili peppers, 4 inches long,
  seeded and minced
½ teaspoon ground coriander
salt and pepper, to taste

1. Preheat the broiler.

2. Cut the tomatoes in half horizontally, squeeze out the seeds, and broil skin-side-up on a broiler pan until the skins are charred and blistered. Peel the skins and chop the pulp.

3. Place the whole chili peppers on a broiler pan and broil until charred on all sides. Peel and discard the skins, ribs, and seeds. Mince.

4. In a saucepan, cook the tomatoes, broiled chili peppers, garlic, and oil, stirring, for 5 minutes or until thickened to a coarse purée.

5. Stir in the tomato paste, tuna, minced chili peppers, coriander, salt, and pepper. Simmer 5 minutes or until the liquid evaporates. Chill.

6. Serve with crusty bread.

▶ Keeps 1 week, refrigerated.

≡ *Potted Braunschweiger*

=== Yield: 1 cup

¼ pound braunschweiger (liverwurst)	1 teaspoon minced parsley
	pinch of thyme
2 tablespoons sour cream	1 teaspoon Cognac
2 tablespoons minced mushrooms	pepper, to taste
	melted clarified butter, optional
2 teaspoons clarified butter	

=== Yield: 1 quart

1 pound braunschweiger (liverwurst)	2 tablespoons minced parsley
½ cup sour cream	¾ teaspoon thyme
½ pound mushrooms, minced	¼ cup Cognac
3 tablespoons clarified butter	pepper, to taste
	melted clarified butter, optional

1. In a food processor, purée the braunschweiger and sour cream. Place in a bowl.

2. In a skillet, sauté the mushrooms in the butter until the liquid evaporates. Add the parsley and thyme and sauté 1 minute. Stir the mushrooms into the braunschweiger and add the Cognac. Correct the seasoning with pepper.

3. Pack into crocks and cover with clarified butter, if desired. Chill.

4. Serve with toast or crackers.

▶ Keeps 1 week, refrigerated.

≡ *Curried Chicken Almond Spread*

═ Yield: 1½ cups

1¼ cups minced cooked
chicken
¼ cup chopped, toasted
almonds
2 teaspoons minced onion

½ teaspoon salt
¼ teaspoon curry powder, or to
taste
pepper, to taste
⅓ cup mayonnaise

═ Yield: 6 cups

5 cups minced cooked chicken
1 cup chopped, toasted
almonds
2 tablespoons minced onion
2 teaspoons salt

1 teaspoon curry powder, or to
taste
pepper, to taste
1½ cups mayonnaise

1. In a bowl, mix the chicken, almonds, onion, salt, curry powder, and pepper. Add just enough mayonnaise to bind.

2. Serve with crackers or bread, or use to fill pastries.

▶ Keeps 3 days, refrigerated.

≡ *Turkey Pâté*

═ Yield: 1½ cups

1 cup ground cooked turkey
¼ cup minced onion
1 hard-cooked egg, minced
¼ cup ground almonds
1 tablespoon Cognac

salt and pepper, to taste
dash of Tabasco sauce
2 to 4 tablespoons mayonnaise
black olives

═ Yield: 6 cups

4 cups ground cooked turkey
1 cup minced onion
4 hard-cooked eggs, minced
1 cup ground almonds
3 tablespoons Cognac

salt and pepper, to taste
¼ teaspoon Tabasco sauce
½ cup mayonnaise
black olives

1. In a bowl, mix the turkey, onion, egg(s), almonds, Cognac, salt, pepper, and Tabasco. Add just enough mayonnaise to bind. Place in a bowl and garnish with the olives.

2. Serve with crackers or breads.

▶ Keeps 3 days, refrigerated.

≡ Lime Steak Spread

═ Yield: 1¼ cups

½ pound raw sirloin
⅓ cup lime juice
½ teaspoon salt
⅓ cup peeled, seeded, and
  chopped tomato

2 tablespoons minced onion
2 tablespoons seeded and
  minced jalapeño peppers
salt and pepper, to taste
¼ cup minced scallions

═ Yield: 6 cups

2 pounds raw sirloin
1⅓ cups lime juice
2 teaspoons salt
1⅓ cups peeled, seeded, and
  chopped tomato

½ cup minced onion
¼ cup seeded and minced
  jalapeño peppers
salt and pepper, to taste
1 cup minced scallions

1. In a food processor, finely chop the sirloin. Add the lime juice and salt. Chill, covered, for 3 hours.

2. Stir in the tomato, onion, jalapeños, salt, and pepper. Place in a bowl and sprinkle scallions over the top.

3. Serve with tortilla chips, crackers, or buttered toast points, or use to fill hollowed French bread loaves.

▶ Refrigerate and serve within 12 hours.

≡ La Carne Cruda Come a Canelli (Raw Beef Spread)

═ Yield: 1 cup

½ pound lean beefsteak
½ garlic clove, peeled
1 tablespoon anchovy paste
pepper, to taste

3 tablespoons lemon juice
3 tablespoons olive oil
cornichons

═ Yield: 1 quart

2 pounds lean beefsteak
2 garlic cloves, peeled
¼ cup anchovy paste
pepper, to taste

½ to ¾ cup lemon juice
¾ cup olive oil
cornichons

1. In a food processor, finely chop the meat and garlic. Do not overprocess to a mush. You may prefer to chop the meat by hand.

2. Put the meat into a bowl and mix in the anchovy paste, pepper, lemon juice, and olive oil. Let stand at room temperature for 3 hours.

3. Pour off any liquid from the meat and correct the seasoning with pepper. Place in a serving dish and garnish with the cornichons.

4. Serve with crisp bread.

▶ Keeps 6 to 8 hours, refrigerated.

≡ *Potted Tongue*

≡ **Yield: 1½ cups**

½ pound smoked tongue	pinch of ground cloves
¾ cup melted butter	salt and pepper, to taste
¼ teaspoon ground nutmeg	

≡ **Yield: 6 cups**

2 pounds smoked tongue	⅛ teaspoon ground cloves
3 cups melted butter	salt and pepper, to taste
1 teaspoon ground nutmeg	

1. In a food processor, purée the tongue, butter, nutmeg, cloves, salt, and pepper.

2. Pack into crocks and chill.

3. Serve with bread or crackers.

▶ Keeps 2 weeks, refrigerated; can be frozen.

≡ *Kibbi (Raw Beef or Lamb Spread)*

≡ **Yield: 3 cups**

1 cup finely grated onion	½ teaspoon dried basil
1 pound very lean beef or lamb, diced	pinch of ground allspice
	Tabasco sauce, to taste
1 teaspoon salt	1 cup bulgur (cracked wheat)
⅛ teaspoon pepper	

≡ **Yield: 6 cups**

2 cups finely grated onion	1 teaspoon dried basil
2 pounds very lean beef or lamb, diced	pinch of ground allspice
	Tabasco sauce, to taste
2 teaspoons salt	2 cups bulgur (cracked wheat)
¼ teaspoon pepper	

1. In a food processor, purée the onions, beef, salt, pepper, basil, allspice, and Tabasco sauce. Add 2 to 4 teaspoons ice water to lighten the texture.

2. Soak the wheat in ice water for 15 minutes. Drain and squeeze out the excess water. Combine with the meat mixture. Correct the seasoning with salt.

3. Serve with lemon wedges and crackers.

▶ Serve within 12 hours.

≡ *Potted Ham*

═ Yield: 1½ cups

½ cup cranberries
¾ cup cubed ham
1 shallot, minced
¼ teaspoon pepper
½ teaspoon dry mustard
¼ teaspoon ground allspice

¼ teaspoon grated nutmeg
pinch of cayenne pepper
¼ cup diced firm ham fat or
   chilled butter
¼ cup butter

═ Yield: 6 cups

2 cups cranberries
3 cups cubed ham
3 shallots, minced
1 teaspoon pepper
2 teaspoons dry mustard
1 teaspoon ground allspice

1 teaspoon grated nutmeg
⅛ teaspoon cayenne pepper
1 cup diced firm ham fat or
   chilled butter
1 cup butter

1. Preheat the oven to 400°F.

2. In a covered baking dish, bake the cranberries for 30 minutes or until they split and soften. Cool, uncovered.

3. In a food processor, coarsely chop half the cubed ham. Turn into a bowl.

4. In the processor, purée the remaining ham, cranberries, shallots, pepper, mustard, allspice, nutmeg, cayenne, and ham fat. Correct the seasoning. Add the cranberry mixture to the chopped ham and mix well. Beat in the butter.

5. Pack into crocks and let ripen for 2 days before serving.

6. Serve with black bread or crackers.

▶ Keeps 2 weeks, refrigerated.

≡ *Ham Mousse*

oil for mold
½ pound boiled ham, ground
¼ pound butter
1 tablespoon Dijon mustard
salt, to taste
1 teaspoon white pepper

1½ tablespoons unflavored
  gelatin
½ cup Madeira
1 cup chicken stock
1 cup heavy cream, whipped
2 teaspoons Cognac

1. Lightly oil a 1½-quart mold.

2. In a food processor, purée the ham, butter, mustard, salt, and pepper.

3. In a small saucepan, soften the gelatin in the Madeira and dissolve over low heat, stirring. Remove from the heat. Add the chicken stock and cool until it thickens to the consistency of raw egg whites.

4. Fold the gelatin and then the cream into the ham mixture. Fold in the Cognac and correct the seasoning. Pour into the mold and refrigerate until set.

5. Unmold and serve with toast, crackers, and dark bread.

▶ Keeps 3 days, refrigerated.

6

Pâtés and Terrines

Pâtés and terrines can mean the same thing. Originally, however, the difference was more distinct. *Terrine* referred to the container as well as the resulting meat loaf. *Pâté* was a terrine mixture baked in a pastry crust. A terrine, the container, can be made of pottery, porcelain, or enameled cast iron, or may be an ordinary loaf pan. Pâtés need not have a pastry crust. Many menus indicate the difference by referring, redundantly, to *pâté en croute*. But no matter what you call them, they are both delicious and easy to make.

Terrines and pâtés can be prepared with a hand-operated meat grinder or by chopping the meats on a board. However, an electric meat grinder or food processor makes the job simpler and faster. For many pâtés, a blender provides the smoothest finish. Some markets will grind the meats for you, but others may refuse to grind pork or livers because public health laws require that the machine be sterilized before grinding another meat, causing extra work.

There are three major categories of pâté: smooth, spreadable mixtures; terrines; and pâtés en croûte. The first two are preferable for cocktail parties, and the latter is best suited for a sit-down affair.

Pâtés and terrines are usually served with cocktail breads or toasts and can be accompanied by those marvelous sour French pickles, cornichons, or with pickled sour cherries.

Smooth, Spreadable Pâtés
Usually based on livers or puréed fish, these pâtés are not often baked. To make them velvety smooth, purée the mixture in a blender (it does a better job of puréeing than a food processor) and then force it through

195

a fine sieve. Chapter 5 contains several recipes for vegetable and fish pâtés of this type; the liver-based versions are given in this chapter.

Smooth, spreadable pâtés can be attractively served by placing them in aspic-decorated molds (see page 215). To lighten the flavor of a liver pâté, fold in an equal quantity or less (by volume) of whipped cream. This not only softens the flavor, but also increases the number of servings.

Terrines

Terrines can be baked in terrines or in ordinary loaf pans. They are cooled in the pan, chilled, and served directly from the container if it is attractive, or unmolded and sliced if it is not. Terrines can be silky smooth or quite coarse. Some may have whole strips of marinated meat, pork fat, fish, or vegetables arranged in the center to create a mosaic design.

Slices of terrine are served on or with bread or toast, or with a plate and fork. Because they are usually baked in pans lined with pork fat, they are often unattractive when unmolded. If you do not do a perfect job lining the pan, there may be unsightly spaces between the strips of pork fat. You can remove the fat, but even so, the meat itself is usually not that pretty. To improve the appearance, sprinkle minced parsley around the edges and place beautiful sprigs of curly-leafed parsley around the base. You can also use cut-out vegetables to make an appealing design. When sliced and arranged in neat rows on a platter, it does look better. If the terrine container is pretty enough to display, leave the pâté in it, pour on a thin layer of aspic, and decorate the top with vegetable flowers or orange or lemon segments for color. Coat with another thin glaze of aspic.

Pâté en Croûte

Pâté en croûte is simply a terrine filling baked in a pastry-lined mold. Fancy molds with removable sides are available for this purpose, but ordinary loaf pans work just as well. Line the pan with parchment paper to make unmolding easier. You can also use a springform pan, or even make the pâté freeform by shaping it directly on a baking sheet. After the pâté has been baked and cooled to room temperature, pour in some cool but still liquid aspic to fill the empty spaces so the slices will hold together when cut. Chill completely before serving.

Pâté en croûte should be served with only about half of the loaf sliced so guests can see how attractively you decorated the top. You must provide plates and forks and serve it only to groups where everyone can be seated.

Rillettes, Cretons

Rillettes and cretons are spreads made from meats cooked for many hours with a lot of fat and seasoning. Although the cooking time is lengthy, they do not require much attention.

Rillettes will keep for a month or longer, refrigerated, if well sealed. This is a good reason to prepare them in quantity. What is not used for a particular occasion can be repacked, sealed, and kept for another event.

Sealing Pâtés and Terrines

Most pâtés are better if made at least one day before serving; many can be made one to two weeks ahead. To keep them longer, many recipes for the smooth, spreadable pâtés suggest that melted clarified butter be poured over the top of the pâté as a seal. This protects the contents and allows it to be stored longer. If the pâté is to be frozen, just cover it with plastic wrap. If you use the butter topping, decoratively score the surface with a fork before presenting it.

Terrines can also be sealed by melting lard and pouring it over the terrine in its container. It will keep a month in the refrigerator. Be sure to scrape off and discard the lard before serving.

Many terrines can be frozen without harming the taste or texture; others get watery. Generally, the smoother the mixture, the better it freezes. Pack smooth, spreadable pâtés in small crocks. You can freeze them and serve one at a moment's notice. Coarse-grained pâtés tend to get watery when frozen; they are best if made and served within 2 weeks.

Keep in mind that most terrines and pâtés taste best if allowed to mellow in the refrigerator for 2 to 3 days before serving.

Lining a Mold with Pork Fat

Ideally, you want to use thin sheets of fresh pork fat to line terrines; salt pork can be used as a substitute. Soak salt pork in cold water for 4 to 6 hours to remove as much salt as possible, then drain it and pat dry. With a thin sharp knife, slice it into sheets ¼ inch thick. If you have an electric meat slicer, this is an easy task — even easier if you can convince a butcher to do the slicing for you. Once cut, place the sheets between pieces of waxed paper and flatten the pork fat slightly with a smooth-headed mallet. Line the bottom and sides of the mold, letting the excess hang over the edge. After the pâté has been packed in the mold, fold the ends over to cover the filling completely. You can also trim the fat so it is even with the top of the pâté. If desired, use a knife or metal cutters to cut out designs from another slice of fat, and arrange these cutouts on top. An easy way to decorate the top is to lay strips of fat in a crosshatched pattern.

To Taste a Pâté Mixture for Seasoning

Never taste an uncooked pâté for seasoning, especially if it contains raw pork. To check it safely, heat a small amount of butter in a skillet and sauté about 1 tablespoon of the pâté mixture shaped into a flat cake. When it is cooked, let it cool and then taste. Remember that pâtés are served cold and chilling dampens the flavor. Therefore, the seasoning should be increased to compensate.

Baking a Terrine

Terrines are usually baked in a bain marie, or water bath. Use an ovenproof container at least an inch larger than the terrine on all sides. Place the terrine in it and fill the container half full of hot water. Cover the terrine tightly with foil or a lid and bake.

Recipes often state "bake until the juices run clear." An easier and more accurate method is to use an instant-read meat thermometer and bake the terrine until it registers 165°F. Pâtés with pork must be baked until well done.

Cooling and Weighting a Terrine

After the terrine is baked, remove it from the oven and the water bath. Let it cool to room temperature on a baking sheet and place a weight on top; 3 to 5 pounds is sufficient. Refrigerate until cold, at least overnight.

Reducing the Fat Content of Terrines and Pâtés

Pâtés were originally created to use all the scraps after pigs were slaughtered just before winter. Over the years this sort of cooking became an art unto itself. Today charcuterie is as prized and admired as ever; however, the types of pâtés have changed. In the past it was not only customary, but necessary, to use a lot of fat. The fat carried the flavor and added valuable calories when food supplies were scarce. The fat was also used to seal the meats so that they could be stored for months in cold rooms. With modern refrigeration, transportation, and the availability of meat year round, this is no longer necessary.

You can reduce the quantity of fat tremendously and not lose any flavor. If you do this, test it first—if too much fat is removed the pâté will be dry and unappealing, rather than unctuous. Read the recipes carefully before proceeding to determine if you wish to prepare a lower fat terrine such as pâté Parisienne (page 227) or a more traditional version such as a terrine du chef (page 235).

You can also reduce the amount of fat in a terrine by using something other than pork fat to line the mold. You may use microwaveable plastic wrap (discard the plastic before serving, of course) or leafy greens such as spinach or Swiss chard. You can also use cabbage, but it will give a different flavor to the pâté. Another alternative is simply to butter the pan well instead of lining it with pork fat.

Servings

How much pâté to prepare, as with so many hors d'oeuvre, depends on the number and type of other items on the menu, whether for dinner or hors d'oeuvre. For 6 to 8 dinner guests, a cup of spreadable pâté should be sufficient. For 20 persons with 6 other hors d'oeuvre on the menu, a cup will also suffice. For large parties, provide about 2 cups for every 30 guests. Sliced terrines are easier to figure. As a first course before dinner, a ½-inch slice is suitable. For a buffet, ¼-inch servings that have been cut in half or quarters are appropriate. With a full menu of 6 or more items, plan on 2 servings per person. To calculate how many a terrine will serve, measure the length of the terrine and multiply by the thickness of the slices. For instance, an 8-inch loaf pan can provide 16 to 64 servings (16 ½-inch servings, or 32 ¼-inch slices cut in half for 64 servings).

≡ Whitefish and Salmon Terrine

≡ **Yield: 1 quart**

1 pound cod or other whitefish fillets	large bunch parsley
2 eggs	10 sorrel or basil leaves
3 ounces fresh bread crumbs	3 scallions, chopped
2 teaspoons green peppercorns	2 ounces butter, softened
6 tablespoons heavy cream	½ pound salmon fillets, cut into
salt, to taste	strips ½ inch wide
	fresh tarragon, optional

1. Preheat the oven to 350°F.

2. In a food processor, purée the cod, eggs, bread crumbs, peppercorns, and cream. Season with salt.

3. In a saucepan of boiling water, blanch the parsley, sorrel or basil, and scallions for 5 minutes, or until just tender. Drain and purée with the butter.

4. Pack half the puréed fish into a buttered 1-quart terrine. Cover with half the herb mixture, the salmon slices, and the remaining herb mixture. Spread the remaining puréed fish on top.

5. Cover with buttered foil and bake in a water bath for 45 minutes, or until a knife inserted in the center comes out clean. Cool, weight, and chill at least 2 hours.

6. Unmold and serve in thin slices. Garnish with tarragon, if desired.

▶ Keeps 3 days, refrigerated.

≡ *Terrine de Saumon Froid (Cold Salmon Pâté)*

== **Yield: 1½ quarts**

2 pounds salmon fillets,
  skinned and boned
½ cup sherry
2 bay leaves
salt and pepper, to taste
⅓ pound whiting or sole

½ pound cod fillets
2 slices stale white bread
milk
2 egg yolks, lightly beaten
¼ cup butter

1. Preheat the oven to 350°F.

2. Cut half the salmon into 1-inch-thick fingers. Reserve the remaining salmon.

3. In a bowl, marinate the salmon fingers with the sherry, bay leaves, salt, and pepper for 2 hours. Drain and pat dry.

4. In a food processor, purée the remaining salmon, whiting, and cod. Soak the bread in the milk and squeeze out the excess moisture. Add the bread, egg yolks, and butter to the fish mixture. Purée again.

5. Correct the seasoning with salt and pepper. This mixture must be very smooth. For the best results, force it through a fine sieve.

6. Butter a 1½-quart terrine. Spread a thin layer of the fish purée and arrange salmon fingers lengthwise. Cover with more fish purée and continue to layer until the terrine is full, ending with a top layer of purée. The salmon fingers will form a mosaic when the terrine is sliced.

7. Cover with buttered parchment, waxed paper, or foil. Place in a water bath and bake for 45 to 60 minutes, or until a knife inserted in the center comes out clean. Cool to room temperature and chill completely before serving. Unmold, if desired.

▶ Keeps 3 days, refrigerated.

≡ *Almond Mushroom Pâté*

== **Yield: 1½ cups**

¼ cup minced onion
3 tablespoons butter
¾ pound mushrooms, minced
2 garlic cloves, minced
2 teaspoons lemon juice
1 teaspoon minced tarragon

½ teaspoon salt
pinch of pepper
¾ cup blanched almonds,
  toasted
⅓ cup sour cream
lemon wedges, optional

═ Yield: 6 cups

1 cup minced onion	2 teaspoons salt
¾ cup butter	½ teaspoon pepper
3 pounds mushrooms, minced	3 cups blanched almonds,
6 garlic cloves, minced	toasted
2 tablespoons lemon juice	1⅓ cups sour cream
1½ tablespoons minced	lemon wedges, optional
tarragon	

1. In a skillet, sauté the onion in one-third of the butter until golden. Add the remaining butter, mushrooms, garlic, lemon juice, tarragon, salt, and pepper. Sauté over high heat until the liquid evaporates.

2. In a food processor, grind the almonds finely, then add the mushroom mixture and sour cream.

3. Pack the mixture into crocks and chill.

4. Serve with crackers or use to fill pastries.

▶ Keeps 4 days, refrigerated.

≡ *Quick Liverwurst Pâté*

═ Yield: 2½ cups

¼ cup butter	pinch of nutmeg
1 pound liverwurst	2 teaspoons grated onion
2 tablespoons minced parsley	2 tablespoons heavy cream
½ teaspoon dried thyme	2 tablespoons Cognac

═ Yield: 5 cups

½ cup butter	⅛ teaspoon nutmeg
2 pounds liverwurst	1½ tablespoons grated onion
¼ cup minced parsley	¼ cup heavy cream
1 teaspoon dried thyme	3 tablespoons Cognac

1. In a food processor, purée the butter, liverwurst, parsley, thyme, nutmeg, onion, cream, and Cognac.

2. Pack into crocks and chill until ready to serve.

3. Serve with crackers or breads, or use to fill pastries.

▶ Keeps 1 week, refrigerated.

☰ *Herbed Chicken Liver Pâté I*

⹀ Yield: 3 cups

1 cup minced onion
¾ cup butter
1 pound chicken livers, cut in
 thirds
1 small bay leaf
1 teaspoon salt

½ teaspoon pepper
½ teaspoon dried thyme
½ teaspoon dried oregano
2 teaspoons Cognac
salt and pepper, to taste

⹀ Yield: 6 cups

2 cups minced onion
1½ cups butter
2 pounds chicken livers, cut in
 thirds
2 bay leaves
2 teaspoons salt

1 teaspoon pepper
1 teaspoon dried thyme
1 teaspoon dried oregano
1 tablespoon Cognac
salt and pepper, to taste

1. In a large skillet, sauté the onion in half the butter until golden. Remove the onions with a slotted spoon and reserve. Add the livers to the skillet with the bay leaves, salt, pepper, thyme, and oregano. Sauté until the livers are medium rare. Discard the bay leaf.

2. Put the livers and onions in a blender and blend until smooth. Force the livers and the remaining butter through a fine sieve. Stir in the Cognac, and correct the seasoning with salt and pepper. Pack into crocks and chill.

3. Serve with crackers or French bread.

▶ Keeps 1 week, refrigerated; can be frozen for up to 4 months.

☰ *Herbed Chicken Liver Pâté II*

⹀ Yield: 3 cups

1¼ pounds chicken livers, cut
 in thirds
1 sprig fresh rosemary
3 tablespoons butter
¼ cup minced onion
2 garlic cloves, crushed

2 tablespoons minced thyme
2 tablespoons minced parsley
1 cup butter, softened
salt and pepper, to taste
½ cup pistachios, chopped
½ cup clarified butter, optional

⹀ Yield: 6 cups

2½ pounds chicken livers, cut
  in thirds
2 sprigs fresh rosemary
⅓ cup butter
½ cup minced onion
4 garlic cloves, crushed

¼ cup minced thyme
¼ cup minced parsley
2 cups butter, softened
salt and pepper, to taste
1 cup pistachios, chopped
1 cup clarified butter, optional

1. In a skillet, sauté the livers and rosemary in the butter until medium rare. Discard the rosemary if it is burned. Put the livers in a food processor.

2. Sauté the onion in the same skillet, scraping up the browned bits. Add the onions, garlic, thyme, and parsley to the livers. Purée and cool.

3. Beat the softened butter into the liver mixture, 2 tablespoons at a time. Correct seasoning with salt and pepper. Fold in the nuts.

4. Pack into crocks and seal with clarified butter, if desired.

▶ Keeps 1 week, refrigerated; can be frozen for up to 2 months.

⹀ *Chicken Liver Mushroom Pâté I*

⹀ Yield: 1 cup

½ pound chicken livers
1 cup chicken stock
½ pound mushrooms, minced
1 garlic clove, minced
½ cup minced scallions
¼ cup butter

1 tablespoon lemon juice
1 tablespoon white wine
2 tablespoons Worcestershire
  sauce
salt and pepper, to taste

⹀ Yield: 1 quart

2 pounds chicken livers
1 quart chicken stock
2 pounds mushrooms, minced
1 garlic clove, minced
2 cups minced scallions

1 cup butter
¼ cup lemon juice
¼ cup white wine
¼ cup Worcestershire sauce
salt and pepper, to taste

1. In a saucepan, simmer the livers in the stock for 5 minutes or until medium rare. Cool and mince finely.

2. In a skillet, sauté the mushrooms, garlic, and scallions in half the butter for 5 minutes. Stir in the lemon juice and white wine, and cook until the liquid evaporates. Cool slightly.

3. Add the livers, the remaining butter, and Worcestershire sauce, and correct seasoning with salt and pepper.

4. Pack into crocks and chill.

▶ Keeps 4 days, refrigerated.

≡ *Chicken Liver Mushroom Pâté II*

= **Yield: 2½ cups**

½ cup minced onion	3 tablespoons minced parsley
3 tablespoons vegetable oil	2 garlic cloves, crushed
1 pound chicken livers, cut in	2 tablespoons butter
half	salt and pepper, to taste
½ pound mushrooms, sliced	pinch of grated nutmeg
2 tablespoons sherry, or to taste	

= **Yield: 5 cups**

1 cup minced onion	⅓ cup minced parsley
⅓ cup vegetable oil	4 garlic cloves, crushed
2 pounds chicken livers, cut in	¼ cup butter
half	salt and pepper, to taste
1 pound mushrooms, sliced	⅛ teaspoon grated nutmeg
¼ cup sherry, or to taste	

1. In a skillet, sauté the onion in the oil until soft but not browned. Add the livers and mushrooms, and sauté until the livers are no longer pink.

2. In a food processor, purée the liver and mushroom mixture. Add the sherry, parsley, garlic, butter, salt, pepper, and nutmeg, and process until well mixed.

3. Pack into crocks and chill.

4. Serve with crackers or toast.

▶ Keeps 4 days, refrigerated.

≡ *Chicken Liver Pâté I*

= **Yield: 2 cups**

½ cup minced onion	2 tablespoons Cognac
¼ cup butter	⅛ teaspoon grated nutmeg
1½ pounds chicken livers	salt and pepper, to taste
2 hard-cooked egg yolks	½ cup minced chives
½ cup butter, softened	

═ **Yield: 1 quart**

1 cup minced onion
½ cup butter
3 pounds chicken livers
4 hard-cooked egg yolks
1 cup butter, softened

¼ cup Cognac
¼ teaspoon grated nutmeg
salt and pepper, to taste
1 cup minced chives

1. In a skillet, sauté the onion in butter until soft but not brown. Add the livers and cook until medium.

2. In a food processor, purée the livers, egg yolks, softened butter, Cognac, nutmeg, salt, and pepper. Fold in the chives.

3. Pack into crocks and chill.

4. Serve with crackers or toast.

▶ Keeps 4 days, refrigerated; can be frozen for 2 months.

≡ *Chicken Liver Pâté II*

═ **Yield: 2 cups**

½ pound chicken livers
2 tablespoons butter
2 hard-cooked egg yolks
6 ounces cream cheese, cut
   into 1-inch cubes

1 to 2 black truffles, minced
3 tablespoons Cognac
salt and pepper, to taste

═ **Yield: 1 quart**

1 pound chicken livers
¼ cup butter
4 hard-cooked egg yolks
12 ounces cream cheese, cut
   into 1-inch cubes

2 to 4 black truffles, minced
⅓ cup Cognac
salt and pepper, to taste

1. In a skillet, sauté the livers in the butter until medium.

2. In a food processor, purée the livers and eggs. With the machine running, add the cream cheese one cube at a time. Stir in the truffles, Cognac, salt, and pepper.

3. Pack into crocks and let ripen at least 12 hours.

4. Serve with bread, crackers, or toast.

▶ Keeps 1 week, refrigerated; can be frozen for 2 months.

≡ *Chicken Liver Pâté III*

=== **Yield: 1 cup**

¼ cup minced onion
¼ cup butter
½ pound chicken livers, cut in
 half
¼ teaspoon ground allspice

2 garlic cloves, crushed
1 tablespoon salt
pepper, to taste
2 tablespoons Cognac

=== **Yield: 1 quart**

1 cup minced onion
1 cup butter
2 pounds chicken livers, cut in
 half
¾ teaspoon ground allspice

4 garlic cloves, crushed
2 tablespoons salt
pepper, to taste
¼ cup Cognac

1. In a skillet, sauté the onion in the butter until soft but not brown. Add the livers, allspice, garlic, salt, and pepper and cook until the livers are medium. Remove from the heat and cool for 10 minutes.

2. In a blender or food processor, purée the mixture. With the machine running, add the Cognac. Force through a sieve for a silkier finish.

3. Pack into crocks and chill.

4. Serve with bread, toast, or crackers.

▶ Keeps 5 days, refrigerated; can be frozen for 2 months.
NOTE: To soften the flavor, fold in an equal volume of whipped cream.

≡ *Leverpostej (Danish Liver Paste)*

=== **Yield: 1¼ cups**

2 tablespoons minced shallots
¼ cup butter
½ pound chicken livers
3 tablespoons warmed brandy

2 tablespoons heavy cream
pinch of dried tarragon
salt and pepper, to taste

=== **Yield: 5 cups**

½ cup minced shallots
1 cup butter
2 pounds chicken livers
⅓ cup warmed brandy

½ cup heavy cream
½ teaspoon dried tarragon
salt and pepper, to taste

1. In a skillet, sauté the shallots in one-fourth the butter until soft but not brown. Remove from the pan and reserve.

2. Add the remaining butter to the skillet and sauté the liver over high heat, stirring, until medium rare.

3. Add the brandy and ignite. When the flames die down, stir in the shallots, cream, tarragon, salt, and pepper. Purée the mixture in a food processor or blender.

4. Pack into crocks and chill.

5. Serve with bread, crackers, or toast.

▶ Keeps 5 days, refrigerated; can be frozen for 2 months.
NOTE: To soften the flavor, fold in an equal volume of whipped cream.

≡ *Pâté Liegeoise (Spicy Chicken Liver Pâté)*

═ **Yield: 3 cups**

1 pound chicken livers	½ teaspoon grated nutmeg
1 cup butter	¼ cup grated onion
2 teaspoons dry mustard	2 tablespoons minced truffles
¼ teaspoon ground cloves	salt and pepper, to taste

═ **Yield: 1½ quarts**

2 pounds chicken livers	1 teaspoon grated nutmeg
2 cups butter	½ cup grated onion
4 teaspoons dry mustard	¼ cup minced truffles
½ teaspoon ground cloves	salt and pepper, to taste

1. In a saucepan, simmer the livers in salted water to cover for 20 minutes. Drain and pat dry.

2. In a food processor, purée the livers, remove, and set aside.

3. Without washing the bowl, purée the butter, mustard, cloves, nutmeg, and onion. With the machine running, add the puréed livers, ⅓ cup at a time. Correct the seasoning with salt and pepper. Fold in the truffles.

4. Pack into crocks and chill for at least 12 hours to allow the flavors to ripen.

5. Serve with bread, crackers, or toast.

▶ Keeps 1 week, refrigerated; can be frozen for 2 months.

≡ Chicken Liver Pâté with Apples and Mushrooms

═ Yield: 1 cup

½ pound chicken livers
1 tablespoon butter
½ cup chicken stock
1 small onion, stuck with 1 clove
¼ teaspoon thyme
½ bay leaf
¼ cup chopped onion
1 tablespoon butter
½ cup minced peeled tart apple

¼ cup mushrooms
1 large anchovy fillet, minced
1 tablespoon rendered chicken fat
1 tablespoon brandy
1 teaspoon lemon juice
½ teaspoon salt
pinch pepper
melted clarified butter, optional

═ Yield: 1 quart

2 pounds chicken livers
¼ cup butter
1½ cups chicken stock
1 large onion, stuck with 3 cloves
1 teaspoon thyme
1 bay leaf
1 cup chopped onion
3 tablespoons butter

1 cup minced peeled tart apple
1 cup mushrooms
2 large anchovy fillets, minced
¼ cup rendered chicken fat
¼ cup brandy
1½ tablespoons lemon juice
2 teaspoons salt
¼ teaspoon pepper
melted clarified butter, optional

1. In a skillet, sauté the livers in the butter until they start to stiffen. Add the stock, whole onion, thyme, and bay leaf and simmer 10 minutes. Strain the liquid and reserve. Set aside the livers and discard the cooked onion and bay leaf.

2. Sauté the chopped onion in the remaining butter until golden. Stir in the apple and mushrooms and sauté until the apple is tender.

3. In a food processor, purée the onion-apple mixture, anchovies, and livers, adding some of the reserved broth to thin the mixture. Cool.

4. Beat in the chicken fat, brandy, lemon juice, salt, and pepper. The mixture should be somewhat fluid; add more broth if necessary.

5. Force through a sieve and pack into crocks. Chill until firm and seal with clarified butter, if desired.

▶ Keeps 5 days, refrigerated; can be frozen for 2 months.

≡ Chicken Liver Pâté with Benedictine

═ Yield: 3 cups

1 pound chicken livers	¼ cup sour cream
1¼ cups butter	1 teaspoon ground allspice
1½ cups minced onion	1 tablespoon Benedictine
1 teaspoon salt	1 tablespoon lemon juice
½ teaspoon black pepper	2 tablespoons minced truffles
2 tablespoons brandy	or pistachios

═ Yield: 6 cups

2 pounds chicken livers	½ cup sour cream
2½ cups butter	2 teaspoons ground allspice
3 cups minced onion	2 tablespoons Benedictine
2 teaspoons salt	2 tablespoons lemon juice
1 teaspoon black pepper	¼ cup minced truffles or
¼ cup brandy	pistachios

1. In a skillet, sauté the livers in ¼ (½) cup butter until brown on the bottom. Add the onion and sauté until the onion is soft. Add more butter if needed.

2. Remove the pan from the heat and add the salt, pepper, and brandy. Ignite the brandy and stir until the flames die. Stir in the sour cream, allspice, and Benedictine.

3. Purée the mixture in a blender or food processor. For a smoother finish, force through a sieve. Chill.

4. Cream the remaining butter and beat into the cold liver mixture, a tablespoon at a time. Correct the seasoning with lemon juice, salt, and pepper. Fold in the truffles.

5. Pack into crocks and chill.

6. Serve with bread, crackers, or toast.

▶ Keeps 5 days, refrigerated; can be frozen for 2 months.

≡ Chicken Liver and Bacon Pâté

═ Yield: 1½ cups

½ pound chicken livers	2 tablespoons Madeira
3 tablespoons Madeira	2 tablespoons sherry
2 tablespoons butter	1 teaspoon brandy
6 slices lean bacon, chopped	salt and pepper, to taste
1 shallot, minced	slivered almonds sautéed in
½ teaspoon dried thyme	butter
¼ cup heavy cream	

══ **Yield: 6 cups**

2 pounds chicken livers
¾ cup Madeira
½ cup butter
1 pound lean bacon, chopped
4 shallots, minced
2 teaspoons dried thyme
1 cup heavy cream

⅓ cup Madeira
⅓ cup sherry
2 tablespoons brandy
salt and pepper, to taste
slivered almonds sautéed in
    butter

1. In a bowl, marinate the livers in the Madeira for 2 hours. Drain and pat dry. Discard the marinade.
2. In a skillet, sauté the livers in the butter until brown.
3. In another skillet, sauté the bacon, shallots, and thyme until half cooked. Add the livers and continue to cook until the livers are medium.
4. In a food processor, purée the liver mixture, cream, remaining Madeira, sherry, brandy, salt, and pepper.
5. Pack into crocks and chill.
6. When ready to serve, garnish the top of each crock with almonds. Serve with bread, crackers, or toast.

▶ Keeps 5 days, refrigerated; can be frozen for 2 months.

══ *Pâté de Foie de Volailles Simple*
   (Easy Chicken Liver Pâté)

══ **Yield: 1 cup**

½ pound chicken livers
½ cup butter, softened
2 tablespoons minced onion
1 teaspoon dry mustard

pinch of ground cloves
pinch of cayenne pepper
pinch of grated nutmeg
salt, to taste

══ **Yield: 1 quart**

2 pounds chicken livers
2 cups butter, softened
½ cup minced onion
1 tablespoon dry mustard

¼ teaspoon ground cloves
¼ teaspoon cayenne pepper
¼ teaspoon grated nutmeg
1 tablespoon salt

1. In a saucepan, simmer the livers in water to cover for 10 minutes. Drain and purée in a food processor.
2. Add the butter, onion, mustard, cloves, cayenne, nutmeg, and salt.
3. Pack into crocks and chill.
4. Serve with bread, crackers, or toast.

▶ Keeps 1 week, refrigerated; can be frozen for 2 months.

≡ Bourbon Pâté

== **Yield: 1½ cups**

¼ pound butter
¼ cup minced onion
½ pound chicken livers
½ cup chicken stock
1 tablespoon sherry
¼ teaspoon paprika

¼ teaspoon ground allspice
¼ teaspoon salt
pinch of cayenne pepper
1 garlic clove, crushed
¼ cup bourbon
½ cup chopped walnuts

== **Yield: 6 cups**

1 pound butter
1 cup minced onion
2 pounds chicken livers
2 cups chicken stock
¼ cup sherry
1 teaspoon paprika

1 teaspoon ground allspice
1 teaspoon salt
¼ teaspoon cayenne pepper
4 garlic cloves, crushed
2 cups bourbon
2 cups chopped walnuts

1. In a skillet, melt the butter and sauté the onion and livers until medium rare. Add the stock, sherry, paprika, allspice, salt, cayenne, and garlic, and simmer 5 minutes. Add the bourbon and ignite. When the flames die down, remove from the heat and let cool for 5 minutes.

2. In a food processor or blender, purée the mixture in batches. Force it through a fine sieve and fold in the nuts.

3. Pack into crocks and chill until set.

▶ Keeps 5 days, refrigerated; can be frozen for 2 months.

≡ Chopped Chicken Livers with Apples

== **Yield: 3 cups**

1 pound chicken livers
½ cup vegetable oil
½ cup minced onion
4 hard-cooked eggs, chopped
2 tablespoons sweet sherry

2 tart apples, peeled and cored
2 tablespoons lemon juice
½ teaspoon curry powder
½ teaspoon salt
¼ teaspoon pepper

== **Yield: 6 cups**

2 pounds chicken livers
1 cup vegetable oil
1 cup minced onion
8 hard-cooked eggs, chopped
¼ cup sweet sherry

4 tart apples, peeled and cored
¼ cup lemon juice
1 teaspoon curry powder
1 teaspoon salt
½ teaspoon pepper

1. In a skillet, sauté the livers in the oil with the onion until medium. Add the eggs, sherry, apples, lemon juice, curry powder, salt, and pepper. Cook until the apples are tender crisp.

2. Remove from the heat and chop coarsely in the pan with two knives, or in a wooden bowl with a rounded chopping blade.

3. Pack into crocks and chill.

4. Serve with bread, crackers, or toast.

▶ Keeps 3 days, refrigerated.

≡ Pâté Maison (Sautéed Chicken Liver Pâté)

Pâté maison means "house special" and can vary from restaurant to restaurant.

══ Yield: 3 cups

½ cup minced onion	¼ cup sherry
½ cup butter	¼ cup Madeira
1 pound chicken livers	salt and pepper, to taste
1 large apple, peeled, cored, and sliced	4 hard-cooked eggs, chopped
	melted clarified butter, optional

══ Yield: 6 cups

1 cup minced onion	⅓ cup sherry
1 cup butter	⅓ cup Madeira
2 pounds chicken livers	salt and pepper, to taste
2 large apples, peeled, cored, and sliced	8 hard-cooked eggs, chopped
	melted clarified butter, optional

1. In a skillet, sauté the onion in the butter until soft but not brown. Add the livers, apples, sherry, and Madeira. Cook, stirring occasionally, until the livers are medium. Season with salt and pepper, and stir in the eggs.

2. Purée in a food processor and force through a fine sieve. Correct the seasoning with salt and pepper.

3. Pack into crocks and chill. Seal with clarified butter, if desired.

▶ Keeps 2 weeks, refrigerated, if sealed. Can be frozen for 2 months.

≡ Potted Chicken Liver

= Yield: 1 cup

½ pound chicken livers, cut in
half
2 tablespoons butter
3 tablespoons minced shallots
⅓ cup Madeira

¼ cup heavy cream
¼ teaspoon ground allspice
pinch of dried thyme
salt and pepper, to taste
¼ cup melted butter

= Yield: 1 quart

2 pounds chicken livers, cut in
half
½ cup butter
¾ cup minced shallots
⅔ cup Madeira

½ cup heavy cream
1 teaspoon ground allspice
½ teaspoon dried thyme
salt and pepper, to taste
1 cup melted butter

1. In a skillet, sauté the livers in the butter until medium. Transfer to a food processor.

2. In the same skillet, sauté the shallots until softened, then deglaze the pan with Madeira. Simmer until reduced to one third of the original quantity.

3. Add the shallots, cream, allspice, thyme, salt, and pepper to the livers and purée.

4. With the machine running, add the melted butter in a slow, steady stream. Force through a fine sieve and pack into crocks. Chill.

▶ Keeps 1 week, refrigerated.

≡ Pâté de Foie de Poulet et Jambon (Ham and Liver Pâté)

= Yield: 2 cups

3 tablespoons minced shallots
1 garlic clove, minced
4 tablespoons butter
½ pound chicken livers
3 tablespoons Cognac

¾ cup diced boiled ham
½ teaspoon salt, or to taste
¼ teaspoon pepper
¼ to ⅓ cup heavy cream

= Yield: 6 cups

⅔ cup minced shallots
3 garlic cloves, minced
¾ cup butter
1½ pounds chicken livers
½ cup Cognac

2¼ cups diced boiled ham
1½ teaspoons salt, or to taste
¾ teaspoon pepper
¾ to 1 cup heavy cream

1. In a skillet, sweat the shallots and garlic in the butter until soft. Add the chicken livers and cook until medium. Add the Cognac and ignite. When the flames die out, add the ham, salt, and pepper and cook 2 minutes longer. Cool.

2. In a food processor, purée the mixture. With the machine running, add the cream in a slow, steady stream.

3. Pack into crocks and chill.

▶ Keeps 5 days, refrigerated; can be frozen up to 2 months.

≡ Chicken Liver Pâté with Aspic

There are two ways of decorating this pâté; read the recipe carefully before proceeding. This decorating method can be used with any smooth pâté.

═ Yield: 2 cups

1 pound chicken livers	pinch of dried thyme
⅓ cup minced shallots	pinch of dried basil
½ cup butter	pinch of dried marjoram
1½ tablespoons sherry	2½ cups simple Madeira aspic
1½ tablespoons brandy	(page 216)
2 teaspoons salt	truffle cutouts
¼ teaspoon grated nutmeg	pimiento cutouts
¼ teaspoon pepper	

═ Yield: 6 cups

3 pounds chicken livers	½ teaspoon dried thyme
1 cup minced shallots	½ teaspoon dried basil
1½ cups butter	½ teaspoon dried marjoram
⅓ cup sherry	5 cups simple Madeira aspic
⅓ cup brandy	(page 216)
2 tablespoons salt	truffle cutouts
¾ teaspoon grated nutmeg	pimiento cutouts
¾ teaspoon pepper	

1. In a skillet, sauté the livers and shallots in the butter until the livers are medium. Transfer to a food processor.

2. Deglaze the skillet with the sherry and brandy. Pour over the livers and season with salt, nutmeg, pepper, thyme, basil, and marjoram. Purée. Force through a fine sieve for a smoother texture.

3. Pack and decorate the mold in one of the following two ways.

▶ Keeps 5 days, refrigerated.

Decorating a Mold with Aspic

One method is to pack the mixture into an attractive terrine or bowl and pour a thin layer of aspic over the top. Chill until almost set, and then arrange aspic-dipped truffle and pimiento cutouts or orange segments on the surface. Chill until set and pour another thin layer of aspic over the top. Chill completely. Serve from the terrine.

The second method requires chilling a metal mold. A fluted brioche mold is particularly attractive. Pour some chilled aspic into the mold, swirling it up around the sides or simply making a layer in the bottom. Chill until set. Continue coating with aspic until there is a layer at least ⅛ inch thick. Dip truffle or pimiento cutouts in aspic and place them on the bottom of the mold and perhaps up the sides. Chill until set. Coat the garnish with more aspic and chill. Pack the pâté into the mold and chill until set. Unmold and serve with bread, crackers, or toast.

NOTE: Instead of making cutouts, stuffed olives are a quick and easy decoration. Slice them crosswise or lengthwise. You can also use tinned black olives.

≡ *Pâté de Foie en Gelée (Liver Pâté with Aspic)*

═ Yield: 3 cups

½ pound bacon, diced
1 pound chicken livers, cut in half
½ cup minced scallions
½ cup Madeira
½ cup heavy cream
¼ teaspoon dried thyme

pinch of ground bay leaf
salt and pepper, to taste
½ cup ripe olives, thinly sliced
½ cup stuffed olives, thinly sliced
2 cups simple Madeira aspic (page 216)

═ Yield: 6 cups

1 pound bacon, diced
2 pounds chicken livers, cut in half
1 cup minced scallions
1 cup Madeira
1 cup heavy cream
½ teaspoon dried thyme

¼ teaspoon ground bay leaf
salt and pepper, to taste
1 cup ripe olives, thinly sliced
1 cup stuffed olives, thinly sliced
4 cups simple Madeira aspic (page 216)

1. In a skillet, sauté the bacon until crisp. Remove the bacon. Add the chicken livers and scallions and sauté in the bacon fat until the livers are medium. Turn into a food processor.

2. Deglaze the pan with Madeira and add the cream. Simmer for 1 minute. Pour into the liver mixture, add the bacon bits, and purée. Force through a fine sieve.

3. Mix in the thyme, bay leaf, salt, and pepper. Chill.

4. Chill a metal mold and thinly coat the sides and bottom of the mold with aspic.

5. Dip olive slices into the aspic and arrange decoratively on the bottom and part way up the sides of the mold. Chill until set.

6. Ladle another layer of aspic along the sides and bottom. Chill. Gently pack in the chilled pâté. Chill until set.

7. Unmold and serve with bread, crackers, or toast.

▶ Keeps 5 days, refrigerated.

☰ *Simple Madeira Aspic*

═ **Yield: 2½ cups**

1 package unflavored gelatin
¾ cup cold water
¾ cup boiling chicken or beef stock

1 cup cold chicken or beef stock
Madeira or sherry, to taste

In a small saucepan, soften the gelatin in cold water. Place over low heat and stir in the boiling stock. Heat, stirring, until the gelatin has dissolved. Remove from the heat and stir in the cold stock. Flavor with Madeira or sherry.

NOTE: The aspic can be reheated if it sets too quickly.

☰ *Roast Chicken and Chicken Liver Pâté*

═ **Yield: 1½ quarts**

4-pound chicken, roasted
½ pound bacon, blanched and diced
½ cup minced onion
¼ cup butter
⅓ cup rendered chicken fat
½ pound chicken livers
2 garlic cloves, crushed
¼ cup gin

¼ teaspoon ground allspice
¾ teaspoon salt
¼ teaspoon mace
¼ teaspoon ground nutmeg
¼ teaspoon pepper
½ cup dry vermouth
¼ cup Cognac
¼ cup melted butter

1. Discard the skin and remove the meat from the chicken. Put it into a bowl.

2. In a skillet, sauté the bacon until crisp. Drain on paper towels and pour off the fat from the skillet.

3. In the same skillet, unwashed, sauté the onion in the butter and chicken fat until soft. Add the livers and sauté until medium.

4. To the bowl of chicken, add the livers, bacon, garlic, gin, allspice, salt, mace, nutmeg, pepper, vermouth, and Cognac. Purée the mixture in batches in a food processor. Beat in the melted butter.

5. Pack into a 1½-quart terrine and chill.

6. Serve from terrine with bread, crackers, or toast.

▶ Keeps 1 week, refrigerated; can be frozen for 2 months.

≡ Duck Liver Pâté

This is best if made with fattened duck livers.

≡ **Yield: 1 cup**

½ pound duck livers	pinch of grated nutmeg
⅓ cup butter	2 tablespoons Cognac or
2 tablespoons minced onion	bourbon
½ teaspoon salt	whole truffles, optional
½ teaspoon dry mustard	

≡ **Yield: 1 quart**

2 pounds duck livers	2 teaspoons dry mustard
1⅓ cups butter	¼ teaspoon grated nutmeg
½ cup minced onion	½ cup Cognac or bourbon
2 teaspoons salt	whole truffles, optional

1. In a saucepan, simmer the livers in enough water to cover for 15 minutes. Drain.

2. In a food processor, purée the livers, butter, onion, salt, mustard, nutmeg, and Cognac. Force through a fine sieve.

3. Pack half the pâté into a mold, arrange the whole truffles down the center, and cover with the remaining pâté. Chill.

▶ Keeps 1 week, refrigerated.

NOTE: The theory behind this arrangement of truffles is that the pâté would be put into a long narrow mold, such as a loaf pan, and the truffles packed into the center, end to end, fully covered by the pâté.

When sliced with a knife dipped in hot water, each portion would have a round slice of truffle, surrounded by pâté as with foie gras. For cocktail hors d'oeuvre, it makes more sense to mince the truffles and fold them into the pâté, so everyone gets a share.

≡ *Duck Pâté*

═ Yield: 2 cups

½ cup butter	salt, to taste
2 duck livers, cut in half	pinch of cayenne pepper
¼ cup Cognac or Calvados	¼ teaspoon lemon juice
1½ cups ground cooked duck	melted butter, optional
3 to 6 tablespoons heavy cream	

═ Yield: 1 quart

1 cup butter	salt, to taste
4 duck livers, cut in half	¼ teaspoon cayenne pepper
½ cup Cognac or Calvados	½ teaspoon lemon juice
3 cups ground cooked duck	melted butter, optional
⅓ to ¾ cup heavy cream	

1. In a skillet, melt one fourth of the butter and sauté the livers until medium. Add the Cognac, ignite, and cook, stirring, until the flames die.

2. In a food processor, purée the livers with the cooked duck, adding enough cream to make a smooth mixture. Beat in the salt, cayenne, and lemon juice.

3. Pack into crocks and seal with melted butter if desired. Chill.

▶ Keeps 5 days, refrigerated; can be frozen.

≡ *Sausage Nut Pâté*

═ Yield: 2 cups

½ pound bulk sausage	1 tablespoon vegetable oil
1 pound mushrooms, sliced	½ teaspoon dried sage
¾ cup chopped onion	¼ teaspoon dried thyme
1 garlic clove, minced	⅛ teaspoon salt, or to taste
¼ cup slivered almonds, toasted	⅛ teaspoon cayenne pepper, or to taste
⅓ cup chopped walnuts, toasted	

=== Yield: 1 quart

1 pound bulk sausage
2 pounds mushrooms, sliced
1½ cups chopped onion
2 garlic cloves, minced
½ cup slivered almonds, toasted
⅔ cup chopped walnuts, toasted

2 tablespoons vegetable oil
1 teaspoon dried sage
½ teaspoon dried thyme
¼ teaspoon salt, or to taste
¼ teaspoon cayenne pepper, or to taste

1. In a saucepan over medium heat, brown the sausage, stirring often for about 8 minutes. Transfer the sausage to a food processor with a slotted spoon.

2. Pour off all but 2 teaspoons of the drippings from the skillet and sauté the mushrooms, onions, and garlic. Cook until the liquid evaporates. Add to the sausage.

3. Add the nuts and mix with on-off turns. Add the oil, sage, thyme, salt, and cayenne. Process until smooth.

4. Transfer to a crock and chill.

▶ Keeps 1 week, refrigerated; does not freeze well.

=== *Rillettes de Canard au Poivre Vert* (*Duck Spread with Green Peppercorns*)

=== Yield: 1 quart

5-pound duck, quartered
½ pound fresh or salted fatback, cut into 1-inch cubes (see note)
1½ cups white wine
2 tablespoons grated gingerroot

1 tablespoon coarse (kosher) salt
1 teaspoon minced garlic
1¾ ounces green peppercorns
salt and pepper, to taste

=== Yield: 1 gallon

20 pounds of duck, quartered
2 pounds fresh or salted fatback, cut into 1-inch cubes (see note)
6 cups white wine

½ cup grated gingerroot
¼ cup coarse (kosher) salt
2 tablespoons minced garlic
7 ounces green peppercorns
salt and pepper, to taste

1. Preheat the oven to 300°F.

2. In a casserole, combine the duck, fatback, wine, gingerroot, salt, and garlic. Bring to a boil on top of the stove, cover, and bake for 4 hours, stirring occasionally.

3. Drain in a colander, saving the fat and liquid. Discard the duck skin and bones. Transfer the meat and fatback to a plate and tear it into shreds using two forks.

4. Crush the peppercorns and add to the meat. Season with salt and pepper. (If it is necessary to use salted fatback, no additional salt should be needed.)

5. Pack the meat into crocks and pour on enough reserved liquid to cover by ¼ inch. Cool to room temperature and chill.

▶ Keeps 6 weeks, refrigerated, if sealed with fat.

NOTE: The saltiness of salted fatback varies. It is best to wash it well before using to eliminate any excess.

≡ *Rillettes de Canard (Duck Rillettes)*

═ **Yield: 1 quart**

5-pound duck, quartered	½ teaspoon ground ginger
¾ pound boneless pork	½ teaspoon ground allspice
¼ pound fresh pork fat	¼ teaspoon cinnamon
3 cups white wine,	salt, to taste
approximately	1 tablespoon minced truffles,
1 teaspoon pepper	optional

═ **Yield: 1 gallon**

20 pounds of duck, quartered	2 teaspoons ground ginger
3 pounds boneless pork	2 teaspoons ground allspice
1 pound fresh pork fat	1 teaspoon cinnamon
3 quarts white wine,	salt, to taste
approximately	¼ cup minced truffles, optional
4 teaspoons pepper	

1. In a casserole, mix the duck, pork, pork fat, and enough wine to cover. Simmer, covered, until the meats are very tender, about 4 hours. Remove the duck and discard the skin and bones. Return the duck meat to the pan and simmer, uncovered, stirring occasionally for 3 hours longer, or until the liquid has evaporated and only the duck, pork, and fat are left. Strain, reserving the duck, pork, and fat.

2. Shred the meat with two forks as finely as possible. Put the meat in a mixer and beat in enough fat to make a heavy paste. Stir in the pepper, ginger, allspice, cinnamon, and salt. Stir in the truffles.

3. Pack into crocks, leaving a ¼-inch space at the top. Heat the remaining fat and pour over the top to seal. Refrigerate for at least 24 hours.

▶ Keeps up to 6 weeks, refrigerated.

≡ Rillettes de Porc I

=== Yield: 1 quart

1 garlic clove, crushed
1 tablespoon coarse (kosher) salt
¼ teaspoon dried thyme
¼ teaspoon ground allspice
2 pounds boneless pork shoulder

1 pound pork fat, cubed
1 tablespoon chopped parsley
2 teaspoons dried thyme
1 bay leaf
¼ teaspoon pepper

=== Yield: 1 gallon

4 garlic cloves, crushed
¼ cup coarse (kosher) salt
1 teaspoon dried thyme
1 teaspoon ground allspice
8 pounds boneless pork shoulder

4 pounds pork fat, cubed
¼ cup chopped parsley
3 tablespoons dried thyme
4 bay leaves
1 teaspoon pepper

1. Preheat the oven to 300°F.

2. In a food processor, purée the garlic, salt, thyme, and allspice. Rub this spice mixture into the pork shoulder. Marinate, covered, in the refrigerator overnight.

3. Cut the pork into 1½-inch pieces, and place in a casserole with the pork fat and enough water to come halfway up the sides of the casserole.

4. Make a bouquet garni from the parsley, thyme, bay leaf, and pepper. Add to the casserole and bring to a boil on top of the stove. Cover and bake for 4 hours. Drain in a colander, reserving the liquid fat.

5. Tear the pork into shreds and correct the seasoning with salt and pepper. Pack into crocks. Strain enough of the reserved liquid fat to cover the rillettes. Seal the crocks and chill.

▶ Keeps 6 weeks, refrigerated.

≡ Rillettes de Porc II

=== Yield: 1½ cups

1½ pounds lean pork, diced
2 pounds fresh pork fat, diced
1 teaspoon pepper
1½ teaspoons salt

pinch of ground allspice
1 bay leaf
1 cup boiling water

== **Yield: 3 quarts**

3 pounds lean pork, diced
4 pounds fresh pork fat, diced
2 teaspoons pepper
1 tablespoon salt

¼ teaspoon ground allspice
2 bay leaves
2 cups boiling water

1. In a casserole, simmer the pork, pork fat, pepper, salt, allspice, bay leaves, and water, stirring occasionally, for 4 hours. When the water evaporates and the meat starts to brown, continue to cook until the pork fat becomes brown and crisp. Drain the meat and cracklings in a colander. Set over a heatproof bowl.

2. Drain off any remaining liquid fat from the casserole and set aside. Discard the bay leaf.

3. Coarsely grind the pork and cracklings. Place in a bowl and gradually add all but one fourth of the fat.

4. Pack into crocks and chill. Melt the reserved fat and pour over the top to seal.

▶ Keeps 6 weeks, refrigerated.

≡ *Cretons*

== **Yield: 1 quart**

1 pound lean pork shoulder,
cut into 2-inch cubes
½ pound lard
1 cup chopped onion
1 tablespoon salt

pepper, to taste
1 garlic clove, minced
1½ teaspoons pickling spices
melted clarified butter, optional

== **Yield: 1 gallon**

4 pounds lean pork shoulder,
cut into 2-inch cubes
2 pounds lard
1 quart chopped onion
¼ cup salt

2 tablespoons pepper
4 garlic cloves, minced
1 tablespoon pickling spices
melted clarified butter, optional

1. Preheat the oven to 325°F.

2. In a casserole, place the pork shoulder, lard, onions, salt, pepper, and garlic. Make a bouquet garni of the pickling spices and push it into the center of the casserole. Bake 3 hours. Cool for 30 minutes and remove the spice bag.

3. In a food processor, chop the pork mixture finely. Return it to the casserole and simmer 15 minutes.

4. Pack into crocks and cover with melted butter to seal.

▶ Keeps 6 weeks, refrigerated.

≡ Cretons Française

═ Yield: 1 quart

¾ pound fatty salt pork, cut into 2-inch cubes
1 pound lean pork, cubed
2 onions, peeled and quartered
½ teaspoon cinnamon

¼ teaspoon ground cloves
¼ teaspoon ground allspice
¼ teaspoon pepper
2 tablespoons bread crumbs
salt, to taste

═ Yield: 1 gallon

3 pounds fatty salt pork, cut into 2-inch cubes
4 pounds lean pork, cubed
8 onions, peeled and quartered
2 teaspoons cinnamon

1 teaspoon ground cloves
1 teaspoon ground allspice
1 teaspoon pepper
½ cup bread crumbs
salt, to taste

1. In a skillet, sauté the salt pork until golden and crisp. Remove the cracklings and reserve the liquid fat.

2. Put the fresh pork, onions, and cracklings into a food processor and chop coarsely. Add the cinnamon, cloves, allspice, and pepper and mix well.

3. Place the pork mixture in a skillet over very low heat, and cook, stirring occasionally, for 1½ hours. Remove from the heat and stir in the bread crumbs. Correct the seasoning with salt.

4. Pour into molds and let stand for 30 minutes. If enough fat has not risen to cover the meats, pour on a thin layer of the reserved fat. Chill.

▶ Keeps 6 weeks, refrigerated.

≡ Baked Chicken Liver Pâté Maison

This recipe demonstrates one method of lowering the fat content of a pâté: Instead of lining the pan with thin slices of fatback, line it with ovenproof plastic wrap.

═ **Yield: 1 quart**

1 cup minced onion
½ cup butter
1 pound chicken livers
1 cup heavy cream
¼ cup Cognac
¼ cup port
1 garlic clove, minced

1 teaspoon dried thyme
1 teaspoon curry powder
salt and pepper, to taste
bay leaf
thin slices of fatback or sheets
of ovenproof plastic wrap

1. Preheat the oven to 325°F.

2. In a skillet, sauté the onions in ¼ cup butter over low heat until tender.

3. In another skillet, sauté the livers in the remaining butter until medium. In a food processor, purée the livers and onions with the cream, Cognac, port, garlic, thyme, curry powder, salt, and pepper. For the smoothest texture, force through a fine sieve.

4. Line the sides of a 1-quart terrine with either fatback or plastic wrap, leaving the ends extended to cover the top. Fill with the liver mixture and place a bay leaf on top. Fold over the ends of the fatback or plastic wrap. Cover with foil and bake in a water bath for 2 hours or until a thermometer registers 165°F.

5. Remove from the water bath, cool, weight, and chill. Unmold to serve.

▶ Keeps 1 week, refrigerated.

≡ *Baked Chicken Liver Pâté*

═ **Yield: 1 quart**

2 tablespoons bread crumbs
1 cup heavy cream
½ pound chicken livers
¼ cup minced onion
2 tablespoons flour

2 eggs
salt and pepper, to taste
2 tablespoons butter, melted
and cooled

═ **Yield: 3 quarts**

⅓ cup bread crumbs
3 cups heavy cream
1½ pounds chicken livers
¾ cup minced onion
⅓ cup flour

6 eggs
salt and pepper, to taste
⅓ cup butter, melted and
cooled

1. Preheat the oven to 350°F.

2. In a bowl, mix the bread crumbs and cream.

3. In a food processor, purée the livers and onion and add the bread crumbs, cream, flour, eggs, salt, pepper, and butter. Force through a fine sieve and pour into one or more molds.

4. Bake in a water bath for 40 to 50 minutes or until a thermometer registers 150°F.

5. Remove from the water bath, cool, weight, and chill. Unmold.

▶ Keeps 1 week, refrigerated.

≡ Chicken Liver and Sausage Pâté

═ **Yield: one 9-inch loaf**

1 pound chicken livers	1 egg, beaten
½ pound pork sausage meat	pinch of mace
½ cup minced parsley	salt and pepper, to taste
½ cup minced celery leaves	8 slices bacon
1 cup minced onion	

1. Preheat the oven to 300°F.

2. In a food processor, purée the chicken livers. In a bowl, combine the livers with the sausage, parsley, celery leaves, onion, egg, mace, salt, and pepper.

3. Sauté 4 bacon slices until crisp. Drain, reserving the fat. Crumble the bacon finely. Mix the bacon and reserved fat into the liver mixture. Pack into a 9″ × 5″ × 3″ loaf pan. Lay the remaining 4 slices of bacon on top. Place the pan in a water bath and bake for 2 hours or until a thermometer registers 165°F.

4. Cool, weight, and chill. Discard the bacon strips and unmold.

▶ Keeps 1 week, refrigerated.

☰ Pâté Maison en Gelée
(Chicken Liver Pâté with Aspic Garnish)

☰ Yield: one 9-inch loaf

⅓ cup chopped onion	2 bay leaves
1 tablespoon dried savory	1 tablespoon unflavored gelatin
1 tablespoon dried tarragon	1 cup white wine
⅓ cup butter	½ teaspoon dried tarragon
3 pounds chicken livers	½ teaspoon minced parsley
6 tablespoons Cognac	1 hard-cooked egg
½ cup light cream	½ teaspoon butter, softened
5 eggs	4 ounces pimiento, drained
1½ tablespoons salt	1 pitted ripe olive
¼ teaspoon pepper	½ green pepper
½ pound bacon slices	2 capers

1. Preheat the oven to 400°F.

2. In a skillet, sauté the onion, savory, and tarragon in the butter until soft. Add the livers and sauté, stirring until medium rare.

3. In a food processor, purée the liver-onion mixture with the Cognac, cream, eggs, salt, and pepper. Force through a sieve.

4. Line a 9″ × 5″ × 3″ loaf pan with bacon and arrange the bay leaves on the bottom. Pour in the liver mixture and place in a water bath. Bake for 1½ hours, or until a thermometer registers 155°F. Cool, weight, and refrigerate.

5. The next day, unmold the pâté, discarding the bacon and bay leaves. With a knife dipped in hot water, smooth the sides of the pâté and chill.

6. To make the glaze, in a small saucepan, sprinkle the gelatin over ¼ cup water and let soften. Add the wine, tarragon, and parsley and stir over low heat until the gelatin is dissolved. Strain. Set over ice until the glaze becomes as thick as raw egg whites and spoon a thin layer over the pâté. Return to the refrigerator.

7. To make the garnishes, cut the pimientos into strips or other shapes with fancy metal cutters. Slice the olive and arrange around the edge of the loaf. Cut the egg in half crosswise and remove the yolk. Mash the yolk to a paste with the butter. Cut 10 ovals from the egg white and arrange 2 daisies on top of the pâté. With a small pastry bag fitted with a no. 30 star tip, pipe the yolk mixture into the center of each daisy and put a caper in the center. With a knife, cut 2 stems and leaves for the daisies from the green pepper.

8. Attach all decorations by dipping them in the semiliquid gelatin glaze.

9. Chill until set. Coat with the remaining glaze and chill again.

▶ Keeps 3 days, refrigerated.

≡ *Pâté Parisienne*

≡ **Yield: one 8-inch loaf**

1½ pounds ground lean veal
1½ pounds ground pork
2 chicken breasts, skinned,
  boned, and cut into ½-inch
  cubes
½ pound chicken livers
⅓ cup pistachios
⅓ cup minced shallots
½ teaspoon dried thyme
salt, to taste

½ teaspoon pepper
⅛ teaspoon ground allspice
⅛ teaspoon cinnamon
⅛ teaspoon cayenne pepper
⅛ teaspoon grated nutmeg
⅛ teaspoon ground cloves
1 egg
¾ pound caul fat or sliced
  unsalted pork fat
1 bay leaf

1. Preheat the oven to 375°F.

2. In a bowl, mix the veal, pork, and chicken.

3. In a food processor, purée the chicken livers and add them to the bowl of meats. Stir in the pistachios, shallots, thyme, salt, pepper, allspice, cinnamon, cayenne, nutmeg, cloves, and egg. Blend well.

4. Line a 9″ × 5″ × 3″ pan with the caul fat or pork fat. Pour in the pâté and smooth the top. Place the bay leaf in the center and cover with any overhanging fat.

5. Bake in a water bath for 1 hour and 45 minutes or until a thermometer registers 165°F.

6. Remove from the oven and let cool for 30 minutes. Weight and chill overnight. Unmold to serve.

▶ Keeps 2 weeks, refrigerated.

≡ *Chicken Terrine*

For a lower fat content, line the pan with plastic wrap instead of fatback.

≡ **Yield: one 9-inch loaf**

4 to 6 chicken livers, cut in half
½ cup Cognac
1 tablespoon minced garlic
½ teaspoon dried savory
¼ teaspoon ground cloves
½ teaspoon ground oregano
1 2½-pound chicken, skinned
  and boned

1 cup fresh bread crumbs
1 egg, lightly beaten
½ cup skinned pistachios
1 teaspoon salt
½ teaspoon pepper
pinch of ground allspice
1 pound fatback, thinly sliced

1. In a bowl, marinate the livers in ¼ cup Cognac for 30 minutes. Drain the livers and save both the livers and the liquid.
2. Meanwhile, marinate the garlic, savory, cloves, and oregano in the remaining ¼ cup of Cognac for 30 minutes.
3. Preheat the oven to 350°F.
4. Coarsely grind the leg and thigh meat of the chicken. Finely grind the white meat.
5. In a large bowl, mix the chicken, herb-Cognac mixture, bread crumbs, egg, pistachios, salt, pepper, and allspice.
6. Line the bottom and sides of a 9" × 5" × 3" loaf pan with fatback. Spread half the chicken mixture in the loaf pan, arrange the livers in a row down the center, and top with the remaining chicken mixture. Cover with fatback, place in a water bath, and bake until a thermometer registers 160°F, about 1½ hours. Remove from the oven and cool.
7. Weight and chill completely. Unmold to serve.

▶ Keeps 1 week, refrigerated.

≡ Veal and Chicken Liver Pâté

=== **Yield: one 9-inch loaf**

1½ pounds chicken livers
1½ pounds veal liver
½ pound lean veal
1 cup heavy cream

1 cup butter, softened
⅓ cup Cognac
salt and pepper, to taste
thin slices of truffles, optional

1. Preheat the oven to 300°F.
2. Blanch the livers in boiling salted water for 5 minutes. Drain. In a food processor, purée the livers and veal, and with the machine running, add the cream.
3. Pour into a buttered 9" × 5" × 3" loaf pan and bake in a water bath for 3 hours.
4. Remove from the water bath, cool, unmold, and force through a fine sieve. Beat in the butter, Cognac, salt, and pepper.
5. In a loaf pan, make layers of the pâté and truffle slices. Chill.

▶ Keeps 1 week, refrigerated.

≡ Goose Liver Pâté

═ Yield: two 9-inch loaves

1½ pounds goose livers
1 tablespoon dried thyme
  leaves, crumbled
2 teaspoons dried sage
2 canned truffles, undrained
½ teaspoon ground allspice
1 teaspoon salt
white pepper, to taste
½ cup Cognac

1 cup minced shallots, sautéed
  in butter
2 garlic cloves, minced
2 pounds unsalted pork fat,
  diced
1½ pounds pork shoulder
fatback, sliced paper-thin
2 bay leaves

1. Preheat the oven to 350°F.

2. In a bowl, marinate the livers, thyme, sage, truffles, truffle liquid, allspice, salt, pepper, and Cognac overnight. Remove the truffle slices and set aside.

3. In a food processor, purée the liver mixture, shallots, and garlic. Put into a bowl.

4. Purée the pork fat and shoulder. Beat into the liver mixture. Force the mixture through a sieve. Fold in the truffle slices.

5. Line two 9-inch loaf pans with sliced fatback. Pack with the liver mixture and arrange a bay leaf on top. Fold the ends of the pork fat over the top.

6. Bake in a water bath for 1½ hours or until a thermometer registers 165°F. Cool, weight, and chill.

▶ Keeps 1 week, refrigerated.

≡ Terrine de Canard (Duck Pâté)

═ Yield: one 9-inch loaf

5-pound duck
½ pound chicken livers,
  approximately
1 carrot, diced
1 turnip, diced
1 onion, diced
1 tomato, diced
bouquet garni of thyme,
  parsley, and bay leaf
1 pound ground pork

1 tablespoon salt
½ teaspoon pepper
¼ cup Armagnac
4 eggs
2 tablespoons heavy cream
3 garlic cloves, minced
6 shallots, minced
1 tablespoon minced parsley
1 black truffle, minced

1. Preheat the oven to 300°F.

2. Bone the duck. Save the fat, bones, liver, and skin as well as the meat. Dice the duck liver and add enough chicken livers to make ½ pound.

3. In a saucepan, simmer the bones, carrot, turnip, onion, tomato, 2 cups water, and bouquet garni until the liquid is reduced to 2 tablespoons. Strain, reserving the liquid. Discard the solids.

4. In a food processor, purée all the duck fat and half the skin. Turn into a large bowl and set aside. Discard the remaining skin.

5. In the processor, coarsely grind the duck flesh and livers. Add to the bowl of duck fat and stir in the broth, ground pork, salt, pepper, Armagnac, eggs, cream, garlic, shallots, parsley, and truffle.

6. Mix well, cover, and let flavors develop for 2 to 3 hours at room temperature. Pack into a 9″ × 5″ × 3″ loaf pan and cover.

7. Bake in a water bath for 1½ hours, remove the cover, and bake until a thermometer registers 165°F.

8. Cool, weight, and chill completely.

▶ Keeps 1 week, refrigerated.

≡ *Leberkäse (Liver Cheese)*

═ **Yield: one 9-inch loaf**

1½ pounds lean pork, cut into 1-inch cubes	2 eggs
1½ cups ice water	¼ pound slab bacon, diced
1 pound pork liver, cut into 1-inch cubes	2 teaspoons salt
1 cup chopped onion	½ teaspoon sugar
1 garlic clove	¼ teaspoon pepper
	¼ teaspoon ground ginger

1. Preheat the oven to 350°F.

2. In a food processor, purée the pork cubes. With the machine running, add the ice water in a slow, steady stream until incorporated. Remove to a bowl.

3. In the processor, purée the liver, onion, and garlic and add to the pork mixture.

4. Without washing the work bowl, purée the eggs, bacon, salt, sugar, pepper, and ginger. Add to the pork mixture and mix well. Pour into a 9″ × 5″ × 3″ loaf pan.

5. Bake in a water bath for 2 hours or until a thermometer registers 165°F.

6. Serve warm, or weight and chill.

▶ Keeps 1 week, refrigerated.

≡ *Pâté du Porc*

Instead of lining the mold with slices of pork fat, use spinach, beet, or chard leaves for a lower fat content.

═ Yield: one 9-inch loaf

½ pound fresh pork fat, cut into ⅛-inch dice
2½ pounds pork shoulder
7 ounces pork liver, trimmed of veins
1 tablespoon olive oil
4 shallots, minced
1 cup white bread crumbs
½ cup white wine
4 garlic cloves, mashed
2 tablespoons minced parsley

⅓ cup skinned pistachios
½ teaspoon ground allspice
½ teaspoon ground bay leaf
½ teaspoon ground oregano
½ teaspoon ground thyme
1½ teaspoons pepper
3 teaspoons salt
¼ teaspoon cayenne pepper
8 to 10 large spinach, beet, or chard leaves, blanched

1. Preheat the oven to 325°F.

2. Lay the pork fat on top of the pork shoulder and chop in 2 batches until you have a forcemeat of fine and coarse bits. Put into a bowl.

3. Chop the liver finely and add to the pork.

4. Heat the oil in a skillet and sauté the shallots until soft but not brown. Add to the pork with the bread crumbs, white wine, garlic, parsley, pistachios, allspice, bay leaf, oregano, thyme, black pepper, salt, and cayenne and mix thoroughly.

5. Line a 9″ × 5″ × 3″ loaf pan with spinach leaves, letting them drape over the edges. Pack the forcemeat into the pan, mounding slightly.

6. Bake in a water bath for 1½ hours or until a thermometer registers 165°F.

7. Cool, weight, and chill.

▶ Keeps 1 week, refrigerated.

≡ *Coarse Pork Liver Terrine I*

= **Yield: one 9-inch loaf**

2 pounds pork liver, minced
1½ cups soft bread crumbs
1 cup sherry
2 teaspoons salt
¼ teaspoon pepper
1½ cups minced onion
3 garlic cloves

3 tablespoons butter
3 eggs
pinch of ground cloves
pinch of dried thyme
1 pound fatback, thinly sliced
½ teaspoon dried thyme leaves
3 bay leaves

1. Preheat the oven to 325°F.

2. In a bowl, marinate the liver, bread crumbs, sherry, salt, and pepper for 1 hour.

3. In a skillet, sauté the onions and garlic in the butter until soft. Add to the livers and beat in the eggs, cloves, and thyme.

4. Line a 9″ × 5″ × 3″ loaf pan with fatback and fill with the pâté mixture. Sprinkle the thyme leaves on top and arrange the bay leaves. Cover.

5. Bake in a water bath for 2 hours or until a thermometer registers 165°F. Cool, weight, and chill.

▶ Keeps 1 week, refrigerated.

≡ *Coarse Pork Liver Terrine II*

= **Yield: one 9-inch loaf**

2 pounds pork liver
1 pound fresh pork fat
2 teaspoons salt
1 teaspoon pepper

½ teaspoon minced garlic
2 tablespoons white wine
2 tablespoons Cognac
½ pound fatback, cut into strips

1. Preheat the oven to 350°F.

2. Coarsely grind the pork liver and pork fat.

3. In a bowl, mix the liver and fat together and add the salt, pepper, garlic, wine, and Cognac. Mix well. Let stand for 1 to 2 hours to let the flavors meld.

4. Pack into a 9″ × 5″ × 3″ loaf pan and arrange strips of fatback in a crisscross pattern. Cover.

5. Bake in a water bath for 1 hour or until a thermometer registers 165°F. Uncover and bake 10 to 15 minutes longer. Cool, weight, and chill.

▶ Keeps 1 week, refrigerated.

≡ Smooth Baked Pork Liver Pâté

This pâté, like many others, can be decorated on top with strips of pork fat. The traditional decoration is a diagonal striping or crosshatching. However, you can also cut out designs from the pork fat and arrange them on the top. The pork fat will shrivel some in baking and turn transparent, but when chilled the design will show.

══ **Yield: two 9-inch loaves**

1 pound pork liver	5 eggs
milk	1½ cups heavy cream
1 pound pork fat	2 teaspoons salt
6 anchovy fillets	1 teaspoon pepper
3 garlic cloves	1 teaspoon dried thyme
¼ cup minced onion	½ cup Cognac
1 tablespoon flour	fatback, thinly sliced

1. Preheat the oven to 300°F.

2. Soak the liver overnight in enough milk to cover. Drain and discard the milk.

3. In a food processor, purée the liver, pork fat, anchovies, garlic, onion, flour, eggs, cream, salt, pepper, thyme, and Cognac. For the smoothest consistency, force the mixture through a sieve.

4. Line two 9″ × 5″ × 3″ loaf pans with fatback and fill with the liver mixture. Top with slices of fatback and cover with foil.

5. Bake in a water bath for 1½ to 2 hours or until a thermometer registers 155°F.

6. Cool, weight, and chill.

▶ Keeps 1 week, refrigerated; can be frozen.

≡ Danish Liver Pâté

══ **Yield: one 9-inch loaf**

1 pound pork or veal liver, chopped	2 teaspoons salt
	1 teaspoon pepper
10 ounces fresh pork fat, chopped	¼ teaspoon ground allspice
	4 slices bacon, cooked and crumbled
½ cup chopped onion	
3 anchovy fillets	¼ pound mushrooms, minced and sautéed in 1 tablespoon butter
¼ cup flour	
¼ cup light cream	
2 eggs, lightly beaten	

1. Preheat the oven to 350°F.

2. In a food processor, purée the liver, pork fat, onion, and anchovies. Add the flour, cream, eggs, salt, pepper, and allspice and mix well.

3. Turn into a buttered 9″ × 5″ × 3″ loaf pan. Bake in a water bath for 1 hour or until a thermometer registers 150°F. Cool and chill.

4. Unmold and garnish with the bacon and mushrooms.

▶ Keeps 1 week, refrigerated; can be frozen for 2 months.

≡ *Rosy Liver Mousse*

═ Yield: one 9-inch loaf

1¼ pounds pork or veal liver, cubed
½ cup port
1 cup dry vermouth
2 tablespoons minced shallots
1 garlic clove, minced
2 cups heavy cream

¾ cup clarified butter
1 egg
2 tablespoons minced parsley
2 tablespoons minced chives
2 teaspoons salt
1½ teaspoons white pepper

1. Preheat the oven to 300°F.

2. In a covered bowl, marinate the liver in the port overnight in the refrigerator.

3. Butter a 9″ × 5″ × 3″ loaf pan.

4. In a saucepan, simmer the vermouth, shallots, and garlic until syrupy. Add the cream and reduce to 1½ cups. Cool.

5. In a food processor, purée the liver, adding enough port to process smoothly. Force through a sieve. Strain the cream into the liver, stirring. Stir in the butter, egg, parsley, chives, salt, and pepper.

6. Pour into the pan and bake in a water bath for 1½ hours or until a thermometer registers 150°F. Chill.

▶ Keeps 1 week, refrigerated; can be frozen.

≡ Veal Liver and Pork Pâté Maison

=== Yield: one 9-inch loaf

¾ pound veal liver, finely ground

½ pound lean pork, finely ground

¼ cup white wine

½ teaspoon dried thyme

¼ teaspoon dried marjoram

1 bay leaf, crushed

pinch of ground cloves

pinch of grated nutmeg

pinch of cayenne pepper

salt and pepper, to taste

1 pound lean pork, cut into ¼-inch-thick slices

¼ pound sliced bacon

1. Preheat the oven to 350°F.

2. In a bowl, mix the liver, ground pork, wine, thyme, marjoram, bay leaf, cloves, nutmeg, cayenne, salt, and pepper.

3. Line a 9″ × 5″ × 3″ loaf pan with strips of bacon, and spoon in half the meat mixture. Cover with half the pork slices, the remaining meat mixture, and the remaining pork slices. Top with the bacon strips. Cover.

4. Bake in a water bath for 2 to 2½ hours or until a thermometer registers 165°F. Cool, weight, and chill.

▶ Keeps 1 week, refrigerated.

≡ Terrine du Chef (Coarse Pork and Veal Terrine)

=== Yield: two 9-inch loaves

1 pound veal, finely diced

1 pound lean pork shoulder, diced

¼ pound pork belly, diced

½ pound pork liver, diced

2 ounces fatback, diced

3 garlic cloves, crushed

1½ teaspoons salt

½ teaspoon coarsely ground pepper

½ teaspoon mace

¼ teaspoon dried thyme

½ teaspoon juniper berries, crushed

¼ teaspoon dried rosemary

¼ teaspoon dried summer savory

¼ teaspoon dried marjoram

¼ teaspoon dried basil

½ cup Armagnac

½ cup white wine

1 egg

3 tablespoons flour

2 to 4 bay leaves

strips of fatback

1. Preheat the oven to 325°F.

2. In a bowl, mix the veal, pork shoulder, pork belly, liver, 2 ounces fatback, garlic, salt, pepper, mace, thyme, juniper berries, rosemary, savory, marjoram, basil, Armagnac, and white wine. Mix well. Marinate, covered, in the refrigerator overnight.

3. Let come to room temperature. Beat in the egg and flour. Butter two 9″ × 5″ × 3″ loaf pans, and fill with the mixture. Arrange the bay leaves on top, and decorate with strips of fatback. Cover.

4. Bake in a water bath for 1½ to 2 hours or until a thermometer registers 165°F. Cool, weight, and chill.

▶ Keeps 1 week, refrigerated.

≡ Pâté de Campagne I (Country Pâté I)

Any pâté can be called campagne, but the term usually refers to coarse pâtés.

═ Yield: two 9-inch loaves

1½ pounds pork fat	½ cup Cognac
1¼ pounds ground pork	6 garlic cloves
1½ pounds lean veal	½ teaspoon cinnamon
1¼ pounds boiled ham	½ teaspoon ground allspice
¾ pound chicken livers	1 tablespoon pepper
4 eggs	1 tablespoon salt
⅓ cup heavy cream	4 tablespoons flour

1. Preheat the oven to 350°F.

2. Slice ½ pound of pork fat very thinly and line two 9″ × 5″ × 3″ loaf pans, letting the long ends hang over the sides.

3. Grind ½ pound of the remaining pork fat with the ground pork and veal.

4. Grind the remaining ½ pound of pork fat and ham with the coarse blade of the grinder. If desired, the ham and this portion of pork fat can be chopped coarsely by hand.

5. In a food processor, purée the chicken livers with the eggs, cream, Cognac, and garlic.

6. In a large bowl, mix the meats and livers with the cinnamon, allspice, pepper, salt, and flour.

7. Fill the molds, fold over the overhanging slices of fat, and cover. Bake in a water bath for 2 to 2½ hours or until a thermometer registers 165°F. Remove the foil and bake 20 minutes longer to brown the top. Cool, weight, and chill.

▶ Keeps 1 week, refrigerated.

≡ *Pâté de Campagne II (Country Pâté II)*

═ **Yield: one 9-inch loaf**

2 garlic cloves, minced
1 cup minced onion
¼ cup butter
¼ pound chicken livers
6 slices bacon, blanched
½ cup parsley, minced
¼ cup bread crumbs
1½ pounds ground pork
1⅓ pounds ground veal
½ pound ground ham

3 eggs
½ cup Cognac
½ cup skinned pistachios
4 teaspoons salt
2 teaspoons mixed minced
    savory, thyme, and oregano
1 teaspoon cinnamon
½ teaspoon ground allspice
½ teaspoon grated nutmeg

1. Preheat the oven to 350°F.

2. In a skillet, sauté the garlic and onion in the butter until soft. Add the livers and cook until medium.

3. In a food processor, purée the livers and onions with 3 bacon slices, parsley, and bread crumbs.

4. In a bowl, mix the pork, veal, ham, eggs, Cognac, pistachios, salt, herbs, cinnamon, allspice, and nutmeg.

5. Turn into a 9″ × 5″ × 3″ loaf pan, top with the remaining bacon slices, and cover. Bake in a water bath for 2½ hours or until a thermometer registers 165°F. Cool, weight, and chill. Remove the bacon slices and unmold.

▶ Keeps 1 week, refrigerated.

≡ *Pâté de Campagne au Poivre Vert (Country Pâté with Green Peppercorns)*

═ **Yield: two 9-inch loaves**

2½ pounds lean pork shoulder,
    cubed
1½ pounds lean veal, cubed
1½ pounds pork fat, cubed
⅔ pounds prosciutto, finely
    diced
½ cup minced onion
6 garlic cloves, crushed
4 eggs

2 teaspoons dried thyme
2 teaspoons ground allspice
1 tablespoon salt
2 teaspoons pepper
1⅓ cups brandy
3 ounces green peppercorns
1 large piece caul fat, cut in 2
    pieces
1 pound fatback, thinly sliced

1. Preheat the oven to 300°F.

2. Cut the pork, veal, and pork fat into ½-inch cubes. Cut the prosciutto into tiny dice, less than ¼ inch.

3. In a bowl, mix the pork shoulder, veal, pork fat, prosciutto, onion, garlic, eggs, thyme, allspice, salt, pepper, brandy, and peppercorns.

4. Line two 9″ × 5″ × 3″ loaf pans with the caul fat and then with the fatback. Pack in the meat mixture, pressing firmly, and fold over-hanging fat over the top; cover.

5. Bake in a water bath for 2½ hours or until a thermometer registers 165°F. Cool, weight, and chill.

▶ Keeps 1 week, refrigerated.

≡ *Pâté with Olives, Pine Nuts, and Prosciutto*

≡ **Yield: one 9-inch loaf**

1 pound ground pork	1½ teaspoons basil
½ pound ground veal	½ teaspoon thyme
¼ pound ground pork fat	¼ teaspoon pepper
⅓ cup chopped ripe olives	1 garlic clove, crushed
¼ cup toasted pine nuts	½ teaspoon salt
¼ cup diced prosciutto	1 egg, beaten
¼ cup soft white bread crumbs	1 pound fatback, thinly sliced
2 tablespoons dry vermouth	

1. Preheat the oven to 350°F.

2. In a bowl, mix the pork, veal, pork fat, olives, pine nuts, prosciutto, bread crumbs, vermouth, basil, thyme, pepper, garlic, salt, and egg.

3. Line a 9″ × 5″ × 3″ loaf pan with fatback and pack in the meat mixture. Cover with slices of fatback. Bake in a water bath for 1½ hours or until a thermometer registers 165°F. Cool, weight, and chill.

▶ Keeps 1 week, refrigerated.

≡ *Pork Pâté with Ham*

═ Yield: one 9-inch loaf

½ pound sliced bacon, blanched
½ cup minced shallots
2 tablespoons butter
1 garlic clove, minced
½ cup Cognac
½ pound prosciutto, cut into ¼-inch cubes
⅓ cup Madeira

¾ pound lean pork
¾ pound ground lean veal
½ pound ground pork fat
2 eggs, beaten
1½ teaspoons salt
½ teaspoon ground allspice
¼ teaspoon dried thyme
¼ cup minced parsley
⅛ teaspoon pepper

1. Preheat the oven to 350°F.

2. Line a 9″ × 5″ × 3″ loaf pan with the bacon, letting the strips overhang the sides.

3. In a skillet, sauté the shallots in the butter until soft. Add the garlic and cook 1 minute. Add the Cognac and cook until most of the liquid has evaporated. Set aside.

4. In a bowl, marinate the prosciutto in the Madeira for 30 minutes.

5. In another bowl, mix the pork, veal, pork fat, eggs, salt, allspice, thyme, parsley, and pepper. Stir in the prosciutto, Madeira, and shallots.

6. Turn into the loaf pan and fold over the bacon slices. Cover. Bake in a water bath for 1 hour, uncover, and bake for 30 minutes longer, or until a thermometer registers 160°F. Cool, weight, and chill.

▶ Keeps 1 week, refrigerated.

≡ *Ham and Fennel Terrine*

The ham batons should create a mosaic pattern when this terrine is sliced.

═ Yield: one 9-inch loaf

fatback, thinly sliced
¾ pound ground veal
¾ pound ground pork
¾ pound ground pork fat
3 eggs
½ cup shelled pistachios, optional

3 tablespoons Pernod
2 teaspoons salt
2 tablespoons fennel seed
1 teaspoon ground allspice
½ teaspoon pepper
¾ pound ham, cut in ½-inch batons

1. Preheat the oven to 350°F.

2. Line a 9″ × 5″ × 3″ loaf pan with the fatback.

3. In a bowl, mix the veal, pork, pork fat, eggs, pistachios, Pernod, salt, fennel, allspice, and pepper.

4. Spread a layer of the pâté in the loaf pan, and arrange ham batons lengthwise on top. Add more pâté and ham until the ingredients are used, ending with pâté mixture.

5. Bake in a water bath for 1 to 1½ hours or until a thermometer registers 160°F. Cool, weight, and chill.

▶ Keeps 1 week, refrigerated.

≡ *Country Veal Pâté*

≡ **Yield: two 9-inch loaves**

6 tablespoons butter
1 cup minced onion
½ cup minced shallots
4 garlic cloves, minced
1½ pounds mushrooms, minced
2 pounds ground veal
1 cup Madeira
1½ cups Spanish olives, chopped, juices reserved
4 teaspoons salt
2 teaspoons pepper

2 teaspoons dried thyme
2 pounds Italian sausage, peeled
4 eggs, beaten
½ cup minced parsley
¼ cup green peppercorns
4 envelopes unflavored gelatin
2 cups veal or beef stock
¼ cup Madeira
parsley or thyme sprigs
mushroom slices

1. Preheat the oven to 350°F.

2. Butter two 9″ × 5″ × 3″ loaf pans.

3. In a large skillet, melt the butter and sweat the onions, shallots, and garlic until soft but not brown. Add the mushrooms and sauté until the juices release and are reduced slightly. Cool.

4. In a mixer, beat the veal, Madeira, 6 tablespoons olive juice, salt, pepper, and thyme. Add the sausage, mushroom mixture, olives, eggs, parsley, and green peppercorns and mix well. Pack into the pans and cover with foil. Bake in a water bath for 1½ hours or until a thermometer registers 160°F. Cool, weight, and chill.

5. To make the aspic, in a small saucepan soften the gelatin in ½ cup stock and heat until dissolved. Add the remaining stock. Stir in the Madeira and cool until syrupy.

6. Unmold the pâtés from the pans, scrape off the excess fat, and arrange on a plate. Fold a sheet of foil, long enough to surround the outside of the pâté in thirds, and wrap tightly around the pâté leaving the top open. Repeat for the second pâté.

7. Coat the top of each pâté with a layer of aspic, chill, and make 3 more layers of aspic, chilling before adding each layer.

8. Arrange a design of parsley sprigs and mushroom slices, and spoon another layer of aspic over the top. Glaze again and chill completely.

▶ Keeps 1 week, refrigerated.

≡ Pork and Veal Pâté Mosaic

== **Yield: one 9-inch loaf**

½ pound veal cutlets, cut into ¼-inch strips
¾ cup Marsala wine
16 juniper berries, crushed
1½ teaspoons dried rosemary, crumbled
4 teaspoons salt
⅛ teaspoon dried oregano, crumbled
¾ teaspoon pepper
1 pound lean ground veal

¾ pound ground pork
½ pound ground pork fat
2 garlic cloves, crushed
5 tablespoons butter
1 onion, thinly sliced
3 eggs, beaten
grated nutmeg, to taste
1 pound thinly sliced bacon
½ pound ham, cut into ¼-inch strips

1. Preheat the oven to 350°F.

2. In a bowl, marinate the veal strips in half the Marsala, half the juniper berries, half the rosemary, half the salt, the oregano, and half the pepper, covered, overnight. Reserve the marinade.

3. In a bowl, mix the ground veal, ground pork, pork fat, and garlic.

4. In a skillet, sauté the onion in the butter until soft, but not brown. Add the remaining Marsala and reduce to 3 tablespoons.

5. Turn into a food processor and add the marinade from the veal strips, the eggs, the remaining juniper berries, salt, rosemary, and pepper, and the nutmeg; purée. Add to the ground meats. If desired, sauté a small amount of the mixture in a skillet to taste for seasoning.

6. Line a 9″ × 5″ × 3″ loaf pan with bacon and spread one-third of the ground meat mixture in the bottom. Top with half of the veal and ham strips and cover with another third of the meat mixture, the remaining veal and ham strips, and then the remaining meat mixture. Fold the overhanging bacon strips over the top and cover with foil.

7. Bake in a water bath for 1½ hours or until a thermometer registers 155°F.

8. Drain a small amount of fat from the pâté, cover with fresh foil, and weight. Chill.

▶ Keeps 1 week, refrigerated.

7

Canapés and Toasts

Canapés are slices of bread, sometimes toasted, spread with butter, and covered with a variety of toppings. They are usually elaborately garnished and sometimes coated with aspic. They are served cold. Toasts are slices of bread toasted on one or both sides, spread with a topping, and then either baked in the oven or deep-fried. They are garnished less elaborately than canapés.

In the past, it was common to coat the tops of canapés with aspic to keep the surfaces shiny and to prevent the toppings from drying out. Pretty, but not too practical. Originally canapés were larger, 2 by 3 inches, and were served as a beginning course in a formal meal. A few different kinds would be passed before the soup. Sometimes, especially in England, they were also served at the end of a formal meal as a "savory," to leave the palate with a salty rather than a sweet taste. With the introduction of cocktail parties, canapés were reduced to bite-size portions that became the bane of guests and hostesses alike. Because the canapés had to be prepared ahead, the bread would become soggy and the toppings would dry out. Worse, some unfortunate guests discovered that the limp bread encouraged the topping to slip onto their clothing or onto the floor, creating awkward moments. Consequently, canapés lost favor, except for very small parties or on those occasions when it was possible to have enough staff to prepare the canapés and serve them immediately.

To avoid soggy canapés, try the following suggestions. If you have serving help, assign one or two people to prepare the canapés as they are needed. Have everything set out on trays for quick assembly, or assemble the toppings on baking sheets as they are to appear on the canapé. Have the bread cut and buttered or ready to toast and butter. Just before serving, toast and butter the bread, and position the assembled topping. This works particularly well if the base of the topping is a slice of meat. If the topping is well chilled, you can use a spatula to quickly transfer it to the toast. You can also arrange the topping on a thin slice of cucumber or zucchini, then quickly slide it onto its bread base. Without the requisite staff to prepare fresh, wonderful canapés, either choose another hors d'oeuvre or invite very few people.

Toasts are hot canapés; however, they are not as precise or labor-intensive as canapés. The bread base may be toasted first. The toasts are heated before serving by baking, broiling, or deep-frying and then served immediately to retain their fresh quality. It is possible to have the bread ready to be toasted on a tray, or even to sauté the bread ahead of time. Spread on the topping, then heat and serve the toasts. One server can do this and, depending on the menu, tend to other responsibilities as well.

Deep-fried toasts, such as Chinese shrimp toast (page 291), can be spread with the filling hours or even the day before serving. They are deep-fried at the last moment and served immediately. It is always a mistake to hold deep-fried foods. In theory, they can be kept warm in a 200°F oven for 20 to 30 minutes, but they will never be as wonderful as when freshly fried and served. Fry them in small batches so that they can be immediately passed around and eaten. If they are not consumed on the first pass, they should be discarded—cold deep-fried food is unpleasant.

In this chapter you will find not only recipes for traditional canapés and toasts, but also some ideas that do not fit into the standard categories, such as tuna wasabi canapés (page 261). Chapter 1 also has recipes for foods that can be used as canapés, such as corn cakes and carrot blinis.

As always, the number of servings depends on the rest of the menu. You can usually assume that people will eat 5 to 6 hors d'oeuvre per hour. For a 4-hour party with a menu of 6 to 8 hors d'oeuvre, plan on 2 to 3 canapés per person. Toasts, however, tend to be particularly popular, and people are apt to eat more of them. Plan on 3 to 4 per person.

—— *Canapés* ——

≡ *Céleri Farci (Stuffed Celery)*

═ Yield: 18 rounds

2 large stalks celery
6 tablespoons butter
2 ounces cream cheese
salt and pepper, to taste

1 teaspoon tomato paste
⅓ cup Roquefort cheese
18 pumpernickel rounds
1 pimiento (see note)

═ Yield: 72 rounds

8 large stalks celery
1½ cups butter
½ pound cream cheese
salt and pepper, to taste

4 teaspoons tomato paste
1⅓ cups Roquefort cheese
72 pumpernickel rounds
2 or 3 pimientos (see note)

1. Wash and dry the celery stalks.

2. In a bowl or food processor, cream half the butter with the cream cheese, salt, pepper, and tomato paste. Cream the remaining butter with the Roquefort cheese.

3. Stuff half the celery stalks with the tomato mixture and the other half with the Roquefort mixture. Press one stalk of each kind together, wrap in waxed paper, and chill. Repeat with the remaining stalks.

4. When ready to serve, cut the celery into thin slices, place on the bread rounds, and garnish with pimiento cutouts.

▶ The stalks can be filled 2 days in advance and assembled just before serving.

NOTE: Cut the pimientos into elaborate shapes using a truffle cutter or into simple diamonds using a knife.

≡ *Stuffed Celery and Cheese Canapés*

═ Yield: 28 rounds

¼ pound blue cheese
¼ cup cream cheese
¼ cup butter
2 tablespoons heavy cream
salt and pepper, to taste

1 bunch celery
28 2½-inch toast rounds,
    toasted on both sides and
    buttered

═ Yield: 84 rounds

¾ pound blue cheese

¾ cup cream cheese

¾ cup butter

⅓ cup heavy cream

salt and pepper, to taste

3 bunches celery

84 2½-inch toast rounds,
    toasted on both sides and
    buttered

1. In a food processor, cream the blue cheese, cream cheese, butter, cream, salt, and pepper.

2. Trim the base of the celery and cut into 7-inch lengths. Separate the stalks. Stuff the stalks with the cheese mixture and then press them together to reassemble the celery stalk. Wrap securely in plastic wrap and chill.

3. Cut into ¼-inch slices and serve on the toasts.

▶ The celery can be prepared 2 days in advance. Make the toast and assemble just before serving. However, if the toast is made by drying it out in a 350°F oven until it turns golden, the toast can be made and buttered several hours ahead. Place the topping on just before serving. **NOTE:** Use small bunches of celery and do not press too many stalks together or else the celery slice will be larger than the bread.

Slices of Stuffed Celery and Cheese Canapés

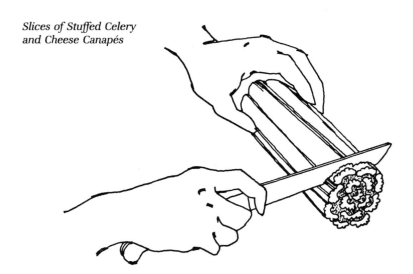

≡ Stuffed Cucumber Canapés

═ Yield: 24 rounds

1 8-inch cucumber, peeled
½ cup drained and mashed
  canned mackerel in oil
1 hard-cooked egg, minced
2 tablespoons mayonnaise
2 tablespoons minced pimiento

1 tablespoon minced scallions
3 tablespoons lemon juice
1½ teaspoons Dijon mustard
salt and pepper, to taste
24 toast rounds, buttered

═ Yield: 72 rounds

3 8-inch cucumbers, peeled
1½ cups drained and mashed
  canned mackerel in oil
3 hard-cooked eggs, minced
⅓ cup mayonnaise
⅓ cup minced pimiento

3 tablespoons minced scallions
½ cup lemon juice
1½ tablespoons Dijon mustard
salt and pepper, to taste
72 toast rounds, buttered

1. Cut off the ends of the cucumbers and cut in half crosswise. With an apple corer, hollow out the seeds. Sprinkle with salt and drain 15 minutes. Pat dry and chill.

2. In a bowl, mix the mackerel, egg(s), mayonnaise, pimiento, scallions, lemon juice, mustard, salt, and pepper. Fill the cucumber hollows and wrap in plastic wrap. Chill 12 hours.

3. Cut the cucumbers into ¼-inch slices and serve on toast rounds.

▶ The cucumbers can be stuffed and chilled 24 hours in advance. Assemble just before serving. The filling can be piped through a pastry bag without a tip.

≡ Smyrnan Ajada (Cucumber with Garlic Spread)

This is a delicious, low-calorie canapé.

═ Yield: 24 rounds

¼ cup fine bread crumbs
1 teaspoon minced garlic, or to
  taste
2 tablespoons olive oil
1 tablespoon lemon juice

salt and pepper, to taste
1 cucumber, peeled and cut
  into ¼-inch slices, skin
  reserved

¾ cup fine bread crumbs
1 tablespoon minced garlic, or
  to taste
6 tablespoons olive oil
3 tablespoons lemon juice

salt and pepper, to taste
3 cucumbers, peeled and cut
  into ¼-inch slices, skins
  reserved

1. In a bowl, mash the bread crumbs with the garlic, olive oil, lemon juice, salt, and pepper to make a paste. Add 1 or more tablespoons of ice water to make it spreadable.

2. Spread on the cucumber slices and decorate with cucumber skin cutouts, if desired. Chill at least 30 minutes before serving, but no longer than 6 hours.

▶ The topping can be prepared one day in advance.

NOTE: For variations use the garlic paste on zucchini slices and peeled, sliced broccoli stems.

═ *Radis au Beurre de Citron (Radishes with Lemon Butter)*

═ **Yield: 24 rounds**

12 large radishes
5 tablespoons unsalted butter
1 teaspoon lemon juice

⅛ teaspoon grated lemon rind
24 pumpernickel rounds,
  optional

═ **Yield: 72 rounds**

36 large radishes
1 cup unsalted butter
1 tablespoon lemon juice

½ teaspoon grated lemon rind
72 pumpernickel rounds,
  optional

1. Wash and dry the radishes. Trim off the roots and any bruised edges, retaining the greens if they are fresh. Cut the radishes in half vertically.

2. In a food processor, cream the butter and add the lemon juice and rind slowly.

3. Fit a pastry bag with a no. 30 star tip and pipe a rosette on the cut surface of each radish. Chill until firm and serve with pumpernickel rounds on the side, or remove the stems from the radishes and place the radish cut-side down on the pumpernickel round. Pipe the butter around the edge.

▶ Can be prepared 6 hours in advance.

☰ *Onion Sandwiches*

═ Yield: 18 sandwiches

36 ¼-inch slices brioche (see note)

¾ cup mayonnaise

18 paper-thin slices raw onion

salt, to taste

¾ cup minced parsley

═ Yield: 72 sandwiches

144 ¼-inch slices brioche (see note)

2 cups mayonnaise

72 paper-thin slices raw onion

salt, to taste

2 cups minced parsley

1. Using a 1½- to 2-inch round cutter, cut the brioche into circles and then cut the onions into circles slightly smaller than the bread rounds. Spread a thin layer of mayonnaise on the brioche slices. Sandwich the onion circles between two brioche rounds.

2. On a sheet of waxed paper, spread a line of mayonnaise about 6 inches long and ½ inch thick. Put the parsley in a small dish. Holding the sandwiches in the center, wheel the edges down the length of mayonnaise and then dip the coated edges in the parsley. Chill.

▶ Keeps 12 hours, refrigerated and covered with damp towels.

NOTE: Substitute any fine-quality bread for the brioche.

☰ *Potato Pancakes (Latkes)*

These are not canapés as served here, but they make an excellent base for many canapé toppings.

═ Yield: 24 pancakes

2 large baking potatoes, peeled

⅓ cup grated onion

½ teaspoon salt

black pepper

1 tablespoon matzo meal or cracker crumbs

1 egg, lightly beaten

vegetable oil

½ cup sour cream

½ cup applesauce, optional

═ Yield: 72 pancakes

6 large baking potatoes, peeled

1 cup grated onion

1½ teaspoons salt

½ teaspoon black pepper

3 tablespoons matzo meal or cracker crumbs

3 eggs, lightly beaten

vegetable oil

1½ cups sour cream

1½ cups applesauce, optional

1. Grate the potatoes into a sieve and press out excess liquid. Discard the liquid. Place the potatoes in a bowl and add the onions. Season with salt and pepper and stir in the matzo meal and egg(s).

2. In a skillet, heat the oil over high heat. Drop tablespoons of the potato mixture to make 2- to 2½-inch cakes and fry for about 2 minutes on each side or until golden and crisp.

3. Drain on baking sheets lined with paper towels. Serve immediately with sour cream and applesauce for dipping.

▶ Make the potato mixture no more than 30 minutes before cooking. Cooked pancakes can be frozen and reheated, though they will not be as good.

NOTE: Grated potatoes darken within a short time. If you need to increase the recipe, it is better to prepare several batches as needed, rather than making the mixture all at one time.

≡ *Courgettes à la Niçoise (Zucchini with Vegetables)*

═ **Yield: 24 rounds**

1 tomato, peeled, seeded, and minced	1 scallion, minced
salt	1½ tablespoons bread crumbs
2 tablespoons cream cheese	pinch of dried thyme
1 tablespoon minced green olives	pinch of minced parsley
1 tablespoon minced black olives	salt and pepper, to taste
	1 6-inch zucchini, cut into ¼-inch slices
	pimiento strips or cutouts

═ **Yield: 72 rounds**

4 tomatoes, peeled, seeded, and minced	⅓ cup bread crumbs
salt	¼ teaspoon dried thyme
½ cup cream cheese	1 teaspoon minced parsley
¼ cup minced green olives	salt and pepper, to taste
¼ cup minced black olives	4 6-inch zucchinis, cut into ¼-inch slices
4 scallions, minced	pimiento strips or cutouts

1. Place the tomatoes in a sieve, sprinkle with salt, and let stand for 30 minutes.

2. In a bowl, cream the cream cheese and beat in the olives, scallions, bread crumbs, thyme, and parsley. Drain the tomatoes well and beat into the cheese mixture. Correct the seasoning with salt and pepper.

3. Mound the filling on top of the zucchini slices. Garnish with pimiento strips.

▶ Keeps 4 hours, refrigerated.

≡ *Horseradish Olive Stars*

This is a particularly colorful canapé. It is delicious in its own right and can also be used as a platter decoration.

═ Yield: 60 stars

1 recipe horseradish
  cream–stuffed olives
  (page 36)
6 ounces cream cheese
¼ cup heavy cream

2 tablespoons drained
  horseradish
salt, to taste
1 loaf Westphalian
  pumpernickel

1. Prepare the olives according to the recipe and set aside.

2. In a food processor, cream the cream cheese, heavy cream, horseradish, and salt.

3. Fit a pastry bag with a no. 30 star tip, fill with the cheese mixture, and set aside.

4. Using a metal cutter, cut the bread into stars and line up on a baking sheet. Place an olive upright in the center of each star and pipe a line of cheese from the olive to each point.

▶ Keeps about 6 hours.

NOTE: Westphalian pumpernickel is sold in 4-inch-square loaves cut into thin slices. Use a knife blade to separate the slices. Other breads can be used, but the black of the olive and the dark brown of the bread set off the white of the cheese best.

Horseradish Olive Stars

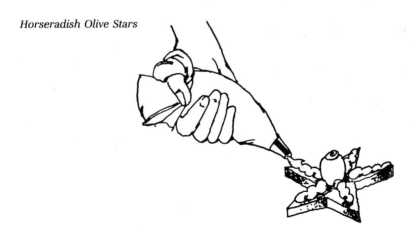

≡ *Camembert Cashew Rounds*

≡ Yield: 24 rounds

⅓ cup ground cashews
1 small Camembert cheese,
   approximately 9 ounces,
   softened

1 to 2 tablespoons white wine
24 melba toast rounds
24 whole cashews

≡ Yield: 72 rounds

1 cup ground cashews
1 large Camembert cheese,
   approximately 27 ounces,
   softened

2 to 4 tablespoons white wine
72 melba toast rounds
72 whole cashews

In a food processor, purée the cashews, Camembert, and wine. Spread on the toast rounds and garnish with a whole cashew.

▶ Keeps 1 to 2 hours.

NOTE: If the cashews are ground fine enough, the mixture can be piped through a star tip or, more reliably, a no. 5 plain tip.

≡ *Anchovy and Pimiento Canapés*

This vibrantly attractive canapé can also be made with sardines instead of anchovies.

≡ Yield: 12 canapés

6 tablespoons butter, softened
1 tablespoon lemon juice
3 slices white bread, crusts
   removed

2 pimientos, sliced
1 to 2 cans anchovy fillets

≡ Yield: 72 canapés

1½ cups butter, softened
⅓ cup lemon juice
18 slices white bread, crusts
   removed

12 pimientos, sliced
6 to 12 cans anchovy fillets

1. In a food processor, cream the butter and gradually beat in the lemon juice.

2. Spread the butter on the bread slices and arrange the pimiento slices and anchovy fillets in alternate rows. Cut the bread slices into 4 triangles.

▶ Keeps 1 hour.

≡ Lucca Augen ("Eyes of Lucca" Oyster Canapés)

== **Yield: 24 canapés**

24 1½-inch circles of thinly
   sliced white bread
¾ cup butter

24 shucked and drained oysters
1½ ounces sevruga caviar
4 thin slices lemon

== **Yield: 72 canapés**

72 1½-inch circles of thinly
   sliced white bread
2¼ cups butter

72 shucked and drained oysters
4½ ounces sevruga caviar
12 thin slices lemon

1. In a skillet, sauté the bread circles in half of the butter until golden on both sides. Drain on paper towels. Spread the remaining butter on the bread, top with an oyster, and surround with the caviar.

2. Cut each lemon slice into 6 wedges and place a wedge on each oyster.

▶ Keeps 1 hour at the most.

≡ Salmon, Mint, and Cucumber Toast

== **Yield: 30 canapés**

½ pound raw salmon fillets,
   finely diced
2 tablespoons minced mint
½ cup peeled, seeded, and
   finely diced cucumber

3 tablespoons olive oil
salt and pepper, to taste
30 slices French bread, sautéed
   in butter
mint leaves

== **Yield: 90 canapés**

2 pounds raw salmon fillets,
   finely diced
½ cup minced mint
1½ cups peeled, seeded, and
   finely diced cucumber

½ to ¾ cup olive oil
salt and pepper, to taste
90 slices French bread, sautéed
   in butter
mint leaves

1. In a bowl, combine the salmon, mint, cucumber, olive oil, salt, and pepper and let marinate for 30 minutes or as long as 5 hours. If you marinate for 5 hours, refrigerate and bring to room temperature before serving.

2. Serve the salmon in a bowl surrounded with the French bread, or spread the salmon on the bread and pass separately. Garnish with the mint leaves.

▶ Do not prepare more than 5 hours ahead.

≡ Curried Smoked Salmon Canapés

Yield: 24 canapés

3 ounces cream cheese
3 tablespoons heavy cream
¼ teaspoon curry powder
1 teaspoon grated onion

6 thin slices smoked salmon
1 cucumber
24 slices black olive
24 toast or cracker rounds

Yield: 72 canapés

½ pound cream cheese
½ cup heavy cream
¾ teaspoon curry powder
1 tablespoon grated onion

18 thin slices smoked salmon
3 cucumbers
72 slices black olive
72 toast or cracker rounds

1. In a food processor, purée the cream cheese, cream, curry powder, and onion.

2. On a sheet of waxed paper arrange the smoked salmon with the edges slightly overlapping to make sheets approximately 6 inches long. Spread with the cheese mixture and roll up like a jelly roll. Chill for 3 hours or until firm.

3. Score the cucumbers with a fork and cut into thin slices. Cut the smoked salmon roll into ¼-inch slices and place on the cucumber slices. Garnish with the olive slices.

4. When ready to serve, lay a cucumber-salmon slice on top of a toast or cracker round.

▶ The salmon keeps 3 days, refrigerated. Assemble before serving.

NOTE: The cucumber can be cut slightly thicker and the cracker omitted.

≡ Smoked Salmon Canapés

Yield: 24 canapés

½ pound smoked salmon
¾ cup butter, softened
1½ teaspoons anchovy paste
1½ teaspoons lemon juice
1 tablespoon minced dill
pepper, to taste

lemon juice, to taste
24 1-inch squares white bread,
    toasted
24 1-inch squares smoked
    salmon
24 capers

═ **Yield: 72 canapés**

1½ pounds smoked salmon
2¼ cups butter, softened
1½ tablespoons anchovy paste
1½ tablepoons lemon juice
3 tablespoons minced dill
pepper, to taste

lemon juice, to taste
72 1-inch squares white bread,
   toasted
72 1-inch squares smoked
   salmon
72 capers

1. In a food processor, purée the salmon, butter, anchovy paste, and lemon juice. Force through a fine sieve and mix in the dill. Season with pepper and lemon juice. Chill until firm but spreadable.

2. Spread generously on the toast squares and top with a square of smoked salmon and a caper.

▶ Keeps 1 to 2 hours, assembled.

≡ *Sardine Canapés*

═ **Yield: 12 canapés**

6 tablespoons butter, softened
1 tablespoon lemon juice
12 ¾- by 3-inch pieces white
   bread, crusts removed

⅓ cup minced parsley
12 sardines
paprika, optional

═ **Yield: 72 canapés**

1¼ pounds butter, softened
⅓ cup lemon juice
72 ¾- by 3-inch pieces white
   bread, crusts removed

2 cups minced parsley
72 sardines
paprika, optional

In a food processor, cream the butter and gradually beat in the lemon juice. Spread the butter on the bread. Sprinkle the parsley around the edges of the bread. Place a sardine on top and dust with paprika.

▶ Keeps 1 to 2 hours.

NOTE: Any leftover butter can be used to make simple designs instead of sprinkling on paprika. A no. 2 plain pastry tip is good for drawing fine lines diagonally across the fish, for example. Keep the decoration simple.

≡ *Sardine and Chive Cheese Canapés*

═ Yield: 30 canapés

1 can skinless, boneless
  sardines, drained
3 ounces cream cheese
1 tablespoon minced chives

dash of Worcestershire sauce
salt and pepper, to taste
1 6-inch pita bread
30 cherry tomato slices

═ Yield: 60 canapés

2 cans skinless, boneless
  sardines, drained
6 ounces cream cheese
2 tablespoons minced chives
¼ teaspoon Worcestershire
  sauce

salt and pepper, to taste
2 6-inch pita breads
60 cherry tomato slices

1. In a food processor, purée the sardines, cream cheese, chives, and Worcestershire sauce. Correct seasoning with salt and pepper.

2. Split the pita bread and spread both halves with the sardine mixture. Roll up each half tightly and wrap in waxed paper. Chill 2 hours.

3. Cut into ¼-inch slices and garnish each piece with a tomato slice.

▶ Keeps overnight, refrigerated, uncut. Slice just before serving.

≡ *Sardines on Anchovy Toast*

═ Yield: 18 canapés

6 tablespoons butter
2 tablespoons anchovy paste
6 slices toasted whole-wheat
  bread, crusts removed

18 skinless, boneless sardines
1 tablespoon lemon juice
lemon wedges

═ Yield: 72 canapés

1½ cups butter
1 can anchovies, mashed
24 slices toasted whole-wheat
  bread, crusts removed

72 skinless, boneless sardines
¼ cup lemon juice
lemon wedges

1. In a food processor, cream the butter and anchovy paste or anchovies.

2. Spread one side of the toast with the anchovy butter and cut into thirds. Top each toast finger with a sardine and sprinkle with a little lemon juice. Serve immediately, with lemon wedges on the side.

▶ Keeps 1 hour.

☰ Canapés Portugaise
(Sardine, Scallion, and Pimiento Canapés)

═ Yield: 20 canapés

2 tablespoons butter
5 slices toast, crusts removed
10 scallions

2 cans sardines
1 pimiento, sliced into thin
   strips

═ Yield: 80 canapés

½ cup butter
20 slices toast, crusts removed
40 scallions

8 cans sardines
4 pimientos, sliced into thin
   strips

1. Butter the toast. Arrange alternate rows of scallions and sardines on the toast, trimming the ends to fit exactly. Cut each slice of toast into 4 triangles.

2. Garnish each triangle with strips of pimiento.

▶ Keeps 1 hour.

☰ Shrimp Canapés

═ Yield: 24 canapés

¾ pound 26-30 size shrimp,
   cooked and peeled
⅓ cup butter
3 tablespoons heavy cream
1 tablespoon lemon juice

2 teaspoons tomato paste
1 teaspoon anchovy paste
salt, to taste
24 1½-inch bread rounds,
   toasted

═ Yield: 72 canapés

2¼ pounds 26-30 size shrimp,
   cooked and peeled
1 cup butter
½ cup heavy cream
3 tablespoons lemon juice

2 tablespoons tomato paste
1 tablespoon anchovy paste
salt, to taste
72 1½-inch bread rounds,
   toasted

1. Cut 12 (for the smaller quantity) or 36 (for the larger quantity) of the shrimp in half lengthwise and reserve the remaining shrimp.

2. Place a shrimp half, cut-side up, in the bottom of well-buttered 1¼-inch muffin tins.

3. In a food processor, purée the remaining shrimp, butter, cream, lemon juice, tomato paste, anchovy paste, and salt. Pack on top of the shrimp halves and chill for 6 hours or until firm.

4. With the tip of a knife, remove the shrimp filling from the molds. When ready to serve, place filling flat-side up on top of the toast rounds.

▶ The shrimp mixture keeps 2 days, refrigerated. Make the toast rounds and assemble just before serving.

≡ *Avocado Shrimp Tostados*

These delicious canapés with a Mexican accent are equally good with a dollop of salmon caviar instead of the shrimp.

═ Yield: 24 canapés

2 tablespoons lime juice
1 garlic clove, crushed
¼ cup vegetable oil
1 tablespoon minced coriander
  (cilantro)
1 teaspoon dry mustard
¼ teaspoon ground cumin
½ teaspoon salt
¼ teaspoon pepper
12 medium shrimp, cooked and
  peeled

3 serrano chilies, seeded and
  minced
3 coriander sprigs, minced
¼ cup minced onion
2 tomatoes, diced
2 avocados, coarsely mashed
salt, to taste
24 round tostados
sour cream
coriander sprigs

═ Yield: 72 canapés

⅓ cup lime juice
3 garlic cloves, crushed
¾ cup vegetable oil
3 tablespoons minced
  coriander (cilantro)
1 tablespoon dry mustard
¾ teaspoon ground cumin
1½ teaspoons salt
¾ teaspoon pepper
36 medium shrimp, cooked and
  peeled

9 serrano chilies, seeded and
  minced
⅓ cup minced coriander
¾ cup minced onion
6 tomatoes, diced
6 avocados, coarsely mashed
salt, to taste
72 round tostados
sour cream
coriander sprigs

1. Mix the lime juice, garlic, vegetable oil, minced coriander, mustard, cumin, salt, and pepper in a bowl. Set aside. Slice the shrimp in half lengthwise, discard the vein, and toss in the marinade. Refrigerate until ready to use.

2. In a bowl, mix the chilies, remaining coriander, onion, tomatoes, avocados, and salt. Cover tightly until ready to use.

3. To serve, top each tostada with 1 teaspoon of the avocado mixture, a dollop of sour cream, and 1 shrimp. Garnish with a sprig of coriander.

▶ The shrimp can be prepared the day before. The avocado mixture should be made within hours of serving and kept tightly sealed, to prevent the avocado from turning black. Assemble just before serving.

≡ Canapés Cardinal (Tomato Shrimp Canapés)

═ Yield: 6 canapés

butter
6 1½- to 2-inch toast rounds
6 tomato slices, 1½ to 2 inches
  in diameter
½ cup mayonnaise
1 tablespoon chili sauce

1 tablespoon mixed minced
  chives, chervil, parsley, and
  tarragon
3 medium shrimp, cooked,
  shelled, and deveined

═ Yield: 72 canapés

1½ cups butter
72 1½- to 2-inch toast rounds
72 tomato slices, 1½ to 2 inches
  in diameter
2 cups mayonnaise

¼ cup chili sauce
¼ cup mixed minced chives,
  chervil, parsley, and tarragon
36 medium shrimp, cooked,
  shelled, and deveined

1. Butter the toast and place a tomato slice on top.

2. In a bowl, mix the mayonnaise, chili sauce, and herbs. Spread on top of the tomatoes. Slice the shrimp in half lengthwise and arrange one on top of each tomato.

▶ Keeps 1 hour, assembled.

NOTE: The tomato-mayonnaise-shrimp topping can be assembled and put on baking sheets 2 to 3 hours ahead. Make the toast, butter it, and slip on the garnish just before serving.

≡ Red Snapper and Salmon Tartare

This is a perfect canapé for today's tastes. It calls for the freshest fish, served marinated, but not cooked, with a light flavorful dressing. It is pretty, delicious, and low in calories.

=== **Yield: 18 canapés**

3 tablespoons Armagnac olive oil dressing (recipe follows)	white pepper, to taste
	2 anchovy fillets
9 ounces salmon fillets, skinned and boned	¼ cup butter, softened
	pinch of paprika
9 ounces red snapper fillets, skinned and boned	black pepper, to taste
	18 slices French bread
1½ teaspoons salt	butter, optional

=== **Yield: 72 canapés**

¾ cup Armagnac olive oil dressing (recipe follows)	white pepper, to taste
	8 anchovy fillets
1½ pounds salmon fillets, skinned and boned	¾ cup butter, softened
	¼ teaspoon paprika
1½ pounds red snapper fillets, skinned and boned	black pepper, to taste
	72 slices French bread
2 tablespoons salt	butter, optional

1. Prepare the dressing a day ahead.

2. Cut the fish into ⅛-inch dice.

3. In a bowl, mix the fish, salt, white pepper, and two-thirds of the dressing. Cover and refrigerate for 4 hours.

4. In a food processor, cream the anchovies, butter, paprika, and black pepper, and add the remaining dressing.

5. Toast the bread on both sides and spread with butter. Top with 1½ tablespoons of the fish mixture. If desired, let guests spread the fish themselves.

▶ Assemble just before serving.

NOTE: Instead of the salmon and red snapper, substitute scallops for an equally attractive and delicious canapé.

☰ *Armagnac Olive Oil Dressing*

=== **Yield: ¾ cup**

½ cup olive oil	2 garlic cloves
¼ cup Armagnac	12 whole cloves
1 tablespoon crushed peppercorns	¼ teaspoon dried tarragon
	¼ teaspoon dried thyme

In a bowl, whisk together the olive oil, Armagnac, pepper, garlic, cloves, tarragon, and thyme. Let stand overnight, refrigerated. Strain.

▶ Can be prepared several days ahead.

NOTE: If you have extra dressing, drizzle it on sliced tomatoes.

≡ *Tuna Wasabi Canapé*

Steve and Carol Wasik of the Cheese Shop in Wellesley, Massachusetts, introduced me to this exciting new hors d'oeuvre. I was so fascinated with it that I practically forgot the rest of their delicious dinner.

═ Yield: 24 canapés

1 1-pound tuna steak, 1 inch thick	1 teaspoon wasabi powder
1 tablespoon lemon juice	½ cup crème fraîche or sour cream
3 tablespoons extra virgin olive oil	1 recipe potato pancakes (page 249)
salt and pepper, to taste	

═ Yield: 72 canapés

3 1-pound tuna steaks, 1 inch thick	1 tablespoon wasabi powder
3 tablespoons lemon juice	1½ cups crème fraîche or sour cream
½ cup extra virgin olive oil	1 recipe potato pancakes (page 249)
salt and pepper, to taste	

1. Marinate the tuna in the lemon juice, olive oil, salt, and pepper for up to 3 hours. Drain.

2. In a bowl, mix the wasabi powder and crème fraîche. Correct the seasoning with salt.

3. Prepare the potato pancakes and cook them in a skillet.

4. Heat a black cast-iron skillet until very hot. Sear the tuna on both sides, keeping it rare in the center. Slice the tuna into ¼-inch slices, about 1 inch wide and as long as the potato pancakes.

5. Place a dollop of wasabi cream on each pancake and top with a slice of tuna. Serve immediately.

▶ The tuna can be marinated 6 hours ahead. The wasabi cream can be prepared the day before. The pancakes should be prepared and cooked immediately.

≡ Polpettone di Tonno e Spinaci (Spinach and Tuna Sausage)

≡ **Yield: 100 canapés**

1½ pounds spinach, cooked	3 tablespoons bread crumbs
1 3½-ounce can Italian tuna, packed in oil	salt and pepper, to taste
	2 carrots
4 anchovy fillets	⅓ cup olive oil
1½ slices white bread	1 tablespoon lemon juice
½ cup milk	100 1½-inch toast rounds
2 eggs	lemon wedges
½ cup grated Parmesan cheese	

1. Drain the spinach, squeeze out any excess liquid, and purée in a food processor with the tuna and anchovies. In a bowl, soak the bread in the milk and squeeze out the excess liquid. Add to the processor and purée. With the machine running, add the eggs, cheese, bread crumbs, salt, and pepper.

2. Arrange two 6- by 12-inch pieces of cheesecloth, 4 layers thick, on a work surface. Shape the mixture on the cloth to form 2 sausages, 1½-inches in diameter and about 12 inches long. Wrap securely, tying the ends with string.

3. Place in a casserole with water to cover and add the carrots. Cover and simmer 30 minutes. Cool in the liquid. Remove and discard the cheesecloth and the cooking liquid, but save the carrots.

4. To serve, cut each sausage into ¼-inch slices and arrange on a tray. Sprinkle with olive oil and lemon juice. Place on toast rounds and top with a thin slice of carrot. Serve with lemon wedges.

▶ The sausage can be made 4 days ahead and the slices of sausage can marinate in the oil and vinegar for several hours. Assemble just before serving.

NOTE: It is impractical to prepare this in smaller quantities; however, the remainder can be sliced and served the next day as a sandwich filling or arranged on lettuce as a first course.

≡ Chicken Liver Canapés

≡ **Yield: 24 canapés**

12 thin slices French bread	½ teaspoon salt
6 tablespoons butter	¼ teaspoon pepper
½ pound chicken livers, minced	2 anchovy fillets, mashed
	2 tablespoons white wine
2 tablespoons minced parsley	black olives

Yield: 72 canapés

36 thin slices French bread
1¼ cups butter
1½ pounds chicken livers,
  minced
⅓ cup minced parsley

1½ teaspoons salt
¾ teaspoon pepper
6 anchovy fillets, mashed
2 tablespoons white wine
black olives

1. In a skillet, sauté the bread slices in half the butter until golden on both sides.

2. Melt the remaining butter in a skillet and sauté the livers, parsley, salt, pepper, anchovies, and white wine until the livers are medium.

3. Cool and spread on the bread slices. Cut the slices in half. Garnish with black olives and serve while still warm.

▶ These are best if prepared and served while still warm.

NOTE: The chicken livers can be cooked whole and the entire mixture chopped finely in a food processor before spreading on the bread. The mixture can be cooled completely, spread on the bread, and served cold as well.

Rolled Chicken Canapés

Yield: 40 canapés

½ cup butter
½ cup chopped onion
1 celery stalk, chopped
1 carrot, chopped
1 tablespoon salt
¼ teaspoon ground allspice
2 large chicken breasts

½ pound boneless pork
¾ pound butter, softened
⅓ cup Cognac
2 tablespoons pistachios
salt and pepper, to taste
1 pound thinly sliced prosciutto

Yield: 80 canapés

1 cup butter
1 cup chopped onion
2 celery stalks, chopped
2 carrots, chopped
2 tablespoons salt
½ teaspoon ground allspice
4 large chicken breasts

1 pound boneless pork
1½ pounds butter, softened
½ cup Cognac
¼ cup pistachios
salt and pepper, to taste
2 pounds thinly sliced
  prosciutto

1. In a casserole, mix the butter, onion, celery, carrot, salt, allspice, chicken breasts, and pork. Cover and cook over medium heat until the meats are tender, about 30 minutes. Remove the chicken and pork and cool.

Rolled Chicken Canapés

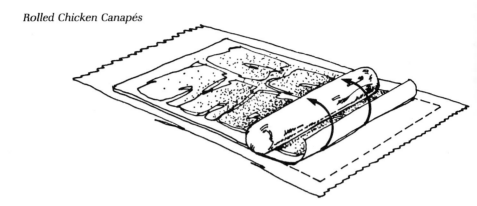

2. In a food processor, chop the chicken and pork finely. With the motor running, add the butter in small amounts and then the Cognac in a slow, steady stream.

3. Remove to a bowl and fold in the pistachios. Taste for seasoning and correct with salt and pepper if necessary.

4. Divide the mixture in half or quarters and shape into logs with the help of waxed paper. Refrigerate.

5. Arrange the slices of prosciutto on sheets of waxed paper to make 10-inch squares. Place a log on each prosciutto square and roll up in the prosciutto. Wrap securely and chill several hours. Cut into ½-inch slices.

▶ Keeps 4 days, refrigerated.

≡ *Curried Chicken Canapés*

This is supposed to be subtly flavored with curry. You can add more for a stronger flavor.

≡ **Yield: 36 canapés**

2 cups poached, finely ground chicken breast	1 teaspoon curry powder, or to taste
¼ cup heavy cream	36 2-inch bread rounds, sautéed in butter
¼ cup chicken stock	pimiento cutouts
salt and pepper, to taste	
1 teaspoon lemon juice	

≡ **Yield: 72 canapés**

4 cups poached, finely ground
   chicken breast
½ cup heavy cream
½ cup chicken stock
salt and pepper, to taste
2 teaspoons lemon juice

2 teaspoons curry powder, or to
   taste
72 2-inch bread rounds,
   sautéed in butter
pimiento cutouts

In a bowl, mix the chicken, cream, stock, salt, pepper, lemon juice, and curry powder. Spread on toast rounds and garnish with pimientos. Serve immediately.

NOTE: Feel free to add some traditional curry accompaniments, such as raisins, minced chutney, chopped cashews, and/or toasted coconut. These can also be used as a garnish.

≡ *Oriental Chicken Roll Canapés*

≡ **Yield: 20 canapés**

1 large chicken breast, skinned
   and boned
1 tablespoon thin soy sauce
1 tablespoon vegetable oil
1 tablespoon sherry
½ garlic clove, crushed
½ teaspoon minced gingerroot
1 tablespoon melted butter

20 bread or cracker rounds
⅓ cup butter, softened
⅓ cup mayonnaise, flavored
   with mustard to taste
pimiento cutouts
green pepper cutouts
parsley sprigs

≡ **Yield: 60 canapés**

3 large chicken breasts, skinned
   and boned
2 tablespoons thin soy sauce
2 tablespoons vegetable oil
¼ cup sherry
1 garlic clove, crushed
2 teaspoons minced gingerroot
3 tablespoons melted butter

60 bread or cracker rounds
1 cup butter, softened
1 cup mayonnaise, flavored
   with mustard to taste
pimiento cutouts
green pepper cutouts
parsley sprigs

1. With a meat pounder, flatten the chicken breasts to ¼-inch thickness. In a bowl, toss the breasts with the soy sauce, oil, sherry, garlic, and ginger. Refrigerate for 4 to 8 hours, turning often.

2. Preheat the oven to 325°F.

3. Roll the chicken breasts into tight rolls and tie with string. Place in a shallow baking dish and pour the marinade and melted butter over them. Bake 30 minutes, basting often. Chill.

4. Slice the rolls ¼ inch thick. Butter each bread round with the softened butter and spread with a layer of mayonnaise. Place a chicken slice on top and garnish with pimiento, green pepper, or parsley.

▶ The chicken rolls can be made several days ahead and refrigerated. Assemble just before serving.

≡ *Steamed Chicken Roll Canapés*

═ **Yield: 20 canapés**

1 large chicken breast, skinned and boned
2 ¼- by ¼-inch carrot sticks, blanched

2 green beans, blanched
½ teaspoon minced gingerroot
1 teaspoon thin soy sauce

═ **Yield: 60 canapés**

3 large chicken breasts, skinned and boned
6 ¼- by ¼-inch carrot sticks, blanched

6 green beans, blanched
1½ teaspoons minced gingerroot
1 tablespoon thin soy sauce

1. With a meat pounder, flatten the breasts until they are ¼ inch thick. Place a carrot stick and a green bean lengthwise on each breast half. Sprinkle with ginger and soy sauce. Roll each breast into a tight log and wrap in plastic wrap, twisting the ends to seal.

2. Place in a steamer and steam for 20 minutes. Let cool for 5 minutes.

3. Carefully unwrap and cut into slices.

▶ Can be prepared the day before.

≡ *Turkey or Chicken Straws in Brazil Nuts*

═ **Yield: 32 canapés**

1 chicken breast, cooked
⅓ cup stiff, lemon tarragon-flavored mayonnaise (see note)

⅓ cup chopped and toasted Brazil nuts, or any other nut of your choice

═ **Yield: 100 canapés**

½ turkey breast, cooked
1 cup stiff, lemon tarragon-
flavored mayonnaise (see
note)

1 cup chopped and toasted
Brazil nuts, or any other nut
of your choice

Cut the chicken or turkey into sticks, ½ by 2½ inches. Dip 2 inches of each stick into the mayonnaise and roll in the nuts.

▶ Can be made 4 to 6 hours ahead and refrigerated.

NOTE: Flavor homemade mayonnaise (page 48) with lemon juice and tarragon to taste.

═ *Syrian Beef Rolls*

═ **Yield: 24 canapés**

3 ounces cream cheese
1 teaspoon minced chives
salt and pepper, to taste
2 6-inch pita breads, split

4 thin slices rare roast beef
½ bunch watercress, minced
24 cherry tomato slices,
optional

═ **Yield: 72 canapés**

½ pound cream cheese
1 tablespoon minced chives
salt and pepper, to taste
6 6-inch pita breads, split
½ pound thinly sliced rare
roast beef

1 bunch watercress, minced
72 cherry tomato slices,
optional

1. In a bowl, cream the cream cheese, chives, salt, and pepper. Spread a thin layer on each bread half. Place a slice of roast beef on top and sprinkle with watercress. Season with salt and pepper.

2. Roll tightly and wrap in waxed paper. Chill.

3. Cut into ½-inch slices and serve topped with a slice of cherry tomato.

▶ Keeps 2 to 3 days, refrigerated.

≡ *English Sandwiches*

= **Yield: 24 canapés**

¼ cup butter
¼ teaspoon curry powder
2 6-inch pita breads, split
½ cup minced watercress

4 thin slices rare roast beef
salt and pepper, to taste
Dijon mustard, to taste

= **Yield: 72 canapés**

¾ cup butter
¾ teaspoon curry powder
6 6-inch pita breads, split
1½ cups minced watercress

½ pound thinly sliced rare
   roast beef
salt and pepper, to taste
Dijon mustard, to taste

1. In a food processor, cream the butter and curry powder and spread on the bread halves. Sprinkle with watercress and place a slice of roast beef on each bread half. Season with salt and pepper and spread thinly with mustard.

2. Roll tightly and wrap in waxed paper. Chill for at least 4 hours. Cut into ½-inch slices.

▶ Keeps 2 to 3 days, refrigerated.

≡ *Lamb Mint Rolls*

= **Yield: 24 canapés**

¼ cup butter, softened
2 6-inch pita breads, split
¼ pound roast lamb, thinly
   sliced

½ cup fresh mint leaves
salt and pepper, to taste

= **Yield: 72 canapés**

¾ cup butter, softened
6 6-inch pita breads, split
¾ pound roast lamb, thinly
   sliced

1½ cups fresh mint leaves
salt and pepper, to taste

1. Butter the bread, top with the lamb slices, and sprinkle with the mint leaves. Season with salt and pepper.

2. Roll tightly and wrap in waxed paper. Chill for at least 4 hours. Cut into ½-inch slices.

▶ Keeps 3 days, refrigerated.

NOTE: To vary the flavor, sprinkle ¼ teaspoon minced garlic on each bread half, or cream minced garlic to taste with the butter.

≡ Sausage Canapés

═ Yield: **48 canapés**

1½ pounds kielbasa, poached and peeled	Dijon mustard, to taste
½ cup sauce ravigote (page 47)	48 cocktail rye rounds
	minced parsley

═ Yield: **96 canapés**

3 pounds kielbasa, poached and peeled	Dijon mustard, to taste
1 cup sauce ravigote (page 47)	96 cocktail rye rounds
	minced parsley

1. Cut the kielbasa into ¼-inch slices.

2. In a bowl, marinate the kielbasa in the ravigote sauce and mustard for 2 hours. Drain.

3. Place a sausage slice on each cocktail round and sprinkle with parsley. Serve immediately.

▶ The sausage can marinate for up to 36 hours. Assemble just before serving.

—— Toasts ——

≡ Potato Skins

Though obviously not toasts in the strict sense, any more than potato pancakes, potato skins are a perfect crispy conveyor of savory toppings and are equally delicious unadorned.

The potato skins most often served are prepared by food purveyors and sold frozen. Generally there is too much potato pulp inside, and instead of being delicious, they are stodgy and uninteresting. To have a properly crisp skin you must remove all of the pulp. Use a flavored butter to make your offerings more distinctive.

═ **Yield: 72 pieces**

6 Idaho potatoes

6 tablespoons melted butter

salt and pepper, to taste

1. Preheat the oven to 400°F.

2. Bake the potatoes until tender; do not wrap in foil or oil the skin. Cut the potatoes in half, lengthwise. Scoop out all the pulp and save for another purpose.

3. Cut each skin into six strips, brush with butter, and season with salt and pepper. Place on baking racks or baking sheets.

4. Lower the oven to 350°F. Bake 15 to 20 minutes or until crisp and brown. Serve immediately.

▶ Baked potato skins can be saved and frozen; bake until crisp just before serving.

≡ *Herbed Toasts*

═ **Yield: 18 toasts**

¼ teaspoon minced parsley

¼ teaspoon minced tarragon

¼ teaspoon minced chervil

¼ teaspoon minced chives

½ cup butter, softened

salt and pepper, to taste

⅛ teaspoon minced garlic

18 thin slices French bread

═ **Yield: 72 toasts**

1 teaspoon minced parsley

1 teaspoon minced tarragon

1 teaspoon minced chervil

1 teaspoon minced chives

2 cups butter, softened

salt and pepper, to taste

½ teaspoon minced garlic

72 slices French bread

1. Preheat the oven to 350°F.

2. In a food processor, purée the parsley, tarragon, chervil, chives, butter, salt, pepper, and garlic until smooth.

3. Spread on the bread slices and bake until golden and crisp. Serve immediately.

▶ The butter can be prepared 2 to 3 days ahead. The bread can be spread with butter several hours before baking.

≡ *Basil, Tomato, and Feta Toasts*

== **Yield: 36 toasts**

1 large pita bread, split	extra virgin olive oil
36 basil leaves	pepper
½ cup crumbled feta cheese	
2 large tomatoes, peeled, seeded, and chopped	

== **Yield: 72 toasts**

2 large pita breads, split	extra virgin olive oil
72 basil leaves	pepper
1 cup crumbled feta cheese	
4 large tomatoes, peeled, seeded, and chopped	

1. Preheat the oven to 350°F.

2. Cut the bread into 2-inch squares. Place a basil leaf on each piece of bread and sprinkle on a little feta and a bit of tomato. Drizzle with olive oil and sprinkle with pepper.

3. Bake until the cheese melts and the bread starts to curl and crisp.

▶ Can be assembled 2 hours ahead.

≡ *Rolled Curried Toasts*

== **Yield: 8 toasts**

8 slices white bread, crusts removed	1 teaspoon curry powder, or to taste
¼ cup butter, softened	¼ cup melted butter

== **Yield: 72 toasts**

72 slices white bread, crusts removed	2 tablespoons curry powder, or to taste
1½ pounds butter, softened	1½ cups melted butter

1. Preheat the oven to 350°F.

2. Flatten the bread slices with a rolling pin.

3. In a food processor, cream the butter and curry powder and spread on the bread slices. Roll tightly and arrange on a baking sheet. Brush with melted butter.

4. Bake until golden, turning often.

▶ Can be assembled 24 hours ahead.

NOTE: This same method can be used with the herbed toasts (page 270).

≡ *Baked Eggplant Sandwiches*

═ **Yield: 24 servings**

2 small eggplants, cut in ¼-inch slices
salt
½ cup fine dry bread crumbs
2 tablespoons grated Parmesan cheese
2 tablespoons minced parsley

¼ pound provolone, thinly sliced
¼ pound mortadella, thinly sliced
1 egg, lightly beaten
2 tablespoons olive oil

═ **Yield: 72 servings**

6 small eggplants, cut in ¼-inch slices
salt
1½ cups fine dry bread crumbs
⅓ cup grated Parmesan cheese
⅓ cup minced parsley

¾ pound provolone, thinly sliced
¾ pound mortadella, thinly sliced
3 eggs, lightly beaten
⅓ cup olive oil

1. Salt the eggplant and drain in a colander with a 2-pound weight on top for 1 hour. Rinse slices, pat dry, and set aside.

2. Preheat the oven to 350°F.

3. In a bowl, mix the bread crumbs, Parmesan, and parsley.

4. Cut circles from the provolone and mortadella slightly smaller than the eggplant slices. Sandwich 1 slice of provolone and 1 slice of mortadella between 2 slices of eggplant. Dip each sandwich in the egg(s), then in the bread crumbs, and let rest on waxed paper.

5. Pour the olive oil in a baking sheet and heat in the oven for 5 minutes. Place the eggplant sandwiches on the sheet and bake 15 minutes on each side. Cut into bite-size servings. Serve hot or at room temperature.

▶ These can be assembled and coated the day before. Once baked they can be held at room temperature for 4 to 6 hours, but they are best fresh from the oven.

≡ *Garlic Toast*

═ Yield: 72 to 144 toasts

1 loaf French bread	1 tablespoon minced parsley
2 garlic cloves, halved	1 teaspoon paprika
½ cup melted butter	2 garlic cloves, crushed
¼ cup grated Parmesan cheese	

1. Preheat the oven to 350°F.

2. Rub the crust of the bread with the garlic halves. Cut the bread in half lengthwise and brush the inside with melted butter.

3. In a bowl, mix the cheese, parsley, paprika, and crushed garlic. Sprinkle evenly over the bread.

4. Bake for 5 to 10 minutes or until hot and just golden. Cut into ¼- to ½-inch slices. Serve immediately.

▶ Can be prepared for baking a day in advance.

NOTE: If you do not need as many toasts as the recipe provides, the extra cheese mixture can be sprinkled on salads or used as a topping for pasta.

≡ *Mushroom Toasts*

═ Yield: 24 toasts

½ pound mushrooms, minced	2 teaspoons minced parsley
2 shallots, minced	½ teaspoon salt
¼ cup butter	12 thin slices white bread,
3 tablespoons fresh bread crumbs	crusts removed

═ Yield: 72 toasts

1½ pounds mushrooms, minced	2 tablespoons minced parsley
1 cup minced shallots	1½ teaspoons salt
¾ cup butter	36 thin slices white bread,
½ cup fresh bread crumbs	crusts removed

1. Preheat the broiler.

2. In a skillet, sauté the mushrooms and shallots in the butter, stirring until the moisture evaporates. Mix in the bread crumbs, parsley, and salt.

3. Spread half the bread with the mushroom mixture. Top with the remaining bread slices. Cut into quarters and place on a baking sheet. Toast, turning once, until golden.

▶ Can be assembled 24 hours ahead. Broil just before serving.

≡ *Mushroom Finger Sandwiches*

Vary the flavor of these sandwiches with different types of breads: white, pumpernickel, rye, or whole grain, for example.

═ **Yield: 12 toasts**

¼ cup butter
3 tablespoons flour
½ cup chicken stock
½ cup heavy cream

salt and pepper, to taste
1½ cups minced mushrooms
9 thin slices bread, crusts
   removed

═ **Yield: 72 toasts**

1½ cups butter
1¼ cups flour
3 cups chicken stock
3 cups heavy cream
salt and pepper, to taste

4¼ pounds mushrooms,
   minced
54 thin slices bread, crusts
   removed

1. Preheat the oven to 400°F.
2. In a saucepan, melt two-thirds of the butter, stir in the flour, and cook until bubbly. Stir in the chicken stock and cream. Cook until thickened and smooth. Season with salt and pepper. Set aside.
3. In a skillet, sauté the mushrooms in the remaining butter until the liquid evaporates. Stir in the cream sauce.
4. Spread two-thirds of the bread slices with the mushroom mixture. Make three-layer sandwiches using two mushroom-topped slices and one plain slice. Cut each sandwich into quarters. Bake until golden.

▶ Can be assembled 24 hours ahead. Bake just before serving.

≡ *Crostini di Funghi (Italian Mushroom Toasts)*

═ **Yield: 48 toasts**

sliced white bread, cut into 48
   crescents
2 cups béchamel sauce
  (page 59)

¼ pound mushrooms, minced
1 tablespoon anchovy paste
grated Parmesan cheese, to
   taste

═ **Yield: 96 toasts**

sliced white bread, cut into 96
crescents
1 quart béchamel sauce
(page 59)

½ pound mushrooms, minced
2 tablespoons anchovy paste
grated Parmesan cheese,
to taste

1. Preheat the oven to 450°F.

2. Bake the crescents in a single layer until golden on top. Do not toast the other side. Set aside. Lower the oven to 400°F.

3. In a bowl, mix the béchamel sauce, mushrooms, and anchovy paste. Spread the untoasted sides of the crescents with the mushroom mixture and sprinkle with the grated cheese.

4. Heat until bubbly and brown. Serve immediately.

▶ The mushroom mixture can be made 2 days ahead. Toast the crescents shortly before assembling.

NOTE: The bread can be cut into any shape.

≡ *Poppy Seed Cubes*

═ **Yield: 50 toasts**

5 thick slices white or dark
bread, crusts removed

¾ cup melted butter
½ cup poppy seeds

═ **Yield: 100 toasts**

10 thick slices white or dark
bread, crusts removed

1½ cups melted butter
1 cup poppy seeds

1. Preheat the oven to 300°F.

2. Cut the bread into cubes and roll the cubes in the butter and then in the poppy seeds. Bake until golden and crisp, about 15 minutes.

▶ Can be made ahead and reheated.

≡ *Käseleckerbissen (Cheese Wedges)*

═ **Yield: 24 toasts**

2½ cups grated Gruyère cheese
½ cup butter, softened
½ cup ground ham
4 egg yolks
1 teaspoon dry mustard
salt, to taste

12 thin slices white bread,
crusts removed
oil for deep-frying
2 eggs, well beaten
1 cup dry bread crumbs
1 cup grated Parmesan cheese

== **Yield: 72 toasts**

7½ cups grated Gruyère cheese
1½ cups butter, softened
1½ cups ground ham
12 egg yolks
1 tablespoon dry mustard
salt, to taste

36 thin slices white bread,
   crusts removed
oil for deep-frying
6 eggs, well beaten
3 cups dry bread crumbs
3 cups grated Parmesan cheese

1. In a bowl, mix the Gruyère, butter, ham, egg yolks, mustard, and salt. Spread a ¼-inch layer on half the bread slices and cover with the remaining slices. Cut the sandwiches into wedges.

2. Heat the oil to 370°F. Dip the sandwiches into the eggs and then into the bread crumbs. Fry until golden and roll in the Parmesan cheese. Serve immediately.

▶ Can be assembled the day before.

≡ *Basler Käseschnitten (Basel Cheese Toasts)*

== **Yield: 20 toasts**

1 medium onion, thinly sliced
1 tablespoon butter

5 slices Emmenthaler cheese
5 slices buttered toast

== **Yield: 80 toasts**

1 quart thinly sliced onion
¼ cup butter

20 slices Emmenthaler cheese
20 slices buttered toast

1. Preheat the broiler.

2. In a skillet, sauté the onion in the butter over low heat, stirring often, until golden.

3. Cut the cheese to fit the toast, lay a slice on top, and broil until bubbly and golden. Trim the crusts from the toasts and cut into quarters. Top each toast with a little of the hot onion mixture. Serve immediately.

▶ The onions can be prepared ahead and reheated.

≡ *Cheddar Parsley Toasts*

═ **Yield: 16 toasts**

¼ cup butter, softened
¼ cup grated Cheddar cheese
¼ cup minced parsley
2 teaspoons minced green
   pepper

2 teaspoons Dijon mustard
4 slices bread, crusts removed

═ **Yield: 64 toasts**

1 cup butter, softened
1 cup grated Cheddar cheese
1 cup minced parsley
3 tablespoons minced green
   pepper

3 tablespoons Dijon mustard
16 slices bread, crusts removed

1. Preheat the broiler.

2. In a bowl, cream the butter, cheese, parsley, green pepper, and mustard. Spread on the bread slices and cut into fingers, squares, or triangles.

3. Broil until golden. Serve immediately.

▶ Can be assembled several hours ahead. Broil just before serving.

≡ *Friar's Toast*

═ **Yield: 24 toasts**

6 slices bacon, cooked until
   crisp and crumbled
1 cup grated Cheddar cheese
Worcestershire sauce, to taste

6 slices toast
72 pickled onion rings
5 tablespoons grated Cheddar
   cheese

═ **Yield: 72 toasts**

½ pound bacon, cooked until
   crisp and crumbled
1 quart grated Cheddar cheese
2 tablespoons Worcestershire
   sauce, or to taste

18 slices toast
216 pickled onion rings
1 cup grated Cheddar cheese

1. Preheat the broiler.

2. In a bowl, mix the bacon with the first measure of cheese and Worcestershire sauce. Spread thickly on the toast and top with overlapping slices of pickled onion rings. Sprinkle with the remaining cheese and broil until the cheese melts. Cut into quarters to serve. Serve immediately.

▶ Can be assembled 1 day ahead. Broil just before serving.

☰ *Gorgonzola Canapés*

══ **Yield: 48 toasts**

48 slices French bread or
cocktail rye
6 ounces imported Gorgonzola
cheese
¼ pound butter, softened

½ teaspoon crushed celery
seed
salt and pepper, to taste
⅓ cup finely chopped pecans

══ **Yield: 96 toasts**

96 slices French bread or
cocktail rye
¾ pound imported Gorgonzola
cheese

½ pound butter, softened
1 teaspoon crushed celery seed
salt and pepper, to taste
⅔ cup finely chopped pecans

1. Preheat the broiler.
2. Toast the bread slices on one side.
3. In a food processor, purée the cheese, butter, celery seed, salt, and pepper. Spread on the untoasted side of the bread and sprinkle with pecans. Broil until bubbly. Serve immediately.

▶ Can be assembled several hours ahead. Broil just before serving.

☰ *Tartines Fribourgeoise (Fribourg Cheese Toasts)*

══ **Yield: 24 toasts**

2 teaspoons butter
1 tablespoon flour
½ cup milk
salt and pepper, to taste
1 egg
½ pound Gruyère cheese,
grated

¼ teaspoon grated nutmeg
pinch of cayenne pepper
2 tablespoons white wine
¾ teaspoon minced garlic
12 slices French bread

══ **Yield: 72 toasts**

2 tablespoons butter
3 tablespoons flour
1½ cups milk
salt and pepper, to taste
3 eggs
1½ pounds Gruyère cheese,
grated

¾ teaspoon grated nutmeg
¼ teaspoon cayenne pepper
⅓ cup white wine
2½ teaspoons minced garlic
36 slices French bread

1. Preheat the oven to 400°F.

2. In a saucepan, melt the butter, stir in the flour, and cook until bubbly and golden. Add the milk and cook, stirring, until thickened and smooth. Season with salt and pepper.

3. Stir in the egg(s), cheese, nutmeg, cayenne, wine, and garlic.

4. Toast the bread on both sides. Spread the cheese on one side and bake until it turns golden. Cut the slices in half. Serve immediately.

▶ The cheese spread can be made 3 days ahead. Toast the bread, assemble, and bake just before serving.

≡ *Diablotin (Spiced Cheese Toasts)*

═ **Yield: 16 toasts**

6 ounces grated Gruyère cheese	pinch of cayenne pepper
2 eggs, lightly beaten	4 slices white toast
pinch of paprika	

═ **Yield: 64 toasts**

1½ pounds grated Gruyère cheese	½ teaspoon paprika
	½ teaspoon cayenne pepper
8 eggs, lightly beaten	16 slices white toast

1. Preheat the oven to 400°F.

2. In a bowl, mix the cheese, eggs, paprika, and cayenne. Spread a layer about ¼ inch thick on the toast.

3. Bake 15 minutes or until bubbly. Trim the crusts and cut into triangles. Serve immediately.

▶ Cheese mixture can be prepared the day before. Spread on bread and toast just before serving.

≡ *Parmesan Cubes*

These are baked cheese-flavored French toast.

═ **Yield: 36 toasts**

4 thick slices bread, crusts removed	2 drops Tabasco sauce
	¼ cup melted butter, cooled
1 egg	⅓ cup grated Parmesan cheese

══ **Yield: 72 toasts**

8 thick slices bread, crusts
  removed
2 eggs

4 drops Tabasco sauce
½ cup melted butter, cooled
⅔ cup grated Parmesan cheese

1. Preheat the oven to 350°F.

2. Cut each bread slice into 9 cubes. Beat the egg(s) with the Tabasco sauce and butter. Toss the cubes in the egg mixture and roll in the cheese. Place on a well-buttered baking sheet and bake 15 minutes or until golden. Serve immediately.

▶ Can be prepared for baking 4 hours ahead.

══ *Parmesan Beer Croutons*

══ **Yield: 36 toasts**

4 slices day-old bread, crusts
  removed
1 cup cold beer

1 cup grated Parmesan cheese
pinch of cayenne pepper
¼ cup melted butter

══ **Yield: 72 toasts**

8 slices day-old bread, crusts
  removed
2 cups cold beer

2 cups grated Parmesan cheese
⅛ teaspoon cayenne pepper
½ cup melted butter

1. Preheat the oven to 450°F.

2. Cut the bread slices into 1-inch cubes. In a bowl, mix the cheese and cayenne. Dip the cubes in the beer, roll in the cheese, and sprinkle with the butter.

3. Bake 10 minutes or until golden. Serve immediately.

▶ Prepare just before serving.

══ *Tomato Cheese Rounds*

══ **Yield: 48 toasts**

48 bread rounds, cut the
  diameter of the tomatoes
½ cup grated sharp Cheddar
  cheese
⅓ cup mayonnaise
¼ cup minced scallions
3 tablespoons minced green
  pepper

pinch of salt
pinch of cayenne pepper
mayonnaise for spreading
48 tomato slices
4 slices bacon, cut into ¼-inch
  pieces
paprika

Yield: 96 toasts

96 bread rounds, cut the
  diameter of the tomatoes
1 cup grated sharp Cheddar
  cheese
⅔ cup mayonnaise
½ cup minced scallions
⅓ cup minced green pepper

¼ teaspoon salt
¼ teaspoon cayenne pepper
mayonnaise for spreading
96 tomato slices
8 slices bacon, cut into ¼-inch
  pieces
paprika

1. Preheat the broiler.

2. Toast the bread rounds on one side and set aside.

3. In a bowl, mix the cheese, mayonnaise, scallions, green pepper, salt, and cayenne. Spread the untoasted sides of the bread with the additional mayonnaise and top with a tomato slice and 1 teaspoon of the cheese mixture.

4. Top each toast with a piece of bacon and a dash of paprika.

5. Broil until bubbly. Serve immediately.

▶ Assemble tomato slices, cheese, and bacon up to 6 hours ahead. Toast bread, assemble, and broil just before serving.

Mozzarella Anchovy Toasts

Yield: 24 toasts

¼ pound mozzarella cheese,
  grated
¼ pound butter, softened
1 ounce anchovy fillets, drained
  and minced

1 tablespoon lemon juice
1 tablespoon minced parsley
½ teaspoon minced garlic
salt and pepper, to taste
24 slices French bread

Yield: 72 toasts

¾ pound mozzarella cheese,
  grated
¾ pound butter, softened
3 ounces anchovy fillets,
  drained and minced

3 tablespoons lemon juice
3 tablespoons minced parsley
1½ teaspoons minced garlic
salt and pepper, to taste
72 slices French bread

1. Preheat the broiler.

2. In a bowl, mix the mozzarella, butter, anchovies, lemon juice, parsley, garlic, salt, and pepper.

3. Toast one side of the bread and spread the untoasted side with the cheese mixture. Broil until bubbly.

▶ The cheese mixture can be made 3 days ahead. Assemble and broil just before serving.

≡ *Broiled Clams with Garlic Butter*

≡ Yield: 12 toasts

2 tablespoons butter
¼ teaspoon minced garlic
1 teaspoon minced parsley

salt and pepper, to taste
12 2-inch bread rounds
12 littleneck clams, shucked

≡ Yield: 72 toasts

¾ cup butter
1½ teaspoons minced garlic
2 tablespoons minced parsley

salt and pepper, to taste
72 2-inch bread rounds
72 littleneck clams, shucked

1. Preheat the broiler.

2. In a food processor, cream the butter and garlic. Add the parsley, salt, and pepper.

3. Lightly toast one side of the bread rounds. Spread the garlic butter on the untoasted side and place a clam on the buttered side. Put a dab of butter on each clam.

4. Broil until hot. Serve immediately.

▶ The butter can be made the day before. Shuck the clams, toast the bread, and assemble just before serving.

≡ *Clam and Beer Appetizers*

≡ Yield: 18 toasts

¼ cup melted butter
¼ cup fresh bread crumbs
2 tablespoons beer
¼ cup minced onion
2 garlic cloves, minced
1 tablespoon minced parsley

¼ teaspoon dried oregano
salt and pepper, to taste
2 6½-ounce cans minced clams
18 2½-inch toast rounds

≡ Yield: 72 toasts

1 cup melted butter
1 cup fresh bread crumbs
½ cup beer
1 cup minced onion
8 garlic cloves, minced

¼ cup minced parsley
1 teaspoon dried oregano
salt and pepper, to taste
1 48-ounce can minced clams
72 2½-inch toast rounds

1. Preheat the oven to 375°F. Lightly butter a baking sheet.

2. In a bowl, mix the butter, bread crumbs, beer, onion, garlic, parsley, oregano, salt, and pepper. Drain the clams, reserving the juice. Add the clams to the beer mixture and moisten with a little juice if too dry. Spread on the toast rounds.

3. Bake 10 minutes then broil until golden. Serve immediately.

▶ The clam mixture can be made the day before. Assemble and broil just before serving.

≡ *Crab Cakes I*

Although these are not toasts, they are similar in appearance. Either anchovy mayonnaise or red pepper watercress sauce can be served as an accompaniment.

═ Yield: 24 cakes

1 egg
2 tablespoons mayonnaise
½ teaspoon dry mustard
⅛ teaspoon cayenne pepper
⅛ teaspoon Tabasco sauce
½ teaspoon salt

½ teaspoon white pepper
1 pound crabmeat, picked over
3 tablespoons minced parsley
1½ tablespoons cracker crumbs
oil for frying
lemon wedges

═ Yield: 72 cakes

3 eggs
⅓ cup mayonnaise
1½ teaspoons dry mustard
½ teaspoon Cayenne pepper
½ teaspoon Tabasco sauce
1½ teaspoons salt
1½ teaspoons white pepper

3 pounds crabmeat, picked
over
½ cup minced parsley
⅓ cup cracker crumbs
oil for frying
lemon wedges

1. In a bowl, beat the egg(s), mayonnaise, mustard, cayenne, Tabasco sauce, salt, and pepper until combined. Mix in the crabmeat, parsley, and cracker crumbs.

2. Shape into small cakes about the size of a half dollar.

3. In a skillet, heat a thin layer of oil and cook the crab cakes until golden, turn, and cook on the other side. Drain on paper towels and keep warm in a 200°F oven if not serving immediately.

4. Serve plain or with anchovy mayonnaise or red pepper watercress sauce (page 49).

▶ Cakes can be prepared for cooking several hours ahead.

≡ *Crab Cakes II*

== **Yield: 24 cakes**

⅓ cup minced green pepper
⅓ cup minced onion
⅓ cup minced celery
1 tablespoon butter
1 pound crabmeat, picked over
½ cup dry bread crumbs

⅓ cup mayonnaise
1 egg white
⅛ teaspoon pepper
dash of Tabasco sauce
bread crumbs for coating
¼ cup melted butter

== **Yield: 72 cakes**

1 cup minced green pepper
1 cup minced onion
1 cup minced celery
3 tablespoons butter
3 pounds crabmeat, picked
   over
1½ cups dry bread crumbs

1 cup mayonnaise
3 egg whites
½ teaspoon pepper
¼ teaspoon Tabasco sauce
bread crumbs for coating
¾ cup melted butter

1. Preheat the oven to 425°F.

2. In a skillet, sauté the pepper, onion, and celery in the butter until soft. Cool.

3. Line baking sheets with waxed paper.

4. In a bowl, combine the vegetable mixture, crabmeat, dry bread crumbs, mayonnaise, egg whites, pepper, and Tabasco sauce. Shape into patties about the size of a half-dollar and twice as thick. Coat with bread crumbs and chill for several hours.

5. Arrange the crab cakes on lightly buttered baking sheets and drizzle with the melted butter. Bake until crisp and golden, 5 to 7 minutes. Drain on paper towels and serve.

▶ Can be prepared for baking the day before.

≡ *Deviled Crabmeat Toasts*

== **Yield: 18 toasts**

½ pound crabmeat, flaked
½ tablespoon minced parsley
½ tablespoon minced chives
¼ teaspoon dried tarragon
Tabasco sauce, to taste

salt and pepper, to taste
3 tablespoons mayonnaise
1 teaspoon dry mustard
1 teaspoon white wine
18 crackers or toast rounds

=== **Yield: 72 toasts**

2 pounds crabmeat, flaked
2 tablespoons minced parsley
2 tablespoons minced chives
1 teaspoon dried tarragon
Tabasco sauce, to taste

salt and pepper, to taste
¾ cup mayonnaise
1 tablespoon dry mustard
4 teaspoons white wine
72 crackers or toast rounds

1. Preheat the broiler.

2. In a bowl, mix the crabmeat, parsley, chives, tarragon, Tabasco sauce, salt, pepper, mayonnaise, mustard, and wine.

3. Spread on the crackers and broil until heated through. Serve immediately.

▶ The crab mixture can be made a day ahead. Assemble and broil just before serving.

≡ *Finnan Haddie Toasts*

=== **Yield: 24 toasts**

2 tablespoons butter
2 tablespoons flour
⅔ cup light cream
1 cup cooked finnan haddie, flaked
½ teaspoon lemon juice

salt and pepper, to taste
6 slices bread, toasted
6 tablespoons bread crumbs
2 tablespoons melted butter
lemon wedges

=== **Yield: 72 toasts**

⅓ cup butter
⅓ cup flour
3 cups light cream
1½ pounds cooked finnan haddie, flaked
1½ teaspoons lemon juice

salt and pepper, to taste
18 slices bread, toasted
1¼ cups bread crumbs
⅓ cup melted butter
lemon wedges

1. Preheat the broiler.

2. In a saucepan, melt the butter, stir in the flour, and cook until the mixture is bubbly. Stir in the cream and cook until the mixture is thick and smooth. Fold in the finnan haddie, lemon juice, salt, and pepper.

3. Spread the fish mixture on the toast and cut into triangles.

4. In a bowl, mix the bread crumbs and melted butter and sprinkle over the fish. Serve with lemon wedges.

▶ The mixture can be made the day before. Toast the bread and assemble just before serving.

≡ *Hot Lobster Toasts*

══ Yield: 18 toasts

½ pound cooked lobster, minced
1 tablespoon grated horseradish
2 tablespoons minced black olives

salt, to taste
mayonnaise
18 2-inch bread rounds
¼ cup grated Parmesan cheese

══ Yield: 72 toasts

2 pounds cooked lobster, minced
¼ cup grated horseradish
½ cup minced black olives

salt, to taste
mayonnaise
72 2-inch bread rounds
¾ cup grated Parmesan cheese

1. Preheat the oven to 375°F.

2. In a bowl, mix the lobster, horseradish, olives, salt, and enough mayonnaise to bind.

3. Spread on the bread rounds and sprinkle with Parmesan cheese. Bake for 10 minutes or until bread is lightly golden around the edges. Serve hot.

▶ The lobster mixture can be made the day before. Assemble and bake shortly before serving.

≡ *Smoked Mussel Toasts*

══ Yield: 16 toasts

3 tablespoons butter
1 garlic clove, minced
1 can smoked mussels, minced
1 tablespoon minced parsley
salt and pepper, to taste

4 thick slices bread, crusts removed
lemon slices
parsley sprigs

══ Yield: 64 toasts

¾ cup butter
4 garlic cloves, minced
4 cans smoked mussels, minced
¼ cup minced parsley

salt and pepper, to taste
16 thick slices bread, crusts removed
lemon slices
parsley sprigs

1. Preheat the oven to 350°F.

2. In a saucepan, melt the butter and simmer the garlic, without browning, for 3 minutes. Add the mussels and parsley and stir gently for 1 minute. Correct the seasoning with salt and pepper. Remove from heat and let cool.

3. Spread on bread and bake until heated. Cut into squares, fingers, or triangles. Garnish each toast with part of a lemon slice and a parsley sprig.

▶ The mussel mixture can be made 2 days before. Assemble and bake just before serving.

≡ *Oyster Roquefort Toasts*

═ Yield: 18 toasts

18 2-inch bread rounds	½ cup Roquefort cheese
¾ cup butter	½ cup butter
1 tablespoon anchovy paste	pepper, to taste
1 pint shucked, undrained oysters	

═ Yield: 72 toasts

72 2-inch bread rounds	2 cups Roquefort cheese
3 cups butter	2 cups butter
¼ cup anchovy paste	pepper, to taste
1 quart shucked, undrained oysters	

1. Preheat the broiler. Toast the bread on one side.

2. In a food processor, cream the butter and anchovy paste. Spread the butter on the untoasted side of the bread.

3. In a saucepan, poach the oysters in their own juices just until the edges begin to curl. Drain the oysters and place one on each bread round.

4. In a food processor, cream the Roquefort cheese, butter, and pepper. Put a bit of Roquefort butter on each oyster and broil until bubbly. Serve immediately.

▶ The butters can be made 2 days ahead. Assemble and broil just before serving.

NOTE: The number of oysters in a pint depends on their size. Half-pints can contain as few as 6 large oysters and as many as 20 small ones. If the oysters are very large, cut them into halves or quarters.

≡ Sardine Puffs

═ Yield: 16 toasts

2 egg whites, beaten until stiff	salt and pepper, to taste
1 cup mayonnaise	4 slices white toast
2 cans sardines, mashed	paprika

═ Yield: 64 toasts

8 egg whites, beaten until stiff	salt and pepper, to taste
1 quart mayonnaise	16 slices white toast
8 cans sardines, mashed	paprika

1. Preheat the broiler.

2. In a bowl, fold the beaten egg whites into the mayonnaise and sardines. Season with salt and pepper.

3. Spread on the toast slices. Cut into quarters and sprinkle with paprika. Broil until puffed and golden, about 3 minutes.

▶ Assemble just before broiling.

≡ Curried Shrimp and Cheese Toasts

For a different flavor, substitute crabmeat or even sardines for the shrimp.

═ Yield: 24 toasts

¼ pound tiny shrimp, cooked and peeled	½ cup mayonnaise
3 ounces cream cheese, softened	¼ cup diced green olives
	2 tablespoons minced onion
¼ cup grated sharp Cheddar cheese	2 tablespoons minced chives
	1 teaspoon curry powder
½ cup grated Parmesan cheese	24 slices French bread

═ Yield: 72 toasts

¾ pound tiny shrimp, cooked and peeled	1½ cups mayonnaise
½ pound cream cheese, softened	¾ cup diced green olives
	⅓ cup minced onion
¾ cup grated sharp Cheddar cheese	⅓ cup minced chives
	1 tablespoon curry powder
1½ cups grated Parmesan cheese	72 slices French bread

1. Preheat the broiler.

2. In a bowl, mix the shrimp, cream cheese, Cheddar, Parmesan, mayonnaise, olives, onion, chives, and curry powder.

3. Toast the bread on one side. Spread the shrimp mixture on the untoasted side and brown under the broiler. Serve immediately.

▶ The shrimp mixture can be prepared 2 days before. Assemble just before broiling.

☰ *Crostini di Formaggio e Gamberetti (Shrimp and Cheese Toasts)*

═ **Yield: 24 toasts**

½ cup grated Parmesan cheese	1 teaspoon Cognac
2 tablespoons butter, softened	½ pound shrimp, cooked,
pinch of salt and pepper	shelled, and chopped
¼ cup heavy cream	6 slices bread, crusts removed

═ **Yield: 72 toasts**

1½ cups grated Parmesan cheese	¾ cup heavy cream
	1 tablespoon Cognac
⅓ cup butter, softened	1½ pounds shrimp, cooked,
½ teaspoon salt	shelled, and chopped
½ teaspoon pepper	18 slices bread, crusts removed

1. Preheat the oven to 350°F.

2. In a food processor, purée the cheese, butter, salt, pepper, cream, and Cognac. Add the shrimp and incorporate with a few on-off turns, or transfer to a bowl and fold in the shrimp. (The shrimp should remain in chunks; do not purée.)

3. Toast the bread on one side and spread the untoasted side with the shrimp. Cut into triangles and heat in the oven for 5 minutes.

▶ The shrimp mixture can be made several days ahead. Toast the bread, assemble, and bake just before serving.

≡ *Hot Shrimp Toasts*

═ Yield: 24 toasts

1 pound shrimp, cooked,
shelled, and chopped
2 tablespoons heavy cream
2 tablespoons fresh bread
crumbs
1 to 2 tablespoons butter,
softened
1 egg
1 teaspoon lemon juice

1 teaspoon Worcestershire
sauce
½ teaspoon dry mustard
¼ teaspoon salt
cayenne pepper, to taste
12 thin slices white bread
3 eggs, well beaten
oil for frying

═ Yield: 72 toasts

3 pounds shrimp, cooked,
shelled, and chopped
⅓ cup heavy cream
⅓ cup fresh bread crumbs
⅓ cup butter, softened
3 eggs
1 tablespoon lemon juice
1 tablespoon Worcestershire
sauce

1½ teaspoons dry mustard
¾ teaspoon salt
¼ teaspoon cayenne pepper, or
to taste
36 thin slices white bread
9 eggs, well beaten
oil for frying

1. In a bowl, blend the shrimp, cream, bread crumbs, butter, eggs, lemon juice, Worcestershire sauce, mustard, salt, and cayenne pepper to a soft, spreadable consistency.

2. Spread half the bread slices thickly with the shrimp mixture and cover with remaining bread. Trim crusts and cut into quarters.

3. Heat the oil to 375°F.

4. Dip the sandwiches in the beaten egg and fry on both sides until golden.

▶ The shrimp filling can be made 2 days before and the sandwiches assembled the day before. Dip and fry just before serving.

Note: Be sure to use very thinly sliced bread. The type sold as ''diet'' bread is the right thickness.

☰ *Chinese Shrimp Toast*

This is a standard from a dim sum menu that has universal appeal.

═ Yield: 24 toasts

1 recipe shrimp paste
  (page 693)
6 water chestnuts, minced
2 teaspoons minced parsley
6 slices white bread, crusts
  removed

oil for frying
salt and pepper, to taste
duck or plum sauce
Chinese mustard (page 73)

═ Yield: 72 toasts

3 recipes shrimp paste
  (page 693)
1 cup minced water chestnuts
2 tablespoons minced parsley
18 slices white bread, crusts
  removed

oil for frying
salt and pepper, to taste
duck or plum sauce
Chinese mustard (page 73)

1. Prepare the shrimp paste and mix in the water chestnuts and parsley. Spread the mixture generously on the bread slices, mounding it in the center. Cut into squares or triangles.
2. Heat the oil to 375°F. Fry the toasts until golden on both sides. Drain and season lightly with salt and pepper. Serve with the sauces.

▶ These can be assembled the day before, or assembled and frozen. Fry and serve immediately.
NOTE: Chicken can be substituted for the shrimp in the shrimp paste recipe. You can also flavor the paste with curry powder.

☰ *Escargots with Wild Mushrooms*

═ Yield: 24 toasts

2 garlic cloves, minced
1 shallot, minced
3 tablespoons butter
½ pound wild mushrooms,
  minced
1 tablespoon lemon juice
4 tablespoons mixed minced
  thyme, basil, and parsley

¼ cup dry vermouth
2 tablespoons hazelnut liqueur
2 cups heavy cream
salt and pepper, to taste
24 snails, rinsed and drained
24 slices French bread, sautéed
  in butter
¼ cup grated Parmesan cheese

== **Yield: 72 toasts**

6 garlic cloves, minced
⅓ cup minced shallot
½ cup butter
1½ pounds wild mushrooms, minced
3 tablespoons lemon juice
¾ cup mixed minced thyme, basil, and parsley

¾ cup dry vermouth
⅓ cup hazelnut liqueur
4 cups heavy cream
salt and pepper, to taste
72 snails, rinsed and drained
72 slices French bread, sautéed in butter
¾ cup grated Parmesan cheese

1. Preheat the oven to 350°F.

2. In a skillet, sauté the garlic and shallot in the butter until soft but not brown. Add the mushrooms and cook over high heat for 2 minutes. Add the lemon juice, herbs, vermouth, and hazelnut liqueur. Reduce by one-fourth. Add the cream and reduce, stirring, until it is thick enough to coat the back of a spoon. Season with salt and pepper.

3. Place a snail on top of each bread slice and coat lightly with the sauce and a sprinkling of Parmesan cheese. Bake for 8 to 10 minutes or until the cheese is golden.

▶ The sauce can be prepared the day before. Assemble and heat just before serving.

NOTE: If the snails are large, cut into halves or quarters.

≡ *Crostini di Fegatini di Pollo (Chicken Livers on Toast)*

This is one version of an Italian favorite. The toasts often accompany roast chicken.

== **Yield: 24 toasts**

4 teaspoons olive oil
2 tablespoons butter
2 tablespoons minced ham fat
⅓ cup minced onion
½ pound chicken livers, chopped

1 stalk sage
salt and pepper, to taste
lemon juice, to taste
4 teaspoons grated Parmesan cheese
6 slices toast

== **Yield: 72 toasts**

4 tablespoons olive oil
½ cup butter
½ cup minced ham fat
1 cup minced onion
1½ pounds chicken livers,
  chopped

3 stalks sage
salt and pepper, to taste
lemon juice, to taste
3 tablespoons grated Parmesan
  cheese
18 slices toast

1. Preheat the oven to 350°F.

2. In a skillet, heat the oil, butter, and ham fat, and sauté the onion until golden brown.

3. Add the livers and sage. Season with salt and pepper and cook over low heat until medium. Add a few drops of lemon juice and the cheese and discard the sage.

4. Spread on the toast and drizzle with the oil in the pan. Heat in the oven until hot.

▶ The livers can be prepared the day before. Assemble and reheat just before serving.

≡ *Grilled Chicken Liver Crostini*

These can be prepared in a broiler, but the best flavor is brought out by grilling over a wood fire.

== **Yield: 24 toasts**

½ pound chicken livers
1 onion, thickly sliced
2 large shiitake mushrooms,
  stems removed
extra virgin olive oil
2 garlic cloves, thinly sliced
¼ cup butter, softened
2 tablespoons grated Parmesan
  cheese

¾ teaspoon minced sage
¼ teaspoon minced rosemary
¼ teaspoon minced gingerroot
salt, to taste
24 slices French bread, toasted
grated Parmesan cheese

═ **Yield: 72 toasts**

1½ pounds chicken livers
3 onions, thickly sliced
6 large shiitake mushrooms,
  stems removed
extra virgin olive oil
6 garlic cloves, thinly sliced
¾ cup butter, softened

⅓ cup grated Parmesan cheese
2 teaspoons minced sage
1 teaspoon minced rosemary
1 teaspoon minced gingerroot
salt, to taste
72 slices French bread, toasted
grated Parmesan cheese

1. Preheat the grill. Preheat the oven to 350°F.

2. Skewer the chicken livers together and brush the livers, onions, and mushrooms with the olive oil. Grill until the livers are rare, the onions are charred and tender, and the mushrooms are softened.

3. In a skillet, brown the garlic in 1 to 2 tablespoons olive oil.

4. Coarsely chop the livers and mushrooms and mince the onion slices.

5. In a bowl, mix the garlic, livers, mushrooms, onion, butter, cheese, sage, rosemary, gingerroot, and salt.

6. Spread on the toast and sprinkle with additional cheese. Heat in the oven until hot.

▶ The mushroom mixture can be prepared the day before. Assemble and reheat just before serving.

≡ *Mushroom Chicken Liver Toasts*

═ **Yield: 18 toasts**

¼ pound chicken livers
¼ cup milk
¼ cup butter
¼ pound mushrooms, minced
dash of Tabasco sauce

1 teaspoon grated onion
salt and pepper, to taste
6 slices bacon, diced
18 2-inch bread rounds,
  buttered

═ **Yield: 72 toasts**

1 pound chicken livers
1 cup milk
½ pound butter
1 pound mushrooms, minced
¼ teaspoon Tabasco sauce

1 tablespoon grated onion
salt and pepper, to taste
18 slices bacon, diced
72 2-inch bread rounds,
  buttered

1. Preheat the oven to 350°F.

2. Marinate the chicken livers in the milk for 30 minutes. Drain and discard the milk. Dry the liver on paper towels.

3. In a skillet, melt the butter and sauté the livers until rare. Remove from the pan and mince.

4. Add the mushrooms to the skillet and sauté until the juices evaporate. Add the liver, Tabasco sauce, and onion, and season with salt and pepper.

5. In a skillet, sauté the bacon until crisp. Drain and crumble.

6. Spread the liver mixture on the bread rounds and sprinkle with the bacon. Heat in the oven until the edges of the toasts start to turn golden.

▶ The liver mixture can be made several days ahead. Assemble and heat just before serving.

☰ *Roman Liver Toasts*

═ **Yield: 24 toasts**

¼ cup butter	salt and pepper, to taste
¼ cup minced onion	24 slices French bread
½ pound chicken livers	minced parsley
pinch of marjoram	

═ **Yield: 72 toasts**

1 cup butter	salt and pepper, to taste
1 cup minced onion	72 slices French bread
2 pounds chicken livers	minced parsley
1 teaspoon marjoram	

1. Preheat the oven to 400°F.

2. In a skillet, melt the butter and sauté the onion until soft. Add the chicken livers and sauté until medium. Season with the marjoram, salt, and pepper.

3. In a food processor, purée the liver mixture and pan juices.

4. Toast the bread slices on one side and spread the untoasted side with the liver paste. Heat in the oven for 5 minutes. Sprinkle with parsley and serve.

▶ The liver mixture can be made several days ahead. Assemble and heat just before serving.

≡ *Swiss Bacon and Mushroom Toasts*

= **Yield: 24 toasts**

2½ cups grated Gruyère cheese
⅔ cup heavy cream
12 slices bread, crusts removed
¼ pound mushrooms, thinly
  sliced
2 tablespoons butter

2 tablespoons lemon juice
12 slices bacon, cooked
4 eggs
⅔ cup milk
½ cup butter

= **Yield: 72 toasts**

7½ cups grated Gruyère cheese
2 cups heavy cream
36 slices bread, crusts removed
¾ pound mushrooms, thinly
  sliced
⅓ cup butter

⅓ cup lemon juice
36 slices bacon, cooked
12 eggs
2 cups milk
1½ cups butter

1. In a bowl, mix the cheese and cream and spread on the bread slices.
2. In a skillet, sauté the mushrooms in the butter. Add the lemon juice. Put 2 bacon slices and 1 to 2 tablespoons of the mushrooms on half the bread slices. Cover with the remaining bread slices, cheese side down.
3. In a bowl, beat the eggs and milk and dip the sandwiches into the egg mixture.
4. In a skillet, heat the remaining butter and sauté the sandwiches until brown on both sides. Cut into quarters.

▶ The sandwiches can be assembled the day before. Dip in the egg and cook just before serving.

≡ *Spinach and Ham Toasts*

= **Yield: 24 toasts**

2 tablespoons minced shallots
1 garlic clove, minced
1 tablespoon butter
½ pound spinach, cooked,
  squeezed dry, and minced
¼ teaspoon rosemary
grated nutmeg, to taste

salt and pepper, to taste
2 ounces cream cheese
¼ cup minced ham
½ teaspoon Dijon mustard
6 slices white toast, buttered
¼ cup grated Gruyère cheese

=== **Yield: 72 toasts**

⅓ cup minced shallots
2 garlic cloves, minced
3 tablespoons butter
1½ pounds spinach, cooked,
    squeezed dry, and minced
¾ teaspoon rosemary
grated nutmeg, to taste

salt and pepper, to taste
6 ounces cream cheese
¾ cup minced ham
1½ teaspoons Dijon mustard
18 slices white toast, buttered
¾ cup grated Gruyère cheese

1. Preheat the broiler.

2. In a skillet, sauté the shallots and garlic in the butter until soft. Add the spinach, rosemary, nutmeg, salt, and pepper. Cook until heated. Stir in the cream cheese, ham, and mustard, and cook until thickened and the cheese is melted.

3. Butter the toast and trim the crusts. Spread with the spinach and sprinkle with the Gruyère. Broil until bubbly. Cut into quarters.

▶ The spinach mixture can be made the day before. Assemble and broil just before serving.

≡ *Crostini Bagheria* *(Mozzarella, Prosciutto, and Tomato Toast)*

=== **Yield: 16 toasts**

8 thin slices Italian bread,
    toasted and cut in half
16 slices mozzarella cheese
16 slices prosciutto

16 slices tomato
16 strips roasted red pepper
2 tablespoons butter
½ teaspoon oregano

=== **Yield: 64 toasts**

32 thin slices Italian bread,
    toasted and cut in half
64 slices mozzarella cheese
64 slices prosciutto

64 slices tomato
64 strips roasted red pepper
½ cup butter
2 teaspoons oregano

1. Preheat the oven to 350°F.

2. Place the bread slices on a baking sheet. If necessary, trim the mozzarella, prosciutto, tomato, and pepper to fit bread. Lay a slice of mozzarella, prosciutto, tomato, and a pepper strip on top. Dot with butter and sprinkle with oregano. Bake 5 minutes.

▶ Can be assembled several hours ahead. Bake just before serving.

≡ *Crostini di Ricotta e Salsiccie* (*Cheese and Sausage Toasts*)

You can perk up the flavor of this toast by using hot Italian sausage instead of sweet. Italian Fontina has a completely different flavor from its imitators. It is important to use the real cheese.

═ Yield: 24 toasts

½ pound ricotta cheese
3 tablespoons cold water
½ teaspoon salt
¼ cup grated Parmesan cheese
3 sweet Italian sausages
⅓ cup olive oil

¼ cup butter
12 slices white bread, crusts removed
¼ pound Italian Fontina cheese, thinly sliced

═ Yield: 72 toasts

1½ pounds ricotta cheese
½ cup cold water
1½ teaspoons salt
¾ cup grated Parmesan cheese
9 sweet Italian sausages
1 cup olive oil

¾ cup butter
36 slices white bread, crusts removed
¾ pound Italian Fontina cheese, thinly sliced

1. Preheat the oven to 350°F.

2. In a bowl, mix the ricotta, water, salt, and Parmesan until smooth and creamy.

3. Prick the sausage skins and put into a skillet with ¼ inch of water. Cook over low heat until the water evaporates, then brown on all sides. Drain, peel, and chop finely. Add to the ricotta mixture.

4. In a skillet, heat the oil and butter and sauté the bread on one side until golden. Drain and keep hot. Spread the sautéed sides of the bread with the sausage mixture.

5. Trim the Fontina to the same size as the bread and place on top of the cheese-sausage mixture. Bake until the Fontina melts. Cut into squares, or triangles.

▶ The cheese-sausage mixture can be made a day ahead. Sauté the bread, assemble, and bake shortly before serving.

NOTE: For variation, add ½ to 1½ pounds minced sautéed mushrooms, flavored with a generous pinch of marjoram, to the cheese-sausage mixture.

≡ Sausage Toasts

═ Yield: 16 toasts

¼ pound sausage meat
1 egg
1 tablespoon minced parsley
½ teaspoon anchovy paste

oil for frying
4 slices white bread, crusts
  removed
minced parsley

═ Yield: 64 toasts

1 pound sausage meat
4 eggs
¼ cup minced parsley
2 teaspoons anchovy paste

oil for frying
16 slices white bread, crusts
  removed
minced parsley

1. Heat the oil to 375°F.

2. In a bowl, mix the sausage meat, egg(s), parsley, and anchovy paste. Spread the sausage mixture on the bread slices, mounding in the center. Cut into triangles. Fry until golden and cooked through, about 3 minutes. Sprinkle with parsley and serve immediately.

▶ Can be assembled the day before. Fry just before serving.

NOTE: Any variety of sausage works well in this recipe.

≡ Beef Emit Silk

═ Yield: 24 toasts

1½ pounds lean ground beef
5 scallions, minced
1 tablespoon brown sugar

2 teaspoons minced gingerroot
⅓ cup thin soy sauce
24 slices French bread

═ Yield: 72 toasts

4½ pounds lean ground beef
15 scallions, minced
3 tablespoons brown sugar

2 tablespoons minced gingerroot
1 cup thin soy sauce
72 slices French bread

1. Preheat the oven to 450°F.

2. In a bowl, beat the beef until smooth. Add the scallions, sugar, gingerroot, and soy sauce. Thickly spread the beef mixture on the bread. Bake for about 8 minutes or until medium rare. Cut in half and serve immediately.

▶ The meat mixture can be prepared several hours ahead. Assemble and bake just before serving.

NOTE: The toast can be broiled instead of baked.

= 8 =

Croquettes and Fritters

Croquettes, perhaps justifiably, suffer from bad press. They are disparaged because, unless they are prepared with care and with the freshest and best of ingredients, they can be quite awful. In the past, it was not uncommon for restaurants and hotels to prepare them from less-than-top-quality leftovers. Further, many cooks did not understand how to cook the basic sauce correctly and produced floury, heavy croquettes bathed in a thick, unpleasant sauce. Properly made with fine, fresh ingredients, croquettes are delicious. Although usually considered to be a main course, made small, they make a luscious hors d'oeuvre. In addition, because they are made with a sauce base, you do not need large quantities of the flavoring ingredient. Making croquettes is a good way to serve an expensive food such as lobster and yet keep within a budget.

Croquettes are simple. They consist of a base, a flavoring ingredient, and an egg–bread crumb coating. The base, a béchamel sauce for croquettes or sauce villeroi, can be made ahead and even frozen. The flavoring ingredients—cheese, meat, fish, or vegetables—are usually chopped finely and folded into the sauce base. The mixture is spread on a buttered platter, chilled for several hours, and then shaped into small corks, balls, sticks, or cones. The croquettes are coated, usually by first rolling in flour, then in beaten egg, and finally in bread crumbs. That is the à l'Anglaise coating. Some of the more delicate preparations require that the croquette be coated a second time. The coating must be allowed to set for at least 30 minutes in the refrigerator, but it can set for 24 to 36 hours, to its advantage. The prepared croquettes can be frozen at this stage. Once the coating has set, the croquettes are deep-fried until golden and served immediately. They can be held in a 250°F oven for a

301

short period, but they lose quality for every minute they wait. They can also be cooled, frozen, and reheated at 350°F, but they are never as wonderful as when freshly cooked.

For the lightest, most delicate croquettes, fresh bread crumbs are required; dried-out crumbs absorb too much moisture and cause the croquette to become heavy. Ideally, the bread should be a day old but not hard. Breads made without fat, such as French and Italian breads, can turn too dry overnight and should be used within 8 hours after baking. Remove the crusts and make the crumbs in a food processor. If it is necessary to keep the crumbs, store them in a freezer; they quickly turn moldy in the refrigerator. Beware of prepackaged crumbs. They usually contain the crusts, which turn dark more quickly and can make dark spots on the croquettes. Seasoned crumbs are not suitable for most croquette recipes.

The oil for deep-frying should be fresh and light. An unflavored oil, such as cottonseed, corn, peanut, or soybean, is preferred. Shortenings have too low a smoking point, as do butter and olive oil, and the latter has too strong a flavor. Oil that has been used for other purposes will give an off-flavor to the croquettes, so it is best to start with fresh oil. For large events, it may be necessary to change the oil one or more times. As soon as the oil stops browning the food nicely, or when too much of the coating falls into the oil and burns, it is time to change the oil. Be sure to fill the kettle no more than half full as the oil bubbles up when the food hits it and can catch fire if it splatters. For the best result, it is crucial to maintain the oil at the correct temperature. Fry the food in batches rather than crowding it, and always let the oil return to the proper temperature between batches. Drain the food on paper towels before serving. If it is fried properly, there will be little oil attached to the food.

Fritters are as delectable as croquettes and share the same problems in preparation. They must be served immediately after cooking. They do not hold at all, and a few minutes delay in serving can be the difference between delicious and disastrous. If you are making them for a few friends, you can cook a few and then pass them, but for a large crowd you need a cook tending to them principally and doing other things as time allows.

There are four types of fritter: (1) The ingredients are blended together to form a dough and fried in deep fat or in a thin layer of oil in a skillet. Some fritters of this kind can be made ahead. (2) The food is coated with a batter made with milk, water, or beer. Beer gives the lightest, crispiest coating, but it is not suitable for every food. These fritters must be served immediately after cooking. (3) English, or *à l'Anglaise,* coating is the same coating used on croquettes. The difference is that the food is not mixed with a sauce base first. (4) *Pâte à chou,* or cream puff pastry, is flavored with savory seasonings and deep-fried. (See Chapter 14 for some other fritter recipes.)

Presentation
Serve croquettes with a dipping sauce on the side, but not poured on top, or the coating will become soggy and guests will have a hard time trying to pick them up.

Serve all deep-fried foods immediately on warm platters lined with a napkin or paper doily—a cold platter will chill the food and make it seem greasy. After a platter has been passed, replace the doily. One method of presenting the food without showing any grease is to line the platters with sprigs of parsley and arrange the food on top. To be attractive, this requires using parsley with tight curls. Use only enough parsley to carpet the surface of the platter and not so much that the guests have to dig through it. Other greens, such as large flat leaves or bunches of kale, make attractive beds for the food.

Linen napkins are perfect, of course, if you change them as soon as they get soiled. A napkin horn arranged at one end of a platter with a fresh napkin on top makes an attractive presentation, especially if a flower is placed inside the horn.

—— *Croquettes* ——

≡ *Brie Balls*

═ **Yield: 24 croquettes**

1 cup béchamel sauce for croquettes (page 60)
¼ pound Brie cheese, rind removed
1½ ounces cream cheese

salt and pepper, to taste
flour for dredging
1 egg, lightly beaten
2 to 3 cups bread crumbs
oil for frying

═ **Yield: 72 croquettes**

3 cups béchamel sauce for croquettes (page 60)
¾ pound Brie cheese, rind removed
5 ounces cream cheese

salt and pepper, to taste
flour for dredging
3 eggs, lightly beaten
6 to 8 cups bread crumbs
oil for frying

1. In a saucepan over low heat, cook the béchamel, Brie, cream cheese, salt, and pepper, stirring until the cheese melts. Transfer to a baking sheet and spread ½ inch thick. Cover with waxed paper. Chill.

2. Shape into 1-inch balls and roll in the flour. Coat with egg and roll in the bread crumbs. Let coating set at least 30 minutes.

3. Heat the fat to 370°F and fry until golden.

▶ Can be prepared for frying 2 days in advance.

≡ *Croquettes de Camembert (Camembert Croquettes)*

═ Yield: 24 croquettes

2 small Camembert cheeses
½ cup sauce Normande (recipe
  follows)
½ cup crème fraîche or heavy
  cream

salt and pepper, to taste
½ cup flour
4 eggs, beaten
2 to 3 cups fresh bread crumbs
oil for frying

═ Yield: 72 croquettes

6 small Camembert cheeses
1½ cups sauce Normande
  (recipe follows)
1½ cups crème fraîche or
  heavy cream

salt and pepper, to taste
1½ cups flour
12 eggs, beaten
6 to 8 cups fresh bread crumbs
oil for frying

1. In a food processor, purée the Camembert, including the rind. Add the sauce Normande and the crème fraîche. Season with salt and pepper.

2. Chill the mixture and shape into bite-size balls. Roll balls in the flour, eggs, and bread crumbs. Let the coating set at least 30 minutes.

3. Heat the oil to 375°F and fry until golden. Serve immediately with the remaining warm sauce Normande for dipping.

▶ Can be prepared for frying 1 day in advance.

≡ *Sauce Normande*
(Apple-Flavored Cream Sauce from Normandy)

═ Yield: 2½ cups

1 tablespoon butter
¼ cup minced onion
2 tablespoons flour
2 cups cider
salt and pepper, to taste

pinch of grated nutmeg
7 tablespoons softened butter
½ cup heavy cream
1 tablespoon lemon juice

= **Yield: 7½ cups**

3 tablespoons butter
¾ cup minced onion
⅓ cup flour
6 cups cider
salt and pepper, to taste

¼ teaspoon grated nutmeg
1¼ cups softened butter
1½ cups heavy cream
3 tablespoons lemon juice

1. In a saucepan, melt the butter and sauté the onion until soft. Stir in the flour and cook until the roux just starts to turn golden.

2. Stir in the cider and cook, stirring, for 7 to 8 minutes, or until smooth, thickened, and the flour taste has cooked away. Season with salt, pepper, and nutmeg.

3. Whisk in the remaining butter in small bits. Add the cream and lemon juice.

▶ Can be made 1 day in advance and reheated.

NOTE: Serve the sauce with skewers of poached chicken and apple.

≡ *Hot Sherry Cheese Balls*

= **Yield: 24 croquettes**

1½ cups grated Cheddar or
  Gruyère cheese
1½ tablespoons flour
3 tablespoons sherry
salt, to taste
paprika, to taste

3 egg whites
cracker crumbs
oil for frying
grated Parmesan cheese,
  optional

= **Yield: 72 croquettes**

1 quart grated Cheddar or
  Gruyère cheese
¼ cup flour
½ cup sherry
salt, to taste
paprika, to taste

8 egg whites
cracker crumbs
oil for frying
grated Parmesan cheese,
  optional

1. In a bowl, mix the cheese, flour, sherry, salt, and paprika.

2. In another bowl, beat the egg whites until stiff but not dry. Fold into the cheese mixture and shape into balls.

3. Roll in the cracker crumbs and let set for at least 30 minutes.

4. Heat the oil to 375°F and fry until golden. Serve immediately, sprinkled with Parmesan, if desired.

▶ Can be prepared for frying 6 hours in advance.

≡ *Cheese Puffs*

= **Yield: 24 puffs**

¾ cup grated Gruyère cheese
2 cups hot béchamel sauce for
croquettes (page 60)

cayenne pepper, to taste
3 egg whites
oil for frying

= **Yield: 72 puffs**

1½ cups grated Gruyère cheese
1 quart hot béchamel sauce for
croquettes (page 60)

cayenne pepper, to taste
6 egg whites
oil for frying

1. Add the cheese to the béchamel and season with cayenne. Cool.

2. Beat the egg whites until stiff but not dry and fold into the sauce.

3. Heat the oil to 390°F and drop the cheese mixture from a teaspoon into the oil. Fry until golden. Serve warm.

▶ Prepare and serve immediately.

NOTE: For an interesting variation, fit a pastry bag with a no. 5 plain or grooved large pastry tip, fill with the croquette mixture, and pipe 1½-inch sections into the hot oil.

≡ *Croquettes Milanaise (Potato, Ham, and Cheese Croquettes)*

= **Yield: 24 croquettes**

2 large baking potatoes
1½ cups béchamel sauce for
croquettes (page 60)
¾ cup grated Gruyère cheese
½ cup ⅛-inch diced ham

salt and pepper, to taste
2 eggs, separated
1 cup bread crumbs
oil for deep frying

= **Yield: 72 croquettes**

6 large baking potatoes
4½ cups béchamel sauce for
croquettes (page 60)
2¼ cups grated Gruyère cheese
1½ cups ⅛-inch diced ham

salt and pepper, to taste
6 eggs, separated
3 cups bread crumbs
oil for frying

1. Peel the potatoes and boil in salted water until tender. Drain and mash.

2. In a bowl, mix the béchamel, potatoes, cheese, and ham. Correct the seasoning with salt and pepper. Beat in the egg yolks. Chill.

3. Beat the egg whites until frothy. Shape the chilled mixture, dip in the egg whites, and roll in the bread crumbs. Let set for at least 30 minutes, refrigerated.

4. Heat the oil to 375°F and fry until golden.

▶ Can be prepared 1 day in advance.

≡ *Gruyère Cheese Croquettes*

═ Yield: 40 croquettes

1 egg white	¼ cup flour
1 pound Gruyère cheese, grated	1 egg
2 tablespoons minced parsley	2 tablespoons milk
¼ teaspoon grated nutmeg	¾ cup fresh bread crumbs
½ teaspoon paprika	oil for frying

═ Yield: 80 croquettes

2 egg whites	½ cup flour
2 pounds Gruyère cheese, grated	2 eggs
¼ cup minced parsley	¼ cup milk
½ teaspoon grated nutmeg	1½ cups fresh bread crumbs
1 teaspoon paprika	oil for frying

1. Beat the egg white(s) until foamy. Mix in the cheese, parsley, nutmeg, and paprika. Chill 2 hours.

2. In a bowl, mix the flour, egg(s), and milk. Shape the cheese mixture into 1-inch balls and dip into the egg mixture. Roll in the bread crumbs. Refrigerate on a baking sheet for 12 hours or longer.

3. Heat the oil to 350°F and fry until golden.

▶ Can be prepared for frying 1 day in advance.

≡ *Croquettes au Fromage (Cheese-Filled Croquettes)*

== **Yield: 24 croquettes**

3 cups hot mashed potatoes	24 ½-inch cubes Gruyère
2 eggs	cheese
1 teaspoon salt	1 egg, lightly beaten
¼ teaspoon pepper	1 tablespoon milk
pinch of nutmeg	2 cups bread crumbs
¼ cup milk	oil for frying
½ cup grated Gruyère cheese	

== **Yield: 72 croquettes**

9 cups hot mashed potatoes	72 ½-inch cubes Gruyère
6 eggs	cheese
1 tablespoon salt	3 eggs, lightly beaten
¾ teaspoon pepper	3 tablespoons milk
¼ teaspoon nutmeg	6 cups bread crumbs
¾ cup milk	oil for frying
1½ cups grated Gruyère cheese	

1. In a bowl, mix the potatoes, egg(s), salt, pepper, nutmeg, milk, and grated cheese.

2. Shape a tablespoon or so of the mixture around a cheese cube to form a small ball. Chill.

3. Beat the remaining egg and milk together. Roll the croquettes in the bread crumbs, egg, and again in the bread crumbs. Let coating set for at least 30 minutes.

4. Heat the oil to 375°F and fry until golden.

▶ Can be prepared 1 day in advance.

≡ *Kaascroquetten (Dutch Cheese Croquettes)*

You can choose any semifirm cheese — Edam, Gouda, or Leerdam, for example — to use in this popular Dutch recipe.

== **Yield: 20 croquettes**

1 cup béchamel sauce for croquettes (page 60)	salt and pepper, to taste
	2 cups fresh bread crumbs
1½ cups grated semifirm cheese	2 eggs, lightly beaten
	oil for frying

═ Yield: 80 croquettes

1 quart béchamel sauce for croquettes (page 60)
1½ quarts grated semifirm cheese

salt and pepper, to taste
8 cups fresh bread crumbs
8 eggs, lightly beaten
oil for frying

1. In a saucepan, heat the béchamel and stir in the cheese until melted. Correct the seasoning with salt and pepper. Spread on a platter and chill.

2. Shape into croquettes. Roll in the bread crumbs, dip in the eggs, and roll in the bread crumbs again.

3. Heat the oil to 375°F and fry until golden.

▶ Can be prepared for frying 1 day in advance.

≡ *Mozzarella Croquettes*

═ Yield: 24 croquettes

½ pound mozzarella, grated
1 cup flour
1 egg

¼ teaspoon salt
pinch of cayenne pepper
¼ cup cornstarch

═ Yield: 72 croquettes

1½ pounds mozzarella, grated
3 cups flour
3 eggs

¾ teaspoon salt
¼ teaspoon cayenne pepper
¾ cup cornstarch

1. In a bowl, mix the cheese, half the flour, and the egg(s), salt, and cayenne and shape into 1-inch balls.

2. In another bowl, whisk the remaining flour and cornstarch together. Roll the balls in the flour mixture and chill for 30 minutes.

3. Heat the oil to 375°F and fry until golden.

▶ Can be prepared for frying 12 hours in advance.

≡ *Petites Fondues, Frites (Little Fried Croquettes)*

═ **Yield: 24 croquettes**

1 cup béchamel sauce for croquettes (page 60)	1 cup flour
1 cup grated Gruyère cheese	1 egg
1 cup grated Parmesan cheese	2 egg whites
½ teaspoon ground sage	1 tablespoon oil
salt and pepper, to taste	1 teaspoon water
nutmeg, to taste	2 cups fresh bread crumbs
	oil for frying

═ **Yield: 72 croquettes**

3 cups béchamel sauce for croquettes (page 60)	3 cups flour
3 cups grated Gruyère cheese	3 eggs
3 cups grated Parmesan cheese	6 egg whites
1½ teaspoons ground sage	3 tablespoons oil
salt and pepper, to taste	1 tablespoon water
¼ teaspoon nutmeg	6 cups fresh bread crumbs
	oil for frying

1. In a saucepan, bring the béchamel to a boil and beat in the Gruyère, Parmesan, sage, salt, pepper, and nutmeg. Spread on a lightly buttered baking sheet and cover with waxed paper. Chill.

2. Put the flour in a pie plate. In a bowl, beat the egg(s), egg whites, oil, and water. Put the bread crumbs in another pie plate.

3. Shape the chilled mixture into croquettes and roll in the flour, egg mixture, and bread crumbs. Chill for at least 30 minutes.

4. Heat the oil to 390°F and fry until golden.

▶ Can be prepared for frying 1 day in advance.

NOTE: The higher cooking temperature immediately sets the bread coating into a crisp crust that holds in the very creamy center.

≡ *Deep-Fried Cheese Balls I*

═ **Yield: 24 croquettes**

1 cup fresh bread crumbs	6 eggs, lightly beaten
½ pound Parmesan cheese, grated	1 tablespoon minced parsley
salt and pepper, to taste	1 cup flour
nutmeg, to taste	oil for frying
	tomato sauce (pages 63–65)

═ **Yield: 72 croquettes**

3 cups fresh bread crumbs	18 eggs, lightly beaten
1½ pounds Parmesan cheese, grated	3 tablespoons minced parsley
	3 cups flour
salt and pepper, to taste	oil for frying
nutmeg, to taste	tomato sauce (pages 63–65)

1. In a bowl, mix the bread crumbs, cheese, salt, pepper, nutmeg, half the eggs, and parsley. Shape into 1-inch balls.

2. Roll in the flour and dip in the remaining eggs.

3. Heat the oil to 390°F and fry until golden. Serve with a tomato sauce on the side.

▶ Can be prepared for dipping in the egg and frying 1 day in advance.

═ *Deep-Fried Cheese Balls II*

═ **Yield: 24 croquettes**

1 cup grated Parmesan cheese	cayenne pepper, to taste
¼ cup soft bread crumbs	fresh bread crumbs
1 egg, separated	oil for frying
¼ teaspoon Dijon mustard	fresh tomato sauce (page 63)
salt, to taste	

═ **Yield: 72 croquettes**

3 cups grated Parmesan cheese	cayenne pepper, to taste
¾ cup soft bread crumbs	fresh bread crumbs
3 eggs, separated	oil for frying
¾ teaspoon Dijon mustard	fresh tomato sauce (page 63)
salt, to taste	

1. In a bowl, mix the cheese, soft bread crumbs, egg yolk(s), mustard, salt, and cayenne. Beat the egg white(s) until stiff and fold into the cheese mixture.

2. Shape into balls and roll in the remaining bread crumbs.

3. Heat the oil to 390°F and fry until golden. Serve the sauce separately.

▶ Can be shaped and coated 1 day in advance. Fry just before serving.

≡ *Palle di Paste (Deep-Fried Fettuccine Balls)*

═ **Yield: 81 croquettes**

1½ cups béchamel sauce for
croquettes (page 60)
¼ cup grated Parmesan cheese
6 ounces fettuccine, cooked *al
dente*
2 eggs, lightly beaten

2 tablespoons water
salt and pepper, to taste
1½ cups bread crumbs
oil for frying
tomato sauce (pages 63–65)

═ **Yield: 162 croquettes**

3 cups béchamel sauce for
croquettes (page 60)
½ cup grated Parmesan cheese
12 ounces fettuccine, cooked *al
dente*
4 eggs, lightly beaten

¼ cup water
salt and pepper, to taste
3 cups bread crumbs
oil for frying
tomato sauce (pages 63–65)

1. Stir the béchamel, cheese, and fettuccine together and pour into one (for the smaller quantity) or two (for the larger quantity) buttered 9-inch square pans. Chill.

2. Cut each pan of fettuccine into 81 squares and shape into balls.

3. In a bowl, mix the eggs, water, salt, and pepper. Dip the balls into the eggs and roll in the bread crumbs. Let the coating set at least 30 minutes.

4. Heat the oil to 375°F and fry until golden. Serve a tomato sauce on the side.

▶ Can be prepared for frying 1 day in advance.

≡ *Falafel I (Chickpea Croquettes I)*

═ **Yield: 24 croquettes**

2 cups canned chickpeas,
drained
1 teaspoon salt
¼ teaspoon white pepper
¼ teaspoon cayenne pepper
¼ teaspoon dried basil,
marjoram, or thyme

2 tablespoons fresh bread
crumbs
1 egg, lightly beaten
1 tablespoon olive oil
flour
oil for frying

=== **Yield: 72 croquettes**

1½ quarts canned chickpeas,
drained
1 tablespoon salt
¾ teaspoon white pepper
¾ teaspoon cayenne pepper
¾ teaspoon dried basil,
marjoram, or thyme

⅓ cup fresh bread crumbs
3 eggs, lightly beaten
3 tablespoons olive oil
flour
oil for frying

1. Purée the chickpeas in a food processor with the salt, white pepper, cayenne, basil, and bread crumbs.

2. With the machine running, add the egg(s) and oil. Shape into croquettes and roll in the flour.

3. Heat the oil to 370°F and fry until golden.

► Can be prepared for frying 1 day in advance.

≡ *Falafel II (Chickpea Croquettes II)*

=== **Yield: 24 croquettes**

1 cup dried chickpeas
1 teaspoon salt
1 egg, beaten
2 teaspoons ground cumin
½ teaspoon baking powder
1 tablespoon flour

½ teaspoon cayenne pepper
½ teaspoon salt, or to taste
1 garlic clove, minced
¼ teaspoon dried oregano
¼ teaspoon dried thyme
oil for frying

=== **Yield: 72 croquettes**

3 cups dried chickpeas
1 tablespoon salt
3 eggs, beaten
2 tablespoons ground cumin
1½ teaspoons baking powder
3 tablespoons flour

1½ teaspoons cayenne pepper
1½ teaspoons salt, or to taste
3 garlic cloves, minced
¾ teaspoon dried oregano
¾ teaspoon dried thyme
oil for frying

1. In a bowl, mix the chickpeas with salt and water to cover. Soak overnight.

2. Simmer the soaked chickpeas in fresh water to cover until tender, about 1½ to 2 hours. Drain.

3. In a food processor, purée the chickpeas with the egg(s), cumin, baking powder, flour, cayenne, salt, garlic, oregano, and thyme. Shape into 1-inch balls.

4. Heat the oil to 390°F and test-fry a croquette. If it does not hold together, add a little more flour and retest. Fry until golden.

▶ Can be prepared for frying 1 day in advance.

≡ Croquettes de Poisson (Fish Croquettes)

These can be made from any leftover fish. Salmon and fresh cod are favorites.

═ Yield: 24 croquettes

3 cups flaked cooked fish
2 tablespoons pickle relish
2 tablespoons butter, softened
2 teaspoons anchovy paste
2 teaspoons capers
1 teaspoon grated onion
Tabasco sauce, to taste

salt, to taste
1 cup sauce villeroi (page 62)
flour
2 eggs, lightly beaten
2 cups fresh bread crumbs
oil for frying

═ Yield: 72 croquettes

2¼ quarts flaked cooked fish
⅓ cup pickle relish
⅓ cup butter, softened
2 tablespoons anchovy paste
2 tablespoons capers
1 tablespoon grated onion
Tabasco sauce, to taste

salt, to taste
3 cups sauce villeroi (page 62)
flour
6 eggs, lightly beaten
6 cups fresh bread crumbs
oil for frying

1. In a bowl, fold the fish, relish, butter, anchovy paste, capers, onion, Tabasco sauce, and salt into the sauce villeroi and mix well. Spread on a buttered baking sheet, cover with waxed paper, and chill.

2. Form into small croquettes and roll in the flour, eggs, and bread crumbs. Chill at least 30 minutes.

3. Heat the oil to 370°F and fry until golden.

▶ Can be prepared for frying the day before.

≡ Beignets de Poisson (Fish Fritters)

The name for these translates as "fish fritters," but the recipe is really for making croquettes.

== **Yield: 24 croquettes**

1 cup béchamel sauce for croquettes (page 60)	2 tablespoons water
	flour
½ teaspoon Worcestershire sauce	fresh bread crumbs
	oil for frying
2 teaspoons grated onion	tomato sauce (pages 63–65)
2 cups flaked cooked fish	rémoulade sauce (page 52)
1 egg	béarnaise sauce (page 57)

== **Yield: 72 croquettes**

3 cups béchamel sauce for croquettes (page 60)	6 tablespoons water
	flour
1½ teaspoons Worcestershire sauce	fresh bread crumbs
	oil for frying
2 tablespoons grated onion	tomato sauce (pages 63–65)
1½ quarts flaked cooked fish	rémoulade sauce (page 52)
3 eggs	béarnaise sauce (page 57)

1. In a bowl, mix the béchamel, Worcestershire sauce, onion, and fish. Spread in a buttered baking pan and chill.

2. Beat the egg(s) with the water.

3. Shape the fish mixture into croquettes and roll in the flour, dip in the eggs, and roll in the crumbs. Chill for at least 30 minutes.

4. Heat the oil to 375°F and fry until golden. Serve with one or all of the above sauces for dipping.

▶ Can be prepared for frying 1 day in advance.

≡ *Fresh Fish and Mushroom Croquettes*

== **Yield: 24 croquettes**

1 pound cod or other flaky white fish	1 tablespoon minced onion
	1 teaspoon paprika
¼ cup butter	2 tablespoons heavy cream
6 tablespoons flour	2 eggs, separated
1½ cups minced mushrooms, sautéed in 3 tablespoons butter	fresh bread crumbs
	oil for frying
	tomato sauce (pages 63–65)
2 tablespoons minced parsley	

═ **Yield: 72 croquettes**

3 pounds cod or other flaky
  white fish
¾ cup butter
1¼ cups flour
6¾ cups minced mushrooms,
  sautéed in ½ cup butter
⅓ cup minced parsley

3 tablespoons minced onion
1 tablespoon paprika
⅓ cup heavy cream
6 eggs, separated
fresh bread crumbs
oil for frying
tomato sauce (pages 63–65)

1. Poach the fish in water to cover until just done. Drain, reserving the cooking liquid. Flake the fish and reduce the liquid by half (see note).

2. In a saucepan, melt the butter, stir in the flour and cook until the roux starts to turn golden. Add the reserved fish stock and cook until thickened and smooth. Stir in the fish, mushrooms, parsley, onion, and paprika. Stir in the heavy cream. Remove from the heat and stir in the egg yolks. Beat the egg whites until stiff and fold into the fish mixture.

3. Spread on a buttered baking sheet, cover with waxed paper, and chill. Shape into balls and roll in bread crumbs. Chill at least 30 minutes.

4. Heat the oil to 380°F and fry until golden. Serve with tomato sauce.

▶ Can be prepared for frying 1 day in advance.

NOTE: You should have 1 cup of reduced fish stock for the smaller quantity and 3 cups for the larger quantity.

═ *Fritots d'Anchois (Anchovy Croquettes)*

These are very delicate and difficult croquettes, but so delicious.

═ **Yield: 24 croquettes**

24 anchovy fillets, rinsed
1 cup thick mornay sauce
  (page 59)
4 eggs, beaten

bread crumbs
oil for frying
lemon quarters

═ **Yield: 72 croquettes**

72 anchovy fillets, rinsed
3 cups thick mornay sauce
  (page 59)
8 eggs, beaten

bread crumbs
oil for frying
lemon quarters

1. Chop the anchovies coarsely and fold into the mornay sauce. Chill until firm.

2. Shape into croquettes, dip into the eggs, and roll in the bread crumbs. Dip again into the egg(s) and roll again in the bread crumbs. Let coating set for at least 30 minutes.

3. Heat the oil to 375°F and fry until golden. Serve immediately.

▶ Can be prepared for frying 1 day in advance.

≡ *Crab Croquettes*

═ Yield: 24 croquettes

¼ pound mushrooms, minced
3 tablespoons minced shallots
2 tablespoons butter
2 teaspoons butter
2 teaspoons flour
1 cup light cream
1 tablespoon lemon juice
¼ teaspoon dry mustard
pinch of grated nutmeg
pinch of dried thyme

pinch of cayenne pepper
salt, to taste
1 pound crabmeat, flaked
3 egg yolks
2 tablespoons sherry
flour
1 egg
2 cups fresh bread crumbs
¼ cup minced chives
oil for frying

═ Yield: 72 croquettes

¾ pound mushrooms, minced
½ cup minced shallots
⅓ cup butter
2 tablespoons butter
2 tablespoons flour
3 cups light cream
3 tablespoons lemon juice
¾ teaspoon dry mustard
¼ teaspoon grated nutmeg
¼ teaspoon dried thyme

¼ teaspoon cayenne pepper
salt, to taste
3 pounds crabmeat, flaked
9 egg yolks
⅓ cup sherry
flour
3 eggs
6 cups fresh bread crumbs
¾ cup minced chives
oil for frying

1. In a skillet, sauté the mushrooms and shallots in the first measure of butter until the liquid evaporates.

2. In a saucepan, melt the remaining butter and stir in the flour. Cook the roux until it just starts to turn golden. Stir in the cream and cook until thickened and smooth. Add the mushrooms, lemon juice, mustard, nutmeg, thyme, cayenne, and salt. Simmer 15 minutes. Stir in the crabmeat.

3. In a bowl, beat the egg yolks with the sherry and fold into the crabmeat mixture. Spread in a buttered pan and chill until firm.

4. Shape into croquettes and roll in the flour. Put on a baking sheet and freeze for 30 minutes.

5. In a bowl, beat the egg(s) and mix the bread crumbs and chives in another bowl. Dip the balls into the egg mixture and then in the bread crumb mixture. Chill at least 30 minutes.

6. Heat the oil to 370°F and fry until golden.

▶ Can be prepared for frying 1 day in advance.

≡ *Shrimp Croquettes*

═ **Yield: 24 croquettes**

1 cup hot béchamel sauce for croquettes (page 60)
1 pound cooked, shelled shrimp, minced
6 mushrooms, minced and sautéed
1 tablespoon minced parsley
salt and pepper, to taste
flour

1 egg
¼ cup milk
1 tablespoon oil
¼ teaspoon salt
fresh bread crumbs
oil for frying
curried béchamel sauce (pages 60–61)

═ **Yield: 72 croquettes**

3 cups hot béchamel sauce for croquettes (page 60)
3 pounds cooked, shelled shrimp, minced
¾ pound mushrooms, minced and sautéed
3 tablespoons minced parsley
salt and pepper, to taste
flour

3 eggs
¾ cup milk
3 tablespoons oil
¾ teaspoon salt
fresh bread crumbs
oil for frying
curried béchamel sauce (pages 60–61)

1. In a saucepan, mix the béchamel, shrimp, mushrooms, and parsley, and cook until the mixture leaves the sides of the pan. Correct the seasoning with salt and pepper. Spread on a buttered baking sheet, cover with waxed paper, and chill.

2. Shape into croquettes and roll in the flour. In a bowl, mix the egg(s), milk, oil, and salt. Dip the croquettes into the egg mixture and roll in the bread crumbs. Let set in the refrigerator for at least 30 minutes.

3. Heat the oil to 390°F and fry until golden. Serve with curried béchamel sauce.

▶ Can be prepared for frying the day before.

≡ *Turkey Croquettes*

These are the perfect hors d'oeuvre for the holidays and a good way to use up leftover turkey.

═ Yield: 24 croquettes

2 cups diced cooked turkey
¼ pound mushrooms, minced and sautéed
3 tablespoons minced black olives
1 cup béchamel sauce for croquettes (page 60)

1 cup puréed cooked chestnuts (see note)
flour
2 eggs, lightly beaten
2 cups fresh bread crumbs
oil for frying

═ Yield: 72 croquettes

1½ quarts diced cooked turkey
¾ pound mushrooms, minced and sautéed
½ cup minced black olives
3 cups béchamel sauce for croquettes (page 60)

3 cups puréed cooked chestnuts (see note)
flour
4 eggs, lightly beaten
6 cups fresh bread crumbs
oil for frying

1. In a bowl, mix the turkey, mushrooms, olives, béchamel, and chestnuts. Chill until firm.

2. Shape into croquettes. Coat them with the flour, dip in the eggs, and roll in the bread crumbs. Let the coating set in the refrigerator at least 30 minutes.

3. Heat the oil to 390°F and fry until golden.

▶ Can be prepared for frying 1 day in advance.

NOTE: Chestnut purée is readily available in cans; be sure to buy the unsweetened kind.

≡ Chicken or Turkey Croquettes

— **Yield: 24 croquettes**

2 tablespoons butter
3 tablespoons minced onion
3 tablespoons flour
1½ cups chicken stock
3½ cups chopped cooked
   chicken or turkey, including
   the skin (see note)
salt and pepper, to taste
¼ teaspoon grated nutmeg

dash of Tabasco sauce, or to
   taste
3 egg yolks
flour
1 egg, lightly beaten
3 tablespoons water
1½ cups fresh bread crumbs
oil for frying
mustard sauce (pages 43–45)

— **Yield: 72 croquettes**

⅓ cup butter
⅓ cup minced onion
⅓ cup flour
4½ cups chicken stock
2½ quarts chopped cooked
   chicken or turkey, including
   the skin (see note)
salt and pepper, to taste
¾ teaspoon grated nutmeg

¼ teaspoon Tabasco sauce, or
   to taste
9 egg yolks
flour
3 eggs, lightly beaten
½ cup water
4½ cups fresh bread crumbs
oil for frying
mustard sauce (pages 43–45)

1. In a saucepan, melt the butter, add the onion, and cook until soft. Add the flour and cook, stirring until the roux just starts to turn golden. Stir in the chicken stock and cook until thickened and smooth. Stir in the chicken, salt, pepper, nutmeg, and Tabasco sauce.

2. Remove from the heat and beat in the egg yolks. Return to the heat and cook 2 minutes, stirring constantly. Pour into a buttered baking sheet, cover with waxed paper, and chill.

3. Shape into croquettes, roll in flour, dip in egg(s) beaten with water, and roll in the bread crumbs. Chill.

4. Heat the oil to 390°F and fry until golden. Serve with mustard sauce.

▶ Can be prepared for frying 1 day in advance.

NOTE: The chicken should be in ¼-inch dice and the skin chopped much finer. The skin intensifies the flavor of the croquettes and is not noticeable if chopped very finely. Try it in other poultry recipes.

≡ Tongue Croquettes

═ **Yield: 24 croquettes**

½ cup seedless raisins, chopped
2½ cups cooked hominy grits
½ cup chopped, cooked, smoked tongue
2 teaspoons Dijon mustard
2 eggs

2 tablespoons flour
pepper, to taste
grated nutmeg, to taste
2 eggs, lightly beaten
2 cups fresh bread crumbs
oil for frying

═ **Yield: 72 croquettes**

1½ cups seedless raisins, chopped
7½ cups cooked hominy grits
1½ cups chopped, cooked, smoked tongue
2 tablespoons Dijon mustard
6 eggs

⅓ cup flour
pepper, to taste
grated nutmeg, to taste
6 eggs, lightly beaten
6 cups fresh bread crumbs
oil for frying

1. In a bowl, mix the raisins, grits, tongue, and mustard.

2. In another bowl, beat the eggs and flour together and stir into the tongue mixture. Correct the seasoning with pepper and nutmeg. Chill.

3. Shape into croquettes, dip in the beaten eggs, and roll in the bread crumbs. Chill at least 30 minutes.

4. Heat the oil to 370°F and fry until golden.

▶ Can be prepared for frying 1 day in advance.

≡ Baked Ham Croquettes

═ **Yield: 24 croquettes**

1 cup ground baked ham
½ cup béchamel sauce for croquettes (page 60)
⅔ cup toasted bread crumbs
1 egg, beaten
1 tablespoon Worcestershire sauce

1 tablespoon minced parsley
½ teaspoon dry mustard
salt and pepper, to taste
fresh bread crumbs
oil for frying

═ **Yield: 72 croquettes**

3 cups ground baked ham
1½ cups béchamel sauce for
croquettes (page 60)
2 cups toasted bread crumbs
3 eggs, beaten
3 tablespoons Worcestershire
sauce

3 tablespoons minced parsley
1½ teaspoons dry mustard
salt and pepper, to taste
fresh bread crumbs
oil for frying

1. In a bowl, mix the ham, béchamel, toasted bread crumbs, egg(s), Worcestershire sauce, parsley, mustard, salt, and pepper. Shape into balls and roll in the fresh bread crumbs. Chill at least 30 minutes.

2. Heat the oil to 370°F and fry until golden.

▶ Can be prepared for frying 1 day in advance.

═ *Ham and Sauerkraut Croquettes*

═ **Yield: 24 croquettes**

¼ cup minced onion
1 tablespoon butter
½ pound sauerkraut, rinsed
and squeezed dry
½ pound cooked ham, finely
ground
½ teaspoon caraway seeds
2 teaspoons dry mustard
salt and pepper, to taste
½ cup béchamel sauce for
croquettes (page 60)

2 egg yolks
1 egg
¼ cup water
flour
1½ cups fresh bread crumbs
oil for frying
lemon wedges
Chinese mustard (page 73)

═ **Yield: 72 croquettes**

¾ cup minced onion
3 tablespoons butter
1½ pounds sauerkraut, rinsed
and squeezed dry
1½ pounds cooked ham, finely
ground
1½ teaspoons caraway seeds
2 tablespoons dry mustard
salt and pepper, to taste
1½ cups béchamel sauce for
croquettes (page 60)

6 egg yolks
3 eggs
¾ cup water
flour
4½ cups fresh bread crumbs
oil for frying
lemon wedges
Chinese mustard (page 73)

1. In a skillet, sauté the onion in the butter until soft. Add the sauerkraut and cook, stirring, until the liquid evaporates. Add the ham, caraway seeds, mustard, salt, pepper, and béchamel. Beat in the egg yolks. Bring just to a boil.

2. Spread on a buttered baking sheet, cover with waxed paper, and chill. Shape into croquettes.

3. Beat the egg(s) and water in a bowl and season with salt and pepper. Roll the croquettes in the flour, dip in the egg, and roll in the crumbs. Let the coating set in the refrigerator for at least 30 minutes.

4. Heat the oil to 375°F and fry until golden. Drain and serve with lemon wedges and mustard.

▶ Can be prepared for frying 1 day in advance.

—— *Fritters* ——

≡ *Beer Batter for Fritters*

⹀ **Yield: 1¾ cups**

½ cup flour	1 egg
¼ teaspoon salt	½ cup flat beer
1 tablespoon melted butter	1 egg white, stiffly beaten

1. In a food processor, mix the flour, salt, butter, and eggs to form a paste. Add the beer in a slow, steady stream and process until smooth.

2. Strain into a bowl, cover with a cloth, and let stand in a warm place for 2 hours or up to 2 days. Just before using, fold in the egg whites.

NOTE: This batter can also be made with milk or water instead of beer. I have found no real difference between using flat and regular beer. The classic recipe specifies that the beer batter will get foamy after standing for 2 hours; however, whether the batter foams or not seems to have no effect on the outcome.

Variation: Beer Batter with Herbs
Add 2 tablespoons minced parsley and 1 teaspoon each of minced tarragon, rosemary, and chives to the beer fritter batter. Or, use one or more other favorite herbs.

≡ *Indonesian Peanut Fritters*

══ Yield: 24 fritters

⅓ cup flour
½ teaspoon salt
¼ teaspoon minced garlic
¼ teaspoon grated gingerroot

2 cups unsweetened coconut
  milk
1 egg
¾ cup unroasted peanuts

══ Yield: 72 fritters

1 cup flour
1½ teaspoons salt
¾ teaspoon minced garlic
¾ teaspoon grated gingerroot

6 cups unsweetened coconut
  milk
3 eggs
2¼ cups unroasted peanuts

1. In a bowl, mix the flour, salt, garlic, gingerroot, coconut milk, and egg(s). Stir the batter until smooth and stir in the nuts.
2. Heat the oil to 375°F. Drop the batter by teaspoonfuls into the oil and fry until golden. Serve immediately.

▶ The batter can be made several hours in advance.

≡ *Deep-Fried Chickpeas*

These can be substituted for seasoned nuts.

══ Yield: 2½ cups

2½ cups canned chickpeas,
  drained
¼ cup flour

1 teaspoon salt
oil for frying

══ Yield: 7½ cups

7½ cups canned chickpeas,
  drained
¾ cup flour

1 tablespoon salt
oil for frying

1. In a bowl, mix the chickpeas, flour, and salt. Shake off the excess flour in a sieve.
2. Heat the oil to 375°F and fry until golden. Drain on paper towels and add additional salt, if desired.

▶ These will keep several days but are best served while still warm.

≡ *Iranian Cauliflower Fritters*

══ Yield: 48 fritters

1 large cauliflower	1 tablespoon water
½ cup flour	1 tomato, peeled, seeded, and
½ teaspoon baking powder	chopped
½ teaspoon salt	3 tablespoons minced parsley
2 eggs	½ cup minced onion
⅓ cup light cream	oil for frying

══ Yield: 144 fritters

2 large cauliflowers	3 tablespoons water
1½ cups flour	3 tomatoes, peeled, seeded, and
1½ teaspoons baking powder	chopped
1½ teaspoons salt	½ cup minced parsley
6 eggs	1½ cups minced onion
1 cup light cream	oil for frying

1. Cook the cauliflower(s) in boiling salted water to cover for 10 minutes. Drain and separate into florets.

2. In a food processor, mix the flour, baking powder, and salt. With the machine running, gradually add the eggs, cream, and water to make a smooth batter. Add the tomato, parsley, and onion with on-off turns.

3. Heat the oil to 375°F. Dip the cauliflower into the batter and fry until golden. Serve immediately.

▶ Prepare the batter no more than 30 minutes before serving.

≡ *Deep-Fried Cauliflower*

══ Yield: 48 fritters

1 large cauliflower	¼ teaspoon curry powder
½ cup flour	2 eggs, well beaten
1 teaspoon salt	fresh bread crumbs
1 teaspoon minced dill	oil for frying
¼ teaspoon pepper	rémoulade sauce (page 52)

══ Yield: 96 fritters

2 large cauliflowers	½ teaspoon curry powder
1 cup flour	4 eggs, well beaten
2 teaspoons salt	fresh bread crumbs
2 teaspoons minced dill	oil for frying
½ teaspoon pepper	rémoulade sauce (page 52)

1. Cook the cauliflower in boiling salted water to cover for 10 minutes. Drain and separate into florets.

2. In a bowl, mix the flour, salt, dill, pepper, and curry powder. Dredge the florets in the flour, dip in the eggs, and roll in the crumbs. Let the coating set for at least 30 minutes.

3. Heat the oil to 375°F and fry until golden. Serve with rémoulade sauce.

▶ Can be prepared for frying 1 day in advance.

☰ *Champignons aux Herbes* (*Breaded Herbed Mushrooms*)

═ Yield: 24 fritters

1 pound mushrooms	¼ teaspoon minced oregano
½ cup flour	¼ teaspoon minced marjoram
2 eggs	½ teaspoon minced thyme
¼ cup water	pinch of cayenne pepper
1 tablespoon olive oil	oil for frying
salt and pepper, to taste	anchovy mayonnaise (see note)
2 cups fresh bread crumbs	

═ Yield: 72 fritters

3 pounds mushrooms	¾ teaspoon minced oregano
1½ cups flour	¾ teaspoon minced marjoram
6 eggs	1½ teaspoons minced thyme
¾ cup water	⅛ teaspoon cayenne pepper
3 tablespoons olive oil	oil for frying
salt and pepper, to taste	anchovy mayonnaise (see note)
6 cups fresh bread crumbs	

1. Wash the mushrooms, drain well, and dredge in the flour.

2. In a bowl, mix the eggs, water, olive oil, salt, and pepper. In another bowl, mix the bread crumbs, oregano, marjoram, thyme, and cayenne.

3. Heat the oil to 360°F. Dip the mushrooms in the egg mixture and then in the crumbs. Fry until golden. Serve immediately with anchovy mayonnaise as a dip.

▶ The mushrooms can be coated several hours in advance.

NOTE: To make anchovy mayonnaise, add anchovy paste and lemon juice to taste to mayonnaise.

≡ Batter-Fried Mushrooms

≡ **Yield: approximately 25 fritters**

1 recipe beer batter, with or   1 pound mushrooms
without herbs (page 323)   oil for frying

1. Heat the oil to 375°F.
2. Prepare the batter and set aside.
3. Remove the stems from the mushroom caps and reserve for another use.
4. Dip the mushrooms into the batter and fry until golden. Serve immediately.

▶ Coat and fry mushrooms just before serving.

≡ Parsnip Chips

≡ **Yield: approximately 2 quarts**

2 pounds firm, thick parsnips   salt
oil for frying

1. Peel the parsnips and cut into paper-thin slices. Soak in cold water for 30 minutes. Drain.
2. Bring 2 quarts salted water to a boil and cook the parsnips 3 minutes. Rinse under cold water and drain well.
3. Heat the oil to 365°F and fry until golden. Sprinkle with salt and serve.

▶ Can be made 1 day in advance and reheated.

≡ Cromesquis Florentine (Spinach-filled Crêpe Fritters)

Cromesquis are small stuffed crêpes dipped in a batter and deep-fried. They lend themselves to many variations. Almost any food can be substituted for the spinach in this recipe. Try cheese fillings, minced chicken or fish, or steak tartare.

== **Yield: 24 fritters**

1 pound spinach, cooked, drained, and minced
1 teaspoon minced onion
1 tablespoon butter
1 cup grated Parmesan cheese
⅓ cup very thick béchamel sauce (page 59)

salt and pepper, to taste
24 3-inch crêpes
beer batter (page 323)
oil for frying

== **Yield: 72 fritters**

3 pounds spinach, cooked, drained, and minced
1 minced onion
3 tablespoons butter
3 cups grated Parmesan cheese
1 cup very thick béchamel sauce (page 59)

salt and pepper, to taste
72 3-inch crêpes
beer batter (page 323)
oil for frying

1. In a skillet, cook the spinach and onion in the butter until the moisture has completely evaporated. Add the cheese and béchamel and season with salt and pepper.

2. Put 1 tablespoon of the spinach mixture on each crêpe and fold like an envelope.

3. Heat the oil to 375°F. Dip the crêpes into the fritter batter and fry until golden. Drain and serve hot.

▶ The crêpes can be assembled several hours in advance, but do not dip in batter and fry until just before serving.

≡ *Crêpes for Hors d'Oeuvre*

== **Yield: 72 3-inch crêpes**

¾ cup sifted flour
3 eggs
1 cup milk

4 tablespoons melted butter
½ teaspoon salt

1. In a bowl, mix the flour and eggs together to form a paste.

2. Gradually beat in the milk, stirring constantly, until mixture is about the consistency of heavy cream. Add the butter and salt.

3. Strain through a fine sieve and let stand for 2 hours.

4. To cook crêpes, heat one or more crêpe pans or a griddle over moderate heat.

5. Butter the pan lightly and pour in enough batter to make a 3-inch crêpe. Cook until just golden, turn with a spatula and cook the second side until golden, and turn out onto a sheet of waxed paper.

▶ The cooked crêpes can be made 2 days in advance and can be frozen.
NOTE: The batter can be prepared in a blender or processor.

≡ *Mucver (Grated Zucchini Fritters)*

═ Yield: 24 fritters

2 small zucchini, peeled and grated
1 egg
2 scallions, minced
2 tablespoons minced dill
2 tablespoons minced parsley
2 tablespoons minced mint leaves

⅓ cup grated Gruyère cheese
⅓ cup flour, approximately
1 teaspoon lemon juice
salt and pepper, to taste
cayenne pepper, to taste
oil for frying

═ Yield: 72 fritters

6 small zucchini, peeled and grated
3 eggs
5 scallions, minced
½ cup minced dill
½ cup minced parsley
½ cup minced mint leaves

1 cup grated Gruyère cheese
1 to 1¼ cups flour
1 tablespoon lemon juice
salt and pepper, to taste
cayenne pepper, to taste
oil for frying

1. In a bowl, mix the zucchini, eggs, scallions, dill, parsley, mint, and cheese. Add the flour a little at a time to give the batter cohesion. Season with lemon juice, salt, pepper, and cayenne.

2. Heat the oil to 365°F. Drop teaspoonfuls of the batter into the fat and fry until golden. Drain and serve hot.

▶ Must be prepared and fried just before serving.

≡ *Kaasballetjes (Dutch Cheese Puffs)*

These can also be made with Gouda, Edam, or Leerdam cheese.

═ **Yield: 24 fritters**

3 tablespoons butter
5 tablespoons flour
1 cup water
1½ cups grated Cheddar or
Gruyère cheese

3 eggs, separated
¼ teaspoon pepper
oil for frying

═ **Yield: 72 fritters**

¾ cup butter
1 cup flour
1 quart water
4½ cups grated Cheddar or
Gruyère cheese

9 eggs, separated
¾ teaspoon pepper
oil for frying

1. In a saucepan, melt the butter, stir in the flour, and cook until roux bubbles and starts to turn golden. Add water and cook, stirring, until thickened and smooth. Stir in the cheese until melted. Remove from the heat and beat in the egg yolks and the pepper.

2. Just before serving, beat the egg whites until stiff but not dry and fold them into the cheese mixture.

3. Heat the oil to 375°F. Drop teaspoonfuls of the batter into the oil and fry until golden. Drain and serve hot.

▶ The cheese mixture can be made ahead and reheated before folding in the egg whites.

═ *Deep-Fried Camembert Balls*

═ **Yield: 24 fritters**

1 recipe beer batter (page 323)
½ pound Camembert cheese

oil for frying

═ **Yield: 72 fritters**

2 recipes beer batter
(page 323)

1½ pounds Camembert cheese
oil for frying

1. Prepare the batter and let it rest.

2. In a food processor, purée the cheese. Shape the cheese into ½-inch balls and set aside.

3. Heat the oil to 375°F. Dip the balls into the batter and fry until golden. Serve immediately.

▶ The cheese can be shaped 1 day in advance and chilled.

≡ *Valesnikis Polonaise (Cheese-Flavored Cromesquis)*

=== **Yield: 24 fritters**

⅔ cup grated Gruyère cheese
⅔ cup butter
salt and pepper, to taste
pinch of grated nutmeg

1 egg, beaten
24 3-inch crêpes (page 328)
1 recipe beer batter (page 323)
oil for frying

=== **Yield: 72 fritters**

2 cups grated Gruyère cheese
2 cups butter
salt and pepper, to taste
¼ teaspoon grated nutmeg

3 eggs, beaten
72 3-inch crêpes (page 328)
2 recipes beer batter (page 323)
oil for frying

1. In a food processor, cream the cheese, butter, salt, pepper, and nutmeg. Add the eggs and process until smooth.

2. Put a tablespoon of filling on each crêpe and fold like an envelope.

3. Heat the oil to 375°F. Dip each crêpe into the beer batter and fry until golden.

▶ The fritters can be prepared and coated with batter 1 day in advance. Do not put into the fritter batter until just ready to serve.

NOTE: The cromesquis can be dipped into eggs and bread crumbs, as for croquettes, instead of beer batter.

≡ *Fried Hot Cheese Rolls*

=== **Yield: 24 fritters**

2 tablespoons butter
½ cup flour
1 cup milk, scalded
1 cup grated Parmesan cheese
2 egg yolks, beaten
½ teaspoon salt

pinch of cayenne pepper
pinch of grated nutmeg
½ loaf thinly sliced white
  bread, crusts removed
oil for frying

=== **Yield: 72 fritters**

⅓ cup butter
1½ cups flour
3 cups milk, scalded
3 cups grated Parmesan cheese
6 egg yolks, beaten
1½ teaspoons salt

½ teaspoon cayenne pepper
¼ teaspoon grated nutmeg
1½ loaves thinly sliced white
  bread, crusts removed
oil for frying

1. In a saucepan, melt the butter, stir in the flour, and cook until the roux just starts to turn golden. Stir in the milk and cook, stirring, until thickened and smooth. Simmer 20 minutes, stirring. Stir in the cheese until melted.

2. Beat in the egg yolks, salt, cayenne, and nutmeg. Bring just to a boil.

3. Spread the cheese mixture on each bread slice and roll like a jelly roll. If necessary, insert a small wooden skewer to hold it together.

4. Heat the oil to 375°F and fry until golden.

▶ Can be prepared for frying 1 day in advance.

≡ *Bifteck Gruyerien-Beignets de Fromage (Cheese Fritters)*

═ **Yield: approximately 20 fritters**

1 pound Gruyère cheese	sauce corail (page 54) or sauce
1 recipe beer batter (page 323)	andalouse (page 51)
oil for frying	

═ **Yield: approximately 80 fritters**

4 pounds Gruyère cheese	sauce corail (page 54) or sauce
2 recipes beer batter (page 323)	andalouse (page 51)
oil for frying	

1. Cut the cheese into fingers 2 inches long and ½ inch thick.

2. Heat the oil to 375°F. Dip the cheese into the batter and fry until golden. Serve immediately with the sauce as a dip.

▶ The cheese and the batter may be prepared hours ahead, but do not combine and cook until ready to serve.

NOTE: If the batter does not adhere to the cheese, roll the fingers in flour first.

≡ *Mozzarella Sticks*

═ **Yield: 24 fritters**

1 pound mozzarella cheese	3 cups fresh bread crumbs
1 cup flour, seasoned with salt and pepper	oil for frying
	grated Parmesan cheese
6 eggs, lightly beaten	tomato sauce (pages 63–65)

== **Yield: 72 fritters**

3 pounds mozzarella cheese

3 cups flour, seasoned with salt
and pepper

18 eggs, lightly beaten

9 cups fresh bread crumbs

oil for frying

grated Parmesan cheese

tomato sauce (pages 63–65)

1. Cut the cheese into sticks, ¼ inch square and 2 inches long. Dredge the cheese in the flour, dip in the eggs, and roll in the crumbs, pressing the crumbs on by hand. Roll again in the crumbs. Let the coating set for at least 30 minutes.

2. Heat the oil to 375°F and fry until golden. Sprinkle with Parmesan cheese and serve with tomato sauce for dipping.

▶ Can be prepared for frying 1 day in advance.

≡ *Mozzarella in Carrozza* *(Deep-Fried Cheese Sandwiches)*

== **Yield: 24 fritters**

1 1-pound loaf French bread

¼ pound prosciutto, thinly
sliced

1 pound mozzarella, sliced ¼
inch thick

4 eggs

2 tablespoons milk

fresh bread crumbs

oil for frying

bagna cauda (pages 111–112)

== **Yield: 72 fritters**

3 1-pound loaves French bread

¾ pound prosciutto, thinly
sliced

3 pounds mozzarella, sliced ¼
inch thick

12 eggs

⅓ cup milk

fresh bread crumbs

oil for frying

bagna cauda (pages 111–112)

1. Cut the bread into ¼-inch slices and then into 2-inch circles. Make sandwiches of bread, prosciutto, and mozzarella. In a bowl, beat the eggs and milk. Dip the sandwiches into the eggs and press the edges together. Roll in the bread crumbs and let set on a pastry rack for at least 30 minutes.

2. Heat the oil to 375°F and fry the sandwiches until golden. Serve with bagna cauda.

▶ Can be prepared for frying 1 day in advance.

≡ Käsekrapfen (Austrian Cheese Fritters)

== **Yield: 24 fritters**

1⅓ cups bread crumbs
1 cup grated Parmesan cheese
½ cup butter
2 egg yolks
salt, to taste

paprika, to taste
2 eggs, lightly beaten
2 cups bread crumbs
oil for frying

== **Yield: 72 fritters**

4 cups bread crumbs
3 cups grated Parmesan cheese
1½ cups butter
6 egg yolks
salt, to taste

1 tablespoon paprika
6 eggs, lightly beaten
6 cups bread crumbs
oil for frying

1. In a bowl, mix the bread crumbs, cheese, butter, egg yolks, salt, and paprika. Work to a paste and shape into balls. Dip in the beaten eggs and roll in the remaining bread crumbs. Let the coating set for 30 minutes.

2. Heat the oil to 360°F and fry until golden.

▶ Can be prepared for frying 1 day in advance.

≡ Fried Fish Puffs

== **Yield: 36 fritters**

2½ cups chopped cooked sole
  or halibut
3 tablespoons lime juice
½ cup minced onion
1 cup evaporated milk
1 cup flour
¾ cup minced cooked parsnips

2 tablespoons soy sauce
½ teaspoon salt
½ teaspoon pepper
½ teaspoon Worcestershire
  sauce
oil for frying

== **Yield: 72 fritters**

5 cups chopped cooked sole or
  halibut
⅓ cup lime juice
1 cup minced onion
2 cups evaporated milk
2 cups flour
1½ cups minced cooked
  parsnips

¼ cup soy sauce
1 teaspoon salt
1 teaspoon pepper
1 teaspoon Worcestershire
  sauce
oil for frying

1. In a bowl, marinate the fish in the lime juice for 15 minutes, turning often. Drain the juice and add the onion, milk, flour, parsnips, soy sauce, salt, pepper, and Worcestershire sauce. Purée in a food processor.

2. Heat the oil to 360°F. Drop teaspoonfuls of the batter into the oil and fry until golden.

▶ Can be prepared for frying 6 hours in advance.

≡ *Ferkedel Ikan Soerabaya* *(Fish and Coconut Fritters)*

═ Yield: 24 fritters

1 pound sole fillets
1 cup grated unsweetened
   coconut
3 eggs, lightly beaten
¼ cup minced scallions
1 tablespoon cornstarch

1 tablespoon ground coriander
1 tablespoon lemon juice
1½ teaspoons ground cumin
salt and pepper, to taste
oil for frying
ketjap manis (see Glossary)

═ Yield: 72 fritters

3 pounds sole fillets
3 cups grated unsweetened
   coconut
9 eggs, lightly beaten
¾ cup minced scallions
3 tablespoons cornstarch

3 tablespoons ground coriander
3 tablespoons lemon juice
4 teaspoons ground cumin
salt and pepper, to taste
oil for frying
ketjap manis (see Glossary)

1. In a food processor, grind the fish to a coarse paste. Mix the fish, coconut, eggs, scallions, cornstarch, coriander, lemon juice, cumin, salt, and pepper.

2. Heat the oil to 350°F. Drop heaping tablespoonfuls of the batter into the oil and fry until golden. Drain and serve hot with the ketjap manis.

▶ Can be prepared for frying 1 day in advance.

☰ *Clam and Olive Fritters*

= Yield: 24 fritters

1 cup drained, minced clams
2 eggs, lightly beaten
1 cup fine dry bread crumbs
1 tablespoon milk
1½ teaspoons minced parsley
1½ tablespoons minced ripe
   olives

1 teaspoon salt
½ teaspoon pepper
1 recipe beer batter (page 323)
oil for frying

= Yield: 72 fritters

3 cups drained, minced clams
6 eggs, lightly beaten
3 cups fine dry bread crumbs
3 tablespoons milk
2 tablespoons minced parsley
5 tablespoons minced ripe
   olives

1 tablespoon salt
1 teaspoon pepper
2 recipes beer batter (page 323)
oil for frying

1. In a bowl, mix the clams, eggs, bread crumbs, milk, parsley, olives, salt, and pepper. Roll into 1-inch balls.
2. Heat the oil to 375°F. Dip the balls into the batter and fry until golden.

▶ The fritters can be shaped 1 day in advance. Dip in batter and cook just before serving.

☰ *Clam Fritters*

= Yield: 24 fritters

1¼ cups sifted flour
1 teaspoon baking powder
¼ teaspoon cayenne pepper
2 eggs
½ cup milk
21 ounces minced canned
   clams, drained

¼ cup minced scallions
1 tablespoon minced parsley
¼ teaspoon salt
pinch of pepper
oil for frying
cocktail sauce (see Glossary) or
   tartar sauce (page 51)

Yield: 72 fritters

3¾ cups sifted flour
1 tablespoon baking powder
½ teaspoon cayenne pepper
6 eggs
1½ cups milk
63 ounces minced canned
    clams, drained

¾ cup minced scallions
3 tablespoons minced parsley
¾ teaspoon salt
¼ teaspoon pepper
oil for frying
cocktail sauce (see Glossary) or
    tartar sauce (page 51)

1. In a bowl, mix the flour, baking powder, and cayenne.

2. In another bowl, beat the eggs and milk. Gradually beat into the flour to make a smooth batter. Let stand for 30 minutes. Stir in the clams, scallions, parsley, salt, and pepper.

3. Heat the oil to 375°F. Drop teaspoonfuls of the batter into the oil and fry until golden. Serve with cocktail sauce or tartar sauce.

▶ Prepare just before serving.

Codfish Balls

This old New England favorite makes a wonderful hors d'oeuvre when made into 1-inch balls. For added flavor, stir in Worcestershire sauce and dry mustard.

Yield: 24 fritters

½ pound boneless, skinless salt
    cod
1 pound potatoes, peeled and
    quartered
¼ cup butter

2 egg yolks
salt and pepper, to taste
oil for frying
tomato sauce (pages 63–65) or
    tartar sauce (page 51)

Yield: 72 fritters

1½ pounds boneless, skinless
    salt cod
3 pounds potatoes, peeled and
    quartered
¾ cup butter

5 egg yolks
salt and pepper, to taste
oil for frying
tomato sauce (pages 63–65) or
    tartar sauce (page 51)

1. Soak the salt cod in cold water for at least 12 hours, changing the water 3 or 4 times. Drain.

2. In a saucepan, cover the salt cod with water and bring to a boil. If the water is very salty, drain, cover with cold water, and bring to a boil again. Simmer 10 minutes. Drain and flake the fish.

3. Boil the potatoes in salted water until tender. Drain, then rice or mash the potatoes.

4. Beat the flaked cod and butter into the potatoes. Beat in the egg yolks, salt, and pepper. Shape into 1-inch balls.

5. Heat the oil to 375°F and fry until golden. Serve with tomato sauce or tartar sauce.

▶ Can be fried in advance and reheated; can also be frozen.

≡ *Accra (West Indian Codfish Balls)*

For many guests these will bring back memories of swaying palms, reggae, and island moonlight.

═ Yield: approximately 50 fritters

1 package dry yeast	1 tablespoon minced garlic
½ cup lukewarm water	1 tablespoon minced chives
2 cups boiling water	1 teaspoon sugar
½ pound salt cod	1 teaspoon red pepper flakes
1 cup flour	½ teaspoon Tabasco sauce
⅓ cup minced onion	oil for frying
¼ cup minced green pepper	

═ Yield: approximately 100 fritters

2 packages dry yeast	2 tablespoons minced garlic
1 cup lukewarm water	2 tablespoons minced chives
1 quart boiling water	2 teaspoons sugar
1 pound salt cod	2 teaspoons red pepper flakes
2 cups flour	¾ teaspoon Tabasco sauce
⅔ cup minced onion	oil for frying
½ cup minced green pepper	

1. In a small bowl, proof the yeast in the lukewarm water.

2. In another bowl, pour the boiling water over the salt cod and let cool. Drain cod, rinse under cold water, and remove the skin and bones. Shred the fish.

3. In another bowl, mix the flour, onion, green pepper, garlic, chives, sugar, red pepper flakes, and Tabasco sauce. Stir in the yeast, its liquid, and the fish and let rise, loosely covered, until double in bulk, about 1½ hours.

4. Heat the oil to 350°F. Drop teaspoonfuls of the batter into the oil and fry until golden. Serve immediately.

▶ Prepare just before serving.

☰ *Moules en Brochettes, Sauce Béarnaise (Skewered Mussels with Béarnaise Sauce)*

━━ **Yield: 24 fritters**

approximately 3 pounds
mussels
½ cup white wine
flour

1 recipe beer batter (page 323)
oil for frying
béarnaise sauce (page 57)

━━ **Yield: 72 fritters**

approximately 10 pounds
mussels
1½ cups white wine
flour

2 recipes beer batter (page 323)
oil for frying
béarnaise sauce (page 57)

1. Scrub, beard, and rinse the mussels. In a covered kettle, bring the wine and mussels to a boil. Boil until the shells open, about 6 minutes. Remove the mussels from the shells, discarding any that have not opened.

2. Thread three mussels on a small wooden skewer.

3. Heat the oil to 375°F. Roll the skewers in the flour, dip in the batter, and fry until golden. Serve with béarnaise sauce.

▶ The mussels can be prepared for coating 1 day in advance. Dip them in batter and fry just before serving.

☰ *Corn and Oyster Fritters*

━━ **Yield: 30 fritters**

¾ cup flour
¼ cup cornmeal
1 teaspoon baking powder
¼ teaspoon salt
¼ teaspoon paprika
¼ teaspoon celery seeds
1 egg, lightly beaten

1 tablespoon sour cream
⅔ cup milk
½ pint shucked oysters, drained
    and chopped
½ cup corn kernels
oil for frying
salt, to taste

━━ **Yield: 90 fritters**

2¼ cups flour
¾ cup cornmeal
1 tablespoon baking powder
¾ teaspoon salt
¾ teaspoon paprika
¾ teaspoon celery seeds
3 eggs, lightly beaten

3 tablespoons sour cream
2 cups milk
1½ pints shucked oysters,
    drained and chopped
1½ cups corn kernels
oil for frying
salt, to taste

1. Sift the flour, cornmeal, baking powder, salt, paprika, and celery seeds into a bowl. Beat in the egg(s) and sour cream and stir in the milk, oysters, and corn kernels.

2. Heat the oil to 375°F. Drop teaspoonfuls of the batter into the oil and fry until golden. Season with salt and serve.

▶ Prepare just before serving; do not try to hold.

≡ *Beignets d'Huitres (Oyster Beignets)*

=== **Yield: 24 fritters**

1 recipe pâte à chou (page 572)	1 tablespoon minced parsley oil for frying
1 pint shucked oysters, drained and chopped	horseradish mustard sauce (page 45)

=== **Yield: 72 fritters**

2 recipes pâte à chou (page 572)	2 tablespoons minced parsley oil for frying
1 quart shucked oysters, drained and chopped	horseradish mustard sauce (page 45)

1. Beat the pâte à chou, oysters, and parsley together.

2. Heat the oil to 375°F. Drop teaspoonfuls of the batter into the oil and fry until puffed and golden. Serve hot with the horseradish sauce.

▶ Can be prepared for frying several hours in advance.

≡ *Cromesquis d'Huitres à la Sauce Tartare*
(Fried Oysters with Creamy Tartar Sauce)

=== **Yield: 24 fritters**

24 large shucked oysters, undrained	2 eggs
24 3-inch crêpes (page 328)	2 cups fresh bread crumbs
1 cup flour	oil for frying
	creamy tartar sauce (page 66)

=== **Yield: 72 fritters**

72 large shucked oysters, undrained	6 eggs
72 3-inch crêpes (page 328)	6 cups fresh bread crumbs
3 cups flour	oil for frying
	creamy tartar sauce (page 66)

1. Drain oyster liquor into a saucepan and bring to a boil. Add the oysters and poach 30 seconds; drain again, reserving the liquid. When the liquid has cooled, return the oysters to keep them plump.

2. Place flour in a pie tin, place the eggs in a second tin, and the bread crumbs in a third tin.

3. Shortly before serving, drain the oysters and wrap each in a crêpe, folding it like an envelope.

4. Dredge in the flour, dip in the eggs, and roll in the bread crumbs. Heat the oil to 370°F and fry until golden. Serve with the tartar sauce.

▶ Can be prepared for frying 3 hours in advance.

NOTE: Any homemade tartar sauce would be acceptable; regrettably few of those prepared commercially are worth serving.

≡ Deep-Fried Oysters with Mushroom Coating

═ Yield: 24 fritters

24 shucked oysters, undrained	2 egg yolks
1 tablespoon butter	salt and pepper, to taste
2 tablespoons flour	lemon juice, to taste
1 cup minced mushrooms,	2 cups fresh bread crumbs
sautéed in 2 tablespoons	oil for frying
butter until dry	lemon wedges

═ Yield: 72 fritters

72 shucked oysters, undrained	6 egg yolks
3 tablespoons butter	salt and pepper, to taste
⅓ cup flour	lemon juice, to taste
3 cups minced mushrooms,	6 cups fresh bread crumbs
sautéed in ⅓ cup butter	oil for frying
until dry	lemon wedges

1. Poach the oysters in their liquor until the edges just begin to curl. Drain.

2. In a saucepan, melt the butter, stir in the flour, and cook the roux until it just starts to turn golden. Stir in the mushrooms and remove from the heat. Beat in the egg yolks. Season with salt, pepper, and lemon juice.

3. Coat the oysters with the mushroom mixture and chill. Roll in the bread crumbs and let the coating set for at least 30 minutes.

4. Heat the oil to 375°F and fry until golden.

▶ Can be prepared for frying 1 day in advance.

≡ Batter-Fried Scallops

≡ **Yield: 24 fritters**

½ cup flour
½ cup cornstarch
1 egg white
1 tablespoon vegetable oil
1 tablespoon rice vinegar
1 teaspoon baking soda

½ cup water, or more
1 pound sea scallops
flour for dredging
oil for frying
1 cup sweet and sour sauce
(pages 77–78)

≡ **Yield: 72 fritters**

1½ cups flour
1½ cups cornstarch
3 egg whites
3 tablespoons vegetable oil
3 tablespoons rice vinegar
1 tablespoon baking soda

1½ cups water, or more
3 pounds sea scallops
flour for dredging
oil for frying
3 cups sweet and sour sauce
(pages 77–78)

1. In a bowl, mix the flour, cornstarch, egg white(s), oil, vinegar, and baking soda. Gradually stir in enough water to make a thick batter.
2. Dredge the scallops in flour.
3. Heat the oil to 375°F. Dip the scallops into the batter and fry until golden. Serve with sweet and sour sauce.

▶ Do not make the batter more than an hour in advance. Coat the scallops and fry just before serving.

NOTE: Test-fry a scallop to see if the batter needs thinning; if it is too thick, add water. The number of servings will depend on the size of the scallops. It is best to use sea scallops for this preparation.

≡ Chinese Butterfly Shrimp

≡ **Yield: 24 fritters**

1 pound large shrimp
3 tablespoons flour
1½ tablespoons cornstarch
1 tablespoon cornmeal
¾ teaspoon baking powder

¾ teaspoon salt
½ cup milk
oil for frying
soy dipping sauce (page 74)
plum sauce

Yield: 72 fritters

3 pounds large shrimp
½ cup flour
⅓ cup cornstarch
3 tablespoons cornmeal
2¼ teaspoons baking powder

2½ teaspoons salt
1½ cups milk
oil for frying
soy dipping sauce (page 74)
plum sauce

1. Peel the shrimp, leaving on the last segment and tail. With a knife, slit the back of the shrimp to remove the vein.
2. In a bowl, mix the flour, cornstarch, cornmeal, baking powder, and salt. Gradually work in the milk to make a thin batter.
3. Heat the oil to 375°F. Dip the shrimp into the batter and fry until golden. Serve immediately with the sauces.

▶ Prepare just before serving; do not try to hold.

Shrimp in Beer Batter with Pungent Fruit Sauce

Yield: 26 to 30 shrimp

1 recipe beer batter (page 323)
oil for frying
1 pound #26–30 shrimp, peeled
    and deveined with tail tips
    left attached

pungent fruit sauce (page 70)

1. Prepare the beer batter.
2. When ready to serve, heat the oil to 375°F. Dip each shrimp by the tail into the beer batter and then into the hot oil. Cook until golden, about 45 seconds. Drain on paper towels and serve immediately with the pungent fruit sauce for dipping.

▶ Fry shrimp just before serving.

Beignets de Crevettes (Shrimp Fritters)

Yield: 30 fritters

1 recipe beer batter, made with
    white wine instead of beer
    (page 323)
30 large shrimp, peeled and
    deveined
2 cups olive oil
¼ cup red wine vinegar

½ tablespoon dried tarragon
1 bay leaf, crumbled
¼ cup thin strips lemon zest
2 garlic cloves, chopped
salt and pepper, to taste
oil for frying

Yield: 90 fritters

2 recipes beer batter, made
  with white wine instead of
  beer (page 323)
90 large shrimp, peeled and
  deveined
3 cups olive oil
⅔ cup red wine vinegar

1½ tablespoons dried tarragon
2 bay leaves, crumbled
½ cup thin strips lemon zest
4 garlic cloves, chopped
salt and pepper, to taste
oil for frying

1. Prepare the fritter batter and set aside.

2. In a bowl, marinate the shrimp in the olive oil, vinegar, tarragon, bay leaf, lemon zest, garlic, salt, and pepper for 2 hours.

3. Heat the oil to 375°F. Dip the shrimp into the batter and fry until golden. Serve immediately.

▶ Fry shrimp just before serving.

Gambal Udang (Indonesian Shrimp Fritters)

These fritters are cooked in a skillet like potato pancakes rather than deep-fried.

Yield: 24 fritters

½ pound diced shrimp
1½ cups bean sprouts
½ cup unsweetened coconut
  milk
1 egg, lightly beaten
5 tablespoons flour
3 scallions, thinly sliced

2 teaspoons ground coriander
salt, to taste
oil for frying
1 bunch fresh coriander
  (cilantro)
ketjap manis (see Glossary)

Yield: 72 fritters

1½ pounds diced shrimp
1 quart bean sprouts
1½ cups unsweetened coconut
  milk
3 eggs, lightly beaten
1 cup flour
9 scallions, thinly sliced

2 tablespoons ground coriander
salt, to taste
oil for frying
3 bunches or more fresh
  coriander (cilantro)
ketjap manis (see Glossary)

1. In a bowl, mix the shrimp, bean sprouts, coconut milk, egg(s), flour, scallions, ground coriander, and salt.

2. Heat a large skillet and add enough oil to film the bottom. When the oil is hot, drop in heaping tablespoons of the batter. The fritter should hold together, spreading 2½ inches. If necessary, add more flour a tablespoon at a time to make a cohesive batter. Fry until golden on both sides. Drain on paper towels.

3. Arrange a bed of coriander on a serving platter and place fritters on top. Serve with ketjap manis as a dip.

▶ Can be prepared for frying several hours in advance.

≡ Cha Ming Hsia (Pom-Pom Prawns)

Fortunately, these taste far better than the translation of their name sounds. When fried, the shrimp look something like giant chrysanthemums, sometimes called "football" mums.

═ Yield: 24 fritters

24 large shrimp
1 teaspoon salt
½ teaspoon pepper
2 tablespoons sherry
¼ cup flour
2 eggs, beaten

2 cups rice stick noodles
  (see note)
oil for frying
sweet and sour sauce or other
  dipping sauces (pages 72–82)

═ Yield: 72 fritters

72 large shrimp
1 tablespoon salt
1½ teaspoons pepper
⅓ cup sherry
¾ cup flour
6 eggs, beaten

6 cups rice stick noodles
  (see note)
oil for frying
sweet and sour sauce or other
  dipping sauces (pages 72–82)

1. Peel and devein the shrimp, leaving the tails attached. Sprinkle with the salt, pepper, and sherry. Dredge in the flour and dip in the eggs.

2. Break the noodles into ½-inch-long sections and roll the shrimp in the noodles.

3. Heat the oil to 360°F and fry until golden. Serve with sauce on the side.

▶ Prepare just before serving; do not try to hold.

NOTE: The finest noodles, called rice sticks, are used here. Although delicate looking, these noodles are quite hard before they are cooked. To break them into smaller sections, separate them into a few strands and then break up the strands. You can also soak the noodles in boiling water for a few minutes and then cut them with a knife. However, the soaked noodles have a tendency to cling to the batter and not fry as crisp as the unsoaked ones.

≡ *Shrimp in Bamboo Shape*

≡ Yield: 24 fritters

1 pound large shrimp	3 eggs
1½ teaspoons salt	oil for frying
½ teaspoon sesame oil	dipping sauces (pages 72–82)
1 cup cornstarch	

≡ Yield: 72 fritters

3 pounds large shrimp	9 eggs
1½ tablespoons salt	oil for frying
1½ teaspoons sesame oil	dipping sauces (pages 72–82)
3 cups cornstarch	

1. Peel the shrimp, leaving the tail segment attached. Sprinkle with the salt and sesame oil and toss to coat. Dip the shrimp into half the cornstarch and place on a platter.

2. In a bowl, beat the remaining cornstarch with the eggs.

3. In a skillet, heat an inch of oil to 375°F. Dip the shrimp into the egg mixture and fry in batches until golden. Serve with dipping sauces.

▶ Prepare just before serving; do not try to hold.
NOTE: The Chinese have a fondness for semideep-fat-frying; this recipe is an example. Do not crowd the pan when frying, and let the oil return to temperature before cooking another batch.

≡ *Parmesan Shrimp*

≡ Yield: 24 fritters

1 pound large shrimp	pepper, to taste
1 tablespoon lemon juice	1 cup flour
1 tablespoon Worcestershire	3 eggs, beaten
sauce	1 cup grated Parmesan cheese
1 teaspoon salt	oil for frying

≡ Yield: 72 fritters

3 pounds large shrimp	¼ teaspoon pepper
3 tablespoons lemon juice	3 cups flour
3 tablespoons Worcestershire	9 eggs, beaten
sauce	3 cups grated Parmesan cheese
1 tablespoon salt	oil for frying

1. Peel the shrimp, leaving the tail segment attached. Devein if necessary. In a bowl, toss the shrimp with the lemon juice, Worcestershire sauce, salt, and pepper. Marinate for 10 minutes to 2 hours.

2. Dredge the shrimp in the flour, dip in the eggs, and roll in the cheese. Place on a baking rack and let the coating set for at least 30 minutes.

3. Heat the oil to 360°F and fry until golden.

▶ Can be prepared for frying 1 day in advance.

≡ *Crispy Fried Shrimp*

≡ Yield: 24 fritters

oil for frying
1 pound shrimp
1½ cups cornmeal
1 teaspoon salt

1 teaspoon celery seeds
2 eggs, lightly beaten
mayonnaise flavored with
  mustard to taste

≡ Yield: 72 fritters

oil for frying
3 pounds shrimp
4 cups cornmeal
1 tablespoon salt

1 tablespoon celery seeds
6 eggs, lightly beaten
mayonnaise flavored with
  mustard to taste

1. Heat the oil to 375°F.

2. In a bowl, mix the cornmeal, salt, and celery seeds.

3. Peel the shrimp, leaving the tail segment attached. Devein. Dip the shrimp into the eggs.

4. Roll the shrimp in the cornmeal and fry until golden. Serve with mustard mayonnaise.

▶ Prepare just before serving; do not try to hold.

≡ *Coconut Fried Shrimp*

≡ Yield: 24 fritters

1 pound shrimp, peeled and
  deveined
¼ cup lemon juice
1 teaspoon curry powder
¼ teaspoon ground ginger
salt, to taste
3 cups flour

1 teaspoon baking powder
1 cup milk
flour for dredging
2 cups shredded unsweetened
  coconut
oil for frying

══ **Yield: 72 fritters**

3 pounds shrimp, peeled and
  deveined
¾ cup lemon juice
1 tablespoon curry powder
¾ teaspoon ground ginger
salt, to taste
9 cups flour

1 tablespoon baking powder
3 cups milk
flour for dredging
6 cups shredded unsweetened
  coconut
oil for frying

1. In a bowl, marinate the shrimp in the lemon juice, curry powder, ginger, and salt for 4 hours. Drain.

2. In a bowl, whisk the flour, baking powder, and a pinch of salt. Slowly beat in the milk and the drained marinade from the shrimp to make a smooth batter.

3. Dredge the shrimp in the flour, dip in the batter, and roll in the coconut.

4. Heat the oil to 375°F and fry until golden.

▶ Prepare just before serving.

══ *Tempura (Assorted Japanese Fritters)*

══ **Yield: 24 fritters**

1 egg
1 cup water
1 cup flour
shrimp, scallops, and/or
  vegetables (see note)

oil for frying
Japanese soy sauce (see
  Glossary)

══ **Yield: 72 fritters**

3 eggs
3 cups water
3 cups flour
shrimp, scallops, and/or
  vegetables (see note)

oil for frying
Japanese soy sauce (see
  Glossary)

1. In a bowl, beat the egg(s) and water and gradually add the flour, stirring lightly; do not overmix. The batter may be lumpy.

2. Heat the oil to 375°F. Dip the foods into the batter and fry until golden. Serve with Japanese soy sauce.

▶ Prepare just before serving.

NOTE: The selection of vegetables and seafood is up to the cook, based on what is available or what best suits the menu. Obviously, shrimp and scallops will be most popular. Vegetables that work well include zucchini, eggplant, cauliflower, broccoli, and carrots.

☰ *Chinese Fried Shrimp Balls*

═ Yield: 36 fritters

1 recipe shrimp paste
  (page 693)
oil for frying

dipping sauces (pages 72–82)
Chinese mustard (page 73)

1. With moistened hands, shape the shrimp paste into 1-inch balls.
2. Heat the oil to 300°F and fry the balls until light and fluffy. Serve immediately with dipping sauces and/or Chinese mustard.

▶ The paste can be made 1 day in advance. The balls puff up when cooked and soon deflate. Therefore, they are best when served immediately.

☰ *Cantonese Fried Chicken*

═ Yield: 24 fritters

1½ pounds boned and skinned
  chicken breasts
3 tablespoons sherry
3 tablespoons soy sauce
½ teaspoon sugar
2 tablespoons ginger syrup
  (see note)

1 cup flour
2 tablespoons cornstarch
1 egg
¾ to 1 cup water
oil for frying
dipping sauces (pages 72–82)

═ Yield: 72 fritters

4½ pounds boned and skinned
  chicken breasts
½ cup sherry
½ cup soy sauce
1½ teaspoons sugar
⅓ cup ginger syrup (see note)

3 cups flour
⅓ cup cornstarch
3 eggs
2 to 3 cups water
oil for frying
dipping sauces (pages 72–82)

1. Cut the chicken into strips ¼ inch wide and 2 inches long.

2. In a bowl, marinate the chicken in the sherry, soy sauce, sugar, and ginger syrup for 1 hour, turning often.

3. In a bowl, mix the flour, cornstarch, egg(s), and enough water to make a thin batter.

4. Heat the oil to 375°F. Dip the chicken into the batter and fry until golden.

▶ Can be prepared for dipping and frying 1 day in advance.

NOTE: Ginger syrup is found in jars of preserved ginger in syrup.

≡ *Sesame Chicken Wings I*

═ Yield: 24 fritters

12 large chicken wings	2 eggs, beaten with 2
1½ teaspoons paprika	tablespoons water
1 teaspoon rubbed sage	1 cup sesame seeds
½ teaspoon salt	oil for frying
flour for dredging	soy dipping sauce (page 74)

═ Yield: 72 fritters

36 large chicken wings	6 eggs, beaten with 6
1½ tablespoons paprika	tablespoons water
1 tablespoon rubbed sage	3 cups sesame seeds
1½ teaspoons salt	oil for frying
flour for dredging	soy dipping sauce (page 74)

1. Cut off the wing tips and discard. Separate the wing sections at the joints.

2. In a bowl, mix the paprika, sage, and salt. Sprinkle on the wings.

3. Dredge chicken in the flour, dip in the eggs, and roll in the sesame seeds. Chill at least 1 hour.

4. Heat the oil to 360°F and fry until golden.

▶ Can be prepared for frying 1 day in advance.

≡ *Sesame Chicken Wings II*

═ Yield: 24 fritters

12 chicken wings	1 cup sesame seeds
1 recipe beer batter (page 323)	oil for frying

═ **Yield: 72 fritters**

36 chicken wings   3 cups sesame seeds
2 recipes beer batter (page 323)   oil for frying

1. Cut off the wing tips and discard. Separate the wing sections at the joints.
2. Prepare the batter.
3. Heat the oil to 375°F. Dip the wings into the batter and sprinkle generously with the sesame seeds. Fry until golden.

▶ Prepare just before serving; do not try to hold.

═ *Batter-Fried Chicken Wing Drumsticks*

═ **Yield: 24 fritters**

12 large chicken wings   1 recipe beer batter (page 323)
¼ cup lemon juice   oil for frying
salt and pepper, to taste   soy dipping sauces (page 74)

═ **Yield: 72 fritters**

36 large chicken wings   2 recipes beer batter (page 323)
¾ cup lemon juice   oil for frying
salt and pepper, to taste   soy dipping sauces (page 74)

1. Cut off the wing tips and discard. Separate the wing sections at the joints.
2. Starting at one end of each wing, gently push the meat to the other end as if turning it inside out; it should look like a tiny chicken leg. Discard the smaller bone.
3. Marinate the wings in the lemon juice, salt, and pepper for 1 hour.
4. Heat the oil to 360°F. Dip the chicken into the batter and fry until golden. Serve with dipping sauce.

▶ Can be prepared for dipping and frying the day before.

≡ Jou Ng Heng Gai
(Chinese Chicken Wing Drumsticks)

═ Yield: 24 fritters

12 chicken wings
1 teaspoon Chinese five-spice
  powder
1½ teaspoons salt
2 garlic cloves, minced
1 tablespoon minced gingerroot
⅓ cup flour
⅓ cup cornstarch

¼ teaspoon white pepper
¼ teaspoon Chinese five-spice
  powder
oil for frying
Chinese mustard, plum sauce,
  or other dipping sauces
  (pages 72–82)

═ Yield: 72 fritters

36 chicken wings
1 tablespoon Chinese five-spice
  powder
1½ tablespoons salt
6 garlic cloves, minced
3 tablespoons minced
  gingerroot
1 cup flour

1 cup cornstarch
¾ teaspoon white pepper
¾ teaspoon Chinese five-spice
  powder
oil for frying
Chinese mustard, plum sauce,
  or other dipping sauces
  (pages 72–82)

1. Prepare the chicken wings as in the previous recipe.

2. In a bowl, mix the first measure of five-spice powder, salt, garlic, and ginger. Rub over the wings and marinate for at least 4 hours.

3. In a bowl, mix the flour, cornstarch, pepper, and remaining five-spice powder.

4. Heat the oil to 375°F. Roll the wings in the cornstarch mixture and fry until golden. Serve with dipping sauces.

► Can be marinated overnight.

≡ Breaded Chicken Wings

═ Yield: 24 fritters

1½ cups fresh bread crumbs
½ cup grated Parmesan cheese
3 tablespoons minced parsley
1 teaspoon dried oregano
12 chicken wings

salt and pepper, to taste
flour for dredging
2 eggs beaten with 2
  tablespoons water
oil for frying

═ **Yield: 72 fritters**

4½ cups fresh bread crumbs
1½ cups grated Parmesan
   cheese
½ cup minced parsley
1 tablespoon dried oregano

36 chicken wings
salt and pepper, to taste
flour for dredging
6 eggs beaten with ⅓ cup water
oil for frying

1. In a bowl, mix the bread crumbs, cheese, parsley, and oregano.
2. Cut off the wing tips and discard. Separate the wing sections at the joints.
3. Season with salt and pepper. Dredge in the flour, dip in the eggs, and roll in the bread crumb mixture. Let coating set for at least 30 minutes.
4. Heat the oil to 360°F and fry until golden.

▶ Can be prepared for frying 1 day in advance.

≡ *Chicken Liver Fritters I*

═ **Yield: 24 fritters**

1 pound chicken livers, cut in
   half
¼ cup soy sauce
2 tablespoons sherry
1 cup flour

½ teaspoon baking powder
1 teaspoon salt
pinch of pepper
⅔ cup water
oil for frying

═ **Yield: 72 fritters**

3 pounds chicken livers, cut in
   half
¾ cup soy sauce
⅓ cup sherry
3 cups flour

1½ teaspoons baking powder
1 tablespoon salt
½ teaspoon pepper
2 cups water
oil for frying

1. In a bowl, marinate the livers in soy sauce and sherry for 30 minutes.
2. In another bowl, mix the flour, baking powder, salt, and pepper. Stir in the water to make a smooth batter.
3. Heat the oil to 375°F. Drain the livers, dip in the batter, and fry until golden.

▶ Can be prepared for frying 1 day in advance.
NOTE: If the batter should slide off the livers, dredge them in flour first.

≡ *Chicken Liver Fritters II*

═ Yield: 24 fritters

1 pound chicken livers, cut in half	salt and pepper, to taste
1 cup dry red wine	flour for dredging
1 tablespoon minced parsley	oil for frying
⅛ teaspoon dried thyme	1 recipe beer batter (page 323)
1 bay leaf	Dijon mustard

═ Yield: 72 fritters

3 pounds chicken livers, cut in half	salt and pepper, to taste
3 cups dry red wine	flour for dredging
3 tablespoons minced parsley	oil for frying
½ teaspoon dried thyme	2 recipes beer batter (page 323)
2 bay leaves	Dijon mustard

1. In a bowl, marinate the livers in the wine, parsley, thyme, bay leaf, salt, and pepper. Drain and dry. Dredge the livers in the flour.

2. Heat the oil to 370°F. Dip the livers into the batter and fry until golden. Serve with the mustard.

▶ Can be marinated overnight.

≡ *Bocconcini Fritti (Mixed Italian Fritters)*

═ Yield: 36 fritters

¼ pound Gruyère cheese, cut in ½-inch cubes	flour for dredging
¼ pound mortadella, cut in ½-inch cubes (see note)	2 eggs, lightly beaten
⅛ pound pancetta, thinly sliced	1 cup fresh bread crumbs
	oil for frying

═ Yield: 72 fritters

½ pound Gruyère cheese, cut in ½-inch cubes	flour for dredging
½ pound mortadella, cut in ½-inch cubes (see note)	4 eggs, lightly beaten
¼ pound pancetta, thinly sliced	2 cups fresh bread crumbs
	oil for frying

1. Wrap half the Gruyère cubes and half the mortadella cubes in the pancetta and secure with wooden skewers. Skewer the remaining cheese and mortadella cubes unwrapped. Roll the cubes in the flour, dip in the eggs, and roll in the bread crumbs. Let the coating set for at least 30 minutes.

2. Heat the oil to 375°F and fry until golden.

▶ Can be prepared for frying 1 day in advance.

NOTE: Mortadella is an Italian cold cut. Order it sliced ½ inch thick, as it is usually sold thinly sliced. Pancetta is an Italian unsmoked bacon; it is usually sold thinly sliced.

≡ *Olive Ripiene (Italian Stuffed Olives)*

These little morsels are truly labor-intensive. It would be a mistake to consider making them for a large crowd.

═ Yield: approximately 50 olives

½ cup ground cooked chicken
½ cup ground ham
1 egg yolk
1 tablespoon grated Parmesan
  cheese
salt and pepper, to taste
pinch of grated nutmeg

1 pound large black olives,
  pitted
flour for dredging
1 egg, lightly beaten
1 cup bread crumbs
oil for frying

1. In a bowl, mix the chicken, ham, egg yolk, cheese, salt, pepper, and nutmeg.

2. Fit a pastry bag with a no. 3 plain tip, fill with the chicken-ham mixture, and stuff the cavities of the olives.

3. Dredge the olives in the flour, dip in the egg, and roll in the crumbs. Let the coating set for at least 30 minutes.

4. Heat the oil to 375°F and fry until golden.

▶ Can be prepared for frying 1 day in advance.

= 9 =

Skewered Foods

Skewers are the cocktail party substitute for forks. They are inexpensive, decorative, and disposable. Skewers come in metal, wood, plastic, or bamboo. Metal skewers are used for heavy cooking only and not for individual cocktail foods. Wooden or bamboo skewers are the most available and the most satisfactory. They range in length from 2½ inches to 10 or 12 inches. Really long skewers are impractical because they can be a danger to others in a crowded room; really short skewers can be a danger to the diner. Guests have been known to pick up a skewered food without seeing or feeling the skewer, only to get stabbed when they bite into it (or, worse, swallow the whole thing). Plastic skewers are not suitable for broiled or other hot foods. Six-inch bamboo skewers work for a number of reasons: they are a reasonable length, they can be used for hot or cold foods, they are festive, and they are easily seen. Shorter skewers work for smaller foods, as long as the skewer is clearly visible. Serve skewers in small containers if guests are to spear the food themselves.

Some caterers choose frilled skewers because they are decorative as well as noticeable. Regrettably, these often come in colors that compete with the food. Use one or two colors that will complement the food: white and dark green are popular choices; purple is not always in the best taste. Of course, these skewers cannot be used near heat.

Asian markets sell short wooden skewers that are decoratively carved at one end. They sound expensive but are not. The carving gives the pick a distinctive feel, and guests seem to notice them more readily. Select the sturdier round skewers instead of the flimsy flat picks found in most markets.

Guests often do not know what to do with used skewers. Caterers should provide clues. If the skewers are short, a small plate with a clean skewer resting in it set on the serving tray signals that used skewers should be placed there. If long skewers are used for sates, for example, one or two laid at the back of the platter away from the food will also give the idea. Of course, servers must be prepared to take used skewers from the guests. Train servers to look for skewers that have fallen to the floor and pick them up quickly before someone falls.

Think of the guests' safety when presenting skewered foods. Arrange the food on the skewers so it will not fall off when guests pick up the skewers. Place the pointed end of the skewer facing the server so the guest reaches for the appropriate end. For food that does not need the skewer to hold it together, such as meatballs, serve the skewers in small containers so the guests can choose the item they wish.

To prevent wooden or bamboo skewers from burning while the food is cooking, soak them in water for 30 minutes or longer. Some charring is acceptable, but if the skewer is burned to the end, replace it before serving the food.

Skewered foods are often accompanied by sauces. Follow the suggestions here, or review Chapters 3 and 4 for other ideas. Of course, other hors d'oeuvre such as meatballs and marinated foods may be served on or with skewers.

An interesting presentation for skewered foods is to insert the sharp end into half a cabbage, orange, or grapefruit. This presentation is best for platters that are to be left on the table rather than passed, so that a hard tug will not topple everything onto the floor.

Arrange the food carefully so that it looks attractive and guests can make their selections easily. Hot foods to be eaten with skewers should be cooked and passed as they are needed, rather than cooked ahead and put out in huge piles. In other words, if you are making chicken livers in bacon, do not dump them all into one large chafing dish. Not only is this unattractive, but it is also difficult for guests to make their selection.

One of the quickest cocktail foods to prepare is a skewer of fruit and meat or cheese. Here are a few quick suggestions. Develop your own ideas and, above all, be creative and adventurous.

- cubes of Gruyère cheese and kumquats
- prunes stuffed with nuts and rolled in cinnamon
- prunes wrapped in bacon and broiled
- grapes with cheese cubes and liverwurst or pâté
- pineapple wrapped in prosciutto or Westphalian ham
- figs wrapped in prosciutto
- salami and cheese cubes
- salami cubes with kumquats

≡ *Involtini di Prosciutto con Asparagi (Asparagus Rolled in Prosciutto)*

≡ Yield: 24 rolls

24 stalks asparagus
12 thin slices prosciutto

½ cup butter
¼ cup grated Parmesan cheese

≡ Yield: 72 rolls

72 stalks asparagus
36 thin slices prosciutto

1 cup butter
½ cup grated Parmesan cheese

1. Preheat the oven to 350°F.

2. Trim the top 3 inches of the asparagus and reserve the bottoms for another use. Cook in boiling salted water until just tender. Drain.

3. Wrap each stalk in half a slice of prosciutto and arrange in a baking dish. Bake for 10 minutes or until heated.

4. Melt the butter and stir in the cheese. Serve the hot butter as a dip. Serve skewers on the side.

▶ Can be prepared for baking 1 day in advance.

NOTE: Make sure that the butter is changed regularly so that it is always liquid. It can be reheated.

≡ *Attereaux au Parmesan (Parmesan Skewers)*

This fritter is made by arranging the ingredients on a skewer. For added flavor, add a thin slice of prosciutto to the skewer.

≡ Yield: 24 skewers

2 cups consommé
⅔ cup semolina
2 tablespoons butter
2 eggs
1 egg yolk
½ cup grated Parmesan cheese

½ pound Gruyère cheese,
  sliced ¼ inch thick
2 eggs, beaten
1½ cups bread crumbs
oil for frying

═ **Yield: 72 skewers**

6 cups consommé
2 cups semolina
⅓ cup butter
6 eggs
3 egg yolks
1½ cups grated Parmesan
 cheese

1½ pounds Gruyère cheese,
 sliced ¼ inch thick
6 eggs, beaten
4½ cups bread crumbs
oil for frying

1. Preheat the oven to 400°F.

2. In a casserole, bring the consommé to a boil and add the semolina in a slow, steady stream, stirring constantly until thickened.

3. Stir in the butter and transfer to the oven. Bake for 25 minutes. Remove from the oven and beat in the eggs, egg yolks, and grated Parmesan cheese.

4. Butter a baking sheet and spread the semolina ¼ inch thick. Cover with waxed paper and chill.

5. Cut semolina into 1-inch circles. Cut the Gruyère cheese into 1-inch circles. Alternate 2 circles of cheese and 2 circles of semolina on a skewer. Dip the skewers in the beaten eggs and roll in the bread crumbs.

6. Heat the oil to 375°F and fry until golden.

▶ Can be prepared for frying 1 day in advance.

═ *Le Grande Fruits de Mer*
  (Assorted Seafood Platter)

This is a display more than it is a single hors d'oeuvre. An alternative to the raw bar when made in large quantities, it can be a truly impressive presentation. Appearance is most important, so arrange the items as creatively as possible, either on a single platter or as an entire buffet. A large sheet of marble, particularly dark green, or a mirror can make an attractive base. However you serve it, it is important to replenish the arrangement easily and neatly. Preparing it in sections allows you to replace those parts that need it, while keeping the display attractive throughout the event. No matter how striking it is in the beginning, if it is dirty-looking at the end, guests will notice.

Even the simplest foods can be made to appear luxurious if presented impressively. Arrange the seafood singularly or in attractive groupings, on platters, in baskets, or in seashells. Needless to say, an ice sculpture can add drama to such a presentation. Place the sauces nearby and serve the skewers separately.

Some of the foods you can select are:

cooked shrimp
chunks of cooked lobster
crab claws
poached, raw, or marinated
   scallops
raw oysters
raw clams
cooked mussels
smoked oysters or mussels
squares of smoked sturgeon
smoked whitefish

rolls of smoked salmon
assorted smoked salmons
chunks of cooked finnan
   haddie
cocktail sauce
sauce Louis
sauce aïllade
sauce horcher
soy dipping sauces
sauce rémoulade

≡ Shellfish en Brochettes

═ Yield: 24 skewers

½ cup olive oil
½ cup sherry
1 teaspoon minced gingerroot
½ teaspoon minced garlic
6 whole cooked lobster tails
¼ pound shrimp, cooked and
   shelled

½ pound raw scallops
3 tablespoons soy sauce
Asian dipping sauces
   (pages 72–82)

═ Yield: 72 skewers

1½ cups olive oil
1 cup sherry
1 tablespoon minced gingerroot
1½ teaspoons minced garlic
18 whole cooked lobster tails
¾ pound shrimp, cooked and
   shelled

1½ pounds raw scallops
½ cup soy sauce
Asian dipping sauces
   (pages 72–82)

1. Preheat the broiler.

2. In a bowl, mix the oil, sherry, gingerroot, and garlic. Cut the lobster into bite-size pieces. If the shrimp are large, cut in half lengthwise; if small, leave whole. Cut the scallops into bite-size pieces. Marinate the seafood in the oil for 1½ hours. Drain.

3. Thread alternating pieces onto skewers and brush lightly with the soy sauce. Broil, turning often, until lightly browned and the scallops are cooked. Serve with dipping sauces.

▶ Can be prepared several hours in advance. Broil just before serving.

≡ *Brochettes de Moules I (Skewers of Mussels I)*

═ Yield: 24 skewers

2 quarts mussels, steamed (see
    page 467)
½ cup bread crumbs
½ teaspoon dried tarragon

salt and pepper, to taste
1½ cups melted butter
1 cup béarnaise sauce
    (page 57)

═ Yield: 72 skewers

6 quarts mussels, steamed (see
    page 467)
1½ cups bread crumbs
1½ teaspoons dried tarragon

salt and pepper, to taste
3 cups melted butter
3 cups béarnaise sauce
    (page 57)

1. Preheat the broiler.

2. Remove the mussels from the shells and set aside; discard the shells. In a bowl, mix the bread crumbs, tarragon, salt, and pepper. Skewer 2 or 3 mussels, dip in the butter, and roll in the crumbs. Let the coating set for at least 30 minutes.

3. Broil until golden, basting with the remaining butter. Serve with the béarnaise sauce.

▶ Can be prepared for broiling 1 day in advance.

≡ *Brochettes de Moules II (Skewers of Mussels II)*

═ Yield: 24 skewers

24 large mussels, steamed
    (see page 467)
24 pork fat squares, ½ inch
    square and ¼ inch thick

½ teaspoon rosemary, crushed

═ Yield: 72 skewers

72 large mussels, steamed
    (see page 467)
72 pork fat squares, ½ inch
    square and ¼ inch thick

1½ teaspoons rosemary,
    crushed

1. Preheat the broiler.

2. Remove the mussels from the shells and set aside; discard the shells. Thread skewers with mussels and pork fat and sprinkle with rosemary. Broil until the fat is crisp.

▶ Can be prepared for broiling 1 day in advance.

NOTE: Slices of bacon can be substituted for the pork fat for more flavor. The rosemary should be crushed almost to a powder.

≡ *Les Anges en Chevaux (Angels on Horseback)*

The name of this classic hors d'oeuvre is a mystery. Perhaps it is a symbol of the best there is.

═ Yield: 24 skewers

24 oysters, shucked
salt and pepper, to taste

paprika, to taste
24 thin slices bacon

═ Yield: 72 skewers

72 oysters, shucked
salt and pepper, to taste

paprika, to taste
72 thin slices bacon

1. Preheat the oven to 375°F.

2. Sprinkle the oysters with salt, pepper, and paprika. Wrap each oyster in a bacon strip and skewer. Bake on a rack until the bacon is crisp.

▶ Can be prepared for baking 1 day in advance.

≡ *Smoked Salmon and Cucumber Skewers*

These look particularly attractive served on a bed of very fresh dill. Once the dill starts to wilt, replace it.

═ Yield: 24 skewers

1 pound smoked salmon, thinly
  sliced
1 cucumber, peeled, seeded,
  and cut into ½-inch cubes

1 cup mayonnaise, seasoned
  with minced dill and black
  pepper to taste

═ Yield: 72 skewers

3 pounds smoked salmon,
  thinly sliced
3 cucumbers, peeled, seeded,
  and cut into ½-inch cubes

3 cups mayonnaise, seasoned
  with minced dill and black
  pepper to taste

Roll the salmon slices into ½-inch-thick rolls and skewer with a cucumber cube. Serve with dill mayonnaise.

▶ Can be prepared for serving 6 hours in advance. Keep covered with a damp cloth.

☰ Marinated Scallops with Coconut Ginger Dressing

═ Yield: 24 skewers

1 onion, chopped
1 pound scallops
1 cup minced scallions
½ cup lemon juice
½ cup lime juice
1 teaspoon salt
¾ cup canned unsweetened
   coconut milk
¾ cup hot milk
1 large garlic clove, quartered
1 teaspoon grated gingerroot

½ teaspoon pepper
¼ teaspoon turmeric
12 cherry tomatoes, cut in half
1 red pepper, cut into 1-inch
   pieces
1 green pepper, cut into 1-inch
   pieces
salt, to taste
minced coriander (cilantro) or
   parsley

═ Yield: 72 skewers

3 onions, chopped
3 pounds scallops
3 cups minced scallions
1½ cups lemon juice
1½ cups lime juice
1 tablespoon salt
2½ cups canned unsweetened
   coconut milk
2½ cups hot milk
3 large garlic cloves, quartered
1 tablespoon grated gingerroot

1½ teaspoons pepper
¾ teaspoon turmeric
36 cherry tomatoes, cut in half
3 red peppers, cut into 1-inch
   pieces
3 green peppers, cut into 1-inch
   pieces
salt, to taste
minced coriander (cilantro) or
   parsley

1. Blanch onion in water to cover for 5 minutes. Drain.

2. In a bowl, gently mix the scallops, onions, scallions, lemon juice, lime juice, and salt. Cover and refrigerate 8 hours or overnight, stirring occasionally.

3. In a blender, purée the coconut milk, hot milk, garlic, ginger, pepper, and turmeric. Chill overnight.

4. Just before serving, drain the marinade from the scallop mixture and discard. Add the tomatoes, green and red peppers, and the coconut mixture. Season with salt. Skewer peppers and scallops alternately and serve sprinkled with the coriander.

▶ Can be prepared 1 day in advance.

≡ *Scallops and Prosciutto*

Many people prefer to eat these at room temperature without baking.

=== Yield: 24 skewers
1½ pounds scallops
1 tablespoon minced garlic
¼ cup lime juice
2 teaspoons salt
pepper, to taste

½ teaspoon minced basil
½ pound prosciutto, thinly sliced
melted butter

=== Yield: 72 skewers
4½ pounds scallops
3 tablespoons minced garlic
¾ cup lime juice
2 tablespoons salt
½ teaspoon pepper

1½ teaspoons minced basil
1½ pounds prosciutto, thinly sliced
melted butter

1. Preheat the oven to 450°F.
2. Cut scallops in half. In a bowl, mix the scallops, garlic, and lime juice. Cover and marinate for several hours.
3. When ready to serve, season with salt, pepper, and basil. Wrap each scallop in a slice of prosciutto and skewer. Brush with butter and bake 10 minutes or until just cooked.

▶ Can be prepared for baking several hours in advance.

≡ *Crevettes Aillade*
(Shrimp with Garlic Walnut Sauce)

This flavorful sauce is a great change from the customary cocktail sauce served with shrimp.

=== Yield: 24 skewers
½ cup chopped walnuts
3 garlic cloves, crushed
1 tablespoon lemon juice
¾ cup olive oil

½ teaspoon salt
2 tablespoons minced parsley
1 pound cooked shrimp, peeled and deveined

═ **Yield: 72 skewers**

1½ cups chopped walnuts
9 garlic cloves, crushed
3 tablespoons lemon juice
2¼ cups olive oil

1½ teaspoons salt
⅓ cup minced parsley
3 pounds cooked shrimp,
    peeled and deveined

1. In a food processor, purée the walnuts, garlic, and lemon juice. With the machine running, slowly add the olive oil and correct the seasoning with the salt. Add the parsley.

2. Serve the shrimp with the walnut sauce as a dip.

▶ The sauce can be prepared 3 days in advance.

═ *Shrimp and Avocado Skewers*

═ **Yield: 25 skewers**

3 avocados
¼ cup lemon juice
1 pound shrimp, cooked,
    peeled, and deveined

sauce horcher (page 53)

═ **Yield: 72 skewers**

9 avocados
¾ cup lemon juice
3 pounds shrimp, cooked,
    peeled, and deveined

sauce horcher (page 53)

1. Using a melon baller, cut the avocados into balls and toss them in the lemon juice.

2. Skewer the balls with the shrimp and serve the sauce as a dip.

▶ The avocado balls should be made no more than 2 hours before serving; keep tightly covered to prevent darkening.

═ *Hot Shrimp and Chicken Skewers*

═ **Yield: 24 skewers**

12 large peeled shrimp, cut in
    half lengthwise
½ pound chicken breast, cut
    into ½-inch strips
3 tablespoons minced shallot
¼ cup minced parsley

1 tablespoon grated lemon rind
2 tablespoons lemon juice
2 garlic cloves, minced
1 jalapeño pepper, minced
1 tablespoon olive oil

══ Yield: 72 skewers

36 large peeled shrimp, cut in
half lengthwise
1½ pounds chicken breasts, cut
into ½-inch strips
½ cup minced shallots
¾ cup minced parsley

3 tablespoons grated lemon
rind
⅓ cup lemon juice
6 garlic cloves, minced
2 jalapeño peppers, minced
3 tablespoons olive oil

1. Preheat the broiler.

2. In a bowl, marinate the shrimp and chicken in the shallots, parsley, lemon rind, lemon juice, garlic, jalapeños, and olive oil for 1 hour.

3. Wrap a strip of chicken around a piece of shrimp and skewer. Broil until just done.

▶ Can be prepared for broiling 1 day in advance.

≡ *Sautéed Shrimp with Garlic Cream Sauce*

This is a wonderfully subtle sauce of garlic in cream.

══ Yield: 24 skewers

2 cups heavy cream
4 garlic cloves, crushed
salt and pepper, to taste
1 pound shrimp, peeled and
deveined

2 garlic cloves, minced
¼ cup olive oil

══ Yield: 72 skewers

6 cups heavy cream
12 garlic cloves, crushed
salt and pepper, to taste
3 pounds shrimp, peeled and
deveined

6 garlic cloves, minced
¾ cup olive oil

1. In a saucepan, reduce the cream and garlic by half. Season with salt and pepper.

2. In a small skillet over medium heat, slowly poach the shrimp and garlic in the oil until the shrimp is just barely cooked; be careful not to brown the garlic or shrimp.

3. Skewer the shrimp and serve with the garlic sauce as a dip.

▶ The sauce can be prepared 1 day in advance and reheated.

≡ *Shrimp in Garlic Wine Sauce*

═ **Yield: 24 shrimp**

1 pound shrimp, peeled and
   deveined
½ cup butter
6 garlic cloves, minced
¼ cup lemon juice

½ teaspoon salt
¼ teaspoon pepper
¾ cup white wine
2 tablespoons minced parsley

═ **Yield: 72 shrimp**

3 pounds shrimp, peeled and
   deveined
1 cup butter
12 garlic cloves, minced
½ cup lemon juice

1 teaspoon salt
½ teaspoon pepper
1½ cups white wine
¼ cup minced parsley

1. In a skillet, sauté the shrimp in the butter for 1 minute. Add the garlic, lemon juice, salt, pepper, and wine and bring to a boil. Sprinkle with parsley.

2. Serve warm with skewers on the side.

▶ Prepare just before serving.

NOTE: The shrimp can be baked in a 450°F oven in gratin dishes. Place the gratins on napkins on serving platters and let the servers pass them while sizzling hot.

≡ *Gambas al Ajillo I (Shrimp in Garlic I)*

═ **Yield: 24 shrimp**

1 pound shrimp, peeled and
   deveined
½ cup olive oil

3 garlic cloves, thinly sliced
1 tablespoon minced parsley
salt and pepper, to taste

═ **Yield: 72 shrimp**

3 pounds shrimp, peeled and
   deveined
1½ cups olive oil

9 garlic cloves, thinly sliced
3 tablespoons minced parsley
salt and pepper, to taste

1. Preheat the oven to 450°F.

2. In a casserole, marinate the shrimp in the olive oil, garlic, parsley, salt, and pepper for 1 hour.

3. Bake for about 5 minutes or until just done. Serve hot or at room temperature.

▶ Can be prepared for baking a day in advance.

NOTE: In Spain these shrimp would be served with their shells on. At a cocktail party this would make eating them too messy.

≡ *Gambas al Ajillo II (Shrimp in Garlic II)*

= **Yield: 24 shrimp**

1 garlic clove, thinly sliced
½ dried hot red chili pepper, broken and seeded
½ bay leaf

⅓ cup olive oil
1 pound shrimp, shelled and deveined
salt, to taste

= **Yield: 72 shrimp**

3 garlic cloves, thinly sliced
1½ dried hot red chili peppers, broken and seeded
1 bay leaf

1 cup olive oil
3 pounds shrimp, shelled and deveined
salt, to taste

1. In a skillet, heat the garlic, chili pepper, bay leaf, and olive oil until the garlic begins to sizzle and turn golden. Add the shrimp (in batches, if necessary) and cook, stirring until they are just cooked, about 2 minutes.

2. Sprinkle with salt and serve with skewers on the side.

▶ Prepare just before serving.

≡ *Broiled Shrimp with Tarragon and Garlic*

= **Yield: 24 shrimp**

1 pound shrimp, peeled and deveined
¼ cup butter
¼ cup olive oil
2 tablespoons lemon juice

2 tablespoons minced shallot
2 teaspoons minced garlic
2 tablespoons minced tarragon
salt and pepper, to taste
1 tablespoon minced parsley

= **Yield: 72 shrimp**

3 pounds shrimp, peeled and deveined
½ cup butter
½ cup olive oil
¼ cup lemon juice

¼ cup minced shallots
3 tablespoons minced garlic
6 tablespoons minced tarragon
salt and pepper, to taste
⅓ cup minced parsley

1. Preheat the broiler.

2. In a baking dish large enough to hold the shrimp in one layer, melt the butter under the broiler. Stir in the olive oil, lemon juice, shallots, garlic, and half the tarragon. Add the shrimp, season with salt and pepper, and stir. Broil until just cooked, about 3 minutes.

3. In a bowl, mix the parsley and remaining tarragon and sprinkle over the shrimp. Serve immediately with skewers on the side.

▶ Can be prepared for broiling several hours in advance.

≡ *Crevettes aux Herbes en Brochettes* (*Broiled Shrimp with Herbs*)

═ **Yield: 24 shrimp**

1 pound shrimp, peeled and deveined with the tails left on	1 teaspoon minced chives
	1 teaspoon crushed garlic
	1 teaspoon minced tarragon
¼ cup extra virgin olive oil	1 teaspoon minced chervil
¼ cup sherry	salt and pepper, to taste
2 teaspoons minced parsley	

═ **Yield: 72 shrimp**

3 pounds shrimp, peeled and deveined with the tails left on	1 tablespoon minced chives
	1 tablespoon crushed garlic
	1 tablespoon minced tarragon
¾ cup extra virgin olive oil	1 tablespoon minced chervil
¾ cup sherry	salt and pepper, to taste
2 tablespoons minced parsley	

1. Preheat the broiler.

2. In a bowl, marinate the shrimp in the olive oil, sherry, parsley, chives, garlic, tarragon, chervil, salt, and pepper for 4 hours, turning often. Drain well.

3. Broil until lightly browned and just cooked.

▶ Can be marinated 1 day in advance.

NOTE: It is imperative not to overcook the shrimp. It is better not to brown them than to risk overcooking them.

≡ Skewered Shrimp and Bacon

═ Yield: 24 skewers

24 shrimp, peeled and deveined
2 tablespoons olive oil
1 tablespoon lemon juice

salt and pepper, to taste
½ teaspoon paprika
24 slices bacon

═ Yield: 72 skewers

72 shrimp, peeled and deveined
⅓ cup olive oil
3 tablespoons lemon juice

salt and pepper, to taste
1½ teaspoons paprika
72 slices bacon

1. Preheat the broiler.
2. In a bowl, marinate the shrimp in the olive oil, lemon juice, salt, pepper, and paprika for up to 24 hours. Drain.
3. Wrap each shrimp in a bacon strip and skewer. Broil until the bacon is crisp and the shrimp is cooked.

▶ Can be prepared for broiling 1 day in advance.
NOTE: For a slightly stronger bacon favor, wrap the shrimp in the bacon first and marinate everything.

≡ Swordfish Brochettes

═ Yield: 24 brochettes

2 pounds swordfish, cut in
1-inch cubes
5 tablespoons olive oil
1 tablespoon lemon juice

2 teaspoons grated onion
½ teaspoon paprika
salt, to taste
lemon wedges

═ Yield: 72 brochettes

6 pounds swordfish, cut in
1-inch cubes
1 cup olive oil
¼ cup lemon juice

2 tablespoons grated onion
2 teaspoons paprika
salt, to taste
lemon wedges

1. Preheat the broiler.
2. In a bowl, marinate the swordfish in the oil, lemon juice, onion, paprika, and salt for at least 2 hours.
3. Broil until barely cooked, about 8 minutes, turning once. Serve with skewers and lemon wedges on the side.

▶ Can be prepared for broiling 1 day in advance.

☰ *Swordfish and Olive Skewers*

═ Yield: 24 skewers

1 pound swordfish, cut in 1-inch cubes	⅓ cup minced parsley
12 green olives, cut in half	¼ cup minced dill
12 black olives, cut in half	2 tablespoons lemon juice
1 cup tomato juice	1 teaspoon minced jalapeño pepper
½ cup chopped scallions	

═ Yield: 72 skewers

3 pounds swordfish, cut in 1-inch cubes	1 cup minced parsley
36 green olives, cut in half	¾ cup minced dill
36 black olives, cut in half	⅓ cup lemon juice
3 cups tomato juice	1 tablespoon minced jalapeño pepper
1½ cups chopped scallions	

1. Preheat the broiler.

2. Thread a swordfish cube, green olive half, swordfish cube, and black olive half onto each skewer. Marinate the skewers in a baking dish with the tomato juice, scallions, parsley, dill, lemon juice, and jalapeño for at least 4 hours.

3. Broil the swordfish until just done, basting with marinade.

▶ Can be prepared for broiling 1 day in advance.

☰ *Teriyaki Ahi (Marinated Tuna Fish)*

Fresh tuna has recently become very popular as well as very expensive. It is important to treat it with care. For the best flavor, it is better to undercook the fish and leave the center medium, if not rare.

═ Yield: 24 tuna cubes

1 pound tuna, cut in 1-inch cubes	¼ cup sugar
1 cup Japanese soy sauce or tamari (see Glossary)	2 garlic cloves, crushed
	1 scallion, minced
	1 teaspoon minced gingerroot

≡ **Yield: 72 tuna cubes**

3 pounds tuna, cut in 1-inch
    cubes
2 cups Japanese soy sauce or
    tamari (see Glossary)

½ cup sugar
4 garlic cloves, crushed
2 scallions, minced
2 teaspoons minced gingerroot

1. Preheat the broiler.
2. In a bowl, marinate the tuna in the soy sauce, sugar, garlic, scallion, and gingerroot for up to 24 hours. Drain.
3. Broil until just cooked. Serve with skewers on the side.

▶ Can be prepared for broiling 24 hours in advance.

≡ *Tuna and Red Pepper Rolls*

≡ **Yield: 24 rolls**

4 roasted red peppers, peeled
3 tablespoons olive oil
3 tablespoons lemon juice
1 7-ounce can Italian tuna
    packed in oil

¼ cup minced parsley
3 tablespoons minced capers
salt and pepper, to taste

≡ **Yield: 72 rolls**

12 roasted red peppers, peeled
½ cup olive oil
9 tablespoons lemon juice
3 7-ounce cans Italian tuna
    packed in oil

¾ cup minced parsley
½ cup minced capers
salt and pepper, to taste

1. Cut the peppers into 1-inch strips and marinate them in the olive oil and one-third of the lemon juice.
2. In a bowl, mix the tuna and its oil, parsley, capers, remaining lemon juice, salt, and pepper. Put 1 teaspoon of the mixture on each pepper strip and roll. Skewer to secure.

▶ Can be prepared 12 hours in advance.

≡ *Sesame Chicken Brochettes*

═ **Yield: 24 skewers**

1½ pounds large chicken
  breasts, skinned, boned, and
  cut into 1½-inch strips
⅓ cup white wine
2 tablespoons minced chutney

3 tablespoons olive oil
1 tablespoon curry powder
1½ cups sesame seeds
½ cup chutney

═ **Yield: 72 skewers**

4½ pounds large chicken
  breasts, skinned, boned, and
  cut into 1½-inch strips
1 cup white wine
⅓ cup minced chutney

½ cup olive oil
3 tablespoons curry powder
4 cups sesame seeds
1½ cups chutney

1. Preheat the broiler.

2. In a bowl, marinate the chicken in the wine, minced chutney, olive oil, and curry for 1 hour, stirring occasionally.

3. Thread onto skewers and roll in the sesame seeds. Broil until cooked through, basting with the marinade.

4. Purée the remaining chutney and serve as a dipping sauce.

▶ Can be prepared for broiling 1 day in advance.

≡ *Chinese Hacked Chicken Skewers with Sesame or Peanut Sauce*

Perhaps no hors d'oeuvre has become as popular as this one since I first wrote it. It has, in fact, become a cliché. Many versions are adaptations of the original without the excitement, so do try the original.

═ **Yield: 24 skewers**

6 cups water
1 pound skinned, boned
  chicken breasts
2 tablespoons sesame paste or
  peanut butter
2 tablespoons Asian sesame oil
1 tablespoon dark soy sauce
1 tablespoon chili paste with
  garlic

1 tablespoon rice vinegar
1½ teaspoons hot chili oil
1½ teaspoons minced
  gingerroot
1½ teaspoons minced scallions
1½ teaspoons minced garlic
3–4 tablespoons minced
  coriander (cilantro)

═ **Yield: 72 skewers**

4½ quarts water
3 pounds skinned, boned
  chicken breasts
⅓ cup sesame paste or peanut
  butter
⅓ cup Asian sesame oil
3 tablespoons dark soy sauce
3 tablespoons chili paste with
  garlic

3 tablespoons rice vinegar
1½ tablespoons hot chili oil
1½ tablespoons minced
  gingerroot
1½ tablespoons minced
  scallions
1½ tablespoons minced garlic
¾ cup minced coriander
  (cilantro)

1. In a saucepan, bring the water to a boil. Add the chicken and simmer 5 to 6 minutes. Turn off the heat and let cool. Drain and chill. Cut the chicken into strips 2 inches long.

2. In a bowl, beat the sesame paste and sesame oil until smooth. Beat in the soy sauce, chili paste, vinegar, chili oil, gingerroot, scallions, and garlic.

3. About 1 to 2 hours before serving, thread the chicken onto skewers and dip 1½ inches of each strip into the sauce. Roll in the minced coriander.

▶ The chicken can be cooked 1 day in advance. The sauce loses potency over time and is best made the day it is to be served.

NOTE: Always advise guests if food is truly hot. Some people have delicate stomachs that just can't tolerate the zestier offerings. If not forewarned, however, those with timid palates may exhibit fiery tempers.

≡ *Chicken and Snow Pea Skewers with Sesame Mayonnaise*

═ **Yield: 24 skewers**

1½ pounds chicken breasts,
  skinned, boned, and cut into
  2-inch strips
¼ cup thin soy sauce
1 garlic clove, sliced

2 tablespoons lemon juice
24 snow peas, blanched
½ cup mayonnaise
2 to 4 teaspoons Asian sesame
  oil

═ **Yield: 72 skewers**

4½ pounds chicken breasts,
  skinned, boned, and cut into
  2-inch strips
¾ cup thin soy sauce
3 garlic cloves, sliced

⅓ cup lemon juice
72 snow peas, blanched
1½ cups mayonnaise
2 to 3 tablespoons Asian sesame
  oil

1. Marinate the chicken in the soy sauce, garlic, and lemon juice for 24 hours.

2. In a saucepan, simmer the chicken, marinade, and enough water to cover until the chicken is just done, about 5 minutes. Drain and chill.

3. Wrap a snow pea around each chicken strip and secure with a skewer.

4. In a bowl, mix enough sesame oil into the mayonnaise to give it a distinctive flavor and serve as a dip.

▶ The sauce can be prepared several days in advance. The chicken can be cooked the day before. Blanch the snow peas and skewer no more than 6 hours before serving.

NOTE: Swordfish cubes, shrimp, and scallops can be prepared in the same fashion.

≡ *Yakitori (Japanese Broiled Chicken)*

═ **Yield: 24 skewers**

1½ pounds skinned, boned
   chicken breasts, cut into
   bite-size cubes
1 bunch scallions, cut into
   2-inch strips

¾ cup soy sauce
¾ cup sake
¼ cup sugar
cayenne pepper, to taste

═ **Yield: 72 skewers**

4½ pounds skinned, boned
   chicken breasts, cut into
   bite-size cubes
3 bunches scallions, cut into
   2-inch strips

2 cups soy sauce
2 cups sake
¾ cup sugar
cayenne pepper, to taste

1. Preheat the broiler.

2. Thread the chicken and scallions onto skewers.

3. In a bowl, mix the soy sauce, sake, and sugar. Dip the skewers into the soy mixture and broil until done, basting with the sauce. Sprinkle with cayenne and serve.

▶ Prepare just before serving.

≡ Indonesian Chicken Sate I

═ Yield: 24 skewers

1½ pounds skinned, boned
  chicken breasts, cut into
  bite-size cubes
¼ pound butter
¼ cup soy sauce

1 teaspoon ground coriander
2 tablespoons lime juice
12 preserved kumquats, halved
coriander (cilantro) sprigs
peanut sauce (page 81)

═ Yield: 72 skewers

4½ pounds skinned, boned
  chicken breasts, cut into
  bite-size cubes
¾ pound butter
¾ cup soy sauce

1 tablespoon ground coriander
⅓ cup lime juice
36 preserved kumquats, halved
coriander (cilantro) sprigs
peanut sauce (page 81)

1. Preheat the broiler.

2. Thread chicken onto skewers.

3. In a saucepan, melt the butter with the soy sauce, ground coriander, and lime juice.

4. Brush the chicken with the sauce and broil until browned, basting often.

5. Thread a kumquat half on each skewer and serve garnished with cilantro.

▶ Can be prepared for broiling a day in advance.

≡ Indonesian Chicken Sate II

═ Yield: 24 sates

1½ pounds skinned, boned
  chicken breasts, cut into
  bite-size cubes
¼ cup soy sauce
2 tablespoons oil
2 garlic cloves, crushed

1 teaspoon sugar
4 slices gingerroot
pinch of pepper
pinch of ground coriander
sate sauce (page 76) or peanut
  sauce (page 81)

═ Yield: 72 sates

4½ pounds skinned, boned
  chicken breasts, cut into
  bite-size cubes
¾ cup soy sauce
⅓ cup oil
6 garlic cloves, crushed

1 tablespoon sugar
12 slices gingerroot
¼ teaspoon pepper
¼ teaspoon ground coriander
sate sauce (page 76) or peanut
  sauce (page 81)

1. Preheat the broiler.

2. In a bowl, marinate the chicken in the soy sauce, oil, garlic, sugar, gingerroot, pepper, and coriander for 1 hour.

3. Thread onto skewers and broil until done. Serve sauce on the side.

▶ Can be prepared for broiling 1 day in advance.

≡ *Chicken Liver and Anchovy Brochettes*

= Yield: 24 brochettes

1 pound chicken livers, cut in half	2 cans anchovy fillets ½ pound sliced bacon

= Yield: 72 brochettes

3 pounds chicken livers, cut in half	6 cans anchovy fillets 1½ pounds sliced bacon

1. Preheat the broiler.

2. Wrap each chicken liver in an anchovy and then in a bacon slice. Skewer. Broil until done.

▶ Can be prepared for broiling 1 day in advance.

≡ *Chicken Liver and Shrimp Brochettes*

= Yield: 24 brochettes

1 pound chicken livers, cut in half ½ pound small shrimp, peeled 12 preserved kumquats, cut in half	1 garlic clove, crushed ½ cup butter, melted

= Yield: 72 brochettes

3 pounds chicken livers, cut in half 1½ pounds small shrimp, peeled	36 preserved kumquats, cut in half 3 garlic cloves, crushed 1½ cups butter, melted

1. Preheat the broiler.

2. Thread one chicken liver and one shrimp on each skewer. Discard the seed cases from the kumquats and thread them on the skewers so that they cup the shrimp.

3. In a saucepan, steep the garlic in the melted butter for 20 minutes. Brush the brochettes with the butter and broil until the chicken liver is medium.

▶ Can be prepared for broiling 1 day in advance.

≡ *Beef Parchment*

= Yield: 24 skewers

8 1-ounce slices raw beef round	4 teaspoons capers
¼ cup extra virgin olive oil	8 anchovy fillets
pepper, to taste	lemon wedges

= Yield: 72 skewers

24 1-ounce slices raw beef round	3 tablespoons capers
¾ cup extra virgin olive oil	24 anchovy fillets
pepper, to taste	lemon wedges

1. Discard any fat from the beef slices. Place between sheets of waxed paper and pound gently until paper-thin.

2. Remove the top layer of the paper and drizzle oil over the meat. Season with pepper, sprinkle with capers, and place an anchovy on top. Roll each slice jellyroll fashion and cut into 2-inch lengths. Skewer. Serve with lemon wedges on the side.

▶ Can be prepared 3 hours in advance.

≡ *Korean Beef Skewers*

= Yield: 24 skewers

1 pound sirloin steak, 1 inch thick	1½ teaspoons soy sauce
2 tablespoons beef stock	1½ teaspoons salt
2 tablespoons Asian sesame oil	1¼ teaspoons sugar
2 garlic cloves, minced	2 pears
1 tablespoon toasted sesame seeds	½ cup lemon juice

═ **Yield: 72 skewers**

3 pounds sirloin steak, 1 inch
  thick
⅓ cup beef stock
⅓ cup Asian sesame oil
6 garlic cloves, minced
3 tablespoons toasted sesame
  seeds

1½ tablespoons soy sauce
1 tablespoon salt
1½ tablespoons sugar
6 pears
1 cup lemon juice

1. Cut the steak into paper-thin slices. Marinate in the stock, sesame oil, garlic, sesame seeds, soy sauce, salt, and sugar for 1 hour.

2. Slice the pears thinly and marinate in the lemon juice for 5 minutes.

3. Wrap each pear slice in a slice of beef and skewer.

▶ Can be prepared 2 hours in advance.

═ *Carpaccio*

This hors d'oeuvre allegedly originated at Harry's Bar in Venice. There are numerous versions, all of them delicious. The principle is the same for each.

Slice a 1 pound raw sirloin or fillet of beef very thinly and pound the slices between sheets of waxed paper or plastic wrap until paper-thin. In the original version the slices would be arranged on a dinner plate and topped with a sauce. To serve at a cocktail party, top each slice with one of the following sauces, roll up, and cut into 2-inch sections. Skewer and serve. (Each slice can also be placed on fingers of buttered white Italian bread.)

Each pound of beef makes approximately 36 hors d'oeuvre. The meat can be pounded and wrapped airtight 1 day in advance. Once sauced, the carpaccio should be served within 4 hours. The sauces are enough for about 36 skewers.

═ *Carpaccio Sauce I*

¼ cup lemon juice
¼ cup olive oil
salt and pepper, to taste

½ cup grated Parmesan cheese
white truffle shavings
minced parsley

Sprinkle the beef slices with the lemon juice, olive oil, salt, pepper, cheese, and truffle shavings. Roll and cut into sections. Dip the ends in the parsley.

≡ *Carpaccio Sauce II*

1 cup mayonnaise	½ teaspoon Tabasco sauce
1 tablespoon Worcestershire sauce	½ teaspoon dry mustard
	⅓ cup very strong beef stock

In a bowl, mix the mayonnaise, Worcestershire sauce, Tabasco, and mustard. Add only enough stock to make the mixture spreadable. Spread on the beef slices, roll, and cut into 2-inch lengths. Skewer. **NOTE:** If desired, the beef can be cut into cubes or strips and threaded onto skewers. Pass the sauce separately.

≡ *Carpaccio Sauce III*

2 tablespoons minced shallots	pepper, to taste
1 cup mayonnaise made with lemon juice (page 48)	lemon wedges

Wrap the shallots in a square of cheesecloth or in the corner of a kitchen towel. Run under cold water and squeeze out the moisture. Fold the shallots into the mayonnaise and season with black pepper. Spread on the beef slices, roll, and skewer. Serve with lemon wedges.

≡ *Carpaccio Sauce IV*

1 cup loosely packed parsley sprigs	2 tablespoons lemon juice
15 anchovy fillets	2 tablespoons red wine vinegar
½ cup chopped onion	1 tablespoon Worcestershire sauce
½ cup olive oil	1 teaspoon dry mustard
2 small gherkins	salt and pepper, to taste
¼ cup capers	

In a food processor, process the parsley, anchovies, onions, olive oil, gherkins, capers, lemon juice, vinegar, Worcestershire, mustard, salt, and pepper to a coarse, creamy-colored paste. Spread on the beef slices, roll, and skewer.

☰ *Cold Fillet of Beef with Dijon Soy Sauce*

═ **Yield: 24 skewers**

1 pound cold cooked beef fillet, thinly sliced
½ cup mayonnaise

2 tablespoons Dijon mustard
1 tablespoon thin soy sauce
½ teaspoon Asian sesame oil

═ **Yield: 72 skewers**

3 pounds cold cooked beef fillet, thinly sliced
1½ cups mayonnaise

⅓ cup Dijon mustard
3 tablespoons thin soy sauce
1½ teaspoons Asian sesame oil

1. Roll the slices of beef and skewer.
2. In a bowl, mix the mayonnaise, mustard, soy sauce, and sesame oil. Serve the beef with the sauce as a dip.

▶ The sauce can be prepared 1 day in advance.

☰ *Beef Rolls Chinoise*

═ **Yield: 24 skewers**

1 teaspoon dry mustard
1½ tablespoons orange marmalade
6 slices very rare roast beef

salt, to taste
2 tablespoons minced chives
2 tablespoons minced parsley

═ **Yield: 72 skewers**

1 tablespoon dry mustard
⅓ cup orange marmalade
18 slices very rare roast beef

salt, to taste
⅓ cup minced chives
⅓ cup minced parsley

1. In a bowl, mix the mustard and marmalade to make a paste. Spread thinly on the beef slices, season with salt, and sprinkle with the chives.
2. Roll and cut into 2-inch lengths. Skewer. Dip the ends into minced parsley.

▶ Can be prepared 6 hours in advance.
NOTE: These can be served on rectangles of thinly sliced, buttered bread as a canapé.

≡ *Roast Beef Rolls with Anchovies*

═ Yield: 24 skewers

1 teaspoon dry mustard
6 thin slices rare roast beef
24 anchovy fillets

2 tablespoons minced onion
minced parsley

═ Yield: 72 skewers

1 tablespoon dry mustard
18 thin slices rare roast beef
72 anchovy fillets

¼ cup minced onion
minced parsley

1. In a bowl, mix the mustard with enough water to make a smooth paste. Spread very thinly on the roast beef slices and top with the anchovy fillets. Sprinkle with the onion.

2. Roll tightly, cut into 2-inch lengths, and skewer. Dip the ends into the parsley.

▶ Can be prepared 6 hours in advance.

≡ *Roast Beef Rolls with Garlic Butter*

═ Yield: 24 skewers

6 thin slices rare roast beef
1 cup garlic butter, softened
(page 72)

minced parsley or gremolata
(recipe follows)

═ Yield: 72 skewers

18 thin slices rare roast beef
3 cups garlic butter, softened
(page 72)

minced parsley or gremolata
(recipe follows)

1. Spread each roast beef slice with the garlic butter and roll tightly.

2. Cut into 2-inch lengths and dip the ends into the minced parsley or gremolata.

▶ Can be prepared 1 day in advance.

≡ *Gremolata*

═ Yield: ⅔ cup

½ cup minced parsley
1 garlic clove

3 tablespoons minced lemon
rind

≡ Yield: 2 cups

1½ cups minced parsley   ½ cup minced lemon rind
3 garlic cloves

In a food processor, finely chop the parsley, garlic, and lemon rind.

▶ Can be prepared 1 day in advance.

≡ *Roquefort Roast Beef Rolls*

≡ Yield: 24 skewers

4 ounces Roquefort cheese   ½ cup minced parsley, optional
4 ounces butter   24 pumpernickel fingers,
1 teaspoon Cognac   optional
6 thin slices rare roast beef

≡ Yield: 72 skewers

¾ pound Roquefort cheese   1½ cups minced parsley,
¾ pound butter   optional
1 tablespoon Cognac   72 pumpernickel fingers,
18 thin slices rare roast beef   optional

1. In a food processor, cream the cheese, butter, and Cognac. Spread on the roast beef slices, roll tightly, and cut into 2-inch lengths.

2. Dip the ends into minced parsley, if desired. These can also be served on pumpernickel fingers.

▶ Can be prepared 1 day in advance.

≡ *Hoisin Broiled Beef*

≡ Yield: 24 skewers

¾ pound beef fillet, cut into 24   salt, to taste
   slices   ½ cup or more hoisin sauce
2 tablespoons dark soy sauce   (see Glossary)
1½ teaspoons rice wine   24 1½-inch pieces scallion
1½ teaspoons Asian sesame oil   24 water chestnuts, cut
1½ teaspoons sugar   crosswise into thirds
¼ teaspoon pepper

== **Yield: 72 skewers**

2¼ pounds beef fillet, cut into
   72 slices
⅓ cup dark soy sauce
1½ tablespoons rice wine
1½ tablespoons Asian sesame
   oil
1½ tablespoons sugar

¾ teaspoon pepper
salt, to taste
1½ cups or more hoisin sauce
   (see Glossary)
72 1½-inch pieces scallion
72 water chestnuts, cut
   crosswise into thirds

1. Preheat the broiler.

2. Marinate the beef in the soy sauce, rice wine, sesame oil, sugar, pepper, and salt for 1 to 2 hours. Pat meat dry and coat both sides with the hoisin sauce.

3. Place 1 piece of scallion and 3 slices of water chestnut in the center of each slice. Roll meat lengthwise and skewer. Broil until medium rare.

▶ Can be prepared for broiling 1 day in advance.

≡ *Indonesian Beef Sates*

== **Yield: 24 sates**

1 cup water
¾ cup minced salted peanuts
½ cup thin soy sauce
¼ cup lime juice
1 teaspoon molasses

1 teaspoon grated gingerroot
½ teaspoon red pepper flakes
2 garlic cloves, crushed
1 pound sirloin steak, cut into
   ½-inch cubes

== **Yield: 72 sates**

2 cups water
1½ cups minced salted peanuts
1 cup thin soy sauce
½ cup lime juice
2 teaspoons molasses

2 teaspoons grated gingerroot
1 teaspoon red pepper flakes
4 garlic cloves, crushed
3 pounds sirloin steak, cut into
   ½-inch cubes

1. Preheat the broiler.

2. In a saucepan, simmer the water, peanuts, soy sauce, lime juice, molasses, gingerroot, red pepper, and garlic for 15 minutes. Cool.

3. Marinate the steak for at least 1 hour. Drain and reserve. Thread the steak onto the skewers and broil, brushing with the marinade, until medium.

4. In a saucepan, heat the remaining marinade and serve as a dipping sauce, if desired.

▶ Can be prepared for broiling 1 day in advance.

≡ *Sweet and Sour Beef Sates*

== **Yield: 24 sates**

2 garlic cloves, crushed	2 tablespoons butter
1 teaspoon brown sugar	1 tablespoon brown sugar
salt and pepper, to taste	1 tablespoon sherry
1 pound lean sirloin steak or	1 tablespoon soy sauce
beef fillet, cut into 1-inch	2 tablespoons lemon juice
cubes	sate sauce (page 76)
½ cup minced onion	

== **Yield: 72 sates**

6 garlic cloves, crushed	1½ cups minced onion
1 tablespoon brown sugar	⅓ cup butter
1 tablespoon salt	3 tablespoons brown sugar
pepper, to taste	3 tablespoons sherry
3 pounds lean sirloin steak or	3 tablespoons soy sauce
beef fillet, cut into 1-inch	⅓ cup lemon juice
cubes	sate sauce (page 76)

1. Preheat the broiler.

2. In a bowl, mix the garlic, brown sugar, salt, and pepper and toss with the beef. Thread the beef onto skewers and set aside.

3. In a skillet, sauté the onion in the butter until soft but not brown. Add the remaining sugar, sherry, and soy sauce and bring to a simmer. Stir in the lemon juice and pour the warm marinade over the beef. Marinate 2 hours, turning often.

4. Broil until medium and serve with a sate sauce.

▶ Can be prepared for broiling 1 day in advance.

≡ *Javanese Steak Sates*

═ **Yield: 24 sates**

6 tablespoons peanut oil
2 tablespoons soy sauce
2 tablespoons lemon juice
1 tablespoon minced onion
1 garlic clove, minced

1 tablespoon ground cumin
pepper, to taste
1 pound rump steak, 1 inch
   thick

═ **Yield: 72 sates**

1 cup peanut oil
⅓ cup soy sauce
⅓ cup lemon juice
3 tablespoons minced onion
3 garlic cloves, minced

2 tablespoons ground cumin
pepper, to taste
3 pounds rump steak, 1 inch
   thick

1. Preheat the broiler.
2. In a bowl, mix the oil, soy sauce, lemon juice, onion, garlic, cumin, and pepper.
3. Cut the steak into strips ¼ inch wide and 3 inches long. Thread onto skewers. Marinate for at least 1 hour.
4. Broil until medium.

▶ Can be prepared for broiling 1 day in advance.
NOTE: The pepper in this recipe is your choice. Black pepper will provide a mildly flavored sate, but cayenne pepper, crushed dried red chili pepper, or fresh chilies of whatever intensity are all options.

≡ *Beef Teriyaki*

═ **Yield: 24 skewers**

1 pound rump steak, cut into
   1-inch cubes
¼ cup chicken stock
¼ cup sake

¼ cup Japanese soy sauce
1 tablespoon honey
pepper, to taste

═ **Yield: 72 skewers**

3 pounds rump steak, cut into
   1-inch cubes
¾ cup chicken stock
¾ cup sake

¾ cup Japanese soy sauce
3 tablespoons honey
pepper, to taste

1. Preheat the broiler.

2. In a bowl, marinate the steak in the stock, sake, soy sauce, and honey for 1 hour.

3. Thread on skewers and broil, brushing with the marinade until medium. Sprinkle with pepper and serve.

▶ Can be prepared for broiling several hours in advance.

☰ *Teriyaki Strips*

☰ Yield: 30 skewers

1 flank steak	½ cup slivered gingerroot
1 cup Japanese soy sauce	⅓ cup sherry
½ cup vegetable oil	1 teaspoon salt
3 garlic cloves, crushed	½ teaspoon Tabasco sauce

☰ Yield: 120 skewers

4 flank steaks	1½ cups slivered gingerroot
1 quart Japanese soy sauce	1⅓ cups sherry
2 cups vegetable oil	1 tablespoon salt
12 garlic cloves, crushed	1 tablespoon Tabasco sauce

1. Preheat the broiler.

2. In a bowl, marinate the steak in the soy sauce, oil, garlic, ginger-root, sherry, salt, and Tabasco sauce for at least 3 hours.

3. Broil the whole steak until medium rare. Cut into thin diagonal slices and thread the slices onto skewers.

▶ Can be prepared for broiling 1 day in advance.

☰ *Pakistan Kebabs*

☰ Yield: 24 kebabs

1½ pounds ground lean beef	½ teaspoon turmeric
1 cup grated onion	½ teaspoon ground coriander
3 tablespoons yogurt	½ teaspoon red pepper flakes
2 garlic cloves, crushed	salt, to taste
1 teaspoon minced parsley	yogurt garlic mint sauce
½ teaspoon minced gingerroot	(page 70)

═ **Yield: 72 kebabs**

4½ pounds ground lean beef
3 cups grated onion
½ cup yogurt
6 garlic cloves, crushed
1 tablespoon minced parsley
1½ teaspoons minced
   gingerroot

1½ teaspoons turmeric
1½ teaspoons ground coriander
1½ teaspoons red pepper flakes
salt, to taste
yogurt garlic mint sauce
   (page 70)

1. Preheat the broiler.

2. In a bowl, mix the beef, onion, yogurt, garlic, parsley, gingerroot, turmeric, coriander, red pepper, and salt.

3. Shape into small sausages and skewer. Broil until crusty and brown. Serve with yogurt mint sauce.

▶ Can be prepared for broiling 1 day in advance.

NOTE: For cocktail food, make these sausages small. They can be made larger when served as part of a main course buffet. Ideally they are cooked over charcoal for additional flavor. These can also be rolled into meatballs and broiled. Serve with skewers on the side.

≡ *Tongue and Watercress Rolls*

═ **Yield: 24 rolls**

¾ pound thinly sliced cold
   tongue
3 tablespoons Dijon mustard

1 bunch watercress
¼ cup vinaigrette (page 46)

═ **Yield: 72 rolls**

2¼ pounds thinly sliced cold
   tongue
½ cup Dijon mustard

3 bunches watercress
¾ cup vinaigrette (page 46)

1. Cut the tongue into 2½-inch squares. Brush each slice with mustard.

2. In a bowl, toss the watercress with the vinaigrette to coat lightly. Arrange a few sprigs of watercress across the tongue slice, letting some of the leaves extend over the edge. Roll and skewer.

▶ Can be prepared 4 to 5 hours in advance.

≡ Tongue Rolls

═ Yield: 24 rolls

3 ounces cream cheese
2 teaspoons horseradish
1 teaspoon minced onion
½ teaspoon dry mustard

salt, to taste
12 thin slices cold tongue
minced parsley

═ Yield: 72 rolls

½ pound cream cheese
2 tablespoons horseradish
1 tablespoon minced onion
1½ teaspoons dry mustard

salt, to taste
36 thin slices cold tongue
minced parsley

1. In a bowl, cream the cream cheese, horseradish, onion, mustard, and salt. Spread on the tongue slices. Roll and skewer.

2. Cut each slice in half and dip the ends in the minced parsley.

▶ Can be prepared 1 day in advance.

≡ Smoked Beef and Pears

═ Yield: 24 skewers

4 Anjou pears, peeled and
   cored
¼ cup lemon juice

¼ pound smoked beef, thinly
   sliced

═ Yield: 72 skewers

12 Anjou pears, peeled and
   cored
¾ cup lemon juice

¾ pound smoked beef, thinly
   sliced

1. Cut the pears into thin slices and toss with the lemon juice.

2. Wrap each pear slice in a beef slice and skewer.

▶ Can be prepared 2 hours in advance.

≡ Lamb Brochettes

== **Yield: 24 brochettes**

1 cup sliced onion
2 teaspoons curry powder
2 tablespoons butter
⅓ cup lemon juice
6 orange segments
2 teaspoons sugar

2 teaspoons mango chutney
⅔ cup unsweetened coconut
  milk
1 pound lamb, cut into 1-inch
  cubes
⅔ cup red wine

== **Yield: 72 brochettes**

3 cups sliced onion
2 tablespoons curry powder
¼ cup butter
⅔ cup lemon juice
18 orange segments
2 tablespoons sugar

2 tablespoons mango chutney
2 cups unsweetened coconut
  milk
3 pounds lamb, cut into 1-inch
  cubes
2 cups red wine

1. Preheat the broiler.

2. In a saucepan, sauté the onion and curry in the butter until the onion is soft. Add the lemon juice, orange sections, sugar, chutney, and milk.

3. Pour over the lamb and toss to coat. Marinate in the refrigerator for 12 hours. Drain; reserve marinade. Skewer and broil until medium rare.

4. Heat the marinade with the wine until hot but not boiling and serve as a dipping sauce.

▶ Can be prepared for broiling 1 day in advance.

≡ Lamb Sates

== **Yield: 24 sates**

1 pound lamb, cut into 1-inch
  cubes
4 scallions, minced
¼ cup ketjap manis (see
  Glossary)
2 garlic cloves, minced

1 tablespoon lemon juice
1 tablespoon minced gingerroot
½ teaspoon grated lemon rind
¼ teaspoon cayenne pepper
hot pepper relish
sambal oelek (see Glossary)

== **Yield: 72 sates**

3 pounds lamb, cut into 1-inch
  cubes
12 scallions, minced
¾ cup ketjap manis (see
  Glossary)
6 garlic cloves, minced
3 tablespoons lemon juice

3 tablespoons minced
  gingerroot
1½ teaspoons grated lemon
  rind
¾ teaspoon cayenne pepper
hot pepper relish
sambal oelek (see Glossary)

1. Preheat the broiler.

2. In a bowl, marinate the lamb, scallions, ketjap manis, garlic, lemon juice, gingerroot, lemon rind, and cayenne for 1 hour.

3. Thread onto skewers and broil until medium rare. Serve with hot pepper relish and sambal oelek for dipping.

▶ Can be prepared for broiling 1 day in advance.

== *Kao Yang Jou Ch'uan (Chinese Lamb Brochettes)*

== **Yield: 24 brochettes**

1 teaspoon Szechuan
  peppercorns
1 pound lamb, cut into 1-inch
  cubes
¼ cup thin soy sauce
2 tablespoons sherry
1 tablespoon minced garlic

1 tablespoon minced gingerroot
2 teaspoons Asian sesame oil
1 teaspoon Chinese five-spice
  powder
¼ teaspoon pepper
sweet bean paste (see Glossary)

== **Yield: 72 brochettes**

1 tablespoon Szechuan
  peppercorns
3 pounds lamb, cut into 1-inch
  cubes
¾ cup thin soy sauce
⅓ cup sherry
3 tablespoons minced garlic

3 tablespoons minced
  gingerroot
2 tablespoons Asian sesame oil
1 tablespoon Chinese five-spice
  powder
¾ teaspoon pepper
sweet bean paste (see Glossary)

1. Preheat the broiler.

2. In a small heavy skillet, toast the peppercorns until fragrant, about 3 minutes. Pulverize in a blender or mortar.

3. In a bowl, marinate the lamb in the peppercorn powder, soy sauce, sherry, garlic, gingerroot, sesame oil, five-spice powder, and pepper for 3 hours.

4. Thread onto skewers and grill until medium rare. Serve with sweet bean paste for dipping.

▶ Can be prepared for broiling 1 day in advance.

NOTE: Any of the dipping sauces in Chapter 3 can be used with or instead of the sweet bean paste. Szechuan peppercorns, five-spice powder, and sweet bean paste are available in Asian markets.

≡ *Lamb Sausage Skewers*

=== **Yield: 24 skewers**

1½ pounds ground lean lamb
⅓ cup minced parsley
3 tablespoons toasted pine nuts
3 garlic cloves, minced

¾ teaspoon rosemary, crushed
⅓ cup olive oil
salt and pepper, to taste
olive oil

=== **Yield: 72 skewers**

4½ pounds ground lean lamb
1 cup minced parsley
½ cup toasted pine nuts
9 garlic cloves, minced
2¼ teaspoons rosemary,
   crushed

1 cup olive oil
salt and pepper, to taste
olive oil

1. Preheat the broiler.

2. In a bowl, mix the lamb, parsley, pine nuts, garlic, rosemary, olive oil, salt, and pepper. Chill 1 hour.

3. Shape the mixture into small sausages and skewer. Broil until medium brushing with olive oil.

▶ Can be prepared for broiling 1 day in advance.

NOTE: These can be rolled into meatballs and broiled. Serve with skewers on the side.

☰ Sosaties (Indonesian Lamb and Pork Sates)

═ Yield: 24 sates

½ cup dried apricots
1 cup minced onion
3 garlic cloves, minced
2 tablespoons oil
3 cups cider vinegar
2 tablespoons sugar

1 tablespoon curry powder
salt and pepper, to taste
1 pound lamb, cut into 1-inch
  cubes
1 pound pork, cut into 1-inch
  cubes

═ Yield: 72 sates

1 cup dried apricots
2 cups minced onion
6 garlic cloves, minced
¼ cup oil
1½ quarts cider vinegar
4 tablespoons sugar

2 tablespoons curry powder
salt and pepper, to taste
3 pounds lamb, cut into 1-inch
  cubes
3 pounds pork, cut into 1-inch
  cubes

1. Preheat the broiler.

2. In a saucepan, simmer the apricots in water to cover until very soft. Purée in a food processor.

3. In a skillet, sauté the onion and garlic in the oil until tender. Stir in the apricot purée, vinegar, sugar, curry powder, salt, and pepper and bring to a boil. Cool.

4. In a large bowl, combine the meats and marinade. Marinate for 4 days, refrigerated, stirring once a day.

5. Drain and thread onto skewers. Broil until medium well done.

▶ Must be prepared for broiling 4 days in advance.

☰ Carnitas (Mexican Pork Cubes)

═ Yield: 24 cubes

1 pound lean pork, cut into
  1-inch cubes

salt and pepper, to taste
avocado sauces (pages 90–91)

═ Yield: 72 cubes

3 pounds lean pork, cut into
  1-inch cubes

salt and pepper, to taste
avocado sauces (pages 90–91)

1. Preheat the oven to 300°F.

2. Season the pork with salt and pepper and place on a baking rack over a baking sheet. Bake for 1½ hours or until the meat is crisp. Pour off the fat as it accumulates.

3. Serve with one of the avocado sauces with skewers on the side.

▶ Can be made ahead and refrigerated, or frozen and reheated.

NOTE: For additional flavor, roll the pork cubes in minced garlic to taste along with the salt and pepper.

≡ *Pork Tenderloin with Guava Grand Marnier Sauce*

═ **Yield: 24 cubes**

1 pork tenderloin
½ cup guava jelly

1 to 2 tablespoons Grand Marnier

═ **Yield: 72 cubes**

3 pork tenderloins
1½ cups guava jelly

3 tablespoons Grand Marnier

1. Preheat the oven to 350°F.

2. Cut the pork tenderloin into 1-inch cubes and roast on a rack until cooked through, about 20 minutes.

3. In a small saucepan, melt the jelly and add just enough Grand Marnier to make the jelly fluid. Serve the pork with the dipping sauce.

▶ The meat can be cut into cubes and the sauce made 1 day in advance. Roast just before serving.

≡ *Hirino Krassato (Pork Cooked in Wine)*

This Greek hors d'oeuvre is similar to a stew. If the meat is cut into larger pieces, it easily can be served as a main course. For those who wish to serve a "casserole" for those who stay late, this with some baked rice would be a perfect answer.

═ **Yield: 24 cubes**

1 pound pork, cut into 1-inch cubes
salt and pepper, to taste
1 teaspoon oregano

1 tablespoon olive oil
2 cups dry red wine
2 tablespoons lemon juice

= **Yield: 72 cubes**

3 pounds pork, cut into 1-inch
cubes
salt and pepper, to taste
1 tablespoon oregano

3 tablespoons olive oil
6 cups dry red wine
⅓ cup lemon juice

1. Remove any fat from the pork and season with salt, pepper, and oregano.

2. In a skillet, heat the oil and brown the meat on all sides. Pour off the fat and add the wine. Cover and simmer until tender. Add the lemon juice and toss to coat.

3. Serve from a chafing dish with skewers.

▶ Can be prepared 1 day in advance and reheated; can be frozen.

= *Korean Pork Skewers*

= **Yield: 24 skewers**

1 pound pork loin
2½ tablespoons sugar
¼ teaspoon cayenne pepper
½ cup soy sauce
¼ cup minced scallions

4 garlic cloves, minced
2 tablespoons toasted sesame
seeds
½ teaspoon ground ginger
2 tablespoons Asian sesame oil

= **Yield: 72 skewers**

3 pounds pork loin
½ cup sugar
¾ teaspoon cayenne pepper
1½ cups soy sauce
¾ cup minced scallions

12 garlic cloves, minced
⅓ cup toasted sesame seeds
1½ teaspoons ground ginger
⅓ cup Asian sesame oil

1. Preheat the broiler.

2. Cut the pork into strips ¼ inch thick, 2 inches long, and ¾ inch wide. In a bowl, mix the sugar and cayenne. Sprinkle over the meat.

3. In a bowl, marinate the meat in the soy sauce, scallions, garlic, sesame seeds, and ginger for 1 hour. Drain.

4. Thread the meat onto skewers and brush with sesame oil. Broil until just done.

▶ Can be prepared for broiling 1 day in advance.

≡ Caribbean Garlic Pork Cubes

== **Yield: 24 cubes**

1 pound boneless pork, cut into
   1-inch cubes
1 tablespoon lime juice
1 head garlic, peeled and
   chopped

⅓ teaspoon dried thyme
salt and pepper, to taste
1 cup white vinegar
oil for frying

== **Yield: 72 cubes**

3 pounds boneless pork, cut
   into 1-inch cubes
3 tablespoons lime juice
¼ pound garlic, peeled and
   chopped

1 teaspoon dried thyme
salt and pepper, to taste
3 cups white vinegar
oil for frying

1. Rub the pork with lime juice. Put into a saucepan with water to cover and simmer for 30 minutes. Drain and discard the water.

2. In a bowl, mix the garlic, thyme, salt, and pepper and rub into the pork cubes. Pack the pork into a large jar or bowl and add the vinegar. Cover and refrigerate for 1 to 2 days. Drain and pat dry.

3. Deep fry at 375°F until golden. Serve with skewers.

▶ Prepare for frying at least 1 day in advance.

≡ Pork Teriyaki

== **Yield: 24 cubes**

1 pound pork loin, cut into
   1-inch cubes
⅔ cup soy sauce

⅓ cup sherry
1 teaspoon brown sugar
1 garlic clove, crushed

== **Yield: 72 cubes**

3 pounds pork loin, cut into
   1-inch cubes
2 cups soy sauce

1 cup sherry
1 tablespoon brown sugar
3 garlic cloves, crushed

1. Preheat the broiler.

2. In a bowl, marinate the pork in the soy sauce, sherry, sugar, and garlic for 1 hour.

3. Thread the pork onto skewers and broil until done.

▶ Can be prepared for broiling 1 day in advance.

≡ Sate Babe Manis (Pork Sates)

═ Yield: 24 sates

1 pound lean pork, cut into
   1-inch cubes
2 tablespoons ketjap manis (see
   Glossary)
2 tablespoons brown sugar
1 tablespoon lemon juice

1 teaspoon ground coriander
1 teaspoon crushed garlic
½ teaspoon ground cumin
salt and pepper, to taste
sate sauce (page 76)

═ Yield: 72 sates

3 pounds lean pork, cut into
   1-inch cubes
⅓ cup ketjap manis (see
   Glossary)
⅓ cup brown sugar
3 tablespoons lemon juice

1 tablespoon ground coriander
1 tablespoon crushed garlic
1½ teaspoons ground cumin
salt and pepper, to taste
sate sauce (page 76)

1. Preheat the broiler.

2. In a bowl, marinate the meat in the ketjap manis, brown sugar, lemon juice, coriander, garlic, cumin, salt, and pepper for 1 hour.

3. Skewer and broil until done. Serve with the sate sauce.

▶ Can be prepared for broiling 1 day in advance.

≡ Marinated Pork Sates

═ Yield: 24 sates

¼ cup ketjap manis (see
   Glossary)
½ cup chopped onion
2 tablespoons lime juice
1 fresh red chili pepper, seeded
   and chopped

1 tablespoon chopped
   gingerroot
1 garlic clove
1 pound lean pork, cut into
   1-inch cubes
peanut oil

═ Yield: 72 sates

¾ cup ketjap manis (see
   Glossary)
1½ cups chopped onion
⅓ cup lime juice
3 fresh red chili peppers,
   seeded and chopped

3 tablespoons chopped
   gingerroot
3 garlic cloves
3 pounds lean pork, cut into
   1-inch cubes
peanut oil

1. Preheat the broiler.

2. In a food processor, purée the ketjap manis, onion, lime juice, red peppers, gingerroot, and garlic. Pour over the pork, mix to combine, and marinate for 2 hours, covered.

3. Thread onto skewers and broil, basting with peanut oil until cooked.

▶ Can be prepared for broiling 1 day in advance.

≡ *Pork Sate with Yogurt Sauce*

═ Yield: 24 sates

1 pound lean pork, cut into
  1-inch cubes
1 cup yogurt
2 tablespoons minced chilies
1 teaspoon salt
1½ teaspoons minced
  gingerroot

½ cup minced onion
1 cup salted cashews
⅔ cup yogurt
1 to 2 garlic cloves

═ Yield: 72 sates

3 pounds lean pork, cut into
  1-inch cubes
3 cups yogurt
⅓ cup minced chilies
1 tablespoon salt
1½ tablespoons minced
  gingerroot

1½ cups minced onion
3 cups salted cashews
2 cups yogurt
3 to 6 garlic cloves

1. Preheat the broiler.

2. In a bowl, marinate the pork in the yogurt, chilies, salt, gingerroot, and onion for 3 hours. Drain the marinade and discard.

3. Thread the meat on skewers and broil until done, turning as needed.

4. In a food processor, purée the cashews, yogurt, and garlic. If too thick, thin with additional yogurt.

5. Serve the sates with the sauce on the side.

▶ Can be prepared for broiling 1 day in advance.

≡ *Hai Shan Jou Ch'uan*
(Barbecued Pork Slices and Chicken Livers)

═ Yield: 24 skewers

12 chicken livers, cut in half	½ cup sherry
1 pound pork loin, cut in 24	3 tablespoons sugar
thin slices	3 garlic cloves, crushed
½ cup hoisin sauce	1 teaspoon Asian sesame oil
¼ cup plum sauce	24 1-inch pieces scallion
¼ cup soy sauce	

═ Yield: 72 skewers

36 chicken livers, cut in half	1½ cups sherry
3 pounds pork loin, cut in 72	½ cup sugar
thin slices	9 garlic cloves, crushed
1½ cups hoisin sauce	1 tablespoon Asian sesame oil
¾ cup plum sauce	72 1-inch pieces scallion
¾ cup soy sauce	

1. Preheat the broiler.

2. In a saucepan, blanch the livers in boiling water to cover for 1 minute. Drain.

3. In a bowl, marinate the livers and the pork in the hoisin sauce, plum sauce, soy sauce, dry sherry, sugar, garlic, and sesame oil for 20 minutes. Drain, reserving the marinade.

4. Wrap a chicken liver and a scallion in a pork slice and skewer. Broil, basting with the marinade.

▶ Can be prepared for broiling 1 day in advance.

≡ *Banana Bacon Skewers*

It would seem that almost anything can be wrapped in bacon, threaded onto a skewer, and broiled or baked until the bacon is crisp. Needless to say, some of these offerings are less than wonderful and others deserve not only a mention but also a place on the most elegant of menus. Here is a small selection of favorites. Additional recipes are located in other chapters because the food wrapped in the bacon seems to predominate; check the index.

═ Yield: 20 skewers

10 slices bacon	3 tablespoons lime juice
5 firm, ripe bananas, peeled	¼ teaspoon ground allspice

1. Preheat the broiler.

2. In a skillet, sauté the bacon slices until the fat is rendered but the bacon is still soft. Drain. (For large quantities, this precooking is most easily done in a 350°F oven.)

3. Cut the bananas into 4 sections and mix with the lemon juice and allspice. Wrap each banana in a bacon slice and skewer.

4. Broil until the bacon is crisp.

▶ Can be prepared 1 hour in advance.

≡ *Figs and Bacon*

≡ **Yield: 48 skewers**

24 fresh figs, not too ripe, cut in half

¼ pound sliced bacon, cut into 4 pieces

1. Preheat the broiler.

2. Wrap each fig half in a bacon slice and thread onto a skewer. Broil until the bacon is cooked.

▶ Can be prepared for broiling 12 hours in advance.

≡ *Marrons à la Diable* *(Spicy Bacon-Wrapped Chestnuts)*

≡ **Yield: 36 skewers**

1 15-ounce can unsweetened chestnuts, drained

¼ pound sliced bacon cayenne pepper, to taste

1. Preheat the broiler.

2. Wrap each chestnut in bacon and thread onto a skewer. Broil until the bacon is crisp. Sprinkle with cayenne.

▶ Can be prepared for broiling 1 day in advance.

≡ *Bacon-Wrapped Olives*

≡ **Yield: 36 skewers**

¼ pound bacon   1 pound green olives, pitted

1. Preheat the broiler.
2. Cut the bacon into sections large enough to cover an olive. Wrap each olive and skewer. Broil until crisp.

▶ Can be prepared 1 day in advance and reheated.

≡ *Olive-Almond-Bacon Brochettes*

≡ **Yield: 24 brochettes**

24 large green olives, pitted   ½ pound sliced bacon
24 blanched almonds

1. Preheat the broiler.
2. Stuff the olives with the almonds, wrap in the bacon, and skewer. Broil until the bacon is crisp.

▶ Can be prepared for broiling 1 day in advance.

≡ *Chutney-Stuffed Bacon-Wrapped Prunes*

≡ **Yield: 24 skewers**

12 ounces pitted prunes   ½ cup mango chutney pieces
½ cup dry port   ½ pound sliced bacon

1. In a bowl, marinate the prunes in the port overnight.
2. Preheat the broiler.
3. Cut the chutney into small strips and stuff each prune with a piece of chutney.
4. Broil the bacon until translucent, drain, and wrap a strip around each prune. Skewer. Broil until crisp.

▶ Can be prepared for broiling 1 day in advance.

☰ Deep-Fried Chicken Liver and Water Chestnut Brochettes

═ Yield: 24 brochettes

½ cup water
⅓ cup sugar
⅓ cup soy sauce
2 tablespoons grated gingerroot
6 star anise
1 garlic clove, crushed

1 bay leaf
1 pound chicken livers, cut in half
12 water chestnuts, cut in half
12 bacon strips, cut in half
oil for frying

═ Yield: 72 brochettes

1½ cups water
1 cup sugar
1 cup soy sauce
⅓ cup grated gingerroot
18 star anise
3 garlic cloves, crushed

1 bay leaf
3 pounds chicken livers, cut in half
36 water chestnuts, cut in half
36 bacon strips, cut in half
oil for frying

1. In a saucepan, simmer the water, sugar, soy sauce, gingerroot, star anise, garlic, and bay leaf for 5 minutes. Add the livers and simmer 2 minutes longer. Drain.

2. Press a chicken liver and water chestnut half together, wrap in bacon, and skewer.

3. Heat the oil to 375°F and fry until the bacon is golden.

▶ Can be prepared for frying 1 day in advance.

☰ Rumaki (Hawaiian Chicken Liver and Bacon Brochettes)

This ever-popular hors d'oeuvre can be served plain or with puréed chutney or duck sauce on the side.

═ Yield: 24 brochettes

8 chicken livers, cut in thirds
24 water chestnuts
12 bacon slices, cut in half

¾ cup soy sauce
1½ teaspoons minced gingerroot

== **Yield: 72 brochettes**

2 pounds chicken livers, cut in
    thirds
72 water chestnuts
1 pound sliced bacon, cut in half

2¼ cups soy sauce
2 tablespoons minced
    gingerroot

1. Preheat the oven to 425°F.

2. Wrap each chicken liver section and a water chestnut half in a slice of bacon and skewer. Marinate the brochettes in the soy sauce and gingerroot for 1 hour.

3. Bake on a rack for 10 minutes or until the bacon is crisp.

▶ Can be prepared for baking 1 day in advance.

NOTE: For a different flavor, add curry powder to taste to the soy marinade.

== *Antipasto Rolls*

== **Yield: 24 rolls**

½ pound mozzarella
24 oval Genoa salami slices
1 7-ounce can Italian tuna
    packed in oil, drained

2 tablespoons extra virgin olive
    oil
2 pepperoncini, minced
24 large stuffed or ripe olives

== **Yield: 72 rolls**

1½ pounds mozzarella
72 oval Genoa salami slices
3 7-ounce cans Italian tuna
    packed in oil, drained

⅓ cup extra virgin olive oil
6 pepperoncini, minced
72 large stuffed or ripe olives

1. Using a slice of salami as a pattern, cut the mozzarella into an oval the same size as the salami. With a cheese slicer, pare off as many cheese slices as there are salami slices. Neatly cover the cheese slices with the salami slices, cheese side up.

2. In a bowl, mix the tuna, olive oil, and pepperoncini. Spread about 1 tablespoon on each cheese-salami slice and place an olive at one end. Roll and skewer.

▶ Can be made 1 day in advance.

≡ Smoked Sausage with Mustard Dressing

═ Yield: 36 slices

1½ pounds smoked sausage
links
1 tablespoon vegetable oil
1 tablespoon Dijon mustard

½ teaspoon mustard seeds
1 tablespoon wine vinegar
½ teaspoon salt
½ teaspoon pepper

═ Yield: 72 slices

3 pounds smoked sausage links
2 tablespoons vegetable oil
2 tablespoons Dijon mustard
1 teaspoon mustard seeds

2 tablespoons wine vinegar
1 teaspoon salt
1 teaspoon pepper

1. In a saucepan, simmer the sausages in boiling water to cover until hot. Remove the sausages from the water and peel and discard the skin. Cut the sausages into chunks and keep warm in the heating water.

2. In a bowl, mix the oil, mustard, mustard seeds, vinegar, salt, and pepper. When ready to serve, toss the sausages in the mustard sauce and serve with skewers on the side.

▶ Can be prepared 2 days in advance and reheated. Can be served from a chafing dish.

≡ Sausage in Wine and Mustard Dressing

═ Yield: 24 slices

⅓ cup red wine
¼ cup Dijon mustard
½ tablespoon minced shallots
½ teaspoon salt

¼ teaspoon pepper
pinch of dried thyme
1 pound kielbasa

═ Yield: 72 slices

1 cup red wine
¾ cup Dijon mustard
1½ tablespoons minced shallots
1 teaspoon salt

¾ teaspoon pepper
½ teaspoon dried thyme
3 pounds kielbasa

1. In a small saucepan, simmer the wine, mustard, shallots, salt, pepper, and thyme for 5 minutes.

2. Peel the sausage and cut into thick slices. Heat in the sauce and serve with skewers on the side.

▶ Can be prepared several days in advance and reheated.

≡ *Sausage in Wine and Grapes*

═ Yield: 24

1 pound kielbasa, peeled and thickly sliced
1 cup seedless grapes
1 cup dry white wine

½ cup brown stock
1 tablespoon Dijon mustard
½ teaspoon dried thyme

═ Yield: 72

3 pounds kielbasa, peeled and thickly sliced
3 cups seedless grapes
3 cups dry white wine

1½ cups brown stock
3 tablespoons Dijon mustard
1½ teaspoons dried thyme

1. Preheat the oven to 400°F.

2. In a baking dish, mix the sausage, grapes, wine, stock, mustard, and thyme. Bake 10 minutes or until heated. Serve with skewers.

▶ Can be prepared for baking 1 day in advance.

≡ *Blue Cheese-Walnut-Ham Rolls*

═ Yield: 24 rolls

¼ pound blue cheese
¼ pound unsalted butter
2 tablespoons finely chopped walnuts

2 teaspoons kirsch
½ pound boiled ham, sliced

═ Yield: 72 rolls

¾ pound blue cheese
¾ pound unsalted butter
½ cup finely chopped walnuts

2 tablespoons kirsch
1½ pounds boiled ham, sliced

1. In a food processor, cream the cheese, butter, walnuts, and kirsch.

2. Spread on the ham slices and roll up jellyroll fashion. Cut into 1-inch lengths and secure with a skewer.

▶ Can be made 2 days in advance and refrigerated.

≡ *Danish Ham and Smoked Salmon Rolls*

== **Yield: 24 rolls**

6 paper-thin slices prosciutto
freshly ground black pepper, to
taste

6 paper-thin slices smoked
salmon

== **Yield: 72 rolls**

18 paper-thin slices prosciutto
freshly ground black pepper, to
taste

18 paper-thin slices smoked
salmon

Place the prosciutto slices on a work surface, dust liberally with freshly ground black pepper, and top with a slice of salmon. Roll tightly and cut into 1-inch sections. Skewer.

▶ Can be made 1 day in advance.

≡ *Mushroom Ham Rolls*

== **Yield: 24 rolls**

½ pound mushrooms, minced
3 tablespoons minced shallots
¼ cup butter
3 ounces cream cheese,
   softened
1 teaspoon Dijon mustard

pinch of cayenne pepper
lemon juice, to taste
salt and pepper, to taste
½ pound baked ham, thinly
   sliced
1 cup minced watercress

== **Yield: 72 rolls**

1½ pounds mushrooms,
   minced
½ cup minced shallots
½ cup butter
9 ounces cream cheese,
   softened
1 tablespoon Dijon mustard

¼ teaspoon cayenne pepper
lemon juice, to taste
salt and pepper, to taste
1½ pounds baked ham, thinly
   sliced
3 cups minced watercress

1. In a skillet, sauté the mushrooms and shallots in the butter until the liquid has evaporated. Remove from the heat and stir in the cream cheese, mustard, cayenne, lemon juice, salt, and pepper. Cool.

2. Spread the ham slices with the cream cheese mixture and sprinkle with the watercress. Roll up jellyroll fashion and chill. Cut into sections and skewer.

▶ Can be made 1 day in advance.

≡ *Fruits Wrapped in Meats*

melons, figs, pineapple, kiwi
  fruit, dates, strawberries

prosciutto, Westphalian ham,
  Smithfield ham, baked ham,
  bundnerfleisch, speck,
  smoked tongue, hard
  salamis, smoked salmon

Choose beautiful fresh fruit. Cut into bite-size pieces and wrap in paper-thin slices of any of the meats or fish listed. If desired, add a generous sprinkle of black pepper. These are usually served alone, but can be served with a ginger soy sauce or sour cream mixed with grated lemon peel.

▶ Prepare and serve immediately. Fruits, especially melons, lose quality quickly.

NOTE: One half pound of meat or fish yields about 60 portions.

≡ *Flamincini Helvia (Prosciutto Veal Rolls)*

≡ **Yield: 24 rolls**

2 cups ground cooked veal
1 cup ground ham
2 tablespoons minced parsley
½ teaspoon dried thyme

½ teaspoon pepper
24 thin slices prosciutto
oil for frying

≡ **Yield: 72 rolls**

1½ quarts ground cooked veal
3 cups ground ham
⅓ cup minced parsley
1½ teaspoons dried thyme

1½ teaspoons pepper
72 thin slices prosciutto
oil for frying

1. In a bowl, mix the veal, ham, parsley, thyme, and pepper. Place a teaspoonful on each prosciutto slice and roll tightly, folding in the ends to make a neat package.

2. Heat the oil to 365°F and fry until hot, about 30 seconds.

▶ Can be prepared for frying 2 days in advance.

═ **10** ═

Cheese Balls, Fish Balls, and Meatballs

Small balls of food have always been a favorite for cocktails. Whether it is because they are convenient to make or easy to eat, they please both the cook and the diner.

For many years individual cheese balls were the hit of every party. But recently caterers and cooks have preferred to serve large cheese balls, logs, or mounds instead. Perhaps this is because a large ball has a greater visual impact or, more likely, because it is a lot faster to make one big ball than numerous small ones. Despite this trend, individual cheese balls are delicious to eat, simple to prepare, and attractive to present. It is important to keep them small, about a teaspoon per serving. Check during preparation that the balls are uniform, or soon they will start to approach the size of golf balls. Once the balls have been shaped, they can be rolled in minced parsley, paprika, ground nuts, or toasted bread crumbs for added flavor, texture, and color. Serve them mounded on paper doilies, arranged on a platter to resemble a bunch of grapes, or threaded on skewers and arranged on styrofoam forms, pineapples, oranges, or cabbages. Use them as an edible garnish on other platters—a lagniappe to any menu.

Fish balls, aside from having an unpleasant, or at least unappealing, name, seem to have little appeal in Western culture. Fortunately, the Asians have many appealing and exciting recipes. Use small chafing dishes when serving hot fish balls in sauce, and plan to replenish them regularly. Deep-fried fish balls should be cooked and passed immediately. Cold fish balls can be served on platters as you would any other cold hors d'oeuvre; serve the skewers separately.

Meatballs are the cliché of cocktail foods. They sometimes represent the worst of cocktail party food, because some caterers opt to serve poor-quality frozen prepared meatballs with a heavy sauce of no particular flavor. Fortunately, this need not be your fate because there are many delicious, freshly made variations that can be a wonderful addition to any menu. Swedish meatballs are no longer *de rigueur*. Your offerings should be exciting and flavorful, with a difference that makes them special and gives a client valid reason for asking you to cater their parties. Because meatballs can be prepared ahead and most freeze well, they are a good way for your staff to make use of slow periods. Some caterers use this as a way of reaching a larger audience by selling their excess to local markets.

Shaping Meatballs
There are several ways to shape meatballs, some of which are faster and more efficient than others. Whatever method you choose, be certain to handle the mixture lightly or you will end up with rocks.

• Roll a tablespoon of meat between the palms of your hands to form a ball.

• Use a set of wooden paddles, rather than your hands, to shape the mixture.

• Gourmet stores sell a small, scissor-like implement that forces a scoop of meat into a ball, extruding the excess through a large hole in the top.

• The Chinese method works well with almost all paste-like substances. With one hand rinsed in cold water, scoop a handful of the mixture. Make a fist, squeezing a knob of the mixture between the thumb and index finger. (See drawing.) Lift off the knob with a tablespoon or with your fingers and set it on a baking sheet. This method sounds more complicated than it is; with a little patience you will get the knack. It is one of the easiest and quickest ways to shape foods into balls.

When preparing meatballs in large quantities, it is more efficient to bake them at 350°F to 400°F than it is to sauté them in a skillet. Once sauced, there is very little difference in flavor and the time saved is enormous.

To freeze fish balls or meatballs, arrange them in single layers on baking sheets and freeze. Once frozen, transfer them to containers. This way you can thaw only the number you need. If the meatballs are to be sauced, freeze the sauce separately in smaller containers. Generally, sauces with cheese, sour cream, or yogurt should not be frozen. As always, review the sauce, dip, and spread recipes (Chapters 3, 4, and 5) to see if you can devise a new offering by using a different sauce.

Shaping Fish Balls and Meatballs

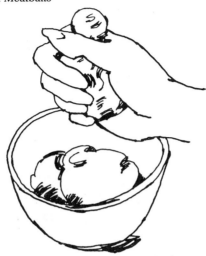

—— *Cheese Balls* ——

≡ *Cream Cheese Balls*

═ Yield: 24

6 tablespoons butter
½ pound cream cheese
1 teaspoon dry mustard
½ teaspoon curry powder
1 tablespoon Worcestershire
    sauce

¼ teaspoon Tabasco sauce
1 teaspoon soy sauce
salt and cayenne pepper, to
    taste
1 cup ground walnuts

═ Yield: 72

½ pound butter
1½ pounds cream cheese
1 tablespoon dry mustard
1½ teaspoons curry powder
3 tablespoons Worcestershire
    sauce

1 teaspoon Tabasco sauce
1 tablespoon soy sauce
salt and cayenne pepper, to
    taste
3 cups ground walnuts

1. In a food processor, cream the butter, cream cheese, mustard, curry powder, Worcestershire sauce, Tabasco sauce, soy sauce, salt, and cayenne until smooth.

2. Chill until firm and shape into small balls. Roll in the walnuts and chill again.

▶ Keeps 2 days, refrigerated.

≡ *Herb Cheese Balls*

=== **Yield: 24**

½ pound cream cheese, softened	3 tablespoons minced chives
3 tablespoons minced parsley	2 tablespoons heavy cream
	salt and pepper, to taste

=== **Yield: 72**

1½ pounds cream cheese, softened	½ cup minced chives
½ cup minced parsley	⅓ cup heavy cream
	salt and pepper, to taste

1. In a food processor, cream the cream cheese, parsley, chives, cream, salt, and pepper.

2. Shape into small balls.

▶ Keeps 2 days, refrigerated.

≡ *Pickled Onion Cheese Balls*

=== **Yield: 24**

½ pound cream cheese	½ cup minced watercress,
24 pickled onions, patted dry	parsley, or dried beef

=== **Yield: 72**

1½ pounds cream cheese	1½ cups minced watercress,
72 pickled onions, patted dry	parsley, or dried beef

1. Cut the cream cheese into as many squares as onions and roll each square into a ball. Poke a hole in the center and insert an onion. Reshape the cheese around the onion.

2. Roll the balls in the watercress, parsley, or beef. Chill.

▶ Keeps 2 days, refrigerated.

NOTE: You can flavor the cheese to taste with curry, creole seasoning, or five-spice powder for added zing.

≡ *Walnut Cheese Olives*

═ **Yield: 24**

¼ cup butter
¼ pound cream cheese
¼ pound Roquefort cheese
2 tablespoons minced shallots
2 teaspoons Cognac

¼ teaspoon dry mustard
salt and pepper, to taste
24 small pitted green olives,
    patted dry
1 cup chopped toasted walnuts

═ **Yield: 72**

¾ cup butter
¾ pound cream cheese
¾ pound Roquefort cheese
⅓ cup minced shallots
2 tablespoons Cognac

¾ teaspoon dry mustard
salt and pepper, to taste
72 small pitted ripe olives,
    patted dry
3 cups chopped toasted walnuts

1. In a food processor, cream the butter, cream cheese, Roquefort, shallots, Cognac, mustard, salt, and pepper. Chill until firm enough to shape.

2. Enclose the olives in teaspoons of the cheese mixture.

3. Roll in the nuts and chill for at least 30 minutes.

▶ Keeps 2 days, refrigerated.

≡ *Walnut Cheese Balls*

═ **Yield: 25**

¼ pound blue cheese
¼ pound butter, softened
¼ cup chopped walnuts
1 to 2 tablespoons heavy cream

paprika, minced parsley,
    minced chives, or ground
    almonds

═ **Yield: 150**

1½ pounds blue cheese
1½ pounds butter, softened
1 cup chopped walnuts
6 to 9 tablespoons heavy cream

paprika, minced parsley,
    minced chives, or ground
    almonds

1. In a mixer, cream the cheese and butter. Fold in the walnuts and enough cream to make a stiff mixture. Chill.

2. Roll into 1-inch balls, then roll the balls in the paprika, parsley, chives, or almonds. For variety, roll in some of each.

▶ Keeps 2 days, refrigerated.

≡ *Cheddar Cheese and Olive Balls*

═ Yield: 24

½ pound Cheddar cheese, grated
¼ cup chopped ripe olives
2 tablespoons butter

1 garlic clove, minced
Tabasco sauce, to taste
cayenne pepper, to taste

═ Yield: 72

1½ pounds Cheddar cheese, grated
¾ cup chopped ripe olives
⅓ cup butter

3 garlic cloves, minced
Tabasco sauce, to taste
cayenne pepper, to taste

1. In a mixer (not a processor), cream the cheese, olives, butter, garlic, Tabasco sauce, and cayenne.
2. Shape into balls and chill.

▶ Keeps 3 days, refrigerated.

≡ *Kaastruffels (Cheese Truffles)*

═ Yield: 24

¼ pound butter
¼ pound Gouda cheese, grated
salt and pepper, to taste
⅛ teaspoon celery seeds

paprika, to taste
2 slices stale pumpernickel, crumbed

═ Yield: 72

¾ pound butter
¾ pound Gouda cheese, grated
salt and pepper, to taste
½ teaspoon celery seeds

paprika, to taste
6 slices stale pumpernickel, crumbed

1. In a food processor, cream the butter, cheese, salt, pepper, celery seeds, and paprika. Chill.
2. Shape into small balls and roll in the pumpernickel crumbs.

▶ Keeps 3 days, refrigerated.

≡ *Chili Cheese Balls*

═ Yield: 24

1½ cups grated Monterey Jack cheese
½ cup grated Fontina cheese
1½ ounces cream cheese
2 teaspoons Dijon mustard
½ teaspoon Worcestershire sauce

¼ teaspoon minced garlic
1 teaspoon chili powder
¼ cup minced parsley or coriander (cilantro)

═ Yield: 72

4½ cups grated Monterey Jack cheese
1½ cups grated Fontina cheese
4½ ounces cream cheese
2 tablespoons Dijon mustard
1½ teaspoons Worcestershire sauce

1¼ teaspoons minced garlic
1 tablespoon chili powder
¾ cup minced parsley or coriander (cilantro)

1. In a mixer or food processor, cream the Monterey Jack cheese, Fontina cheese, cream cheese, mustard, Worcestershire sauce, garlic, and chili powder.

2. Shape into balls and roll in the parsley or coriander.

▶ Keeps 2 days, refrigerated.

≡ *Labanee (Yogurt Cheese Balls)*

═ Yield: 30

1 quart plain yogurt
pinch of salt

1 cup Greek olive oil
paprika, to taste

═ Yield: 90

3 quarts plain yogurt
1 teaspoon salt

3 cups Greek olive oil
paprika, to taste

1. In a bowl, mix the yogurt and salt.

2. Rinse a double layer of cheesecloth in cold water and wring it out well. Line a sieve with the cheesecloth and suspend over a bowl. Pour in the yogurt, cover, and let drain overnight, refrigerated. Pour off the liquid and drain another day.

3. Use 2 teaspoons to shape the thickened yogurt into balls. The balls will be soft. Arrange on platters and sprinkle with the oil and paprika.

▶ Keeps 2 days, refrigerated.

—— *Fish Balls* ——

≡ *Scandinavian Fish Balls in Dill Sauce*

This hors d'oeuvre is based on the national dish of Norway, *fiske-pudding*, one of the less appealing names for a food. It is not only a delicious hors d'oeuvre, it also makes a superb buffet dish. To make for a buffet, pack the mixture into a buttered mold and bake it in a hot water bath at 350°F, or until a knife inserted in the center comes out clean. Unmold and serve it hot or cold with any of the sauces listed below or your own favorite.

≡ **Yield: 36**

1 pound haddock or halibut fillets, chopped	1½ quarts water
1 tablespoon cornstarch	1 tablespoon butter
1 teaspoon salt	1½ tablespoons water
pinch of grated nutmeg	1 tablespoon cornstarch
3 tablespoons light cream	1½ tablespoons lemon juice
3 tablespoons milk	1½ tablespoons minced dill
	pinch of pepper

≡ **Yield: 100**

3 pounds haddock or halibut fillets, chopped	3 quarts water
⅓ cup cornstarch	3 tablespoons butter
1 tablespoon salt	¼ cup water
¼ teaspoon grated nutmeg	3 tablespoons cornstarch
½ cup light cream	⅓ cup lemon juice
½ cup milk	⅓ cup minced dill
	½ teaspoon pepper

1. In a food processor, purée the fish, cornstarch, salt, nutmeg, cream, and milk. Chill and shape into 1-inch balls.

2. In a kettle, bring the water to a simmer and poach the balls for 10 minutes or until cooked. Drain, reserving the liquid.

3. In a saucepan, heat 2 cups *(6 cups)* of the broth with the butter.

4. In a bowl, mix the water with the cornstarch and add to the simmering broth, stirring constantly, until it boils and the liquid clears.

5. Add the lemon juice, dill, and salt and pepper, to taste. Pour over the fish balls and serve in a chafing dish.

▶ Can be prepared 2 days in advance; can be frozen.

NOTE: Other sauce options include soy dipping sauce, egg lemon sauce, tomato sauce, béarnaise, hollandaise, or spinach dill dip.

☰ Crab Balls

These crab balls differ from the crab cake recipes in Chapter 7 because they are rolled into balls and deep-fried instead of shaped into flat cakes and sautéed.

☰ Yield: 36

1 pound crabmeat, flaked	½ cup fresh bread crumbs
¼ cup melted butter	1 egg
1 tablespoon salt	flour for dredging
1 tablespoon Dijon mustard	oil for frying
⅛ teaspoon grated nutmeg	mustard sauce (pages 43–45)
⅛ teaspoon cayenne pepper	

☰ Yield: 108

3 pounds crabmeat, flaked	1½ cups fresh bread crumbs
¾ cup melted butter	3 eggs
2 tablespoons salt	flour for dredging
3 tablespoons Dijon mustard	oil for frying
½ teaspoon grated nutmeg	mustard sauce (pages 43–45)
½ teaspoon cayenne pepper	

1. In a bowl, mix the crabmeat, butter, salt, mustard, nutmeg, cayenne, bread crumbs, and egg(s). Chill.

2. Roll into small balls and dredge in the flour.

3. Heat the oil to 390°F and fry until golden. Serve with the mustard sauce.

▶ Can be prepared for frying 2 days in advance.

≡ *Maryland Crab Balls*

═ Yield: 36

1 pound crabmeat	½ cup fresh bread crumbs
¼ cup cracker meal	oil for frying
¼ cup mayonnaise	anchovy mayonnaise (page 49),
1 tablespoon minced onion	tartar sauce (page 51), or
1 egg	tomato sauce (pages 63–65)
½ teaspoon dry mustard	
¼ teaspoon Worcestershire sauce	

═ Yield: 108

3 pounds crabmeat	1½ cups fresh bread crumbs
¾ cup cracker meal	oil for frying
¾ cup mayonnaise	anchovy mayonnaise (page 49),
3 tablespoons minced onion	tartar sauce (page 51), or
3 eggs	tomato sauce (pages 63–65)
1½ teaspoons dry mustard	
1 teaspoon Worcestershire sauce	

1. In a bowl, mix the crabmeat, cracker meal, mayonnaise, onion, egg(s), mustard, and Worcestershire sauce. Shape into balls and roll in the bread crumbs.

2. Heat the oil to 375°F and fry until golden. Serve with one of the sauces.

▶ Can be prepared for frying 1 day in advance.

NOTE: If cracker meal is not available, crush any mildly flavored cracker such as Bremmer wafers or saltines.

≡ *Hundred-Corner Crab Balls*

The crab balls are rolled into tiny cubes of bread to make "100 corners."

═ Yield: 36

12 slices white bread, crusts removed and cut into ⅛-inch cubes	1 teaspoon salt
	⅓ pound crabmeat, flaked
	½ cup chopped water
⅔ pound shrimp, peeled and deveined	chestnuts
	2 tablespoons cornstarch
1 egg white	oil for frying
1 tablespoon rice wine	plum sauce
2 teaspoons minced gingerroot	Chinese mustard (page 73)
1½ teaspoons Asian sesame oil	

═ Yield: 144

48 slices white bread, crusts removed and cut into ⅛-inch cubes	2 tablespoons Asian sesame oil
	1 tablespoon salt
	1⅓ pounds crabmeat, flaked
2⅔ pounds shrimp, peeled and deveined	2 cups chopped water chestnuts
4 egg whites	½ cup cornstarch
¼ cup rice wine	oil for frying
3 tablespoons minced gingerroot	plum sauce
	Chinese mustard (page 73)

1. Spread the bread cubes on a baking sheet and let dry for 2 hours, turning occasionally.

2. In a food processor, chop the shrimp until it forms a coarse paste. Add the egg white(s), rice wine, gingerroot, sesame oil, and salt, and process until it forms a fine paste. Transfer to a bowl and add the crabmeat, water chestnuts, and cornstarch.

3. Shape into ¾-inch balls and roll in the bread cubes to coat, pressing lightly.

4. Heat the oil to 350°F and fry until golden. Serve with plum sauce and/or Chinese mustard.

▶ Can be prepared for frying 1 day in advance.

≡ *Pork and Crabmeat Balls I*

═ **Yield: 36**

1½ pounds ground pork	1½ teaspoons salt
6 ounces crabmeat	1 teaspoon minced gingerroot
2 tablespoons minced scallions	¼ teaspoon white pepper
2 tablespoons cornstarch	cabbage leaves for steaming
1 tablespoon sherry	dipping sauces (pages 72–82)

═ **Yield: 144**

6 pounds ground pork	1½ tablespoons minced
1½ pounds crabmeat	gingerroot
½ cup minced scallions	1 teaspoon white pepper
½ cup cornstarch	cabbage leaves for steaming
¼ cup sherry	dipping sauces (pages 72–82)
2 tablespoons salt	

1. In a bowl, mix the pork, half the crabmeat, scallions, cornstarch, sherry, salt, gingerroot, and pepper until smooth. Form into balls.

2. Poke a hole in the center of each ball and fill with the remaining crabmeat.

3. Place on cabbage leaves over a steamer and steam until cooked (see page 684). Serve with one of the dipping sauces.

▶ Can be prepared for steaming 1 day in advance.

≡ *Pork and Crabmeat Balls II*

═ **Yield: 36**

½ pound lean ground pork	1 tablespoon soy sauce
½ pound crabmeat, flaked	½ garlic clove, crushed
½ cup minced water chestnuts	½ teaspoon salt
1 egg, lightly beaten	flour, optional
1 scallion, minced	peanut oil, optional
1 tablespoon minced gingerroot	dipping sauces (pages 72–82)

══ **Yield: 100**

1½ pounds lean ground pork
1½ pounds crabmeat, flaked
1½ cups minced water
  chestnuts
3 eggs, lightly beaten
3 scallions, minced
3 tablespoons minced
  gingerroot

3 tablespoons soy sauce
2 garlic cloves, crushed
1½ teaspoons salt
flour, optional
peanut oil, optional
dipping sauces (pages 72–82)

1. In a bowl, mix the pork, crabmeat, water chestnuts, egg(s), scallion(s), gingerroot, soy sauce, garlic, and salt. Shape into small balls.

2. Arrange on a baking sheet and bake 20 minutes at 350°F, or roll in the flour and sauté in the peanut oil until cooked. Serve with one of the dipping sauces, such as duck sauce, Chinese mustard, or soy dipping sauce.

▶ Cooked balls can be frozen or refrigerated for 2 days.

══ *Crab Cakes with Shrimp*

══ **Yield: 36**

¾ pound shrimp, peeled and
  deveined
1 egg
¾ cup heavy cream
salt and pepper, to taste
1 pound crabmeat

½ cup minced scallions
1 tablespoon Dijon mustard
1 teaspoon Worcestershire
  sauce
¼ teaspoon Tabasco sauce
½ cup vegetable oil

══ **Yield: 144**

3 pounds shrimp, peeled and
  deveined
4 eggs
3 cups heavy cream
salt and pepper, to taste
4 pounds crabmeat

2 cups minced scallions
¼ cup Dijon mustard
4 teaspoons Worcestershire
  sauce
1 teaspoon Tabasco sauce
2 cups vegetable oil

1. In a food processor, purée the shrimp, egg(s), cream, salt, and pepper. Transfer to a bowl.

2. Add the crabmeat, scallions, mustard, Worcestershire, and Tabasco. Shape into 2-inch cakes about ¼ inch thick.

3. In a skillet, heat a thin layer of oil and sauté cakes on both sides until golden.

▶ Can be prepared for sautéing 1 day ahead.

NOTE: These can be served plain, but using a spicy sauce such as a tartar, sate, mustard, or peppery sauce adds excitement.

≡ *Crab, Shrimp, and Scallop Cakes*

═ **Yield: 36**

½ pound scallops	1 teaspoon minced chives
¼ pound peeled shrimp	pinch cayenne pepper
½ cup heavy cream	salt and pepper, to taste
1 egg yolk	½ pound crabmeat
1 tablespoon Dijon mustard	vegetable oil

═ **Yield: 144**

2 pounds scallops	2 tablespoons minced chives
1 pound peeled shrimp	¼ teaspoon cayenne pepper
2 cups heavy cream	salt and pepper, to taste
4 egg yolks	2 pounds crabmeat
¼ cup Dijon mustard	vegetable oil

1. In a food processor, purée the scallops and shrimp. With the machine running, add the cream, egg yolk(s), mustard, chives, cayenne, salt, and pepper. Transfer to a bowl and fold in the crabmeat. Chill.

2. With floured hands, shape the crabmeat into small cakes about ½ inch thick.

3. Sauté on both sides in oil until golden. Serve with a spicy dipping sauce.

▶ Can be prepared for sautéing 1 day ahead.

☰ *Louisiana Crab Cakes*

═ Yield: 36

1 pound lump crabmeat
⅓ cup mayonnaise
⅓ cup bread crumbs
1 egg
2 tablespoons diced green pepper
2 tablespoons diced scallions
1 tablespoon Worcestershire sauce
1½ teaspoons hot green pepper sauce
1 teaspoon creole seasoning (page 65)

3 cups bread crumbs
⅓ cup grated Romano cheese
1 tablespoon dried basil, crumbled
1 tablespoon dried oregano, crumbled
1 teaspoon garlic powder
1 teaspoon onion powder
1 teaspoon cayenne pepper
1 teaspoon salt
¼ cup butter
creole sauce (page 65)

═ Yield: 144

4 pounds lump crabmeat
1⅓ cups mayonnaise
1⅓ cups bread crumbs
4 eggs
½ cup diced green pepper
½ cup diced scallions
¼ cup Worcestershire sauce
2 tablespoons hot green pepper sauce
4 teaspoons creole seasoning (page 65)

12 cups bread crumbs
1⅓ cups grated Romano cheese
¼ cup dried basil, crumbled
¼ cup dried oregano, crumbled
4 teaspoons garlic powder
4 teaspoons onion powder
4 teaspoons cayenne pepper
4 teaspoons salt
1 cup butter
creole sauce (page 65)

1. In a bowl, blend the crabmeat, mayonnaise, bread crumbs, egg(s), green pepper, scallions, Worcestershire sauce, hot pepper sauce, and creole seasoning. Shape mixture into 1-inch balls.

2. In a bowl, mix the bread crumbs, Romano cheese, basil, oregano, garlic powder, onion powder, cayenne, and salt.

3. Roll the crab balls in the bread crumb mixture and flatten into rounds ½ inch thick.

4. In a skillet, sauté the crab cakes in the butter on both sides until golden. Serve with creole sauce.

▶ Can be prepared for sautéing 1 day in advance.

≡ *Salmon Cakes with Jalapeño Sauce*

=== Yield: 36

3 cups fresh bread crumbs	1 tablespoon mayonnaise
1 tablespoon minced onion	2 teaspoons creole mustard (see
1 teaspoon ground thyme	note)
½ teaspoon salt	1 teaspoon lemon juice
¼ teaspoon cayenne pepper	1½ cups flaked cooked salmon
3 large shallots, minced	vegetable oil
½ cup grated Asiago cheese	jalapeño sauce (page 50)
1 egg	

=== Yield: 144

12 cups fresh bread crumbs	¼ cup mayonnaise
¼ cup minced onion	2½ tablespoons creole mustard
1½ tablespoons ground thyme	(see note)
2 teaspoons salt	4 teaspoons lemon juice
1 teaspoon cayenne pepper	6 cups flaked cooked salmon
1 cup minced shallots	vegetable oil
2 cups grated Asiago cheese	jalapeño sauce (page 50)
4 eggs	

1. In a bowl, mix the bread crumbs, onion, thyme, salt, and cayenne.

2. In another bowl, mix half the bread crumb mixture with the shallots, cheese, egg(s), mayonnaise, mustard, and lemon juice. Fold in the salmon and roll into 1-inch balls, then flatten to ½-inch rounds. Roll cakes in the remaining bread crumb mixture.

3. In a skillet, sauté salmon cakes in oil until crisp and brown on both sides. Serve hot.

▶ Can be prepared for sautéing 1 day in advance.

NOTE: Creole mustard is found in specialty stores. It is flavored with spices. Whole-grain Dijon mustard can be substituted.

≡ *Smoked Salmon Balls*

=== Yield: 24

½ pound smoked salmon	1 tablespoon light cream
¼ pound cream cheese	salt and pepper, to taste
½ teaspoon lemon juice	minced dill

══ **Yield: 72**

1½ pounds smoked salmon   3 tablespoons light cream
¾ pound cream cheese   salt and pepper, to taste
1½ teaspoons lemon juice   minced dill

1. In a food processor, purée the salmon, cream cheese, lemon juice, cream, salt, and pepper.
2. Shape into balls and roll in the dill. Chill.

▶ Keeps 2 days, refrigerated.

≡ *Steamed Shrimp Balls*

══ **Yield: 36**

1½ pounds shrimp, peeled   ½ teaspoon minced gingerroot
⅓ cup minced water chestnuts   ⅛ teaspoon pepper
1½ teaspoons sherry   1 egg white
1½ teaspoons salt   peanut oil
1½ teaspoons cornstarch   hot mustard, oyster sauce,
1 teaspoon minced scallions   plum sauce, or hoisin sauce

══ **Yield: 100**

4½ pounds shrimp, peeled   2 teaspoons minced gingerroot
1 cup minced water chestnuts   ½ teaspoon pepper
2 tablespoons sherry   3 egg whites
2 tablespoons salt   peanut oil
2 tablespoons cornstarch   hot mustard, oyster sauce,
1 tablespoon minced scallions   plum sauce, or hoisin sauce

1. In a food processor, purée the shrimp. Transfer to a bowl and beat in the water chestnuts, sherry, salt, cornstarch, scallions, gingerroot, and pepper.
2. Beat the egg white(s) until frothy. Stir into the shrimp until the mixture leaves the sides of the bowl.
3. Oil your hands and shape the paste into small balls. Steam (see page 684) until cooked, about 10 minutes. Serve with one of the sauces.

▶ Can be steamed 1 or 2 days in advance and reheated.

≡ *Rolos do Cararaos à Portuguêsa*
(Shrimp Crab Balls)

== **Yield: 50**

1½ pounds crabmeat, flaked
¾ pound shrimp, cooked and
   minced
½ cup minced onion
½ cup minced green pepper
1 hard-cooked egg, minced
1 tablespoon Worcestershire
   sauce

1 tablespoon Madeira
½ teaspoon dry mustard
salt and pepper, to taste
fine dry bread crumbs
oil for frying

== **Yield: 150**

4½ pounds crabmeat, flaked
2¼ pounds shrimp, cooked and
   minced
1½ cups minced onion
1½ cups minced green pepper
3 hard-cooked eggs, minced

¼ cup Worcestershire sauce
¼ cup Madeira
2 teaspoons dry mustard
salt and pepper, to taste
fine dry bread crumbs
oil for frying

1. In a bowl, mix the crabmeat, shrimp, onion, green pepper, egg(s), Worcestershire sauce, Madeira, mustard, salt, pepper, and enough bread crumbs to bind. Shape into balls.

2. Heat the oil to 375°F and fry until golden.

▶ Can be prepared for frying 1 day in advance.

≡ *Pa Chiao Hsia Ch'iu*
(Hundred-Corner Shrimp Balls)

This is a favorite of the dim sum lunch. The tiny cubes of bread give a delightful texture to these balls.

== **Yield: 36**

10 thin slices white bread, cut
   into ⅛-inch cubes
1 recipe shrimp paste
   (page 693)

1½ teaspoons minced scallions
oil for frying

= **Yield: 108**

30 thin slices white bread, cut
into ⅛-inch cubes
3 recipes shrimp paste
(page 693)

1½ tablespoons minced
scallions
oil for frying

1. Place the bread cubes in a single layer on baking sheets and let dry for several hours.

2. Combine the shrimp paste and the scallions and shape into small balls. Roll the balls in the dry bread cubes, lightly pressing the cubes into the shrimp.

3. Heat the oil to 325°F and fry until balls start to turn golden. Drain. Raise the oil to 375°F and fry until dark golden.

▶ Can be refrigerated for 1 day after the first frying.

☰ *Banana Shrimp Balls*

= **Yield: 36**

1 pound shrimp, cooked and
minced
2 ripe bananas, mashed
¾ cup chopped peanuts
2 tablespoons minced chives
½ teaspoon minced gingerroot

salt, to taste
Tabasco sauce, to taste
fresh bread crumbs
oil for frying
soy dipping sauces (page 74)

= **Yield: 108**

3 pounds shrimp, cooked and
minced
6 ripe bananas, mashed
2¼ cups chopped peanuts
⅓ cup minced chives
2 teaspoons minced gingerroot

salt, to taste
Tabasco sauce, to taste
fresh bread crumbs
oil for frying
soy dipping sauces (page 74)

1. In a bowl, mix the shrimp, bananas, peanuts, chives, gingerroot, salt, and Tabasco sauce. Shape into balls and coat in the bread crumbs. Chill 30 minutes.

2. Heat the oil to 365°F and fry until golden. Serve with one of the soy dipping sauces.

▶ Can be prepared for frying 6 hours in advance.

≡ Shrimp Balls with Mustard Pineapple Sauce

== **Yield: 36**

1 pound shrimp, cooked and
    finely chopped
⅓ cup minced water chestnuts
1 tablespoon cornstarch
2 teaspoons sherry

1 egg, lightly beaten
oil for frying
⅓ cup pineapple juice
1 cup water
⅓ cup dry mustard

== **Yield: 108**

3 pounds shrimp, cooked and
    finely chopped
1 cup minced water chestnuts
3 tablespoons cornstarch
2 tablespoons sherry

3 eggs, lightly beaten
oil for frying
1 cup pineapple juice
3 cups water
1 cup dry mustard

1. The shrimp should be chopped almost to a paste.

2. In a bowl, mix the shrimp, water chestnuts, cornstarch, sherry, and egg(s). Shape into balls.

3. Heat the oil to 375°F and fry until golden.

4. In a small saucepan, bring the pineapple juice and water to a boil and stir in the mustard to form a smooth paste. Serve with the shrimp balls.

▶ Can be prepared for frying 1 day in advance. The sauce can be reheated.

≡ Japanese Prickly Shrimp Balls

== **Yield: 24**

1 pound shrimp, cooked and
    peeled
2 teaspoons sherry
1 egg white
¼ teaspoon salt
6 tablespoons flour, or more

12 water chestnuts, cut in half
3 ounces thin udon noodles,
    broken into ½-inch lengths
    (see Glossary)
oil for frying

== **Yield: 72**

3 pounds shrimp, cooked and
    peeled
2 tablespoons sherry
3 egg whites
¾ teaspoon salt
1 cup flour, or more

36 water chestnuts, cut in half
1 package thin udon noodles,
    broken into ½-inch lengths
    (see Glossary)
oil for frying

1. In a food processor, purée the shrimp and sherry. With the machine running, add the egg white(s), salt, and enough flour to make a smooth paste. Roll the mixture into balls.

2. Press a water chestnut half into the center of each ball and cover with the paste. Roll the balls in the broken noodles, letting pieces of noodle stick out.

3. Heat the oil to 375°F and fry until golden.

▶ Can be prepared for frying 1 day in advance.

☰ *Shrimp and Pork Balls*

═ **Yield: 24**

½ pound ground pork
½ pound shrimp, cooked and minced
½ cup minced water chestnuts
½ cup minced scallions
3 tablespoons soy sauce

⅛ teaspoon sugar
1 egg, lightly beaten
1 teaspoon salt
oil for frying
dipping sauces (pages 72–82)

═ **Yield: 72**

1½ pounds ground pork
1½ pounds shrimp, cooked and minced
1½ cups minced water chestnuts
1½ cups minced scallions

½ cup soy sauce
½ teaspoon sugar
3 eggs, lightly beaten
1 tablespoon salt
oil for frying
dipping sauces (pages 72–82)

1. In a bowl, mix the pork, shrimp, water chestnuts, onion, soy sauce, sugar, egg(s), and salt. Shape into balls and chill 1 hour.

2. Heat the oil to 360°F and fry until golden. Serve with one of the dipping sauces.

▶ Can be prepared for frying 1 day in advance.

—— *Meatballs* ——

≡ *Indian Chicken Balls*

= **Yield: 50**

½ pound cream cheese	1 tablespoon minced chutney
1 cup minced cooked chicken	1 tablespoon curry powder
1 cup blanched, sliced almonds	½ teaspoon salt, or to taste
2 tablespoons mayonnaise	grated unsweetened coconut

= **Yield: 150**

1½ pounds cream cheese	3 tablespoons minced chutney
3 cups minced cooked chicken	3 tablespoons curry powder
3 cups blanched, sliced almonds	1½ teaspoons salt, or to taste
⅓ cup mayonnaise	grated unsweetened coconut

1. In a bowl, mix the cream cheese, chicken, almonds, mayonnaise, chutney, curry powder, and salt.
2. Shape into balls and roll in the coconut.

▶ Keeps 2 days, refrigerated.

NOTE: For a slightly different flavor and more color, toast some or all of the coconut. Serve on banana leaves.

≡ *Chicken and Liver Balls*

These are like individual liver pâtés and can be picked up easily.

= **Yield: 24**

½ pound skinned and boned chicken breast, cooked	1 tablespoon minced onion
¼ pound chicken livers	1 tablespoon sherry
2 tablespoons butter	salt and pepper, to taste
	minced black olives

= **Yield: 72**

1½ pounds skinned and boned chicken breast, cooked	3 tablespoons minced onion
¾ pound chicken livers	3 tablespoons sherry
⅓ cup butter	salt and pepper, to taste
	minced black olives

1. In a food processor, mince the chicken breast.

2. In a skillet, sauté the livers in the butter and onions until the livers are cooked to medium. Pour into the food processor and purée. Correct the seasoning with the sherry, salt, and pepper. Chill.

3. Shape into balls and roll in the olives.

▶ Keeps 2 days, refrigerated.

NOTE: Sherry can overpower other flavors; add only enough to enhance the mixture.

☰ *Turkey-Oyster Balls*

=== **Yield: 50**

½ pint shucked oysters and their liquid
2 cups minced cooked turkey
2 tablespoons butter
2 tablespoons minced shallots
2 egg yolks
1 tablespoon minced celery leaves

4 tablespoons heavy cream
1 teaspoon lemon juice
½ teaspoon Tabasco sauce
salt and pepper, to taste
2 eggs
½ cup dry bread crumbs
½ cup ground almonds
oil for frying

=== **Yield: 144**

1½ pints shucked oysters and their liquid
1½ quarts minced cooked turkey
⅓ cup butter
⅓ cup minced shallots
6 egg yolks
3 tablespoons minced celery leaves

⅔ cup heavy cream
1 tablespoon lemon juice
1½ teaspoons Tabasco sauce
salt and pepper, to taste
6 eggs
1½ cups dry bread crumbs
1½ cups ground almonds
oil for frying

1. In a saucepan, poach oysters until the edges start to curl. Chop the oysters finely and mix with the turkey.

2. In a skillet, melt the butter and sauté the shallots until soft. Add the turkey-oyster mixture and heat. Stir in the egg yolks, celery leaves, half the cream, lemon juice, and Tabasco sauce. Correct the seasoning with salt and pepper. Chill. Shape into balls and chill again.

3. In a bowl, mix the eggs and remaining cream. In another bowl, mix the bread crumbs and the almonds. Roll each ball in the eggs and then in the bread crumbs. Chill.

4. Heat the oil to 375°F and fry until golden.

▶ Can be prepared for frying 1 day in advance.

≡ *Mexican Meatballs*

═ Yield: 36

1 pound ground beef	1 to 2 tablespoons minced hot
1 cup fresh bread crumbs	or mild chilies
¾ cup light cream	½ teaspoon dried oregano
1 egg	salt and pepper, to taste
½ cup minced onion	½ cup butter, optional
1 tablespoon butter, softened	salsa (page 68)

═ Yield: 144

4 pounds ground beef	¼ to ½ cup minced hot or mild
1 quart fresh bread crumbs	chilies
3 cups light cream	1 tablespoon dried oregano
4 eggs	salt and pepper, to taste
2 cups minced onion	2 cups butter, optional
¼ cup butter, softened	salsa (page 68)

1. In a bowl, mix the beef, bread crumbs, cream, egg(s), onion, softened butter, chilies, oregano, salt, and pepper. Shape into small balls.

2. Sauté in butter in a skillet or bake in a 400°F oven for 5 to 10 minutes until just cooked. Serve with Mexican salsa, if desired.

▶ Can be prepared for cooking up to 2 days in advance; cooked meatballs can be frozen.

≡ Albondigas (Spanish Meatballs)

=== **Yield: 36**

¼ pound ham fat, chopped (see note)	1 teaspoon salt
3 garlic cloves, chopped	⅛ teaspoon pepper
1 teaspoon chopped parsley	⅛ teaspoon chili powder
½ teaspoon dried sage	flour for dredging
1 pound beef, pork, or veal	vegetable oil
1 slice stale bread	1 bay leaf
3 eggs	1 cup water
	1 cup white wine

=== **Yield: 108**

¾ pound ham fat, chopped (see note)	1 tablespoon salt
9 garlic cloves, chopped	½ teaspoon pepper
1 tablespoon chopped parsley	½ teaspoon chili powder
1½ teaspoons dried sage	flour for dredging
3 pounds beef, pork, or veal	vegetable oil
3 slices stale bread	2 to 3 bay leaves
9 eggs	3 cups water
	3 cups white wine

1. In a food processor, purée the ham fat, garlic, parsley, and sage. Transfer to a bowl.

2. In a food processor, finely chop the meat and bread. Add to the ham fat mixture with the eggs, salt, pepper, and chili powder. Shape into balls and dredge in flour.

3. In a skillet, sauté the balls in ½ inch of oil with the bay leaf, turning until cooked. Drain the fat from the meatballs and add the water. Bring to a boil, scraping up the browned bits. Stir in the wine and reduce by half. Serve the meatballs in the sauce.

▶ Cooked meatballs can be frozen or kept 2 days, refrigerated.

NOTE: Markets that sell prosciutto often sell the fat separately. Try to obtain that fat for this recipe because of its greater flavor.

≡ Olive-Stuffed Meatballs

=== **Yield: 36**

1 pound ground beef	½ teaspoon salt
½ cup minced onion	½ teaspoon pepper
½ cup bread crumbs	36 medium-size stuffed olives
1 egg, lightly beaten	vegetable oil for frying, optional

== **Yield: 108**

3 pounds ground beef	1½ teaspoons salt
1½ cups minced onion	1½ teaspoons pepper
1½ cups bread crumbs	108 medium-size stuffed olives
3 eggs, lightly beaten	vegetable oil for frying, optional

1. In a bowl, mix the beef, onion, bread crumbs, egg(s), salt, and pepper.

2. Shape into balls. Poke a hole in the center of each and insert an olive. Reshape the meat around the olive. Sauté in oil or bake at 350°F.

▶ Cooked meatballs can be frozen or kept 2 days, refrigerated.

== *Akta Svensk Köttbullar med Gradd Sås*
   (Swedish Meatballs I with Cream Sauce)

There are possibly as many recipes for Swedish, or Scandinavian, meatballs as there are Scandinavians. Here are a few favorites. Although similar, each is different.

== **Yield: 70**

2 pounds lean ground beef	1 tablespoon butter
1 pound ground veal	½ teaspoon salt
2 eggs	½ teaspoon pepper
½ cup bread crumbs	½ cup butter
3 tablespoons milk	2 cups heavy cream
3 tablespoons minced onion	

== **Yield: 210**

6 pounds lean ground beef	3 tablespoons butter
3 pounds ground veal	1½ teaspoons salt
6 eggs	1½ teaspoons pepper
1½ cups bread crumbs	1½ cups butter
⅓ cup milk	6 cups heavy cream
⅓ cup minced onion	

1. In a bowl, mix the beef, veal, eggs, bread crumbs, and milk.

2. In a skillet, sauté the onion in the butter until soft but not brown. Mix into the meat with salt and pepper. Shape into small balls.

3. In a skillet, heat the remaining butter and sauté the balls until cooked. Remove from the pan. Stir in the cream and cook over high heat, scraping up the browned bits. Correct the seasoning with salt and pepper.
4. Simmer the meatballs in the sauce for 5 minutes.

▶ Cooked meatballs can be frozen or kept 2 days, refrigerated.
NOTE: For additional flavor, add nutmeg or cinnamon to taste to the sauce.

≡ Swedish Meatballs II

═ Yield: 70

2 pounds ground beef	½ teaspoon ground cloves
1 pound ground pork	½ teaspoon ground allspice
2 eggs, beaten	½ teaspoon ground ginger
1 cup dry bread crumbs	1 cup milk
1 cup mashed potatoes	flour for dredging
2 teaspoons salt	¼ cup butter
1 teaspoon brown sugar	2 cups light cream
1 teaspoon pepper	

═ Yield: 210

6 pounds ground beef	1½ teaspoons ground cloves
3 pounds ground pork	1½ teaspoons ground allspice
6 eggs, beaten	1½ teaspoons ground ginger
3 cups dry bread crumbs	3 cups milk
3 cups mashed potatoes	flour for dredging
2 tablespoons salt	¾ cup butter
1 tablespoon brown sugar	6 cups light cream
1 tablespoon pepper	

1. Preheat the oven to 325°F.
2. In a bowl, mix the beef, pork, eggs, bread crumbs, potatoes, salt, sugar, pepper, cloves, allspice, ginger, and milk. Work the mixture together and shape into balls.
3. Dredge in the flour and sauté in the butter until well browned.
4. Transfer to a casserole, pour in the cream, and bake for 35 minutes.

▶ Cooked meatballs can be frozen or kept 2 days, refrigerated.

≡ *Svensk Köttbullar (Swedish Meatballs III)*

=== **Yield: 70**

3 pounds ground beef
2¼ cups grated potatoes
⅓ cup grated onion
1½ tablespoons salt

2 teaspoons ground allspice
4 cups beef broth
½ cup butter

=== **Yield: 210**

9 pounds ground beef
7 cups grated potatoes
1 cup grated onion
⅓ cup salt

2 tablespoons ground allspice
12 cups beef broth
1½ cups butter

    1. In a bowl, mix the beef, potatoes, onion, salt, and allspice. Shape into balls.

    2. Bring the broth to a simmer, and poach the meatballs for 5 minutes.

    3. Drain and sauté in the butter until browned.

▶ Cooked meatballs can be frozen or kept 2 days, refrigerated.

≡ *Norwegian Meatballs*

=== **Yield: 70**

1 pound ground beef
1 pound ground veal
1 pound ground pork
2 eggs
⅓ cup milk
2 cups grated potatoes
1 cup grated onion
½ teaspoon grated nutmeg

½ teaspoon ground ginger
¼ teaspoon ground cloves
salt and pepper, to taste
½ cup butter
4 cups sour cream
3 cups beef consommé
⅛ teaspoon dill seed

=== **Yield: 210**

3 pounds ground beef
3 pounds ground veal
3 pounds ground pork
6 eggs
1 cup milk
6 cups grated potatoes
3 cups grated onion
1½ teaspoons grated nutmeg

1½ teaspoons ground ginger
¾ teaspoon ground cloves
salt and pepper, to taste
1½ cups butter
12 cups sour cream
9 cups beef consommé
½ teaspoon dill seed

1. In a bowl, mix the beef, veal, pork, eggs, milk, potatoes, onion, nutmeg, ginger, cloves, salt, and pepper. Shape into balls.

2. In a skillet, sauté the meatballs in the butter. Drain off the excess fat and stir in sour cream, consommé, and dill seed. Heat without simmering for 20 minutes to develop the flavor.

▶ Can be cooked 2 days in advance and reheated.

≡ *Bitterballen (Dutch Meatballs)*

The Dutch are as proud of their *bitterballen* as the Scandinavians are of their *köttbullar*.

═ Yield: 36

1 cup béchamel sauce for
   croquettes (page 60)
grated nutmeg, to taste
pepper, to taste
¼ cup minced onion
2 tablespoons butter
½ teaspoon minced garlic
1¼ cups minced ham
1 cup minced cooked chicken,
   veal, pork, or beef
2 teaspoons minced parsley

1 teaspoon Worcestershire
   sauce
½ teaspoon dried thyme
¼ teaspoon Tabasco sauce
salt and pepper, to taste
fine, dry bread crumbs
1 egg, lightly beaten with 1 egg
   yolk
oil for frying
hot mustard

═ Yield: 108

3 cups béchamel sauce for
   croquettes (page 60)
grated nutmeg, to taste
pepper, to taste
¾ cup minced onion
⅓ cup butter
1½ teaspoons minced garlic
4 cups minced ham
3 cups minced cooked chicken,
   veal, pork, or beef

2 tablespoons minced parsley
1 tablespoon Worcestershire
   sauce
1½ teaspoons dried thyme
¾ teaspoon Tabasco sauce
salt and pepper, to taste
fine, dry bread crumbs
6 eggs, lightly beaten
oil for frying
hot mustard

1. In a bowl, mix the béchamel sauce, nutmeg, and pepper. Set aside.

2. In a skillet, sauté the onion in the butter until soft. Add the garlic and sauté 1 minute. Add the ham and chicken and sauté 3 minutes. Stir into the béchamel sauce with the parsley, Worcestershire sauce, thyme, Tabasco sauce, salt, and pepper. Chill.

3. Shape into balls and roll in the bread crumbs, dip in the eggs, and roll in the crumbs again. Let the coating set for at least 30 minutes.
4. Heat the oil to 350°F and fry until golden. Serve with hot mustard.

▶ Can be prepared for frying 2 days in advance or frozen.

≡ *Cheese Meatballs*

═ **Yield: 25**

1 pound ground beef	1 egg
½ cup fresh bread crumbs	2 tablespoons minced onion
⅓ cup crumbled Roquefort	¾ teaspoon salt
cheese	¼ teaspoon pepper
3 tablespoons milk	butter

═ **Yield: 200**

8 pounds ground beef	8 eggs
1 quart fresh bread crumbs	1 cup minced onion
3 cups crumbled Roquefort	3 tablespoons salt
cheese	2 teaspoons pepper
1½ cups milk	butter

1. In a bowl, mix the beef, bread crumbs, cheese, milk, egg(s), onion, salt, and pepper.
2. Shape into balls and sauté in the butter.

▶ Cooked meatballs can be frozen or kept 2 days, refrigerated.

≡ *Viennese Sweet and Sour Meatballs*

═ **Yield: 50**

3 slices white bread, crusts	½ teaspoon pepper
removed	¼ teaspoon dried thyme
2 pounds ground beef	1-pound can Italian plum
1 egg, beaten	tomatoes
½ cup minced onion	⅓ cup brown sugar
½ cup beef broth	⅓ cup sugar
1 garlic clove, minced	½ cup crumbled gingersnaps
1 teaspoon salt	⅓ cup lemon juice
1 teaspoon paprika	

═ **Yield: 200**

12 slices white bread, crusts
   removed
8 pounds ground beef
4 eggs, beaten
2 cups minced onion
2 cups beef broth
4 garlic cloves, minced
3 tablespoons salt
3 tablespoons paprika

2 tablespoons pepper
2 teaspoons dried thyme
4 pounds canned Italian plum
   tomatoes
1⅓ cups brown sugar
1⅓ cups sugar
2 cups crumbled gingersnaps
1⅓ cups lemon juice

1. Preheat the oven to 350°F.

2. In a bowl, soak the bread in cold water to cover for 3 minutes, drain, and squeeze out the excess liquid.

3. Mix in the beef, egg(s), onion, broth, garlic, salt, paprika, pepper, and thyme. Shape into balls and bake on baking sheets until cooked.

4. Drain the tomatoes, force through a sieve, and heat with the brown sugar, sugar, gingersnaps, and lemon juice until the sugars dissolve. Add the meatballs and simmer until glazed and the sauce thickens slightly.

▶ Cooked meatballs can be frozen or kept 2 days, refrigerated.

═ *Boulettes aux Herbes (Meatballs with Herbs)*

═ **Yield: 35**

4 slices white bread, crusts
   removed
½ cup minced onion
2 tablespoons butter
1½ pounds ground beef
2 eggs

salt and pepper, to taste
4 garlic cloves, minced
1 teaspoon crumbled tarragon
½ cup minced dill
2 tablespoons butter
1½ cups sour cream

═ **Yield: 200**

1 loaf white bread, crusts
   removed
3 cups minced onion
¾ cup butter
9 pounds ground beef
12 eggs
salt and pepper, to taste

1 large head garlic, minced
2 tablespoons crumbled
   tarragon
3 cups minced dill
¾ pound butter
9 cups sour cream

1. In a bowl, soak the bread in cold water to cover for 3 minutes, drain, and squeeze out the excess liquid.

2. In a skillet, sauté the onion in the butter until soft but not brown. Add the onion to the bread and mix in the beef, eggs, salt, and pepper. Shape into balls.

3. Heat a kettle of salted water and bring to a boil. Poach the balls for 10 minutes.

4. In a skillet, sauté the garlic, tarragon, and dill in the butter until fragrant, about 2 minutes. Add the meatballs and cook, stirring, until well coated and hot.

5. Stir in the sour cream and heat, without boiling. Correct the seasoning with salt and pepper.

▶ Cooked meatballs can be frozen or kept 2 days, refrigerated. Make the sauce just before serving.

≡ *Parmesan Beef Balls*

═ Yield: 25

1 pound ground beef	1 egg, lightly beaten
½ cup fresh dry bread crumbs	¼ teaspoon crumbled rosemary
¼ cup grated Parmesan cheese	¼ teaspoon pepper
¼ cup white wine	salt, to taste
1 tablespoon minced parsley	butter
1 garlic clove, minced	

═ Yield: 200

8 pounds ground beef	8 eggs, lightly beaten
1 quart fresh dry bread crumbs	2 teaspoons crumbled rosemary
2 cups grated Parmesan cheese	2 teaspoons pepper
2 cups white wine	salt, to taste
½ cup minced parsley	butter
8 garlic cloves, minced	

1. In a bowl, mix the beef, bread crumbs, cheese, wine, parsley, garlic, egg(s), rosemary, pepper, and salt. Shape into balls.

2. Sauté the balls in the butter until golden and cooked.

▶ Cooked meatballs can be frozen or kept 2 days, refrigerated.

≡ *Batter-Fried Meatballs*

=== **Yield: 25**

1 pound ground beef	1½ teaspoons baking powder
1 tablespoon grated onion	1 egg, lightly beaten
1 teaspoon salt	½ cup water
½ teaspoon black pepper	salt and pepper, to taste
1 garlic clove, minced	oil for frying
1½ cups flour	tomato sauce (pages 63–65)

=== **Yield: 200**

8 pounds ground beef	3 tablespoons baking powder
½ cup grated onion	8 eggs, lightly beaten
3 tablespoons salt	1 quart water
1½ tablespoons pepper	salt and pepper, to taste
8 garlic cloves, minced	oil for frying
10 cups flour	tomato sauce (pages 63–65)

1. In a bowl, mix the beef, onion, salt, pepper, and garlic. Shape into balls.

2. In a bowl, mix the flour and baking powder. Add the egg(s), water, salt, and pepper and stir to make a batter.

3. Heat the oil to 375°F. Dip the meatballs into the batter and fry until golden. Serve immediately with tomato sauce as a dip.

▶ The meatballs can be prepared 1 day in advance. Make the batter and fry just before serving.

≡ *Keftedes I (Greek Meatballs I)*

=== **Yield: 40**

2 slices white bread, crusts removed	¼ teaspoon cinnamon
	¼ teaspoon ground allspice
1½ pounds ground beef	salt and pepper, to taste
1 cup minced onion	vegetable oil
2 eggs, lightly beaten	avgolemonou sauce (page 71)
2 tablespoons parsley	yogurt garlic mint sauce
1 tablespoon minced mint	(page 70)

══ **Yield: 200**

10 slices white bread, crusts
    removed
7½ pounds ground beef
5 cups minced onion
10 eggs, lightly beaten
⅔ cup minced parsley
⅓ cup minced mint

1¼ teaspoons cinnamon
1¼ teaspoons ground allspice
salt and pepper, to taste
vegetable oil
avgolemonou sauce (page 71)
yogurt garlic mint sauce
    (page 70)

1. Cut the bread into ¼-inch cubes.
2. In a bowl, mix the bread cubes, beef, onion, eggs, parsley, mint, cinnamon, allspice, salt, and pepper. Chill.
3. Shape into balls and sauté in the oil. Serve with avgolemonou sauce or yogurt garlic mint sauce.

▶ Cooked meatballs can be frozen or kept 2 days, refrigerated.

══ *Keftedes II (Greek Meatballs II)*

══ **Yield: 20**

½ pound ground veal
⅓ pound ground beef
⅓ cup bread crumbs
1 tablespoon grated onion
1 egg
1 tablespoon hot water
1 teaspoon vinegar

1 teaspoon salt
½ teaspoon oregano
¼ teaspoon minced garlic
pepper, to taste
flour for dredging
olive oil

══ **Yield: 200**

5 pounds ground veal
3 pounds ground beef
3½ cups bread crumbs
¾ cup grated onion
10 eggs
¾ cup hot water
3 tablespoons vinegar

3 tablespoons salt
1½ tablespoons oregano
2½ teaspoons minced garlic
pepper, to taste
flour for dredging
olive oil

1. In a bowl, mix the veal, beef, bread crumbs, onion, egg(s), water, vinegar, salt, oregano, garlic, and pepper. Shape into 1-inch balls and dredge in the flour.
2. In a skillet, sauté the meatballs in the olive oil until cooked.

▶ Cooked meatballs can be frozen or kept 2 days, refrigerated.

≡ *Soutzoukakia (Greek Meatballs III)*

== **Yield: 40**

3 slices white bread, crusts
  removed
¾ pound ground veal
¾ pound ground beef
1 cup minced onion
2 garlic cloves, minced
2 tablespoons minced parsley

2 tablespoons minced mint
pinch of ground cumin
salt and pepper, to taste
olive oil for frying
1 cup tomato sauce
  (pages 63–65)

== **Yield: 200**

15 slices white bread, crusts
  removed
4 pounds ground veal
4 pounds ground beef
5 cups minced onion
10 garlic cloves, minced
⅓ cup minced parsley

⅓ cup minced mint
1¼ teaspoons ground cumin
salt and pepper, to taste
olive oil for frying
5 cups tomato sauce
  (pages 63–65)

1. In a bowl, soak the bread in cold water to cover for 3 minutes, drain, and squeeze out the excess liquid.

2. In another bowl, mix the veal, beef, onion, garlic, parsley, mint, cumin, bread, salt, and pepper. Shape into balls.

3. In a skillet, sauté the balls in the olive oil until cooked. Drain the excess fat and add the tomato sauce. Heat.

▶ Cooked meatballs can be frozen or kept 2 days, refrigerated.

≡ *Veal Balls*

== **Yield: 50**

2 pounds ground veal
4 anchovy fillets
½ garlic clove, crushed
2 teaspoons Dijon mustard
salt and pepper, to taste

butter
hollandaise sauce (page 54) or
  warm mayonnaise (page 48)
  flavored with lemon to taste

═ **Yield: 200**

8 pounds ground veal	butter
16 anchovy fillets	hollandaise sauce (page 54) or
4 garlic cloves, crushed	warm mayonnaise (page 48)
3 tablespoons Dijon mustard	flavored with lemon to taste
salt and pepper, to taste	

1. In a bowl, mix the veal, anchovies, garlic, mustard, salt, and pepper. Shape into 1-inch balls.
2. In a skillet, sauté the balls in the butter until cooked. Serve with hot lemon-flavored mayonnaise.

▶ The cooked meatballs can be frozen or kept 2 days, refrigerated, but make the sauce just before serving.

NOTE: To make hot mayonnaise, heat the oil for the mayonnaise to 130°F and make the mayonnaise in the usual manner. Keep warm in a double boiler.

≡ *Lamb Meatballs Avgolemonou (with Egg Lemon Sauce)*

═ **Yield: 25**

1½ cups beef consommé	½ teaspoon salt
¼ cup rice	pinch of pepper
1 pound ground lamb	olive oil
⅓ cup chopped ripe olives	avgolemonou sauce (page 71)
1 tablespoon minced mint	mint leaves

═ **Yield: 200**

8 cups beef consommé	4 teaspoons salt
2 cups rice	pepper, to taste
8 pounds ground lamb	olive oil
3 cups chopped ripe olives	avgolemonou sauce (page 71)
½ cup minced mint	mint leaves

1. In a saucepan, bring the consommé to a boil, add the rice, and cook until tender. Drain.
2. In a bowl, mix the rice, lamb, olives, mint, salt, and pepper. Shape into balls and sauté in the olive oil until cooked. Serve in the sauce, garnished with the mint leaves.

▶ Cooked meatballs can be frozen or kept 2 days, refrigerated. Make the sauce just before serving.

≡ *Minted Lamb Meatballs*

═ Yield: 25

1 pound ground lamb
1 egg, beaten
3 tablespoons minced onion
2 tablespoons bread crumbs
2 tablespoons minced mint
2 tablespoons minced parsley
1 teaspoon salt

¼ teaspoon ground cumin
¼ teaspoon pepper
½ pint cherry tomatoes, cut in half
yogurt garlic mint sauce (page 70)

═ Yield: 200

8 pounds ground lamb
8 eggs, beaten
1½ cups minced onion
1 cup bread crumbs
1 cup minced mint
1 cup minced parsley
3 tablespoons salt

2 teaspoons ground cumin
2 teaspoons pepper
6 pints cherry tomatoes, cut in half
yogurt garlic mint sauce (page 70)

1. Preheat the oven to 400°F or preheat a grill.

2. In a bowl, mix the lamb, egg(s), onion, bread crumbs, mint, parsley, salt, cumin, and pepper. Shape into balls. Arrange on a baking sheet and bake at 400°F for 15 minutes, or arrange on skewers and cook on a grill.

3. Thread a meatball and half a cherry tomato on a skewer and serve with the dip.

▶ Cooked meatballs can be frozen or kept 2 days, refrigerated.

≡ *Lamb and Leek Meatballs*

═ Yield: 25

1 cup minced leeks
1½ cups ground roast lamb
1 tablespoon minced parsley
1 tablespoon lemon juice
½ teaspoon minced garlic
½ teaspoon salt
pepper, to taste
2 egg yolks

2 to 4 tablespoons heavy cream
2 eggs
1½ tablespoons oil
½ cup flour
1 cup bread crumbs
oil for frying
yogurt cucumber sauce (page 71)

⟆ **Yield: 200**

2 quarts minced leeks	1 to 2 cups heavy cream
3 quarts ground roast lamb	16 eggs
½ cup minced parsley	¾ cup oil
½ cup lemon juice	4 cups flour
4 teaspoons minced garlic	2 quarts bread crumbs
4 teaspoons salt	oil for frying
pepper, to taste	yogurt cucumber sauce
12 eggs	(page 71)

1. In a saucepan, blanch the leeks in boiling salted water for 8 minutes, drain, and refresh under cold water. Squeeze out the excess liquid.

2. In a bowl, mix the leeks, lamb, parsley, lemon juice, garlic, salt, pepper, egg yolks, and enough cream to bind. Shape into balls and chill 1 hour.

3. In a bowl, lightly beat the eggs with the oil. Dredge the balls in the flour, dip in the egg mixture, and roll in the bread crumbs. Let the coating set at least 30 minutes.

4. Heat the oil to 375°F and fry until golden. Serve with cucumber yogurt sauce.

▶ Can be prepared for frying 2 days in advance.

☰ *Lamb Meatballs*

⟆ **Yield: 25**

1 pound ground lamb	¾ teaspoon Dijon mustard
½ cup minced onion	¾ teaspoon ground coriander
⅓ cup pine nuts, chopped	¼ teaspoon crumbled rosemary
1 egg	Tabasco sauce, to taste
2 garlic cloves, minced	pepper, to taste
2 tablespoons minced parsley	pinch of ground allspice
2 tablespoons lemon juice	olive oil
1 teaspoon salt, or to taste	ginger soy dip (page 74)

⟆ **Yield: 200**

8 pounds ground lamb	3 tablespoons Dijon mustard
1 quart minced onion	3 tablespoons ground coriander
3 cups pine nuts, chopped	2 teaspoons crumbled rosemary
8 eggs	Tabasco sauce, to taste
16 garlic cloves, minced	pepper, to taste
1 cup minced parsley	½ teaspoon ground allspice
1 cup lemon juice	olive oil
2½ tablespoons salt, or to taste	ginger soy dip (page 74)

1. In a bowl, mix the lamb, onion, pine nuts, egg(s), garlic, parsley, lemon juice, salt, Dijon mustard, coriander, rosemary, Tabasco sauce, pepper, and allspice.

2. Shape into balls and sauté in the oil until cooked. Serve with ginger soy dipping sauce on the side.

▶ Cooked meatballs can be frozen.

≡ Cevabcici (Serbian Meatballs)

These sausage-like meatballs from Serbia are an interesting change.

═ **Yield: 36**

1½ pounds ground pork	oil
salt and pepper, to taste	thin slices dark bread
flour for dredging	1 cup minced onion

═ **Yield: 180**

8 pounds ground pork	oil
salt and pepper, to taste	thin slices dark bread
flour for dredging	8 cups minced onion

1. In a bowl, mix the pork, salt, and pepper. Roll the meat into sausages 2½ inches long and ¾ inch thick.

2. Dredge in the flour and sauté in a lightly oiled skillet until cooked. Serve on the bread with the onion on the side.

▶ Can be prepared for cooking 1 day in advance.

≡ Pork-Clam Balls

═ **Yield: 36**

2 7½-ounce cans minced clams	3 tablespoons butter
1 pound ground pork	3 tablespoons flour
1 egg, beaten	1½ cups half-and-half
2 tablespoons bread crumbs	1 tablespoon minced dill
1 tablespoon minced parsley	1 tablespoon sherry
½ teaspoon rubbed sage	salt and pepper, to taste
¼ teaspoon pepper	

═ **Yield: 180**

5 pints minced clams	1 cup butter
5 pounds ground pork	1 cup flour
5 eggs, beaten	2 quarts half-and-half
¾ cup bread crumbs	⅓ cup minced dill
⅓ cup minced parsley	¼ cup sherry
1 tablespoon rubbed sage	salt and pepper, to taste
1¼ teaspoons pepper	

1. Preheat the oven to 400°F.

2. Drain the clams, reserving the liquid.

3. In a bowl, mix the clams, pork, egg(s), bread crumbs, 2 table-spoons (¾ *cup*) clam liquid, parsley, sage, and pepper. Shape into balls and place on baking sheets. Bake for about 15 minutes or until cooked.

4. In a saucepan, melt the butter, stir in the flour, and cook, stirring until the roux starts to foam and turn golden. Add ½ cup (*3 cups*) clam liquid and the half-and-half. Cook until thickened and smooth. Stir in the dill and sherry. Correct the seasoning with salt and pepper.

▶ Meatballs and sauce can be cooked 2 days in advance and refrigerated or frozen.

═ *Pork Balls with Ginger*
_____

═ **Yield: 25**

1 pound ground pork	1 teaspoon salt
1 cup chopped water chestnuts	cornstarch
¼ cup minced crystallized	oil for frying
ginger	dipping sauces (pages 72–82)
1 egg, lightly beaten	

═ **Yield: 200**

8 pounds ground pork	8 eggs, lightly beaten
2 quarts chopped water	3 tablespoons salt
chestnuts	cornstarch
2 cups minced crystallized	oil for frying
ginger	dipping sauces (pages 72–82)

1. In a bowl, mix the pork, water chestnuts, ginger, egg(s), and salt. Shape into balls and dredge in the cornstarch.

2. Heat the oil to 375°F and fry until golden. Serve with dipping sauces.

▶ Can be fried a day in advance and reheated; can be frozen.

≡ *Fat Horses*

My brother, a long-time resident of Bangkok, introduced me to this and many other Thai recipes. These are not truly meatballs, but because the method of eating them is so similar, they seem to belong in this chapter.

═ Yield: 36

10 ounces pork loin, cubed	2 eggs, separated
10 ounces chicken breast, cubed	3 tablespoons coconut cream
4 garlic cloves	1 tablespoon nam pla (see Glossary)
1 teaspoon minced coriander (cilantro)	½ teaspoon brown sugar
¼ teaspoon pepper	½ teaspoon molasses
	minced scallions

═ Yield: 180

3 pounds pork loin, cubed	10 eggs, separated
3 pounds chicken breasts, cubed	1 cup coconut cream
20 garlic cloves	⅓ cup nam pla (see Glossary)
2 tablespoons minced coriander (cilantro)	1 tablespoon brown sugar
2 tablespoons pepper	1 tablespoon molasses
	minced scallions

1. Oil miniature muffin tins.

2. In a food processor, finely grind the pork, chicken, garlic, coriander, and pepper. In a bowl, beat the egg whites with half the yolks and add to the pork mixture. With off-on turns, blend in the coconut cream, nam pla, brown sugar, and molasses until the mixture forms a thick paste.

3. Divide the mixture among the tins. Lightly beat the remaining yolks and brush the tops of the meat cakes. Sprinkle with the scallions.

4. Place the muffin tins in a Chinese steamer and steam until firm, about 20 minutes. Serve warm.

▶ Can be steamed 1 day in advance and reheated.

NOTE: For details on steaming, see Chapter 18.

≡ *Mu Sarong I (Lady in a Sarong I)*

There are many recipes for mu sarong. The fanciful name comes from the wrapping of each meatball in strands of noodles. This is tedious work, but the results are worth the effort.

═ **Yield: 36**

¾ pound ground beef
¼ pound ground pork
½ cup minced scallions
2 tablespoons minced
coriander (cilantro)
2 tablespoons nam pla (see
Glossary)
1 tablespoon minced garlic

½ teaspoon grated nutmeg
¼ teaspoon salt
¼ teaspoon pepper
1 egg
12 ounces fresh Chinese
noodles
oil for frying
plum sauce

═ **Yield: 180**

4 pounds ground beef
1¼ pounds ground pork
2½ cups minced scallions
⅔ cup minced coriander
(cilantro)
⅔ cup nam pla (see Glossary)
5 tablespoons minced garlic

2½ teaspoons grated nutmeg
1¼ teaspoons salt
1¼ teaspoons pepper
5 eggs
4 pounds fresh Chinese noodles
oil for frying
plum sauce

1. In a bowl, mix the beef, pork, scallions, coriander, nam pla, garlic, nutmeg, salt, and pepper. Shape into 1-inch balls.

2. Dip each meatball into the egg(s) and wrap one or more noodles around the ball as you would wind a ball of yarn. The meatball should be completely enclosed.

3. Heat the oil to 375°F and fry until golden. Serve with plum sauce.

▶ Can be prepared for frying 1 day in advance.

NOTE: It is faster to take two to four strands of noodles and wrap them at one time around the meatball.

═ *Mu Sarong II (Lady in a Sarong II)*

═ **Yield: 36**

1 4-ounce package rice stick
noodles
1 pound ground pork
2 teaspoons minced garlic
1½ teaspoons pepper
1 teaspoon salt

½ cup nam pla (see Glossary)
1 egg, beaten
oil for frying
sweet hot dipping sauce
(page 80)

== **Yield: 180**

5 4-ounce packages rice stick	2½ cups nam pla (see Glossary)
noodles	5 eggs, beaten
5 pounds ground pork	oil for frying
3 tablespoons minced garlic	sweet hot dipping sauce
2½ tablespoons pepper	(page 80)
2 tablespoons salt	

1. In a bowl, soak the noodles in boiling water to cover for 10 minutes. Drain and set aside.

2. In a bowl, mix the pork, garlic, pepper, salt, and nam pla. Shape into balls.

3. Dip each meatball into the egg(s) and wrap the rice stick noodles around the ball as you would wind a ball of yarn. The meatball should be completely enclosed.

4. Heat the oil to 375°F and fry until golden. Drain.

▶ Can be prepared for frying 1 day in advance.

≡ *Pearl Balls*

This is another Asian specialty with a magical name. The glutinous rice cooks to a translucency reminiscent of pearls. Regular white rice is not acceptable. Glutinous rice, also called sweet rice, is available in Asian markets.

== **Yield: 36**

½ cup glutinous rice	1½ teaspoons salt
4 dried Chinese mushrooms	1 teaspoon minced gingerroot
1 pound ground pork	½ teaspoon sugar
1 egg, lightly beaten	duck sauce, Chinese mustard
½ cup minced water chestnuts	(page 73), or soy dipping
1 scallion, minced	sauces (page 74)
1 tablespoon soy sauce	

== **Yield: 180**

2½ cups glutinous rice	2½ tablespoons salt
20 dried Chinese mushrooms	2 tablespoons minced
5 pounds ground pork	gingerroot
5 eggs, lightly beaten	2½ teaspoons sugar
2½ cups minced water	duck sauce, Chinese mustard
chestnuts	(page 73), or soy dipping
5 scallions, minced	sauces (page 74)
⅓ cup soy sauce	

1. Cover the rice with cold water and soak for 2 hours. Drain.

2. Soak the mushrooms in boiling water for 30 minutes. Drain. Remove the stems from the mushrooms and discard. Mince the caps.

3. In a bowl, mix the mushrooms, pork, egg(s), water chestnuts, scallions, soy sauce, salt, ginger, and sugar. Shape into 1-inch balls. Roll each ball in the drained rice.

4. Steam about 20 minutes (see Chapter 18) or until cooked. Serve with one of the sauces.

▶ Can be steamed 1 day in advance and reheated; can be frozen.

≡ *Deep-Fried Meatballs with Sesame Seeds*

═ **Yield: 25**

1 pound ground pork	oil for frying
¼ teaspoon minced gingerroot	2 tablespoons ketchup
¼ teaspoon pepper	1 tablespoon vinegar
1 tablespoon sherry	1 tablespoon sugar
1 tablespoon soy sauce	2 tablespoons toasted sesame
1 egg	seeds
2 tablespoons cornstarch	

═ **Yield: 200**

8 pounds ground pork	1 cup cornstarch
2 tablespoons minced	oil for frying
gingerroot	1 cup ketchup
2 tablespoons pepper	½ cup vinegar
½ cup sherry	½ cup sugar
½ cup soy sauce	1 cup toasted sesame seeds
8 eggs	

1. In a bowl, mix the pork, gingerroot, pepper, sherry, soy sauce, egg(s), and cornstarch. Shape into balls.

2. Heat the oil to 360°F and fry until golden.

3. In a saucepan, simmer the ketchup, vinegar, and sugar until the sugar dissolves. Add the fried balls and toss to coat. Sprinkle with sesame seeds. Serve hot or cold.

▶ Can be fried 1 day in advance and reheated.

≡ Rempah (Indonesian Meatballs)

═ Yield: 25

1 pound pork sausage meat
2 cups grated fresh coconut
½ cup minced onion
2 garlic cloves, minced
2 eggs
1 teaspoon brown sugar

1 teaspoon ground coriander
½ teaspoon lemon juice
½ teaspoon ground caraway
    seeds
salt, to taste
vegetable oil

═ Yield: 200

8 pounds pork sausage meat
2 quarts grated fresh coconut
4 cups minced onion
16 garlic cloves, minced
16 eggs
3 tablespoons brown sugar

3 tablespoons ground coriander
4 teaspoons lemon juice
4 teaspoons ground caraway
    seeds
salt, to taste
vegetable oil

1. In a bowl, mix the sausage meat, coconut, onion, garlic, eggs, brown sugar, coriander, lemon juice, caraway seeds, and salt.

2. Shape into balls and sauté in the oil until golden.

▶ Can be cooked 1 day in advance and reheated; can be frozen.

≡ Ginger Sausage Rounds

═ Yield: 36

1½ pounds pork sausage meat
1 garlic clove, crushed
1 tablespoon minced candied
    ginger

3 eggs, separated
oil for frying

═ Yield: 180

7½ pounds pork sausage meat
5 garlic cloves, crushed
⅓ cup minced candied ginger

15 eggs, separated
oil for frying

1. In a bowl, mix the sausage, garlic, ginger, and egg yolks.

2. Beat the egg whites until stiff but not dry. Fold into the sausage mixture and shape into balls.

3. Heat the oil to 375°F and fry until golden. Serve hot.

▶ Can be prepared for frying 1 day in advance.

NOTE: When making the larger quantity, it is easier to fold in the egg whites if the sausage mixture is divided into 5 batches. Beat the egg whites and fold in just before shaping.

≡ *Ching Tong Har Gow*
(Ham and Shrimp Balls in Broth)

═ **Yield: 35**

1 pound shrimp, peeled	1 teaspoon salt
½ cup chopped ham	1 teaspoon sugar
3 egg whites	chicken stock
1 tablespoon cornstarch	dipping sauces (pages 72–82)
2 teaspoons soy sauce	

═ **Yield: 200**

5 pounds shrimp, peeled	2½ tablespoons salt
2½ cups chopped ham	2½ tablespoons sugar
15 egg whites	chicken stock
⅓ cup cornstarch	dipping sauces (pages 72–82)
2½ tablespoons soy sauce	

1. In a food processor, purée the shrimp and ham. With the motor running, add the egg whites, cornstarch, soy sauce, salt, and sugar. Shape into balls.

2. In a casserole, bring 3 inches of chicken stock to a simmer and poach the balls until they float to the surface. Serve with one of the dipping sauces.

▶ Can be prepared 2 days in advance, refrigerated in the stock; reheat to serve.

☰ *Hot Ham and Cheese Balls*

═ Yield: 25

2 cups ground ham	¼ cup minced parsley
2 cups toasted fine bread crumbs	oil for frying
1 cup grated Parmesan cheese	Chinese mustard (page 73), sour cream or puréed chutney
4 eggs, beaten	
½ cup minced onion	

═ Yield: 200

4 quarts ground ham	1 quart minced onion
4 quarts toasted fine bread crumbs	2 cups minced parsley
2 quarts grated Parmesan cheese	oil for frying
2½ dozen eggs, beaten	Chinese mustard (page 73), sour cream or puréed chutney

1. In a bowl, mix the ham, 1½ cups *(3 quarts)* bread crumbs, cheese, eggs, onion, and parsley. Shape into balls and roll in the remaining bread crumbs.

2. Heat the oil to 360°F and fry until golden. Serve with one of the sauces.

▶ Can be prepared for frying 2 days in advance.

═ **11** ═

Marinated and
Pickled Foods

Marinating can produce some extraordinarily good cocktail foods. Foods can be marinated from a few hours to several weeks or even longer. Buy produce when it is in ready supply, fresh and cheap, and marinate it so you can serve it out of season. Marinated hors d'oeuvre can be as simple as commercial pickles or olives, or as elaborate as pickled fish. Many restaurants, especially those offering regional specialties, make their reputations in part on their pickles and relishes.

The recipes in this chapter avoid the readily available; they emphasize the preparation of marinated foods that are different as well as delicious. Suitable for the cocktail hour, they can also be served as a summer luncheon or supper, or as a side dish to fill out an otherwise replete buffet. Think of these foods as replacements for the ubiquitous crudités. Since many caterers go halfway by blanching raw vegetables, why not go a step further and prepare the vegetables and their sauce all at one time. This saves the effort of preparing different dips as well as supplies a refreshing change.

Marinated vegetables, fish, and meat are the most common, but fruits can also be macerated or served on their own. Many combinations of fruits macerated in liqueur are delightful. Serve them to provide a light counterpoint to a menu. Try pineapple in gin, rum, or white crème de menthe (green crème de menthe turns the fruit an unappealing color); melon balls in port or red wine; apple slices in rum; or pears in Poire William. Liqueur manufacturers introduce new flavors and combinations continually, so be adventurous. Just remember that the liqueur should complement the fruit, not overwhelm it. Use it sparingly. An hour is generally sufficient for the flavors to meld. If you macerate the fruits too long, they will become mushy.

The recipes for pickled vegetables are given for only one quantity; determine how much you want to prepare and increase the ingredients accordingly.

≡ *Raw Vegetables Vinaigrette*

The combination of vegetables listed here is only a suggestion. You can mix vegetables to your liking for a colorful and inviting presentation.

═ Yield: 8 cups

1 cup carrots	1 cup snow peas
1 cup tiny beets	1 cup celery
1 cup seeded cucumber	1 cup Belgian endive
1 cup cherry tomatoes, peeled	1 cup vinaigrette (page 46)

1. Prepare the vegetables as you choose: slice into rounds; cut into balls with a melon baller; cut into batons, or fingers; leave whole if tiny; slice across or on the diagonal; or make fancy cuts to shape them into flower-like designs.

2. In separate bowls, marinate the vegetables with vinaigrette for 1 hour. Drain well and arrange on a platter.

3. Serve with triangles of toasted pita bread, so guests can create their own canapés, or serve with skewers, so they can select their favorites.

▶ Can be prepared 1 day in advance.

NOTE: Although peeling cherry tomatoes is tedious, the tomatoes will absorb the marinade more readily and, perhaps most important, guests will be able to bite into them without causing the juices to spurt.

≡ *Légumes à la Grecque (Vegetables Greek Style)*

These are vegetables in the Greek style, but with a French accent.

═ Yield: 1 quart

½ cup olive oil	4 stalks chervil
¼ cup lemon juice	2 sprigs tarragon
3 tablespoons wine vinegar	2 sprigs thyme
1 teaspoon salt	1 bay leaf
2 garlic cloves, cut in half	1 quart assorted vegetables (see
¼ teaspoon peppercorns	note)
4 stalks parsley	

Yield: 2 gallons

1 quart olive oil
2 cups lemon juice
1½ cups wine vinegar
2½ tablespoons salt
1 head garlic, chopped
2 teaspoons peppercorns
small bunch parsley

large bunch chervil
large bunch tarragon
large bunch thyme
4 bay leaves
2 gallons assorted vegetables
(see note)

1. In a saucepan, mix the olive oil, lemon juice, wine vinegar, salt, and garlic. With a cheesecloth bag, make a bouquet garni of the peppercorns, parsley, chervil, tarragon, thyme, and bay leaf. Add to the pan.

2. Add the vegetables of your choice, cover with boiling water, and cook until barely tender. Drain the vegetables and reduce the liquid by half. Pour the hot liquid over the vegetables and let cool. Best if served at room temperature.

▶ Keeps 1 week, refrigerated.

NOTE: To cook a number of different vegetables, cook each vegetable in the liquid separately, drain, and place in separate bowls. When the liquid is reduced, divide it among the vegetables.

An interesting combination of the following vegetables would make an appealing assortment:

small artichokes
celery hearts
cauliflower florets
asparagus tips
sliced carrots
small white onions

tiny beets
tiny squashes
eggplant cubes or sticks
cucumber slices
zucchini slices or sticks
mushroom caps

Be wary of cooking green beans, broccoli, and other green vegetables because they turn grayish if prepared more than 2 to 3 hours in advance.

≡ Pickled Green Beans

Yield: 1 quart

1 pound green beans, trimmed
¼ cup salt
2 dried red chili peppers
1 tablespoon mustard seeds
1 tablespoon celery seeds

3 cups vinegar
½ cup brown sugar
2 ¼-inch-thick slices fresh
horseradish or 1 tablespoon
prepared horseradish

1. In a noncorrosible bowl, soak the green beans and salt overnight in cold water to cover. Drain and rinse under cold water. Pat dry.

2. Pack the beans into a 1-quart jar and add the chili peppers, mustard seeds, and celery seeds. Bring the vinegar to a boil with the brown sugar and pour over the beans. Insert the horseradish and seal the jar. Let stand, 1 week, shaking the jar once a day.

▶ Keeps 6 months, refrigerated.

NOTE: You can substitute wax beans or zucchini for the green beans.

≡ *Pickled Baby Carrots I*

═ Yield: 1 quart

1 cup white vinegar
½ cup chopped onion
1 teaspoon sugar
1 teaspoon salt

1 teaspoon pickling spices
1 pound baby carrots, scrubbed
   and trimmed

1. In a saucepan, bring the vinegar, onion, sugar, salt, and spices to a boil.

2. Add the carrots and simmer until tender crisp. Cool in the liquid and chill.

▶ Keeps 2 weeks, refrigerated.

NOTE: You can substitute green or wax beans, zucchini, or cauliflower for the carrots.

≡ *Pickled Baby Carrots II*

═ Yield: 1 quart

1 quart baby carrots, scrubbed
   and trimmed
4 cups white vinegar

1½ cups sugar
3 tablespoons pickling spices

1. If the carrots are tiny, keep them whole, or trim larger carrots to the size of the preserving jars.

2. In a saucepan, simmer the vinegar, sugar, and pickling spices (wrapped in cheesecloth) for 10 minutes.

3. In a large, noncorrosible bowl, mix the carrots and the hot liquid and let stand overnight.

4. In a saucepan, simmer the carrots and liquid until the carrots are tender crisp. Pack into sterilized jars, adding hot syrup to overflow the top. Screw on the top of the jar to seal.

▶ Keeps 6 months, sealed.

NOTE: You can substitute beets or tiny turnips for the carrots.

≡ *Marinated Carrots*

═ Yield: 1 quart

1 pound carrots, peeled
½ cup olive oil
¼ cup white wine vinegar
1 small onion, sliced
2 garlic cloves, split

1 teaspoon dried basil
1 teaspoon salt
½ teaspoon pepper
2 tablespoons lemon juice

═ Yield: 8 quarts

8 pounds carrots, peeled
4 cups olive oil
2 cups white wine vinegar
4 cups sliced onion
1 head garlic cloves, split

3 tablespoons dried basil
3 tablespoons salt
4 teaspoons pepper
1 cup lemon juice

1. Cut the carrots into batons, ¼ to ½ inch thick and 2 inches long.

2. Simmer in boiling water to cover for 3 to 5 minutes or until just tender. Drain.

3. In a bowl, mix the oil, vinegar, onion, garlic, basil, salt, and pepper. Add the carrots and toss. Refrigerate for 12 hours. Remove and discard the onion and garlic.

4. When ready to serve, drain and sprinkle with the lemon juice.

▶ Keeps 6 days, refrigerated.

NOTE: You can substitute beets, beans, broccoli, cauliflower, or zucchini for the carrots.

≡ *Pickled Cauliflower*

═ Yield: 2 quarts

3 large cauliflowers, cut into
  florets
1 teaspoon whole cloves
1 teaspoon black peppercorns
1 teaspoon whole allspice

1 teaspoon mustard seeds
4 cups cider vinegar
½ cup sugar
1 tablespoon brown mustard

1. Cook the cauliflower in boiling salted water to cover until tender crisp. Drain and pack into sterilized jars, leaving room for ½ inch of liquid above the cauliflower.

2. In a cheesecloth bag, tie the cloves, peppercorns, allspice, and mustard seeds. Put into a saucepan with the vinegar, sugar, and mustard. Simmer 15 minutes. Remove and discard the spices.

3. Pour the hot liquid into the jars and seal.

▶ Keeps 6 months, sealed.

NOTE: You can substitute beets, carrots, or beans for the cauliflower.

≡ *Marinated Cauliflower*

═ Yield: 1 quart

1 large cauliflower, cut into florets	2 tablespoons white wine
	1 tablespoon lemon juice
2 garlic cloves, minced	salt, to taste
6 tablespoons olive oil	paprika, optional

═ Yield: 4 quarts

4 large cauliflowers, cut into florets	1 cup white wine
	½ cup lemon juice
8 garlic cloves, minced	salt, to taste
2 cups olive oil	paprika, optional

1. Cook the cauliflower in boiling salted water to cover until tender crisp. Plunge into cold water to stop the cooking and drain.

2. In a saucepan, sauté the garlic in the olive oil until just golden but not burned. Pour over the cauliflower and sprinkle with the wine and lemon juice. Season with salt and marinate for at least 1 hour. Serve dusted with paprika, if desired.

▶ Keeps 4 days, refrigerated. Serve at room temperature.

NOTE: You can substitute broccoli, beets, carrots, or zucchini for the cauliflower.

≡ *Marinated Mushrooms I*

Marinated mushrooms have become a staple for many restaurants. Try one of these versions for a change. Since they are so popular, it makes sense to prepare them in quantity. Use them not only on their own, but also in salads.

═ **Yield: 1 quart**

2 pounds button mushrooms,
    trimmed and cleaned
2 tablespoons lemon juice
salt, to taste
½ cup wine vinegar
½ cup olive oil

2 garlic cloves, crushed
2 sprigs parsley
1 sprig thyme
1 bay leaf
½ teaspoon coriander seeds
¼ teaspoon peppercorns

═ **Yield: 5 quarts**

10 pounds button mushrooms,
    trimmed and cleaned
⅔ cup lemon juice
salt, to taste
2½ cups wine vinegar
2½ cups olive oil

1 head garlic, crushed
10 sprigs parsley
5 sprigs thyme
5 bay leaves
2 tablespoons coriander seeds
1 tablespoon peppercorns

1. Simmer the mushrooms, lemon juice, and salt in water to cover for 10 minutes. Drain and put into a bowl.

2. In a saucepan, simmer the vinegar, olive oil, garlic, parsley, thyme, bay leaf, coriander seeds, and peppercorns for 20 minutes. Pour over the mushrooms and marinate for 12 hours.

▶ Keeps 4 days, refrigerated.

≡ *Marinated Mushrooms II*

The beauty of this recipe is that it is so simple. You can enhance the flavor of the mushrooms by adding sliced garlic cloves, crumbled thyme, or summer savory. You can vary it every time you prepare it.

═ **Yield: 2 cups**

1 pound mushrooms
¼ cup lemon juice

1 cup olive oil
salt and pepper, to taste

═ **Yield: 5 quarts**

10 pounds mushrooms
3 cups lemon juice

2 quarts olive oil
salt and pepper, to taste

In a container, marinate the mushrooms, lemon juice, olive oil, salt, and pepper for at least 2 hours.

▶ Keeps 3 days, refrigerated.

≡ *Dilled Okra*

=== Yield: 2 quarts

2 pounds young okra   2⅔ cups water
celery leaves   1⅔ cups white vinegar
4 garlic cloves   2 tablespoons salt
4 sprigs dill

1. Scrub the okra and pack into four sterilized 1-pint jars. Insert a few celery leaves, 1 garlic clove, and 1 dill sprig into each jar.

2. In a saucepan, simmer the water, vinegar, and salt for 3 minutes. Pour over the okra and seal. Let stand 1 month.

▶ Keeps 6 months, sealed.

≡ *Cold Curried Potato Balls*

This is a truly different hors d'oeuvre that gains favor readily. Your melon baller becomes a handy potato baller.

=== Yield: 2 quarts

8 cups potato balls   salt and pepper, to taste
1 cup mayonnaise   ¾ cup minced red onion
¾ cup sour cream   ½ cup minced green pepper
⅓ cup beef stock   ⅓ cup minced parsley
1½ tablespoons curry powder

=== Yield: 10 quarts

10 quarts potato balls   salt and pepper, to taste
1 quart mayonnaise   1 quart minced red onion
1 quart sour cream   2½ cups minced green pepper
1⅔ cups beef stock   1½ cups minced parsley
½ cup curry powder, or to taste

1. In boiling salted water, cook the potatoes until just done. Drain and cool.

2. In a bowl, mix the mayonnaise, sour cream, stock, curry powder, salt, and pepper. Fold in the potato balls, onion, and green pepper. Refrigerate for 2 hours.

3. Sprinkle with parsley and serve skewers on the side.

▶ Keeps 2 days, refrigerated.

≡ Pickled Fish

== **Yield: 2 quarts**

1½ pounds salmon or
   swordfish fillets
1 pound sea scallops, quartered
2 tablespoons salt
1½ cups white wine vinegar
1¼ cups water
2 tablespoons sugar
2 teaspoons coriander seeds,
   crushed

2 bay leaves, crumbled
½ cinnamon stick
½ teaspoon whole allspice
½ teaspoon peppercorns
¼ teaspoon dried thyme
⅓ cup olive oil
4 scallions, thinly sliced
1 carrot, thinly sliced

== **Yield: 1 gallon**

3 pounds salmon or swordfish
   fillets
2 pounds sea scallops,
   quartered
¼ cup salt
3 cups white wine vinegar
2½ cups water
¼ cup sugar
4 teaspoons coriander seeds,
   crushed

4 bay leaves, crumbled
1 cinnamon stick
1 teaspoon whole allspice
1 teaspoon peppercorns
½ teaspoon dried thyme
⅔ cup olive oil
8 scallions, thinly sliced
2 carrots, thinly sliced

1. Cut the fish into 1½-inch cubes. Sprinkle the fish and the scallops with salt and let stand 1 hour. Drain, rinse under cold water, and drain again.

2. In a saucepan, simmer the vinegar, water, sugar, coriander, bay leaves, cinnamon stick, allspice, peppercorns, and thyme for 10 minutes. Add the olive oil, fish, and scallops. Bring to a simmer and remove from the heat. Remove the fish and scallops with a slotted spoon; set aside. Drain the spices and herbs from the liquid, reserving both.

3. Ladle the seafood into 1-quart canning jars in layers, separating the layers with slices of scallions and carrots. Divide the spices among the jars and pour the liquid over the fish. Cool. Cover and refrigerate for 3 days.

▶ Keeps 5 days, refrigerated.

≡ *Seafood in Dill Sauce*

═ **Yield: 1 quart**

½ cup white wine	1 pound shrimp, peeled
½ cup water	1 pound scallops
½ cup sliced onion	1½ cups dill, firmly packed
1 bay leaf	½ cup olive oil
1 teaspoon salt	4 garlic cloves
¼ teaspoon peppercorns	

═ **Yield: 1 gallon**

2 cups white wine	4 pounds shrimp, peeled
2 cups water	4 pounds scallops
2 cups sliced onion	6 cups dill, firmly packed
2 bay leaves	2 cups olive oil
1 tablespoon salt	8 garlic cloves
1 teaspoon peppercorns	

1. In a saucepan, simmer the wine, water, onion, bay leaf, salt, and peppercorns for 5 minutes. Add the shrimp and cook until just pink. Remove the shrimp. Add the scallops and cook until just done. Remove the scallops. Reduce the cooking liquid by two-thirds.

2. In a food processor, purée the dill, olive oil, and garlic, gradually adding the reduced cooking liquid. Correct the seasoning with salt and pepper. Pour over the shellfish and marinate for 1 hour.

▶ Keeps 2 days, refrigerated.

NOTE: You can substitute salmon and swordfish for the shellfish.

≡ *Mussels Marinara*

The popularity of mussels increases as they become better known.

═ **Yield: 2 cups**

5 pounds mussels, scrubbed and bearded	¾ cup olive oil
½ cup water	¼ cup tomato paste
2 garlic cloves, split	2 tablespoons wine vinegar
¼ teaspoon peppercorns	pinch of ground cloves
	salt and pepper, to taste

═ **Yield: 2 quarts**

20 pounds mussels, scrubbed
and bearded
2 cups water
8 garlic cloves, split
1 teaspoon peppercorns

1½ cups olive oil
½ cup tomato paste
¼ cup wine vinegar
⅛ teaspoon ground cloves
salt and pepper, to taste

1. In a large covered kettle, steam the mussels in the water, garlic, and peppercorns until the mussels open, about 5 minutes. Remove the mussels from the shells and discard the shells and any unopened mussels.

2. In a bowl, mix the oil, tomato paste, vinegar, cloves, salt, and pepper. Mix with the mussels and marinate for 1 hour. Serve with skewers.

▶ Keeps 2 days, refrigerated.

═ *Marinated Mussels with Herbs*

═ **Yield: 2 cups**

5 pounds mussels, scrubbed
and bearded
½ cup water
½ cup heavy cream
1 cup mayonnaise

2 tablespoons sherry
2 tablespoons minced tarragon
2 tablespoons minced parsley
2 tablespoons minced scallions
2 tablespoons minced capers

═ **Yield: 2 quarts**

20 pounds mussels, scrubbed
and bearded
2 cups water
1 cup heavy cream
2 cups mayonnaise

¼ cup sherry
¼ cup minced tarragon
¼ cup minced parsley
¼ cup minced scallions
¼ cup minced capers

1. In a large covered kettle, steam the mussels in the water until they open, about 5 minutes. Remove the mussels from the shells and discard the shells and any unopened mussels. Reduce the cooking liquid to a syrupy glaze, about ¼ cup for the smaller quantity and 1 cup for the larger. Cool.

2. Whip the cream to the soft peak stage and fold into the mayonnaise with the sherry, tarragon, parsley, scallions, capers, and enough mussel liquor to make a fluid sauce. Fold in the drained mussels and chill 1 hour.

▶ Keeps 2 days, refrigerated.

≡ *Ceviche (Marinated Scallops)*

This recipe is equally good when made with firm-fleshed fish. Choose one or more varieties and cut them into cubes before marinating.

═ **Yield: 1 quart**

2 pounds scallops
1 cup lime juice
2 tablespoons lemon juice

1 large red onion, thinly sliced
1 tablespoon wine vinegar
pinch of cayenne

═ **Yield: 4 quarts**

10 pounds scallops
3 cups lime juice
½ cup lemon juice

4 large red onions, thinly sliced
¼ cup wine vinegar
pinch of cayenne

1. Rinse the scallops and drain.

2. In a noncorrosible container, marinate the scallops, lime juice, lemon juice, onion, vinegar, and pepper. Chill at least 6 hours. Serve with skewers.

▶ Keeps 3 days refrigerated.

NOTE: For best results, use fresh, not frozen, scallops. The lime juice "cooks" the scallops, and the longer they stand, the firmer they become. For the best flavor, do not marinate them too long—6 to 12 hours is best.

≡ *Marinated Scallop Cocktail*

═ **Yield: 1 quart**

2 pounds scallops
½ cup olive oil
¼ cup minced onion

2 tablespoons vinegar
1 tablespoon minced parsley
salt and pepper, to taste

═ **Yield: 5 quarts**

10 pounds scallops
2 cups olive oil
1 cup minced onion

½ cup vinegar
⅓ cup minced parsley
salt and pepper, to taste

1. Rinse the scallops and drain.
2. In a bowl, marinate the scallops, olive oil, onion, vinegar, parsley, salt, and pepper for at least 4 hours.

▶ Keeps 2 days, refrigerated.

NOTE: For best results, use only fresh, not frozen, fish and marinate no longer than 12 hours.

≡ Coquilles St. Jacques Froid (Cold Scallops)

═ **Yield: 1 quart**

2 pounds scallops, cooked
⅓ cup capers

1 cup mayonnaise
cherry tomatoes, cut in half

═ **Yield: 4 quarts**

8 pounds scallops, cooked
1 cup capers

3 cups mayonnaise
cherry tomatoes, cut in half

1. In a bowl, mix the scallops, capers, and mayonnaise. Chill 1 hour.
2. Serve on skewers with cherry tomato halves.

▶ Keeps 2 days, refrigerated.

NOTE: The number of portions will depend on the type of scallop. Calico bay scallops, for example, are so tiny that you would want to skewer several with each cherry tomato half. Sea scallops may need to be cut into halves or quarters.

≡ Coquilles St. Jacques, Sauces Varies (Scallops with Various Sauces)

═ **Yield: 1 quart**

2 pounds scallops, cooked
1 cup sauce of your choice
  (see note)

═ **Yield: 4 quarts**

8 pounds scallops, cooked
4 cups sauce of your choice
  (see note)

1. In a bowl, mix the scallops and just enough sauce to bind.
2. Refrigerate for 1 hour and serve on skewers.

▶ Keeps 2 days, refrigerated.

NOTE: There are any number of sauces in Chapter 3 from which to choose. Try sauce verte, tartar sauce, horcher sauce, or mustard mayonnaise, for example. Or marinate the scallops in a lemon-flavored vinaigrette or yogurt-based sauce for an hour.

≡ Pickled Shrimp I

The number of shrimp for this or any other shrimp recipe depends on the size you use. The sizes best suited for hors d'oeuvre are 21 to 25's and 26 to 30's. Larger shrimp are too big and the smaller ones look stingy.

≡ Yield: 20 to 30 shrimp

1 pound shrimp, peeled	⅓ cup chopped onion
⅓ cup white wine vinegar	2 whole cloves
⅓ cup olive oil	1 dried hot chili pepper
⅔ cup white wine	¼ cup chopped celery leaves
1 teaspoon salt	pinch of dried thyme
⅔ cup water	½ bay leaf
1 teaspoon sugar	¼ teaspoon peppercorns

≡ Yield: 100 to 150 shrimp

5 pounds shrimp, peeled	2 cups chopped onion
2 cups white wine vinegar	½ teaspoon whole cloves
2 cups olive oil	4 dried hot chili peppers
1 quart white wine	1 cup chopped celery leaves
2 tablespoons salt	1 teaspoon dried thyme
1 quart water	2 bay leaves
2 tablespoons sugar	1 teaspoon peppercorns

1. In a saucepan, combine the shrimp, vinegar, olive oil, wine, salt, water, sugar, onion, cloves, chili pepper(s), celery leaves, thyme, bay leaf, and peppercorns.
2. Bring just to a simmer, stirring occasionally, until the shrimp are cooked. Cool in the liquid. Drain. Serve with or without skewers.

▶ Keeps 1 week, refrigerated.

≡ *Pickled Shrimp II*

═ Yield: 20 to 30 shrimp

2 teaspoons pickling spices
1 dried hot red chili pepper
2 cups water
1 pound shrimp
2 bunches scallions, thinly
sliced

1 bay leaf
⅓ cup olive oil
¼ cup tarragon vinegar
⅔ teaspoon salt
⅓ teaspoon dry mustard

═ Yield: 100 to 150 shrimp

¼ cup pickling spices
2 dried hot red chili peppers
3 quarts water
5 pounds shrimp
12 bunches scallions, thinly
sliced

4 bay leaves
2 cups olive oil
1½ cups tarragon vinegar
1 tablespoon salt
2 teaspoons dry mustard

1. Tie the pickling spices and chili pepper(s) in a cheesecloth bag. In a kettle, simmer the water and the pickling spices for 5 minutes. Add the shrimp and cook until just done. Drain, shell, and devein.

2. In a casserole, layer the shrimp with the scallions, ending with scallions. Place the bay leaves in the middle layer.

3. In a bowl, whisk the oil, vinegar, salt, and mustard until well combined. Pour over the shrimp and marinate for 24 hours.

▶ Keeps 3 days, refrigerated.

≡ *Pickled Shrimp III*

═ Yield: 25 shrimp

1 garlic clove, crushed
½ cup chopped onion
2 tablespoons plus ¼ cup olive
oil
1 pound shrimp
1 onion, thinly sliced

¼ cup vinegar
⅛ teaspoon dry mustard
⅛ teaspoon cayenne pepper
¾ teaspoon salt
¼ teaspoon pepper

═ **Yield: 125 shrimp**

6 garlic cloves, crushed

2 cups chopped onion

1½ cups olive oil

5 pounds shrimp

4 onions, thinly sliced

1 cup vinegar

½ teaspoon dry mustard

½ teaspoon cayenne pepper

1 tablespoon salt

1 teaspoon pepper

1. In a skillet, sauté the garlic and onion in 2 tablespoons (½ *cup*) olive oil until soft but not brown. Stir in the shrimp and cook until just done. Remove from the heat and cool. Peel and devein the shrimp.

2. In a bowl, mix the onion slices, remaining oil, vinegar, mustard, cayenne, salt, and pepper. Marinate the shrimp for 24 hours.

▶ Keeps 3 days, refrigerated.

≡ *Marinated Balinese Shrimp*

═ **Yield: 25 shrimp**

1 small onion, thinly sliced

3 slices gingerroot

2 garlic cloves, sliced

1 tablespoon peanut oil

1 pound shrimp, peeled and
    deveined

1 cup vinegar

1 teaspoon turmeric

salt, to taste

═ **Yield: 125 shrimp**

2 large onions, thinly sliced

10 slices gingerroot

8 garlic cloves, sliced

2 tablespoons peanut oil

5 pounds shrimp, peeled and
    deveined

1 quart vinegar

2 tablespoons turmeric

salt, to taste

1. In a skillet, sauté the onion, gingerroot, and garlic in the oil until soft but not brown. Add the shrimp, vinegar, turmeric, and salt. Simmer until the shrimp are just cooked.

2. Cool and marinate for 24 hours.

▶ Keeps 4 days, refrigerated.

≡ *Marinated Shrimp and Cucumber*

═ Yield: 25 shrimp

2 cucumbers, peeled, seeded,
and cubed
1 pound shrimp, cooked and
peeled

¾ cup vinegar
2 tablespoons minced dill
¼ cup vegetable oil
salt and pepper, to taste

═ Yield: 125 shrimp

10 cucumbers, peeled, seeded,
and cubed
5 pounds shrimp, cooked and
peeled

4 cups vinegar
⅔ cup minced dill
1¼ cups vegetable oil
salt and pepper, to taste

In a bowl, marinate the cucumbers, shrimp, vinegar, dill, oil, salt, and pepper for 6 hours.

▶ Keeps 2 days, refrigerated.

≡ *Shrimp in Red Rioja Wine*

═ Yield: 25 shrimp

½ cup minced onion
1 garlic clove, minced
2 tablespoons olive oil
1 cup red Rioja wine

1 pound shrimp, cooked and
peeled
salt and pepper, to taste

═ Yield: 125 shrimp

2½ cups minced onion
5 garlic cloves, minced
⅔ cup olive oil
5 cups red Rioja wine

5 pounds shrimp, cooked and
peeled
salt and pepper, to taste

In a skillet, sauté the onions and garlic in the olive oil until soft but not brown. Add the wine and reduce by one fourth. Add the shrimp and heat. Correct the seasoning with salt and pepper. Serve hot or cold.

▶ Keeps 2 days, refrigerated.
NOTE: If serving warm, reheat very carefully to avoid overcooking the shrimp.

≡ *Gambretti al'Olio e Limone (Shrimp in Lemon Oil)*

=== **Yield: 25 shrimp**

1 stalk celery, chopped	1 pound shrimp, peeled and
1 carrot, chopped	deveined
2 tablespoons red wine vinegar	½ cup olive oil
1 tablespoon salt	¼ cup lemon juice
2 quarts water	salt and pepper, to taste

=== **Yield: 125 shrimp**

2½ cups chopped celery	5 pounds shrimp, peeled and
2½ cups chopped carrots	deveined
⅔ cup red wine vinegar	2½ cups olive oil
⅓ cup salt	1¼ cups lemon juice
10 quarts water	salt and pepper, to taste

1. In a saucepan, simmer the celery, carrot(s), vinegar, salt, and water for 5 minutes. Add the shrimp and cook until just done. Drain.

2. In a bowl, marinate the shrimp with the oil, lemon juice, salt, and pepper for 2 hours.

▶ Keeps 3 days, refrigerated.

≡ *Dilled Shrimp*

=== **Yield: 25 shrimp**

1 quart water	5 dill sprigs
½ lemon, sliced	1 pound shrimp
2 teaspoons salt	

=== **Yield: 125 shrimp**

5 quarts water	1 large bunch dill sprigs
3 lemons, sliced	5 pounds shrimp
3 tablespoons salt	

1. In a kettle, simmer the water, lemon slices, salt, and dill for 10 minutes. Add the shrimp and cook until just done. Cool in the broth.

2. Peel and devein.

▶ Keeps 4 days, refrigerated in the broth.

≡ Shrimp in Dill

== Yield: 25 shrimp

1 pound shrimp, cooked and
    peeled
2 tablespoons minced dill
4 tablespoons olive oil

1 tablespoon lime juice
1 tablespoon lemon juice
salt, to taste
pinch of cayenne pepper

== Yield: 125 shrimp

5 pounds shrimp, cooked and
    peeled
⅔ cup minced dill
1¼ cups olive oil

¼ cup lime juice
¼ cup lemon juice
salt, to taste
cayenne pepper, to taste

In a bowl, marinate the shrimp in the dill, olive oil, lime juice, lemon juice, salt, and cayenne for 12 hours.

▶ Keeps 2 days, refrigerated.

≡ Hunan Hsia (Shrimp Hunan Style)

== Yield: 25 shrimp

1 pound shrimp, cooked,
    peeled, and deveined
1 cup minced scallions
1 garlic clove, minced
1 tablespoon chili paste with
    garlic
1 tablespoon hot chili oil
1½ teaspoons Asian sesame oil

1 teaspoon seeded and minced
    chili pepper
1 teaspoon minced gingerroot
1 teaspoon sherry
1 teaspoon Chinese five-spice
    powder
½ teaspoon white pepper
salt, to taste

== Yield: 125 shrimp

5 pounds shrimp, cooked,
    peeled, and deveined
1 quart minced scallions
5 garlic cloves, minced
¼ cup chili paste with garlic
¼ cup hot chili oil
2½ tablespoons Asian sesame
    oil

2 tablespoons seeded and
    minced chili pepper
2 tablespoons minced gingerroot
2 tablespoons sherry
2 tablespoons Chinese five-spice
    powder
1 tablespoon white pepper
salt, to taste

In a bowl, marinate the shrimp in the scallions, garlic, chili paste, chili oil, sesame oil, chili pepper, gingerroot, sherry, five-spice powder, white pepper, and salt for 1 hour.

▶ Keeps 3 days, refrigerated.

≡ *Shrimp in Beer*

== **Yield: 25 shrimp**

1 pound shrimp	½ bay leaf
18 ounces beer	pinch of dried thyme
1 dried red pepper	

== **Yield: 125 shrimp**

5 pounds shrimp	2 bay leaves
3 quarts beer	½ teaspoon dried thyme
3 dried red peppers	

1. In a saucepan, bring the shrimp, beer, red pepper(s), bay leaves, and thyme to a boil. Cook until shrimp are just done. Remove from heat and cool in the liquid.

2. Peel and devein the shrimp.

▶ Keeps 3 days, refrigerated.

≡ *Huîtres Marinées (Marinated Oysters)*

== **Yield: 25 servings**

2 tablespoons vinegar	2 garlic cloves, chopped
2 tablespoons olive oil	¼ teaspoon dried thyme
1 cup water	1 teaspoon minced parsley
1½ cups white wine	50 small oysters, shucked
salt and pepper, to taste	½ cup minced parsley
½ cup chopped carrots	½ cup minced chives
½ cup chopped onion	lemon wedges

═ **Yield: 125 servings**

⅓ cup vinegar

⅓ cup olive oil

5 cups water

7 cups white wine

salt and pepper, to taste

2½ cups chopped carrots

2½ cups chopped onion

10 garlic cloves, chopped

1 teaspoon dried thyme

2 tablespoons minced parsley

250 small oysters, shucked

2½ cups minced parsley

2½ cups minced chives

lemon wedges

1. In a saucepan, simmer the vinegar, olive oil, water, wine, salt, pepper, carrot, onion, garlic, thyme, and parsley, uncovered, for 1 hour. Strain.

2. Poach the oysters in the broth until the edges begin to curl. Cool in the liquid.

3. In a bowl, mix the parsley and chives. When ready to serve, drain the oysters and roll in the herbs. Serve on skewers with lemon wedges.

▶ Keeps 2 days, refrigerated.

═ *Tarragon Chicken Wings*

Chicken wings are a delicious, albeit somewhat messy appetizer. Plan to serve them at informal functions where people are prepared for less fastidious food, such as at barbecues, cookouts, and clambakes. Most of the following recipes can be served hot or at room temperature, which makes them a good appetizer to prepare ahead and transport.

To prepare the wings, cut off the wing tips and discard. Separate the two joints.

═ **Yield: 24 servings**

¾ cup butter, softened

⅓ cup Dijon mustard

2 tablespoons lemon juice

¾ teaspoon minced tarragon

salt and pepper, to taste

12 large chicken wings, cut up

fresh bread crumbs

═ **Yield: 120 servings**

2 pounds butter, softened

1⅔ cups Dijon mustard

⅔ cup lemon juice

½ cup minced tarragon

salt and pepper, to taste

60 large chicken wings, cut up

fresh bread crumbs

1. Preheat the broiler.

2. In a food processor, cream the butter, mustard, lemon juice, tarragon, salt, and pepper.

3. Butter the wings and broil on a rack for 15 minutes. Turn, baste with more butter, and broil 10 minutes longer. Sprinkle generously with the bread crumbs and broil until brown, about 2 minutes. Serve hot or at room temperature.

▶ Can be prepared 1 day in advance and reheated.

≡ Chinese Sesame Chicken Wings

≡ **Yield: 24**

1 tablespoon salted black beans (see Glossary)	3 tablespoons dark soy sauce
1 tablespoon water	1½ tablespoons sherry
1 tablespoon oil	2 tablespoons minced scallions
2 garlic cloves, crushed	1 tablespoon toasted sesame seeds
1 slice gingerroot	¼ teaspoon black pepper
12 chicken wings, cut up	

≡ **Yield: 120**

⅓ cup salted black beans (see Glossary)	60 chicken wings, cut up
⅓ cup water	1 cup dark soy sauce
⅓ cup oil	½ cup sherry
10 garlic cloves, crushed	⅔ cup minced scallions
5 slices gingerroot	⅓ cup toasted sesame seeds
	1 teaspoon black pepper

1. In a bowl, crush the black beans and soak in the water until needed.

2. In a wok, heat the oil and stir-fry the garlic and ginger for 30 seconds. Add the wings and stir-fry until lightly browned. Add the soy sauce and sherry and cook 30 seconds. Stir in the soaked, drained black beans. Cover and simmer 8 to 10 minutes. Uncover and cook until the liquid almost evaporates. Remove from the heat and stir in the scallions, sesame seeds, and pepper.

▶ Can be prepared 1 day in advance and reheated; can be frozen.

≡ *Barbecued Chicken Wings*

Every backyard cook has the perfect barbecue sauce. I do not make such claims for this sauce, but it does make damn good chicken wings!

═ Yield: 24 servings

12 large chicken wings, cut up
¾ cup tomato purée
¼ cup molasses
¼ cup cider vinegar
2 tablespoons oil

1½ tablespoons Dijon mustard
2 garlic cloves, minced
2 teaspoons Worcestershire
  sauce
½ teaspoon Tabasco sauce

═ Yield: 120 servings

60 large chicken wings, cut up
1 quart tomato purée
1¼ cups molasses
1½ cups cider vinegar
⅔ cup oil

½ cup Dijon mustard
10 garlic cloves, minced
3 tablespoons Worcestershire
  sauce
2 teaspoons Tabasco sauce

1. Preheat the broiler.

2. In a bowl, marinate the chicken wings in the tomato purée, molasses, vinegar, oil, mustard, garlic, Worcestershire sauce, and Tabasco sauce for 1 hour, turning every 15 minutes.

3. Broil about 15 minutes, basting often. Turn and broil 10 minutes longer, basting often. Serve hot or at room temperature.

▶ Can be prepared 2 days in advance; can be frozen.

≡ *Chicken Wings with Oyster Sauce*

═ Yield: 24 servings

½ cup peanut oil
1 slice gingerroot
12 chicken wings, cut up
3 tablespoons oyster sauce

2½ tablespoons soy sauce
1 teaspoon sherry
1 teaspoon sugar

═ Yield: 120 servings

2 cups peanut oil
5 slices gingerroot
60 chicken wings, cut up
1 cup oyster sauce

¾ cup soy sauce
2 tablespoons sherry
2 tablespoons sugar

1. In a wok, heat the oil and gingerroot. Brown the wings in the oil, in batches if necessary. Pour off and discard the oil.

2. Add the wings to the pan with the oyster sauce, soy sauce, sherry, and sugar. Add enough water to half cover the wings and simmer, covered, for 10 minutes. Baste and simmer 10 minutes, uncovered. Serve hot or cold.

▶ Can be prepared 1 day in advance.

☰ *Indonesian Chicken Wings*

═ Yield: 24 servings

1½ cups walnuts	½ teaspoon salt
⅓ cup lime juice	½ cup plain yogurt
¼ cup chopped scallions	salt and pepper, to taste
2 tablespoons chicken stock	12 chicken wings, cut up
2 garlic cloves	3 tablespoons vegetable oil

═ Yield: 120 servings

7½ cups walnuts	2½ teaspoons salt
1⅔ cups lime juice	2½ cups plain yogurt
1¼ cups chopped scallions	salt and pepper, to taste
⅔ cup chicken stock	60 chicken wings, cut up
10 garlic cloves	1 cup vegetable oil

1. Preheat the broiler.

2. In a food processor, purée the walnuts, lime juice, scallions, chicken stock, garlic, and salt. Mix one fourth of the walnut mixture into the yogurt with salt and pepper to taste and set aside.

3. In a bowl, mix the wings with the oil and add the remaining puréed walnut mixture. Marinate for 3 hours.

4. Broil the wings for 15 minutes on one side. Turn and broil 10 minutes longer. Serve the reserved walnut yogurt sauce as a dip.

▶ The wings can be made 2 days in advance and reheated; can be frozen. Do not freeze the sauce.

≡ Chicken Wings Shanghai Style

═ Yield: 24 servings

12 chicken wings, cut up
⅓ cup soy sauce
2 tablespoons sugar
1 tablespoon sherry

2 slices gingerroot
1 whole star anise
⅓ cup water

═ Yield: 120 servings

60 chicken wings, cut up
1⅔ cups soy sauce
⅔ cup sugar
¼ cup sherry

10 slices gingerroot
5 whole star anise
1⅔ cups water

In a saucepan, simmer the chicken wings in the soy sauce, sugar, sherry, gingerroot, anise, and water, covered for 20 minutes, stirring several times. Uncover and simmer until the liquid is reduced to a glaze. Serve hot or cold.

▶ Can be prepared 2 to 3 days in advance and reheated.

≡ Chinese Chicken Livers

═ Yield: 24 servings

1 pound chicken livers, cut in
 half
½ cup soy sauce
½ cup water
¼ cup sherry

1 tablespoon sugar
1 scallion, minced
2 slices gingerroot
¼ teaspoon peppercorns
1 whole star anise

═ Yield: 120 servings

5 pounds chicken livers, cut in
 half
2½ cups soy sauce
2½ cups water
1¼ cups sherry

⅓ cup sugar
5 scallions, minced
10 slices gingerroot
1¼ teaspoons peppercorns
5 whole star anise

1. In a saucepan, simmer the livers in water to cover for 5 minutes. Drain, rinse, and drain again.

2. In a casserole, simmer the chicken livers in the soy sauce, water, sherry, sugar, scallion(s), gingerroot, peppercorns, and star anise for 10 minutes. Cool in the broth.

▶ Can be made 2 to 3 days in advance.

≡ Curried Beef Appetizer

═ Yield: 24 cubes

1 pound round steak, broiled
   and cut into 1-inch cubes
1 cup olive oil
½ cup soy sauce
½ cup thinly sliced onion
½ cup thinly sliced celery

¼ cup vinegar
1 tablespoon peppercorns
½ cup mayonnaise
1 teaspoon curry powder
⅛ teaspoon dry mustard

═ Yield: 120 cubes

5 pounds round steak, broiled
   and cut into 1-inch cubes
2 cups olive oil
1 cup soy sauce
1 cup thinly sliced onion
1 cup thinly sliced celery

½ cup vinegar
2 tablespoons peppercorns
1½ cups mayonnaise
1 tablespoon curry powder
¼ teaspoon dry mustard

1. In a bowl, marinate the beef in the olive oil, soy sauce, onion, celery, vinegar, and peppercorns for 12 hours. Drain.

2. In a bowl, mix the mayonnaise, curry powder, and mustard. Fold in the beef and mix to coat. Serve on skewers.

▶ The beef can be marinated 3 days in advance. Mix with the mayonnaise shortly before serving.

≡ Tuscany Beef

═ Yield: 24 servings

1 cup minced onion
¼ cup minced celery
3 garlic cloves, minced
⅓ cup olive oil
1½ cups red wine
1½ cups beef stock

¼ cup wine vinegar
1¾ cups minced parsley
1 bay leaf, crumbled
salt and pepper, to taste
2 pounds raw beef tenderloin,
   thinly sliced

═ Yield: 120 servings

5 cups minced onion
1¼ cups minced celery
15 garlic cloves, minced
1⅔ cups olive oil
2 quarts red wine
2 quarts beef stock

1¼ cups wine vinegar
6¼ cups minced parsley
5 bay leaves, crumbled
salt and pepper, to taste
10 pounds raw beef tenderloin,
   thinly sliced

1. In a skillet, sauté the onion, celery, and garlic in the oil until soft. Add the wine, stock, and vinegar and reduce by one third. Add ¼ cup (*1¼ cups*) parsley, bay leaf, salt, and pepper.

2. Spoon some of the liquid in a deep dish, add a layer of beef, and then more liquid. Repeat the layers. Cover and refrigerate for 24 hours. Drain the slices, roll, and skewer. Dip the ends into the remaining parsley.

▶ Keeps 3 days, refrigerated.

≡ Kao P'ai Ku (Barbecued Spareribs) Cha Shu (Roast Pork Strips)

These ever-popular stars of Chinese cookery are easy to prepare and make excellent hors d'oeuvre on any menu.

There are dozens of marinade variations, including one that gives the meat a bright red color. Red signifies happiness in China, and the Chinese extend that connotation to the reddish browns of soy, oyster, and hoisin sauces. The recipe that follows provides a reddish brown, exquisitely flavored version. You can produce a redder finish by adding red food coloring.

═ Yield: 24 spareribs or about 50 pork strips

2 pounds small spareribs or
  pork tenderloin
¼ cup hoisin sauce
2 tablespoons soy sauce
2 tablespoons honey
2 tablespoons oil
1 tablespoon chicken stock

1 tablespoon sherry
2 teaspoons sugar
1 teaspoon crushed gingerroot
½ teaspoon crushed garlic
plum sauce, duck sauce, or
  mustard

═ Yield: 120 spareribs or about 250 pork strips

10 pounds small spareribs or
  pork tenderloin
1¼ cups hoisin sauce
⅔ cup soy sauce
⅔ cup honey
⅔ cup oil
⅓ cup chicken stock

⅓ cup dry sherry
3 tablespoons sugar
1½ tablespoons crushed
  gingerroot
1 tablespoon crushed garlic
plum sauce, duck sauce, or
  mustard

1. Preheat the oven to 375°F.

2. Marinate the pork in the hoisin sauce, soy sauce, honey, oil, chicken stock, sherry, sugar, gingerroot, and garlic for 3 hours.

3. Place the meat on a rack over a pan of boiling water, and roast for 45 minutes to 1 hour, or until cooked through. It should register 165°F on a meat thermometer. Serve with one of the sauces or with mustard.

▶ Can be prepared 2 days ahead and reheated.

NOTE: To vary the flavor, add ½ (2½) teaspoons Chinese five-spice powder to the marinade. For a brighter color, add ⅛ (¾) teaspoon red food coloring to the marinade.

There are two methods of roasting in the Chinese manner. Position an oven rack at the top of the oven. Place a pan of hot water on the oven floor, and hang the meat from curtain hooks suspended from the rack over the pan of water. The other method is to place a roasting rack over a pan of hot water and arrange the meat on the rack. Both methods allow the fat to drip from the meat into the water.

≡ *Indonesian Pork Riblets*

═ Yield: 20 ribs

20 pork loin back ribs
1 tablespoon dark soy sauce
1 tablespoon rice wine
1 tablespoon sugar
1½ teaspoons curry powder
1½ teaspoons minced garlic
1 teaspoon salt

½ teaspoon Chinese five-spice
   powder
¼ teaspoon pepper
3 egg yolks, beaten
¼ cup cornstarch
8 tablespoons vegetable oil

═ Yield: 120 ribs

120 pork loin back ribs
⅓ cup dark soy sauce
⅓ cup rice wine
⅓ cup sugar
3 tablespoons curry powder
3 tablespoons minced garlic
2 tablespoons salt

1 tablespoon Chinese five-spice
   powder
1½ teaspoons pepper
18 egg yolks, beaten
1½ cups cornstarch
3 cups vegetable oil

1. In a bowl, marinate the pork ribs in the soy sauce, rice wine, sugar, curry powder, garlic, salt, five-spice powder, and pepper at room temperature for 1 hour, or refrigerate overnight.

2. Dip each rib into the egg yolks and roll in the cornstarch.

3. Heat the oil in a skillet and fry the ribs in batches until golden on all sides. Add additional oil as needed.

▶ Can be prepared for frying 2 days ahead.

≡ *Korean Marinated Pork Strips*

≡ **Yield: approximately 50 pork strips**

2 pounds pork tenderloin	2 tablespoons minced onion
¾ cup sesame seeds	2 garlic cloves, minced
½ cup soy sauce	2 teaspoons crushed gingerroot
3 tablespoons sugar	2 tablespoons oil

≡ **Yield: approximately 200 pork strips**

10 pounds pork tenderloin	8 garlic cloves, minced
3 cups sesame seeds	3 tablespoons crushed
2 cups soy sauce	gingerroot
¾ cup sugar	⅔ cup olive oil
⅔ cup minced onion	

1. Preheat the oven to 375°F.

2. Trim the fat from the pork. In a bowl, marinate the pork in the sesame seeds, soy sauce, sugar, onion, garlic, and gingerroot for 3 hours. Drain the pork, reserving the marinade.

3. Oil a roasting pan and roast the pork about 45 minutes or until a thermometer registers 165°F.

4. In a saucepan, simmer the marinade for 10 minutes. Slice the pork thinly, and serve the marinade as a dipping sauce.

▶ Can be prepared ahead and reheated. Can be frozen.

≡ *Spiced Cherries*

≡ **Yield: 1 quart**

3 pounds cherries, pitted	1 pound sugar, approximately
1 quart cider vinegar, approximately	

≡ **Yield: 1 gallon**

12 pounds cherries, pitted	4 pounds sugar, approximately
1 gallon cider vinegar, approximately	

1. In a noncorrosible container, soak the cherries in vinegar to cover for 8 days, stirring twice a day.

2. Drain the cherries and arrange in layers, sprinkling on 1 cup of sugar for each cup of cherries. Let stand 8 days, stirring twice a day. Pack into sterilized jars and seal.

▶ Keeps 6 months, sealed.

≡ *Pineapple with Preserved Ginger*

≡ **Yield: 3 cups**

1 large pineapple, cut into bite-size pieces	1 tablespoon syrup from the ginger
3 tablespoons preserved ginger, minced	

≡ **Yield: 1 gallon**

5 large pineapples, cut into bite-size pieces	1 cup preserved ginger, minced
	⅓ cup syrup from the ginger

In a bowl, macerate the pineapple, ginger, and syrup for 2 hours.

▶ Do not keep more than 6 hours.

≡ *Melon à l'Indienne (Curried Melon)*

≡ **Yield: 1 quart**

1 cantaloupe, cut into balls	1 cup minced onion
1 honeydew melon, cut into balls	4 teaspoons curry powder
¼ cup butter	¾ cup mayonnaise
	¼ cup heavy cream

≡ **Yield: 1 gallon**

4 cantaloupes, cut into balls	1 quart minced onion
4 honeydew melons, cut into balls	⅓ cup curry powder
1 cup butter	4 cups mayonnaise
	1¼ cups heavy cream

1. In a bowl, mix the melons.

2. In a skillet, sauté the onion in the butter until soft. Add the curry and cook, stirring over low heat for 5 minutes. Force through a sieve. Add the mayonnaise and cream and fold into the melon. Serve with skewers.

▶ Can be prepared 8 hours in advance.

≡ *Melon con Anis (Melon with Anisette)*

═ Yield: approximately 3 cups

1 Spanish melon, cut into balls
3 tablespoons anisette

2 tablespoons confectioners' sugar
2 tablespoons water

═ Yield: approximately 1 gallon

5 Spanish melons, cut into balls
1 cup anisette

⅔ cup confectioners' sugar
⅔ cup water

In a bowl, macerate the melon in the anisette, sugar, and water for 2 hours.

▶ Can be prepared 8 hours in advance.

== 12 ==

Stuffed Vegetables, Fish, Meats, Breads, and Fruits

*F*or many hosts, hostesses, and caterers, vegetables as an hors d'oeuvre are limited to raw crudités served with a dip. Massive arrangements of raw or blanched vegetables are displayed with one or more dips at *every* party, ad nauseam. Vegetables do have broader uses, however, and stuffing them is one of the best. Some foods, like grape leaves, are obvious, but many vegetables can be filled to provide attractive and colorful hot or cold hors d'oeuvre. In addition, they can be passed quickly and easily. If there is not space in the buffet for a vegetable display, pass or set out trays of carefully arranged filled vegetables. As with most filled hors d'oeuvre, the fillings are limited only by your imagination; those suggested here are just a few of the possibilities. The fillings used in other hors d'oeuvre such as pastries can also work in vegetables.

Choose fresh, blemish-free vegetables as containers. Peel the vegetables if the skins are tough or cut off strips of skin in a decorative design. Some vegetables, such as baby beets, squashes, or potatoes, are better if blanched or fully cooked before filling. Whatever the preparation, the stuffed vegetables must be dry when passed or they will slip from the fingers onto the nearest carpet or dress. Some vegetables cannot be served completely risk-free, however. Hot stuffed mushrooms are a perfect example. They are usually slippery, messy, and difficult to eat neatly. Experienced guests put their thumb in the filling and their fingers on the cap to stabilize them. Less experienced guests ask the staff for soda water or another cleaning fluid. If the party is small, pass plates and forks; at larger gatherings, if you must serve stuffed mushrooms, place them stuffing side down on small rounds of toast.

For a small menu, fill several different vegetables with different fillings, but if the menu is large and there are already many flavors, use the same filling in a variety of vegetables. For example, a crabmeat filling can be used to stuff black olives, cucumber cups, raw mushroom caps, cherry tomatoes, and Belgian endives. Or use the filling warm in steamed hollowed tiny potatoes, Brussels sprouts, beets, and tiny onions. The same filling can also be used to fill small puffs or tartlets. If you are serving beets, by the way, pass them with a small container of skewers for those who want to avoid staining their fingers. Of course, beets and any other vegetables that are apt to roll should have a slice cut off their bottoms so they will sit upright. (Cherry tomatoes are a special case. See the instructions for cherry tomatoes, page 508.)

Stuffed fish and meat hors d'oeuvre are usually made by wrapping thin slices of fish or meat around pieces of melon or by shaping them into horns or cornucopias that are then filled. Preparing these requires less skill but more patience. You can fill hollowed-out lengths of hard sausages with cheese or pâté as you would stuffed bread loaves.

Bread loaves are ideal for stuffing. These hearty hors d'oeuvre are particularly suited for large parties that require something filling, simple, and relatively inexpensive. Long French bread loaves, either ficelles or baguettes, are hollowed, filled, wrapped in foil, and chilled, then sliced for serving. Stuffed bread loaves are best made a day in advance so the filling can become firm enough to slice. Certain filled breads are best heated briefly in the oven before slicing. Some of the fillings for pastries can be used, and some of the cheese fillings, especially when used to stuff the smaller ficelles rather than the larger baguettes, work well for the most sophisticated affair. They are also perfect for a box lunch or other picnic meal.

Stuffed fruits provide a vibrant note in any hors d'oeuvre menu. In addition to a cool, refreshing taste, they supply bright color. Serve stuffed fruits on their own or use them to garnish an otherwise uninteresting platter. For instance, a loaf of liver pâté is much more appealing accompanied by a few stuffed bright orange kumquats.

—— *Stuffed Vegetables* ——

≡ *Artichoke Hearts and Caviar*

≡ Yield: 12 artichokes

12 artichoke bottoms, cooked	1 to 2 tablespoons lemon juice
¼ cup fresh caviar	1 egg yolk, sieved

100 artichoke bottoms, cooked   1 cup lemon juice
2 cups fresh caviar   8 egg yolks, sieved

Drain the artichoke hearts, dry, and fill with caviar. Sprinkle with lemon juice and garnish with egg yolk.

▶ Keeps approximately 4 hours.

≡ Stuffed Celery with Cheese and Caviar

══ **Yield: 25 pieces**

½ pound cream cheese,   ⅓ cup salmon caviar
    softened   salt and pepper, to taste
3 tablespoons minced parsley   8 celery stalks, cut into 2-inch
1 tablespoon grated onion   lengths

══ **Yield: 150 pieces**

3 pounds cream cheese,   1 pound salmon caviar
    softened   salt and pepper, to taste
1 cup minced parsley   2 bunches celery, cut into
⅓ cup grated onion   2-inch lengths

1. In a food processor, cream the cream cheese, parsley, and onion. Fold in the caviar and correct the seasoning with salt and pepper.

2. Fit a pastry bag with a no. 3 plain tip, fill it with the cream cheese, and pipe the filling into the celery sections.

▶ Keeps overnight, refrigerated.

NOTE: This filling can be used with other vegetables and pastries. You may prepare the cheese without the caviar and then place a dab of caviar on top of the piped cheese.

≡ Cucumber Cups Filled with Smoked Fish

Use smoked salmon, trout, whitefish, sablefish, mackerel, finnan haddie, oysters, or mussels.

═ **Yield: 25 cups**

12 ounces cream cheese, softened	lemon juice, to taste
	salt and pepper, to taste
4 ounces smoked fish, skinned and boned	4 small cucumbers, cut into cups
2½ tablespoons grated onion	

═ **Yield: 100 cups**

3 pounds cream cheese, softened	lemon juice, to taste
	salt and pepper, to taste
1 pound smoked fish, skinned and boned	16 small cucumbers, cut into cups
⅔ cup grated onion	

1. In a food processor, purée the cream cheese, fish, onion, lemon juice, salt, and pepper.

2. Fit a pastry bag with a no. 4B tip, fill with the cream cheese mixture, and pipe the filling into the cucumber cups.

▶ Keeps overnight, refrigerated.

NOTE: The filling can be used to fill salmon cornucopias, or small beets, or it can be wrapped in small leaves of Boston lettuce to form little rolls. It can also be used as a pastry filling.

Preparing Cucumber Containers

There are several ways of shaping cucumbers to hold stuffings.

Cups Score the cucumber if desired. Cut into ½-inch sections and with a melon baller, scoop out most of the seeds, leaving a thin base. Fill.

Petalled Cups To make a pretty container, cut off both ends of the cucumber; score the sides if desired. With a paring knife, cut into the side of the cucumber starting about 1 inch above one end. Cut down towards that end to make a curved slice, halfway through the cucumber. (This is similar to making a radish rose.) Remove the knife, give the cucumber a slight turn, and continue around the base of the cucumber. You will have a cup shaped like a flower. Cut the bottom of the cucumber evenly and repeat, continuing up the cucumber until used.

Slices Score the cucumber if desired and cut off both ends. Use an apple or zucchini corer to remove the seeds to make a hollow tube. Fill a pastry bag either without a tip or with a large plain tip and pipe in the filling. Chill until set and cut into slices.

Half Slices, or Boats Score or peel the cucumber if desired. Cut in half lengthwise and scoop out the seeds with a spoon. Cut a thin slice off the rounded side of each cucumber so it does not roll. With a pastry bag fitted with a grooved tube, pipe small mounds of filling every ½ inch. Cut between the mounds of filling.

≡ Yogurt-Mint-Filled Cucumbers

═ Yield: 30 cups

1 cup minced, seeded
   cucumber
1 teaspoon lemon juice
1 teaspoon minced mint
salt and pepper, to taste

plain yogurt
3 cucumbers, peeled and cut
   into ½-inch cups
mint sprigs

═ Yield: 90 cups

3 cups minced, seeded
   cucumber
1 tablespoon lemon juice
1 tablespoon minced mint
salt and pepper, to taste

plain yogurt
9 cucumbers, peeled and cut
   into ½-inch cups
mint sprigs

1. In a bowl, mix the minced cucumber, lemon juice, mint, salt, and pepper. Add just enough yogurt to bind the mixture.

2. Fill the cups and garnish with a sprig of mint.

▶ Keeps about 4 hours.

≡ Gurkas Dronningen (Stuffed Cucumber Cups)

═ Yield: 25 cups

¾ cup cream cheese, softened
12 anchovy fillets, minced
2 tablespoons mayonnaise
1 tablespoon minced dill
1 tablespoon minced chives

salt and pepper, to taste
4 small cucumbers, cut into
   cups
½ cup sour cream
4 tablespoons caviar

== **Yield: 100 cups**

3 cups cream cheese, softened	salt and pepper, to taste
½ cup anchovy fillets, minced	16 small cucumbers, cut into
½ cup mayonnaise	cups
¼ cup minced dill	2 cups sour cream
¼ cup minced chives	1 cup caviar

1. In a bowl, mix the cream cheese, anchovies, mayonnaise, dill, chives, salt, and pepper. Fill the cucumber cups and chill.

2. Just before serving, top each cup with a dollop of sour cream and a dab of caviar.

▶ Keeps 1 day, refrigerated.

≡ *Salmon-Stuffed Cucumber Slices*

== **Yield: 25 slices**

2 large cucumbers	1 tablespoon minced celery
1 cup flaked cooked salmon	1 teaspoon tomato paste
3 hard-cooked eggs	1 teaspoon lemon juice
½ cup butter, softened	salt and pepper, to taste
¼ cup mayonnaise	dill sprigs
1 tablespoon grated horseradish	

== **Yield: 100 slices**

8 large cucumbers	¼ cup minced celery
4 cups flaked cooked salmon	4 teaspoons tomato paste
12 hard-cooked eggs	4 teaspoons lemon juice
2 cups butter, softened	salt and pepper, to taste
1 cup mayonnaise	dill sprigs
¼ cup grated horseradish	

1. Prepare the cucumbers for slicing (see page 492) and set aside.

2. In a food processor, purée the salmon, eggs, butter, mayonnaise, horseradish, celery, tomato paste, lemon juice, salt, and pepper.

3. Fit a pastry bag with a no. 5 large plain tip and fill it with the salmon filling. Pipe the mixture firmly into each section. Wrap in waxed paper or foil and chill for at least 2 hours. Cut into ¼-inch slices and garnish with dill sprigs.

▶ Keeps 2 days, refrigerated.

NOTE: The filling works well in other vegetables, especially cherry tomatoes.

Stuffed Cucumber

1. *Score cucumber or zucchini with a fork.*

2. *Cut off ends and use an apple corer to hollow out center.*

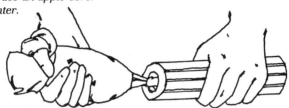

3. *Pipe filling through a pastry bag.*

≡ Stuffed Cucumber Cups

═ Yield: 25 cups

7 ounces canned tuna	2 cucumbers, scored and cut
¼ cup butter	into petalled cups
2 gherkins, chopped	2 gherkins, thinly sliced

═ Yield: 100 cups

35 ounces canned tuna	10 cucumbers, scored and cut
1¼ cups butter	into petalled cups
10 gherkins, chopped	10 gherkins, thinly sliced

In a food processor, purée the tuna, butter, and chopped gherkins. Fill the cucumber cups and top with a slice of gherkin.

▶ Keeps 1 day, refrigerated.

≡ Tuna in Cucumbers

═ Yield: 36 boats

7 ounces canned tuna packed in olive oil	3 small cucumbers, cut into boats
¼ cup mayonnaise, flavored to taste with mustard	capers
	black olives

== **Yield: 100 boats**

21 ounces canned tuna packed in olive oil	9 small cucumbers, cut into boats
¾ cup mayonnaise, flavored to taste with mustard	capers
	black olives

1. In a bowl, flake the tuna and mix with the mayonnaise.

2. Pack lightly into the cucumber boats and cut into 1-inch segments. Garnish with black olives and capers.

▶ Keeps 1 day, refrigerated.

== *Roquefort-Filled Belgian Endive*

== **Yield: 30 endives**

1 cup butter, softened	½ cup light cream
4 ounces Roquefort cheese, crumbled	salt and pepper, to taste
	2 heads Belgian endive

== **Yield: 120 endives**

2 pounds butter, softened	2 cups light cream
1 pound Roquefort cheese, crumbled	salt and pepper, to taste
	8 heads Belgian endive

1. In a food processor, purée the butter, cheese, cream, salt, and pepper. Fit a pastry bag with a no. 2 star tip and fill with the cheese mixture.

2. Separate the endive leaves and place on baking sheets. Pipe the filling in a shell design on each leaf. Chill.

▶ Keeps 1 day, refrigerated.

NOTE: The filling can be used to fill cherry tomatoes, artichoke hearts, olives, cocktail puffs, or tarts.

== *Belgian Endive Stuffed with Tongue*

== **Yield: 25 endives**

½ pound cold cooked tongue, minced	1½ teaspoons minced chives
1 hard-cooked egg, minced	1 teaspoon Dijon mustard
1 tablespoon minced parsley	mayonnaise
1½ teaspoons minced gherkins	2 heads Belgian endive

═ **Yield: 100 endives**

2 pounds cold cooked tongue, minced
4 hard-cooked eggs, minced
¼ cup minced parsley
2 tablespoons minced gherkins

2 tablespoons minced chives
4 teaspoons Dijon mustard
mayonnaise
8 heads Belgian endive

1. In a bowl, mix the tongue, egg, parsley, gherkins, chives, and mustard. Add just enough mayonnaise to bind.

2. Separate the endive leaves and fill with the mixture.

▶ Keeps 4 hours.

NOTE: The filling can be prepared in a food processor and piped through a large open star tip.

═ *Dolmadakia Yialandi (Stuffed Grape Leaves)*

═ **Yield: 50 grape leaves**

2 cups minced onion
1 teaspoon salt
2 cups minced scallions
⅔ cup rice
¾ cup olive oil
½ cup minced parsley, stems reserved

¼ cup minced mint
¼ cup minced dill
salt and pepper, to taste
¼ cup lemon juice
1 pound grape leaves
¼ cup lemon juice
1 cup boiling water

1. In a covered skillet, sprinkle the onions with the salt and steam over low heat, stirring until soft. Remove from heat and stir in the scallions, rice, ½ cup olive oil, minced parsley, mint, dill, salt, pepper, and lemon juice. Stuff the grape leaves.

2. Place the parsley stems in the bottom of a saucepan and arrange the dolma in layers. Add the remaining ¼ cup olive oil, lemon juice, and water.

3. Top with plate and weight, cover, and simmer 20 minutes. Add more water if needed and simmer 25 minutes longer. Serve cold, sprinkled with lemon juice.

Preparing Stuffed Grape Leaves

Dolma, dolmadakia, and *dolmades* are only a few of the Greek words for stuffed grape leaves. The Azerbaijanis refer to them as *dolmasy* and Iranians call them *dolmeh.* Whatever you call them, they are found in those areas and throughout the Middle East, and they are stuffed with as many different fillings as there are cooks. Dolma can be filled with

Stuffed Grape Leaves

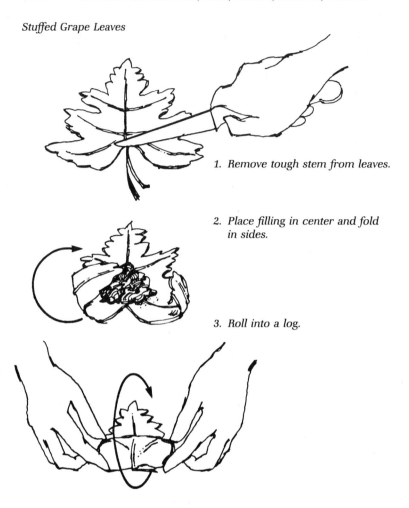

1. *Remove tough stem from leaves.*

2. *Place filling in center and fold in sides.*

3. *Roll into a log.*

herbs and rice, beef, chicken, lamb, and even fish. Whatever you fill them with, they are prepared in the same fashion. Rinse the leaves in cold water and drain well. Place each leaf on a work surface, dull side up, and cut off any remaining stem. Place the filling in the center, and fold the sides over the filling. Roll into a small, firmly packed log. Do not fill it too full, or the filling will swell and burst during cooking. The usual way to cook grape leaves is to put them seam-side down in a saucepan, separating the layers with a single layer of unfilled grape leaves. Place a plate smaller than the pan on top of the leaves, and put a 2- to 3-pound weight on the plate. Add barely enough liquid (water, lemon juice, and olive oil) to cover the grape leaves, and simmer until tender, about 45 minutes.

Grape leaves keep several days, refrigerated. Bring them to room temperature before serving. They can also be frozen.

A pound jar of leaves makes about 50 stuffed leaves, with enough leaves left for layering in the casserole. The recipes can be doubled or tripled without difficulty.

☰ *Dolmades*
(Stuffed Grape Leaves with Rice and Spices)

☰ **Yield: 50 grape leaves**

¼ cup currants	2 tablespoons lemon juice
2 tablespoons white wine	¼ cup minced parsley
1 cup minced onion	3 tablespoons pine nuts
¼ cup olive oil	1 tablespoon minced mint
salt and pepper, to taste	1½ teaspoons dried oregano
1 cup rice	¼ teaspoon ground allspice
1½ cups water	¼ teaspoon cinnamon

1. Soak the currants in the wine for 1 hour.

2. In a skillet, sauté the onion in the olive oil until soft but not brown. Season with salt and pepper.

3. Stir in the rice, water, and lemon juice, and simmer until the rice is almost tender, about 15 minutes. Stir in the currants, parsley, pine nuts, mint, oregano, allspice, and cinnamon. Taste for seasoning.

4. Stuff the grape leaves and place in a saucepan. Top with a plate and weight, cover, and simmer for about 45 minutes.

☰ *Salmon-Stuffed Grape Leaves*

☰ **Yield: 50 grape leaves**

½ cup minced onion	salt and pepper, to taste
½ cup butter	1 pound grape leaves
1 cup minced mushrooms	dill stalks
½ pound raw salmon, finely	2 tablespoons lemon juice
chopped	2 tablespoons olive oil
1 cup cooked rice	boiling water
¼ cup minced dill	

1. In a skillet, sauté the onion in the butter until wilted. Add the mushrooms and cook until the liquid evaporates. Stir in the salmon, rice, dill, salt, and pepper.

2. Stuff the grape leaves. Place a layer of unrolled grape leaves in a saucepan, top with a layer of dill stalks, and cover with a layer of stuffed grape leaves. Continue layering, using all the dill stalks.

3. Add the lemon juice, olive oil, and boiling water barely to cover. Top with a plate and weight, and simmer for about 30 minutes. Serve at room temperature.

≡ Chicken-Stuffed Grape Leaves

══ **Yield: 50 grape leaves**

3 cups ground cooked chicken	pinch of ground cloves
1 cup half-cooked rice	salt and pepper, to taste
½ cup minced scallions	1 pound grape leaves
½ cup minced parsley	2 cups chicken stock
¼ cup butter, melted	½ cup lemon juice
¼ teaspoon turmeric	1 tablespoon tomato paste
¼ teaspoon saffron	plain yogurt

1. In a bowl, mix the chicken, rice, scallions, parsley, butter, turmeric, saffron, cloves, salt, and pepper. Stuff the grape leaves.

2. Place the stuffed leaves in a saucepan with a layer of grape leaves between each layer of stuffed leaves. Add the stock, lemon juice, and tomato paste. Top with a plate and weight, and simmer 45 minutes. Cool and serve with yogurt.

≡ Beef-Stuffed Grape Leaves

══ **Yield: 50 grape leaves**

½ pound ground beef	pinch of pepper
½ cup minced onion	1 cup bouillon
½ cup raw rice	¼ cup olive oil
1 tablespoon minced parsley	3 lemon slices
1 teaspoon salt	1 pound grape leaves

1. In a skillet, sauté the beef and onion until the meat loses its color. Add the rice, parsley, salt, pepper, and bouillon, and cook until the liquid is absorbed.

2. Stuff the grape leaves and place in a saucepan with the olive oil and lemon slices. Top with a plate and weight, and add water to cover. Simmer for 45 minutes.

☰ *Pork and Beef Filling for Grape Leaves*

═ Yield: 50 grape leaves

1 pound ground beef	¾ tablespoon fresh basil
½ pound ground pork	¾ teaspoon dried marjoram
¾ cup minced onion	salt and pepper, to taste
½ cup minced parsley	1 pound grape leaves
1½ tablespoons lemon juice	5 lemon slices
1 tablespoon raw rice	½ cup olive oil

1. In a bowl, mix the beef, pork, onion, parsley, lemon juice, rice, basil, marjoram, salt, and pepper. Stuff the grape leaves.

2. Place the stuffed leaves in a saucepan with the lemon slices, olive oil, and water to cover. Top with a plate and weight, and simmer until tender, about 45 minutes.

☰ *Lamb Stuffing for Grape Leaves*

═ Yield: 50 grape leaves

1 pound ground lamb	1 teaspoon crushed garlic
1 cup peeled, seeded, and	½ teaspoon dried oregano
chopped tomatoes	½ teaspoon dried thyme
¼ cup pine nuts	salt and pepper, to taste
¼ cup minced onion	1 pound grape leaves
2 tablespoons tomato paste	½ cup olive oil
2 tablespoons minced parsley	5 lemon slices
2 tablespoons minced mint or	
dill	

1. In a bowl, mix the lamb, tomatoes, pine nuts, onion, tomato paste, parsley, mint, garlic, oregano, thyme, salt, and pepper. Stuff the grape leaves. Place in a saucepan, top with a plate and weight.

2. Add water to cover, olive oil, and lemon slices. Simmer until tender, about 45 minutes.

☰ *Mushroom-Filled Mushrooms*

═ Yield: 25 mushrooms

25 mushrooms	salt and pepper, to taste
¼ cup vinaigrette (page 46)	sour cream
1 tablespoon minced dill	dill sprigs

== **Yield: 100 mushrooms**

100 mushrooms
1 cup vinaigrette (page 46)
¼ cup minced dill

salt and pepper, to taste
sour cream
dill sprigs

1. Remove the stems from the mushrooms and mince the stems. Season each cap with a little vinaigrette.

2. In a bowl, mix the stems, dill, salt, and pepper with just enough sour cream to bind. Fill the caps and garnish with the dill sprigs.

▶ Keeps 6 hours, refrigerated.

≡ *Champignons au Roquefort (Roquefort-Stuffed Mushrooms)*

== **Yield: 30 mushrooms**

½ pound butter
¼ pound Roquefort cheese
2 tablespoons Cognac
¼ teaspoon Worcestershire
sauce

1 pound mushrooms
green pepper cutouts, optional

== **Yield: 90 mushrooms**

1½ pounds butter
¾ pound Roquefort cheese
⅓ cup Cognac
¾ teaspoon Worcestershire
sauce

3 pounds mushrooms
green pepper cutouts, optional

1. In a food processor, purée the butter, cheese, Cognac, and Worcestershire sauce. Fit a pastry bag with a no. 30 star tip and fill with the cheese mixture.

2. Remove the stems from the mushrooms. Pipe the filling into each cap. Garnish with green pepper.

▶ Keeps 1 day, refrigerated.

≡ Herb Cheese-Filled Mushrooms

=== Yield: 25 mushrooms

½ pound cream cheese, softened
¼ cup minced parsley
1 shallot, minced
1 garlic clove, minced

1 tablespoon sour cream
½ teaspoon salt
¼ teaspoon pepper
25 mushroom caps
parsley sprigs

=== Yield: 100 mushrooms

2 pounds cream cheese, softened
1 cup minced parsley
4 shallots, minced
4 garlic cloves, minced

¼ cup sour cream
2 teaspoons salt
1 teaspoon pepper
100 mushroom caps
parsley sprigs

1. In a food processor, cream the cream cheese and add the parsley, shallots, garlic, sour cream, salt, and pepper.

2. Stuff the caps and garnish with the parsley.

▶ The filling keeps 3 days, refrigerated. Do not stuff the caps until a few hours before serving.

≡ Smoked Salmon-Stuffed Mushrooms

=== Yield: 25 mushrooms

¼ pound smoked salmon, minced
½ cup heavy cream, whipped
½ teaspoon minced dill

25 mushroom caps
lemon juice, to taste
paprika

=== Yield: 100 mushrooms

1 pound smoked salmon, minced
2 cups heavy cream, whipped
2 teaspoons minced dill

100 mushroom caps
lemon juice, to taste
paprika

In a bowl, fold the salmon and dill into the whipped cream. Sprinkle the caps with lemon juice and fill with the salmon mixture. Sprinkle with paprika.

▶ Keeps 6 hours, refrigerated.

≡ Champignons Farci Provençal
(Stuffed Mushrooms Provence-Style)

═ Yield: 20 mushrooms

20 mushroom caps	1 tablespoon minced parsley
¼ cup butter	1 teaspoon minced garlic
4 chicken livers, cut in half	lemon juice, to taste
¼ cup minced gherkins	salt and pepper, to taste
3 tablespoons heavy cream	minced parsley

═ Yield: 120 mushrooms

120 mushroom caps	⅓ cup minced parsley
1½ cups butter	2 tablespoons minced garlic
1½ pounds chicken livers, cut in half	lemon juice, to taste
	salt and pepper, to taste
1½ cups minced gherkins	minced parsley
1¼ cups heavy cream	

1. In a skillet, sauté the mushrooms in the butter until tender. Remove and cool. In the same skillet, sauté the livers until medium.

2. Transfer the livers and their juices to a food processor and purée, adding the gherkins, cream, parsley, garlic, lemon juice, salt, and pepper.

3. Stuff the caps and garnish with the parsley.

▶ Keeps 1 day, refrigerated.

≡ Mushroom Caps with Horseradish,
Cheese, and Ham

═ Yield: 30 mushrooms

½ pound cream cheese, softened	3 tablespoons minced chives
	2 tablespoons minced parsley
¼ cup drained horseradish	salt, to taste
¼ cup minced ham or salami	30 mushroom caps

═ Yield: 90 mushrooms

1½ pounds cream cheese, softened	
¾ cup drained horseradish	⅔ cup minced chives
¾ cup minced ham or salami	⅓ cup minced parsley
	salt, to taste
	90 mushroom caps

In a bowl, mix the cream cheese, horseradish, ham, chives, parsley, and salt. Stuff the mushroom caps.

▶ Keeps 1 day, refrigerated.

≡ *Stuffed Pepper Slices*

=== **Yield: 50 slices**

1 pound cream cheese	1½ teaspoons salt
½ cup minced chives	¼ cup minced Gruyère cheese
2 teaspoons Dijon mustard	6 to 8 Italianelle peppers

=== **Yield: 150 slices**

3 pounds cream cheese	1½ tablespoons salt
1½ cups minced chives	¾ cup minced Gruyère cheese
2 tablespoons Dijon mustard	18 to 24 Italianelle peppers

1. In a food processor, cream the cream cheese, chives, mustard, and salt. Transfer to a bowl and stir in the Gruyère cheese.

2. Cut off the tops of the peppers and remove the seeds. Fit a pastry bag with a no. 8 large plain tip, fill with the cheese mixture, and pipe the filling into the peppers, packing the mixture firmly. Chill at least 2 hours. Cut into ¼-inch slices to serve.

▶ Keeps 2 days, refrigerated.

≡ *Green Peppers Stuffed with Feta Cheese*

=== **Yield: 50 slices**

1 pound feta cheese, crumbled	2 to 3 tablespoons minced ripe
½ pound cream cheese	olives
1 egg yolk	6 to 8 Italianelle peppers

=== **Yield: 100 slices**

2 pounds feta cheese, crumbled	⅓ cup minced ripe olives
1 pound cream cheese	12 to 16 Italianelle peppers
2 egg yolks	

1. In a bowl, mix the feta cheese, cream cheese, egg yolk(s), and olives.

2. Fit a pastry bag with a no. 8 large plain tip, fill with the cheese mixture, and pipe the filling into the peppers. Chill 3 hours. Cut into slices to serve.

▶ Keeps 2 days, refrigerated.

≡ *Roses d'Hiver, Armenonville (Stuffed Radishes)*

═ Yield: 12 radishes

12 large bright radishes with stems	1 teaspoon port
⅓ cup Roquefort cheese	minced parsley

═ Yield: 100 radishes

100 large bright radishes with stems	3 tablespoons port
2⅔ cups Roquefort cheese	minced parsley

1. Cut the radishes into roses, leaving on a section of the stem. Soak in ice water until the petals open. Remove the center section of the radish.

2. In a food processor, purée the Roquefort and the port; force through a sieve if not perfectly smooth. Fit a pastry bag with a no. 30 star tip, fill with the cheese mixture, and pipe the filling into the center of each radish. Dip the center into the parsley and chill.

▶ Keeps 1 day, refrigerated.

≡ *Stuffed Snow Peas*

The tender-crisp quality of blanched snow peas makes them a taste treat. The cool snap in the mouth makes them a joy to eat and the bright green color a pleasure to see.

═ Yield: 25 snow peas

½ pound snow peas	⅓ cup minced chives
¾ pound cream cheese, softened	Worcestershire sauce, to taste
	salt and pepper, to taste

═ Yield: 100 snow peas

2 pounds snow peas	1⅓ cups minced chives
3 pounds cream cheese, softened	Worcestershire sauce, to taste
	salt and pepper, to taste

1. String the snow peas and blanch in boiling water for 45 seconds. Drain, cool in ice water, and drain again. Slit one side of each pea.

2. In a food processor, purée the cream cheese, chives, Worcestershire sauce, salt, and pepper. Fit a pastry bag with a no. 30 star tip, fill with the cheese mixture, and pipe the filling into each snow pea through the slit.

▶ Keeps 1 day, refrigerated.

NOTE: There are several points to success with this hors d'oeuvre. The strings must be removed, the snow peas must be blanched only long enough to make them pliable, and they must be drained and patted dry before filling.

This filling is the simplest, but virtually any cheese spread can be used. Try some of the other spread recipes in Chapter 5, especially the smooth spreads with fish or liver.

≡ Caviar-Stuffed Cherry Tomatoes

Stuffed cherry tomatoes make an attractive addition to any hors d'oeuvre tray. They add bright color and are easily eaten. The fillings can be as varied as your imagination permits.

≡ **Yield: 25 tomatoes**

1 pint cherry tomatoes, hollowed for filling	4 ounces salmon caviar
12 ounces cream cheese, softened	2½ tablespoons grated onion
	salt and pepper, to taste

≡ **Yield: 100 tomatoes**

4 pints cherry tomatoes, hollowed for filling	1 pound salmon caviar
3 pounds cream cheese, softened	⅔ cup grated onion
	salt and pepper, to taste

1. Sprinkle the tomatoes with salt and pepper and turn upside down to drain for 20 minutes.

2. In a food processor, purée the cream cheese, caviar, onion, salt, and pepper.

3. Fit a pastry bag with a no. 4B tip, fill with the cheese mixture, and pipe the filling into the tomatoes.

▶ Keeps 1 day, refrigerated.

NOTE: The filling can be used to stuff artichoke hearts and cocktail puffs, or to spread on crackers. Try it also as a filling for thin slices of smoked salmon.

How to Hollow Cherry Tomatoes

Preparing cherry tomatoes is tedious, but this method makes the job simpler. Remove the stem, if any, and cut a slice off the bottom. The tomato will rest on its "shoulders" and stand upright, rather than roll around on the tray. Use a small spoon or a tomato corer to scoop out the seeds and fill the tomato.

Try to find small cherry tomatoes—many are too large for hors d'oeuvre. Remember that it should be possible to consume any hors d'oeuvre in one or two polite bites.

☰ Cherry Tomatoes with Horseradish Mayonnaise

═ **Yield: 25 tomatoes**

1 pint cherry tomatoes, hollowed for filling	1 cup mayonnaise
salt and pepper, to taste	1 to 2 tablespoons grated horseradish

═ **Yield: 100 tomatoes**

4 pints cherry tomatoes, hollowed for filling	1 quart mayonnaise
salt and pepper, to taste	¼ to ½ cup grated horseradish

1. Sprinkle the tomatoes with salt and pepper and turn upside down to drain for 20 minutes.

2. In a bowl, mix the mayonnaise with horseradish to taste and fill the tomatoes.

▶ Keeps 1 day, refrigerated.

☰ Cherry Tomatoes with Pesto

The affinity of tomatoes for basil is always pleasing, and pesto sauce is certainly the ultimate basil flavoring. However, there are many other sauces, dips, and spreads that are equally appealing. Anchoïade, per bacco, or aïoli, for example, make stunning fillings.

═ **Yield: 25 tomatoes**

1 pint cherry tomatoes, hollowed for filling	salt and pepper, to taste
	1 recipe pesto (page 68)

═ **Yield: 100 tomatoes**

4 pints cherry tomatoes, hollowed for filling	salt and pepper, to taste
	4 recipes pesto (page 68)

1. Season the inside of the tomatoes with salt and pepper and turn upside down to drain for 20 minutes.

2. Fill with the pesto.

▶ Keeps 12 hours, refrigerated.

═ *Cherry Tomatoes Stuffed with Avocado*

═ **Yield: 25 tomatoes**

1 pint cherry tomatoes, hollowed for filling	4 teaspoons lime juice
salt, to taste	2 teaspoons lemon juice
sugar, to taste	2 teaspoons minced chives
2 ripe avocados	½ teaspoon salt
2 tablespoons sour cream	¼ teaspoon Tabasco sauce
2 tablespoons minced parsley	¼ teaspoon sugar

═ **Yield: 100 tomatoes**

4 pints cherry tomatoes, hollowed for filling	¼ cup lime juice
salt, to taste	2 tablespoons lemon juice
sugar, to taste	2 tablespoons minced chives
8 ripe avocados	2 teaspoons salt
½ cup sour cream	1 teaspoon Tabasco sauce
½ cup minced parsley	1 teaspoon sugar

1. Sprinkle the inside of the tomatoes with salt and sugar and turn upside down onto paper towels to drain for 20 minutes.

2. In a food processor, purée the avocado, sour cream, parsley, lime juice, lemon juice, chives, salt, Tabasco sauce, and sugar. Fit a pastry bag with a no. 4 plain tip, fill with the avocado mixture, and pipe the filling into the tomatoes.

▶ Keeps 4 hours, tightly covered and refrigerated.

≡ Cherry Tomatoes Niçoise

=== Yield: 25 tomatoes

1 pint cherry tomatoes,
  hollowed for filling
salt and pepper, to taste
6 hard-cooked egg yolks
4 anchovy fillets, minced
1 tablespoon minced capers

1 tablespoon minced ripe olives
1 teaspoon Dijon mustard
1 teaspoon Cognac
1 teaspoon olive oil
1 to 2 tablespoons mayonnaise
capers

=== Yield: 100 tomatoes

4 pints cherry tomatoes,
  hollowed for filling
salt and pepper, to taste
24 hard-cooked egg yolks
16 anchovy fillets, minced
¼ cup minced capers

¼ cup minced ripe olives
1½ tablespoons Dijon mustard
1½ tablespoons Cognac
1½ tablespoons olive oil
¼ to ½ cup mayonnaise
capers

1. Season the tomatoes with salt and pepper and turn upside down to drain for 20 minutes.

2. In a bowl, mash the egg yolks, anchovies, capers, olives, Dijon mustard, Cognac, and olive oil. Add just enough mayonnaise to bind. Fit a pastry bag with a no. 4 plain tip, fill with the anchovy mixture, and pipe the filling into the tomatoes. Garnish with capers.

▶ Keeps 1 day, refrigerated.

≡ Cherry Tomatoes Filled with Crab Cream

=== Yield: 25 tomatoes

½ pound crabmeat, flaked
¼ cup lime juice
1 pint cherry tomatoes,
  hollowed for filling
3 ounces cream cheese
¼ cup heavy cream
2 tablespoons mayonnaise
1 tablespoon minced onion

½ teaspoon minced garlic
1 teaspoon minced dill
Tabasco sauce, to taste
1 teaspoon Worcestershire
  sauce
salt, to taste
dill sprigs

== **Yield: 100 tomatoes**

2 pounds crabmeat, flaked
1 cup lime juice
4 pints cherry tomatoes,
  hollowed for filling
¾ pound cream cheese
1 cup heavy cream
½ cup mayonnaise
¼ cup minced onion

2 teaspoons minced garlic
1½ tablespoons minced dill
Tabasco sauce, to taste
1 tablespoon Worcestershire
  sauce
salt, to taste
dill sprigs

1. In a bowl, marinate the crabmeat in the lime juice for 1 hour; drain. Drain the cherry tomatoes for 20 minutes.

2. In a food processor, cream the cream cheese, cream, and mayonnaise. Add the onion, garlic, dill, Tabasco sauce, Worcestershire sauce, and salt. Fold in the crabmeat and fill the tomatoes. Garnish with dill sprigs.

▶ Keeps 1 day, refrigerated.

≡ *Cherry Tomatoes with Pickled Herring*

== **Yield: 25 tomatoes**

¼ pound cream cheese,
  softened
2 ounces herring in cream
  sauce, minced

¼ cup minced scallions
1 pint cherry tomatoes,
  hollowed for filling
minced parsley

== **Yield: 100 tomatoes**

1 pound cream cheese,
  softened
½ pound herring in cream
  sauce, minced

1 cup minced scallions
4 pints cherry tomatoes,
  hollowed for filling
minced parsley

1. In a bowl, mix the cream cheese, herring in cream sauce, and scallions.

2. Fit a pastry bag with a no. 5 plain tip, fill with the herring mixture, and pipe the filling into the tomatoes. Garnish with parsley.

▶ Keeps 1 day, refrigerated.

≡ *Tomates Farcies aux Moules* (*Mussels in Tomato Shells*)

═ Yield: 25 tomatoes

1 pint cherry tomatoes,
hollowed for filling
salt and pepper, to taste
1 small recipe marinated
mussels with herbs
(page 467)

½ cup mayonnaise
1 tablespoon mixed minced
tarragon, chervil, chives, and
parsley
parsley sprigs

═ Yield: 100 tomatoes

4 pints cherry tomatoes,
hollowed for filling
salt and pepper, to taste
1 large recipe marinated
mussels with herbs
(page 467)

2 cups mayonnaise
4 tablespoons mixed minced
tarragon, chervil, chives, and
parsley
parsley sprigs

1. Season the tomatoes with salt and pepper and turn upside down to drain for 20 minutes.

2. Discard the mussel shells. Mix just enough mayonnaise with the mussels to bind. Fold in the minced herbs.

3. Put a mussel in each tomato and garnish with a parsley sprig.

▶ Keeps 12 hours, refrigerated.

≡ *Smoked Salmon-Stuffed Cherry Tomatoes*

═ Yield: 25 tomatoes

1 pint cherry tomatoes,
hollowed for filling
salt and pepper, to taste
3 ounces cream cheese, softened
⅓ pound smoked salmon,
minced

1½ tablespoons lemon juice
1 tablespoon minced onion
heavy cream
dill sprigs and capers

═ Yield: 100 tomatoes

4 pints cherry tomatoes,
hollowed for filling
salt and pepper, to taste
¾ pound cream cheese, softened
1 pound smoked salmon,
minced

4½ tablespoons lemon juice
¼ cup minced onion
heavy cream
dill sprigs and capers

1. Season the tomatoes with salt and pepper and turn upside down to drain for 20 minutes.

2. In a food processor, cream the cream cheese, salmon, lemon juice, and onion. Add just enough heavy cream to make it smooth. Correct the seasoning with salt and pepper.

3. Fit a pastry bag with a no. 6 large star tip, fill with the cream cheese mixture, and pipe the filling into the tomatoes. Garnish with dill sprigs and capers.

▶ Keeps 1 day, refrigerated.

≡ *Shrimp and Olive-Stuffed Tomatoes*

═ Yield: 25 tomatoes

1 pint cherry tomatoes,
 hollowed for filling
salt and pepper, to taste
½ pound shrimp, cooked,
 peeled, and minced

1 scallion, minced
2 tablespoons minced black
 olives
1 tablespoon soy sauce

═ Yield: 100 tomatoes

4 pints cherry tomatoes,
 hollowed for filling
salt and pepper, to taste
2 pounds shrimp, cooked,
 peeled, and minced

4 scallions, minced
½ cup minced black olives
¼ cup soy sauce

1. Season the tomatoes with salt and pepper and turn upside down to drain for 20 minutes.

2. In a bowl, mix the shrimp, scallion(s), olives, and soy sauce. Stuff the tomatoes.

▶ Keeps 1 day, refrigerated.

≡ *Cherry Tomatoes Stuffed with Steak Tartare*

This is a highly seasoned version of steak tartare. For another example, see page 531.

Yield: 25 tomatoes

1 pint cherry tomatoes,
    hollowed for filling
salt and pepper, to taste
½ pound sirloin or beef fillet
1 egg yolk
2 tablespoons minced onion
1 tablespoon minced parsley

1½ teaspoons Cognac
1 teaspoon Dijon mustard
½ teaspoon curry powder
salt and pepper, to taste
25 asparagus tips, blanched,
    optional

Yield: 100 tomatoes

4 pints cherry tomatoes,
    hollowed for filling
salt and pepper, to taste
2 pounds sirloin or beef fillet
4 egg yolks
½ cup minced onion
¼ cup minced parsley

⅓ cup Cognac
1½ tablespoons Dijon mustard
2 teaspoons curry powder
salt and pepper, to taste
100 asparagus tips, blanched,
    optional

1. Season the tomatoes with salt and pepper, and turn upside down to drain for 20 minutes.

2. Remove any fat or membrane from the meat and chop finely in a food processor. Do not overprocess. (This works best when the meat is very cold but not frozen.)

3. In a bowl, mix the meat with the egg yolk(s), onion, parsley, Cognac, mustard, curry powder, salt, and pepper. Fill the tomatoes and top with an asparagus tip, if desired.

▶ Keeps 12 hours, refrigerated.

NOTE: Other toppings are possible. The most luxurious is a lavish dollop of fresh caviar. Sevruga will do nicely.

≡ *Zucchini Stuffed with Salmon Salad*

Yield: 25 sections

1 pound salmon, cooked and
    flaked
¼ cup mayonnaise
1 tablespoon lime juice
2 tablespoons minced dill
¼ teaspoon pepper
¼ teaspoon salt
pinch of cayenne pepper

⅔ cup minced celery
2 tablespoons minced red
    pepper
4 zucchini
salt
parsley sprigs
red pepper strips

= **Yield: 100 sections**

4 pounds salmon, cooked and
   flaked
1 cup mayonnaise
¼ cup lime juice
½ cup minced dill
1 teaspoon pepper
1 teaspoon salt

¼ teaspoon cayenne pepper
2⅔ cups minced celery
½ cup minced red pepper
16 zucchini
salt
parsley sprigs
red pepper strips

1. In a bowl, mash the salmon with the mayonnaise, lime juice, dill, pepper, salt, and cayenne pepper. Fold in the celery and minced red pepper; chill.

2. Cut a thin lengthwise slice from opposite sides of each zucchini. Cut each zucchini in half lengthwise, and scoop out the seeds to make a hollow shell. Sprinkle the shells with salt and drain for 15 minutes.

3. Fill the shells with the salmon mixture, piling it loosely. Cut each zucchini into ¾-inch-wide sections, and garnish each section with parsley and red pepper strips.

▶ Keeps 1 day, refrigerated.

—— *Hot Stuffed Vegetables* ——

One of the most popular vegetables to serve as a hot hors d'oeuvre is the mushroom. However, they are messy and difficult to eat, so plan to serve them with plates and forks, or serve the mushrooms, filling side down, on small rounds of toast.

≡ *Hot Cheese-Stuffed Mushrooms*

= **Yield: 25 mushrooms**

25 mushroom caps
¼ cup butter
⅓ cup grated Cheddar cheese
¼ cup grated Parmesan cheese
2 tablespoons minced pitted
   green olives

2 anchovy fillets, minced
2 tablespoons lime juice
2 tablespoons soy sauce

= **Yield: 100 mushrooms**

100 mushroom caps
1 cup butter
1⅓ cups grated Cheddar cheese
1 cup grated Parmesan cheese

½ cup minced pitted green olives
8 anchovy fillets, minced
½ cup lime juice
½ cup soy sauce

1. Preheat the oven to 350°F.

2. In a skillet, sauté the mushrooms in the butter until tender.

3. In a bowl, mix the Cheddar, Parmesan, olives, anchovies, lime juice, and soy sauce. Stuff the caps and bake 12 to 15 minutes, or until heated and the cheeses have melted.

▶ Can be prepared for baking 1 day in advance.

≡ *Blue Cheese-Stuffed Mushrooms*

═ Yield: 25 mushrooms

25 mushrooms	¼ cup bread crumbs
½ cup minced scallions	salt and pepper, to taste
½ cup butter	⅓ cup bread crumbs
½ cup crumbled blue cheese	

═ Yield: 100 mushrooms

100 mushrooms	1 cup bread crumbs
2 cups minced scallions	salt and pepper, to taste
2 cups butter	1⅓ cups bread crumbs
2 cups crumbled blue cheese	

1. Preheat the oven to 350°F.

2. Remove the stems from the mushrooms and mince the stems.

3. In a skillet, sauté the stems and scallions in the butter until soft. Stir in the cheese and ¼ cup (*1 cup*) bread crumbs. Correct the seasoning with salt and pepper. Stuff the mushroom caps and sprinkle with the remaining bread crumbs. Bake 12 minutes.

▶ Can be prepared for baking 1 day in advance.

≡ *Clam-Stuffed Mushrooms*

═ Yield: 25 mushrooms

25 mushrooms	1 cup minced clams
½ cup minced scallions	¼ cup cracker crumbs
½ cup butter	3 tablespoons minced parsley
½ teaspoon dried thyme	salt and pepper, to taste
½ teaspoon minced garlic	melted butter

== **Yield: 100 mushrooms**

100 mushrooms	1 quart minced clams
2 cups minced scallions	1 cup cracker crumbs
2 cups butter	¾ cup minced parsley
2 teaspoons dried thyme	salt and pepper, to taste
2 teaspoons minced garlic	melted butter

1. Preheat the oven to 350°F.

2. Remove the stems from the mushrooms and mince the stems.

3. In a skillet, sauté the scallions in the butter until soft. Add the mushroom stems, thyme, and garlic and cook until the liquid evaporates. Stir in the clams, cracker crumbs, parsley, salt, and pepper.

4. Place the mushroom caps on a baking sheet, brush with butter, and bake for 10 minutes. Mound the clam mixture in the caps. Sprinkle with butter and bake until light brown.

▶ Can be prepared for the final baking 1 day in advance.

≡ *Oyster-Stuffed Mushrooms*

== **Yield: 25 mushrooms**

25 mushroom caps	salt and pepper, to taste
¼ cup butter	cayenne pepper, to taste
25 oysters, shucked	

== **Yield: 100**

100 mushroom caps	salt and pepper, to taste
1 cup butter	cayenne pepper, to taste
100 oysters, shucked	

1. Preheat the oven to 425°F.

2. In a skillet, sauté the caps in the butter for 2 minutes. Place stem side up on a baking sheet and place an oyster in each cap. Drizzle the butter from the skillet over the caps, adding more if needed. Season with salt, pepper, and cayenne.

3. Bake 3 to 5 minutes or until the oysters just start to curl around the edges.

▶ Can be prepared for baking 1 day in advance.

≡ *Snail and Smoked Oyster-Stuffed Mushrooms*

═ **Yield: 24 mushrooms**

24 mushroom caps	12 smoked oysters, drained
½ cup garlic butter (page 72)	½ cup grated Gruyère cheese
12 snails, rinsed and drained	½ cup buttered bread crumbs

═ **Yield: 100 mushrooms**

100 mushroom caps	50 smoked oysters, drained
2 cups garlic butter (page 72)	2 cups grated Gruyère cheese
50 snails, rinsed and drained	2 cups buttered bread crumbs

1. Preheat the oven to 350°F.

2. Place the caps on baking sheets and dot with the garlic butter. Fill half the caps with snails and the other half with the smoked oysters. Dot with the remaining butter. Sprinkle with cheese and bread crumbs. Bake until very hot, about 7 minutes.

▶ Can be prepared for baking 1 day in advance.

≡ *Shrimp-Stuffed Mushrooms I*

═ **Yield: 25 mushrooms**

1 cup minced cooked shrimp	1 teaspoon minced tarragon
1 tablespoon cracker crumbs	salt, to taste
1 tablespoon minced onion	1 egg
1 tablespoon minced parsley	25 mushroom caps
1 tablespoon softened butter	½ cup buttered bread crumbs

═ **Yield: 100 mushrooms**

1 quart minced cooked shrimp	1 tablespoon minced tarragon
¼ cup cracker crumbs	salt, to taste
¼ cup minced onion	4 eggs
¼ cup minced parsley	100 mushroom caps
¼ cup softened butter	2 cups buttered bread crumbs

1. Preheat the oven to 350°F.

2. In a bowl, mix the shrimp, cracker crumbs, onion, parsley, butter, tarragon, salt, and egg(s). Stuff the caps and sprinkle with the buttered bread crumbs.

3. Bake for 15 to 20 minutes or until the mushrooms are tender.

▶ Can be prepared for baking 1 day in advance.

≡ Shrimp-Stuffed Mushrooms II

== **Yield: 25 mushrooms**

25 mushrooms
1 pound shrimp, cooked and
  minced
¼ cup bread crumbs
3 tablespoons melted butter
1 egg

1 tablespoon lemon juice
1 tablespoon minced shallots
1 tablespoon minced parsley
salt and pepper, to taste
1 cup mornay sauce (page 59)

== **Yield: 100 mushrooms**

100 mushrooms
4 pounds shrimp, cooked and
  minced
1 cup bread crumbs
¾ cup melted butter
4 eggs

¼ cup lemon juice
¼ cup minced shallots
¼ cup minced parsley
salt and pepper, to taste
1 quart mornay sauce (page 59)

1. Preheat the oven to 400°F.

2. Remove the stems from the mushrooms and mince the stems.

3. In a bowl, mix the stems, shrimp, bread crumbs, melted butter, egg(s), lemon juice, shallots, parsley, salt, and pepper. Fill the caps and bake for 10 minutes.

4. Remove from the oven and top with a little mornay sauce. Broil until golden.

▶ Can be prepared for baking 1 day in advance.

≡ Liver-and-Cheese-Stuffed Mushrooms

== **Yield: 25 mushrooms**

25 mushroom caps
1 cup grated Fontina cheese
⅔ cup liver pâté
¼ cup sour cream
2 teaspoons minced chives

1 teaspoon Worcestershire
  sauce
¼ cup butter
2 tablespoons lemon juice
salt and pepper, to taste

== **Yield: 100 mushrooms**

100 mushroom caps
1 quart grated Fontina cheese
2⅔ cups liver pâté
1 cup sour cream
3 tablespoons minced chives

1½ tablespoons Worcestershire
  sauce
1 cup butter
½ cup lemon juice
salt and pepper, to taste

1. Preheat the broiler.

2. Remove the stems from the caps and mince the stems.

3. In a bowl, mix the stems, cheese, pâté, sour cream, chives, and Worcestershire sauce.

4. In a skillet, heat the butter and lemon juice and sauté the caps for 5 minutes. Remove from the heat and let cool.

5. Season the caps with salt and pepper. Stuff with the liver mixture. Broil until browned.

▶ Can be prepared for broiling 1 day in advance.

≡ *Ham-Filled Mushrooms*

═ Yield: 25 mushrooms

25 mushrooms	⅔ cup sour cream
⅓ cup butter	3 tablespoons minced chives
2 cups ground ham	

═ Yield: 100 mushrooms

100 mushrooms	2⅔ cups sour cream
1⅓ cups butter	¾ cup minced chives
2 quarts ground ham	

1. Preheat the oven to 350°F.

2. Remove the stems from the caps, and mince the stems.

3. In a skillet, sauté the caps in butter for 3 minutes and arrange on a baking sheet.

4. In a bowl, mix the mushroom stems, ham, sour cream, and chives. Fill the caps. Bake for 10 minutes.

▶ Can be prepared for baking 1 day in advance.

≡ *Cherry Tomatoes, Grand Corniche*

═ Yield: 25 tomatoes

25 cherry tomatoes	¾ cup fine bread crumbs
3 cans rolled anchovy fillets	dried oregano, to taste

═ Yield: 100 tomatoes

100 cherry tomatoes	3 cups fine bread crumbs
12 cans rolled anchovy fillets	dried oregano, to taste

1. Preheat the oven to 400°F.
2. Hollow the tomatoes (see page 508 for instructions).
3. Drain the anchovies, reserving the oil. Place an anchovy in each tomato.
4. In a bowl, mix the bread crumbs, oregano, and enough reserved anchovy oil to moisten. Fill the tomatoes and drizzle with more oil. Bake for 10 minutes, until warmed.

▶ Can be prepared for baking 1 day in advance.

—— *Stuffed Fish* ——

≡ *Saumon Fumée à la Moscovite* (*Smoked Salmon Moscow-Style*)

This sophisticated hors d'oeuvre deserves the best of everything—fine silver or crystal platters and the best caviar you can afford. Save it for the truly special occasion.

≡ **Yield: 25 cornets**

½ pound smoked salmon, thinly sliced	1 hard-cooked egg
2 ounces fresh caviar	2 tablespoons minced parsley

≡ **Yield: 100 cornets**

2 pounds smoked salmon, thinly sliced	4 hard-cooked eggs
½ pound fresh caviar	½ cup minced parsley

1. Cut the salmon slices into triangles and shape into cornets. Put a dab of caviar in the center of each cornet.
2. Separate the white and yolk from the egg(s) and sieve separately. In a small bowl toss the egg yolk(s), egg white(s), and parsley to make a mimosa garnish. Sprinkle the caviar with some of the mimosa.

▶ Keeps 12 hours, refrigerated.
NOTE: To serve as a canapé, place a salmon cornet on a toast finger and garnish with the caviar and mimosa.

Salmon Rolls

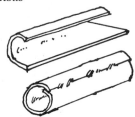

≡ *Lachstuten mit Rahm*
(Smoked Salmon Rolls with Horseradish Cream)

═ Yield: 25 rolls

1 envelope unflavored gelatin	25 slices smoked salmon, cut
⅔ cup cold water	into 3″ × 3″ squares
2 tablespoons sugar	25 pumpernickel slices, cut into
¼ cup grated horseradish	1″ × 3″ pieces, optional
⅔ cup heavy cream	capers

═ Yield: 100 rolls

4 envelopes unflavored gelatin	100 slices smoked salmon, cut
2⅔ cups cold water	into 3″ × 3″ squares
½ cup sugar	100 pumpernickel slices, cut
1 cup grated horseradish	into 1″ × 3″ pieces, optional
2⅔ cups heavy cream	capers

1. In a saucepan, soften the gelatin in the water. Over low heat, dissolve the gelatin and stir in the sugar. Refrigerate until cool but not set. Stir in the horseradish. Beat the cream until stiff and fold into the gelatin mixture. Refrigerate until almost set.

2. Roll the smoked salmon into tubes.

3. Fit a pastry bag with a no. 6 large open star tip, fill with the horseradish-cream mixture, and pipe the filling into the salmon rolls. Place the rolls seam-side down on a baking sheet and refrigerate until set. If desired, serve on pumpernickel fingers and garnish with capers.

▶ Keeps 1 day, covered and refrigerated.

NOTE: The salmon can also be cut into triangles and shaped into cornets instead of tubes.

Salami, Ham, or Fish Cornets

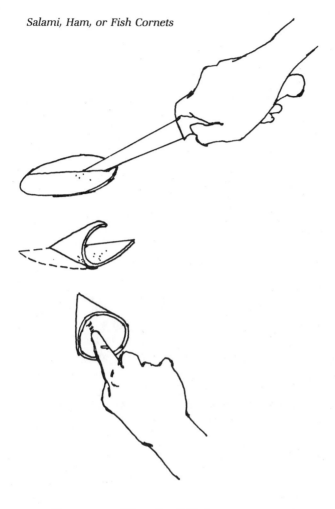

≡ *Cornets of Smoked Salmon*

═ Yield: 25 cornets
¼ pound smoked salmon
½ cup butter
1 tablespoon Cognac

dash of white pepper
¼ pound smoked salmon,
  thinly sliced

═ Yield: 100 cornets
1 pound smoked salmon
½ pound butter
¼ cup Cognac

white pepper, to taste
1 pound smoked salmon, thinly
  sliced

1. In a food processor, purée the smoked salmon, butter, Cognac, and pepper.

2. Cut the sliced salmon into 1½-inch squares and roll into cornets.

3. Fit a pastry bag with a no. 99 tip, fill with the salmon filling, and pipe the purée into the cornets.

▶ Keeps 2 days, refrigerated.

NOTE: The salmon used for the purée can be prepared from trimmings from whole salmon or purchased as smoked salmon bits.

≡ Smoked Salmon Rolls

=== **Yield: 25 rolls**

¼ pound smoked salmon, thinly sliced	2 tablespoons minced dill
	salt and pepper, to taste
¼ pound cream cheese	bread or cracker rounds,
1 tablespoon heavy cream	optional

=== **Yield: 100 rolls**

1 pound smoked salmon, thinly sliced	½ cup minced dill
	salt and pepper, to taste
1 pound cream cheese	bread or cracker rounds,
¼ cup heavy cream	optional

1. Arrange the salmon slices, edges slightly overlapping, on sheets of waxed paper, in 6″ × 8″ rectangles.

2. In a food processor, cream the cream cheese, cream, dill, salt, and pepper. Spread over the salmon slices. With the help of the waxed paper, roll the salmon, jellyroll fashion, into a tight roll. Wrap in waxed paper and chill until firm. Cut into ¼-inch slices. If desired, serve on bread or crackers.

▶ Keeps 3 days, refrigerated.

—— Stuffed Meats ——

≡ Stuffed Chicken Breast Slices

This highly flavored hors d'oeuvre is also low calorie. If desired, serve it with a sesame oil–flavored mayonnaise as a dip.

= **Yield: 25 slices**

2 chicken breasts, skinned and
  boned
4 red pepper batons
4 carrot batons, blanched
4 green beans, blanched

1½ teaspoons seeded and
  minced jalapeño peppers
1 teaspoon minced gingerroot
4 sage leaves, minced, or ½
  teaspoon dried sage

= **Yield: 100 slices**

8 chicken breasts, skinned and
  boned
16 red pepper batons
16 carrot batons, blanched
16 green beans, blanched
2 tablespoons seeded and
  minced jalapeño peppers

2 tablespoons minced
  gingerroot
16 sage leaves, minced, or 1½
  tablespoons dried sage

1. Pound the chicken breasts ¼ inch thick.

2. Place 1 baton of each vegetable in the center of each breast and sprinkle with jalapeño, ginger, and sage. Fold the chicken over and roll tightly.

3. Wrap tightly in plastic wrap and steam over boiling water for 15 minutes. Unwrap and cut into slices. Can be served hot or cold.

▶ Keeps 2 days, refrigerated.

☰ *Ham and Chive Roll*

= **Yield: 25 rolls**

¼ pound cream cheese
¼ cup minced chives
1½ tablespoons sour cream

salt, to taste
4 thin slices boiled ham

= **Yield: 100 rolls**

1 pound cream cheese
1 cup minced chives
⅓ cup sour cream

salt, to taste
16 thin slices boiled ham

1. In a food processor, purée the cream cheese, chives, sour cream, and salt.

2. Arrange the ham on a work surface. Spread with the cheese mixture. Starting from the long side, roll into long thin tubes. Chill. Cut into 1½-inch sections.

▶ Keeps 2 days, refrigerated.
NOTE: These are similar to several recipes in Chapter 9. Check there for other ideas.

≡ Cornets de Jambon (Ham Cornets)

═ **Yield: 25 cornets**

6 thin slices boiled ham	1 teaspoon salt
6 ounces boiled ham	¼ teaspoon grated nutmeg
¼ pound butter	⅛ teaspoon mace
3 tablespoons Madeira	pinch of cayenne pepper
1 teaspoon Dijon mustard	watercress, optional
1 teaspoon dry mustard	

═ **Yield: 100 cornets**

24 thin slices boiled ham	1 tablespoon salt
1½ pounds boiled ham	1 teaspoon grated nutmeg
1 pound butter	½ teaspoon mace
½ cup Madeira	¼ teaspoon cayenne pepper
1½ tablespoons Dijon mustard	watercress, optional
1½ tablespoons dry mustard	

1. Cut the ham slices into 3-inch squares and cut the squares into triangles. Shape into cornets. Reserve any trimmings or scraps.

2. In a food processor, purée the trimmings, ham, butter, Madeira, Dijon mustard, dry mustard, salt, nutmeg, mace, and cayenne. Fit a pastry bag with a no. 6 large star tip, fill with the ham mixture, and pipe the purée into each cornucopia. Garnish with watercress.

▶ Keeps 1 day, refrigerated. Garnish just before serving.

≡ Salami Cornets

═ **Yield: 25 cornets**

½ pound Genoa salami, sliced	¼ teaspoon salt
¼ cup butter	¼ teaspoon pepper
¼ pound liver pâté	black olives or parsley sprigs
1 tablespoon brandy	

═ Yield: 100 cornets

2 pounds Genoa salami, sliced	1 teaspoon salt
1 cup butter	1 teaspoon pepper
1 pound liver pâté	black olives or parsley sprigs
¼ cup brandy	

1. If necessary, remove the skin from the salami slices. Cut each slice in half. Fold the slices to form cornets and pinch the ends together to secure; skewer if necessary. Chill.

2. In a food processor, cream the butter and beat in the pâté, brandy, salt, and pepper.

3. Fit a pastry bag with a no. 30 star tip, fill with the pâté mixture, and pipe the filling into the cornets. Garnish with black olives or parsley sprigs.

▶ Keeps 1 day, covered and refrigerated.

═ *Cornets de Saucisse au Roquefort (Cornets of Salami with Roquefort)*

═ Yield: 24 cornets

12 thin slices Genoa salami	2 teaspoons sherry
3 ounces sieved Roquefort cheese	pepper, to taste
⅓ cup butter	24 raisins

═ Yield: 100 cornets

50 thin slices Genoa salami	2 tablespoons sherry
¾ pound sieved Roquefort cheese	pepper, to taste
1⅓ cups butter	100 raisins

1. Cut the salami slices in half and fold into cornets.

2. In a food processor, cream the cheese, butter, sherry, and pepper.

3. Fit a pastry bag with a no. 30 star tip, fill with the cheese mixture, and pipe the filling into the cornets. Garnish with a raisin.

▶ Keeps 1 day, covered and refrigerated.

Stuffed French Bread

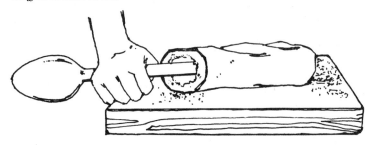

—— *Stuffed Breads* ——

This is a handy way of dealing with hors d'oeuvre for large crowds. The last-minute work entails only slicing and arranging the slices on platters. The fillings are usually colorful and the flavors are appealing. You can use any filling that will hold its shape when it is cold. Be sure to consider the fillings in the chapters on spreads, pastries, and dim sum.

To stuff a French bread loaf, first cut off the ends of the loaf and slice it into 6-inch sections for ease in handling. Use the handle of a wooden spoon to push out the inside of the loaf, leaving a hollow tube. Pack the bread firmly with the filling, using your hands or by forcing the filling through a pastry bag without a tip. Wrap in waxed paper and chill.

The recipes that follow make enough to fill baguettes about 2½ inches in diameter and 36 inches long. Each loaf yields about 60 slices. All of the fillings can be doubled or tripled without difficulty.

Once filled, the loaves keep for about 2 days, refrigerated, but the longer they are kept, the less crisp the crust will be. You can heat the loaf for about 5 minutes in a 500°F to crisp the crust before slicing. Be careful that you do not heat the loaf too long and melt the filling.

≡ *Chèvre and Sun-Dried Tomato Stuffing for French Bread*

1 pound chèvre	1 teaspoon minced rosemary or
½ cup minced sun-dried	summer savory
tomatoes	1 teaspoon coarsely ground
¼ cup extra virgin olive oil	black pepper
2 teaspoons minced garlic	

In a bowl, mix the chèvre, tomatoes, olive oil, garlic, rosemary, and black pepper.

≡ *Gruyère and Pistachio Filling for French Bread*

½ pound grated Gruyère
    cheese
¼ pound butter, softened
½ teaspoon Dijon mustard

½ cup chopped pistachios
½ cup Gruyère cheese, cut into
    ¼-inch dice

In a bowl, mix the grated Gruyère cheese, butter, mustard, nuts, and diced Gruyère cheese.

≡ *Olive Stuffing for French Bread*

crumbs from hollowed bread
    loaf
1 cup pitted ripe olives
1 cup Spanish olives
4 tomatoes, peeled, seeded, and
    chopped

½ cup grated Gruyère cheese
2 tablespoons olive oil
1½ teaspoons minced parsley
½ teaspoon dried tarragon
½ teaspoon dried chervil
salt and pepper, to taste

In a bowl, mix the crumbs, olives, Spanish olives, tomatoes, cheese, olive oil, parsley, tarragon, chervil, salt, and pepper.

≡ *Anchovy Cheese Stuffing for French Bread*

This method of stuffing the bread is different from the other recipes. An alternative method is explained in the note.

9 ounces cream cheese,
    softened
1 can anchovy fillets, mashed
2 tablespoons chili sauce
1 tablespoon capers
1 teaspoon grated onion
1 teaspoon Worcestershire
    sauce

Tabasco sauce, to taste
salt, to taste
½ cup butter
½ cup minced watercress
1 tablespoon crumbs from the
    hollowed bread loaf

1. In a food processor, cream the cheese, anchovies, chili sauce, capers, onion, Worcestershire sauce, Tabasco sauce, and salt. Set aside.

2. In a food processor, cream the butter, watercress, and bread crumbs. Fit a pastry bag with a no. 5 plain tip, fill with the watercress mixture, and pipe a solid line of filling down the bottom of each bread section. Chill.

3. Fill a pastry bag, without a tip, with the soft anchovy-cheese mixture and stuff the loaf firmly. Chill until firm. Each slice should have a core of watercress butter surrounded by the anchovy-cheese mixture. **NOTE:** The alternative method is to split the loaf in half and remove all the crumbs. Prepare the two mixtures. Spread the watercress butter on one half and spread the anchovy cheese, mounding it down the center, in the other half. Press the sides together, wrap, and chill until firm.

≡ Smoked Scallop Stuffing for French Bread

1 pound cream cheese, softened	½ teaspoon Tabasco sauce
½ cup minced onion	½ pound smoked scallops, minced
2 tablespoons lemon juice	
1 tablespoon Worcestershire sauce	

In a food processor, cream the cheese, onion, lemon juice, Worcestershire sauce, and Tabasco sauce. Fold in the scallops.

≡ Shrimp and Green Olive Stuffing for French Bread

1 pound shrimp, cooked, shelled, and diced	¼ cup sherry wine vinegar
¾ cup extra virgin olive oil	¾ cup chopped Spanish olives
½ cup minced parsley	2 celery stalks, minced
	salt and pepper, to taste

In a bowl, mix the shrimp with the oil, parsley, vinegar, olives, celery, salt, and pepper.

≡ Liverwurst Stuffing for French Bread

½ pound liverwurst	1 teaspoon Worcestershire sauce
2 hard-cooked eggs	
¼ cup grated Gruyère cheese	1 teaspoon Dijon mustard
¼ cup mayonnaise	1 teaspoon grated onion

In a bowl, coarsely mash the liverwurst and eggs. Beat in the cheese, mayonnaise, Worcestershire sauce, mustard, and onion. Correct the seasoning with mustard and onion.

≡ Ham and Chicken Stuffing for French Bread

2 cups diced cooked chicken	¼ cup mayonnaise
1 cup ground ham	1 tablespoon Dijon mustard
½ cup butter	2 teaspoons minced tarragon
¼ cup minced gherkins	

In a bowl, mix the chicken, ham, butter, gherkins, mayonnaise, mustard, and tarragon.

≡ Ham, Cheese, and Tongue-Filled French Bread

6 anchovy fillets, mashed	½ cup cubed cooked tongue
3 tablespoons butter	3 cornichons, sliced
1 cup cubed ham	2 tablespoons caviar
1 cup cubed Edam cheese	

In a bowl, mash the anchovies and butter to form a paste, and mix in the ham, cheese, and tongue. Fold in the cornichons and caviar.

≡ Beef Tartare Stuffing for French Bread

2 cups lean beef, finely chopped	3 tablespoons minced parsley
¼ cup minced dill pickles	1 tablespoon Worcestershire sauce
2 hard-cooked eggs, minced	Tabasco sauce, to taste
3 tablespoons minced onion	softened butter

In a bowl, mix the beef, pickles, eggs, onion, parsley, Worcestershire sauce, and Tabasco sauce with just enough butter to bind. **NOTE:** Also see the recipe for steak tartare on page 513.

≡ Veal and Tongue Stuffing for French Bread

1¼ cups butter	¼ cup chopped pistachios
¾ cup ground ham	¼ cup minced dill pickles
¾ cup ground cooked veal	5 sardines, mashed
¾ cup ground cooked tongue	3 slices bacon, crumbled
2 hard-cooked eggs, chopped	

In a bowl, cream the butter and beat in the ham, veal, tongue, eggs, pistachios, pickles, sardines, and bacon.

≡ Rye Bread Rolls

This Scandinavian delight seems weird at first, but it produces a lovely morsel.

Finn Crisp is one brand of very thin slices of crisp rye bread from Scandinavia. The bread slices are usually less than ⅛ inch thick. Any bread like it will work as well.

═ Yield: 25 rolls

3 cups water
25 Finn Crisp
¼ pound butter, softened
1 tablespoon grainy mustard

1 tablespoon minced dill
½ pound Emmenthaler cheese,
  grated

═ Yield: 100 rolls

3 cups water
100 Finn Crisp
1 pound butter, softened
¼ cup grainy mustard

¼ cup minced dill
2 pounds Emmenthaler cheese,
  grated

1. Bring the water to a boil, and quickly dip each piece of crisp bread into it. Place the bread on waxed paper.

2. In a bowl, mix the butter with the mustard and dill. Spread some of the mixture over the softened bread and cover with the grated cheese. Roll up the bread slices and arrange them, seam-side down, on a baking sheet. Chill until ready to serve.

▶ Keeps 2 days, refrigerated and covered with plastic wrap and a damp towel.

—— Stuffed Fruits ——

≡ Stuffed Kumquats

These are not only good to eat, they also brighten any platter. Use them to garnish pâtés and other foods that are not particularly attractive.

═ Yield: 24 kumquats

12 preserved kumquats
1 cup cream cheese, softened
1 teaspoon minced crystallized
  ginger

salt and pepper, to taste
minced parsley

=== **Yield: 100 kumquats**

50 preserved kumquats

2 pounds cream cheese

2 tablespoons minced
  crystallized ginger

salt and pepper, to taste

minced parsley

1. Cut the kumquats in half lengthwise and discard the centers.

2. In a food processor, cream the cream cheese, ginger, salt, and pepper. Fill the kumquat halves and sprinkle with the parsley.

Note: For a fancier looking filling, cream the cream cheese, salt, and pepper, and pipe into the kumquats through a pastry tip. Decorate with the ginger and set on a bed of parsley sprigs.

≡ *Stuffed Pineapple*

When cut, a large pineapple and a cantaloupe should produce about 50 pieces. Be prepared to replenish the shell with additional fruit, or arrange several pineapples on the buffet. A pretty presentation is to set the pineapples in beds of ice surrounded with tropical flowers.

1 large pineapple

½ cup diced preserved ginger
  in syrup

1 cantaloupe, cut into balls

Stuffed Pineapple

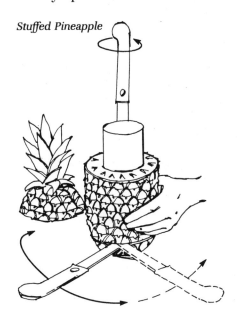

1. Cut off the top of the pineapple and reserve. Insert a long sharp knife to about 1 inch from the bottom. Cut around the inside edge to make a shell. Alternatively, insert a pineapple corer to within 1 inch from the bottom. With the knife 1 inch from the bottom of the pineapple, held horizontally, cut into the pineapple and slide the knife toward one side. Remove the knife, turn the blade in the opposite direction, and reinsert in the same hole. Swivel the blade to the opposite side of the pineapple. (See illustration page 533.) You should be able to remove the pineapple center in a solid piece. To seal the hole, dab a bit of butter against the inside of the pineapple where the knife went through the side of the shell.

2. Cut the pineapple core into bite-size pieces. In a bowl, mix the pineapple pieces, ginger in its syrup, and cantaloupe. Macerate for 2 hours. Pack into the shell and replace the top, askew. Serve with toothpicks.

= 13 =

Short Pastry, Cream Cheese Pastry, Yogurt Pastry, and Sour Cream Pastry

English is not the language of pastry. *Pâte brisée*, or short pastry, is also called tart pastry, flaky pastry, and pie pastry. They all refer to doughs most often used for pies. *Pâte feuilletée*, also called flaky pastry, puff pastry, or French puff pastry, is the flaky multi-layered dough used to make napoleons, bouchées, vol-au-vents, and palmiers (elephant ears). Puff pastry can also mean *pâte à chou*, or cream puff pastry.

This chapter concerns the quickly made pastry used for tart shells, turnovers, and other pastry-based hors d'oeuvre. Included are versions of the classic pâte brisée, as well as a food processor version, and recipes for *pâte pour pâté en croûte*, the pastry for wrapping pâtés. In addition, there are recipes for cream cheese and sour cream or yogurt pastries. All of these doughs can be prepared ahead and kept refrigerated for up to 4 days. They can be frozen raw, unshaped or shaped, or frozen after they have been baked.

Pastries made with cream cheese, sour cream, or yogurt are more substantial than short pastry, but produce a similar result. These doughs are usually rolled slightly thicker and have a higher ratio of pastry to filling. Generally, you can substitute fillings at will, and by changing the pastry produce a slightly different hors d'oeuvre using the same filling.

It is foolish to make pastry in very large amounts because of the tendency to overwork the dough. It is far better to make several smaller batches. I have included a large quantity recipe for pâte brisée, but the volume of dough is quite manageable. Some caterers have equipment for preparing and rolling dough in large quantities. This usually produces a commercial type of pastry. If you prefer to use this equipment, then follow the recipes suggested with the machinery. The average caterer or hostess will find that smaller quantities produce a more delicate pastry.

The pastry doughs in this chapter can be made in a food processor. Mix the flour and seasoning. Cut in the fat until the mixture resembles a coarse meal. Add the liquid and process until just moistened; do not overwork the dough.

—— *Rolling the Dough* ——

Fraisage (Smearing)

To make flaky pastry successfully it is necessary to join the flour and fat. The French method of accomplishing this is called *fraisage*. Turn the mixed dough onto a counter in a pile. With the heel of your hand, smear a small amount, about 3 tablespoons, 6 inches or more across the surface. Bring the heel of your hand back to the dough and repeat until all of it has been smeared.

Hints on Rolling Pastry

1. Work quickly and lightly. If you want a flaky, delicate product, you must treat it gently.

2. Shape the dough into a flat cake before chilling or freezing it. Shaping it into a ball is worthless, since the first step in rolling the dough is to flatten it.

3. Pastry need not look perfectly smooth when wrapped for chilling. In fact, it can look a mess. It is far better to have it underworked than overworked.

4. If the chilled pastry is very hard, do not try to roll it immediately. Pound it with the rolling pin until it starts to give. The pounding softens the fats, and the pastry is less likely to crack and separate.

5. If the pastry *does* crack and separate, stack the pieces and roll them into a long rectangle, fold into thirds, and turn an open end toward you and roll again. A few of these turns will make the pastry pliable while keeping it flaky and tender.

6. Roll the pastry from the center to, but not over, one edge (the one farthest from you). After each stroke, pick up the rolling pin, return it to the center of the pastry, and roll to the opposite edge (the one closest to you), applying even pressure so the pastry moves uniformly. Do not roll the pin back and forth. Pick up the pin and roll with an outward pressure, gently stretching the dough to the desired size and thickness.

7. Roll the pastry in a rectangle or square, no matter what the desired final shape. Think of it as a woven fabric with a warp and woof.

Roll a few times in one direction, turn the pastry one quarter, and roll again. If you try to roll the dough in a circle you will be pushing the pastry into too many directions at once.

Any pastry scraps can be rolled again. Do not press these into a ball, but rather stack the pieces on top of each other. Then roll gently but firmly. Keep the idea of layers in mind to ensure flaky and tender pastry.

—— *Shaping the Dough* ——

Tiny Tarts or Barquettes

Use 1½- to 2-inch tart molds for tiny tart shells, or 2½-inch boat-shaped molds (*barquettes*) for hors d'oeuvre. The quickest method for lining the molds is to arrange them next to each other in a large square. Roll the pastry into a slightly larger square, about ⅛ inch thick. Roll the pastry around the rolling pin and unroll it over the tops of the molds. Let it "rest" in position for 3 to 5 minutes. With a small ball of dough, press the pastry into each mold. Roll a rolling pin over the top of the pastry, using the edges of the molds to cut the pastry to fit.

Lining Barquette Molds

Rounds or Pillows

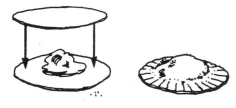

Turnovers

Crescents

Stack two pastry-lined molds and place an empty mold on top. Arrange the molds on a baking sheet about 1 inch apart, cover with another baking sheet, and weight with a 2- to 4-pound brick or heavy pot. Do not use food cans—they could explode. Bake at 375°F until golden brown, about 25 minutes.

Turnovers
Roll the pastry ⅛ inch thick and cut into 3-inch circles. Place a teaspoon of filling off center. Moisten the edges with cold water and fold one side over the filling to form a half-circle. Press the edges to seal with your fingertips or with the tines of a fork. With the point of a knife or the tines of a fork, prick the pastries to allow steam to escape. The pastry can also be cut into squares and folded into triangles or rectangles. Brush with egg wash, or dorure (see page 539). Bake at 400°F for 20 minutes or until golden. These can also be cooked as rissoles (see page 540).

Rolls or Logs

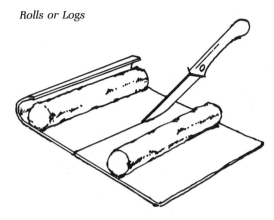

Rounds or Pillows

Roll the pastry ⅛ inch thick and cut into 2- to 3-inch circles. Brush the edges with cold water. Put 1 teaspoon of filling in the center and top with another circle of pastry. Press the edges to seal. Prick the tops to let steam escape. Brush with dorure. Bake at 400°F for 20 minutes or until golden. These can also be cooked as rissoles (see page 540).

Crescents

Roll the pastry ⅛ inch thick and cut it into 3-inch triangles. Put 1 teaspoon of filling on one side and roll toward the opposite point. Place on a baking sheet with the middle point underneath. Curve the ends to form a crescent. Brush with dorure. Bake at 400°F for 20 minutes.

Rolls or Logs

For the busy professional kitchen, this is the fastest method of making filled pastries. Roll the pastry into a rectangle, ⅛ inch thick. Arrange a strip of filling about 1 inch thick, 2 inches from one edge. Brush the pastry with cold water and roll just to encircle the filling once. Cut off the remaining dough and place the filled log, seam-side down, on a baking sheet. Brush with dorure. Continue with the remaining dough and filling. You can cut three quarters of the way through the roll to indicate the slices, or bake and slice afterward.

Dorure (Egg Wash, or Gilding)

A dorure is a wash brushed onto pastries to help them brown and to give them a sheen. The richer the dorure, the deeper the color and the glossier the finish. Dorures can be prepared from salted water; water and egg white; whole egg and salt; water, salt, and whole egg; milk and whole egg; milk and egg yolks; cream and whole egg; and cream and egg yolks. For the pastries in this book, an equal mixture of milk or cream and whole egg or egg yolk makes the most attractive glaze. When the pastries have been shaped, brush with the dorure, refrigerate for 10 minutes, and brush again. For a more decorative finish, use the point of a small knife to score the surface of the pastry after the second brushing. After it is baked, the scoring will show through the glaze.

Rissoles

When short pastries are deep-fried rather than baked, they are called rissoles. In effect, this doubles your repertoire, because the flavor and appearance of a deep-fried pastry are quite different from those of the same pastry baked. Do not offer both on the same menu. To make rissoles, deep-fry turnovers or pillows at 375°F until golden, about 2 minutes.

—— Fillings ——

This chapter contains a few suggestions for fillings, but throughout the book there are dozens, if not hundreds, of other possibilities. The chapters on dips, spreads, pâtés, canapés, and meatballs offer excellent ideas for other fillings.

Remember that the pastry is merely the container for the filling. The pastry must be wonderful, but the filling must be fully flavored and able to stand up to the pastry. Avoid making pastries so small that the filling—what there is of it—can barely be tasted. Tiny quiches are often in this category.

Quiches

Quiches are perhaps a symbol of the sophistication of the American palate. When we accepted this "foreign" food (hot custard pie with cheese!), we were then able to consider other "exotic" foods. Now, of course, no cuisine is safe from our curiosity. In the process, it has become common to try to force certain foods into roles for which they are not suited. Quiche is one. When a large round tart shell is filled with a mixture of custard and other wonderful ingredients, it is a perfect luncheon dish. However, when miniaturized to a cocktail food, it loses a lot. Tiny 2-inch quiches require enough pastry to support a filling, which means that there is little room left for the filling.

If quiche must be served, roll the pastry into a large rectangle to line a 1-inch-deep jellyroll pan. Add the filling and bake. After it has cooled about 5 minutes, cut it into 1- or 1½-inch squares.

—— *Pastry Doughs* ——

≡ *Pâte Brisée I (Short Pastry or Flaky Pastry I)*

= **Yield: about 75 pastries**

4 cups flour	1¼ cups butter
2 teaspoons salt	5 tablespoons lard
¼ teaspoon sugar	1 cup ice water, approximately

= **Yield: about 400 pastries**

5 pounds flour	2¾ pounds butter
3½ tablespoons salt	¾ pound lard
1½ teaspoons sugar	6 cups ice water, approximately

1. In a bowl, mix the flour, salt, and sugar. Cut the butter and lard into 1-inch pieces and add to the flour. With your fingertips or a pastry blender, crumble the mixture to form a coarse meal. Work quickly and lightly.

2. Add three-fourths of the water and mix to combine. Add more water, if required, until the mixture is crumbly and just holds together. Do not add too much water and do not stir to make a neat dough.

3. Turn the pastry onto a work surface (it will be messy). With the heel of your hand, starting at the edge of the pile farthest from you, smear about 3 tablespoons of dough about 6 inches across the surface (see Fraisage, page 536). Repeat until all of the pastry has been smeared.

4. Form the dough into a flat cake about 1 inch thick and wrap it in waxed paper, parchment paper, plastic wrap, or a plastic bag. Chill for at least 20 minutes.

▶ Can be frozen before or after shaping and baking.

NOTE: The lard provides flakiness and the butter provides flavor. If necessary, vegetable shortening can be substituted for the lard, but the flavor and texture will not be the same (just as margarine is no substitute for butter).

≡ *Pâte Brisée II (Short Pastry or Flaky Pastry II)*

This recipe produces an even flakier pastry.

= **Yield: 18 pastries**

1½ cups sifted flour	3½ tablespoons water
8 tablespoons butter	1 teaspoon salt
4 tablespoons lard	

══ **Yield: 72 pastries**

6 cups sifted flour   ¾ to 1 cup water
2 cups butter   4 teaspoons salt
1 cup lard

Put the flour into a bowl and cut in the butter and lard until the mixture resembles coarse meal. Add three fourths of the water and the salt and mix to form a soft dough, adding more water if needed. Perform the fraisage (smearing; see page 536). Form the dough into a flat cake about 1 inch thick and wrap in waxed paper or plastic. Chill at least 20 minutes.

▶ Can be frozen before or after shaping and baking.

══ *Pâte Brisée III (Short Pastry or Flaky Pastry III, Processor Method)*

Make sure that your food processor has the capacity to handle the larger quantity of dough.

══ **Yield: 20 pastries**

2 cups flour   4 tablespoons cold lard, cut up
½ teaspoon salt   5 tablespoons cold water
7 tablespoons cold butter, cut
  up

══ **Yield: 80 pastries**

8 cups flour   1 cup cold lard, cut up
2 teaspoons salt   1¼ cups cold water
1¾ cups cold butter, cut up

1. In a food processor, mix the flour and salt for 2 seconds. Add the butter and lard, and process with on-off turns until the mixture resembles coarse meal. With the machine running, add the water and process until the particles are just moistened and start to clump together.

2. Do not let the dough form a ball on top of the blades or it will be overworked. If you are not sure if it has been processed enough, remove the lid and pick up a handful and press it. If it holds its shape, it is ready. Turn it onto a counter and form it into a flat cake. Wrap in paper or plastic and chill for at least 20 minutes.

▶ Can be frozen before or after shaping and baking.

≡ *Pâte pour Pâté en Croûte*
(Pastry for Pâté in Pastry)

This somewhat more substantial pastry will stand up to the require-
ments of pâtés. It is not recommended for other uses.

== **Yield: enough for 1 loaf**

4 cups flour	1 cup lard
1 teaspoon salt	1 egg, beaten
1 cup butter	½ cup water, approximately

In a bowl, mix the flour and salt together. Cut in the butter and lard
until the mixture resembles coarse meal. In a cup, mix the egg and
water and add to the dough, adding more water if needed to make it
manageable. Shape into a flat cake and wrap. Chill at least 1 hour.

▶ Keeps 4 days, refrigerated. Can be frozen.

≡ *Cream Cheese Pastry*

== **Yield: 50 pastries**

1 cup butter, softened	2½ cups flour
1 cup cream cheese, softened	1 teaspoon salt
¼ cup heavy cream	

== **Yield: 100 pastries**

1 pound butter, softened	½ cup heavy cream
1 pound cream cheese,	5 cups flour
softened	2 teaspoons salt

In a food processor, cream the butter and cream cheese. Gradually
beat in the cream. Add the flour and salt and blend well. Wrap in waxed
paper and refrigerate for 1 hour before using.

▶ Can be made 4 days in advance.

≡ *Sour Cream or Yogurt Pastry*

== **Yield: 50 pastries**

1 cup butter, softened	2½ cups flour
1 cup sour cream or yogurt	1¼ teaspoons salt

= **Yield: 100 pastries**

1 pound butter, softened	5–6 cups flour
1 quart sour cream or yogurt	2½ teaspoons salt

In a bowl, beat the butter and sour cream or yogurt together. Stir in the flour and salt. If the dough is too sticky, add a little more flour. Shape into a flat cake and wrap. Chill at least 2 hours.

▶ Can be made 1 day in advance.

—— *Fillings* ——

☰ *Käse Algeriennes (Cheese Algerians or Turbans)*

= **Yield: 36 tarts**

½ pound Roquefort cheese	salt, to taste
2 tablespoons butter, softened	paprika
cayenne pepper, to taste	36 round 1-inch tart shells,
½ cup heavy cream	baked

= **Yield: 72 tarts**

1 pound Roquefort cheese	salt, to taste
¼ cup butter, softened	paprika
cayenne pepper, to taste	72 round 1-inch tart shells,
1 cup heavy cream	baked

1. In a food processor, cream the cheese, butter, and cayenne. In a bowl, whip the cream until it forms medium firm peaks and season with salt. Fold the cream into the cheese.

2. Fit a pastry bag with a large open star tip, fill with the cheese mixture, and pipe "turbans" of the cheese into the pastry shells. Sprinkle with paprika.

▶ Can be assembled 6 hours in advance, refrigerated.

☰ *Barquettes au Salade Russe (Mixed Vegetable Salad Pastry Boats)*

= **Yield: 12 barquettes**

2 cups mixed vegetables (finely diced carrots, green beans, peas, potatoes, and turnips, poached separately in salted water)	½ cup mayonnaise 12 barquettes, baked ¼ cup minced parsley

═══ Yield: 72 barquettes

12 cups mixed vegetables (finely diced carrots, green beans, peas, potatoes, and turnips, poached separately in salted water)

3 cups mayonnaise
72 barquettes, baked
1½ cups minced parsley

In a bowl, fold the cooled, well-drained vegetables into the mayonnaise. Correct the seasoning with salt and pepper. Fill the barquettes and sprinkle with parsley.

▶ Serve within 2 hours.

═══ Caviar Barquettes

═══ Yield: 12 barquettes

12 barquettes, baked
4 ounces caviar or salmon roe

½ cup sour cream
parsley sprigs

═══ Yield: 72 barquettes

72 barquettes, baked
1½ pounds caviar or salmon roe

3 cups sour cream
parsley sprigs

Fill the barquettes with caviar, top with a dollop of sour cream, and garnish with parsley. Serve immediately.

NOTE: You can fill the barquettes with a single kind of caviar, or alternate black and salmon roes, arranging them on a diagonal, straight down the center, or horizontally.

If the budget is limited, place the sour cream in the barquette and garnish with a healthy dollop of caviar.

═══ Basic Cold Seafood Filling for Tarts and Pastries

═══ Yield: 24 tarts

2 cups minced cooked seafood (such as lobster, scallops, shrimp, crab, or whitefish)
1 tablespoon minced onion
pinch of dried thyme
salt and pepper, to taste

½ cup mayonnaise, approximately
24 tart shells, baked
parsley, pimiento, or black olives, optional

══ **Yield: 72 tarts**

6 cups minced cooked seafood
(such as lobster, scallops,
shrimp, crab, or whitefish)
¼ cup minced onion
½ teaspoon dried thyme
salt and pepper, to taste

1½ cups mayonnaise,
approximately
72 tart shells, baked
parsley, pimiento, or black
olives, optional

In a bowl, mix the seafood with the onion, thyme, salt, pepper, and just enough mayonnaise to bind. Fill the tart shells and garnish with parsley, pimiento, or black olives.

▶ Fill just before serving.

NOTE: The flavor of this filling can be varied *ad infinitum*. Add Dijon or dry mustard, Worcestershire sauce, or a generous spoonful of horse-radish. Try adding a favorite herb such as marjoram, tarragon, chervil, or savory. Instead of mayonnaise, use a small amount of vinaigrette to moisten the fish.

══ *Hot or Cold Ham Filling for Tarts*

══ **Yield: 30 tarts**

1 cup minced onion
3 tablespoons butter
2 cups minced ham
1 cup sour cream

4 egg yolks
¼ cup minced parsley
pepper, to taste

══ **Yield: 90 tarts**

3 cups minced onion
⅔ cup butter
1½ quarts minced ham
3 cups sour cream

12 egg yolks
¾ cup minced parsley
pepper, to taste

In a skillet, sauté the onion in the butter until soft. Add the ham and heat. Stir in the sour cream and egg yolks and heat almost to a boil. Remove from the heat and stir in the parsley. Season liberally with the pepper.

▶ Can be prepared 1 day in advance.

NOTE: This filling can be spooned into barquettes and served cold, garnished with minced chutney, or used to fill turnovers or rissoles and served at room temperature or hot.

≡ Cabbage Filling I

Cabbage may seem a prosaic food to serve at a sophisticated party, but when handled with élan it can become an imaginative and interesting filling.

═ Yield: 36 pastries

½ pound fresh pork fat, minced
6 cups minced cabbage
1 cup minced onion

4 Chinese mushrooms, soaked
  in hot water until soft
salt and pepper, to taste

═ Yield: 144 pastries

2 pounds fresh pork fat,
  minced
6 quarts minced cabbage
1 quart minced onion

16 Chinese mushrooms, soaked
  in hot water until soft
salt and pepper, to taste

1. In a casserole, fry the pork fat until golden brown. Add the cabbage and onion.

2. Drain the mushrooms, reserving the liquid. Cut off and discard the stems. Mince the caps.

3. Add the mushroom liquid and the mushrooms to the cabbage and simmer over low heat until lightly browned, about 30 to 45 minutes, stirring often. Correct the seasoning with salt and pepper. Cool.

4. Use to fill tarts, turnovers, or logs.

▶ Can be prepared 2 days in advance.

≡ Cabbage Filling II

═ Yield: 36 pastries

6 cups finely chopped cabbage
1 tablespoon salt
2 cups minced onion
5 tablespoons butter

2 hard-cooked eggs, chopped
1 tablespoon minced dill
salt and pepper, to taste

═ Yield: 144 pastries

6 quarts finely chopped
  cabbage
¼ cup salt
2 quarts minced onion

1½ cups butter
8 hard-cooked eggs, chopped
¼ cup minced dill
salt and pepper, to taste

1. In a colander, sprinkle the cabbage with salt and let drain for 15 minutes. Squeeze the cabbage dry. Transfer to a bowl, pour boiling water over the cabbage, and let stand 3 minutes. Drain.

2. In a skillet, sauté the onion in the butter until soft but not brown. Add the cabbage and sauté until soft but not brown. Stir in the eggs, dill, salt, and pepper. Cool.

3. Use to fill turnovers or logs. This filling is especially suitable for cream cheese or sour cream pastry.

▶ Can be prepared 2 days in advance.

≡ Mushroom Quiche

=== Yield: 50 quiches

1½ cups minced mushrooms	1½ cups sour cream
3 tablespoons butter	1 tablespoon minced parsley
¾ cup minced onion	salt and pepper, to taste
4 eggs	50 tart shells, partially baked

=== Yield: 200 quiches

6 cups minced mushrooms	6 cups sour cream
¾ cup butter	¼ cup minced parsley
3 cups minced onion	salt and pepper, to taste
16 eggs	200 tart shells, partially baked

1. Preheat the oven to 350°F.

2. In a skillet, sauté the mushrooms in 2 tablespoons (½ cup) butter until soft. In another skillet, sauté the onion in the remaining butter until soft. Combine the mushrooms and onion and divide among the tart shells.

3. In a bowl, mix the eggs, sour cream, parsley, salt, and pepper. Pour over the vegetables and bake until set, about 15 minutes.

▶ Best baked and served immediately.

NOTE: The filling can also be baked in pastry-lined jellyroll pans.

≡ *Sauerkraut Turnovers*

═ Yield: 36 turnovers

¼ cup minced onion
2 tablespoons butter
1 pound sauerkraut, drained
    and rinsed
1 cup cooked ground beef or
    ham
2 teaspoons minced dill pickle

2 teaspoons minced thyme
½ teaspoon dried marjoram
½ teaspoon minced dill
salt and pepper, to taste
2 eggs
2 tablespoons sour cream

═ Yield: 100 turnovers

¾ cup minced onion
⅓ cup butter
3 pounds sauerkraut, drained
    and rinsed
3 cups cooked ground beef or
    ham
2 tablespoons minced dill
    pickle

2 tablespoons minced thyme
1½ teaspoons dried marjoram
1½ teaspoons minced dill
salt and pepper, to taste
6 eggs
⅓ cup sour cream

1. In a skillet, sauté the onion in the butter until golden. Add the sauerkraut, ground beef or ham, pickle, thyme, marjoram, dill, salt, and pepper; heat.

2. Mix in the eggs and sour cream and stir. Cool.

3. Use to fill turnovers.

▶ Can be prepared 2 days in advance.

≡ *Hot Basic Seafood Filling*

═ Yield: 25 pastries

¾ cup white wine
½ teaspoon salt
3 peppercorns
1 small bay leaf
½ teaspoon dried thyme
1 small stalk celery, chopped
1 sprig parsley
1 pound scallops, shrimp, or
    fish

1 tablespoon butter
1 tablespoon flour
½ cup heavy cream
1 egg yolk
1 tablespoon minced parsley
salt and pepper, to taste

═ **Yield: 100 pastries**

3 cups white wine
2 teaspoons salt
1 tablespoon peppercorns
1 bay leaf
2 teaspoons dried thyme
4 small stalks celery, chopped
4 sprigs parsley
4 pounds scallops, shrimp, or
  fish

¼ cup butter
¼ cup flour
2 cups heavy cream
4 egg yolks
⅓ cup minced parsley
salt and pepper, to taste

1. In a saucepan, simmer the wine, salt, peppercorns, bay leaf, thyme, celery, and parsley for 5 minutes. Add the seafood and simmer until just cooked. Drain, reserving the fish and the broth. Mince the fish. Reduce the liquid by one third.

2. In a saucepan, melt the butter, stir in the flour, and cook until the roux just starts to turn golden. Stir in the fish stock and cream, and cook until thick and smooth. Stir some of the hot sauce into the egg yolk(s) and return it to the sauce. Heat, stirring until it just reaches a boil.

3. Fold in the seafood and parsley. Correct the seasoning with salt and pepper. Cool.

4. Use to fill barquettes, turnovers, logs, or rissoles.

▶ Can be prepared 2 days in advance.

═ *Clam Quiche*
───

═ **Yield: 36 quiches**

8 ounces minced clams
3 tablespoons shallots
½ cup minced bacon
2 tablespoons butter
36 tartlet shells, baked

1½ cups heavy cream
3 eggs
salt and pepper, to taste
Tabasco sauce, to taste

═ **Yield: 72 quiches**

1 pound minced clams
⅓ cup minced shallots
1 cup minced bacon
¼ cup butter
72 tartlet shells, baked

3 cups heavy cream
6 eggs
salt and pepper, to taste
Tabasco sauce, to taste

1. Preheat the oven to 350°F.

2. Drain the clams, reserving the liquid. In a saucepan, reduce the liquid to 2 (4) tablespoons.

3. In a skillet, sauté the shallots and bacon in the butter until the shallots are soft but not brown. Drain the fat from the pan. Add the clams and heat. Put some of the clam mixture into each tart shell.
4. In a bowl, mix the cream, eggs, salt, pepper, Tabasco sauce, and reduced clam juice. Strain. Spoon a little into each tart shell. Bake for 15 minutes or until set.

▶ Best baked and served immediately.

☰ Rissoles d'Huîtres (Deep-Fried Oyster Turnovers)

═ **Yield: 24 turnovers**

24 small oysters, shucked and drained	¼ teaspoon celery seeds
	pâte brisée (pages 541–542)
⅛ teaspoon pepper	dorure
¼ teaspoon salt	oil for frying

═ **Yield: 72 turnovers**

72 small oysters, shucked and drained	¾ teaspoon celery seeds
	pâte brisée (pages 541–542)
½ teaspoon pepper	dorure
¾ teaspoon salt	oil for frying

1. In a bowl, marinate the oysters, pepper, salt, and celery seeds for 30 minutes.
2. Roll the pastry ⅛ inch thick, cut into 3-inch circles, and fill with an oyster. Shape into turnovers and brush with dorure.
3. Heat the oil to 375°F and fry until golden.

▶ Can be prepared for frying 6 hours in advance.

☰ Smoked Oyster Crescents

═ **Yield: 24 pastries**

1 can smoked oysters	Dijon mustard
pâte brisée (pages 541–542)	dorure

═ **Yield: 72 pastries**

3 cans smoked oysters	Dijon mustard
pâte brisée (pages 541–542)	dorure

1. Preheat the oven to 375°F. Drain the oysters.

2. Roll the pastry ⅛ inch thick and cut into 3-inch triangles. Brush each triangle with Dijon mustard and top with a smoked oyster. Roll and shape into crescents.

3. Brush with dorure and bake for 15 minutes or until golden.

▶ Can be baked 2 days in advance and reheated; can be frozen.

≡ *Smoked Oyster–Wild Rice Filling*

═ **Yield: 36 pastries**

2 garlic cloves, minced
1 cup minced mushrooms
2 tablespoons butter
1 can smoked oysters, drained and minced
1 cup cooked wild rice

3 tablespoons grated Gruyère cheese
salt and pepper, to taste
pâte brisée (pages 541–542)
dorure

═ **Yield: 144 pastries**

8 garlic cloves, minced
1 quart minced mushrooms
½ cup butter
4 cans smoked oysters, drained and minced

1 quart cooked wild rice
¾ cup grated Gruyère cheese
salt and pepper, to taste
pâte brisée (pages 541–542)
dorure

1. Preheat the oven to 400°F.

2. In a skillet, sauté the garlic and mushrooms in the butter until soft. Stir in the oysters, wild rice, cheese, salt, and pepper.

3. Fill the pastry, brush with dorure, and bake until golden, about 20 minutes.

4. Use to fill logs or turnovers, or fry as rissoles.

▶ Can be prepared for cooking 1 day in advance.

≡ *Salmon Turnovers*

═ **Yield: 36 turnovers**

2 cups flaked cooked salmon
½ cup minced dill
¼ cup butter, softened
2 tablespoons lemon juice
1½ tablespoons Dijon mustard
salt and pepper, to taste

pâte brisée (pages 541–542)
dorure
sesame seeds
1 cup sour cream
¼ cup minced dill

═ **Yield: 144 turnovers**

2 quarts flaked cooked salmon	pâte brisée (pages 541–542)
2 cups minced dill	dorure
1 cup butter, softened	sesame seeds
½ cup lemon juice	1 quart sour cream
⅓ cup Dijon mustard	1 cup minced dill
salt and pepper, to taste	

1. Preheat the oven to 425°F.

2. In a bowl, mix the salmon, dill, butter, lemon juice, mustard, salt, and pepper. Make turnovers, brush with dorure, and sprinkle with sesame seeds. Bake for 20 minutes or until golden. Serve warm.

3. In a bowl, mix the sour cream and dill. Serve as a dip for the turnovers.

▶ Can be prepared several days in advance; can be frozen.

≡ *Chicken-Chutney Filling*

═ **Yield: 25 pastries**

1 cup minced cooked chicken	3 tablespoons heavy cream
3 tablespoons minced chutney	salt and pepper, to taste
1 to 3 teaspoons curry powder	

═ **Yield: 100 pastries**

1 quart minced cooked chicken	¾ cup heavy cream
¾ cup minced chutney	salt and pepper, to taste
1 to 3 tablespoons curry powder	

1. In a bowl, mix the chicken, chutney, and curry to taste. Add just enough cream to bind. Season with salt and pepper.

2. Use to fill turnovers, rissoles, or logs.

▶ Can be prepared 1 day in advance.

≡ *Basic Meat Filling for Short Pastry*

═ **Yield: 50 pastries**

½ cup minced onion	2 eggs
½ cup butter	½ cup minced parsley
½ cup minced scallions	salt and pepper, to taste
2 cups ground meat or poultry	

═ **Yield: 200 pastries**

2 cups minced onion	8 eggs
2 cups butter	2 cups minced parsley
2 cups minced scallions	salt and pepper, to taste
2 quarts ground meat or poultry	

1. In a skillet, sauté the onion in the butter until soft. Add the scallions and cook until soft. Stir in the meat and remove from the heat. Stir in the eggs, parsley, salt, and pepper. Cool.

2. Use to fill turnovers, logs, rounds, or rissoles.

▶ Can be prepared 2 days in advance.

Meat Filling Variations

Season with 1 tablespoon (*¼ cup*) curry powder, ½ cup (*2 cups*) minced black olives, and ¼ cup (*1 cup*) minced chutney.

Season with 2 tablespoons (*½ cup*) paprika, ¼ cup (*2 cups*) sour cream, and 1 teaspoon (*4 teaspoons*) tomato paste.

Season with 1 tablespoon (*¼ cup*) chili powder, ½ cup (*2 cups*) cooked mashed pinto beans, 2 tablespoons (*½ cup*) grated Cheddar cheese, and 1 teaspoon (*4 teaspoons*) tomato paste.

Season with 2 cups (*2 quarts*) finely minced mushrooms sautéed until brown, ¼ cup (*1 cup*) minced dill, and ½ cup (*2 cups*) sour cream.

═ *Meat Filling for Rissoles or Turnovers*
___

═ **Yield: 25 pastries**

1 cup cooked ground beef, ham, lamb, or veal	2 tablespoons minced onion
¼ cup thick velouté (page 62) or sour cream	1 tablespoon minced parsley
	¼ teaspoon dry mustard mixed with 1 teaspoon water

═ **Yield: 100 pastries**

1 quart cooked ground beef, ham, lamb, or veal	½ cup minced onion
1 cup thick velouté (page 62) or sour cream	¼ cup minced parsley
	1 teaspoon dry mustard mixed with 1 tablespoon water

In a bowl, mix the meat, velouté, onion, parsley, and mustard.

▶ Can be prepared 2 days in advance.

≡ Beef and Dill Filling

═ Yield: 36 pastries

¼ cup minced onion	¼ cup minced dill
¼ cup butter	1 cup cooked rice
1 pound lean ground beef	salt and pepper, to taste
1 egg, beaten	

═ Yield: 144 pastries

1 cup minced onion	1 cup minced dill
1 cup butter	1 quart cooked rice
4 pounds lean ground beef	salt and pepper, to taste
4 eggs, beaten	

1. In a skillet, sauté the onion in the butter until soft but not brown. Add the meat and egg(s) and cook, stirring, until the meat loses its color. Stir in the dill, rice, salt, and pepper.

2. Use to fill turnovers, logs, or rounds. This filling is especially good with cream cheese or sour cream pastry. It can also be used to fill cocktail puffs.

▶ Can be prepared 2 days in advance.

≡ Empanadilla Filling I (Argentinian Turnovers)

In Argentina empanadas are a street food usually made from 6- or 8-inch circles of dough. They are the equivalent of a sandwich or an egg roll — a neat package of food to be eaten on the run. For hors d'oeuvre, shape them into small turnovers (empanadillas). See page 566 for empanadillas made with veal and sausage.

═ Yield: 36 turnovers

½ cup minced onion	3 tablespoons chopped raisins
2 tablespoons olive oil	1 tablespoon beef extract
1 pound ground beef	1 teaspoon paprika
¼ cup minced pitted green olives	¼ teaspoon oregano
2 hard-cooked eggs, minced	Tabasco sauce, to taste

═ **Yield: 144 turnovers**

2 cups minced onion	¾ cup chopped raisins
½ cup olive oil	¼ cup beef extract
4 pounds ground beef	1½ tablespoons paprika
1 cup minced pitted green	1 teaspoon oregano
olives	Tabasco sauce, to taste
8 hard-cooked eggs, minced	

1. In a skillet, sauté the onion in the olive oil until lightly browned. Add the beef and cook, stirring, until the meat loses its color.

2. Add the olives, eggs, raisins, beef extract, paprika, oregano, and Tabasco sauce. If the mixture seems dry, add a little water to moisten. Fill turnovers.

3. Bake at 400°F until golden, about 20 minutes, or deep-fry at 375°F.

▶ Filling can be prepared 2 days in advance.

Variation: Empanadilla Filling II

═ **Yield: 36**

To the original recipe add 1 minced garlic clove to the onion. To the meat mixture add 1 peeled, seeded, and chopped tomato, 2 teaspoons chili powder, and ½ teaspoon sugar.

═ **Yield: 144**

To the original recipe add 4 minced garlic cloves to the onion. To the meat mixture add 4 peeled, seeded, and chopped tomatoes, 3 tablespoons chili powder, and 2 teaspoons sugar.

Variation: Empanadilla Filling III

═ **Yield: 36**

To the original mixture add 1 cup minced cooked potato and ½ cup minced ham.

═ **Yield: 144**

To the original mixture add 1 quart minced cooked potato and 2 cups minced ham.

≡ *Spiced Meat Filling*

== **Yield: 20 pastries**

½ cup minced onion
1 tablespoon butter
½ pound ground beef
1 tablespoon tomato paste

1 tablespoon minced basil
dash of cayenne pepper
salt and pepper, to taste

== **Yield: 80 pastries**

2 cups minced onion
¼ cup butter
2 pounds ground beef
¼ cup tomato paste

¼ cup minced basil
dash of cayenne pepper
salt and pepper, to taste

In a skillet, sauté the onion in the butter until soft. Add the beef and cook, stirring until the meat loses its color. Stir in the tomato paste, basil, cayenne, salt, and pepper. Use to fill logs, turnovers, or rounds.

▶ Can be prepared 2 days in advance.

≡ *Petites Pâtes de Provence* *(Small Provençal Pastries)*

== **Yield: 25 pastries**

1 can anchovy fillets
¼ cup minced onion
2 garlic cloves
¼ to ½ cup olive oil
⅓ cup minced parsley

2 cups cooked ground ham or veal
2 eggs
salt and pepper, to taste

== **Yield: 100 pastries**

4 cans anchovy fillets
1 cup minced onion
8 garlic cloves
1 to 2 cups olive oil
1⅓ cups minced parsley

2 quarts cooked ground ham or veal
8 eggs
salt and pepper, to taste

1. In a food processor, purée the anchovies, onion, and garlic. With the motor running, add just enough oil to make a smooth mixture. Add the parsley and ham with on-off turns. Transfer to a bowl and add the eggs. Correct the seasoning with salt and pepper.

2. Use to fill pillows or turnovers.

▶ Can be prepared 2 days in advance.

≡ *Veal Pasties*

Pasties are an edible lunch box for English workmen, especially those from Cornwall—meat and potatoes wrapped in pastry for easy eating. This version leaves out the potatoes but contains fruits and spices reminiscent of the trade routes.

═ Yield: 20 pasties

¾ pound cooked ground veal
2 hard-cooked eggs, chopped
3 tablespoons currants
3 tablespoons pine nuts
3 tablespoons minced prunes
3 tablespoons minced dates
1 teaspoon brown sugar
¼ teaspoon crushed fennel
   seed

¼ teaspoon cinnamon
¼ teaspoon salt
⅛ teaspoon ground cloves
⅛ teaspoon ground ginger
⅛ teaspoon grated nutmeg
cream cheese pastry (page 543)

═ Yield: 80 pasties

3 pounds cooked ground veal
8 hard-cooked eggs, chopped
1½ cups currants
1½ cups pine nuts
1½ cups minced prunes
1½ cups minced dates
4 teaspoons brown sugar

1 teaspoon crushed fennel seed
1 teaspoon cinnamon
1 teaspoon salt
½ teaspoon ground cloves
½ teaspoon ground ginger
½ teaspoon grated nutmeg
cream cheese pastry (page 543)

1. In a bowl, mix the veal, eggs, currants, pine nuts, prunes, dates, brown sugar, fennel, cinnamon, salt, cloves, ginger, and nutmeg.

2. Use to fill turnovers or logs.

▶ Can be prepared 2 days in advance.

≡ *Veal Turnovers*

═ Yield: 36 turnovers

½ cup minced onion
3 tablespoons butter
1 pound ground veal
1 tablespoon flour
¾ cup beef stock

2 hard-cooked eggs, minced
2 tablespoons minced parsley
1 teaspoon salt
½ teaspoon rosemary
¼ teaspoon pepper

== **Yield: 72 turnovers**

1 cup minced onion	4 hard-cooked eggs, minced
⅓ cup butter	¼ cup minced parsley
2 pounds ground veal	2 teaspoons salt
2 tablespoons flour	1 teaspoon rosemary
1½ cups beef stock	½ teaspoon pepper

1. In a skillet, sauté the onion in the butter until golden. Add the veal and cook, stirring until lightly browned. Transfer to a bowl with a slotted spoon.

2. Stir the flour into the pan and cook, stirring up the browned bits until golden. Add the beef stock and cook until it thickens. Stir into the veal and add the eggs, parsley, salt, rosemary, and pepper.

3. Use to fill turnovers, logs, rounds, or rissoles.

► Can be prepared 2 days in advance.

≡ *Samosas (Curried Meat Pastries)*

These pastries are the Indian version of rissoles. Note the different method of shaping them. They can be formed into traditional turnovers and log shapes as well.

== **Yield: 36 pastries**

¾ cup minced onion	1 teaspoon chili powder
2 garlic cloves, minced	1 teaspoon curry powder
2 tablespoons oil	¼ cup tomato paste
1 pound ground lamb	salt, to taste
1 tablespoon ground coriander	yogurt pastry (page 543)
1 teaspoon grated gingerroot	oil for frying

== **Yield: 144 pastries**

3 cups minced onion	1½ tablespoons chili powder
8 garlic cloves, minced	1½ tablespoons curry powder
½ cup oil	1 cup tomato paste
4 pounds ground lamb	salt, to taste
¼ cup ground coriander	yogurt pastry (page 543)
1½ tablespoons grated gingerroot	oil for frying

1. In a skillet, sauté the onion and garlic in the oil until soft and golden. Add the lamb, coriander, gingerroot, chili powder, and curry powder. Cook, stirring until the lamb loses its color. Stir in the tomato paste and season with salt. Chill.

2. Roll the dough into a large rectangle and cut out 4-inch circles. Cut the circles in half and moisten the edges. Shape into cones and fill. Pinch the edges closed.

3. Heat the oil to 375°F and fry until golden.

▶ Can be prepared for filling 1 day in advance.

≡ Sanbusak (Baked Lamb Pastries)

These are similar to samosas, except that they are baked.

≡ **Yield: 36 pastries**

¾ cup minced onion
2 tablespoons oil
1 pound ground lamb
½ cup minced parsley
½ cup toasted pine nuts
⅓ cup minced raisins
3 tablespoons lemon juice

2 tablespoons minced
 coriander (cilantro)
2 tablespoons tomato paste
cayenne pepper, to taste
salt and pepper, to taste
yogurt pastry (page 543)
dorure

≡ **Yield: 144 pastries**

3 cups minced onion
½ cup oil
4 pounds ground lamb
2 cups minced parsley
2 cups toasted pine nuts
1⅓ cups minced raisins
¾ cup lemon juice

½ cup minced coriander
 (cilantro)
½ cup tomato paste
cayenne pepper, to taste
salt and pepper, to taste
yogurt pastry (page 543)
dorure

1. Preheat the oven to 400°F.

2. In a skillet, sauté the onion in the oil until soft and golden. Stir in the lamb, parsley, pine nuts, raisins, lemon juice, and coriander. Cook, stirring until the lamb loses its color. Stir in the tomato paste, cayenne, salt, and pepper. Chill.

3. Make turnovers, brush with dorure, and bake for about 25 minutes or until golden.

▶ The filling can be prepared 2 days in advance. The baked pastries can be frozen.

≡ Lamb Turnovers

═ Yield: 36 turnovers

2 cups cooked ground lamb
½ cup cooked rice
¼ cup minced parsley
1 hard-cooked egg, minced
2 tablespoons softened butter
2 tablespoons sour cream

1½ tablespoons minced chives
½ teaspoon grated lemon rind
salt and pepper, to taste
cream cheese pastry (page 543)
dorure

═ Yield: 144 turnovers

2 quarts cooked ground lamb
2 cups cooked rice
1 cup minced parsley
4 hard-cooked eggs, minced
½ cup softened butter
½ cup sour cream

⅓ cup minced chives
2 teaspoons grated lemon rind
salt and pepper, to taste
cream cheese pastry (page 543)
dorure

1. Preheat the oven to 375°F.

2. In a bowl, mix the lamb, rice, parsley, egg(s), butter, sour cream, chives, lemon rind, salt, and pepper.

3. Roll the dough between sheets of waxed paper to ⅛-inch thickness. Cut out 3-inch squares and fill for turnovers. Brush with dorure. Bake until golden, about 24 to 30 minutes.

▶ The filling can be prepared 2 days in advance.

≡ Lamb Filling for Turnovers, Puffs, and Phyllo

═ Yield: 36 pastries

3 tablespoons butter
1 pound finely ground lamb
1 egg, beaten
1 teaspoon salt
⅛ teaspoon grated nutmeg

⅛ teaspoon ground allspice
⅛ teaspoon cinnamon
¼ cup currants
½ cup cooked rice

═ Yield: 144 pastries

¾ cup butter
4 pounds finely ground lamb
4 eggs, beaten
4 teaspoons salt
½ teaspoon grated nutmeg

½ teaspoon ground allspice
½ teaspoon cinnamon
1 cup currants
2 cups cooked rice

In a skillet, melt the butter and sauté the meat and egg(s), tossing with a fork until the meat loses its red color. Add the salt, nutmeg, allspice, cinnamon, currants, and rice. Cool.

▶ Can be prepared 2 days in advance.

≡ Lebanese Barquettes of Lamb

═ Yield: 25 barquettes

1½ cups minced onion
½ cup butter
1 pound cooked ground lamb
½ cup golden raisins
¼ cup currants
½ cup pine nuts

2 tablespoons tomato paste
2 garlic cloves, minced
½ cup minced parsley
25 barquettes, baked
½ cup crisp fried onions

═ Yield: 100 barquettes

1½ quarts minced onion
2 cups butter
4 pounds cooked ground lamb
2 cups golden raisins
1 cup currants
2 cups pine nuts

½ cup tomato paste
8 garlic cloves, minced
2 cups minced parsley
100 barquettes, baked
2 cups crisp fried onions

1. In a skillet, sauté the onion in the butter until brown. Add the lamb, raisins, currants, pine nuts, tomato paste, and garlic and heat. Stir in the parsley.

2. Spoon the mixture into warm barquettes and sprinkle with the fried onions.

▶ Filling can be prepared 2 days in advance and reheated.

≡ Pork and Crab or Shrimp Pastry Rolls

═ Yield: 36 pastries

½ pound lean ground pork
¼ cup flaked crabmeat or
  minced cooked shrimp
¼ cup minced water chestnuts
2 tablespoons minced scallions
2 tablespoons bread crumbs
1 tablespoon soy sauce

1 teaspoon minced gingerroot
1 egg, beaten
½ teaspoon minced garlic
¼ teaspoon salt
¼ teaspoon Asian sesame oil
cream cheese pastry (page 543)

═ **Yield: 144 pastries**

2 pounds lean ground pork
1 cup flaked crabmeat or
   minced cooked shrimp
1 cup minced water chestnuts
½ cup minced scallions
½ cup bread crumbs
¼ cup soy sauce

1½ tablespoons minced
   gingerroot
4 eggs, beaten
2 teaspoons minced garlic
1 teaspoon salt
1 teaspoon Asian sesame oil
cream cheese pastry (page 543)

1. In a skillet, sauté the pork until it loses its color; do not brown. Add the crab or shrimp, water chestnuts, scallions, bread crumbs, soy sauce, gingerroot, egg(s), garlic, salt, and sesame oil. If the mixture is too runny, add more bread crumbs.

2. Use to fill turnovers, logs, or rissoles.

▶ Can be prepared 2 days in advance.

═ *Ham and Chicken Tarts*

═ **Yield: 25 tarts**

1 cup diced ham
1 cup diced cooked chicken
1 cup béchamel sauce
   (page 59)
½ cup minced onion

grated rind of 1 lemon
pinch of mace
salt and pepper, to taste
25 tart shells, baked

═ **Yield: 100 tarts**

1 quart diced ham
1 quart diced cooked chicken
1 quart béchamel sauce
   (page 59)
2 cups minced onion

grated rind of 4 lemons
1 teaspoon mace
salt and pepper, to taste
100 tart shells, baked

1. Preheat the oven to 375°F.

2. In a bowl, mix the ham, chicken, béchamel, onion, lemon rind, mace, salt, and pepper. Fill the tarts and bake until hot.

▶ Filling can be prepared 2 days in advance.

☰ *Curried Ham Filling for Rissoles or Turnovers*

= **Yield: 25 pastries**

1 cup ground lean ham	1 teaspoon minced onion
½ cup thick velouté (page 62),	½ teaspoon dry mustard
or ½ cup sour cream and 1	¼ teaspoon salt
tablespoon mayonnaise	pinch of cayenne pepper
1 teaspoon curry powder	pinch of minced garlic

= **Yield: 100 pastries**

1 quart ground lean ham	1½ tablespoons minced onion
2 cups thick velouté (page 62),	2 teaspoons dry mustard
or 2 cups sour cream and ¼	1 teaspoon salt
cup mayonnaise	½ teaspoon cayenne pepper
1½ tablespoons curry powder	½ teaspoon minced garlic

1. In a bowl, mix the ham, velouté, curry powder, onion, mustard, salt, cayenne pepper, and garlic.

2. Use to fill turnovers, logs, rissoles, or small puffs.

▶ Can be prepared 2 days in advance.

☰ *Mozzarella and Salami Rounds*

= **Yield: 36 pastries**

1 cup diced Genoa salami	pâte brisée (pages 541–542)
1 cup diced mozzarella cheese	dorure

= **Yield: 144 pastries**

1 quart diced Genoa salami	pâte brisée (pages 541–542)
1 quart diced mozzarella	dorure
cheese	

1. Preheat the oven to 400°F.

2. In a bowl, mix the salami and cheese. Cut the pastry into 3-inch circles and place a few squares of cheese and salami on top. Shape into turnovers or pillows. Brush with dorure and bake until golden, about 20 minutes.

▶ Can be frozen and reheated.

NOTE: Can also be used to fill rissoles.

≡ *Chausson à la Napolitaine (Neapolitan Turnover)*

This is a slightly more elaborate version of the preceding recipe. It can be further enhanced by adding minced oregano to taste.

═ Yield: 36

1 cup ricotta cheese	¼ pound salami, diced
1 cup diced mozzarella cheese	1 egg
⅔ cup grated Romano cheese	salt and pepper, to taste

═ Yield: 144

1 quart ricotta cheese	1 pound salami, diced
1 quart diced mozzarella cheese	4 eggs
	salt and pepper, to taste
2⅔ cup grated Romano cheese	

1. Preheat the oven to 400°F.

2. In a bowl, beat the ricotta until smooth and fold in the mozzarella, Romano, salami, egg(s), salt, and pepper.

3. Shape into turnovers or pillows. Bake or deep-fry.

▶ Can be frozen and reheated.

≡ *Saucisses en Croûte (Sausages in Pastry)*

If you use miniature hot dogs, these are called "pigs in a blanket."

═ Yield: 24 to 60 pieces

8 to 12 smoked links or 1 pound kielbasa or other sausage	mustard or mustard sauce (pages 41–45)
pâte brisée (pages 541–542), cream cheese pastry (page 543), or pâte feuilletée (page 601)	dorure

1. Preheat the oven to 375°F.

2. If necessary, cook the sausage and peel before wrapping in the pastry.

3. Roll the pastry ¼ inch thick and cut into rectangles large enough to enclose the sausages and overlap slightly. If desired, brush the pastry with mustard before wrapping. Wrap the sausages and brush with dorure. Bake until golden. If the sausages are small, serve whole; if large, cut into bite-size pieces. Serve with mustard or mustard sauce.

▶ Can be frozen after baking and reheated.

≡ *Empanadilla Filling IV (Sausage Filling)*

== **Yield: 25 pastries**

½ pound garlic sausage (chorizo), peeled	1 egg

== **Yield: 100 pastries**

2 pounds garlic sausage (chorizo), peeled	1 egg

In a food processor, chop the sausage finely. Transfer to a bowl and beat in the egg. Use to fill turnovers.

▶ Serve warm. Can be prepared 1 day in advance.

≡ *Empanadilla Filling V (Veal and Tomato Filling)*

== **Yield: 36 pastries**

½ cup minced onion	1 pimiento, chopped
1 garlic clove, minced	1 tablespoon minced parsley
1 tablespoon olive oil	1 tablespoon minced Spanish
2 ounces chorizo, chopped	olives
1 pound ground veal	salt and pepper, to taste
¼ cup dry white wine	oil for frying
3 tablespoons tomato paste	

= **Yield: 144 pastries**

2 cups minced onion	¾ cup tomato paste
4 garlic cloves, minced	4 pimientos, chopped
¼ cup olive oil	¼ cup minced parsley
½ pound chorizo, chopped	¼ cup minced Spanish olives
4 pounds ground veal	salt and pepper, to taste
1 cup dry white wine	oil for frying

1. In a skillet, sauté the onion and garlic in the oil until soft. Add the chorizo and cook, stirring, for 5 minutes. Increase the heat, add the veal, and cook until browned.

2. Lower the heat and add the wine, tomato paste, pimiento(s), parsley, olives, salt, and pepper. Simmer, covered, for 20 minutes.

3. Use to fill turnovers.

▶ Can be prepared 1 day in advance.

14

Pâte à Chou

Cocktail puffs are one of the most appealing hors d'oeuvre—guests enjoy the variety of fillings and luscious flavors and cooks appreciate their simple, quick preparation. Literally translated, *pâte à chou* means cabbage paste (once baked, the puffs resemble little cabbages). In the United States they are called puff pastry, cream puffs, cocktail puffs, and on rare occasion, chou pastry. The pastry itself should not be confused with *pâte feuilletée*, or French puff pastry.

The recipe is simplicity itself. Bring a liquid to a full rolling boil, add the flour all at once and cook, stirring until it forms a ball. Remove from the heat and let cool a few minutes. By hand or with a food processor or mixer, beat in the eggs, preferably one at a time. The pastry is then ready to shape and bake. Refrigerated, it will hold for several hours without difficulty. I have found no difference in using buttered or unbuttered baking sheets; therefore I do not butter the sheets.

Shaping Pâte à Chou

Round Puffs
With a pastry bag fitted with a no. 5 large plain tip, pipe small mounds about the size of walnuts, about ½ inch apart.

Eclairs
With a pastry bag fitted with a no. 5 large plain tip, pipe fingers about ½ inch thick and 2½ inches long.

Cocktail Puff Swans

1. Pipe pâte à chou into S curves with a no. 2 large plain tip and into ovals with a no. 5 large plain tip.

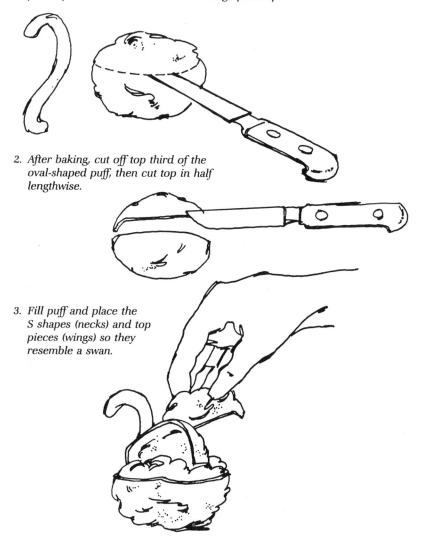

2. After baking, cut off top third of the oval-shaped puff, then cut top in half lengthwise.

3. Fill puff and place the S shapes (necks) and top pieces (wings) so they resemble a swan.

Swans

With a pastry bag fitted with a no. 5 large open star tip, pipe 3-inch-long ovals. With a no. 1 or 2 plain pastry tip, pipe figure S's. Bake until crisp.

When baked, cut off the top third from the ovals and then cut the cap in half lengthwise.

Fill the bottom and insert an S-shaped pastry into the larger end of the oval. Place the cut sides of the cap into the cream at an angle to simulate wings.

—— *Baking* ——

Bake at 400°F until puffed, golden, and cooked. To test, remove one from the oven. It should feel light. Break it open and examine the center. It should be almost completely dry. If the center is moist, let another puff sit out of the oven for a few minutes. If it collapses, it needs to bake longer. With this recipe one or two test puffs is not a serious loss.

There are two schools of thought on how long to bake puffs. My preference is to cook them until the insides are barely moist and the outside no longer has beads of moisture. After they cool, the shells will have a soft, not soggy, finish. The other method is to dry them out completely; these will be crisp. The choice is yours.

—— *Freezing* ——

Although a recipe may make more puffs than you think you need, make them all. Puffs are one of the best pastries to freeze for emergency use. Pack them loosely in plastic bags and freeze. They will thaw quickly at room temperature.

—— *Deep-Frying* ——

As with other pastries, pâte à choux can be deep-fried. The pastry is usually mixed with other ingredients and deep-fried to make beignets, or fritters. Although it is not customary, if the pastries are fried until the centers are fully cooked, they can be filled. As with all deep-fried food, they are best when fried and served immediately.

—— *Fillings* ——

Don't be limited by just using the fillings in this chapter. Whatever can be used to fill a pastry can be used to fill a puff. Review the recipes for dips, spreads, and fillings for other pastries to give you additional ideas for creating your own specialties.

The puffs can usually be filled several hours before serving. If they are to be served warm, arrange the filled puffs on baking sheets and heat in a 350°F oven. Beware of filling puffs too early if the filling is very moist.

To fill baked puffs, cut three quarters of the way through, horizontally, about half way up the puff. Lift the cap without removing it completely and fill with a teaspoonful of filling, or, if the mixture is not too coarse, use a pastry bag fitted with a large tip. Gently press the top of the puff over the filling. A small amount of filling showing is not only attractive, but also gives an idea of what is to come. Take care not to overstuff the puff so the filling spills over the sides. This looks messy and makes it hard to pick up. Attempts to completely hide the filling often leave a puff with too little filling for the amount of pastry.

≡ Pâte à Chou (Cocktail Pastry)

═ Yield: 50 to 90 puffs

1 cup water	1 cup flour
½ cup butter	4 eggs
½ teaspoon salt	

═ Yield: 200 to 360 puffs

1 quart water	1 quart flour
2 cups butter	16 eggs
2 teaspoons salt	

1. Preheat the oven to 400°F.

2. In a saucepan, bring the water, butter, and salt to a full rolling boil. When the butter has melted, dump in the flour all at once and cook, stirring vigorously until the mixture forms a ball and leaves the side of the pan. There should be a thin film of the paste on the bottom of the pan. Remove from the heat and let cool for about 5 minutes.

3. Place the dough in a food processor and add all the eggs. Turn on the machine and process until completely blended. or place the dough in a mixer and add the eggs, one at a time, fully incorporating each egg before adding the next. Or, beat the eggs in by hand one at a time, fully incorporating each egg before adding the next. This is especially important if you are making the dough by hand. Powerful mixers or food processors can handle several eggs at a time, but the mixture must be beaten thoroughly until the eggs are fully incorporated.

4. The dough can be used immediately, or it can rest at room temperature or in the refrigerator for 4 to 5 hours.

5. Shape into puffs or eclairs. Bake until light and golden, about 30 minutes depending on the size. The surface will look dry, with no beads of moisture.

▶ Can be frozen after baking.

NOTE: Some cooks like to apply a dorure (page 539) to the tops of the puffs before baking for added gloss, but this is not necessary.

☰ *Cornmeal Puffs*

═ Yield: 75 puffs

1 cup water	¾ cup flour
½ cup butter	2 tablespoons yellow cornmeal
½ teaspoon salt	4 eggs

═ Yield: 300 puffs

1 quart water	3 cups flour
2 cups butter	⅓ cup yellow cornmeal
2 teaspoons salt	16 eggs

1. In a saucepan, bring the water, butter, and salt to a full rolling boil. Add the flour and cornmeal all at once and cook, stirring until the mixture forms a ball and leaves the sides of the pan. Remove from the heat and let cool for 5 minutes. In a food processor or mixer, beat in the eggs one at a time, beating well after each addition.

2. Shape and bake as for pâte à chou.

☰ *La Gougère (Cheese Pastry Ring)*

This specialty from Burgundy makes an attractive, delicious hors d'oeuvre. You can arrange it on a baking sheet several hours ahead. Shortly before guests arrive, pop it into the oven and serve steaming hot. Tell guests to pull it apart with their fingers.

═ Yield: one 12-inch ring

1 small recipe pâte à chou (page 572)	¾ cup grated Gruyère cheese

═ Yield: four 10-inch rings

1 large recipe pâte à chou (page 572)	3 cups grated Gruyère cheese

1. Preheat the oven to 400°F.

2. Prepare the pastry and beat in three-fourths of the cheese. With a spoon, drop large dollops of the pastry onto a buttered baking sheet in a large circle. Drawing the spoon away from the center will give it a star-like shape.

3. Sprinkle the top with the remaining cheese. Bake about 45 minutes. It will be puffed and browned. Without removing it from the oven, pierce around the edges with the point of a knife to let the steam escape and bake 5 minutes longer. Serve immediately.

▶ Cannot be made in advance.

NOTE: For a sharper flavor, add cayenne pepper, white pepper, grated nutmeg, and Dijon mustard to taste to the pâte à chou batter.

For large events where serving large rings would be impractical, make individual gougères by dropping tablespoonfuls of dough onto buttered sheets. Bake and serve immediately. These should not be baked ahead.

≡ *Cheese Filling*

═ **Yield: 25 puffs**

3 tablespoons cream cheese	1 teaspoon Dijon mustard
5 tablespoons butter	¼ cup ground ham
1 tablespoon minced parsley	salt and pepper, to taste
1 tablespoon minced chives	
1 tablespoon minced watercress	

═ **Yield: 100 puffs**

¾ cup cream cheese	¼ cup minced watercress
1¼ cups butter	1½ tablespoons Dijon mustard
¼ cup minced parsley	1 cup ground ham
¼ cup minced chives	salt and pepper, to taste

1. In a bowl, cream the cream cheese, butter, parsley, chives, watercress, and mustard. Beat in the ham and season with salt and pepper.

2. Use to fill puffs and barquettes, or as a spread.

▶ Can be prepared 2 days in advance.

≡ Ramequins de Crème de Camembert (Cheese Cases with Camembert Cream)

═ Yield: 75 puffs

1 small recipe pâte à chou (page 572)	1 ripe Camembert cheese
	1 cup white wine
1 cup grated Gruyère cheese	¼ cup softened butter

═ Yield: 300 puffs

1 large recipe pâte à chou (page 572)	4 ripe Camembert cheeses
	4 cups white wine
1 quart grated Gruyère cheese	1 cup softened butter

1. Prepare the pâte à chou, beat in the Gruyère, and bake as usual.
2. In a food processor, purée the Camembert, wine, and butter.
3. Fill the puffs and serve; warm them in the oven if desired.

▶ Filling can be prepared 2 days in advance.

≡ Cold Cheese Filling for Puffs

═ Yield: 25 puffs

1 cup heavy cream, whipped	1 egg yolk
½ cup grated Gruyère or Cheddar cheese	salt, to taste

═ Yield: 100 puffs

1 quart heavy cream, whipped	4 egg yolks
2 cups grated Gruyère or Cheddar cheese	salt, to taste

In a bowl, fold the cream into the cheese, egg yolks, and salt.

▶ Will not keep more than a few hours, refrigerated.

≡ Fondue de Fromage pour Pâtisseries (Cheese Filling for Puffs)

═ Yield: 50 puffs

1 cup béchamel sauce for croquettes (page 60)	pinch of grated nutmeg
	Tabasco sauce, to taste
1 cup grated Gruyère cheese	3 to 4 tablespoons heavy cream,
⅓ cup grated Parmesan cheese	if needed

═ **Yield: 200 puffs**

1 quart béchamel for
  croquettes (page 60)
1 quart grated Gruyère cheese
1⅓ cups grated Parmesan
  cheese

½ teaspoon grated nutmeg
Tabasco sauce, to taste
¾ to 1 cup heavy cream, if
  needed

1. In a saucepan, bring the béchamel to a boil, stir in the cheeses, nutmeg, and Tabasco sauce. Let cool. If the mixture is too thick, thin with heavy cream. It should hold its shape on a spoon.

2. Use to fill puffs or barquettes, or as a base for croquettes.

▶ Can be prepared 2 days in advance.

═ *Choux Mexicains (Avocado-Filled Puffs)*

═ **Yield: 20 puffs**

1 cup mashed ripe avocado
1 tablespoon lemon or lime
  juice

1½ teaspoons grated onion
salt and cayenne pepper, to
  taste

═ **Yield: 80 puffs**

1 quart mashed ripe avocado
¼ cup lemon or lime juice
2 tablespoons minced onion

salt and cayenne pepper, to
  taste

In a food processor, purée the avocado, lemon juice, onion, salt, and cayenne. Use to fill puffs.

▶ Keep tightly covered and use within 2 hours.

═ *Cucumber Filling*

This is a light, refreshing, summery filling.

═ **Yield: 25 puffs**

2 cups peeled, seeded, and
  diced cucumber
¼ cup minced onion

1 tablespoon minced parsley
salt and pepper, to taste
mayonnaise

== **Yield: 100 puffs**

2 quarts peeled, seeded, and
diced cucumber
1 cup minced onion

¼ cup minced parsley
salt and pepper, to taste
mayonnaise

In a bowl, mix the cucumber, parsley, onion, salt, and pepper. Add just enough mayonnaise to bind. Use to fill puffs or barquettes.

▶ Filling can be made 2 hours in advance; fill puffs just before serving.

≡ *Clam Filling I*

== **Yield: 25 puffs**

2 10½-ounce cans minced
clams, drained with liquid
reserved
1 cup mayonnaise
½ cup minced celery
1 tablespoon minced green
pepper

1 tablespoon minced onion
1 envelope unflavored gelatin
1 teaspoon Worcestershire
sauce
½ teaspoon dry mustard
salt and pepper, to taste

== **Yield: 100 puffs**

1 48-ounce can minced clams,
drained with liquid reserved
1 quart mayonnaise
2 cups minced celery
¼ cup minced green pepper
¼ cup minced onion

4 envelopes unflavored gelatin
1½ tablespoons Worcestershire
sauce
2 teaspoons dry mustard
salt and pepper, to taste

1. In a bowl, mix the clams, mayonnaise, celery, pepper, and onion.
2. In a saucepan, soften the gelatin in ½ (2) cups reserved clam juice and dissolve over low heat. Add the dissolved gelatin mixture, Worcestershire sauce, mustard, salt, and pepper.
3. Cool until almost set and fill puffs.

▶ Filled puffs can be kept overnight, refrigerated.

≡ *Clam Filling II*

= Yield: 25 puffs

½ pound cream cheese,
softened
1 6½-ounce can minced clams,
drained
1 tablespoon minced onion

2 teaspoons lemon juice
1½ teaspoons Worcestershire
sauce
1 garlic clove, minced
¼ to ½ cup sour cream

= Yield: 100 puffs

2 pounds cream cheese,
softened
4 6½-ounce cans minced
clams, drained
¼ cup minced onion

3 tablespoons lemon juice
2 tablespoons Worcestershire
sauce
4 garlic cloves, minced
1 to 2 cups sour cream

In a bowl, mix the cheese, clams, onion, lemon juice, Worcestershire sauce, and garlic. Add enough sour cream to bind. Use to fill puffs or barquettes.

▶ Filling can be made 2 days in advance.
NOTE: This filling can also be used as a spread.

≡ *Clam-Filled Clam Puffs*

These clam puffs can also be filled with any other compatible filling.

= Yield: 25 puffs

1¾ cups minced clams, drained
and ½ cup liquor reserved
¼ cup butter
1½ teaspoons minced dill
pinch of cayenne pepper

½ cup flour
2 eggs
½ cup sour cream
2 tablespoons minced chives
salt and pepper, to taste

= Yield: 100 puffs

7 cups minced clams, drained
and 2 cups liquor reserved
1 cup butter
2 tablespoons minced dill
¼ teaspoon cayenne pepper

2 cups flour
8 eggs
2 cups sour cream
½ cup minced chives
salt and pepper, to taste

1. Preheat the oven to 400°F.

2. In a saucepan, combine the reserved clam liquor, butter, dill, and cayenne. Bring to a full rolling boil and add the flour all at once. Stir until the mixture leaves the sides of the pan.

3. Remove from the heat and beat in the eggs one at a time until fully incorporated. Beat in ½ cup (*2 cups*) of the minced clams.

4. Shape into puffs and bake until puffed and golden. Cool.

5. In a bowl, mix the sour cream, remaining clams, chives, salt, and pepper.

▶ Puffs and filling can be prepared 2 days in advance. Fill shortly before serving.

≡ Crabmeat Avocado Filling

═ Yield: 25 puffs

8 ounces crabmeat, picked over	1 tablespoon mayonnaise
2 tablespoons lemon juice	1 scallion, minced
½ avocado, mashed	½ to 1 teaspoon horseradish
1 tablespoon sour cream	salt and pepper, to taste

═ Yield: 100 puffs

2 pounds crabmeat, picked over	¼ cup mayonnaise
½ cup lemon juice	4 scallions, minced
2 avocados, mashed	2 to 4 teaspoons horseradish
¼ cup sour cream	salt and pepper, to taste

In a bowl, toss the crabmeat with the lemon juice. Add avocado, sour cream, mayonnaise, scallion(s), horseradish, salt, and pepper. Use to fill puffs or barquettes.

▶ Prepare the filling and fill puffs no more than 2 hours in advance.

≡ Smoked Oyster Puffs

═ Yield: 25 puffs

1 can smoked oysters	lemon juice, to taste
3 tablespoons horseradish	

= **Yield: 100 puffs**

4 cans smoked oysters

¾ cup horseradish

lemon juice, to taste

Split the puffs, insert a smoked oyster, and dab with horseradish and a sprinkle of lemon juice. Serve immediately. Can also be used to fill barquettes.

▶ Fill just before serving.

= *Mousse de Saumon Fumé*
(Smoked Salmon Mousse Filling)

= **Yield: 40 puffs**

6 ounces smoked salmon

⅓ cup butter

pinch of cayenne pepper

pinch of grated nutmeg

salt, to taste

1½ teaspoons unflavored
gelatin

½ cup chicken stock

2 tablespoons lemon juice

¼ cup Cognac

½ cup heavy cream, whipped

red food coloring, optional

= **Yield: 200 puffs**

1⅔ pounds smoked salmon

1⅔ pounds butter

½ teaspoon cayenne pepper

½ teaspoon grated nutmeg

salt, to taste

2½ tablespoons unflavored
gelatin

2½ cups chicken stock

⅔ cup lemon juice

1 cup Cognac

2½ cups heavy cream, whipped

red food coloring, optional

1. In a food processor, purée the salmon, butter, cayenne, nutmeg, and salt.

2. In a saucepan, soften the gelatin in the stock and dissolve over low heat. Cool. Add to the salmon mixture and correct the seasoning with the lemon juice and Cognac.

3. In a large bowl, fold the whipped cream into the salmon. If desired, tint with the food coloring. Use to fill puffs or barquettes.

▶ Filled puffs can be kept for 6 hours.

NOTE: Only use the food color if the mixture is too pale, and use it sparingly. Remember that food color tends to intensify in the air, so add barely enough to hint at the color you want. In a few hours it will darken to the shade you wish.

≡ Shrimp and Avocado Filling

═ Yield: 50 puffs

1 pound shrimp, cooked and minced
2 cups minced avocado
4 hard-cooked eggs, sieved
1 cup mayonnaise

½ cup minced scallions
¼ cup lemon juice
½ tablespoon minced tarragon
Tabasco sauce, to taste
salt and pepper, to taste

═ Yield: 200 puffs

4 pounds shrimp, cooked and minced
2 quarts minced avocado
16 hard-cooked eggs, sieved
1 quart mayonnaise

2 cups minced scallions
1 cup lemon juice
2 tablespoons minced tarragon
Tabasco sauce, to taste
salt and pepper, to taste

In a bowl, mix the shrimp, avocado, eggs, mayonnaise, scallions, lemon juice, tarragon, Tabasco sauce, salt, and pepper. Use to fill puffs or barquettes.

▶ Filling can be kept 4 to 6 hours, refrigerated.
NOTE: Avocado can turn dark easily. It helps to toss it with lemon juice before mixing it with the other ingredients.
This recipe is a good use for very tiny shrimp.
This filling should not look like a paste. The colors of shrimp, avocado, and egg should all be distinct.

≡ Curried Shrimp Filling

═ Yield: 25 puffs

¾ cup butter
1 tablespoon curry powder
½ pound shrimp, cooked, peeled, and deveined

lemon juice, to taste
salt and pepper, to taste

═ Yield: 100 puffs

3 cups butter
¼ cup curry powder
2 pounds shrimp, cooked, peeled, and deveined

lemon juice, to taste
salt and pepper, to taste

In a saucepan, melt the butter, add the curry powder, and let simmer for 5 minutes. In a food processor, mince the shrimp, and with the machine running, pour in the hot curry butter, lemon juice, salt, and pepper. Cool. Use to fill puffs, barquettes, or vegetables.

▶ Can be prepared 2 days in advance, refrigerated.

☰ *Deviled Filling*

═ Yield: 50 puffs

2 cups ground cooked chicken	1 tablespoon Dijon mustard
1 cup ground ham	1 tablespoon minced dill
½ cup butter	4 teaspoons minced gherkins

═ Yield: 200 puffs

2 quarts ground cooked chicken	¼ cup Dijon mustard
1 quart ground ham	¼ cup minced dill
2 cups butter	⅓ cup minced gherkins

In a bowl, beat the chicken, ham, and butter until light and fluffy. Beat in the mustard, dill, and gherkins. Correct the seasoning with salt and pepper. Use to fill puffs, barquettes, or vegetables.

▶ Filling can be prepared 1 day in advance.

☰ *Mulligatawny Filling*

═ Yield: 25 puffs

2 cups finely diced cooked chicken	¼ cup raisins
	2 tablespoons chopped walnuts
¼ cup finely diced unpeeled apple	½ cup mayonnaise
¼ cup finely diced celery	curry powder, to taste

═ Yield: 100 puffs

2 quarts finely diced cooked chicken	1 cup raisins
	½ cup chopped walnuts
1 cup finely diced unpeeled apple	2 cups mayonnaise
1 cup finely diced celery	curry powder, to taste

In a bowl, mix the chicken, apple, celery, raisins, walnuts, and just enough mayonnaise to bind. Add curry powder to taste. Use to fill puffs, barquettes, or vegetables.

▶ Filling can be prepared 1 day in advance.

≡ Lamb Filling I

=== Yield: 25 puffs
2 cups cooked ground lamb   salt and pepper, to taste
¼ cup minced green pepper   mayonnaise

=== Yield: 100 puffs
2 quarts cooked ground lamb   salt and pepper, to taste
1 cup minced green pepper   mayonnaise

In a bowl, mix the lamb, green pepper, salt, pepper, and mayonnaise. Use to fill puffs, barquettes, or vegetables.

▶ Can be prepared 2 days in advance.

≡ Lamb Filling II

=== Yield: 25 puffs
1 cup cooked ground lamb   ¼ cup mayonnaise
½ cup chopped black olives   salt and pepper, to taste
2 tablespoons ketchup

=== Yield: 100 puffs
1 quart cooked ground lamb   1 cup mayonnaise
2 cups chopped black olives   salt and pepper, to taste
½ cup ketchup

In a bowl, mix the lamb, olives, ketchup, and just enough mayonnaise to bind. Correct the seasoning with salt and pepper. Use to fill puffs, barquettes, or vegetables.

▶ Can be prepared 2 days in advance.

≡ Lamb Filling III

= Yield: 25 puffs

1 cup cooked ground lamb	1 teaspoon minced mint
1 tablespoon capers	1 teaspoon salt
1 tablespoon lemon juice	pepper, to taste

= Yield: 100 puffs

1 quart cooked ground lamb	1½ tablespoons minced mint
¼ cup capers	1 tablespoon salt
¼ cup lemon juice	pepper, to taste

In a bowl, mix the lamb, capers, lemon juice, mint, salt, and pepper. Use to fill puffs, barquettes, or vegetables.

▶ Can be prepared 2 days in advance.
NOTE: If desired, add yogurt to bind.

≡ Tongue Filling

= Yield: 25 puffs

2 cups minced cooked tongue	3 to 4 tablespoons mayonnaise
3 tablespoons capers	salt and pepper, to taste

= Yield: 100 puffs

2 quarts minced cooked tongue	¾ to 1 cup mayonnaise
¾ cup capers	salt and pepper, to taste

In a bowl, mix the tongue, capers, and enough mayonnaise to bind. Correct the seasoning with salt and pepper. Use to fill puffs, barquettes, or vegetables.

▶ Can be prepared 2 days in advance.

≡ Mortadella Cucumber Filling

= Yield: 40 puffs

1 cup peeled, seeded, and minced cucumber	¼ pound mortadella, minced
1 tablespoon salt	½ pound cream cheese
	pepper, to taste

= **Yield: 160 puffs**

1 quart peeled, seeded, and
  minced cucumber
¼ cup salt

1 pound mortadella, minced
2 pounds cream cheese
pepper, to taste

1. In a colander, mix the cucumber and salt and drain for 30 minutes. Press out excess moisture. Taste for salt and if too salty, rinse under cold water and press out excess moisture.

2. In a bowl, mix the cucumber, mortadella, cream cheese, and pepper.

3. Use to fill puffs, barquettes, or vegetables.

▶ Prepare shortly before serving.

—— *Hot Cocktail Puffs* ——

= *Pignatelles (Pine Cones)*

These fancifully named pastries are reminiscent of pine cones.

= **Yield: 100 puffs**

1 cup finely diced ham
1 cup finely diced Gruyère
  cheese

1 small recipe pâte à chou
  (page 572)
oil for frying

= **Yield: 400 puffs**

1 quart finely diced ham
1 quart finely diced Gruyère
  cheese

1 large recipe pâte à chou
  (page 572)
oil for frying

1. Beat the ham and cheese into the pâte à chou.

2. Heat the oil to 375°F. Fry teaspoonfuls of the paste until puffed and golden, about 2 minutes. Serve very hot.

▶ The paste can be prepared 6 hours in advance.

NOTE: For an Italian accent, substitute prosciutto and grated Parmesan; for a Dutch flavor, use ham, Edam, and caraway seeds.

≡ *Beignets de Fromage (Cheese Fritters)*

== **Yield: 100 fritters**

1 small recipe pâte à chou
(page 572)
⅔ cup grated Parmesan cheese
1 teaspoon dry mustard

1 teaspoon Dijon mustard
½ teaspoon baking powder
1 egg white
oil for frying

== **Yield: 400 fritters**

1 large recipe pâte à chou
(page 572)
2⅔ cups grated Parmesan
cheese
1½ tablespoons dry mustard

1½ tablespoons Dijon mustard
2 teaspoons baking powder
4 egg whites
oil for frying

1. While the pâte à chou is still warm, beat in the cheese, dry mustard, Dijon mustard, and baking powder.

2. Beat the egg white(s) until soft peaks form and fold into the dough.

3. Heat the oil to 375°F. Fry teaspoonfuls of the paste until puffed and golden. Serve at once.

▶ Can be prepared for frying 2 hours in advance.

≡ *Cheddar Puffs*

== **Yield: 100 puffs**

¾ cup grated sharp Cheddar
cheese
2 tablespoons sesame seeds,
fennel seeds, or caraway
seeds

1 small recipe pâte à chou
(page 572)
oil for frying

== **Yield: 400 puffs**

3 cups grated sharp Cheddar
cheese
½ cup sesame seeds, fennel
seeds, or caraway seeds

1 large recipe pâte à chou
(page 572)
oil for frying

1. Beat the cheese and seeds into the pâte à chou.

2. Heat the oil to 375°F. Fry teaspoonfuls of the paste until puffed and golden brown, about 1 minute. Serve immediately.

▶ Can be prepared for frying 6 hours in advance.

NOTE: This recipe can be baked in the same manner as la gougère (page 573).

≡ *Hot Cheese Filling*

=== **Yield: 50 puffs**

2 tablespoons butter	⅔ cups grated Gruyère or
3 tablespoons flour	sharp Cheddar cheese
1 cup heavy cream	salt and pepper, to taste
3 egg yolks	

=== **Yield: 200 puffs**

½ cup butter	2⅔ cups grated Gruyère or
¾ cup flour	sharp Cheddar cheese
1 quart heavy cream	salt and pepper, to taste
12 egg yolks	

1. In a saucepan, melt the butter, stir in the flour, and cook until the roux just begins to turn golden. Stir in the cream and cook until thick and smooth. Beat in the egg yolks and cheese and cook, over low heat, stirring, until the cheese melts. Correct seasoning with salt and pepper. Cool.

2. Reheat in a 350°F oven just before serving. Use to fill puffs or barquettes.

NOTE: The filling can be made more piquant by adding Tabasco sauce or cayenne pepper to taste. Gruyère filling can be flavored with tarragon, oregano, or marjoram to taste; Cheddar filling can be seasoned with caraway or fennel seeds.

≡ *Onion Fritters*

=== **Yield: 100 fritters**

½ pound onion, minced	oil for frying
1 small recipe pâte à chou	salt
(page 572)	

=== **Yield: 400 fritters**

2 pounds onion, minced	oil for frying
1 large recipe pâte à chou	salt
(page 572)	

1. Beat the onion into the pâte à chou.

2. Heat the oil to 375°F. Fry teaspoonfuls of the paste until puffed and golden. Sprinkle with salt and serve immediately.

▶ Can be prepared for frying 6 hours in advance.

NOTE: The fried puffs can be split and filled with salmon, caviar, or shrimp butter.

≡ Beignets d'Huitres (Oyster Fritters)

═ Yield: 100 fritters

1 small recipe pâte à chou (page 572)	1 tablespoon minced parsley oil for frying
1 pint shucked oysters, drained and chopped	horseradish mustard sauce (page 45)

═ Yield: 400 fritters

1 large recipe pâte à chou (page 572)	¼ cup minced parsley oil for frying
2 quarts shucked oysters, drained and chopped	horseradish mustard sauce (page 45)

1. In a bowl, beat the pâte à chou, oysters, and parsley together.

2. Heat the oil to 375°F. Fry teaspoonfuls of the paste until puffed and golden. Serve immediately with horseradish sauce.

▶ Can be prepared for frying 2 hours in advance.

≡ Beignets de Saumon (Salmon Fritters)

═ Yield: 100 fritters

1 cup flaked cooked salmon	1 teaspoon salt
3 tablespoons grated Parmesan cheese	pinch of cayenne pepper
1 tablespoon minced anchovy fillets	1 small recipe pâte à chou (page 572)
	oil for frying

═ Yield: 400 fritters

1 quart flaked cooked salmon	¼ teaspoon cayenne pepper
¾ cup grated Parmesan cheese	1 large recipe pâte à chou (page 572)
¼ cup minced anchovy fillets	oil for frying
4 teaspoons salt	

1. In a bowl, mix the salmon, cheese, anchovies, salt, and cayenne into the paste.

2. Heat the oil to 375°F. Fry teaspoonfuls of the paste until puffed and golden.

▶ Can be prepared for frying 5 hours in advance.

≡ *Shrimp and Water Chestnut Filling*

═ Yield: 50 puffs

2 tablespoons butter	3 tablespoons white wine
1½ cups minced cooked	½ cup minced water chestnuts
shrimp	1 tablespoon minced chives
2 teaspoons flour	1 tablespoon minced parsley
½ cup light cream	salt and pepper, to taste
1 tablespoon tomato paste	

═ Yield: 200 puffs

½ cup butter	¾ cup white wine
6 cups minced cooked shrimp	2 cups minced water chestnuts
3 tablespoons flour	¼ cup minced chives
2 cups light cream	¼ cup minced parsley
¼ cup tomato paste	salt and pepper, to taste

1. In a skillet, heat the butter and shrimp until hot. Sprinkle with the flour and cook, stirring, for 3 minutes. Stir in the cream, tomato paste, and wine and cook until lightly thickened. Stir in the water chestnuts, chives, parsley, salt and pepper.

2. Fill puffs, barquettes, or vegetables. Reheat in a 350°F oven, if necessary.

▶ Filling can be prepared 1 day in advance.

≡ *Hot Chicken-Cheese Filling*

═ Yield: 50 puffs

¼ cup minced onion	½ teaspoon salt
¼ pound mushrooms, minced	¼ teaspoon white pepper
2 tablespoons butter	1 egg, beaten
2 cups minced cooked chicken	¾ cup grated Gruyère cheese
2 tablespoons minced parsley	
1 tablespoon minced tarragon	
or basil	

═ Yield: 200 puffs

1 cup minced onion	¼ cup minced tarragon or basil
1 pound mushrooms, minced	2 teaspoons salt
½ cup butter	1 teaspoon white pepper
2 quarts minced cooked chicken	4 eggs, beaten
½ cup minced parsley	3 cups grated Gruyère cheese

1. In a skillet, sauté the onion and mushrooms in the butter until soft but not brown. Stir in the chicken, parsley, tarragon, salt, pepper, egg(s) and cheese. Cook, stirring, over low heat until the cheese is melted.
2. Use warm to fill puffs or barquettes.

▶ Can be prepared 1 day in advance and reheated.

≡ *Westphalian Ham Fritters*

═ Yield: 100 fritters

½ cup minced onion
2 tablespoons olive oil
½ cup minced Westphalian
   ham

1 small recipe pâte à chou
   (page 572)
oil for frying
mustard sauce (pages 43–45)

═ Yield: 400 fritters

2 cups minced onion
¼ cup olive oil
2 cups minced Westphalian
   ham

1 large recipe pâte à chou
   (page 572)
oil for frying
mustard sauce (pages 43–45)

1. In a skillet, sauté the onion in the oil until it just starts to turn golden.
2. Beat the onion and ham into the paste.
3. Heat the oil to 375°F. Fry teaspoonfuls of the paste until puffed and golden. Serve immediately with the sauce as a dip.

▶ Can be prepared for frying 6 hours in advance.

≡ *Ham and Swiss Cheese Puffs*

═ Yield: 50 puffs

1 cup finely diced Gruyère
   cheese
1½ small recipes pâte à chou
   (page 572)

⅓ pound ham, diced
2 tablespoons Dijon mustard
1⅓ cups grated Gruyère cheese
1½ tablespoons bread crumbs

═ Yield: 200 puffs

1 quart finely diced Gruyère
   cheese
1½ large recipes pâte à chou
   (page 572)

1⅓ pounds ham, diced
½ cup Dijon mustard
5⅓ cups grated Gruyère cheese
6 tablespoons bread crumbs

1. Preheat the oven to 375°F.

2. Fold the diced cheese into the paste. Set aside one third of the mixture.

3. Pipe the remaining mixture into mounds 1½ inches wide onto a baking sheet. Dip a finger into cold water and make an indentation in each mound.

4. In a bowl, mix the ham and mustard and put a little into each indentation. Cover with the remaining pastry.

5. In a bowl, mix the grated cheese and bread crumbs and sprinkle over the puffs. Bake until puffed and browned, about 35 minutes. Serve warm.

▶ Can be prepared for baking 6 hours in advance.

NOTE: This unusual way of filling the puffs can be used with any filling. Try using shrimp, flaked salmon, or smoked oysters in place of the ham.

15

Pâte Feuilletée, Strudel, and Phyllo

Pâte Feuilletée

Pâte feuilletée, also called puff pastry or flaky pastry, is difficult, but not impossible, to make successfully. Even the most skilled chefs often leave this pastry to experts rather than prepare it themselves. It requires a touch and a feel that you may not be able to achieve without personal instruction, and even then, you may not produce perfect results. Properly made, the pastry will consist of hundreds of light, delicate, and tender layers. There is no shame in not being able to achieve perfect puff pastry, but if you can, be justifiably proud.

If you cannot prepare the pastry or are hesitant to try, you can make an easier, quick puff pastry that is well suited to hors d'oeuvre. If you are pressed for time, many markets sell good-quality frozen puff pastry. Caterers and other commercial operations often buy it from their regular suppliers.

The instructions for making pâte feuilletée are slightly different from those found in many books. To be light and flaky, the pastry must be handled as lightly and as sparingly as possible. Therefore, when you first assemble the dough, do not be disturbed if the dough is a crumbly mess. (Many books have photographs of perfectly smooth dough at this point. This is not only misleading, but to have achieved that look, you probably would have overworked and toughened the dough.) It will come together as you proceed with the necessary rolling and folding. Never allow the butter to get oily—it will be absorbed by the flour and the pastry will not bake into separate layers. If the dough starts to get warm or feels very soft, put it in the refrigerator to firm up before proceeding.

Jalousies (Open Turnovers)
1. *Roll pastry into 3- × 4-inch rectangles.*
2. *Place filling on one half and cut slits in remaining half.*

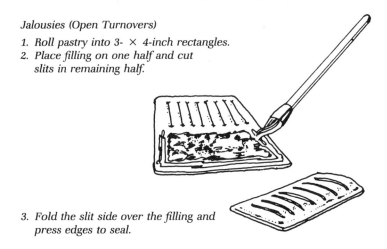

3. *Fold the slit side over the filling and press edges to seal.*

Reread the instructions on rolling pastry in Chapter 13. With puff pastry, it is extremely important to keep the dough as square as possible. When rolling it into a rectangle, keep the edges straight and fold it together evenly so that the pastry will rise evenly. If the pastry seems elastic during the rolling, let it rest in the refrigerator before proceeding. By the sixth turn there will be some elasticity, but the dough should not be rubbery.

The pastry will keep in the refrigerator, unshaped and unbaked, for 3 to 4 days, after which it tends to turn gray. You can store it in the freezer for 2 to 3 months. It can be shaped and refrigerated for 1 day before baking, or shaped and frozen for 2 to 3 months. Bake it from the frozen state, allowing a longer baking time. (Lower the temperature about 50 degrees after the first 10 minutes of baking.) Or the pastries can be shaped, baked, and then frozen.

Shaping Puff Pastry
Like short pastry, puff pastry can be shaped into turnovers, pillows, crescents, or logs. It can also be deep-fried for rissoles. Some methods of shaping are particularly associated with puff pastry; these are described below.

Jalousies   These are open turnovers. The pastry is rolled ⅛ inch thick and cut into rectangles, twice as wide as the desired finished size. For example, cut a 3- by 4-inch rectangle. Place a scant teaspoon of filling on one half of the rectangle along the 3-inch side. Brush the edges with cold water. Cut a few slits vertically toward the filling. Fold the slit side over the filling to form a turnover. Brush with dorure and chill 10 minutes. Brush again and bake on wet baking sheets.

Talmouses ("Little Purses") Roll the pastry ⅛ inch thick and cut into 3-inch squares. Place the filling in the center of each square. Pick up all four corners and pinch together. Brush with dorure.

Sacristans (Spirals) Roll the pastry very thinly, brush with egg yolk, and sprinkle with grated cheese and possibly ground nuts. Run a rolling pin over the surface to press the cheese lightly into the pastry. Cut into strips about ½ inch wide. Holding one end, twist the other end to form a long corkscrew. Place on a wet baking sheet and press the ends to the sheet. Although these can be cut to any length, it is easiest and quickest to make them as long as the baking sheet. After they have been baked, you can cut them to the desired size with a serrated knife.

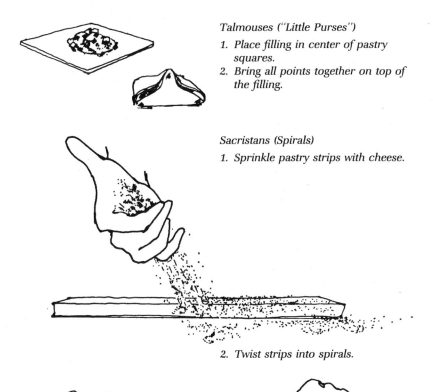

Talmouses ("Little Purses")
1. *Place filling in center of pastry squares.*
2. *Bring all points together on top of the filling.*

Sacristans (Spirals)
1. *Sprinkle pastry strips with cheese.*

2. *Twist strips into spirals.*

Allumettes (Matchsticks)
1. Brush pastry with beaten egg.
2. Fold pastry over filling.

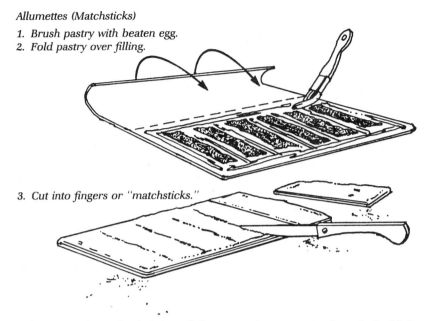

3. Cut into fingers or "matchsticks."

Allumettes (Matchsticks) Roll the pastry into a rectangle ⅛ inch thick, about 5 inches wide, and as long as desired. Fit a pastry bag with a no. 3 plain tip and pipe strips of the filling ½ inch apart, 2 inches long, ¼ inch from the edge to ¼ inch from the center. The filling will look like a ladder running up one side of the pastry. Fold the unfilled pastry over the filling and cut off the folded edge. Cut between the mounds of filling, pressing the edges to seal. Brush with dorure and bake on wet baking sheets.

Bouchées (Small Pastry Cases) These little pastry cups hold delicate fillings. Roll the pastry ¼ to ⅜ inch thick. With a 1½- to 2-inch grooved cutter, cut out pastry circles and turn them over onto wet baking sheets. With a smaller cutter, press halfway down into each circle. Brush the top with dorure, and chill for 20 minutes. Brush again and bake. When baked, carefully lift out the center section. Remove any uncooked center. Fill with the desired filling and reheat if necessary.

Baking Puff Pastry
Puff pastry is baked on baking sheets that have been run under cold water. Pour off the excess water and place the pastries on the sheet. The moisture creates steam in the oven that helps the pastry to puff. Bake at 400°F until puffed, cooked through, and golden. Turn the baking pan once during the baking to compensate for the heating variances found in most ovens. Once baked, the pastries can be frozen and reheated. Reheat them just before serving, unless they have a cold filling.

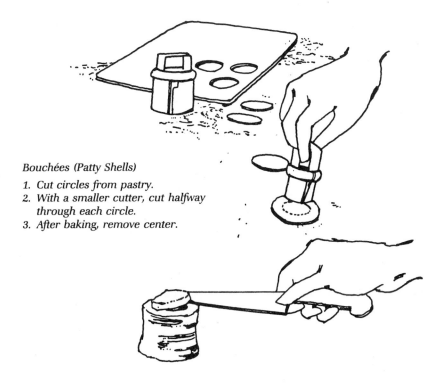

Bouchées (Patty Shells)
1. *Cut circles from pastry.*
2. *With a smaller cutter, cut halfway through each circle.*
3. *After baking, remove center.*

Fillings

Most fillings used in other hors d'oeuvre will probably work in puff pastry. If the filling is moist, do not fill the pastry too far in advance or it will become soggy.

Leftover Pastry

Because of the time and effort required to make puff pastry, every scrap should be used — carefully. Stack the scraps; do not bunch them in a ball. Treat the scraps as layers, and roll them gently but firmly. Use the leftover pastry for hors d'oeuvre that will not suffer from a slightly tough dough. Hors d'oeuvre that are crisp, such as cheese sticks, or batons, or cheese palmiers, are fine if made from scraps.

Dorure

Puff pastry, like short pastry, is coated with a dorure before baking, usually egg yolk mixed with heavy cream (see Chapter 13 for other combinations). When applying the dorure to puff pastry, never allow it to dribble over the edges of the pastry. It will act like glue and prevent the pastry from rising. Strain the dorure to make it easier to apply.

Brush on a light coating, chill the pastries for 20 minutes, and brush on a second light coat. If desired, decoratively score the surface of the pastries with a sharp knife.

—— *Strudel and Phyllo Dough* ——

Strudel, phyllo, fillo, or filo—no matter what you call them or how you spell them—are delectable, thin-layered pastry doughs. Making this pastry by hand is difficult and frankly not worth the effort when prepared dough is so readily available fresh or frozen. Use whichever is available for these recipes; no recipe is offered here.

Handling Strudel or Phyllo Dough

Unwrap the dough onto a sheet of waxed paper. Top with another sheet of waxed paper and cover with a towel wrung out in cold water. Keep the pastry covered—the dampened towel prevents it from drying and cracking. Also, if the pastry is a little brittle, the dampened towel remoistens it and makes it easier to use.

Place one sheet at a time onto a work surface and brush with melted butter or olive oil. Use a very soft pastry brush, preferably of goose feathers, to avoid tearing the pastry. Depending on the moistness of the filling, you may need two buttered sheets of phyllo for each pastry. If the filling is particularly moist or apt to ooze during baking, sprinkle the buttered pastry with dry bread crumbs before adding the filling.

There are several methods of shaping the pastry for hors d'oeuvre. No matter what method the recipe indicates, you can shape the pastries in any way that best suits your needs.

Large Logs or Rolls Butter two sheets of pastry, placing one on top of the other. Arrange a strip of filling, about 1 inch in diameter, along one side of the pastry, about 1 inch from the edge. Fold in the sides about 1 inch. Brush with butter. Lift the edge of the pastry closest to the filling and roll up like a jellyroll. Place on a baking sheet and brush with melted butter. With a sharp knife, cut three-quarters of the way through the pastry, either straight across or on a diagonal, at 1-inch intervals. Finish cutting the sections after the pastries are baked. This precutting is important; if it is baked and then cut, the pastry will crumble.

Small Logs Use one sheet of pastry. Butter it and cut into 3-inch-wide strips. Put a generous teaspoonful of filling at one end. Fold in the edges about ½ inch, then roll like a jellyroll. Place on a baking sheet and brush with butter. These are individual servings, so precutting is not required. If the filling is moist, you can layer two sheets of pastry.

Strudel or Phyllo Logs
1. *Place filling along one edge of phyllo.*
2. *Fold in sides and roll into a log.*

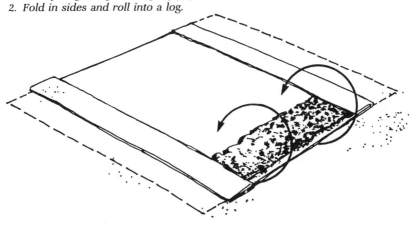

3. *Cut into 1-inch sections.*

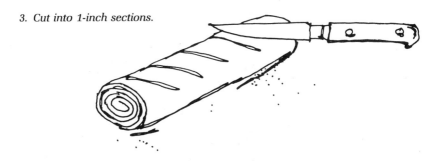

Triangles This is just like folding the American flag. Butter one sheet of phyllo and cut into 3-inch-wide strips. Place a generous teaspoonful of filling at one end of the pastry. Pick up one corner and fold it over the filling, aligning the short edge with one of the long edges to form a triangle. Continue folding until you reach the end of the strip. Place, seam-side down, on a baking sheet and brush with butter.

Purses Butter two sheets of phyllo and stack. Cut the sheets into 3-inch squares or circles. Place a teaspoonful of filling in the center of each square or circle and lift the dough up around the filling. Give the top a slight twist to make a small round sack. Brush with melted butter.

Barquettes Butter two sheets of phyllo and stack. Cut the dough into ovals and line barquette pans with the pastry, cutting to fit. Stack molds as

Strudel or Phyllo Triangles

1. Place filling on one corner of the pastry.

2. Fold the adjacent corner over the filling to form a triangle.

3. Continue folding, keeping the triangular shape.

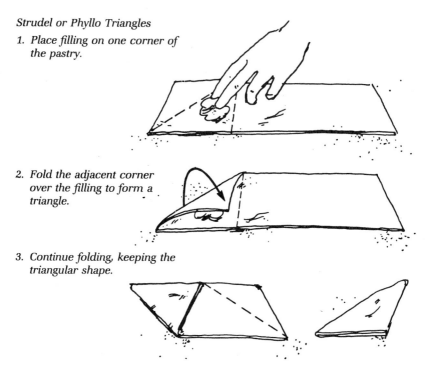

described on page 538. Bake, unfilled, until golden, about 6 to 8 minutes at 425°F. Cool. Just before serving, fill with either a hot or a cold filling.

Fillings

Only a few fillings are offered here, but you can choose from many of the fillings in other chapters. Just make sure that the filling can be heated (unless it is to be used in barquettes) and that it is not too fluid.

Baking Phyllo

Phyllo is baked at 375°F until puffed and golden—from 20 to 40 minutes depending on the size of the pastry. Since you determine the size and shape of the pastry, you must be careful to avoid overbaking.

Once the pastry is shaped, it can be frozen and baked later, or it can be baked and then frozen. Reheat at 350°F.

Deep-Frying

Although it is not commonly done, phyllo pastries can be deep-fried to great advantage. Shape individually as logs, purses, or triangles, but do not brush the surface with melted butter. Keep the filled pastries protected under waxed paper topped with a towel wrung out in cold water until ready to fry. Heat the oil to 375°F and fry until golden. Drain well before serving.

—— *Puff Pastries* ——

≡ *Pâte Feuilletée (Puff Pastry, Flaky Pastry)*

== Yield: 2½ pounds pastry

4 cups flour	1 pound cold unsalted butter
2 teaspoons salt	1 cup water, approximately

== Yield: 12½ pounds pastry

5 pounds flour	5 pounds cold unsalted butter
1 ounce salt	6 cups water, approximately

1. In a bowl, mix the flour and salt and cut in ¼ pound (*1 pound*) butter until the mixture resembles coarse meal. Make a well in the flour and add just enough water to make a medium-firm, pliable dough, pulling together with a fork until the ingredients are just moistened. Do not mix or beat. Work quickly and lightly.

2. Turn onto a board—the dough should be a crumbly mess. With a pastry scraper or broad-bladed putty knife, pick up the dough from the bottom and press it onto itself about 8 to 10 times, going around the edge. Use the blade of the scraper to cut through the dough, repeatedly chopping it into sections to incorporate the ingredients. The process should take no more than a few minutes. It will still be crumbly.

3. With a pastry scraper, push and shape the dough into a rough square. Put it into a plastic bag and press into a square about 1½ inches thick. Chill for 20 minutes.

4. Meanwhile, work the remaining butter with your hands to form a pliable, waxy mass. Do not let it get warm or oily. (One way to work the butter is to immerse it in a bowl of cold water. Be sure to press out the excess moisture when done. Another way is to put the butter in a plastic bag and work it from outside the bag.) Shape the butter into a square about 1 inch thick. Chill until the pastry and the butter are equally firm.

5. Remove the pastry from the refrigerator and take it out of the bag. Place it on a lightly floured board and roll into a square large enough to enclose the butter. It will be about 1 inch thick and still look crumbly. Place the butter on top of the pastry so that the corners of the butter point to the sides of the pastry. Fold the corners of the pastry over the butter to form a package, letting the pastry edges just meet. Pinch the edges together.

6. With a lightly floured rolling pin, gently roll the pastry into a rectangle 10 inches wide by 18 inches long (20 inches wide by 30 inches long for the larger quantity). Keep the pastry edges as straight as possible. Fold the pastry into thirds like a business letter.

Pâte Feuilletée

1. *Place butter on pastry with butter corners pointing to sides of pastry.*

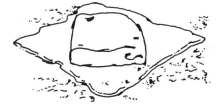

2. *Fold corners of pastry over butter and pinch edges to seal.*

3. *Roll into a rectangle 10 × 18 inches (or, for the larger quantity of dough, 20 × 30 inches).*

4. *Fold in thirds and turn so open end faces you. Roll again.*

7. Turn the pastry so an open end faces you. Roll the pastry into a rectangle again and fold into thirds. You will have just made two turns. Return the pastry to the plastic bag and chill for 40 minutes.

8. Remove from the refrigerator and roll and fold two more times. Put it back into the plastic bag and return it to the refrigerator. Repeat the process one more time to make a total of six turns.

NOTE: If the dough is too firm to roll, soften it by banging it with a rolling pin until it starts to give. Always keep the pastry cold. Never do more than two turns at one time, and allow it to rest after each set of turns. Keep the pastry as square as possible, and be sure that an open end faces you before rolling.

For the greatest lift or puff, use the pastry as soon as possible after preparing it. The longer it waits, the less it will rise. If you cannot use it immediately, freeze it.

≡ *Demi-Feuilletée (Quick or Rough Puff Pastry)*

This is a quick and acceptable substitute for the classic pastry.

═ Yield: 2 pounds pastry

4 cups flour	1¾ cups cold unsalted butter
2 teaspoons salt	1 cup ice water

═ Yield: 10 pounds pastry

5 pounds flour	4¾ pounds cold unsalted butter
1 ounce salt	5 cups ice water

1. In a large bowl, mix the flour and salt. Cut in the butter until the mixture resembles coarse meal. Add the ice water and form the dough into a flat cake. Dust lightly with flour and wrap in plastic. Chill 1 hour.

2. On a lightly floured board, roll the dough into a large rectangle about ½ inch thick. Fold it in thirds like a business letter. Turn so an open end faces you and roll again. Fold in thirds. This completes two turns. Chill for 20 minutes and roll again, making two more turns. Chill 30 minutes. The pastry is ready to use.

≡ *Talmouses Saint Denis (Cheese "Purses")*

═ **Yield: 40 purses**

1 pound puff pastry	dorure
6 ounces cream cheese	
salt and cayenne pepper, to taste	

═ **Yield: 200 purses**

5 pounds puff pastry	dorure
2 pounds cream cheese	
salt and cayenne pepper, to taste	

1. Preheat the oven to 400°F.

2. Roll the pastry ⅛ inch thick and cut into 3-inch squares.

3. In a food processor, cream the cream cheese, salt, and cayenne. Put ½ teaspoon of cheese in the center of each square. Lift the corners and pinch together. Brush with dorure.

4. Place on a wet baking sheet and chill 20 minutes. Bake until golden, about 20 minutes.

▶ Can be assembled and frozen before baking. Best if served shortly after baking.

NOTE: Many cheese spreads from other chapters can be substituted.

≡ *Roquefort Circles*

═ **Yield: 70 pastries**

3 ounces cream cheese	1 tablespoon butter
1½ ounces Roquefort cheese	pinch of cayenne pepper
¼ cup minced scallions or chives	1 pound puff pastry

═ **Yield: 210 pastries**

9 ounces cream cheese	3 tablespoons butter
5 ounces Roquefort cheese	¼ teaspoon cayenne pepper
¾ cup minced scallions or chives	3 pounds puff pastry

1. Preheat the oven to 350°F.
2. In a bowl, cream the cream cheese, Roquefort, scallions, butter, and cayenne.
3. Roll the pastry into a rectangle about 6 by 17 inches. (Make additional rectangles for the larger quantity.) Spread the filling over the dough, leaving a ½-inch border on one long side. Brush the border with cold water. Roll the sheet jellyroll fashion toward the border, wrap, and chill until firm.
4. Cut into ¼-inch slices and place, cut side down, on wet baking sheets. Bake until golden, about 15 to 20 minutes.

▶ Can be frozen baked or unbaked.

≡ *Allumettes au Roquefort (Roquefort Bars)*

= **Yield: 50 pastries**

⅔ cup Roquefort cheese
¼ cup ground walnuts
1 egg yolk
1 teaspoon minced parsley

¼ teaspoon pepper
1 to 2 tablespoons heavy cream
1 pound puff pastry

= **Yield: 100 pastries**

1⅓ cups Roquefort cheese
½ cup ground walnuts
2 egg yolks
2 teaspoons minced parsley

½ teaspoon pepper
2 to 4 tablespoons heavy cream
2 pounds puff pastry

1. Preheat the oven to 400°F.
2. In a bowl, mix the cheese, walnuts, egg yolk(s), parsley, pepper, and enough cream to make a smooth mixture. Use to fill allumettes, turnovers, pillows, or crescents.
3. Bake until golden on wet baking sheets.

▶ Can be frozen baked or unbaked.

≡ *Cheese Sticks*

= **Yield: 50 sticks**

½ pound puff pastry
1 egg, beaten

½ cup shredded Cheddar
cheese

— **Yield: 100 sticks**

1 pound puff pastry
2 eggs, beaten

1 cup shredded Cheddar
cheese

1. Preheat the oven to 375°F.

2. Roll the pastry into a rectangle ¼ inch thick. Trim evenly.

3. Brush with egg and sprinkle with the cheese. With a rolling pin, lightly press the cheese into the dough.

4. Cut into strips ½ inch wide by 3 inches long and bake until golden. Or cut into ¼-inch-wide strips and twist into spirals.

▶ Can be frozen baked or unbaked.

≡ *Corniottes Bourguignonnes (Cheese Tricorns)*

— **Yield: 25 pastries**

8 ounces cream cheese
6 ounces diced Gruyère cheese
2 eggs
salt and pepper, to taste

½ pound puff pastry
½ cup grated Gruyère cheese
dorure

— **Yield: 100 pastries**

2 pounds cream cheese
1½ pounds diced Gruyère
cheese
8 eggs

salt and pepper, to taste
2 pounds puff pastry
2 cups grated Gruyère cheese
dorure

1. Preheat the oven to 400°F.

2. In a bowl, beat the cream cheese, diced Gruyère, eggs, salt, and pepper.

3. Roll the pastry ⅛ inch thick and cut into 4-inch circles with a pastry cutter. Put a spoonful of the filling in the center of each round and brush the edges of the pastry with dorure. Lift the edges of the dough from three directions to make a triangle and pinch the edges to seal. They will look like tricorn hats. Chill 15 minutes until firm.

4. Brush the pastries with the dorure and bake 15 minutes. Sprinkle with the grated cheese and bake 10 to 15 minutes longer or until golden brown. Serve hot or at room temperature.

▶ Can be frozen unbaked.

≡ Palmiers de Fromage (Cheese Elephant Ears)

═ Yield: 24 palmiers

½ pound puff pastry	cayenne pepper, to taste
¾ cup grated Parmesan cheese	1 egg, beaten
½ cup grated Gruyère cheese	

═ Yield: 100 palmiers

2 pounds puff pastry	cayenne pepper, to taste
3 cups grated Parmesan cheese	4 eggs, beaten
2 cups grated Gruyère cheese	

1. Preheat the oven to 400°F.

2. Roll the pastry ⅛ inch thick and about 12 inches wide. Brush with water. Sprinkle with two-thirds of the Parmesan, the Gruyère, and sprinkle with cayenne.

3. Fold 3 inches of one long side of the pastry to the middle. Fold again so the fold is just at the middle of the pastry. Repeat with the other side. Fold the sides on top of each other and press together. Cut into ½-inch slices and place on a wet baking sheet. Flatten each palmier with your hand and chill for 30 minutes.

4. Bake for 15 minutes. Turn and brush with egg and sprinkle with the remaining Parmesan and a little cayenne. Bake 10 minutes longer.

▶ Can be baked, frozen, and reheated.

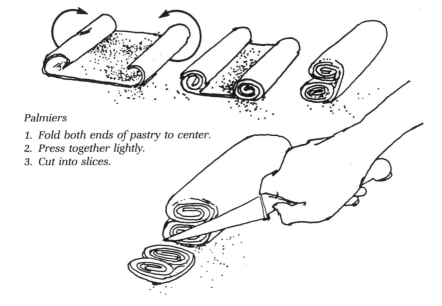

Palmiers
1. *Fold both ends of pastry to center.*
2. *Press together lightly.*
3. *Cut into slices.*

☰ *Allumettes aux Anchois I (Anchovy Matchsticks I)*

══ Yield: 25 pastries

½ cup tuna, mashed
3 tablespoons béchamel sauce
(page 59)
2 teaspoons anchovy paste

anchovy fillets
½ pound puff pastry
dorure

══ Yield: 100 pastries

2 cups tuna, mashed
¾ cup béchamel sauce
(page 59)
3 tablespoons anchovy paste

anchovy fillets
2 pounds puff pastry
dorure

1. In a bowl, mix the tuna, béchamel, and anchovy paste.
2. Roll the pastry as for allumettes and make strips of the tuna filling.
Top each strip with an anchovy fillet. Fold as for allumettes, brush with
dorure, and bake.

▶ Can be frozen baked or unbaked.

☰ *Allumettes aux Anchois II (Anchovy Matchsticks II)*

══ Yield: 25 pastries

½ pound puff pastry
25 anchovy fillets

1 hard-cooked egg, minced
½ cup minced parsley

══ Yield: 100 pastries

2 pounds puff pastry
100 anchovy fillets

4 hard-cooked eggs, minced
2 cups minced parsley

Roll the pastry for allumettes. Roll the anchovy fillets in the egg(s) and
parsley and place on the pastry. Shape into allumettes and bake.

▶ Can be frozen baked or unbaked.

≡ Crabmeat and Pecan Filling

═ Yield: 40 pastries

2 tablespoons minced scallions
2 tablespoons butter
2 tablespoons flour
½ cup light cream
½ cup crabmeat
⅓ cup finely chopped pecans

¼ teaspoon Worcestershire
  sauce
pinch of cayenne pepper
salt and pepper, to taste
1 pound puff pastry

═ Yield: 200 pastries

⅔ cup minced scallions
⅔ cup butter
⅔ cup flour
2½ cups light cream
2½ cups crabmeat
1⅔ cups finely chopped pecans

1¼ teaspoons Worcestershire
  sauce
¼ teaspoon cayenne pepper
salt and pepper, to taste
5 pounds puff pastry

1. In a saucepan, sauté the scallions in the butter until soft. Stir in the flour and cook until the roux just starts to turn golden. Stir in the cream and cook until thick and smooth. Stir in the crabmeat, pecans, Worcestershire sauce, cayenne, salt, and pepper.

2. Use to make turnovers, or to fill cocktail puffs or strudel.

▶ Filling can be made 2 days in advance.

≡ Lobster Filling

═ Yield: 25 pastries

½ pound cooked lobster meat,
  minced
2 tablespoons butter
salt and cayenne pepper, to
  taste

2 tablespoons Cognac
1 tablespoon flour
⅓ cup sour cream
2 teaspoons minced dill
1 pound puff pastry

═ Yield: 100 pastries

2 pounds cooked lobster meat,
  minced
½ cup butter
salt and cayenne pepper, to
  taste

¼ cup Cognac
¼ cup flour
1⅓ cups sour cream
3 tablespoons minced dill
4 pounds puff pastry

1. In a saucepan, melt the butter and heat the lobster, salt, and cayenne pepper. Add the Cognac, ignite, and cook until the flames go out. Add the flour, sour cream, and dill and mix well.

2. Use to fill jalousies, talmouses, turnovers, bouchées, or cocktail puffs.

▶ Filling can be made 2 days iln advance.

≡ *Bouchées aux Moules (Mussel-Filled Pastry Cases)*

≡ Yield: 48 bouchées

1 small recipe mussels marinara (page 466)	½ cup heavy cream
	3 tablespoons butter
¼ pound shrimp, unpeeled	1 cup finely diced mushrooms
½ cup butter	1 tablespoon lemon juice
1½ tablespoons flour	48 bouchées
1 cup milk	

≡ Yield: 200 bouchées

1 large recipe mussels marinara (page 466)	2 cups heavy cream
	⅔ cup butter
1 pound shrimp, unpeeled	1 quart finely diced mushrooms
2 cups butter	¼ cup lemon juice
⅓ cup flour	200 bouchées
1 quart milk	

1. Preheat oven to 350°F.

2. Strain the juices from the mussels and reserve. Reserve mussels and discard the shells. Heat the mussel liquid and cook the shrimp until just done. Remove the shrimp, peel, and return the shells to the cooking liquid. Simmer until reduced to ¾ cup (*3 cups*).

3. Strain and reduce to ⅓ cup (*1½ cups*). In a saucepan, melt the butter and stir in the flour. Cook until the roux just starts to turn golden. Add the milk and mussel liquor, and cook until reduced to ¾ cup (*3 cups*). Stir in the cream.

4. In a skillet, sauté the mushrooms in the remaining butter and lemon juice until the liquid evaporates.

5. Dice the mussels and shrimp into ¼-inch pieces. Add the shellfish and mushrooms to the sauce.

6. Fill the bouchées and heat before serving.

▶ Filling can be made 2 days in advance.

≡ *Talmouses Boston (Boston "Purses")*

There is no clear reason why this delicious hors d'oeuvre has its name, other than perhaps because salmon and good cooking are synonymous with this city.

═ Yield: 25 pastries

½ pound puff pastry
1 cup flaked cooked salmon
¼ cup mornay sauce (page 59)

½ cup grated Gruyère cheese
dorure

═ Yield: 100 pastries

2 pounds puff pastry
1 quart flaked cooked salmon
1 cup mornay sauce (page 59)

2 cups grated Gruyère cheese
dorure

1. Preheat the oven to 400°F.
2. Roll the puff pastry ⅛ inch thick and cut into 3-inch squares.
3. In a bowl, mix the salmon with enough mornay sauce to bind. Put 1 teaspoon of filling in the center of each square and sprinkle with the cheese. Pick up the corners and pinch together. Brush with dorure.
4. Bake until golden, about 20 minutes. Serve warm.

▶ Can be frozen and baked.

≡ *Petites Pâtes à l'Indienne (Curried Chicken Filling)*

═ Yield: 25 pastries

2 cups ground cooked chicken
1 cup curry sauce (page 66)

2 tablespoons minced chutney

═ Yield: 100 pastries

2 quarts ground cooked
chicken

1 quart curry sauce (page 66)
½ cup minced chutney

1. In a bowl, mix the chicken, curry sauce, and chutney.
2. Use to fill turnovers, logs, talmouses, or rissoles.

▶ Can be prepared 2 days in advance.

≡ Chicken and Sausage-Filled Palmiers

== **Yield: 60 palmiers**

¾ pound Italian sausage,
  peeled
2 garlic cloves, minced
1 pound chicken breasts,
  skinned and boned
½ cup grated Parmesan cheese

⅓ cup heavy cream
¼ cup tomato paste
¼ cup minced basil
½ teaspoon pepper
¼ pound puff pastry

== **Yield: 120 palmiers**

1½ pounds Italian sausage,
  peeled
4 garlic cloves, minced
2 pounds chicken breasts,
  skinned and boned
1 cup grated Parmesan cheese

⅔ cup heavy cream
½ cup tomato paste
½ cup minced basil
1 teaspoon pepper
½ pound puff pastry

1. Preheat the oven to 400°F.

2. In a large skillet, cook the sausage and garlic, crumbling the meat, until it loses its color and is fully cooked. Remove with a slotted spoon and put into a bowl.

3. In the fat left in the pan, sauté the chicken breasts until cooked, about 10 minutes. Remove and cool.

4. In a food processor, purée the sausage, chicken, cheese, cream, tomato paste, basil, and pepper.

5. Roll the pastry into a rectangle about ⅛ inch thick. Spread the filling over the surface and fold as for palmiers. Cut into thin slices and arrange on wet baking sheets. Bake until puffed and golden, about 20 minutes. Serve warm.

▶ The filling can be prepared 2 days in advance. Pastries can be frozen baked or unbaked.

≡ Spinach and Prosciutto Crescents

== **Yield: 25 pastries**

½ pound puff pastry
2 egg yolks beaten with 1
  tablespoon heavy cream

¼ pound prosciutto, julienned
½ pound spinach, cooked,
  drained, and chopped

== **Yield: 100 pastries**

2 pounds puff pastry
8 egg yolks beaten with ¼ cup
   heavy cream

1 pound prosciutto, julienned
2 pounds spinach, cooked,
   drained, and chopped

1. Preheat the oven to 400°F.

2. Roll the pastry ⅛ inch thick and cut into 3-inch-wide strips. Cut the strips into triangles and brush the triangles with the egg wash. Spread strips of prosciutto and ½ teaspoon spinach in the center of each triangle. Roll toward one point and shape into crescents.

3. Place on wet baking sheets, brush with the remaining egg wash, and chill 30 minutes. Brush again and bake until golden, about 20 minutes. Serve hot.

▶ Can be frozen baked or unbaked.

≡ *Saucijzebroodjes (Dutch Sausage Rolls)*

Another street food that has made its way into the smartest salons, these Dutch delights are easy and delicious.

== **Yield: 50 rolls**

½ pound puff pastry
1 pound fresh pork sausage
   meat

dorure

== **Yield: 200 rolls**

2 pounds puff pastry
4 pounds fresh pork sausage
   meat

dorure

1. Preheat the oven to 400°F.

2. Roll the pastry ⅛ inch thick and cut into 3-inch-wide strips.

3. Shape the sausage into rolls ½ inch thick and lay on the pastry. Brush the pastry with dorure, wrap around the sausage, and seal. Brush the surface with dorure and cut into 2-inch lengths. Bake until golden.

▶ Can be frozen baked or unbaked.

——— *Strudel and Phyllo Pastries* ———

≡ *Bourekakia I (Cheese Logs I)*

═ **Yield: 36 logs**

½ cup crumbled feta cheese
6 ounces cream cheese,
  softened
1 egg

pinch of grated nutmeg
½ pound phyllo dough
½ cup melted butter

═ **Yield: 144 logs**

2 cups crumbled feta cheese
1½ pounds cream cheese,
  softened
4 eggs

¼ teaspoon grated nutmeg
2 pounds phyllo dough
2 cups melted butter

1. Preheat the oven to 350°F.

2. In a bowl, mix the feta cheese, cream cheese, egg(s), and nutmeg.

3. Lay a sheet of phyllo on the counter and brush with butter. Cut into 3-inch-wide strips. Place a teaspoonful of the mixture on one end and fold over the dough. Fold over the sides the full length of the strip and roll into a log. Brush with butter.

4. Place on a baking sheet and bake 20 minutes or until puffed and browned. Serve warm.

▶ Can be frozen baked or unbaked. If frozen unbaked, bake immediately from the freezer.

≡ *Bourekakia II (Cheese Logs II)*

═ **Yield: 36 logs**

½ pound feta cheese, crumbled
½ cup minced parsley
1 egg, lightly beaten
½ teaspoon dried thyme
½ teaspoon dried oregano

½ teaspoon ground cumin
¼ teaspoon cayenne pepper
½ pound phyllo dough
½ cup melted butter

═ **Yield: 144 logs**

2 pounds feta cheese, crumbled
2 cups minced parsley
4 eggs, lightly beaten
2 teaspoons dried thyme
2 teaspoons dried oregano

2 teaspoons ground cumin
1 teaspoon cayenne pepper
2 pounds phyllo dough
2 cups melted butter

1. In a bowl, mix the cheese, parsley, egg(s), thyme, oregano, cumin, and cayenne.
2. Use to fill triangles or large or small logs.

▶ Can be prepared 2 days in advance.

≡ Feta-Walnut Filling

== **Yield: 25 pastries**

½ cup finely crumbled feta cheese
⅓ cup chopped walnuts
⅓ cup cottage cheese

½ teaspoon pepper
6 sheets phyllo dough
⅓ cup melted butter

== **Yield: 100 pastries**

2 cups finely crumbled feta cheese
1⅓ cups chopped walnuts
1⅓ cups cottage cheese

2 teaspoons pepper
1 pound phyllo dough
1⅓ cups melted butter

1. In a bowl, mix the feta, walnuts, cottage cheese, and pepper.
2. Use to fill phyllo shapes of your choice.

▶ Can be prepared 2 days in advance.

≡ Baked Sesame Triangles

== **Yield: 25 pastries**

¼ cup sesame paste
3 tablespoons water
½ tablespoon lemon juice
salt and pepper, to taste
1 pound bean curd, cut into
  ½-inch cubes

1 tablespoon minced parsley
½ teaspoon cumin
½ pound phyllo dough
¼ pound melted butter
½ cup sesame seeds, toasted

== **Yield: 100 pastries**

1 cup sesame paste
¾ cup water
2 tablespoons lemon juice
salt and pepper, to taste
4 pounds bean curd, cut into
  ½-inch cubes

¼ cup minced parsley
2 teaspoons cumin
2 pounds phyllo dough
1 pound melted butter
2 cups sesame seeds, toasted

1. Preheat the oven to 400°F.

2. In a bowl, mix the sesame paste, water, lemon juice, salt, and pepper. In another bowl, mix the bean curd with the parsley and cumin.

3. Brush a sheet of phyllo with some of the sesame mixture and butter. Repeat with two more sheets. Cut the stack into 4 long strips.

4. Place a piece of bean curd at one end and fold into a triangle. Brush the top with butter and sprinkle with sesame seeds. Bake for 30 minutes or until golden. Serve hot.

▶ Can be prepared for baking 1 day in advance.

≡ *Cabbage Strudel I*

═ **Yield: 36 pastries**

⅔ cup butter   1 cup minced onion
1½ pounds cabbage, minced   salt and pepper, to taste

═ **Yield: 144 pastries**

2⅔ cups butter   1 quart minced onion
6 pounds cabbage, minced   salt and pepper, to taste

1. In a skillet, cook the butter, cabbage, and onion, stirring until well coated with the butter. Cover and simmer over very low heat until the vegetables wilt.

2. Uncover and cook, stirring occasionally, until the cabbage is soft and lightly browned. Season with salt and pepper. Cool. Use to fill phyllo dough or short pastry.

▶ Can be prepared 2 days in advance.

≡ *Cabbage Strudel II*

═ **Yield: 48 pastries**

2 pounds cabbage, shredded   1 tablespoon sugar
2 teaspoons salt   1 teaspoon caraway seeds
1 cup minced onion   1 teaspoon cinnamon
¼ cup vegetable oil   ¼ teaspoon pepper

≡ **Yield: 144 pastries**

6 pounds cabbage, shredded	3 tablespoons sugar
2 tablespoons salt	1 tablespoon caraway seeds
3 cups minced onion	1 tablespoon cinnamon
¾ cup vegetable oil	1 teaspoon pepper

1. Sprinkle the cabbage with the salt and let stand for 30 minutes. Squeeze out the liquid.

2. In a skillet, sauté the onion in the oil until golden. Remove the onion with a slotted spoon.

3. In the same pan, sauté the cabbage in batches over low heat until golden. In a bowl, mix the cabbage, onion, sugar, caraway seeds, cinnamon, and pepper.

4. Use to fill phyllo sheets or short pastry.

▶ Can be prepared 2 days in advance.

≡ *Mushroom Filling I*

≡ **Yield: 36 pastries**

1 pound mushrooms, minced	3 tablespoons flour
½ cup minced scallions	½ teaspoon salt
¼ cup butter	¼ teaspoon curry powder
2 tablespoons butter	1 cup light cream

≡ **Yield: 144 pastries**

4 pounds mushrooms, minced	¾ cup flour
2 cups minced scallions	2 teaspoons salt
1 cup butter	1 teaspoon curry powder
½ cup butter	1 quart light cream

1. In a skillet, sauté the mushrooms and scallions in the butter until the liquid evaporates. Stir in the remaining butter and sprinkle with the flour, salt, and curry powder. Cook, stirring for 3 minutes. Stir in the cream and cook, stirring until the mixture thickens. Cool.

2. Use to fill phyllo, puff pastry, or cocktail puffs.

▶ Can be prepared 2 days in advance.

≡ Mushroom Filling II

≡ **Yield: 36 pastries**

1 pound mushrooms, minced
½ cup minced onion
3 tablespoons butter
½ cup sour cream

2 tablespoons minced dill,
    optional
salt and pepper, to taste

≡ **Yield: 144 pastries**

4 pounds mushrooms, minced
2 cups minced onion
¾ cup butter

2 cups sour cream
½ cup minced dill, optional
salt and pepper, to taste

1. Place the mushrooms in a clean kitchen towel and squeeze out the moisture.

2. In a skillet, sauté the mushrooms and onion in the butter until the liquid evaporates. Stir in the sour cream, dill, salt, and pepper. Set aside to cool.

3. Use to fill phyllo dough, short pastry, puff pastry, or cocktail puffs.

▶ Can be prepared 2 days in advance.

≡ Spinach-Cheese Filling I

≡ **Yield: 50 pastries**

2 10-ounce packages frozen
    chopped spinach, thawed
1 cup minced onion
¾ cup minced scallions
¼ cup butter
½ cup minced dill

¼ cup minced parsley
salt, to taste
½ pound feta cheese, crumbled
¼ cup grated Parmesan cheese
4 eggs

≡ **Yield: 200 pastries**

8 10-ounce packages frozen
    chopped spinach, thawed
1 quart minced onion
1½ cups minced scallions
1 cup butter
2 cups minced dill

1 cup minced parsley
1 teaspoon salt
2 pounds feta cheese, crumbled
1 cup grated Parmesan cheese
16 eggs

1. Squeeze the excess moisture from the spinach.
2. In a skillet, sauté the onion and scallions in the butter until golden. Add the dill and parsley and sauté for 5 minutes. Add the spinach and salt and sauté for 10 minutes or until almost dry.
3. Transfer to a bowl and cool. Stir in the feta, Parmesan, and eggs.
4. Use to fill phyllo dough or cocktail puffs.

▶ Can be prepared 2 days in advance.

☰ Spinach-Cheese Filling II

═ Yield: 50 pastries

½ cup minced onion
¼ cup olive oil
1 10-ounce package frozen
   chopped spinach, thawed

½ pound feta cheese, crumbled
6 ounces pot cheese
3 eggs, beaten
¼ cup bread crumbs

═ Yield: 200 pastries

2 cups minced onion
1 cup olive oil
4 10-ounce packages frozen
   chopped spinach, thawed

2 pounds feta cheese, crumbled
1½ pounds pot cheese
12 eggs, beaten
1 cup bread crumbs

1. Squeeze the excess moisture from the spinach.
2. In a skillet, sauté the onion in the olive oil until soft. Stir in the spinach and simmer, stirring occasionally, until the moisture evaporates.
3. Stir in the feta, pot cheese, eggs, and bread crumbs.
4. Use to fill phyllo or cocktail puffs.

▶ Can be prepared 2 days in advance.

☰ Seafood Filling I

Select a variety of fish and shellfish for this filling. Shrimp, scallops, and lobster are most popular, but salmon, sole, and mussels are another possibility.

== **Yield: 36 pastries**

½ cup minced onion
1 tablespoon butter
1½ cups mixed cooked seafood
1 cup sour cream
2 tablespoons minced scallions
2 tablespoons minced parsley

½ teaspoon salt
¼ teaspoon pepper
½ cup fine bread crumbs
½ cup grated Parmesan cheese
2 teaspoons dry mustard

== **Yield: 144 pastries**

2 cups minced onion
¼ cup butter
6 cups mixed cooked seafood
1 quart sour cream
½ cup minced scallions
½ cup minced parsley

2 teaspoons salt
1 teaspoon pepper
2 cups fine bread crumbs
2 cups grated Parmesan cheese
3 tablespoons dry mustard

1. In a skillet, sauté the onion in the butter until soft but not brown. Stir in the seafood, sour cream, scallions, parsley, salt, and pepper.

2. In a bowl, mix the bread crumbs, cheese, and mustard.

3. Spread phyllo sheets on a counter, brush with butter, and sprinkle with the bread crumb mixture. Arrange the filling on top and roll into logs. Use to fill short pastry, puff pastry, or cocktail puffs.

▶ Filling can be prepared 2 days in advance.

≡ *Seafood Filling II*

== **Yield: 50 pastries**

1½ cups white wine
½ cup chopped celery, with leaves
2 tablespoons chopped parsley
1 teaspoon salt
1 bay leaf
¼ teaspoon peppercorns

¼ teaspoon dried thyme
2 pounds mixed seafood
1 cup heavy cream
2 tablespoons butter
2 tablespoons flour
2 egg yolks, beaten
1 tablespoon minced parsley

=== **Yield: 200 pastries**

6 cups white wine
2 cups chopped celery, with
   leaves
½ cup chopped parsley
4 teaspoons salt
2 bay leaves
1 teaspoon peppercorns
1 teaspoon dried thyme

8 pounds mixed seafood
1 quart heavy cream
½ cup butter
½ cup flour
8 egg yolks, beaten
¼ cup minced parsley
salt and pepper, to taste

1. In a saucepan, simmer the wine, celery, parsley, salt, bay leaf, peppercorns, and thyme for 5 minutes. Add each seafood separately and poach until just done, 2 to 3 minutes as a rule.

2. Strain the stock and reduce by half. Mince the fish if large.

3. In a saucepan, reduce the cream by one half.

4. In another saucepan, melt the butter, stir in the flour, and cook the roux until it starts to turn golden. Add the reduced stock and cream and cook, stirring until thick and smooth. Stir one fourth of the sauce into the egg yolks and then add the yolks to the sauce. Heat until hot but not boiling. Remove from the heat and stir in the parsley. Fold in the seafood. Correct the seasoning with salt and pepper.

5. Use to fill phyllo and other pastries.

▶ Can be prepared 2 days in advance.

=== *Crabmeat Filling I*

=== **Yield: 25 pastries**

½ pound crabmeat
1 cup minced mushrooms,
   sautéed in 1 tablespoon
   butter

½ to ¾ cup béchamel sauce
   (page 59)
salt and pepper, to taste

=== **Yield: 100 pastries**

2 pounds crabmeat
1 quart minced mushrooms,
   sautéed in ¼ cup butter

2 to 3 cups béchamel sauce
   (page 59)
salt and pepper, to taste

1. In a bowl, mix the crabmeat, mushrooms, and enough béchamel to bind. Correct the seasoning with salt and pepper.

2. Use to fill phyllo and other pastries.

▶ Can be prepared 1 day in advance.

☰ Crabmeat Filling II

═ Yield: 50 pastries

1½ pounds crabmeat	1 tablespoon minced dill
2 cups béchamel sauce	1 tablespoon minced pimiento
(page 59)	1 tablespoon A-1 sauce
½ cup minced mushrooms	1 teaspoon sherry
2 hard-cooked eggs, chopped	dash of Tabasco sauce
1 tablespoon minced parsley	salt, to taste

═ Yield: 200 pastries

6 pounds crabmeat	¼ cup minced dill
2 quarts béchamel sauce	¼ cup minced pimiento
(page 59)	¼ cup A-1 sauce
2 cups minced mushrooms	1½ tablespoons sherry
8 hard-cooked eggs, chopped	¼ teaspoon Tabasco sauce
¼ cup minced parsley	salt, to taste

1. In a bowl, mix the crabmeat, béchamel, mushrooms, eggs, parsley, dill, pimiento, A-1 sauce, sherry, Tabasco sauce, and salt.

2. Use to fill buttered phyllo or other pastries.

▶ Can be prepared 2 days in advance.

☰ Chicken Liver Strudel Pastries

═ Yield: 50 pastries

3 cups minced onion	2 tablespoons Cognac
1 large garlic clove, minced	2 tablespoons minced parsley
⅓ cup butter	1½ teaspoons grated Parmesan
½ pound mushrooms, chopped	cheese
1 pound chicken livers	salt and pepper, to taste
1 egg, lightly beaten	1 cup sour cream
¼ cup bread crumbs	2 tablespoons minced dill
¼ cup sour cream	

— **Yield: 200 pastries**

3 quarts minced onion
4 large garlic cloves, minced
1⅓ cups butter
2 pounds mushrooms, chopped
4 pounds chicken livers
4 eggs, lightly beaten
1 cup bread crumbs
1 cup sour cream

½ cup Cognac
½ cup minced parsley
2 tablespoons grated Parmesan
  cheese
salt and pepper, to taste
1 quart sour cream
½ cup minced dill

1. In a skillet, sauté the onion and garlic in the butter until golden. Stir in the mushrooms and cook 5 minutes. Add the chicken livers and cook until medium.

2. In a food processor, purée the chicken liver mixture, egg(s), bread crumbs, sour cream, Cognac, parsley, cheese, salt, and pepper.

3. Use to fill phyllo or other pastries.

4. In a bowl, mix the sour cream and dill and serve as a dip for the pastries.

▶ Can be prepared 2 days in advance.

≡ *Lamb Filling I*

— **Yield: 50 pastries**

2 cups minced onion
2 tablespoons olive oil
1½ pounds ground lamb
4 teaspoons dried mint
1 teaspoon cinnamon

pinch of nutmeg
salt, to taste
¾ cup pine nuts
2 tablespoons butter

— **Yield: 200 pastries**

2 quarts minced onion
½ cup olive oil
6 pounds ground lamb
⅓ cup dried mint
4 teaspoons cinnamon

¼ teaspoon nutmeg
salt, to taste
3 cups pine nuts
½ cup butter

1. In a skillet, sauté the onion in the oil until soft but not brown. Add the lamb and cook, stirring until the meat loses its color. Stir in the mint, cinnamon, nutmeg, and salt.

2. In another skillet, sauté the pine nuts in the butter until golden, then stir into the lamb mixture.

3. Use to fill phyllo.

▶ Can be prepared 2 days in advance.

≡ Apricot Pork Filling

= **Yield: 50 pastries**

½ pound dried apricots, chopped
¼ cup white wine
2 cups chopped scallions
3 garlic cloves, minced
½ cup butter

¾ cup pine nuts
1 tablespoon dried thyme
1 pound ground pork
2 eggs
salt and pepper, to taste

= **Yield: 200 pastries**

2 pounds dried apricots, chopped
1 cup white wine
2 quarts chopped scallions
12 garlic cloves, minced
2 cups butter

3 cups pine nuts
¼ cup dried thyme
4 pounds ground pork
8 eggs
salt and pepper, to taste

1. In a bowl, soak the apricots in the wine for 20 minutes.

2. In a skillet, sauté the scallions and garlic in the butter until soft but not brown. Add the pine nuts and thyme and sauté until the nuts are golden. Add the pork and cook, stirring, until it loses its color.

3. Add the eggs to the apricot mixture and season with salt and pepper. Stir in the pork.

4. Use to fill phyllo or other pastries.

▶ Can be prepared 2 days in advance.

≡ Sausage-Mushroom Strudel

= **Yield: 50 pastries**

1 pound Italian sausage, peeled
1 pound mushrooms, minced
¼ cup minced shallots

⅓ cup butter
salt and pepper, to taste
½ pound ricotta cheese

═ Yield: 200 pastries

4 pounds Italian sausage, peeled

4 pounds mushrooms, minced

1 cup minced shallots

1⅓ cups butter

salt and pepper, to taste

2 pounds ricotta cheese

1. In a skillet, sauté the sausage, breaking it into bits, until it loses its color.

2. In a separate skillet, sauté the mushrooms and shallots in the butter until the liquid evaporates. Correct the seasoning with salt and pepper.

3. In a bowl, mix the sausage, mushroom mixture, and cheese.

4. Use to fill buttered phyllo and other pastries, or to stuff French bread.

▶ Can be prepared 2 days in advance.

= 16 =

Yeast Doughs

Yeast doughs are not often used for hors d'oeuvre because they tend to be too heavy. There are exceptions, however. Bread, of course, is a base for many hors d'oeuvre, and there are doughs baked with fillings, such as calzone, that are served as hors d'oeuvre as well.

As any professional baker knows, yeast doughs are easy and trouble-free for the most part, needing only the necessary time to rise. The two areas of failure usually involve the yeast. It can be too old, so check the package date, or the liquid added to the yeast can be too hot and kill it.

As with many of the other doughs, yeast doughs can be deep-fried as well as baked. The dough can be shaped into turnovers or into small filled balls.

When preparing baked flat breads such as pizza or lahmajoon (an Armenian pizza), you can make them in rounds 2 to 12 inches and serve them individually or by the slice. For larger affairs, you may wish to line a baking sheet with the dough and make large rectangles that can be cut into bite-size pieces.

Preparing the Dough
After the dough has been prepared, knead it by hand, in an electric mixer, or in a food processor. If using a mixer, be sure it is a heavy-duty machine. If using a food processor, use the proper blade for the machine. Kneading by hand, even in commercial operations, is simple, pleasurable, and satisfactory. Knead with vigor and firmness for the best result. Put the dough on a lightly floured surface and, with the heels of your hands, push the dough away from you about 6 to 10 inches. Pick up the far edge with your fingertips and lift it part way over the top of the dough, giving the dough a slight turn. Repeat. Once you get the

knack, this becomes a smooth rocking motion. Knead the dough until it is smooth, elastic, and no longer sticks to your fingers. Take care not to add too much flour during the kneading. Depending on the energy you expend and the amount of dough, the kneading can take 5 to 20 minutes.

Place the dough in an oiled or floured bowl, cover with a damp cloth, and let rise until doubled in bulk. To test, push a finger into the dough. If the hole remains, it has doubled; if it fills in within a minute, it needs to rise longer. Any yeast dough benefits from long, slow rising if you have the time. Dough can be refrigerated overnight to slow the rising.

The fillings and toppings in this chapter, as with many of the other chapters, are only a few of the possibilities. Changing a filling or topping from one pastry or vegetable to another can create a new dimension. For yeast doughs, be sure to use full-flavored fillings or toppings that can stand up to the dough.

≡ Buckwheat Blinis

These puffy little pancakes are the classic accompaniment to fresh beluga caviar. They are worth the effort if you are serving the best of those sumptuous little eggs.

═ Yield: 36 blinis

1 package dry yeast	1 teaspoon salt
¼ cup warm water	3 tablespoons melted butter
¾ cup lukewarm milk	1¼ cups sifted buckwheat flour
¾ cup sifted buckwheat flour	2 cups lukewarm milk
4 egg yolks	4 egg whites
1 tablespoon sugar	

═ Yield: 144 blinis

4 packages dry yeast	4 teaspoons salt
1 cup warm water	¾ cup melted butter
3 cups lukewarm milk	5 cups sifted buckwheat flour
3 cups sifted buckwheat flour	2 quarts lukewarm milk
16 egg yolks	16 egg whites
¼ cup sugar	

1. In a bowl, sprinkle the yeast over the water and let prove. Add the milk and buckwheat flour and stir until smooth. Cover and let stand in a warm place for 2 hours.

2. Beat in the egg yolks, sugar, salt, and melted butter. Beat in the remaining flour and milk.

3. In another bowl, beat the egg whites until stiff but not dry. Fold into the batter.

4. Pour just enough batter onto a buttered griddle to make cakes the size of a silver dollar. Brown on both sides and serve warm.

▶ These can be baked and reheated. However, they are best when freshly baked.

NOTE: If desired, prepare the batter the day before, except for the egg whites. Chill overnight, stirring down once or twice. Shortly before using, beat and fold in the egg whites.

—— *Pizza* ——

Americans adore pizza and will eat it on every occasion. This is the basic dough; a selection of toppings and variations follow.

≡ *Pizza Dough*

≡ **Yield: 100 1-inch pieces or six 5-inch pizzas**

2½ cups flour	½ teaspoon salt
1 package dry yeast	1 cup warm water

1. In a bowl or a food processor, mix the flour, yeast, salt, and water to form a dough.

2. Turn out onto a board and knead until smooth, adding as little extra flour as possible.

3. Place in a bowl rubbed with olive oil, cover with a damp towel, and let rise until doubled in bulk, about 1 hour. Punch down and knead until elastic. Let rise again.

4. Preheat the oven to 450°F.

5. Punch down and roll into circles or a rectangle ¼ inch thick. Place on an oiled baking pan. Spread with a topping and bake for 20 minutes or until golden. Cut into squares and serve warm.

▶ Pizzas can be reheated, but they are never as good as when served warm right after baking.

NOTE: With the current dietary interest, you can make a whole wheat dough by substituting 1 cup whole wheat flour for 1 cup white flour.

As with any hors d'oeuvre, pizza should be served in bite-size pieces. Cutting a 5-inch circle into quarters makes a somewhat large, but still acceptable serving. You may prefer to cut it into sixths. Beware of cutting them too thin, however, or the strips will flop over as guests try to eat them.

If desired, partially bake the pizza shell for 15 minutes or until it sets its shape. Remove and let cool. When ready to serve, put it in the oven on the rack without a baking sheet to crisp the bottom and finish the cooking.

Pizza Toppings

The original topping for pizza—tomato sauce with a tracery of anchovy fillets or a generous sprinkling of mozzarella—has given way to more exotic combinations. Many chefs now prepare pizza fantasies that do not always work, such as rare duck breast with fresh raspberries. However, there is room for great imagination, and I encourage you to be inventive.

My good friend, the Boston architect Daniel Sugarman, often gives parties with small pizzas as the principal form of food. He rolls the dough into 5-inch circles and partially bakes them. When the guests arrive, he starts putting on different toppings and finishes the baking. Quickly cut into quarters, the pizzas are served hot and often.

This is easy for any professional kitchen to accomplish. Line up the topping components and bake trays of different varieties as the party progresses.

Here are a few standard suggestions, but let your imagination soar and create your own. These pizzas could be one of *the* reasons why people select your firm over others.

≡ Pissaladière

This pizza is from the south of France, where it is a popular street food.

≡ Yield: 100 1-inch pieces

1¼ pounds onions, thinly sliced	salt and pepper, to taste
¼ cup olive oil	12 anchovy fillets
2 tomatoes, peeled, seeded, and chopped	12 pitted black olives
3 garlic cloves, chopped	1 recipe pizza dough (page 629)

1. Preheat oven to 450°F.

2. In a skillet, sweat the onions in the olive oil very slowly, covered, until very soft and pale gold. Stir in the tomatoes, garlic, salt, and pepper and simmer until almost dry. Cool slightly.

3. Roll the pastry ¼ inch thick and spread with the topping. Crisscross the anchovy fillets over the topping and insert black olives into the interstices.

4. Bake 20 minutes, lower the heat to 350°F, and bake 20 minutes longer. Serve warm.

Variations: Thinly slice two green peppers and cook with the onions. After assembling, sprinkle either grated Parmesan or Gruyère cheese over the top, or omit the cheese and sprinkle 3 tablespoons capers.

≡ *Pizza Marinara (Pizza with Tomato Sauce)*

≡ **Yield: 100 1-inch pieces**

3 pounds plum tomatoes
⅔ cup olive oil
1 recipe pizza dough (page 629)

salt
6 garlic cloves, thinly sliced
1 tablespoon minced oregano

1. Preheat the oven to 450°F.

2. In a saucepan, cook the tomatoes in ⅓ cup olive oil until thickened. Cool.

3. Spread tomatoes on the pizza dough and sprinkle with salt, garlic, and oregano. Drizzle the remaining oil over the top. Let rise 10 minutes, then bake 20 minutes or until golden and crisp.

≡ *Pizza Margherita*
(Pizza with Tomatoes, Mozzarella, and Parmesan)

≡ **Yield: 100 1-inch pieces**

3 pounds tomatoes, peeled,
   seeded, and chopped
⅔ cup olive oil
1 recipe pizza dough (page 629)

½ pound grated mozzarella
   cheese
¼ cup grated Parmesan cheese

1. Preheat the oven to 450°F.

2. In a saucepan, cook the tomatoes in ⅓ cup olive oil until thickened. Cool.

3. Spread tomatoes on the pizza dough and sprinkle with the mozzarella and Parmesan. Drizzle the remaining oil over the top. Let rise 10 minutes, then bake 20 minutes or until golden and crisp.

≡ *Leek and Chèvre Topping*

≡ **Yield: 100 1-inch pieces**

¼ cup walnut oil
2 cups minced white parts of
   leeks
salt and pepper, to taste
1 recipe pizza dough (page 629)
½ pound Bucheron cheese,
   crumbled

1 tablespoon minced fresh
   summer savory or 1
   teaspoon crumbled dried
   savory

1. Preheat the oven to 450°F.
2. In a skillet, heat the oil and cook the leeks over low heat until soft. Season with salt and pepper.
3. Spread the mixture over the pizza dough and sprinkle with the cheese and savory. Let rise 10 minutes, then bake 20 minutes or until golden.

≡ *Pizza Calabrese (Tomato, Tuna, and Olive Pizza)*

≡ **Yield: 100 1-inch pieces**

3 pounds tomatoes, peeled,
   seeded, and chopped
¼ cup olive oil
8 ounces canned tuna, drained
1 cup pitted ripe olives,
   chopped

4 anchovy fillets, chopped
1 tablespoon capers
salt and pepper, to taste
1 recipe pizza dough (page 629)

1. Preheat the oven to 450°F.
2. In a saucepan, cook the tomatoes in the olive oil until thickened. Stir in the tuna, olives, anchovies, and capers. Season with salt and pepper.
3. Spread topping on the pizza dough, let rise 10 minutes, then bake 20 minutes or until golden and crisp.

≡ *Mascarpone and Smoked Scallop Topping*

≡ **Yield: 100 1-inch pieces**

½ pound mascarpone cheese
2 tablespoons horseradish
salt and pepper, to taste

1 recipe pizza dough (page 629)
½ pound smoked scallops,
   diced

1. In a bowl, mix the cheese and horseradish and season with salt and pepper. Spread over the pizza dough.
2. Let rise 10 minutes, then bake about 20 minutes or until golden. Scatter the scallops over the top and bake 1 minute longer. Serve immediately.

☰ Ricotta and Salami Topping

☰ **Yield: 100 1-inch pieces**

4 tablespoons olive oil
½ cup thinly sliced onion
salt and pepper, to taste
1 recipe pizza dough (page 629)

⅔ cup diced Genoa salami
⅔ cup diced Italian Fontina
  cheese
½ cup ricotta cheese

1. Preheat the oven to 450°F.
2. In a skillet, sauté the onions in the oil until dark golden. Season with salt and pepper. Cool.
3. Spread the onions over the dough and sprinkle with the salami, Fontina, and ricotta.
4. Let rise 10 minutes, then bake for 20 minutes or until golden.

☰ Tomato, Provolone, and Bresaola Topping

☰ **Yield: 100 pieces**

1 recipe pizza dough (page 629)
⅔ cup extra virgin olive oil
¼ cup minced sage leaves
¼ cup minced basil leaves
1 tablespoon minced oregano

⅓ pound provolone cheese,
  sliced
4 large tomatoes, thinly sliced
¼ pound thinly sliced bresaola
  or shredded prosciutto

1. Prick the pizza dough in the pan. Preheat the oven to 450°.
2. In a bowl, mix the olive oil, sage, basil, and oregano, and drizzle half of it over the dough.
3. Lay the provolone slices on top and arrange the tomatoes on top of the provolone. Drizzle with the remaining oil mixture.
4. Let rise 10 minutes, then bake 20 minutes or until golden.
5. Sprinkle the bresaola over the top and bake 1 minute longer.

—— *Lahmajoon (Armenian Pizzas)* ——

The Italians are not the only ones who spread a topping on thin bread dough and then bake it into a luscious snack. Traditionally, these are made in 5-inch circles, although making them in 2- to 3-inch rounds is more attractive for hors d'oeuvre.

≡ *Lahmajoon Dough*

Roll the dough almost paper-thin to provide a crisp, thin "plate" for the topping.

═ Yield: 100 bite-size pieces or 50 tartlets

1 package dry yeast	¼ cup olive oil
½ cup warm water	½ teaspoon salt
2 cups flour	½ teaspoon sugar

1. Preheat the oven to 425°F.

2. In a bowl, mix the yeast and water and let prove. Add the flour, oil, salt, and sugar. Knead until smooth and elastic. Form into a ball, sprinkle with flour, and cover with a towel. Let rise for about 2 hours or until doubled in bulk. Punch down and let rest 10 minutes.

3. Roll ¼ inch thick and cut into 2½-inch circles or into a rectangle to fit an 11″ × 16″ baking sheet. Top with one of the fillings that follow.

4. Bake for 20 minutes or until crisp and brown.

▶ Can be frozen and reheated.

≡ *Lahmajoon Filling I*

═ Yield: 100 bite-size pieces or 50 tartlets

1 cup ground roast lamb	1 tablespoon minced mint
¾ cup tomatoes, peeled, seeded, and finely chopped	4 teaspoons tomato paste
	1 teaspoon minced garlic
¼ cup minced onion	¾ teaspoon salt
3 tablespoons minced green pepper	¼ teaspoon Tabasco sauce
	1 recipe lahmajoon dough
2 tablespoons minced parsley	(preceding recipe)

1. In a bowl, mix the lamb, tomatoes, onion, green pepper, parsley, mint, tomato paste, garlic, salt, and Tabasco sauce.

2. Spread thickly onto the prepared dough and bake as directed.

≡ Lahmajoon Filling II

═ Yield: 200 bite-size pieces or 100 tartlets

⅓ cup pine nuts
2 tablespoons olive oil
1 pound ground raw lamb
   shoulder
1 cup minced onion
1 cup peeled, seeded, and
   chopped tomatoes
⅓ cup minced parsley
¼ cup minced mint leaves
¼ cup minced green pepper

1 tablespoon tamarind juice,
   optional
2½ teaspoons salt
½ teaspoon cayenne pepper
½ teaspoon ground allspice
¼ teaspoon pepper
2 recipes lahmajoon dough
   (page 634)
plain yogurt, optional

1. In a skillet, sauté the pine nuts in the oil until golden. Drain on paper towels.

2. In a bowl, mix the lamb, onion, tomatoes, parsley, mint, green pepper, tamarind juice, salt, cayenne, allspice, pepper, and pine nuts.

3. Spread topping on the dough and bake as directed. Serve with yogurt as a dip.

▶ Can be frozen and reheated.

NOTE: Tamarind juice is available in Middle Eastern markets.

—— Focaccia (Italian Flat Bread) ——

Focaccia, or *caccia* in dialect, is the latest addition to the pizza craze. It is the same dough, pressed flat (but not as thinly as pizza), flavored with extra virgin olive oil, and sprinkled with a very light topping. The topping is pressed into the dough with the fingertips. Once baked, the bread is cut into squares and served warm. It can be made ahead and reheated, but is best when freshly baked.

≡ Focaccia al Salvia, Rosamarino, o Oregane (Sage, Rosemary, or Oregano Flat Bread)

═ Yield: 80 1-inch pieces

1 recipe pizza dough (page 629)
5 tablespoons extra virgin olive
   oil

2 tablespoons minced sage,
   rosemary, or oregano
salt and pepper, to taste

1. Preheat the oven to 400°F.

2. Knead 2 tablespoons olive oil into the dough. Shape the dough into a large flat loaf, about 8 by 10 inches and ½ inch thick. Using your fingertips, make small impressions in the dough over the entire surface.

3. Drizzle the remaining olive oil and sprinkle with the herb. Season with salt and pepper.

4. Let rise 10 minutes, then bake 15 to 20 minutes or until puffed and golden.

≡ Focaccia à la Nanza (Flat Bread with Garlic and Rosemary)

Prepare the above recipe and sprinkle 2 thinly sliced garlic cloves over the surface, pressing them into the dough with your fingers.

≡ Focaccia con Pesto (Flat Bread with Pesto)

≡ **Yield: 80 pieces**

1 recipe pizza dough (page 629)	⅓ cup grated Parmesan cheese
½ cup pesto (page 68)	¼ cup grated Italian Fontina
½ cup shredded mozzarella cheese	cheese

1. Preheat the oven to 400°F.

2. Press the dough ½ inch thick into a rectangle about 8 by 10 inches. Spread with the pesto and sprinkle the mozzarella, Parmesan, and Fontina cheeses over the top.

3. Let rise 10 minutes, then bake 20 minutes or until golden.

—— Calzone ——

As pizza and focaccia have caught the imagination, so has calzone. Calzone is another Italian specialty that is usually made in large loaves and cut into thick slices to be eaten for lunch or carried around as a snack food. It can be made smaller and cut into thinner sections to serve as a luscious hors d'oeuvre. Or it can be made into small turnovers, although the problem with turnovers is that there is often more dough than filling.

≡ Calzone Dough

≡ **Yield: 60 1-inch slices**

1 package dry yeast	2½ to 3 cups flour
1 cup warm water	1½ teaspoons salt
¼ cup olive oil	

1. In a bowl, proof the yeast in the water and stir in the olive oil.

2. In a food processor, mix the flour and salt. With the machine running, add the yeast in a stream and process until the dough is smooth. Turn the dough onto a lightly floured board and knead briefly. Place in a lightly oiled bowl and let rise until doubled in bulk, about 1 hour.

3. Roll the dough into a large oval or cut it into four pieces and roll each piece into a 9-inch circle. Let the dough rise for 30 minutes before filling if possible.

4. For hors d'oeuvre, divide the dough into four pieces and roll into long rectangles, about 3 inches wide and 16 inches long.

5. Place the filling in the center, moisten the edges, and seal by pinching the seams. Place seam-side down on a baking sheet, let rise 15 minutes, and bake. Let calzone rest for 10 minutes before cutting into 1-inch slices.

≡ Calzone Margherita (Tomato Mozzarella Filling)

≡ **Yield: 60 1-inch slices**

calzone dough (preceding recipe)	¼ cup grated Parmesan cheese
1 cup thinly sliced onions	2 tablespoons olive oil
3 tablespoons olive oil	2 garlic cloves, minced
35-ounce can Italian tomatoes, drained and chopped	8 basil leaves, minced
	½ teaspoon dried oregano
8 ounces mozzarella cheese, diced	⅛ teaspoon pepper

1. Preheat the oven to 450°F.

2. While the dough is rising, make the filling. In a skillet, sauté the onions in the oil until golden. Add the tomatoes and cook until the liquid evaporates.

3. In a bowl, mix the mozzarella, Parmesan, oil, garlic, basil, oregano, and pepper. Add the tomatoes and mix gently.

4. Roll and shape the calzone and fill with the tomato mixture, pinching the seams to seal. Place it on an oiled baking sheet and bake

20 to 25 minutes or until puffed and brown. Let it rest 10 minutes before cutting into 1-inch slices.

▶ Can be baked and reheated.

≡ Calzone Siciliano

≡ **Yield: 60 1-inch slices**

calzone dough (page 637)
3 tablespoons olive oil
1 cup thinly sliced onions
35-ounce can Italian tomatoes,
   drained and chopped

1½ teaspoons dried oregano
pinch of salt and pepper
⅓ cup calamata olives, pitted
   and chopped
1 can anchovy fillets

  1. Preheat the oven to 450°F.

  2. While the dough is rising, make the filling. In a large skillet, heat the oil and sauté the onions until golden. Add the tomatoes, oregano, salt, and pepper and simmer, stirring until the liquid evaporates, about 20 minutes. Cool.

  3. Roll and shape the calzone and fill with the tomato mixture. Arrange the olives and anchovies on top. Bake until puffed and golden, about 20 to 25 minutes. Let rest 10 minutes before cutting into 1-inch slices.

▶ Can be baked and reheated.

≡ Calzone con Salsicci

≡ **Yield: 60 1-inch slices**

calzone dough (page 637)
¾ pound Italian sausage
2 red peppers, thinly sliced
2 green peppers, thinly sliced

3 tablespoons olive oil
3 cups thinly sliced onions
½ to 1 teaspoon salt
pinch of pepper

  1. Preheat the oven to 450°F.

  2. While the dough is rising, make the filling. Prick the sausages with a fork and place in a skillet with ½ inch of water. Simmer, covered, until the water evaporates, about 20 minutes. Uncover and cook, turning occasionally until the sausages are browned. Let cool and chop finely.

  3. In a skillet, sauté the red and green peppers in the oil for 5 minutes. Add the onions, salt, and pepper. Cook until the peppers are soft and the onions are lightly browned, about 15 to 20 minutes. Remove from the heat, stir in the sausages, and cool.

4. Roll and shape the calzone and fill with the sausage mixture, pinching the seams to seal. Bake about 20 minutes or until puffed and golden. Let cool 10 minutes before cutting into 1-inch slices.

▶ Can be baked and reheated.

≡ Calzone Italiano (Meat and Cheese Filling)

≡ **Yield: 60 1-inch slices**

calzone dough (page 637)
¼ pound mortadella, sliced
¼ pound salami, sliced
¼ pound boiled ham, sliced
¼ pound Gruyère cheese, sliced

¼ pound mozzarella cheese, sliced
3 sun-dried tomatoes, sliced
1 cup thinly sliced onion
1 egg, beaten
2 tablespoons water
sesame seeds

1. Preheat the oven to 450°F.

2. Roll the dough and fill as follows: Arrange the mortadella, salami, ham, Gruyère, mozzarella, tomatoes, and onion in the center.

3. Brush the edges of the dough with the egg beaten with the water, and fold over and pinch the edges to seal.

4. Brush the top of the dough with the egg wash and sprinkle with the sesame seeds. Bake 20 minutes or until puffed and golden. Let rest 10 minutes before cutting into 1-inch slices.

▶ Can be baked and reheated.

—— Pirozhki (Stuffed Pastries) ——

The Slavic countries are justifiably famous for their version of turnovers made with a yeast dough. The fillings can also be used to fill short pastry, cream cheese dough, and phyllo.

≡ Pirozhki Dough

≡ **Yield: 60 pirozhki**

1 package dry yeast
1 cup scalded milk
5 cups flour
3 eggs
½ cup melted butter

2 teaspoons sugar
1 teaspoon salt
pirozhki filling (see following recipes)
1 egg yolk

1. In a large bowl, dissolve the yeast in the milk. Stir in half the flour and let prove, covered, for 1 hour.

2. In another bowl, beat the eggs, butter, sugar, and salt, and add to the yeast mixture. Add the remaining flour and mix well.

3. Knead until smooth and elastic. Form into a ball and place in a large buttered bowl. Cover and let rise until doubled in bulk.

4. Preheat the oven to 400°F.

5. Roll the dough ¼ inch thick and cut into 3-inch circles. Place 1 tablespoon of filling in the center of each circle. Brush the edges with cold water and fold to form turnovers. Let rise 12 to 15 minutes.

6. Brush the turnovers with egg yolk beaten with a little water and bake 12 to 15 minutes. Lower heat to 350°F and bake 10 minutes longer. Or deep-fry at 375°F until golden.

▶ Can be baked, frozen, and reheated.

≡ *Mushroom and Onion Filling*

≡ **Yield: 60 pirozhki**

4 cups thinly sliced mushrooms
4 tablespoons butter
1 cup minced onion

salt and pepper, to taste
3 tablespoons sour cream

Sauté the mushrooms in 2 tablespoons butter until tender. In a separate skillet, sauté the onion in the remaining butter until soft but not browned. Combine the mushrooms and onions and season with salt and pepper. Stir in the sour cream.

▶ Can be prepared 2 days in advance.

≡ *Salmon-Egg-Rice Filling*

≡ **Yield: 60 pirozhki**

½ cup minced onion
½ cup minced mushrooms
2 tablespoons butter
2 cups cooked rice
½ pound salmon, cooked and
  flaked

1 hard-cooked egg, chopped
1 tablespoon minced dill
salt and pepper, to taste
2 tablespoons sour cream

In a skillet, sauté the onion and mushrooms in the butter until soft. Add the rice, salmon, egg, dill, salt, and pepper. Remove from the heat and stir in the sour cream. Cool.

▶ Can be prepared 2 days in advance.

═ Beef Filling

═ **Yield: 60 pirozhki**

1 cup minced onion	2 tablespoons minced dill
5 tablespoons butter	1 tablespoon flour
1 pound ground beef	¼ cup water
salt and pepper, to taste	2 hard-cooked eggs, chopped

In a skillet, sauté the onion in the butter until lightly browned. Add the beef and sauté until browned. Season with salt and pepper. Remove the beef. In the same pan, add the dill and flour. Cook, stirring until the flour is golden brown. Add the water and bring to a boil, stirring. Return the beef to the pan and add the eggs.

▶ Can be prepared 2 days in advance.

═ Lamb and Cabbage Filling

═ **Yield: 60 pirozhki**

2 cups chopped cabbage	1 tablespoon minced dill
½ cup minced onion	1 teaspoon lemon juice
3 tablespoons butter	salt and pepper, to taste
1 pound ground lamb	¼ cup sour cream

In a skillet, sauté the cabbage and onion in the butter until soft. Stir in the lamb and cook, stirring, until the lamb loses its color. Add the dill, lemon juice, salt, and pepper. Mix well. Stir in the sour cream.

▶ Can be prepared 2 days in advance.

── Faggottini (Fried Italian Turnovers) ──

Faggottini are little bundles. They can be little bundles of anything, such as crêpes wrapped around a filling, or slices of prosciutto wrapped around bunches of green beans, but here they are a yeast dough wrapped around a filling and made into small turnovers. They are usually deep-fried, but there is no reason why they could not be brushed with a dorure and baked at 375°F until golden. The fillings for calzone and faggottini are interchangeable.

≡ *Faggottini Dough*

== **Yield: 25 turnovers**

1 package dry yeast	2 cups sifted flour
1½ cups warm water	oil for frying

== **Yield: 100 turnovers**

2 packages dry yeast	8 cups sifted flour
1½ quarts warm water	oil for frying

1. In a bowl, dissolve the yeast in one third of the water and let prove.

2. Stir in the flour and the remaining water. Turn dough onto a board and knead until smooth and elastic. Clean the bowl, brush with oil, return the dough to it, and let the dough rise for 2 hours or until doubled in bulk.

3. Turn the dough onto a floured board. Roll out very thinly, about ⅛ inch thick. Cut into 2- to 3-inch circles. Place 1 tablespoon of filling on each circle and shape into turnovers. Pinch edges to seal.

4. Heat the oil to 375°F and fry until crisp and golden. Serve immediately.

▶ The dough should be filled and fried within 1 hour of being made.

≡ *Faggottini Filling I*

== **Yield: 25 turnovers**

½ cup minced onion	¼ cup minced Spanish olives
2 tablespoons butter	1½ tablespoons pickle relish
2 ounces ground pork	1 tablespoon tomato purée
2 ounces ground beef	1 tablespoon minced capers
½ cup diced green pepper	1 egg, lightly beaten
1 hot green chili pepper, seeded and minced	1 small recipe faggottini dough (preceding recipe)
¼ cup raisins	

≡ Yield: 100 turnovers

2 cups minced onion
½ cup butter
½ pound ground pork
½ pound ground beef
2 cups diced green pepper
4 hot green chili peppers,
   seeded and minced
1 cup raisins

1 cup minced Spanish olives
⅓ cup pickle relish
¼ cup tomato purée
¼ cup minced capers
4 eggs, lightly beaten
1 large recipe faggottini dough
   (preceding recipe)

1. In a skillet, sauté the onion in the butter until soft. Add the pork and beef and cook, breaking up the chunks until the meats lose their color.

2. Add the green pepper and cook 5 minutes. Stir in the chili pepper, raisins, olives, relish, tomato purée, and capers. Stir in the egg and cook until it just begins to set.

3. Fill and fry the faggottini as directed.

▶ Can be prepared 2 days in advance.

≡ *Faggottini Filling II*

≡ Yield: 25 turnovers

½ pound mozzarella cheese,
   diced
10 anchovy fillets, diced
1 tablespoon minced parsley

salt and pepper, to taste
1 small recipe faggottini dough
   (page 642)
oil for frying

≡ Yield: 100 turnovers

2 pounds mozzarella cheese,
   diced
40 anchovy fillets, diced
¼ cup minced parsley

salt and pepper, to taste
1 large recipe faggottini dough
   (page 642)
oil for frying

1. In a bowl, mix the cheese, anchovies, parsley, salt, and pepper.

2. Fill the dough as directed.

3. Heat the oil to 375°F and fry until crisp and golden. Serve hot.

▶ Can be prepared 2 days in advance.

≡ *Faggottini Filling III*

This recipe can be easily multiplied.

═ Yield: 20

1 small recipe faggottini dough
(page 642)
2 tomatoes, diced
4 ounces mozzarella cheese,
cut into 20 pieces

20 basil leaves
10 anchovy fillets, cut in half
oil for frying

1. Prepare the dough, roll thinly, and cut into 3-inch circles. Put a piece of tomato, mozzarella, 1 basil leaf, and half an anchovy fillet on half of the circles.

2. Brush the edges with cold water, top with the remaining circles, and press to seal. Let rise until puffy, about 30 minutes.

3. Heat the oil to 375°F and fry until puffed and golden.

▶ Fill and fry just before serving.

—— *Brioche* ——

≡ *Brioche, Processor Method*

One of the great advantages of the food processor is its speed. Using the processor to make several batches of brioche dough in minutes is more efficient than making one large batch using ordinary methods.

═ Yield: 3 pounds dough

1 package dry yeast
¼ cup warm milk
1 tablespoon sugar
2 cups flour

1 teaspoon salt
½ cup very cold butter cut into
pieces
2 eggs, lightly beaten

1. In a bowl, mix the yeast, milk, and sugar and let prove.

2. In a food processor, process the flour, salt, and butter until the mixture resembles coarse meal. With the machine running, add the yeast and eggs and process until blended.

3. Turn onto a board and knead until smooth. Put into a buttered bowl and let rise until doubled in bulk. Punch down. The dough is ready to shape and bake.

≡ *Brie en Croûte (Brie Baked in Brioche Dough)*

≡ **Yield: 100 or more servings**

2-kilo Brie cheese   dorure

1 recipe brioche dough
   (preceding recipe)

1. Preheat the oven to 375°F. Unwrap the Brie and remove any labels.

2. Divide the dough into two parts. Roll one half into a large circle about 2 inches larger than the cheese. Place the cheese on the dough and lift the edges up over the top of the dough.

3. With a sharp knife, cut off the extra dough, leaving enough to make a ½-inch edge around the top of the cheese. Brush with dorure.

4. Roll the remaining dough into a circle larger than the cheese. Place the circle on top of the cheese and trim the edge to fit. Use the scraps to make a design on top of the cheese. Brush with dorure.

5. Bake for 35 minutes or until puffed and golden.

▶ Bake as close to serving time as possible. Ideally, the cheese should be hot and runny when served.

NOTE: The design I use most often is to roll bits of the dough into small balls and assemble them to look like a bunch of grapes on the center of the pastry. With the remaining scraps, I cut out leaves and shape stems. Very thin strings of the dough can be wrapped around buttered pencils and placed on the baking sheet. When they are golden, remove them from the pan and let cool. Twist the pencil in place to loosen them and withdraw. Arrange these "tendrils" at the top of the bunch of grapes after the cheese is baked.

Other cheeses can be used, such as Camembert and St. André. Fairly soft, very rich cheeses with high butter content work best. They tend not to get as rubbery as quickly.

≡ *Fried Brie en Croûte*

Cut the cheese into tiny ½-inch cubes and wrap in small squares of the pastry. Heat oil to 375°F and deep-fry until golden.

≡ *Saucisson en Croûte (Sausage in Pastry)*

≡ **Yield: 50 slices**

2½ pounds pork shoulder,
  coarsely ground
½ pound fresh pork fat,
  coarsely ground
½ cup bourbon
4 garlic cloves, minced
2 tablespoons dried rosemary

1 tablespoon dried thyme
1 tablespoon salt
1 tablespoon pepper
1 recipe brioche dough
  (page 644)
dorure

≡ **Yield: 200 slices**

10 pounds pork shoulder,
  coarsely ground
2 pounds fresh pork fat,
  coarsely ground
2 cups bourbon
16 garlic cloves, minced
½ cup dried rosemary

¼ cup dried thyme
¼ cup salt
¼ cup pepper
4 recipes brioche dough
  (page 644)
dorure

1. Preheat the oven to 375°F.

2. In a bowl, mix the pork, pork fat, bourbon, garlic, rosemary, thyme, salt, and pepper.

3. Shape into 1½-inch-thick sausages and wrap in double layers of cheesecloth. Twist ends to secure and tie with string. Poach in boiling salted water for 35 to 40 minutes, or until the juices run clear when pricked with a fork. Remove from the pan and chill. Unwrap the sausages.

4. Roll the pastry ¼ inch thick and enclose the sausages. Brush with dorure and let rise until they look puffy, about 30 minutes.

5. Brush again with dorure and bake until golden, about 35 minutes. Cut into slices.

▶ Can be frozen and reheated.

= 17 =

Crackers, Salt Pastries, Cheese Pastries, and Sponge Rolls

Although there are many commercial crackers available, making your own is a new flavor treat. Since making crackers is admittedly uninteresting, you may want to prepare them for a small group rather than a large crowd. Of course, once you understand the basics, you will be able to flavor and season them to suit yourself.

Salt pastries are very popular in Europe. When served a drink, you are most likely to be offered a salt pastry rather than some of the more elaborate hors d'oeuvre that Americans proffer. Salt pastries are a delicious nibble when your goal is to provide something light and subtle to accompany a glass of wine or a soup or salad course.

Cheese pastries are similar to biscuits or crackers. They usually stand on their own, although some can be filled. A selection of these in the freezer will allow you to be always ready for unexpected company. The bed and breakfast, small inn, or elite restaurant may find these the perfect offering while guests are relaxing with a cocktail. Cheese pastries have many advantages: They can be made ahead, they freeze beautifully, and are generally quick to make.

Almost all of the pastries in this chapter can be prepared in advance. Store them at room temperature for 2 to 3 days or prepare them in quantity and freeze. If they are to be kept frozen, store them in plastic or metal containers to protect them—they are delicate. When ready to serve, thaw as many as you need and warm them in a 350°F oven for a few minutes to give them a more inviting flavor.

Sponge rolls are unsweetened sponge cakes that are filled and rolled like a jellyroll. They are very delicate and are usually subtly seasoned. Add them to those menus where elegance reigns. The fillings suggested here are just some of the possibilities. Many of the spreads also can be used to fill these delicious, light hors d'oeuvre. Just choose a filling that has some adhesion in order to keep the rolls rolled.

—— *Crackers* ——

≡ *Soda Crackers*

═ Yield: 50 crackers

½ cup sour milk	1 teaspoon butter
½ teaspoon baking soda	1 teaspoon lard
3 cups flour	coarse (kosher) salt

═ Yield: 200 crackers

2 cups sour milk	4 teaspoons butter
2 teaspoons baking soda	4 teaspoons lard
12 cups flour	coarse (kosher) salt

1. Preheat the oven to 350°F.

2. In a bowl, mix the milk and soda. Stir in the flour to make a stiff dough. Knead in the butter and lard.

3. Roll the dough ⅛ inch thick and cut into shapes. Sprinkle with salt and prick with a fork.

4. Place on unbuttered baking sheets and bake until crisp, about 12 to 15 minutes.

▶ Keeps 1 week in an airtight container.

NOTE: Cut these crackers into squares, rectangles, triangles, diamonds, circles, crescents, or animal or seasonal shapes.

Both the butter and lard are necessary. The butter provides the flavor and the lard the flakiness. Vegetable shortening can be used, but the crackers will not be as flaky.

≡ *Whole Wheat Crackers*

═ Yield: 30 crackers

1½ cups whole wheat flour	2½ tablespoons vegetable oil
½ cup cornmeal	1½ tablespoons honey
1 teaspoon salt	⅓ to ½ cup water

═ **Yield: 120 crackers**

6 cups whole wheat flour

2 cups cornmeal

4 teaspoons salt

10 tablespoons vegetable oil

6 tablespoons honey

1⅓ to 2 cups water

1. Preheat the oven to 375°F.

2. In a bowl, mix the flour, cornmeal, salt, oil, honey, and just enough water to make a workable dough.

3. Roll as thinly as possible, about 14 by 16 inches for the smaller quantity, and cut into 1½-inch squares. Divide the larger quantity into 4 pieces and roll.

4. Bake 15 to 20 minutes. Transfer the crackers individually to a rack as they brown, rather than waiting for the whole tray.

▶ Keeps 1 week in an airtight container; can be frozen.

—— *Salt Pastries* ——

═ *Haselnuss Salzgebäck (Salted Hazelnut Crackers)*

═ **Yield: 100 crackers**

2½ cups flour

½ teaspoon salt

¾ cup butter

1 egg yolk

2 tablespoons ice water, approximately

1 egg yolk beaten with 1 teaspoon water

2 tablespoons salt

2 tablespoons cinnamon

1 cup ground hazelnuts

═ **Yield: 400 crackers**

10 cups flour

2 teaspoons salt

3 cups butter

4 egg yolks

½ cup ice water, approximately

4 egg yolks beaten with 4 teaspoons water

½ cup salt

½ cup cinnamon

1 quart ground hazelnuts

1. Preheat the oven to 350°F.

2. In a bowl, mix the flour and salt. Cut in the butter and work in the egg yolk(s) and just enough water to make a smooth dough. Shape into a flat cake and wrap in waxed paper. Chill 30 minutes.

3. On a lightly floured board, roll the dough ⅛ inch thick and cut into 1½-inch circles. Brush with the beaten egg yolk(s) and water.

4. In a bowl, mix the salt and cinnamon and sprinkle over the circles. Sprinkle on the hazelnuts.

5. Bake on an unbuttered baking sheet for 15 minutes or until golden.

▶ Keeps 1 week in an airtight container; can be frozen.

≡ *Salzschiffen (Salt Boats)*

≡ **Yield: approximately 50 barquettes**

1 small recipe haselnuss
 salzgebäck (see preceding
 recipe)

Use the pastry to line barquette molds (see page 537) and bake until golden. Fill with a cheese filling or spread, or any other savory filling.

≡ *Salztangen I (Salt Sticks I)*

≡ **Yield: 50 sticks**

½ cup butter	1 teaspoon salt
1 cup flour	1 egg, beaten
¼ pound potatoes, boiled and riced	coarse (kosher) salt

≡ **Yield: 200 sticks**

2 cups butter	4 teaspoons salt
4 cups flour	4 eggs, beaten
1 pound potatoes, boiled and riced	coarse (kosher) salt

1. Preheat the oven to 350°F.

2. In a bowl, work the butter, flour, potatoes, and salt to form a smooth dough. Shape into a flat cake, wrap in waxed paper, and chill for 15 minutes.

3. Roll to less than ¼ inch thick and cut into strips ½ inch wide and 6 inches long. Brush with beaten egg and sprinkle generously with salt.

4. Bake about 15 minutes or until golden.

▶ Keeps 1 week in an airtight container; can be frozen.

≡ Salztangen II (Salt Sticks II)

═ Yield: 50 sticks

1½ cups flour
½ teaspoon salt
¼ teaspoon baking powder
⅓ cup butter
2 egg yolks

¼ cup heavy cream
1 egg yolk beaten with 1
    teaspoon water
coarse (kosher) salt
caraway, poppy, or celery seeds

═ Yield: 200 sticks

6 cups flour
2 teaspoons salt
1 teaspoon baking powder
1⅓ cups butter
8 egg yolks

1 cup heavy cream
4 egg yolks beaten with 4
    teaspoons water
coarse (kosher) salt
caraway, poppy, or celery seeds

1. Preheat the oven to 350°F.

2. In a bowl, mix the flour, salt, and baking powder. Cut in the butter. Add the egg yolks and cream and work into a smooth dough. Shape into a flat cake, wrap in waxed paper, and chill 2 hours.

3. Roll 1½-tablespoon portions of the dough into pencil-thin sticks, about 14 inches long. Brush the sticks with the beaten egg yolk(s) and water and sprinkle with salt and seeds.

4. Bake on unbuttered baking sheets for 15 minutes or until golden.

▶ Keeps 1 week in an airtight container; can be frozen.

≡ Kartoffelteig (Potato Dough)

═ Yield: 25 pastries

1 cup sifted flour
½ cup butter
1 cup grated Parmesan cheese

½ teaspoon salt
½ cup riced boiled potatoes
¼ cup grated Parmesan cheese

═ Yield: 100 pastries

4 cups sifted flour
2 cups butter
4 cups grated Parmesan cheese

2 teaspoons salt
2 cups riced boiled potatoes
1 cup grated Parmesan cheese

1. In a bowl, mix the flour, butter, 1 cup (*4 cups*) cheese, salt, and potatoes. Roll the dough ¼ inch thick, fold in thirds, and chill 30 minutes.

2. Roll ½ inch thick and sprinkle with half the remaining cheese. Fold in thirds and chill again. Roll ½ inch thick and sprinkle with the rest of the cheese. Fold in thirds again. Chill before rolling and cutting.

▶ Can be prepared 1 day in advance.

☰ *Kartoffelstangen (Potato Sticks)*

═ Yield: 25 sticks

1 small recipe kartoffelteig (see preceding recipe)	⅓ cup grated Parmesan cheese

═ Yield: 100 sticks

1 large recipe kartoffelteig (see preceding recipe)	1⅓ cups grated Parmesan cheese

1. Preheat the oven to 350°F.
2. Roll the dough ⅛ inch thick on a lightly floured board. Cut into strips ½ inch wide and 6 inches long. Place on an unbuttered baking sheet and sprinkle with the cheese.
3. Bake 15 minutes or until golden.

▶ Keeps 1 week in an airtight container; can be frozen.

☰ *Plätzchen (Potato Disks)*

═ Yield: 25 disks

1 small recipe kartoffelteig (page 651)	1 cup hazelnuts salt, to taste

═ Yield: 100 disks

1 large recipe kartoffelteig (page 651)	4 cups hazelnuts salt, to taste

1. Preheat the oven to 350°F.
2. Roll the dough ⅛ inch thick and cut into 1-inch circles. Press one hazelnut into each circle and sprinkle with salt. Place on an unbuttered baking sheet and bake for 15 minutes or until golden.

▶ Keeps 1 week in an airtight container; can be frozen.

≡ *Poppy Seed Twists*

═ Yield: 100 twists

⅓ cup poppy seeds	¼ cup minced parsley
2⅔ cups flour	1 egg
1 cup butter, softened	2 tablespoons heavy cream
4 egg yolks, lightly beaten	coarse (kosher) salt
3 hard-cooked eggs, sieved	coarsely ground black pepper
1 teaspoon salt	dorure

═ Yield: 300 twists

1 cup poppy seeds	¾ cup minced parsley
8 cups flour	3 eggs
3 cups butter, softened	⅓ cup heavy cream
12 egg yolks, lightly beaten	coarse (kosher) salt
9 hard-cooked eggs, sieved	coarsely ground black pepper
1 tablespoon salt	dorure

1. Preheat the oven to 350°F.

2. In a bowl, soak the poppy seeds in water to cover by 1 inch for 3 hours.

3. In a food processor, blend the flour, butter, egg yolks, hard-cooked eggs, and salt just until they form a dough. Shape into a flat cake and chill 1 hour.

4. Drain the poppy seeds, dry on paper towels, and pulverize in a blender. Mix in the parsley.

5. On a lightly floured board, roll the dough into rectangles 7 inches wide. Beat the egg(s) and cream together and brush over the dough. Spread the poppy seed mixture on top and season with salt and pepper. Cut into ½-inch-wide strips. Twist each strip 3 or 4 times and put on a lightly buttered baking sheet. Brush with dorure.

6. Bake about 15 minutes or until golden.

▶ Keeps 1 week in an airtight container; can be frozen.

≡ Sesame Seed–Cheese Crackers

═ Yield: 40 crackers

¼ pound grated Cheddar
cheese
5 tablespoons butter
3 tablespoons water
2 tablespoons sesame seeds
1 teaspoon dry mustard

1 teaspoon Tabasco sauce
1 teaspoon salt
1 cup flour
1 teaspoon baking powder
1 egg
sesame seeds

═ Yield: 160 crackers

1 pound grated Cheddar cheese
1½ pounds butter
¾ cup water
½ cup sesame seeds
4 teaspoons dry mustard
4 teaspoons Tabasco sauce

4 teaspoons salt
4 cups flour
4 teaspoons baking powder
4 eggs
sesame seeds

1. Preheat the oven to 350°F.

2. Butter two baking sheets and sprinkle with cold water. Set aside.

3. In a bowl, mix the cheese, butter, water, sesame seeds, mustard, Tabasco sauce, and half the salt. Add the flour and baking powder and work to form a dough. Wrap in waxed paper and chill for 30 minutes.

4. Roll the dough ¼ inch thick and cut into 1-inch circles. Place on the baking sheet.

5. In a bowl, mix the egg(s) and the remaining salt, and brush the tops of the crackers. Sprinkle with sesame seeds.

6. Bake about 15 minutes or until golden.

▶ Keeps 1 week in an airtight container; can be frozen.

≡ Sesame Seed Cocktail Biscuits

═ Yield: 100 crackers

2 cups flour
1 teaspoon baking powder
½ teaspoon salt
½ cup butter, softened

½ cup sesame seeds, toasted
⅓ cup milk
coarse (kosher) salt

═ **Yield: 200 crackers**

4 cups flour
2 teaspoons baking powder
1 teaspoon salt
1 cup butter, softened

1 cup sesame seeds, toasted
⅔ cup milk
coarse (kosher) salt

1. Preheat the oven to 350°F.
2. In a bowl, mix the flour, baking powder, and salt. Cut in the butter and sesame seeds, then stir in the milk to make a dough.
3. On a lightly floured board, roll the dough ⅛ inch thick and cut into 2-inch circles. Transfer to a baking sheet.
4. Bake 10 to 12 minutes or until lightly browned. Sprinkle with salt.

▶ Keeps 1 week in an airtight container; can be frozen.

—— *Cheese Pastries* ——

≡ *Hot Cheese Balls I*

═ **Yield: 30 1-inch balls**

¼ pound grated Cheddar or
   Edam cheese
½ cup sifted flour
¼ cup butter
1½ tablespoons sesame,
   caraway, or cumin seeds

1 tablespoon bacon fat
pinch of cayenne pepper
salt, to taste

═ **Yield: 120 1-inch balls**

1 pound grated Cheddar or
   Edam cheese
2 cups sifted flour
1 cup butter
⅓ cup sesame, caraway, or
   cumin seeds

¼ cup bacon fat
¼ teaspoon cayenne pepper
salt, to taste

1. Preheat the oven to 450°F.
2. In a bowl, mix the cheese, flour, butter, sesame seeds, bacon fat, cayenne, and salt. Cover and refrigerate for 2 hours.
3. Roll into 1-inch balls and place on ungreased baking sheets.
4. Bake 15 minutes or until golden. Serve hot.

▶ Keeps 1 week in an airtight container; can be frozen.

≡ *Bals de Fromage (Hot Cheese Balls II)*

═ **Yield: 25 1-inch balls**

6 ounces grated Gruyère or
  Edam cheese
1 cup flour

¼ pound butter
3 egg yolks
salt and pepper, to taste

═ **Yield: 100 1-inch balls**

1½ pounds grated Gruyère or
  Edam cheese
4 cups flour

1 pound butter
12 egg yolks
salt and pepper, to taste

1. Preheat the oven to 400°F.

2. In a bowl, mix the cheese, flour, butter, egg yolks, salt, and pepper to form a dough. Chill for 30 minutes.

3. Shape into 1-inch balls and bake on ungreased baking sheets for 15 to 20 minutes or until golden.

▶ Keeps 1 week in an airtight container; can be frozen.

≡ *Almond-Cheese Rounds*

═ **Yield: 50 crackers**

2 cups flour
½ cup grated Parmesan cheese
2 eggs
½ teaspoon salt

½ cup chilled butter, thinly
  sliced
coarse (kosher) salt
blanched, slivered almonds

═ **Yield: 200 crackers**

8 cups flour
2 cups grated Parmesan cheese
8 eggs
2 teaspoons salt

2 cups chilled butter, thinly
  sliced
coarse (kosher) salt
blanched, slivered almonds

1. Preheat the oven to 375°F.

2. In a bowl, mix the flour and cheese.

3. In another bowl, beat the eggs and set aside 3 tablespoons (¾ *cup*). Add the remaining eggs and salt to the flour-cheese mixture. Cut in the butter, working lightly until the mixture holds together. Chill for 1 hour.

4. On a lightly floured board, roll the dough ⅛ inch thick and cut out designs of your choice (for example, circles, rectangles, diamonds, squares, and crescents). Place on unbuttered baking sheets.

5. Brush with the reserved egg mixture and sprinkle with coarse salt and almonds.

6. Bake 15 minutes or until golden.

▶ Keeps 1 week in an airtight container; can be frozen.

≡ Baked Cheddar Cheese Olives

=== **Yield: 25 pastries**

1 cup shredded Cheddar	½ cup flour
cheese	dash of cayenne pepper
2 tablespoons butter	25 large Spanish olives

=== **Yield: 100 pastries**

1 quart shredded Cheddar	2 cups flour
cheese	¼ teaspoon cayenne pepper
½ cup butter	100 large Spanish olives

1. Preheat the oven to 400°F.

2. In a bowl, work the cheese and butter together. Add the flour and cayenne and mix well.

3. Use about 1 teaspoon of dough to wrap around each olive, enclosing it completely. Flour your hands to make molding easier. Place on buttered baking sheets.

4. Bake about 15 minutes or until golden. Serve warm.

▶ Keeps 3 days in an airtight container; can be frozen.

≡ Cheese Thins

=== **Yield: 60 pastries**

1 cup sifted flour	2 tablespoons grated Parmesan
½ teaspoon salt	cheese
¼ teaspoon paprika	¼ cup cold beer
pinch of cayenne pepper	1 egg yolk
¾ cup grated sharp Cheddar	2 tablespoons beer
cheese	caraway or poppy seeds
⅓ cup butter	

== **Yield: 240 pastries**

4 cups flour	1⅓ cups butter
2 teaspoons salt	½ cup grated Parmesan cheese
1 teaspoon paprika	1 cup cold beer
¼ teaspoon cayenne pepper	4 egg yolks
3 cups grated sharp Cheddar	½ cup beer
cheese	caraway or poppy seeds

1. Preheat the oven to 450°F.

2. In a bowl, mix the flour, salt, paprika, and cayenne. Add the Cheddar, butter, and Parmesan and mix again. Add the beer and mix until the mixture forms a dough. With the aid of waxed paper, shape the dough into rolls 1 inch in diameter. Wrap in waxed paper and freeze until firm, about 45 minutes.

3. Slice the rolls ⅛ inch thick and arrange on buttered baking sheets. In a bowl, mix the egg yolk(s) and beer and brush the top of each round. Sprinkle with seeds. Bake 12 to 15 minutes or until lightly golden.

▶ Keeps 1 week in an airtight container; can be frozen.

☰ *Cheddar Cheese Sticks*

== **Yield: 50 sticks**

½ cup butter	1¼ teaspoons salt
¼ pound sharp Cheddar	pinch of cayenne pepper
cheese, grated	1⅓ cups flour

== **Yield: 200 sticks**

2 cups butter	5 teaspoons salt
1 pound sharp Cheddar cheese,	¼ teaspoon cayenne pepper
grated	5⅓ cups flour

1. Preheat the oven to 400°F.

2. In a bowl, mix the butter, cheese, salt, and cayenne. Stir in the flour to form a dough.

3. Shape the dough into 3- by 5-inch rectangles, about 1 inch thick. Wrap in waxed paper and chill 30 minutes. Between sheets of waxed paper, roll each section ⅛ inch thick and place on a baking sheet, still in the waxed paper. Chill 30 minutes longer. Remove from the refrigerator, remove the top sheet of paper, and turn onto a buttered baking sheet. Peel off the remaining paper. Cut into strips ½ inch wide and 3 inches long, separating as you cut.

4. Bake 12 to 15 minutes or until golden.

▶ Keeps 1 week in an airtight container; can be frozen.

≡ *Paillettes au Pistaches (Pistachio Rounds)*

≡ **Yield: 100 rounds**

1 large recipe Cheddar cheese sticks dough (preceding recipe)	dorure blanched, chopped pistachios

1. Preheat the oven to 375°F.

2. Roll the Cheddar cheese pastry ⅛ inch thick and cut into 1½-inch circles. Place on a baking sheet, brush with dorure, and sprinkle center with the pistachios.

3. Bake 12 to 15 minutes or until golden.

▶ Keeps 1 week in an airtight container; can be frozen.

≡ *Almond Sticks or Salt Sticks*

≡ **Yield: 100 sticks**

1 large recipe Cheddar cheese sticks dough (page 658) chopped blanched almonds or coarse (kosher) salt	dorure

1. Preheat the oven to 375°F.

2. Roll about 1 tablespoon of the Cheddar cheese pastry into sticks 2 inches long by ⅓ inch thick. Put on baking sheets and freeze for 15 minutes.

3. Spread chopped blanched almonds or coarse salt on a sheet of waxed paper. Brush the chilled sticks with dorure and roll in the almonds or salt.

4. Bake 12 to 15 minutes or until golden.

▶ Keeps 1 week in an airtight container; can be frozen.

≡ *Cheese Stars*

═ Yield: 60 stars

2 cups flour
½ cup butter, softened
¼ pound Gruyère cheese, grated
2 ounces Parmesan cheese, grated
¼ cup heavy cream

1 egg yolk
½ teaspoon salt
pinch of cayenne pepper
1 egg
1 tablespoon water
1 cup chopped salted pistachios

═ Yield: 240 stars

8 cups flour
2 cups butter, softened
1 pound Gruyère cheese, grated
½ pound Parmesan cheese, grated
1 cup heavy cream
4 egg yolks

2 teaspoons salt
¼ teaspoon cayenne pepper
4 eggs
¼ cup water
1 quart chopped salted pistachios

1. Preheat the oven to 325°F.

2. In a bowl, mix the flour, butter, Gruyère, Parmesan, cream, egg yolk(s), salt, and cayenne into a dough.

3. Divide the dough into manageable pieces and chill 30 minutes.

4. On a lightly floured board, roll the dough ⅛ inch thick and cut into 1½-inch stars. Arrange on buttered baking sheets.

5. Beat the egg(s) with water and brush on the stars. Sprinkle with the pistachios.

6. Bake 20 minutes or until lightly colored.

▶ Keeps 1 week in an airtight container; can be frozen.

≡ *Käse Beilage (Cheese Pastries)*

These crisp, light, delicate pastries must be baked and served at the last moment. If this is possible, they truly make the effort worthwhile.

═ Yield: 25 pastries

2 cups flour
1 teaspoon baking powder
1 teaspoon salt
1 cup heavy cream, chilled

1 cup grated Parmesan cheese
2 tablespoons butter
2 tablespoons olive oil

═ **Yield: 100 pastries**

8 cups flour
4 teaspoons baking powder
4 teaspoons salt
1 quart heavy cream, chilled

1 quart grated Parmesan
   cheese
½ cup butter
½ cup olive oil

1. Preheat the oven to 400°F.

2. In a bowl, mix the flour, baking powder, salt, cream, and cheese.

3. In a jellyroll pan, heat the butter and olive oil in the oven. Drop the batter by the tablespoonful onto the pan and bake for 10 minutes or until crisp and lightly browned. Drain on paper towels and serve hot.

▶ These cannot be made in advance.

═ *Herb-Parmesan Biscuits*

═ **Yield: 50 biscuits**

1¼ cups grated Parmesan
   cheese
1 cup flour
½ cup butter
¾ teaspoon dried marjoram

¾ teaspoon dried oregano
¾ teaspoon dried basil
½ teaspoon Worcestershire
   sauce
2 to 3 tablespoons white wine

═ **Yield: 200 biscuits**

5 cups grated Parmesan cheese
4 cups flour
2 cups butter
1 tablespoon dried marjoram
1 tablespoon dried oregano

1 tablespoon dried basil
2 teaspoons Worcestershire
   sauce
½ to ¾ cup white wine

1. Preheat the oven to 400°F.

2. In a bowl, mix the cheese, flour, butter, and herbs until they resemble coarse meal. Add the Worcestershire sauce and wine and mix to form a dough. Shape into a log 1½ inches in diameter, wrap in waxed paper, and chill until firm.

3. Slice into ¼-inch pieces and arrange ½ inch apart on lightly buttered baking sheets.

4. Bake 12 to 15 minutes or until lightly browned.

▶ Keeps 1 week in an airtight container; can be frozen.

☰ *Nussrolle (Nut Cheese Roll)*

☰ **Yield: 50 slices**

2 cups flour	¼ cup minced green olives
1 teaspoon baking powder	2 tablespoons chopped
⅓ cup grated Cheddar cheese	anchovies
1 teaspoon salt	½ teaspoon salt
½ cup butter	1 egg yolk beaten with 1
½ cup cream	teaspoon water
1 cup chopped almonds	grated Parmesan cheese
1 egg	slivered almonds

☰ **Yield: 200 slices**

8 cups flour	4 eggs
4 teaspoons baking powder	1 cup minced green olives
1⅓ cups grated Cheddar	½ cup chopped anchovies
cheese	2 teaspoons salt
4 teaspoons salt	4 egg yolks beaten with 4
2 cups butter	teaspoons water
2 cups cream	grated Parmesan cheese
1 quart chopped almonds	slivered almonds

1. Preheat the oven to 300°F.

2. In a bowl, mix the flour, baking powder, Cheddar, and salt. Cut in the butter until the mixture resembles coarse meal. Add the cream and work the ingredients into a smooth dough. Chill ½ hour wrapped in waxed paper.

3. In a bowl, mix the almonds, egg(s), olives, anchovies, and salt. Roll the dough ¼ inch thick and spread with the filling. Roll jellyroll fashion and chill 15 minutes. Brush the roll with the beaten egg.

4. Bake the rolls on lightly buttered baking sheets for 30 minutes.

5. Brush again with the egg, and sprinkle with the grated Parmesan and slivered almonds.

6. Bake 15 minutes longer or until golden. Slice and serve warm.

▶ Can be frozen.

≡ *Cheese Straws I*

═ Yield: 50 straws

1 cup grated Cheddar cheese	2 tablespoons milk
2 tablespoons butter	salt and cayenne pepper, to
1 cup soft bread crumbs	taste
⅔ cup flour	

═ Yield: 200 straws

4 cups grated Cheddar cheese	½ cup milk
½ cup butter	salt and cayenne pepper, to
1 quart soft bread crumbs	taste
2⅔ cups flour	

1. Preheat the oven to 375°F.

2. In a food processor, cream the cheese and butter. Add the bread crumbs, flour, milk, salt, and cayenne with on-off turns until just combined.

3. On a lightly floured board, roll ¼ inch thick. Cut into ½-inch-wide strips or small circles.

4. Bake on buttered baking sheets for 15 minutes or until golden.

▶ Can be frozen.

≡ *Cheese Straws II*

═ Yield: 50 straws

½ pound grated Cheddar cheese	2 cups flour
½ pound butter, cut into small pieces	coarse (kosher) salt caraway seeds

═ Yield: 200 straws

2 pounds grated Cheddar cheese	8 cups flour
2 pounds butter, cut into small pieces	coarse (kosher) salt caraway seeds

1. Preheat the oven to 350°F.

2. In a food processor, blend the cheese, butter, and flour. Roll the dough ⅛ inch thick and cut into strips 2 inches long and ¼ inch wide.

3. Sprinkle with salt and caraway seeds.

4. Bake on a lightly buttered baking sheet for 15 minutes or until golden.

▶ Keeps 1 week in an airtight container; can be frozen.

☰ *Cheese Straws III*

══ **Yield: 100 straws**

2 cups sifted flour	⅓ cup beer
½ teaspoon salt	¼ cup heavy cream
2 teaspoons chili powder	½ cup ground pecans or
¾ cup butter	walnuts
1 cup grated Cheddar cheese	

══ **Yield: 400 straws**

8 cups sifted flour	1⅓ cups beer
2 teaspoons salt	1 cup heavy cream
3 tablespoons chili powder	2 cups ground pecans or
3 cups butter	walnuts
1 quart grated Cheddar cheese	

1. Preheat the oven to 425°F.

2. In a bowl, mix the flour, salt, and chili powder. Cut in the butter and cheese with a pastry blender or use your fingertips. Stir in just enough beer to make the particles adhere. Shape into a flat cake, wrap in waxed paper, and chill for 2 hours.

3. On a lightly floured board, roll the dough ⅛ inch thick and cut into strips ½ inch wide and 3 inches long. Arrange on unbuttered baking sheets. Brush with cream and sprinkle with nuts.

4. Bake 10 minutes or until golden.

▶ Keeps 1 week in an airtight container; can be frozen.

☰ *Walnut Cheese Circles*

══ **Yield: 36 circles**

¾ cup flour	½ cup butter
½ cup ground walnuts	½ cup grated Cheddar cheese
½ teaspoon baking powder	½ cup grated Gruyère cheese
¼ teaspoon salt	1 egg, beaten
¼ teaspoon dry mustard	

== **Yield: 144 circles**

3 cups flour

2 cups ground walnuts

2 teaspoons baking powder

1 teaspoon salt

1 teaspoon dry mustard

2 cups butter

2 cups grated Cheddar cheese

2 cups grated Gruyère cheese

2 to 3 eggs, beaten

1. Preheat the oven to 350°F.

2. In a bowl, mix the flour, nuts, baking powder, salt, and mustard. Cut in the butter until the mixture resembles coarse meal. Add the Cheddar, Gruyère, and enough egg to make a stiff dough. Roll into logs 1¼ inches in diameter. Wrap in waxed paper and refrigerate for 2 hours.

3. Slice the dough into ¼-inch circles and place on unbuttered baking sheets.

4. Bake 18 to 20 minutes or until lightly browned.

▶ Keeps 1 week in an airtight container; can be frozen.

≡ *Baked Cheese Balls*

== **Yield: 40 1-inch balls**

¼ pound grated sharp Cheddar cheese

¾ cup flour

1 tablespoon melted butter

1 teaspoon Dijon mustard

1 teaspoon Worcestershire sauce

¼ teaspoon salt

Tabasco sauce, to taste

¼ cup sesame seeds

== **Yield: 160 1-inch balls**

1 pound grated sharp Cheddar cheese

3 cups flour

¼ cup melted butter

4 teaspoons Dijon mustard

4 teaspoons Worcestershire sauce

1 teaspoon salt

Tabasco sauce, to taste

1 cup sesame seeds

1. Preheat the oven to 375°F.

2. In a bowl, mix the cheese, flour, butter, mustard, Worcestershire sauce, salt, and Tabasco sauce. Shape into 1-inch balls and roll them in the sesame seeds.

3. Bake on lightly buttered baking sheets for 20 minutes or until golden.

▶ Keeps 1 week in an airtight container; can be frozen.

≡ *Wiener Zigaretten (Viennese Cheese Cigarettes)*

═ Yield: 30 pastries

1½ cups sifted flour
1 teaspoon salt
¼ teaspoon paprika
1 cup grated Gruyère cheese
½ cup butter
3 tablespoons cream

½ cup flour
½ cup grated Parmesan cheese
1 egg yolk beaten with 1
   teaspoon water
grated Parmesan cheese

═ Yield: 120 pastries

6 cups flour
4 teaspoons salt
1 teaspoon paprika
1 quart grated Gruyère cheese
2 cups butter
¾ cup cream

2 cups flour
2 cups grated Parmesan cheese
4 egg yolks beaten with 4
   teaspoons water
grated Parmesan cheese

1. Preheat the oven to 375°F.

2. In a bowl, mix the sifted flour, salt, paprika, and cheese. Cut in the butter until it resembles a coarse meal. Add the cream and gently work to form a dough. Shape into a flat cake, wrap in waxed paper, and chill 30 minutes.

3. In another bowl, mix the remaining flour and Parmesan. Use this to roll the dough.

4. Sprinkle some of the flour-cheese mixture onto a work surface and roll the pastry into a long rectangle. Fold into thirds and roll again. Sprinkle with the flour-cheese, fold in thirds, and roll again. Sprinkle with the flour-cheese and fold in thirds. Chill at least 15 minutes.

5. Roll the dough ⅛ inch thick and cut into strips ¾ inch wide and 10 inches long. Coil each strip, overlapping slightly, around a well-buttered ¼-inch-thick dowel about 6 inches long. Brush with the egg yolk and water and roll in the grated Parmesan.

6. Bake on a lightly buttered baking sheet until golden, about 20 minutes. While the pastries are still hot, twist the dowel in place and gently withdraw.

▶ Keeps 1 week in an airtight container; can be frozen.

NOTE: Chopsticks make good dowels. For a more elaborate pastry, roll the pastry around a ½-inch-thick dowel and bake. When cooled, pipe in the Parmesan filling for cheese pastries (page 667).

≡ *Salatini al Parmigiano (Parmesan Crackers)*

These delicate little crackers are delicious on their own, but become truly special when filled.

═ **Yield: 25 crackers**

½ cup butter	½ teaspoon salt
½ cup grated Parmesan cheese	Parmesan filling for cheese
1 cup sifted flour	pastries (recipe follows),
½ teaspoon baking powder	optional

═ **Yield: 100 crackers**

2 cups butter	2 teaspoons salt
2 cups grated Parmesan cheese	Parmesan filling for cheese
4 cups sifted flour	pastries (recipe follows),
2 teaspoons baking powder	optional

1. Preheat the oven to 400°F.

2. In a food processor, cream the butter and cheese. Add the flour, baking powder, and salt and process to form a dough. If the dough is too soft to roll, chill for 20 minutes.

3. On a lightly floured board, roll the dough ⅛ inch thick and cut into 1-inch circles.

4. Bake on a lightly buttered baking sheet for 8 to 10 minutes or until lightly browned. Serve plain or make cheese sandwiches with the following filling.

▶ Keeps 1 week in an airtight container; can be frozen. Fill no more than 1 hour in advance.

≡ *Parmesan Filling for Cheese Pastries*

═ **Yield: enough for 12 sandwiches**

2 tablespoons butter	2 tablespoons heavy cream
¼ cup grated Parmesan cheese	

═ **Yield: enough for 48 sandwiches**

½ cup butter	½ cup heavy cream
1 cup grated Parmesan cheese	

1. In a food processor, cream the butter, cheese, and cream. Spread on half the crackers and top with the remaining halves.

2. Alternately, the filling can be doubled and put into a pastry bag, fitted with a no. 30 star tip, and piped on top of each cracker.

▶ Can be made 1 day in advance.

≡ Käsestangen I (Cheddar Cheese Sticks I)

═ **Yield: 100 sticks**

2¼ cups flour
1¼ cups grated Cheddar
cheese
1 cup butter, softened

salt and paprika, to taste
1 egg beaten with 1 teaspoon
water
½ cup grated Parmesan cheese

═ **Yield: 400 sticks**

9 cups flour
5 cups grated Cheddar cheese
2 pounds butter, softened
salt and paprika, to taste

4 eggs beaten with 4 teaspoons
water
2 cups grated Parmesan cheese

1. Preheat oven to 350°F.

2. In a bowl, mix the flour, Cheddar, butter, salt, and paprika to form a dough. Shape into a flat cake, wrap in waxed paper, and chill for 30 minutes.

3. On a lightly floured board, roll the dough ¼ inch thick. Brush with the beaten egg and sprinkle with the Parmesan. Cut into 1¼-inch squares or any other shape.

4. Bake on unbuttered baking sheets about 15 minutes or until golden.

▶ Keeps 1 week in an airtight container; can be frozen.

Gefüllte Käsestangen (Stuffed Cheese Sticks)
Roll the käsestangen I pastry ⅛ inch thick and cut into strips 1 inch wide by 4 inches long. Bake in a 350°F oven for 15 minutes or until golden. Sandwich with cheese filling for puffs (page 575).

≡ Käsebatons I (Cheese Pencils I)

Roll the käsestangen I pastry (preceding recipe) into pencil-thin sticks, about 6 inches long. Brush with the egg wash and roll in poppy seeds. Bake in a 350°F oven for 15 minutes or until golden.

▶ Keeps 1 week in an airtight container; can be frozen.

≡ *Käsestangen II (Cheddar Cheese Sticks II)*

=== **Yield: 50 sticks**

1 cup flour
¾ cup grated Parmesan cheese
¼ cup grated Cheddar cheese
½ teaspoon salt
¼ teaspoon paprika
½ cup butter, cut into pieces

1 tablespoon heavy cream
1 egg yolk beaten with 1
   teaspoon water
salt
caraway seeds

=== **Yield: 200 sticks**

4 cups flour
3 cups grated Parmesan cheese
1 cup grated Cheddar cheese
2 teaspoons salt
1 teaspoon paprika
2 cups butter, cut into pieces

¼ cup heavy cream
4 egg yolks beaten with 4
   teaspoons water
salt
caraway seeds

1. Preheat the oven to 325°F.

2. In a bowl, mix the flour, Parmesan, Cheddar, salt, and paprika. Cut in the butter and add the cream to make a smooth dough.

3. Shape into a flat cake, wrap in waxed paper, and chill 1 hour.

4. Roll the pastry ⅛ inch thick and cut into strips ½ inch wide by 4 inches long. Brush with the egg wash and sprinkle with salt and caraway seeds.

5. Bake on unbuttered baking sheets for 15 minutes or until golden.

▶ Keeps 1 week in an airtight container; can be frozen.

≡ *Käsebatons II (Cheese Pencils II)*

With your hands, roll the käsestangen II pastry (preceding recipe) into thin sticks. Brush with the egg wash and roll in caraway seeds. Bake in a 325°F oven for 15 minutes or until golden.

▶ Keeps 1 week in an airtight container; can be frozen.

≡ Käsestangen III (Cheese Sticks III)

Yield: 30 sticks

1 cup grated Parmesan cheese	7 tablespoons sour cream
1 cup flour	salt, to taste
¼ cup butter	paprika, to taste

Yield: 120 sticks

4 cups grated Parmesan cheese	1¾ cups sour cream
4 cups flour	salt, to taste
1 cup butter	paprika, to taste

1. Preheat the oven to 350°F.

2. In a bowl, mix the cheese, flour, butter, sour cream, salt, and paprika. Shape into a flat cake and chill 1 hour.

3. On a lightly floured board, roll the pastry ¼ inch thick and cut into strips ½ inch wide by 6 inches long. Twist into spirals.

4. Bake on unbuttered baking sheets for 15 minutes or until golden.

▶ Keeps 1 week in an airtight container; can be frozen.

≡ Anchovy Rolls

Yield: 50 rolls

1 cup sifted flour	⅓ cup butter
¾ teaspoon dry mustard	3 tablespoons water
½ teaspoon salt	2 tablespoons melted butter
¼ teaspoon crushed garlic	1 tube anchovy paste
pinch of cayenne pepper	¼ cup grated Parmesan cheese

Yield: 200 rolls

4 cups sifted flour	1⅓ cups butter
3 teaspoons dry mustard	¾ cup water
2 teaspoons salt	½ cup melted butter
1 teaspoon crushed garlic	4 tubes anchovy paste
¼ teaspoon cayenne pepper	1 cup grated Parmesan cheese

1. Preheat the oven to 400°F.

2. In a bowl, mix the flour, mustard, salt, garlic, and cayenne. Cut in the butter until the mixture resembles coarse meal. Sprinkle with the water and mix to form a dough. Shape into a flat cake, wrap in waxed paper, and chill 1 hour.

3. On a lightly floured board, roll the pastry into rectangles ⅛ inch thick, and spread with the melted butter and anchovy paste. Sprinkle with the cheese and roll jellyroll fashion. Chill until firm.

4. Cut into ¼-inch-thick slices. Bake on a lightly buttered baking sheet for 12 to 15 minutes or until lightly browned. Serve warm.

▶ Keeps 1 week in an airtight container; can be frozen.

≡ Date Cheese Balls

≡ **Yield: 25 balls**

1 pound dates	2 cups sifted flour
1 cup pecan halves	¼ cup milk
2 cups grated Cheddar cheese	1 teaspoon salt
½ cup butter	pinch of cayenne pepper

≡ **Yield: 100 balls**

4 pounds dates	8 cups sifted flour
1 quart pecan halves	1 cup milk
2 quarts grated Cheddar cheese	4 teaspoons salt
2 cups butter	¼ teaspoon cayenne pepper

1. Preheat the oven to 375°F.

2. Stuff the dates with the pecan halves and set aside.

3. In a saucepan over medium heat, melt the cheese and butter. Stir in the flour, milk, salt, and cayenne. Cool.

4. Flatten tablespoonfuls of the dough into small rounds and enclose the dates.

5. Bake on lightly buttered baking sheets for 30 minutes or until golden.

▶ Keeps 1 week in an airtight container; can be frozen.

≡ Käsetaschen (Cheese Hats or Turnovers)

≡ **Yield: 25 turnovers**

1 cup butter, softened	½ pound Cheddar cheese, cut
6 ounces cream cheese	into sticks
2 cups flour	

=== **Yield: 100 turnovers**

2 pounds butter, softened
1½ pounds cream cheese
8 cups flour

2 pounds Cheddar cheese, cut
    into sticks

1. Preheat the oven to 375°F.
2. In a food processor, mix the butter, cream cheese, and flour to form a dough.
3. Roll the dough ¼ inch thick and chill for 30 minutes.
4. Cut into 2-inch circles. Place a stick of cheese on each round and fold to form a turnover. Press edges to seal.
5. Bake on unbuttered baking sheets for 10 minutes or until golden.

▶ Keeps 1 week in an airtight container; can be frozen.

=== *Petites Tartines au Fromage (Austrian Cheese Cakes)*

These may well have been a gift to the French from their most notorious queen, the Austrian-born Marie Antoinette.

=== **Yield: 25 pastries**

1¼ cups flour
¾ cup butter
⅔ cup grated Parmesan cheese
1 hard-cooked egg yolk, sieved

2 ounces ground almonds
½ teaspoon salt
pinch of cayenne pepper
1 egg yolk beaten with
    1 tablespoon ice water

=== **Yield: 100 pastries**

5 cups flour
3 cups butter
2⅔ cups grated Parmesan
    cheese
4 hard-cooked egg yolks, sieved

½ pound ground almonds
2 teaspoons salt
¼ teaspoon cayenne pepper
4 egg yolks beaten with ¼ cup
    ice water

1. Preheat the oven to 350°F.
2. In a bowl, crumble the flour and butter until the mixture resembles coarse meal. Add the cheese, hard-cooked egg yolks, almonds, salt, and cayenne. Stir in the egg yolks and water to make a firm dough.
3. Roll ¼ inch thick and cut into 1-inch circles.
4. Bake on unbuttered baking sheets for 20 minutes or until golden.

▶ Keeps 1 week in an airtight container; can be frozen.

≡ Rags and Tatters

This pastry is supposed to be cut into irregular shapes, but you may be as neat as you desire.

═ Yield: 30 pastries

¾ cup flour
pinch of cayenne pepper
¼ cup butter
1 teaspoon Dijon mustard
¼ cup grated Cheddar cheese

⅓ cup grated Parmesan cheese
1 egg, beaten
2 tablespoons anchovy paste
milk

═ Yield: 120 pastries

3 cups flour
¼ teaspoon cayenne pepper
1 cup butter
4 teaspoons Dijon mustard
1 cup grated Cheddar cheese

1⅓ cups grated Parmesan cheese
4 eggs, beaten
½ cup anchovy paste
milk

1. Preheat the oven to 450°F.
2. In a bowl, mix the flour and cayenne. Cut in the butter and mustard until the mixture resembles coarse meal. Work in the Cheddar and Parmesan to make a stiff dough.
3. On a lightly floured board, roll the pastry ⅛ inch thick. Brush half the pastry with the egg(s); then spread anchovy paste mixed with enough milk to make a thin paste. Fold the remaining pastry over the top and brush with more of the egg. Press together and cut into irregular shapes.
4. Bake on unbuttered baking sheets for 10 minutes or until golden.

▶ Keeps 1 week in an airtight container; can be frozen.

≡ Galettes au Camembert (Camembert Biscuits)

═ Yield: 60 biscuits

8 ounces Camembert cheese
3 ounces butter, softened
2 eggs
½ teaspoon salt

pinch of pepper
pinch of cayenne pepper
2 cups sifted flour
dorure

═ **Yield: 240 biscuits**

2 pounds Camembert cheese	¼ teaspoon pepper
¾ pound butter, softened	¼ teaspoon cayenne pepper
8 eggs	8 cups sifted flour
2 teaspoons salt	dorure

1. Preheat the oven to 350°F.

2. Scrape the rind from the Camembert.

3. In a food processor, cream the cheese and butter. Add the eggs, salt, pepper, and cayenne. Add the flour and process until it forms a smooth dough. Add a little more flour if needed. Shape into a flat cake, wrap in waxed paper, and chill until firm.

4. Roll the pastry ¼ inch thick and cut into 1½-inch circles. Brush with dorure.

5. Bake on lightly buttered baking sheets for 15 minutes or until golden.

▶ Keeps 1 week in an airtight container; can be frozen.

═ *Petites Tartes Danoise (Danish Cheese Tarts)*

═ **Yield: 25 tarts**

3 ounces cream cheese	2 tablespoons butter
⅓ cup crumbled blue cheese	½ pound blue cheese,
2 tablespoons butter	crumbled
1 tablespoon butter	3 eggs, beaten
1 cup flour	1 cup heavy cream
3 scallions, minced	salt and pepper, to taste

═ **Yield: 100 tarts**

¾ pound cream cheese	2 pounds blue cheese,
1⅓ cups crumbled blue cheese	crumbled
¼ cup butter	12 eggs, beaten
4 cups flour	1 quart heavy cream
12 scallions, minced	salt and pepper, to taste
½ cup butter	

1. Preheat the oven to 375°F.

2. In a food processor, blend the cream cheese, blue cheese, butter, and flour to form a dough. Shape into a flat cake, wrap in waxed paper, and chill for 1 hour.

3. On a lightly floured board, roll the pastry ⅛ inch thick and line tiny tartlet pans. Prick and bake 10 minutes or until the dough is set.

4. In a small skillet, sauté the scallions in the remaining butter and divide among the tarts. Put a little crumbled blue cheese into each shell. Beat the eggs with the cream and season with salt and pepper. Pour a little into each shell.

5. Bake 10 to 15 minutes or until the eggs are set.

▶ Can be reheated, but best baked and served immediately.

≡ *Bouchées Parmentier au Fromage* *(Potato-Cheese Fritters)*

=== **Yield: 60 fritters**

½ pound potatoes, boiled, riced, and hot	pinch of white pepper
1 cup flour	pinch of nutmeg
¼ cup butter, softened	pinch of cayenne pepper
4 eggs	salt, to taste
¼ pound Gruyère cheese, grated	

=== **Yield: 240 fritters**

2 pounds potatoes, boiled, riced, and hot	1 pound Gruyère cheese, grated
4 cups flour	¼ teaspoon white pepper
1 cup butter, softened	¼ teaspoon nutmeg
16 eggs	¼ teaspoon cayenne pepper
	salt, to taste

1. Preheat the oven to 425°F.

2. In a food processor, mix the potatoes, flour, butter, eggs, cheese, pepper, nutmeg, cayenne, and salt to form a dough resembling pâte à chou paste.

3. Fit a pastry bag with a no. 5 open star tip and pipe the mixture onto buttered baking sheets in 2½-inch strips.

4. Bake until puffed and light brown, about 20 minutes.

▶ Best made and served immediately.

NOTE: For a different effect, heat oil to 375°F and deep-fry the fritters until puffed and golden.

☰ *Cheese Biscuits*

═ Yield: 75 biscuits

¼ pound Edam cheese, diced
6 ounces butter
1½ cups flour
⅔ cup finely ground walnuts
1 tablespoon salt

1 egg white, lightly beaten
cayenne pepper, to taste, or
   poppy, sesame, or caraway
   seeds or paprika

═ Yield: 300 biscuits

1 pound Edam cheese, diced
1½ pounds butter
6 cups flour
2⅔ cups finely ground walnuts
¼ cup salt

4 egg whites, lightly beaten
cayenne pepper, to taste, or
   poppy, sesame, or caraway
   seeds or paprika

1. Preheat the oven to 375°F.

2. In a food processor, cream the cheese until smooth. Add the butter; cream until fluffy. Add the flour, walnuts, and salt and process to form a dough. Shape into a flat cake, wrap in waxed paper, and chill 30 minutes.

3. Roll the pastry between sheets of waxed paper and cut into shapes with cookie cutters.

4. Spread with the beaten egg whites and sprinkle with the cayenne pepper, seeds, or paprika.

5. Bake on unbuttered baking sheets for 10 minutes or until golden.

▶ Keeps 1 week in an airtight container; can be frozen.

☰ *Gruyère Rolls*

═ Yield: 30 rolls

¾ pound Gruyère cheese,
   shredded
1½ cups flour
¾ cup butter, softened

½ teaspoon salt
pinch of cayenne pepper
1 egg, lightly beaten

═ Yield: 120 rolls

3 pounds Gruyère cheese,
   shredded
6 cups flour
3 cups butter, softened

2 teaspoons salt
¼ teaspoon cayenne pepper
4 eggs, lightly beaten

1. Preheat the oven to 425°F.

2. In a bowl, knead 2½ cups (*6 cups*) of the cheese, flour, butter, salt, and cayenne to form a dough. Roll into 1-inch balls.

3. Place the balls, 2 inches apart, on unbuttered baking sheets and flatten into ¼-inch-thick circles. Brush tops with beaten egg and sprinkle with the remaining cheese.

4. Bake 10 to 12 minutes or until browned. Serve warm.

▶ Keeps 1 week in an airtight container; can be frozen.

≡ Cheese Wafers

═ Yield: 60 wafers

¼ pound sharp Cheddar cheese, grated	½ cup butter
	½ teaspoon salt
1½ cups flour	½ teaspoon cayenne pepper

═ Yield: 240 wafers

1 pound sharp Cheddar cheese, grated	2 cups butter
	2 teaspoons salt
6 cups flour	2 teaspoons cayenne pepper

1. Preheat the oven to 375°F.

2. In a food processor, blend the cheese, flour, butter, salt, and cayenne to form a smooth paste. Chill 20 minutes.

3. Fit a pastry bag with a ½-inch-wide ribbon tip and fill with the dough. Pipe long strips of pastry onto lightly buttered baking sheets. Cut the strips at 1-inch intervals (they will separate while baking).

4. Bake 10 minutes or until golden.

▶ Keeps 1 week in an airtight container; can be frozen.

—— Sponge Rolls ——

≡ Basic Sponge Roll for Hors d'Oeuvre

The most practical way to make these is described here. Do not try to multiply the recipe and make large trays of sponge roll; it will become dry and crisp and be impossible to roll.

= **Yield: 60 ½-inch slices**

softened butter to grease pan	2 cups hot milk
¼ cup butter	4 eggs, separated
½ cup sifted flour	pinch of salt

1. Preheat the oven to 400°F.

2. Line a 10″ × 15″ jellyroll pan with foil, pressing neatly into the corners. Brush with softened butter and set aside.

3. In a saucepan, melt the butter, stir in the flour, and cook the roux until it starts to turn golden. Whisk in the milk and cook until thickened and smooth. Simmer, stirring, for 1 minute.

4. In a bowl, beat the egg yolks to blend and add one fourth of the hot sauce. Return the egg yolks to the sauce, stirring constantly, and add the salt.

5. Beat the egg whites until stiff but not dry and fold into the hot sauce.

6. Pour into the prepared baking sheet and bake 15 to 18 minutes, or until the cake is just golden and springs back to the touch.

7. Cool in the pan. Turn out onto a clean towel and carefully remove the foil. The cake is now ready to be spread with a filling and rolled.

▶ Can be wrapped in damp towels and kept 2 days, refrigerated, or wrapped in foil and frozen.

≡ *Smoked Salmon-Filled Sponge Roll*

= **Yield: 60 ½-inch slices**

1 basic sponge roll (preceding recipe)	¼ pound smoked salmon, thinly sliced
3 ounces cream cheese, softened	¼ cup minced dill
1 cup sour cream	dill sprigs

1. Cut the sponge roll in half lengthwise.

2. In a bowl, mix the cream cheese and ¼ cup sour cream and spread over the roll. Arrange the salmon in rows along the length of the roll, leaving a 1-inch cheese-coated border along one long side. Sprinkle with minced dill.

3. With the aid of the towel, roll the cake jellyroll fashion toward the exposed cheese border. Wrap securely in waxed paper and chill 1 hour.

4. When ready to serve, cut the roll into ½-inch slices and top each slice with a dollop of sour cream and a sprig of dill.

▶ Can be prepared 1 day in advance.

≡ *Caviar-Filled Sponge Roll*

═ Yield: 60 ½-inch slices

1 basic sponge roll (page 677)
3 ounces cream cheese
1 cup sour cream

½ pound salmon caviar
½ cup minced chives

1. Cut the sponge roll in half lengthwise.

2. In a bowl, mix the cream cheese and ¼ cup sour cream. Spread over the roll. Scatter half of the caviar over the cream cheese and sprinkle with the chives, leaving a 1-inch border along one long edge.

3. With the aid of the towel, roll the cake jellyroll fashion toward the cheese border. Wrap securely in waxed paper and chill 1 hour.

4. When ready to serve, cut the roll into ½-inch slices and garnish each slice with a dollop of sour cream, topped with a spoonful of caviar.

▶ Can be prepared 1 day in advance.

≡ *Shrimp and Blue Cheese-Filled Sponge Roll*

═ Yield: 60 ½-inch slices

1 basic sponge roll (page 677)
2 tablespoons cream cheese
2 tablespoons blue cheese
1 cup sour cream
1 tablespoon minced onion
1 tablespoon mayonnaise

1 tablespoon minced parsley
2 teaspoons lemon juice
¼ pound shrimp, cooked and
finely chopped
60 tiny shrimp, cooked, peeled,
and deveined

1. Cut the sponge roll in half lengthwise.

2. In a bowl, mix the cream cheese, blue cheese, 1 tablespoon sour cream, onion, mayonnaise, parsley, and lemon juice and spread over the roll.

3. Sprinkle the chopped shrimp over the cheese, leaving a 1-inch border along one long edge.

4. With the aid of the towel, roll the sponge roll jellyroll fashion toward the cheese border. Wrap securely in waxed paper and chill 1 hour.

5. When ready to serve, cut the roll into ½-inch slices and garnish each slice with a dollop of sour cream, topped with a tiny shrimp.

▶ Can be prepared 1 day in advance.

≡ Käserolle (Cheese-Filled Sponge Roll)

This sponge roll is different from the preceding rolls. You could use the basic sponge roll with this filling if desired.

== **Yield: 60 ½-inch slices**

6 eggs	¾ cup butter
1 cup sifted flour	2 cups grated Cheddar cheese
1 cup grated Parmesan or	¼ cup minced almonds
Gruyère cheese	¼ cup minced chives
½ teaspoon salt	

1. Preheat the oven to 350°F.

2. Prepare a jellyroll pan as for the basic sponge roll (page 677).

3. Place the bowl of the mixer over hot, not boiling, water and heat the eggs until hot to the touch. Remove from the heat, place the bowl in the mixer, and beat until thick, foamy, and tripled in bulk. Fold in the flour, Parmesan, and salt, and pour into the prepared baking sheet.

4. Bake 20 minutes or until golden. Cool in the pan.

5. Turn out onto a clean towel, carefully remove the foil, and cut in half lengthwise.

6. In a bowl, mix the butter, Cheddar, almonds, and chives and spread over the sponge roll. With the aid of the towel, roll the cake jellyroll fashion from the long side. Wrap securely in waxed paper and chill 1 hour.

7. When ready to serve, cut into ½-inch slices.

▶ Can be prepared 1 day in advance.

≡ Käseschaumschnitten (Cheese-Filled Sponge Slices)

This cheese-flavored sponge layer is split and filled rather than rolled.

== **Yield: 88 sandwiches**

flour for dusting the pan	1½ cups grated Parmesan
1 cup butter, softened	cheese
6 eggs, separated	salt and pepper, to taste
½ teaspoon salt	paprika, to taste
½ teaspoon paprika	¾ cup heavy cream
1½ cups grated Gruyère cheese	toasted almonds
⅔ cup sifted flour	
1 teaspoon baking powder	

1. Preheat the oven to 350°F.

2. Prepare a jellyroll pan as for the basic sponge roll (page 677). Sprinkle the baking sheet with flour and shake off the excess.

3. In a bowl, cream half the butter, then beat in the egg yolks, salt, and paprika until foamy.

4. In another bowl, beat the egg whites until stiff but not dry. Fold the beaten whites, Gruyère, flour, and baking powder into the yolks. Pour into the prepared pan.

5. Bake 18 minutes or until the roll springs back when touched. Cool in the pan.

6. In a food processor, cream the Parmesan, remaining butter, salt, pepper, and paprika. In a bowl, beat the cream until stiff and fold into the cheese mixture.

7. Turn out onto a work surface and cut into 1- by 2-inch fingers. Split the fingers in half.

8. Spread half of the filling on the bottom halves of the fingers, then replace the tops to make sandwiches. Chill 20 minutes.

9. Fit a pastry bag with a no. 30 star tip. Fill with remaining filling and pipe rosettes on top of each sandwich. Garnish with almonds.

▶ Can be prepared 1 day in advance. Keeps in the refrigerator for 1 day.

= 18 =

Asian Hors d'Oeuvre

The foods of the Far East have long held Westerners in thrall. Whether we recall the spice routes of the Middle Ages, or the subtle marriage of flavors of the "Young Turks" of current French cooking, the foods appear to us as exotic and the cooking methods as almost mysterious.

Whether from the plains of China, the isles of Japan, or the mountains of Afghanistan, the food is different and almost universally appealing. Over the years I have found that adding one or two of these to a menu has created the necessary excitement to have people remember us.

Other chapters in this book contain Asian recipes that are so well known as to have become part of Western cooking, or at least Western culinary thought. Teriyaki, sates, and various meatballs are common, almost to the point of being hackneyed. This chapter focuses on the less familiar hors d'oeuvre, or those that, no matter how well known, are still "foreign," such as sushi. Among certain groups, sushi is as ordinary as Swedish meatballs, but for most people it still carries a hint of the exotic.

The Chinese devote an entire cuisine to small bites of food suitable to serve with cups of tea. Dim sum, or "tea lunch" as some restaurants refer to it, consists of small delicacies that are superb with cocktails as well as tea. Many Chinese restaurants feature these items as an ongoing lunch, and others serve them as appetizers. The recipes in this chapter are for filled pastries made with noodle doughs and wrappers, such as wheat starch dough and wonton skins. Recipes for spare ribs and pork strips are found in other chapters, as are sesame meatballs, pearl balls, hundred-corner crab balls, shrimp toast, and so on.

The techniques and equipment required for dim sum and other Asian hors d'oeuvre are somewhat different from those in Western cooking, but not so exotic that you cannot easily prepare the recipes.

683

Most special equipment is readily available, but you can do very well with standard kitchen equipment. A food processor certainly makes dough preparation, mincing, and chopping easier. A set of steamer baskets is a great help, but you can improvise. A tortilla press helps to flatten doughs that are difficult to roll otherwise.

The ingredients are available in Asian markets, by mail order, and at many supermarkets. If you are unsure of where to buy something specific, call your local Chinese restaurant and ask them. To prepare the recipes properly, it is important to use genuine ingredients and not substitutes. Ground ginger is not an acceptable replacement for fresh gingerroot. The soy sauce should be correct for the cuisine and the country. Domestic soy sauce has an unsuitable flavor and should not be used with any of these recipes. Use Japanese soy sauce with Japanese dishes and Chinese soy sauce for all others. Unless a recipe specifies thick or dark soy, use thin or light soy. (Do not confuse light soy with the "lite" soy containing less sodium.) Bean sprouts should be fresh, as should all vegetables, except perhaps water chestnuts and bamboo shoots.

Descriptions of the Asian ingredients used in this and other chapters are given in the Glossary of Ingredients following this chapter. Please refer to those pages for more information on where to buy foreign foods and what to look for.

Steaming
Steaming is the principal method of cooking dim sum. Ideally, purchase a bamboo or metal steamer basket set from an Asian market. A set consists of three layers: a lid and two steaming baskets. You can purchase additional steaming baskets and stack them as high as you desire. If you do not have a steamer set and do not wish to buy one, improvise as follows. Use a large kettle and place about 1½ inches of water in the bottom. Cut both ends out of a large tuna fish can and set it in the center of the pot. Arrange the food on a plate and set it on top of the can. There should be about 1 inch of space between the sides of the plate and the kettle. Cover the kettle and steam.

If you have a steamer set, place the steamer baskets over a wok, or any other large pot, filled with an inch or more of water. Check the water often during steaming, and replenish when it looks low. Place the pastries on lightly oiled plates about an inch smaller than the diameter of the basket, or line the baskets with cabbage leaves and arrange the food directly on the leaves. If you place the pastries directly on the bamboo or metal, they are apt to stick.

Serving

Most steamed dim sum are served hot and can be prepared in advance and reheated with no loss of quality. Serve them with hot mustard, duck sauce, or any one of the dipping sauces listed in Chapter 4.

Storing

To store steamed dim sum, wrap them in plastic bags and freeze for up to 2 months. Shaping the various pastries can be tedious, so make large quantities at one time, cook, and keep them in the freezer. You can reheat the pastries in the steamer from the frozen state. Baked dim sum can be reheated in a 350°F oven after thawing. Since fried food is always best served immediately, freeze the uncooked dim sum and partially thaw before frying.

—— *Doughs for Chinese Pastries* ——

≡ *Lard Pastry for Turnovers*

≡ **Yield: 36 turnovers**

2 cups flour	⅔ cup lard
½ teaspoon salt	⅓ cup ice water

≡ **Yield: 144 turnovers**

8 cups flour	2⅔ cups lard
2 teaspoons salt	1⅓ cups ice water

1. In a bowl, cut the flour, salt, and lard together until it resembles coarse meal. Add enough water to make a dough. Shape into a flat cake, wrap in waxed paper, and chill for 15 minutes.

2. Roll and shape into turnovers, as with short pastry (see Chapter 13).

≡ *Chinese Yeast Dough*

This dough differs from other yeast doughs in that baking powder is kneaded in after the dough has risen to give it additional "lift."

≡ **Yield: 36 pastries**

1¼ teaspoons dry yeast	3½ cups flour
1¼ cups lukewarm milk	1 teaspoon baking powder
2 tablespoons sugar	

≡ Yield: 144 pastries

2 packages dry yeast

5 cups lukewarm milk

½ cup sugar

14 cups flour

4 teaspoons baking powder

1. In a bowl, sprinkle the yeast over ¼ cup (*1 cup*) milk and sprinkle on the sugar. Let prove.

2. Add the remaining milk and stir in the flour to make a soft dough, adding more flour if needed. Turn onto a board and knead until smooth and elastic.

3. Place the dough in an oiled bowl and let rise 1 hour or until doubled in bulk. Roll into a circle, ½ inch thick, and sprinkle the baking powder over the dough. Fold dough in half and then shape into a ball. Knead for 10 minutes.

4. Let rise for 20 minutes longer. Punch down and knead for 3 minutes. Use for filled pastries.

≡ *Egg Roll Skins*

Egg roll skins are made from egg noodle dough, rolled thinly and cut into large squares, about 5 inches. They can be bought ready-made. Spring roll skins and rice paper skins are also available ready-made. Any of them can be used to make egg rolls. Once made and cooked, they can be cut into bite-size servings.

Since these skins are readily available in Asian markets, and the home-made product is not remarkably better (and often not as good), buying them makes sense. They can be kept in the freezer for months.

To Shape and Fry Egg Rolls Place the egg roll skin on a board with one corner pointing toward you. Put a generous amount of filling on the skin, about 1½ inches from the corner nearest you. Lift that corner and fold it over the filling. Brush the opposite corner with beaten egg. Fold in each side to enclose the filling (it will look something like an open envelope) and roll tightly toward the egg-coated point. Set the egg roll on a baking sheet until ready to fry.

Heat the oil to 375°F and fry until golden. One pound of wrappers yields about 25 egg rolls. The fillings also yield about 25 egg rolls.

Wonton Skins and Gyoza Skins (Square or Round Noodle Dough Wrappers)

These skins are used to make wontons, shao mai, miniature egg rolls, and many other pastries. They are made from a noodle dough that is sometimes made with egg. The 2½-inch square wonton wrappers and

Filling Egg Roll Skins

1. *Place filling on egg roll wrapper.*

2. *Fold over one end and both sides.*

3. *Brush point with beaten eggs and roll.*

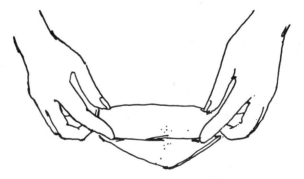

the 2½-inch round gyoza wrappers can be used interchangeably. The difference is how the final pastry looks, not how it tastes. Each package yields about 50 wrappers.

Miniature Egg Rolls Use either wonton or gyoza skins and fill as for standard egg rolls. A 1-pound package makes about 50 miniature egg rolls.

Wontons Place a skin on the counter with one corner pointing toward you. Place 1 teaspoon of filling in the center of each skin. Dip a finger in beaten egg and moisten the edges of the pastry. Lift the corner closest

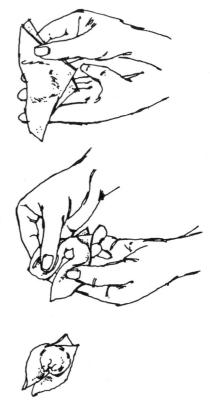

Wontons

1. *Place filling on a wonton/pastry square.*
2. *Fold one corner over filling, placing points adjacent to, but not on top of, each other. Pinch to seal.*
3. *Bring outside points together at the opposite end and pinch to seal.*

to you over the top of the filling to within ¼ inch of the opposite corner, so the points are side by side. Press the edges to seal. Bring the two points on either side of the filling together under the filling, opposite the other corners, and pinch to seal.

Heat the oil to 375°F and fry until golden. Wontons can be frozen after frying.

Shao Mai, Siu Mai These round, squat dumplings are shaped to expose the filling. Use gyoza skins or wonton skins cut into circles. Put 1 tablespoon of filling in the center of each circle. Lift up the sides of the dough, pinching and pleating around the outside, leaving the top of the filling exposed. Squeeze in the sides to give the pastry a waist, then drop it lightly on a counter to flatten the bottom. Place in a steamer and steam until cooked.

Shao Mai

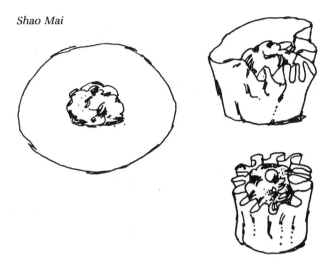

≡ *Chiao Tzu Wrappers*

These round noodle dough wrappers are similar to gyoza skins. If you don't have time to make them, substitute purchased gyoza skins.

═ Yield: 50 wrappers

2 cups flour   ¾ cup cold water

═ Yield: 200 wrappers

8 cups flour   3 cups cold water

1. Place the flour in a food processor and with the machine running, gradually add the water to make a stiff dough. Process for 2 minutes to knead. Let rest for 30 minutes.

2. Shape the dough into logs, 12 inches long and 1½ inches in diameter. Cut into ½-inch slices.

3. Place each slice on a lightly floured tortilla press and press into 3-inch circles. Place the circles on a baking sheet and keep covered with a damp towel until ready to fill.

To Fill Chiao Tzu Place 2 teaspoons of filling in the center of each dumpling. Lift the sides up over the filling and give a twist to the ends. This should make a purse-like pastry with a series of pleats gathered at the top and a rounded bottom. Stand it on its bottom on a lightly floured baking sheet.

Chiao Tzu
1. *Place filling in center of dough.*
2. *Lift edges and pinch to seal.*

These can also be shaped in the same manner as the wheat starch dough (see following page), in which case they are most commonly known as Peking ravioli, or pot stickers.

To Boil Chiao Tzu Bring 2 quarts of water to a boil in a saucepan. Add the dumplings and stir. Cover and return to a boil. Add 1 cup cold water and return to the boil again. Repeat twice. Drain. These can be reheated by steaming or by plunging them into boiling water.

To Fry Chiao Tzu Heat 2 tablespoons of oil in a large skillet and place the dumplings, pleated side up, with the sides just touching. Cook over low heat until they brown lightly on the bottom. Add 1 cup chicken stock and cook until the liquid evaporates. Add 1 more tablespoon of oil and fry, covered, for 2 minutes. Remove from the pan and serve. These are called pot stickers with good reason.

To Deep-Fry Chiao Tzu Heat oil to 375°F and fry until golden.

≡ *Wheat Starch Wrappers*

This is an especially resilient dough. When properly made, the finished pastries will have a silvery translucent covering that allows the filling to show through delicately.

═══ **Yield: 80 wrappers**

2 cups wheat starch	4 teaspoons oil
1⅓ cups tapioca starch	2¼ cups rapidly boiling water
1 teaspoon salt	

═══ **Yield: 320 wrappers**

8 cups wheat starch	5½ tablespoons oil
5⅓ cups tapioca starch	10 cups rapidly boiling water
4 teaspoons salt	

1. In a food processor, mix the wheat starch, tapioca starch, and salt. With the motor running, add the oil and gradually pour in the boiling water. Process until the dough forms a ball on top of the blades. Let rest 15 minutes.

2. Knead on a lightly oiled surface until smooth. Divide the dough into portions. Roll into ½-inch-wide strips and cut the strips into ¾-inch lengths.

3. In a tortilla press, stamp out 3-inch rounds.

Wheat Starch Dough Bonnets Put 1 teaspoon of filling on each round and press the opposite sides of the circle together to seal. On one side of the center joint, pinch 3 pleats, heading towards the joint. Repeat on the other side. The pastry should resemble a poke bonnet with a smooth back and a series of pleats on the front.

The illustration on the next page shows how to pleat the dough. Some Asian markets sell a small plastic gadget that creates a reasonable facsimile in one stroke.

Rabbit-Shaped Dim Sum These are most often made with wheat starch dough, but gyoza wrappers can be used as well. Place a circle of dough in one hand, put 1 teaspoon of filling in the center, and gather the dough up and around the filling. Pinch the dough over the top of the filling and twist to form a long point. The pastry should look like a teardrop. Using scissors, cut the point in half toward the filling. Bend the ends back over the dumpling to resemble rabbit ears. With your thumb and index finger, press into the base of the ears to make indentations for

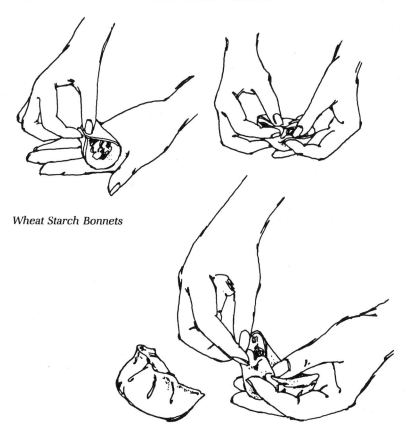

Wheat Starch Bonnets

eyes. The eyes can be left empty, but for added realism, fill with tiny cubes of ham or shrimp.

Wheat Starch Dough Slices Roll the dough into rectangles, fill, and roll into logs as with short pastry (see Chapter 13). After the logs are cooked, cut them into slices.

To Cook Wheat Starch Dough Steam until the filling is cooked, about 20 minutes. The dough will look translucent and will disintegrate if steamed too long. Once cooked, it is better to remove the pastries immediately and reheat them later, rather than hold them over the steam to keep them warm.

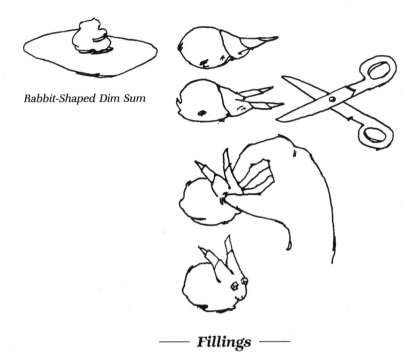

Rabbit-Shaped Dim Sum

—— *Fillings* ——

As with so many other pastries in this book, the fillings are interchangeable. Although a particular wrapper is suggested for each filling, a different wrapper or dough can be substituted to suit your needs. In order to make these switches intelligently, I recommend that you prepare them as suggested first and then decide if you prefer another wrapper.

≡ *Hsia Chiu Jung (Shrimp Paste)*

This is one of the most versatile recipes in the book. Shrimp paste can be spread on shrimp toast, wrapped around crab claws, made into deep-fried balls, or used to fill wonton, chiao tzu, or wheat starch wrappers, which may be steamed, sautéed, stir-fried, or baked. In addition, it can be further flavored with sesame oil and given a different texture and taste by adding minced Chinese mushrooms, bamboo shoots, or water chestnuts.

═ Yield: 3 cups

1 pound shrimp, peeled
¼ pound pork fat, ground
2 egg whites
1 tablespoon cornstarch
1 tablespoon sherry

1½-inch piece gingerroot, minced
1½ teaspoons salt
pinch of white pepper

= **Yield: 12 cups**

4 pounds shrimp, peeled	¼ cup sherry
1 pound pork fat, ground	¼ cup minced gingerroot
8 egg whites	2 tablespoons salt
¼ cup cornstarch	¼ teaspoon white pepper

In a food processor, process the shrimp and pork fat to form a paste. With the machine running, add the egg whites, cornstarch, sherry, gingerroot, salt, and pepper.

▶ Can be frozen.

NOTE: For large quantities, it is easier to grind the shrimp and pork finely and beat in the remaining ingredients with an electric mixer.

≡ *Baked Curried Turnovers*

= **Yield: 36 turnovers**

1 pound ground pork	2 teaspoons curry powder
1 teaspoon oil	1 cup minced onion
1½ tablespoons soy sauce	1 cup mashed potatoes
1½ teaspoons salt	lard pastry for turnovers
1½ teaspoons sugar	(page 685)
1 teaspoon sherry	dorure (page 539)

= **Yield: 144 turnovers**

4 pounds ground pork	3 tablespoons curry powder
2 tablespoons oil	1 quart minced onion
⅓ cup soy sauce	1 quart mashed potatoes
2 tablespoons salt	lard pastry for turnovers
2 tablespoons sugar	(page 685)
1½ tablespoons sherry	dorure (page 539)

1. Preheat the oven to 400°F.

2. In a skillet, stir-fry the pork in the oil, breaking up the lumps, until it loses its color. Add the soy sauce, salt, sugar, sherry, and curry powder. Spoon into a bowl.

3. Stir-fry the onion in the remaining fat in the pan until wilted. Add the onion and potatoes to the pork and mix well. Cool.

4. Fill and shape into turnovers. Brush with dorure and bake 15 minutes or until golden.

▶ Can be frozen and reheated.

≡ *Chiu Ts'ai Su P'ing*
(Pork, Shrimp, and Mushroom Turnovers)

It is easiest to stir-fry in smaller amounts. Prepare the larger quantity in batches.

══ **Yield: 36 turnovers**

4 Chinese mushrooms, soaked	2 teaspoons minced gingerroot
½ pound ground pork	1½ teaspoons cornstarch
6 ounces finely chopped	1 teaspoon rice wine or sherry
shrimp	1 teaspoon minced garlic
½ cup minced scallions	½ teaspoon sugar
1 teaspoon soy sauce	½ teaspoon salt
½ teaspoon rice wine or sherry	peanut oil
½ teaspoon Asian sesame oil	lard pastry for turnovers
2 tablespoons chicken stock	(page 685)
2 teaspoons soy sauce	1 egg, beaten
2 teaspoons Asian sesame oil	

══ **Yield: 144 turnovers**

16 Chinese mushrooms, soaked	2 tablespoons cornstarch
2 pounds ground pork	1½ tablespoons rice wine
1½ pounds finely chopped	or sherry
shrimp	1½ tablespoons minced garlic
2 cups minced scallions	2 teaspoons sugar
4 teaspoons soy sauce	2 teaspoons salt
2 teaspoons rice wine or sherry	peanut oil
2 teaspoons Asian sesame oil	lard pastry for turnovers
½ cup chicken stock	(page 685)
3 tablespoons soy sauce	4 eggs, beaten
3 tablespoons Asian sesame oil	
3 tablespoons minced	
gingerroot	

1. Preheat the oven to 400°F.

2. Remove the stems from the mushrooms and discard. Mince the caps.

3. In a bowl, mix the pork, shrimp, scallions, soy sauce, wine, and sesame oil.

4. In another bowl, mix the chicken stock, second measure of soy sauce, sesame oil, gingerroot, cornstarch, wine, garlic, sugar, and salt.

5. Heat a wok, add enough peanut oil to film the bottom, and stir-fry the pork-shrimp mixture until the pork separates and loses its color. Transfer to a sieve and drain. Heat the wok and add 1 tablespoon (¼ *cup*) peanut oil. Stir-fry the mushrooms for 30 seconds or until well coated. Stir in the pork mixture and add the cornstarch mixture. Cook, stirring, until thickened. Put into a bowl and chill.

6. Fill and shape into turnovers, brush with beaten egg, and bake for 20 minutes or until golden.

▶ Can be frozen and reheated.

≡ *Chia Li Chiao (Curried Beef Turnovers)*

═ Yield: 36 turnovers

½ pound ground beef	1 tablespoon cornstarch
1 teaspoon soy sauce	4 tablespoons peanut oil
1 teaspoon rice wine or sherry	½ cup minced onion
½ teaspoon Asian sesame oil	1 tablespoon curry powder
½ cup chicken stock	lard pastry for turnovers
2 teaspoons sugar	(page 685)
1 teaspoon salt	dorure (page 539)
2 tablespoons water	

═ Yield: 144 turnovers

2 pounds ground beef	¼ cup cornstarch
4 teaspoons soy sauce	1 cup peanut oil
4 teaspoons rice wine or sherry	2 cups minced onion
2 teaspoons Asian sesame oil	¼ cup curry powder
2 cups chicken stock	lard pastry for turnovers
3 tablespoons sugar	(page 685)
1½ tablespoons salt	dorure (page 539)
½ cup water	

1. Preheat the oven to 400°F.

2. In a bowl, mix the beef, soy sauce, wine, and sesame oil. In a second bowl, mix the chicken stock, sugar, and salt. In a third bowl, stir the water into the cornstarch.

3. In a wok, heat 2 tablespoons oil and sauté the meat mixture until the mixture separates and loses its color. Transfer to a sieve and drain. In the same wok, heat 2 tablespoons oil and stir-fry the onion until soft. Add the curry powder and stir-fry for 1 minute. Return the meat and stir-fry for 1 minute. Add the stock and bring to a boil. Stir the cornstarch mixture and add it to the wok and cook, stirring, until thickened. Transfer to a bowl and chill.

4. Fill and shape into turnovers and brush with the dorure.

5. Bake for 20 minutes or until golden.

▶ Can be frozen and reheated.

NOTE: Prepare the large quantity in batches.

≡ *Bao Tzu (Pork and Bok Choy-Filled Buns)*

═ **Yield: 40 buns**

2 pounds roast pork, minced	4 teaspoons grated gingerroot
6 cups chopped bok choy	½ cup soy sauce
6 scallions, minced	2 tablespoons Asian sesame oil
4 garlic cloves, minced	Chinese yeast dough (page 685)
4 teaspoons salt	

═ **Yield: 160 buns**

8 pounds roast pork, minced	⅓ cup grated gingerroot
6 quarts chopped bok choy	2 cups soy sauce
3 cups minced scallions	½ cup Asian sesame oil
½ cup minced garlic	Chinese yeast dough (page 685)
⅓ cup salt	

1. In a bowl, mix the pork, bok choy, scallions, garlic, salt, ginger-root, soy sauce, and sesame oil.

2. Roll the dough into logs, 1½ inches in diameter, and cut into 40 pieces (*160 pieces*). Roll each piece into 3-inch circles, or press in a tortilla press. Put 3 tablespoons of filling in the center of each circle and pull the edges together over the filling, pinching the edges together and giving a final twist.

3. Place the buns, seam-side down, 2 inches apart on lightly oiled baking sheets. Cover and let rise 1 hour.

4. Steam 20 minutes or until puffed and dry on the inside.

▶ Can be reheated in the steamer, but best if freshly made.

NOTE: These become somewhat large when steamed. I have found cutting them in half and exposing the filling makes them more appealing and a better size for hors d'oeuvre. If left whole, the tops can be decorated by dipping the end of a chopstick into red food coloring and putting a dot on top of each bun.

≡ *Cha Siu Bao (Roast Pork Steamed Buns)*

═ Yield: 36 buns

3 tablespoons oyster sauce
3 tablespoons sugar
2 tablespoons soy sauce
1 tablespoon Asian sesame oil
2 teaspoons flour
2 teaspoons cornstarch

⅓ cup water
2 tablespoons lard
½ pound roast pork, finely diced
2 tablespoons minced garlic
2 tablespoons minced scallions
Chinese yeast dough (page 685)

═ Yield: 144 buns

¾ cup oyster sauce
¾ cup sugar
½ cup soy sauce
¼ cup Asian sesame oil
3 tablespoons flour
3 tablespoons cornstarch

1⅓ cups water
½ cup lard
2 pounds roast pork, finely diced
½ cup minced garlic
½ cup minced scallions
Chinese yeast dough (page 685)

1. In a bowl, mix the oyster sauce, sugar, soy sauce, and sesame oil. In another bowl, mix the flour, cornstarch, and water.

2. In a wok, heat the lard and cook the pork, stirring, until hot. Add the garlic and scallions and stir-fry for 15 minutes. Add the oyster sauce mixture and cook, stirring, until simmering. Stir the cornstarch mixture and add it to the wok. Cook, stirring, until thickened. Cool.

3. Pinch off sections of the dough and shape into 2-inch balls. Roll into 3½-inch circles, or press in a tortilla press. Fill the circles and gather up the edges, pinching to seal.

4. Place on a floured surface, seam-side down, and cover. Let rise 15 to 20 minutes.

5. Steam until puffed and dry on the inside, about 15 minutes.

▶ Can be reheated, but best if freshly made.

≡ *Steamed Flower Rolls with Mongolian Lamb*

═ Yield: 36 rolls

Chinese yeast dough (page 685)
3 tablespoons minced scallions
¼ cup sesame oil
¼ cup toasted sesame seeds
1 pound boned leg of lamb
¼ cup soy sauce
¼ cup rice wine
2 tablespoons sweet bean sauce
   or hoisin sauce

2 tablespoons water
1 tablespoon sugar
1 tablespoon Asian sesame oil
1 tablespoon minced garlic
1½ teaspoons minced gingerroot
sesame oil
4 leeks, julienned
2 red peppers, julienned
2 mild chili peppers, julienned

═ Yield: 144 rolls

Chinese yeast dough (page 685)
¾ cup minced scallions
1 cup sesame oil
1 cup toasted sesame seeds
4 pounds boned leg of lamb
1 cup soy sauce
1 cup rice wine
½ cup sweet bean sauce or
   hoisin sauce

½ cup water
¼ cup sugar
¼ cup Asian sesame oil
¼ cup minced garlic
2 tablespoons minced gingerroot
sesame oil
16 leeks, julienned
8 red peppers, julienned
8 mild chili peppers, julienned

1. To make the rolls, allow the dough to rise for 2 hours or until tripled in bulk before adding the baking powder. Sprinkle on the scallions at the same time as the baking powder.

2. Line a steamer with parchment paper and brush with sesame oil.

3. Roll the dough into 1½-inch-diameter rope and cut into 36 pieces (*144 pieces*). Press into 3-inch rounds and brush with sesame oil. Fold in half and with a chopstick press the edge at ¼-inch intervals to make ⅛-inch indentations. Score surface from the indentations on top of the roll to the center of the folded edge. Brush lightly with water and sprinkle with sesame seeds. The pastries should look a little like flowers.

4. Place on the parchment-lined racks, ½ inch apart, and let rise for 10 minutes.

5. Steam for 12 to 15 minutes.

6. To make the filling, slice the lamb into paper-thin 2-inch squares.

7. In a bowl, marinate the lamb in the soy sauce, wine, sweet bean sauce, water, sugar, sesame oil, garlic, and ginger for at least 4 hours. Drain the lamb.

8. Brush a cast iron skillet with sesame oil and heat until hot.

9. Arrange the lamb in one layer and cook until no longer pink. Add some of the leeks, red peppers, and chili peppers and stir-fry until tender. Transfer vegetables to a platter and continue until all are cooked.

10. Open the flower rolls and fill with the lamb mixture.

▶ The unfilled buns can be steamed the day before and reheated. The filling is best if used immediately.

≡ Wontons I
(Shallow-Fried Dumplings or Pot Stickers I)

These can also be deep-fried.

≡ **Yield: 50 wontons**

10 ounces frozen spinach, thawed	1 tablespoon peanut oil
1 pound ground pork	1 teaspoon salt
1 egg	50 wonton wrappers
1 tablespoon soy sauce	garlic soy dipping sauce
1 tablespoon cornstarch	(page 74)

≡ **Yield: 200 wontons**

40 ounces frozen spinach, thawed	¼ cup peanut oil
4 pounds ground pork	4 teaspoons salt
4 eggs	200 wonton wrappers
¼ cup soy sauce	garlic soy dipping sauce
¼ cup cornstarch	(page 74)

1. Chop the spinach finely and squeeze out the excess moisture. Place in a bowl and mix in the pork, egg(s), soy sauce, cornstarch, oil, and salt.

2. To fill, place 1 teaspoon of filling just below the center and above one corner of the wrapper. Fold the corner over the filling and place it next to the opposite point. Moisten the two ends on either side of the filling and bring them together underneath the flat side of the triangle. Pinch to seal.

3. Bring a kettle of water to a boil, add the wontons, return to a boil, add ½ cup water, and bring to a boil again. Add ½ cup water and repeat once more. The wontons are done when they float to the surface. Drain and cool.

4. Pan-fry the wontons in a little oil in a skillet until they form a crust on both sides.

5. Drain and serve with garlic soy dipping sauce.

▶ Can be frozen; fry just before serving.

≡ *Wontons II*

═ Yield: 25 wontons

½ pound ground pork
¼ cup water chestnuts, chopped
1 egg
1 tablespoon minced scallions

1 teaspoon salt
⅛ teaspoon pepper
25 wonton wrappers
oil for frying

═ Yield: 100 wontons

2 pounds ground pork
1 cup water chestnuts, chopped
4 eggs
¼ cup minced scallions

1 tablespoon salt
½ teaspoon pepper
100 wonton wrappers
oil for frying

1. In a bowl, mix the pork, water chestnuts, egg(s), scallions, salt, and pepper.

2. Fill wonton wrappers and fold.

3. Heat oil to 375°F and fry until golden.

▶ Filling can be prepared 1 day in advance, but do not fill and fry until shortly before serving.

NOTE: To boil wontons to serve in soup, cook them in boiling water for 5 minutes, drain, run under cold water to stop cooking, and store covered with water in the refrigerator for several days, or freeze them after they have been cooked.

≡ *Wontons III (Deep-Fried Dumplings)*

═ Yield: 50 wontons

4 Chinese mushrooms, soaked
½ pound ground pork
½ cup minced water chestnuts
2 teaspoons minced scallions
1½ teaspoons cornstarch
1 teaspoon soy sauce

1 teaspoon minced gingerroot
½ teaspoon sherry
½ teaspoon Asian sesame oil
½ teaspoon salt
50 wonton wrappers
oil for frying

= **Yield: 200 wontons**

16 Chinese mushrooms, soaked
2 pounds ground pork
2 cups minced water chestnuts
3 tablespoons minced scallions
2 tablespoons cornstarch
1½ tablespoons soy sauce
1½ tablespoons minced
  gingerroot

2 teaspoons sherry
2 teaspoons Asian sesame oil
2 teaspoons salt
200 wonton wrappers
oil for frying

1. Remove and discard the mushroom stems. Mince the caps.

2. In a bowl, mix the mushrooms, pork, water chestnuts, scallions, cornstarch, soy sauce, gingerroot, sherry, sesame oil, and salt.

3. Fill wonton wrappers and fold.

4. Heat the oil to 375°F and fry until golden. Serve with duck sauce, Chinese mustard, or soy dipping sauces.

▶ Can be fried, frozen, and reheated, but best if freshly fried.

≡ *Wontons with Shrimp and Pork Filling*

= **Yield: 50 wontons**

½ pound ground pork
½ pound shrimp, peeled and
  minced
½ cup minced water chestnuts
2 scallions, minced

1 teaspoon soy sauce
1 teaspoon cornstarch
½ teaspoon salt
50 wonton wrappers
oil for frying

= **Yield: 200 wontons**

2 pounds ground pork
2 pounds shrimp, peeled and
  minced
2 cups minced water chestnuts
8 scallions, minced

4 teaspoons soy sauce
4 teaspoons cornstarch
2 teaspoons salt
200 wonton wrappers
oil for frying

1. In a bowl, mix the pork, shrimp, water chestnuts, scallions, soy sauce, cornstarch, and salt until the mixture holds together.

2. Fill wonton wrappers and fold.

3. Heat the oil to 375°F and fry until golden.

▶ Can be fried, frozen, and reheated, but best if freshly fried.

≡ *Hsien Shui Chiao*
(Deep-Fried Pork and Shrimp Turnovers)

─────────────────────────────────

═ **Yield: 50 turnovers**

½ pound pork, finely diced, not ground

1 tablespoon soy sauce

2 teaspoons rice wine or sherry

1½ teaspoons cornstarch

1 teaspoon Asian sesame oil

¼ pound shrimp, finely diced, not ground

1 teaspoon rice wine or sherry

½ teaspoon salt

1 slice gingerroot

6 Chinese mushrooms, soaked

½ cup chicken stock

1 tablespoon soy sauce

1 teaspoon cornstarch

1 teaspoon Asian sesame oil

½ teaspoon sugar

½ teaspoon salt

¼ cup peanut oil

2 tablespoons minced scallions

50 wonton wrappers

═ **Yield: 200 turnovers**

2 pounds pork, finely diced, not ground

¼ cup soy sauce

3 tablespoons rice wine or sherry

2 tablespoons cornstarch

1 tablespoon Asian sesame oil

1 pound shrimp, finely diced, not ground

4 teaspoons rice wine or sherry

2 teaspoons salt

4 slices gingerroot

24 Chinese mushrooms, soaked

2 cups chicken stock

¼ cup soy sauce

4 teaspoons cornstarch

4 teaspoons Asian sesame oil

2 teaspoons sugar

2 teaspoons salt

1 cup peanut oil

½ cup minced scallions

200 wonton wrappers

1. In a bowl, marinate the pork in the soy sauce, wine, cornstarch, and sesame oil for 20 minutes.

2. In another bowl, marinate the shrimp in the wine, salt, and gingerroot for 20 minutes.

3. Remove and discard the mushroom stems. Mince the caps.

4. In a small bowl, mix the chicken stock, soy sauce, cornstarch, sesame oil, sugar, and salt.

5. Heat a wok and add 2 tablespoons oil. Stir-fry the pork and shrimp, discarding the ginger, for 2 minutes or until the pork and shrimp pieces separate and change color. Transfer to a plate. (Fry larger quantity in batches, adding oil as necessary.)

6. Reheat the wok, add 2 more tablespoons oil, and stir-fry the mushrooms and scallions for 15 seconds. Stir the cornstarch mixture and add to the wok with the pork and shrimp. Stir-fry until well coated and the sauce thickens. Cool.

7. Fill the wonton wrappers and shape as turnovers.

8. Heat the oil to 375°F and fry until golden.

▶ Can be frozen and reheated.

≡ *Shrimp Paste–Filled Wontons*

Fill wonton wrappers with the shrimp paste filling (page 693) and fry at 375°F until golden.

≡ *Kuo Tieh, Chiao Tzu (Pot Stickers II)*

═ Yield: 50 dumplings

¾ pound ground pork
1 cup finely shredded celery
   cabbage
¼ cup minced scallions
1½ teaspoons minced garlic
1 teaspoon minced gingerroot
½ teaspoon salt

½ teaspoon rice vinegar
½ teaspoon Asian sesame oil
¼ teaspoon pepper
⅛ teaspoon chili oil
wonton wrappers or chiao tzu
   wrappers (page 689)
peanut oil

═ Yield: 200 dumplings

3 pounds ground pork
1 quart finely shredded celery
   cabbage
1 cup minced scallions
2 tablespoons minced garlic
2 tablespoons minced
   gingerroot
2 teaspoons salt

2 teaspoons rice vinegar
2 teaspoons Asian sesame oil
1 teaspoon pepper
½ teaspoon chili oil
wonton wrappers or chiao tzu
   wrappers (page 689)
peanut oil

1. In a bowl, mix the pork, cabbage, scallions, garlic, ginger, salt, vinegar, sesame oil, pepper, and chili oil.

2. Fill and cook like fried chiao tzu (see page 690). Serve drizzled with more hot oil, or use a dipping sauce (pages 72–82).

▶ Can be frozen before cooking.

≡ *Bulanee Kachalou*
(Turnovers with Ground Beef and Green Pepper)

The Chinese are not the only people who use a thin noodle dough. Here are a few examples from Afghanistan.

═ Yield: 50 turnovers

½ cup minced onion
3 tablespoons oil
½ pound ground beef
¼ cup boiling water
1 teaspoon minced garlic
1 teaspoon pepper

salt, to taste
1 potato, cooked and grated
⅓ cup minced green pepper
50 wonton wrappers
oil for frying
1 cup chilled yogurt

═ Yield: 200 turnovers

2 cups minced onion
½ cup oil
2 pounds ground beef
1 cup boiling water
4 teaspoons minced garlic
4 teaspoons pepper

salt, to taste
4 potatoes, cooked and grated
1⅓ cups minced green pepper
200 wonton wrappers
oil for frying
1 quart chilled yogurt

1. In a skillet, sauté half the onion in the oil until golden. Add the beef and cook, breaking up the lumps, until it loses its color. Add the water, garlic, pepper, and salt. Cook, stirring, until the liquid evaporates. Drain to remove excess oil.

2. Stir in the potato, remaining onion, and green pepper.

3. Fill the wontons, brush the edges with water, and fold into turnovers. Press the edges to seal.

4. In a skillet, heat ½ inch oil and fry the turnovers until golden on both sides. Drain and serve with yogurt.

▶ Filling can be prepared 1 day in advance. Do not fill until shortly before frying.

≡ *Aushak (Scallion Dumplings, Afghan)*

═ Yield: 36 dumplings

1½ cups minced scallions
½ teaspoon minced garlic
¼ teaspoon pepper
2 tablespoons corn oil
salt, to taste

36 gyoza wrappers
1 cup yogurt
1 tablespoon minced garlic
2 teaspoons crumbled dried
  mint

== **Yield: 144 dumplings**

6 cups minced scallions
2 teaspoons minced garlic
1 teaspoon pepper
½ cup corn oil
salt, to taste

144 gyoza wrappers
1 quart yogurt
¼ cup minced garlic
3 tablespoons crumbled dried
  mint

1. In a bowl, mix the scallions, garlic, pepper, oil, and salt.

2. Rub the edges of the gyoza skins with cold water and fill each with a teaspoon of the scallion mixture. Shape into turnovers, pressing the edges to seal.

3. Steam for 15 minutes.

4. In a bowl, mix the yogurt, garlic, and mint. Serve the hot dumplings with the yogurt sauce as a dip.

▶ Filling can be prepared 1 day in advance.

≡ *Bulanee Gandana (Scallion Turnovers)*

== **Yield: 36 turnovers**

1½ cups minced scallions
¾ teaspoon pepper
2 teaspoons minced garlic
salt, to taste

1 tablespoon vegetable oil
36 wonton wrappers
oil for frying
chilled yogurt

== **Yield: 144 turnovers**

6 cups minced scallions
1 tablespoon pepper
3 tablespoons minced garlic
salt, to taste

¼ cup vegetable oil
144 wonton wrappers
oil for frying
chilled yogurt

1. In a bowl, mix the scallions, pepper, garlic, salt, and oil.

2. Rub the edges of the wonton wrappers with water and fill each with a teaspoon of the filling. Fold into triangles and press the edges to seal.

3. In a skillet, heat ½ inch oil and cook the turnovers until golden on both sides.

4. Serve with the yogurt or with the yogurt garlic sauce from the previous recipe.

▶ Can be prepared 1 day in advance.

≡ *Spicy Crab-Stuffed Wontons*

═ Yield: 50 wontons

½ cup minced shallots
2 tablespoons olive oil
¼ cup white wine
2 tablespoons minced black
  olives
2 tablespoons horseradish
1 teaspoon minced garlic
½ teaspoon cayenne pepper

½ teaspoon thyme
1 cup heavy cream
1½ pounds crabmeat
¼ cup grated Parmesan cheese
50 wonton wrappers
oil for frying
garlic cream sauce (page 367)

═ Yield: 200 wontons

2 cups minced shallots
½ cup olive oil
1 cup white wine
½ cup minced black olives
½ cup horseradish
4 teaspoons minced garlic
1 teaspoon cayenne pepper

2 teaspoons thyme
1 quart heavy cream
6 pounds crabmeat
1 cup grated Parmesan cheese
200 wonton wrappers
oil for frying
garlic cream sauce (page 367)

1. In a skillet, sauté the shallots in the oil until soft. Add the wine, olives, horseradish, garlic, cayenne, and thyme and deglaze. Add the cream and reduce by half. Stir in the crabmeat and cheese. Cool.

2. Fill the wontons and shape like turnovers, or fold into the traditional wonton shape.

3. Heat the oil to 350°F and fry until golden. Serve hot. Serve with garlic cream sauce if desired.

▶ Filling can be made 1 day in advance.

≡ *Curried Lamb Wontons*

═ Yield: 50 wontons

2 tablespoons butter
1½ cups minced onion
1 teaspoon minced garlic
1 teaspoon minced ginger
1 tablespoon lemon juice
2 teaspoons curry powder
½ teaspoon salt
¾ pound ground lamb
1 tablespoon minced mint

1 tablespoon minced coriander
  (cilantro)
1 teaspoon garam masala or
  curry powder
1½ cups minced onion
50 wonton wrappers
oil for frying
plum sauce or pungent fruit
  sauce (page 70)

=== **Yield: 200 wontons**

½ cup butter
6 cups minced onion
2 tablespoons minced garlic
2 tablespoons minced ginger
¼ cup lemon juice
3 tablespoons curry powder
2 teaspoons salt
3 pounds ground lamb
¼ cup minced mint

¼ cup minced coriander
  (cilantro)
4 teaspoons garam masala or
  curry powder
6 cups minced onion
200 wonton wrappers
oil for frying
plum sauce or pungent fruit
  sauce (page 70)

1. In a skillet, heat the butter and sauté the onion, garlic, and ginger until softened. Add the lemon juice, curry, and salt and increase heat. Add the lamb and sauté until it loses its color. Add the mint, coriander, garam masala, and remaining onion. Cover and cook 2 minutes. Cool.

2. Fill the wrappers and shape into turnovers.

3. Heat the oil to 375°F and fry until golden. Serve hot with one of the sauces.

▶ Filling can be prepared 1 day in advance.

≡ *Mushroom-Filled Shao Mai*

=== **Yield: 25 dumplings**

5 Chinese mushrooms, soaked
1 pound mushrooms, minced
1 tablespoon minced gingerroot
1 tablespoon vegetable oil
¼ pound pork fat

1 tablespoon soy sauce
1 tablespoon Asian sesame oil
1 egg white
wheat starch or gyoza wrappers
dipping sauces (pages 72–82)

=== **Yield: 100**

20 Chinese mushrooms, soaked
4 pounds mushrooms, minced
¼ cup minced gingerroot
¼ cup vegetable oil
1 pound pork fat

¼ cup soy sauce
¼ cup Asian sesame oil
4 egg whites
wheat starch or gyoza wrappers
dipping sauces (pages 72–82)

1. Remove and discard the Chinese mushroom stems, reserving the soaking liquid and the caps. Mince the caps and strain the liquid.

2. In a wok, stir-fry the plain mushrooms and gingerroot in the oil until the liquid evaporates. Add the mushroom soaking liquid and the minced caps to the wok and reduce until dry.

3. In a food processor, process the fat, the mushroom mixture, soy sauce, sesame oil, and egg white(s) until the mixture holds together.

4. Fill wrappers and shape into shao mai. Steam for 20 minutes. Serve with a dipping sauce.

▶ Can be prepared for steaming 2 hours in advance. Can be reheated after steaming.

≡ Shao Mai I, Siu Mai (Steamed Pork and Shrimp Dumplings I)

Shao mai are delicious little dumplings, wrapped in dough, with the filling showing out of the top. Once steamed, they can be refrigerated or frozen and resteamed. Do not keep them too long before steaming, or the pastry will dissolve.

═ Yield: 40 dumplings

1 pound ground pork	2 teaspoons minced scallions
6 ounces shrimp, minced	1 teaspoon Asian sesame oil
¼ cup minced water chestnuts	1 teaspoon minced gingerroot
1 egg white	½ teaspoon sugar
1 tablespoon sherry	¼ teaspoon pepper
1 tablespoon cornstarch	wheat starch or gyoza wrappers
2 teaspoons soy sauce	½ cup grated carrot

═ Yield: 200 dumplings

4 pounds ground pork	1½ tablespoons Asian sesame oil
1½ pounds shrimp, minced	
1 cup minced water chestnuts	2 tablespoons minced gingerroot
4 egg whites	2 teaspoons sugar
¼ cup sherry	1 teaspoon pepper
¼ cup cornstarch	wheat starch or gyoza wrappers
3 tablespoons soy sauce	2 cups grated carrot
3 tablespoons minced scallions	

1. In a bowl, mix the pork, shrimp, water chestnuts, egg white(s), sherry, cornstarch, soy sauce, scallions, sesame oil, gingerroot, sugar, and pepper.

2. Fill and cook as directed for shao mai, placing the carrot on top for color.

▶ Keeps refrigerated for 2 days; can be frozen and reheated.

≡ Shao Mai II
(Steamed Pork and Shrimp Dumplings II)

= Yield: 50 dumplings

½ pound ground pork
½ pound shrimp, minced
¼ cup minced scallions
3 tablespoons chicken stock
1 tablespoon soy sauce
1 tablespoon sherry
2 teaspoons Asian sesame oil
1 teaspoon cornstarch
½ teaspoon sugar

¼ teaspoon salt
wheat starch or gyoza wrappers
2 tablespoons minced ham
2 tablespoons minced water
  chestnuts
2 tablespoons Chinese
  mushroom caps, soaked and
  minced
½ cup frozen peas, thawed

= Yield: 200 dumplings

2 pounds ground pork
2 pounds shrimp, minced
1 cup minced scallions
¾ cup chicken stock
¼ cup soy sauce
¼ cup sherry
2 tablespoons Asian sesame oil
4 teaspoons cornstarch

2 teaspoons sugar
1 teaspoon salt
wheat starch or gyoza wrappers
½ cup minced ham
½ cup minced water chestnuts
½ cup Chinese mushroom
  caps, soaked and minced
2 cups frozen peas, thawed

1. In a bowl, mix the pork, shrimp, scallions, chicken stock, soy sauce, sherry, sesame oil, cornstarch, sugar, and salt.

2. Fill as for shao mai, pressing the edges to the center on four sides to shape the top into four petals like a clover. Fill the openings with ham, water chestnuts, mushroom caps, or frozen peas.

▶ Filling can be prepared 1 day in advance.

≡ Shao Mai III (Shrimp and Pork Dumplings III)

= Yield: 50 dumplings

1 pound shrimp, minced
⅔ cup diced pork
½ cup minced bamboo shoots
2 tablespoons sugar

1 tablespoon cornstarch
1 teaspoon salt
¼ teaspoon pepper
gyoza wrappers

≡ Yield: 200 dumplings

4 pounds shrimp, minced
2⅔ cups diced pork
2 cups minced bamboo shoots
½ cup sugar

¼ cup cornstarch
4 teaspoons salt
1 teaspoon pepper
gyoza wrappers

1. In a bowl, mix the shrimp, pork, bamboo shoots, sugar, cornstarch, salt, and pepper.

2. Fill and cook as for shao mai.

▶ Filling can be prepared 1 day in advance.

≡ *Szu Fang Chiao (Four-Flavor Dumplings)*

≡ Yield: 50 dumplings

2 eggs
2 teaspoons water
¾ teaspoon salt
peanut oil
½ cup soaked and minced
   Chinese mushroom caps

½ cup minced ham
½ cup minced scallions
shao mai filling I, II, or III
   (pages 709–710)
wheat starch or gyoza wrappers

≡ Yield: 200 dumplings

8 eggs
3 tablespoons water
1 tablespoon salt
peanut oil
2 cups soaked and minced
   Chinese mushroom caps

2 cups minced ham
2 cups minced scallions
shao mai filling I, II, or III
   (pages 709–710)
wheat starch or gyoza wrappers

1. In a bowl, mix the eggs, water, and salt.

2. Brush a 9-inch skillet with peanut oil and heat until very hot. Remove from the heat and cool 1 minute. Pour in ¼ cup of the egg mixture and twirl to coat the bottom of the pan. Cook until set but not brown. Turn and cook the second side until just done but not brown. Transfer to a board and continue making egg sheets. Cool the sheets and mince.

3. Fill as for shao mai, pressing the edges to the center on four sides to shape the top into four petals like a clover. Fill the openings with egg, mushrooms, ham, or scallions.

4. Steam until cooked.

▶ Filling can be prepared 1 day in advance.

≡ Chicken and Shrimp Filling for Shao Mai

= Yield: 50 dumplings

6 Chinese mushrooms, soaked
1 cup ground raw chicken or
 turkey
¼ pound shrimp, minced
½ cup minced water chestnuts
¼ cup minced scallions

3 tablespoons soy sauce
1 tablespoon Asian sesame oil
1 tablespoon sherry
1 teaspoon salt
wheat starch or gyoza wrappers

= Yield: 200 dumplings

24 Chinese mushrooms, soaked
4 cups ground raw chicken or
 turkey
1 pound shrimp, minced
2 cups minced water chestnuts
1 cup minced scallions

¾ cup soy sauce
¼ cup Asian sesame oil
¼ cup sherry
4 teaspoons salt
wheat starch or gyoza wrappers

1. Remove and discard the mushroom stems and mince the caps.

2. In a bowl, mix the mushrooms with the chicken, shrimp, water chestnuts, scallions, soy sauce, sesame oil, sherry, and salt.

3. Fill and steam as for shao mai.

▶ Can be refrigerated for 2 days; can be frozen and reheated.

≡ Feng Yen Chiao (Phoenix Eye Dumplings)

The fanciful name of some Chinese dishes adds to their allure. Since not many have met a phoenix, I trust that the explicit folding instructions will give you your first glimpse.

= Yield: 36 dumplings

4 Chinese mushrooms, soaked
¾ pound ground pork
6 ounces shrimp, minced
¼ cup minced water chestnuts
¼ cup grated carrot
2 tablespoons minced scallions
1 tablespoon cornstarch
2 teaspoons soy sauce

2 teaspoons minced gingerroot
1 teaspoon sherry
1 teaspoon Asian sesame oil
½ teaspoon salt
¼ teaspoon pepper
36 chiao tzu (page 689) or gyoza
 wrappers
dipping sauces (pages 72–82)

══ **Yield: 144 dumplings**

16 Chinese mushrooms, soaked
3 pounds ground pork
1½ pounds shrimp, minced
1 cup minced water chestnuts
1 cup grated carrot
½ cup minced scallions
¼ cup cornstarch
3 tablespoons soy sauce
3 tablespoons minced
    gingerroot

1 tablespoon sherry
1 tablespoon Asian sesame oil
2 teaspoons salt
½ cup minced scallions
1 teaspoon pepper
144 chiao tzu (page 689) or
    gyoza wrappers
dipping sauces (pages 72–82)

1. Remove and discard the mushroom stems. Mince the caps.

2. In a bowl, mix the mushrooms, pork, shrimp, water chestnuts, carrot, scallions, cornstarch, soy sauce, gingerroot, sherry, sesame oil, salt, and pepper.

3. To fill, put 1 teaspoon of filling into the center of each wrapper. Bring the opposite sides together as if making a turnover and pinch in the center only. Push one end toward the center point, making a U-shaped indentation. Repeat at the opposite end. The pastry should have four sections of the dough meeting in the center and four "wings." Gather two wings and pinch them together at the end; repeat on the opposite side of the center.

4. Steam the pastries for about 20 minutes or until the filling is cooked. Serve with dipping sauces.

▶ Cooked pastries can be refrigerated for one day or frozen and reheated.

≡ *Chiao Tzu (Meat Dumplings)*

══ **Yield: 50 dumplings**

1½ cups minced celery
    cabbage
1 teaspoon salt
¾ pound ground pork
1 cup minced scallions
2 tablespoons soy sauce

2 tablespoons Asian sesame oil
1 tablespoon sherry
1 teaspoon minced gingerroot
½ teaspoon minced garlic
50 chiao tzu (page 689) or gyoza
    wrappers

═══ **Yield: 200 dumplings**

6 cups minced celery cabbage
4 teaspoons salt
3 pounds ground pork
1 quart minced scallions
½ cup soy sauce
½ cup Asian sesame oil

¼ cup sherry
1½ tablespoons minced
  gingerroot
2 teaspoons minced garlic
200 chiao tzu (page 689) or
  gyoza wrappers

1. In a colander, toss the cabbage with the salt and let drain for 30 minutes. Squeeze out the excess moisture.

2. In a bowl, mix the cabbage, pork, scallions, soy sauce, sesame oil, sherry, gingerroot, and garlic.

3. Fill as for chiao tzu. Steam for 15 to 20 minutes or boil until tender.

▶ Filling can be prepared 1 day in advance.

═══ *Crab-Filled Chiao Tzu*

═══ **Yield: 36 dumplings**

6 Chinese mushrooms, soaked
½ pound ground pork
½ pound crabmeat
⅔ cup minced bamboo shoots
1 tablespoon sherry
1 tablespoon soy sauce

2 teaspoons cornstarch
½ teaspoon sugar
salt, to taste
36 chiao tzu (page 689) or gyoza
  wrappers

═══ **Yield: 144 dumplings**

24 Chinese mushrooms, soaked
2 pounds ground pork
2 pounds crabmeat
2⅔ cups minced bamboo
  shoots
¼ cup sherry

¼ cup soy sauce
3 tablespoons cornstarch
2 teaspoons sugar
salt, to taste
144 chiao tzu (page 689) or
  gyoza wrappers

1. Remove and discard the mushroom stems. Mince the caps. In a bowl, mix the mushrooms, pork, crabmeat, bamboo shoots, sherry, soy sauce, cornstarch, sugar, and salt.

2. Fill and shape as for chiao tzu.

3. Steam, boil, pan-fry, or deep-fry.

▶ Filling can be prepared 1 day in advance.

—— *Egg Rolls and Spring Rolls* ——

Not only the Chinese, but also the peoples of most Asian countries have a form of food wrapped in a noodle dough and fried. The wrappers can be made of egg noodle dough, crêpe dough, or rice sheets. The fillings can be as simple as spiced shrimp or involve a number of ingredients including fish, meat, and vegetables. There is no set filling for egg rolls. Select your favorite from the recipes here. Not all fillings are rolled in the dough; some versions are made in flat layers that are cut into sections and fried in serving pieces. Although most egg rolls are deep-fried, some are shallow-fried in an inch or so of oil, often starting with cold oil.

Some guests love the filling, but would prefer not to eat the fried container. For a lower-calorie option, you can fully cook the fillings in a wok or skillet, then serve them with lettuce leaves. The guests put a spoonful of the filling in a leaf, roll it, and eat it like an egg roll. Unfortunately, for a cocktail party this can be a bit messy. The staff can wrap small portions in the leaves and tie them with a scallion to make attractive small packets. If you choose to prepare these, be sure to assemble them very shortly before serving. Also make the packets small lest the filling drip.

≡ *Egg Rolls with Roast Pork Filling*

≡ Yield: 20 egg rolls cut into 80 pieces or 75 small egg rolls

6 Chinese mushrooms, soaked	½ cup minced water chestnuts
1 tablespoon soy sauce	½ cup shredded bamboo
1 tablespoon cornstarch	shoots
1 teaspoon Asian sesame oil	2 cups shredded celery cabbage
1 teaspoon salt	or bean sprouts, or a
1 teaspoon sugar	mixture
2 tablespoons peanut oil	20 egg roll wrappers or 75
1 pound roast pork, shredded	wonton wrappers
2 scallions, minced	

Yield: 80 egg rolls cut into 320 pieces or 300 small egg rolls

24 Chinese mushrooms, soaked
¼ cup soy sauce
¼ cup cornstarch
4 teaspoons Asian sesame oil
4 teaspoons salt
4 teaspoons sugar
¼ to ½ cup peanut oil
4 pounds roast pork, shredded
8 scallions, minced

2 cups minced water chestnuts
2 cups shredded bamboo
shoots
2 quarts shredded celery
cabbage or bean sprouts, or
a mixture
80 egg roll wrappers or 300
wonton wrappers

1. Remove and discard the mushroom stems. Shred the caps.
2. In a bowl, mix the soy sauce, cornstarch, sesame oil, salt, and sugar.
3. In a wok, heat 2 tablespoons oil and stir-fry the pork for 3 minutes or until heated.
4. Transfer to a bowl. Add the scallions, water chestnuts, bamboo shoots, and cabbage. Stir-fry 2 minutes. Add the mushroom shreds and pork and stir-fry 1 minute. Stir the cornstarch mixture and add to the wok. Cook, stirring, until well coated and the sauce thickens. Drain in a strainer until cool.
5. Fill the egg roll skins to make large servings or the wonton wrappers to make cocktail-size rolls.

▶ Filling can be prepared 1 day in advance.
NOTE: Fry the large quantity in batches.

Egg Rolls with Shrimp and Pork

Yield: 20 egg rolls cut into 80 pieces or 75 small egg rolls

3 Chinese mushrooms, soaked
3 tablespoons oil
1 slice gingerroot
½ pound ground pork
½ pound raw shrimp, minced
1 tablespoon sherry
1 tablespoon soy sauce
½ teaspoon sugar

2 cups minced celery
½ pound bean sprouts
¼ cup minced water chestnuts
2 teaspoons salt
1 tablespoon cornstarch mixed
with 2 tablespoons water
20 egg roll wrappers or 75
wonton wrappers

=== **Yield: 80 egg rolls cut into 320 pieces or 300 small egg rolls**

12 Chinese mushrooms, soaked
¾ cup oil
4 slices gingerroot
2 pounds ground pork
2 pounds raw shrimp, minced
¼ cup sherry
¼ cup soy sauce
2 teaspoons sugar

2 quarts minced celery
2 pounds bean sprouts
1 cup minced water chestnuts
2 tablespoons salt
¼ cup cornstarch mixed with
    ½ cup water
80 egg roll wrappers or 300
    wonton wrappers

1. Remove and discard mushroom stems and mince the caps.

2. In a wok, heat the oil and cook the gingerroot for 20 seconds. Add the pork and cook until it loses its color. Add the shrimp, sherry, soy sauce, sugar, and mushrooms. Stir-fry until the shrimp are pink and cooked. Transfer to a bowl.

3. Add 2 tablespoons oil to the wok and stir-fry the celery for 5 minutes. Add the sprouts, water chestnuts, and salt. Add the shrimp and pork mixture. Discard the ginger.

4. Cook over moderate heat until the liquid starts to boil. Stir the cornstarch and water and add to the mixture. Cook until thickened. Cool.

5. Use to fill egg rolls.

6. Fry at 375°F until golden and crisp.

▶ Filling can be prepared 1 day in advance.

≡ *Beef in Monks' Robes*

These are little sandwiches made with an egg pancake that is similar to the crêpe-like wrapper used in some areas of Asia to make egg rolls.

=== **Yield: approximately 100 sandwiches**

5 eggs, beaten
1 tablespoon cornstarch
1 tablespoon water
1 teaspoon vegetable oil
salt, to taste
¾ pound lean ground beef
2 tablespoons minced scallions
2 tablespoons water
1 tablespoon Chinese
    pepper-salt (page 72)

1 tablespoon soy sauce
1 tablespoon cornstarch
1 teaspoon grated gingerroot
1 egg
1 tablespoon cornstarch
2 teaspoons water
oil for sautéing
Chinese pepper-salt
soy sauce

═ **Yield: approximately 400 sandwiches**

20 eggs, beaten
¼ cup cornstarch
¼ cup water
4 teaspoons vegetable oil
salt, to taste
3 pounds lean ground beef
½ cup minced scallions
½ cup water
¼ cup Chinese pepper-salt
    (page 72)

¼ cup soy sauce
¼ cup cornstarch
1½ tablespoons minced
    gingerroot
4 eggs
¼ cup cornstarch
3 tablespoons water
oil for sautéing
Chinese pepper-salt
soy sauce

1. In a bowl, beat together the eggs, cornstarch, water, oil, and salt. Set aside for 30 minutes.

2. In another bowl, mix the beef, scallions, water, pepper-salt, soy sauce, cornstarch, and gingerroot. Let stand for at least 30 minutes. Chill while preparing the pancakes.

3. Wipe a 9-inch omelet pan with oil and heat over moderate heat. Pour in enough egg batter to coat the bottom of the pan in a thin layer. Cook until small bubbles appear and the underside is speckled with brown. Turn. Cook until very lightly colored and remove from the pan. Continue with remaining batter.

4. In a bowl, mix the remaining egg(s), cornstarch, and water, and brush over one side of each pancake.

5. Spread a thick layer of beef over half the pancakes and cover with remaining pancakes, coated side down, to make sandwiches. Cut the pancakes into 1½-inch-wide strips and then into diagonals. Heat ¼ inch oil in a skillet and sauté until golden on both sides. Drain and serve with pepper-salt and soy sauce for dipping.

▶ Can be prepared for frying 1 day in advance.

NOTE: If desired, add red and orange food coloring to the egg mixture to give it the saffron color of a Buddhist monk's robes.

═ *Thai Spring Rolls*

Thai spring rolls are quite different from the customary Chinese version and are served with a truly intriguing sweet-hot sauce that can accompany other foods, such as wontons and shao mai.

== **Yield: 50 pieces**

4 ounces bean thread noodles
3 small cloud ear mushrooms
oil
2 eggs, lightly beaten
2 tablespoons nam pla (see
  Glossary)
1 teaspoon pepper
1 teaspoon sugar

1 tablespoon oil
1 tablespoon minced garlic
¼ cup minced shallots
½ pound ground pork
½ pound shrimp, chopped
10 spring roll wrappers
oil for frying
dipping sauce (pages 72–74)

== **Yield: 200 pieces**

1 pound bean thread noodles
12 small cloud ear mushrooms
oil
8 eggs, lightly beaten
½ cup nam pla (see Glossary)
4 teaspoons pepper
4 teaspoons sugar
¼ cup oil

¼ cup minced garlic
1 cup minced shallots
2 pounds ground pork
2 pounds shrimp, chopped
40 spring roll wrappers
oil for frying
dipping sauce (pages 72–74)

1. Soak the noodles in hot water for 15 minutes, drain, and cut into 1-inch pieces.

2. Soak the cloud ears in hot water for 10 minutes, drain, and cut off and discard the stems. Cut into very fine julienne.

3. Brush a wok with oil and heat over medium heat. Pour in ¼ cup of the eggs and swirl to coat the bottom evenly. Cook until set into a large, thin pancake. Turn out and repeat with the remaining eggs. Cut the pancake into julienne.

4. In a bowl, mix the nam pla, pepper, and sugar.

5. In a wok, heat the oil and stir-fry the garlic until golden. Add the shallots and cook until wilted. Add the pork and stir-fry until no longer pink.

6. Add the shrimp and stir-fry until pink. Add the nam pla mixture and toss well.

7. Add the noodles, cloud ears, and egg strips, and mix well. Cool.

8. Fill the spring roll wrappers. Heat the oil to 375°F and fry until golden. Cut each roll into 5 slices. Serve with a dipping sauce.

▶ Fill shortly before frying.

≡ *Thai Crystal Spring Rolls*

This spring roll recipe is another fascinating version from Thailand. The extremely thin circular or rectangular skins are sold in Asian markets. They have to be peeled apart. They make a crispier egg roll and can always be substituted for the more common egg roll skin.

═ Yield: 72 pieces

1 bunch coriander (cilantro), including the roots
1 garlic clove, minced
¼ teaspoon pepper
1 pound shrimp, chopped
1 tablespoon nam pla (see Glossary)

1 recipe beer batter (page 323)
1 package spring roll skins
oil for frying
dipping sauce (pages 72–82)

═ Yield: 288 pieces

4 bunches coriander (cilantro), including the roots
4 garlic cloves, minced
1 teaspoon pepper
4 pounds shrimp, chopped
¼ cup nam pla (see Glossary)

2 recipes beer batter (page 323)
4 packages spring roll skins
oil for frying
dipping sauce (pages 72–82)

1. In a food processor, purée 2 teaspoons (*3 tablespoons*) of the chopped coriander root, garlic, and pepper. Add the shrimp and nam pla and process until the shrimp is finely minced.

2. Cover spring rolls with a damp towel.

3. Peel off two skins and brush one with batter and a thin layer of the shrimp mixture. Arrange 4 to 5 coriander sprigs on top of the shrimp, top with second skin, and brush the top with more batter.

4. In a skillet large enough to hold one package flat, heat 2 tablespoons oil.

5. Fry one package, batter side down, and brush the top with more batter. Turn and brown the second side. Drain and cut into bite-size pieces. Serve with a dipping sauce.

▶ The packages can be prepared for frying 2 hours before cooking. Serve immediately.

≡ Cha Gio (Vietnamese Spring Rolls)

The Vietnamese not only use a different filling and wrapper, they eat their spring rolls differently too. Traditionally, the rolls are served on top of vegetable salads. Another way to serve them is to wrap the rolls in lettuce leaves before eating. For hors d'oeuvre, cutting them into bite-size pieces is more suitable. Serve them with the appropriate dipping sauces.

═ Yield: 80 pieces

2 tablespoons tree ears soaked in warm water for 30 minutes, drained and minced

2 ounces cellophane noodles, soaked in warm water for 20 minutes and cut into 1-inch lengths

1 pound ground pork

½ pound crabmeat, flaked

1 cup bean sprouts

½ cup minced onion

¼ cup minced shallots or scallions

3 garlic cloves, minced

1 teaspoon nuoc mam (see Glossary)

½ teaspoon pepper

20 13-inch sheets rice paper (banh trang)

bowl of warm water

oil for frying

nuoc cham (see Glossary)

hoisin-peanut sauce (page 79)

Vietnamese mint dipping sauce (page 79)

═ Yield 320 pieces

½ cup tree ears soaked in warm water for 30 minutes, drained and minced

½ pound cellophane noodles, soaked in warm water for 20 minutes and cut into 1-inch lengths

4 pounds ground pork

2 pounds crabmeat, flaked

1 quart bean sprouts

2 cups minced onion

1 cup minced shallots or scallions

½ cup minced garlic

2 tablespoons nuoc mam (see Glossary)

2 teaspoons pepper

80 13-inch sheets rice paper (banh trang)

bowl of warm water

oil for frying

nuoc cham (see Glossary)

hoisin-peanut sauce (page 79)

Vietnamese mint dipping sauce (page 79)

1. In a bowl, mix the tree ears, drained noodles, pork, crabmeat, bean sprouts, onion, shallots, garlic, nuoc mam, and pepper.

2. Cut the rice papers into quarters and lay out on a counter. Dip the rice papers into the water and let stand until the paper softens, about 2 minutes.

3. Place about ½ teaspoon of filling ½ inch from the wide end of the triangle. Fold over both sides and roll toward the point. Place on a baking sheet and continue with the remaining filling and triangles.

4. Heat oil to 325°F and fry until golden and crisp, about 10 minutes (see note). Serve egg rolls with one or more of the dipping sauces.

▶ If prepared ahead, the rolls can be recrisped in hot oil.

NOTE: Because none of the ingredients in the filling is precooked, you may prefer this alternative method: Put the rolls into cold oil and cook for 20 to 30 minutes over moderate heat until golden brown.

≡ Chicken and Shrimp Filling

Substitute chicken for the pork and shrimp for the crabmeat in the preceding recipe and add ¼ pound (*1 pound*) ground pork fat.

≡ Lumpia Wrappers

This wrapper for Philippine egg rolls is more like a crêpe, but the filling can be put into egg roll wrappers for convenience.

═ Yield: 24 wrappers

2 cups flour	oil
2 cups water	

═ Yield: 100 wrappers

8 cups flour	oil
2 quarts water	

1. Place the flour in a food processor or mixer and, with the motor running, add the water in a slow, steady stream to make a smooth, fluid batter the consistency of heavy cream. If necessary, force through a sieve.

2. Heat an 8-inch skillet over moderate heat and brush with vegetable oil.

3. Ladle about 3 tablespoons of batter into the pan and swirl to thinly coat the bottom of the pan. Cook a few seconds until the edges of the sheet begin to curl away from the sides of the pan. Transfer to a sheet of waxed paper dusted with flour. Repeat, oiling the pan between each sheet.

4. Stack the sheets until ready to fill, preferably no longer than 2 hours.

≡ *Lumpia Filling*

═ Yield: 25 rolls

¼ pound bacon, cut into
¼-inch dice
½ cup minced onion
2 teaspoons minced garlic
1 cup diced cooked chicken
1 cup diced cooked pork
1½ pounds green beans, cut
French-style
2 cups shredded cabbage

¼ pound bean sprouts
1 cup minced celery
½ cup chicken stock
2 tablespoons Japanese soy
sauce
salt, to taste
25 lumpia or egg roll wrappers
oil for frying

═ Yield: 100 rolls

1 pound bacon, cut into ¼-inch
dice
2 cups minced onion
2 tablespoons minced garlic
1 quart diced cooked chicken
1 quart diced cooked pork
6 pounds green beans, cut
French-style
2 quarts shredded cabbage

1 pound bean sprouts
1 quart minced celery
2 cups chicken stock
½ cup Japanese soy sauce
salt, to taste
100 lumpia or egg roll
wrappers
oil for frying

1. In a wok or skillet, cook the bacon until crisp. Remove with a slotted spoon and drain.

2. Add the onion and garlic to the skillet and cook, stirring until soft but not brown. Add the chicken and pork and cook until the meat browns lightly. Add the green beans, cabbage, bean sprouts, and celery. Cook, stirring 1 minute. Add the bacon bits, chicken stock, soy sauce, and salt to taste. Cook, stirring, until the vegetables are tender-crisp.

3. Transfer to a colander and let drain for 10 to 15 minutes. Discard the liquid.

4. Fill the lumpia wrappers and fold like egg rolls.

5. Heat oil to 375°F and fry until golden. Serve immediately.

▶ Can be reheated.

≡ *Wheat Starch Dough Dumplings*

══ **Yield: 80 dumplings**

6 Chinese mushrooms, soaked
¼ pound raw ground pork
1 tablespoon cornstarch
½ cup minced raw shrimp
¼ cup lard or peanut oil
¾ cup minced bamboo shoots
½ cup minced roast pork
salt, to taste

1 tablespoon sherry
½ teaspoon sugar
1 tablespoon soy sauce
1 teaspoon Asian sesame oil
¼ teaspoon pepper
80 coriander (cilantro) leaves
80 wheat starch wrappers (page
  691) or wonton wrappers

══ **Yield: 320 dumplings**

24 Chinese mushrooms, soaked
1 pound raw ground pork
¼ cup cornstarch
2 cups minced raw shrimp
1 cup lard or peanut oil
3 cups minced bamboo shoots
2 cups minced roast pork
salt, to taste

¼ cup sherry
2 teaspoons sugar
¼ cup soy sauce
4 teaspoons Asian sesame oil
1 teaspoon pepper
320 coriander (cilantro) leaves
320 wheat starch wrappers (page
  691) or wonton wrappers

1. Remove and discard the mushroom stems. Mince the caps.
2. In a bowl, mix the ground pork with half the cornstarch.
3. In another bowl, mix the shrimp with the remaining cornstarch.
4. In a wok, heat the lard until hot, add the ground pork, and cook, stirring until it loses its color. Add the shrimp, bamboo shoots, roast pork, mushrooms, salt, sherry, sugar, and soy sauce. Cook, stirring, until hot. Add the sesame oil and pepper.
5. Fill the wheat starch wrappers, placing a coriander leaf on top of each filling before pleating the wrapper closed.

▶ Steam just until done. Let cool and reheat if necessary.

≡ *Filling for Rabbit-Shaped Dumplings*

══ **Yield: 20 dumplings**

¾ cup minced fresh pork fat
⅔ cup minced shrimp
⅓ cup minced water chestnuts
½ teaspoon sugar
¼ teaspoon salt
pinch of pepper

¼ teaspoon Asian sesame oil
40 ¼-inch cubes of ham
¼ small recipe wheat starch
  wrappers (page 691) or 20
  shao mai or gyoza wrappers

☰ Yield: 80 dumplings

3 cups minced fresh pork fat
2⅔ cups minced shrimp
1⅓ cups minced water
   chestnuts
2 teaspoons sugar
1 teaspoon salt

¼ teaspoon pepper
1 teaspoon Asian sesame oil
160 ¼-inch cubes of ham
1 small recipe wheat starch
   wrappers (page 691) or 80
   shao mai or gyoza wrappers

1. Place the fat in a sieve, put into a pan of boiling water, and let stand for 10 seconds. Drain, run under cold water, and drain again.

2. In a bowl, mix the pork fat, shrimp, water chestnuts, sugar, salt, pepper, sesame oil, and ham.

3. Fill and shape the wrappers into rabbits (see page 691). Use any remaining wheat starch dough for other fillings.

4. Steam for 8 minutes or just until the filling is cooked. The wrapper will disintegrate if steamed too long.

▶ These freeze well once they are cooked and can be reheated in the steamer.

☰ *Har Gow (Shrimp Bonnets)*

☰ Yield: 50 dumplings

¾ pound shrimp, minced
¾ cup minced bamboo shoots
½ cup minced pork fat,
   blanched
1 scallion, minced
2½ tablespoons cornstarch
4 teaspoons sugar

1 teaspoon Asian sesame oil
1 teaspoon oil
1 teaspoon soy sauce
½ teaspoon salt
¼ teaspoon white pepper
50 wheat starch wrappers
   (page 691)

☰ Yield: 200 dumplings

3 pounds shrimp, minced
3 cups minced bamboo shoots
2 cups minced pork fat,
   blanched
4 scallions, minced
⅔ cup cornstarch
⅓ cup sugar

4 teaspoons Asian sesame oil
4 teaspoons oil
4 teaspoons soy sauce
2 teaspoons salt
1 teaspoon white pepper
200 wheat starch wrappers
   (page 691)

Wheat Starch Dumplings
(Alternate Shaping Method)

1. *Place filling in center of dough round.*

2. *Pinch one-third of circle into pleats.*

3. *Lift pleats over filling and press against pastry.*
4. *Twist ends in front and pinch to seal.*

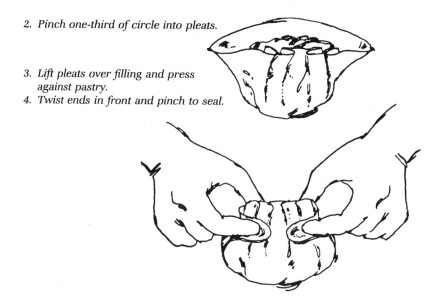

1. In a bowl, mix the shrimp, bamboo shoots, pork fat, scallion(s), cornstarch, sugar, sesame oil, oil, soy sauce, salt, and pepper.

2. Use to fill wheat starch wrappers and shape into bonnets (as above; also see page 692).

3. Steam 15 minutes.

▶ Steam just until cooked. Let cool and reheat if necessary.

Phoenix Rolls

1. *Spread shrimp mixture on waxed paper in 4½- × 7-inch rectangle. Arrange egg wedges.*
2. *Roll pork mixture over eggs to seal.*

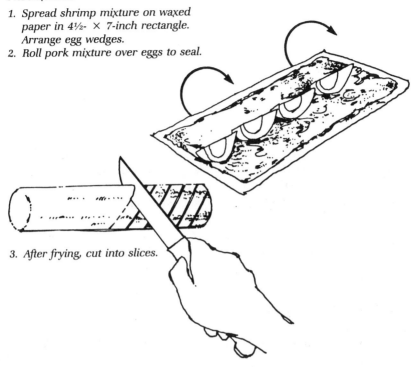

3. *After frying, cut into slices.*

≡ *Phoenix Rolls*

== Yield: 50 slices

1 large Chinese mushroom, soaked
½ pound shrimp, minced
1 cup ground pork
1 egg
salt, to taste
1½ tablespoons cornstarch
1 teaspoon sherry

1 teaspoon oil
¼ teaspoon Asian sesame oil
2 tablespoons minced ham
2 hard-cooked eggs, each cut into 3 wedges
1 egg
½ cup wheat starch
oil for frying

== **Yield: 200 slices**

4 large Chinese mushrooms,
  soaked
2 pounds shrimp, minced
1 quart ground pork
4 eggs
salt, to taste
⅓ cup cornstarch
4 teaspoons sherry

4 teaspoons oil
1 teaspoon Asian sesame oil
½ cup minced ham
8 hard-cooked eggs, each cut
  into 3 wedges
4 eggs
2 cups wheat starch
oil for frying

1. Remove and discard the mushroom stem(s). Mince the cap(s).

2. In a bowl, mix the mushroom(s), shrimp, pork, egg(s), salt, corn-starch, sherry, oil, sesame oil, and ham until the ingredients hold together.

3. On a sheet of waxed paper, shape half (one eighth for the larger quantity) of the mixture into a 4½″ × 7″ rectangle. Place 3 egg wedges lengthwise down the rectangle and, with the aid of the waxed paper, roll into a log. Press to seal the ends and sides. Repeat with the remaining ingredients.

4. Place on a steamer rack and steam 20 minutes. Remove from the heat, cool, and unwrap.

5. Beat the remaining egg(s) and brush over the log. Sprinkle with the wheat starch.

6. Heat the oil to 375°F and fry until golden. Drain and cool 5 minutes. Cut into ¼-inch-thick slices.

▶ Can be steamed 1 day in advance or frozen. Deep-fry just before serving.

≡ *Deep-Fried Shrimp Wrapped in Rice Paper*

== **Yield: 25 shrimp**

25 large shrimp, peeled and
  deveined
2 teaspoons sugar
2 teaspoons minced gingerroot
1 teaspoon salt
1 teaspoon Chinese five-spice
  powder

½ cup sherry
25 sheets rice paper (banh
  trang), 12 inches in diameter
2 eggs, beaten
oil for frying

☰ Yield: 100 shrimp

100 large shrimp, peeled and
   deveined
3 tablespoons sugar
3 tablespoons minced
   gingerroot
4 teaspoons salt
4 teaspoons Chinese five-spice
   powder

1 cup sherry
100 sheets rice paper (banh
   trang), 12 inches in diameter
6 eggs, beaten
oil for frying

1. In a bowl, marinate the shrimp in the sugar, gingerroot, salt, five-spice powder, and sherry for 15 minutes, turning often. Drain and pat dry.

2. Dip each rice sheet into hot water or sprinkle a sheet of rice paper with water and rub in until the paper is moist and pliable. Place a shrimp on one end of the paper and roll, folding in the sides in a butcher fold. Brush with beaten egg to seal.

3. Place in a covered container until ready to cook. Do not let the shrimp touch.

4. Heat the oil to 375°F and fry until golden.

☰ *Wor Teap Har (Butterflied Shrimp with Ham)*

☰ Yield: 24 shrimp

24 large shrimp, peeled, with
   tail section on
4 eggs, beaten
¼ cup flour
24 thin triangles Smithfield ham

24 thin triangles bacon
oil for frying
sweet and sour sauce
   (pages 77–78)

☰ Yield: 100 shrimp

100 large shrimp, peeled, with
   tail section on
16 eggs, beaten
1 cup flour
100 thin triangles Smithfield
   ham

100 thin triangles bacon
oil for frying
sweet and sour sauce
   (pages 77–78)

1. Butterfly the shrimp and press to flatten.

2. In a bowl, mix the eggs and flour into a batter. Dip each piece of ham into the batter and place on the cut side of the shrimp. Dip each piece of bacon into the batter and place on the ham.

3. Heat 2 tablespoons oil in a skillet and put the shrimp into the pan, bacon-side down. Fry 2 to 3 minutes. Gently turn and fry 1 to 2 minutes more. Serve immediately with the sauce for dipping.

▶ Can be prepared for frying 1 day in advance.

≡ *Spicy Shrimp Fritters*

═ Yield: 36 fritters

10 Chinese mushrooms, soaked	¼ teaspoon salt
½ pound shrimp, peeled and deveined	⅛ teaspoon white pepper
	¾ cup oil
6 garlic cloves, minced	1 cup diced water chestnuts
2 scallions, thinly sliced	1½ tablespoons sugar
1 egg	1 tablespoon chili paste with
1-inch piece gingerroot, minced	garlic
1½ tablespoons cornstarch	2 teaspoons rice vinegar
1 tablespoon Asian sesame oil	2 teaspoons soy sauce
2 teaspoons rice wine or sherry	oil for frying

═ Yield: 144 fritters

40 Chinese mushrooms, soaked	1 teaspoon salt
2 pounds shrimp, peeled and deveined	½ teaspoon pepper
	1½ cups oil
½ cup minced garlic	2 cups diced water chestnuts
8 scallions, thinly sliced	3 tablespoons sugar
4 eggs	2 tablespoons chili paste with
¼ cup minced gingerroot	garlic
6 tablespoons cornstarch	4 teaspoons rice vinegar
¼ cup Asian sesame oil	4 teaspoons soy sauce
2 tablespoons rice wine or sherry	oil for frying

1. Remove and discard the mushroom stems. Mince the caps.

2. In a food processor, process the shrimp until it forms a paste.

3. In a bowl, mix the shrimp paste, garlic, scallions, egg(s), gingerroot, cornstarch, sesame oil, wine, salt, and pepper.

4. In a wok, heat the oil and stir-fry the water chestnuts and mushrooms 1 minute. Mix in the sugar, chili paste, vinegar, and soy sauce. Keep warm.

5. Heat the oil to 375°F and fry tablespoonfuls of the shrimp mixture until golden brown. Drain and serve with the sauce.

▶ The sauce and shrimp paste can be prepared 1 day in advance.

≡ *Crab Dates*

≡ Yield: 36 dates

salt
1½ pounds shrimp, peeled
2 ounces fatback
2 egg whites
1 tablespoon tapioca flour
1 teaspoon Asian sesame oil
1 teaspoon rice wine or sherry
½ teaspoon sugar
pepper, to taste
½ pound crabmeat

¼ cup minced water chestnuts
2 scallions, minced
2 tablespoons minced ham
¼ teaspoon minced coriander
  (cilantro)
¼ cup cornstarch
¼ cup bread crumbs
oil for frying
dipping sauces (pages 72–82)

≡ Yield: 144 dates

salt
6 pounds shrimp, peeled
½ pound fatback
8 egg whites
¼ cup tapioca flour
4 teaspoons Asian sesame oil
4 teaspoons rice wine or sherry
2 teaspoons sugar
pepper, to taste
2 pounds crabmeat

1 cup minced water chestnuts
8 scallions, minced
½ cup minced ham
1 teaspoon minced coriander
  (cilantro)
1 cup cornstarch
1 cup bread crumbs
oil for frying
dipping sauces (pages 72–82)

1. In a colander, rub 1 tablespoon (*¼ cup*) salt into the shrimp. Rinse shrimp under cold water for 2 minutes. Repeat the salting, rinse again, and drain shrimp on a single layer of paper towels. Pat shrimp dry and wrap in towel. Refrigerate for at least 1 hour.

2. In a saucepan, blanch the fatback in boiling water for 5 minutes. Drain, put into a bowl of ice water and chill until firm. Pat dry and cut into ⅛-inch dice.

3. Chop the cold shrimp and season with 1 teaspoon (*4 teaspoons*) salt. In a food processor, chop until it forms a coarse paste. Transfer to a bowl and add the egg whites, tapioca flour, sesame oil, wine, sugar, and pepper. Beat until it forms a firm, elastic paste.

4. Fold in the diced fatback, crabmeat, water chestnuts, scallions, ham, and coriander.

5. Form tablespoonfuls of the mixture into the shape of large dates. In a flat pan, mix the cornstarch and bread crumbs and roll the crab dates to coat.

6. Heat the oil to 375°F and fry until golden. Serve with dipping sauces.

▶ Can be prepared for frying 1 day in advance.

≡ *Crystal Shrimp*

≡ **Yield: 25 shrimp**

1 pound shrimp, peeled and
   deveined
1 teaspoon salt
1 egg white
¾ to 1 cup cornstarch
2 tablespoons oil
1 scallion, minced

1 slice gingerroot, minced
6 tablespoons ketchup
1 tablespoon sugar
2 tablespoons chicken stock
1 teaspoon chili oil
oil for frying

≡ **Yield: 125 shrimp**

5 pounds shrimp, peeled and
   deveined
4 teaspoons salt
4 egg whites
3 to 4 cups cornstarch
½ cup oil
4 scallions, minced

4 slices gingerroot, minced
1½ cups ketchup
4 tablespoons sugar
½ cup chicken stock
4 teaspoons chili oil
oil for frying

1. In a bowl, mix the shrimp, salt, and egg white(s). Coat heavily with the cornstarch. Shake off the excess.

2. In a wok, heat the oil and stir-fry the scallion(s) and gingerroot 30 seconds. Add the ketchup, sugar, stock, and chili oil. Bring to a boil. Keep warm.

3. In a kettle heat the oil to 375°F and fry the shrimp one at a time for 1 minute. Drain and remove. Fry again for 30 seconds; drain and remove. Serve immediately with the warm sauce for dipping.

▶ These do not keep; prepare just before serving. The sauce can be prepared 1 day in advance.

≡ *Red-Cooked Anise Beef*

≡ **Yield: 100 skewers**

2 tablespoons peanut oil
3½ pounds beef stew meat
1½ cups water
¼ cup soy sauce
3 tablespoons sherry

2 tablespoons sugar
4 slices gingerroot, minced
3 garlic cloves, minced
2 star anise

═ **Yield: 400 skewers**

½ cup peanut oil

14 pounds beef stew meat

6 cups water

1 cup soy sauce

¾ cup sherry

½ cup sugar

¾ cup minced gingerroot

12 garlic cloves, minced

8 star anise

1. In a wok or casserole over high heat, heat the oil and brown the meat in batches, adding more oil if needed.

2. Return the meat to the wok and stir in the water, soy sauce, sherry, sugar, gingerroot, garlic, and star anise. Bring to a boil and simmer until very tender, 1½ to 2 hours.

3. Remove the meat from the wok, and skim the sauce of any fat. Cool the meat in the liquid.

4. When cold, cut into thin slices and serve on skewers.

▶ Can be prepared 2 days in advance; can be frozen.

═ *Garlic Cold Pork*

═ **Yield: 60 slices**

1 pound pork tenderloin

2 slices gingerroot

1 scallion, quartered

3 cloves garlic, minced

2 tablespoons soy sauce

1 tablespoon chicken stock

1 tablespoon chili oil

1 tablespoon Asian sesame oil

¼ teaspoon salt

═ **Yield: 240 slices**

4 pounds pork tenderloin

8 slices gingerroot

4 scallions, quartered

12 garlic cloves, minced

½ cup soy sauce

¼ cup chicken stock

¼ cup chili oil

¼ cup Asian sesame oil

1 teaspoon salt

1. In a kettle, simmer the pork, gingerroot, and scallion(s) in water to cover for 30 minutes or until tender. Cool and cut into very thin slices.

2. In a bowl, mix the garlic, soy sauce, chicken stock, chili oil, sesame oil, and salt. Serve as a dip for the pork.

▶ Can be prepared 2 days in advance; can be frozen.

≡ Crisp-Fried Smoked Chicken

= **Yield: 32 pieces**

4 smoked chicken breast halves
(recipe follows)
2½ tablespoons sweet bean
paste
1¼ teaspoons Chinese
pepper-salt (page 72)

1½ teaspoons sugar
2 tablespoons cornstarch
oil for frying
coriander (cilantro) sprigs for
garnish
soy dipping sauce (page 74)

= **Yield: 128 pieces**

16 smoked chicken breast
halves (recipe follows)
⅔ cup sweet bean paste
1½ tablespoons Chinese
pepper-salt (page 72)
2 tablespoons sugar

½ cup cornstarch
oil for frying
coriander (cilantro) sprigs for
garnish
soy dipping sauce (page 74)

1. Tear each chicken breast along the grain into about 8 fingers.

2. In a bowl, marinate the chicken with the bean paste, Chinese pepper-salt, and sugar for 20 minutes. Add the cornstarch and mix well.

3. Heat the oil to 375°F and fry the chicken until crisp and golden.

4. Pile onto a serving plate and surround with coriander. Serve extra Chinese pepper-salt and a soy dipping sauce as dips.

▶ Best if served immediately after frying.

≡ Indoor Smoked Cooked Chicken

Smoked chicken can be eaten as part of a main course, or at a picnic. Try using it in chicken salad.

= **Yield: 4 chicken breasts**

4 chicken breasts, skinned and
boned
¾ cup soy sauce
½ cup sherry
2 teaspoons sugar
1 onion, cut into wedges

1 tablespoon minced gingerroot
1 teaspoon crushed fennel
seeds
1 piece dried tangerine peel
2 tablespoons gin
3 tablespoons brown sugar

1. In a bowl, marinate the chicken in the soy sauce, sherry, sugar, onion, gingerroot, fennel seeds, and tangerine peel for 2 hours, turning every 30 minutes.

2. Place the chicken on a plate in a steamer and steam for 20 to 30 minutes or until just done.

3. To smoke, line a skillet with foil, turn the heat to medium, add the gin, and ignite. When the flame dies, add the sugar and stir until the sugar melts. Fit a cake rack into the skillet, and when the sugar begins to get dark and bubbly, place the chicken on the rack, cover, and smoke 10 to 15 minutes.

▶ Can be prepared 2 days in advance or frozen.

NOTE: To line the pan, spread a sheet of foil over the bottom, up over the sides, and fold over the edge. Do the same with the cover. The two pieces should fit together tightly. This is a very smoky process and is more pleasantly done by putting the frying pan over an outdoor grill.

☰ *Crispy Orange Beef*

When Maureen Lerner of Hollis, New Hampshire, told me that this was one of her favorite Chinese dishes, I turned this popular main course into a remarkably fine appetizer.

☰ Yield: 100 skewers

3 pounds flank steak, thinly sliced into long strips
½ teaspoon baking soda
⅔ cup plus 3 tablespoons water
3 tablespoons sherry
1 egg white
1½ tablespoons cornstarch
2 tablespoons oil
2 scallions, cut into ½-inch lengths
3 tablespoons dried orange peel

3 slices gingerroot, minced
1 long hot red chili pepper, minced
2 tablespoons cornstarch mixed with 3 tablespoons water
¼ cup chicken stock
3 tablespoons light soy sauce
2 tablespoons sugar
1 teaspoon Asian sesame oil
4 cups oil for frying
10 dried hot red chili peppers

1. In a bowl, mix the steak, baking soda, and water, and refrigerate overnight. Rinse beef and pat dry.

2. Transfer to a dry bowl. Add 1 tablespoon sherry and the egg white and stir until the white is foamy. Add 1½ tablespoons of cornstarch and the oil.

3. In a second bowl, mix the scallions, orange peel, gingerroot, and chili pepper.

4. In a third bowl, mix the cornstarch-water mixture, remaining sherry, chicken stock, soy sauce, sugar, and sesame oil. Set aside.

5. In a wok, heat the oil to 375°F. Add the beef and cook, stirring, for 45 seconds. Drain. Reheat the oil and cook the beef 15 seconds. Drain and fry again. Drain all but 2 tablespoons oil from the wok.

6. Reheat the wok, add the dried peppers, and stir until almost black. Remove the peppers and discard. Add the scallion mixture and stir-fry. Add the beef and heat. Add the sherry-cornstarch mixture and stir until the beef is coated and hot. Serve on skewers.

▶ The beef and sauce can be prepared 1 day in advance and reheated. **NOTE:** The success of this dish depends on cooking the beef three times. This gives the beef the crisp, yet chewy quality that is so appealing. Be sure to let the oil return to temperature before each frying. Fry the meat in batches and do not crowd the pan. The recipe can be increased without difficulty.

≡ *Chicken Walnut Rolls*

≡ **Yield: 32 rolls**

2 chicken breasts, skinned and boned
1 egg white, lightly beaten
1 tablespoon cornstarch
1 tablespoon water
¼ teaspoon salt
1 tablespoon minced scallion
¼ teaspoon minced gingerroot
¼ teaspoon minced garlic
2 tablespoons peanut oil
½ cup chicken stock
2 tablespoons water

1 tablespoon sherry
1 tablespoon soy sauce
¼ teaspoon salt
½ teaspoon sugar
¼ teaspoon white pepper
½ teaspoon cornstarch
1 teaspoon Asian sesame oil
½ teaspoon white vinegar
1 cup walnuts, blanched and drained
oil for frying

═ **Yield: 128 rolls**

8 chicken breasts, skinned and
   boned
4 egg whites, lightly beaten
¼ cup cornstarch
¼ cup water
1 teaspoon salt
¼ cup minced scallions
1 teaspoon minced gingerroot
1 teaspoon minced garlic
¼ cup peanut oil
2 cups chicken stock
½ cup water

¼ cup sherry
¼ cup soy sauce
1 teaspoon salt
2 teaspoons sugar
1 teaspoon white pepper
2 teaspoons cornstarch
4 teaspoons Asian sesame oil
2 teaspoons white vinegar
4 cups walnuts, blanched and
   drained
oil for frying

1. Cut the chicken breasts across the grain into thin slices and flatten slightly. Marinate in the egg white(s), 1 tablespoon (¼ *cup*) cornstarch, 1 tablespoon (¼ *cup*) water, and ¼ teaspoon (*1 teaspoon*) salt for 20 minutes.

2. In a saucepan, sauté the scallions, gingerroot, and garlic in the oil for 30 seconds. Add the chicken stock, 2 tablespoons (½ *cup*) water, sherry, soy sauce, salt, sugar, pepper, and ½ teaspoon (*2 teaspoons*) cornstarch. Bring to a boil and simmer until thickened slightly. Add the sesame oil and vinegar and set aside.

3. Heat the oil to 375°F and fry the walnuts until lightly colored. Drain and cool.

4. Wrap a walnut in a chicken slice and squeeze gently into a compact bundle. Fry the chicken rolls until the skin whitens. Drain and serve with the sauce as a dip.

▶ The chicken rolls and the sauce can be prepared 1 day in advance.

≡ *Deep-Fried Bean Curd, Shrimp, and Chicken Fritters*

═ **Yield: 81 cubes**

2 pounds soft bean curd
2½ ounces ground shrimp
2 ounces ground chicken
2 ounces ground pork fat
2 egg whites, beaten
1½ tablespoons cornstarch
1 tablespoon scallion-ginger
   infusion (recipe follows)

1 teaspoon salt
oil for frying
2 ounces pine nuts or peanuts
cornstarch for dredging
salt and pepper, to taste

=== **Yield: 324 cubes**

8 pounds soft bean curd	4 teaspoons salt
10 ounces ground shrimp	oil for frying
½ pound ground chicken	½ pound pine nuts or peanuts
½ pound ground pork fat	cornstarch for dredging
8 egg whites, beaten	salt and pepper, to taste
⅓ cup cornstarch	
¼ cup scallion-ginger infusion (recipe follows)	

1. Mash the bean curd with a fork and mix with the shrimp, chicken, and pork fat. Add the egg whites, cornstarch, scallion-ginger infusion, and salt.

2. Heat the oil to 350°F and fry the pine nuts until golden. Drain and chop finely. Stir into the bean curd mixture.

3. Press the mixture into an oiled 9-inch-square baking pan (or 4 pans, for the larger quantity) and steam for 15 to 20 minutes or until firm. Remove and cool.

4. Cut the mixture into cubes and dredge in the cornstarch. Fry until golden. Season with salt and pepper and serve.

▶ Can be steamed 1 day in advance.

≡ *Scallion-Ginger Infusion*

3 scallions, minced	½ cup boiling water
5 thick slices gingerroot, minced	

In a bowl, mix the ingredients and cool rapidly. Store in the refrigerator until ready to use. Drain the liquid, discard the solids, and store in a screw-top jar after 24 hours.

▶ Can be prepared 2 days in advance.

—— *Sushi* ——

Certain foods at one time considered inedible because they were so unfamiliar can become a cult food in the next generation. Sushi is a perfect example. Not so many years ago, crude jokes were made about eating raw fish, and anybody who did so was ranked as a barbarian.

Since then, sushi has not only become acceptable, it has even developed into a fad food. Certain aficionados constantly search for more and more esoteric fish.

Fortunately for the average host, hostess, and caterer, it is not necessary to hunt far and wide for a luscious assortment of sushi. A local fish market can supply salmon, tuna, sole, and shrimp, as well as other fish. It is vital, of course, that the fish be *absolutely* fresh. If it is not, make something else.

Making sushi is not difficult; what it requires is the ability to slice the fish paper-thin and an artistic eye.

Sushi is composed of a specially prepared rice base, wasabi (a Japanese horseradish sauce), and a slice of fresh fish. It may also include vegetables and sheets of nori (seaweed). There are three basic types of sushi.

Nigirisushi This is made of blocks of rice, covered with slices of fish. It can be garnished in several ways.

Makisushi This is sushi rolled inside sheets of nori (see note, page 740).

Kansai-Style Sushi This is a more elaborate means of shaping the rice and fish. Often the ingredients are put into a sushi box and compressed into a block that is then sliced.

≡ *Sushi Rice*

≡ **Yield: 6 cups, or about 50 sushi**

3 cups short-grain white rice	¼ cup vinegar
3⅓ cups water	¼ cup sugar

≡ **Yield: 24 cups, or about 200 sushi**

12 cups short-grain white rice	1 cup vinegar
13⅓ cups water	1 cup sugar

1. Rinse the rice in several changes of cold water until the water runs almost clear. Drain.

2. In a heavy pot, mix the rice and water and cover tightly. Bring to a boil over high heat. Reduce the heat to low and, without removing the lid, cook the rice 8 minutes more or until the water has been absorbed and the rice is fluffy.

3. Cover the top of the pot with a kitchen towel, replace the lid, and let rest for 10 to 15 minutes.

4. In a bowl, mix the vinegar and sugar. Using a dampened wooden spatula, transfer the rice to a large stainless steel baking pan. Cut the spatula through the rice in a slicing motion to separate the grains, slowly adding the vinegar and sugar mixture as you work, spreading the mixture. Cover the rice with a towel and let stand at room temperature until ready to use.

▶ Sushi rice must not be refrigerated and should be used on the day it is made.

NOTE: Dampen the wooden spatula periodically to prevent the rice from sticking to the wood.

While the vinegar mixture is added to the rice, it should be fanned to help cool it. Set an electric fan on the counter to cool the rice, or have an assistant wave a fan over it. Fanning the rice makes it glossy.

≡ *Nigirisushi*

1 small recipe sushi rice
    (preceding recipe)
½ cup white vinegar
2 cups water
50 thin slices assorted fish
    (about 2½ pounds)

wasabi (page 73)
lemon slices, optional
nori strips, optional
pickled ginger
Japanese soy sauce

1. Prepare the sushi rice.

2. In a bowl, mix the vinegar and water. (This is to moisten your hands to prevent the rice from sticking to them.) Dip your hands in the vinegar. Put 2 tablespoons of rice into your right hand and shape it into a compact oval using two fingers of your left hand.

3. Thinly slice the fish (directions follow). Brush a stripe of wasabi over the fish, place the rice oval on top, and press to join. Place on a tray with the fish upright.

4. The finished sushi can be garnished with slices of lemon or strips of nori.

5. Serve the sushi on lacquer trays with small piles of pickled ginger and saucers of soy sauce for dipping. The ginger is used to freshen the palate between various sushi.

NOTE: Nori is a seaweed that comes in sheets. Wave a sheet over a gas flame for about 5 seconds to toast it and make it papery. Cut it into thin strips and place it horizontally, vertically, or diagonally over the sushi as a garnish. Moisten the ends and join under the rice.

Maguro (Tuna)
Slice raw tuna about ¼ inch thick.

Saba (Mackerel)
Cut unskinned mackerel in ¼-inch slices and place on the rice with the skin along one side.

Sake (Salmon)
Slice salmon fillets ¼ inch thick and garnish with lemon wedges. (Do not confuse this with the beverage. The difference is in the pronunciation. Salmon is pronounced sah-keh and the beverage is pronounced sah-kay.)

Hirame (Halibut)
Cut into paper-thin slices and garnish with a strip of nori.

Suzuki (Sea Bass)
Cut into paper-thin slices and garnish with scallion slices.

Kaibashira (Scallop)
Cut sea scallops into thin slices and garnish with nori strips.

Ebi (Shrimp)
Shrimp are not served raw for sushi. Run a skewer lengthwise into each unshelled shrimp to straighten it. Cook in boiling, salted water until just done, about 1 minute. Cool, peel, remove the skewer, and cut almost through the underside of the shrimp to butterfly it. Place the opened shrimp on the rice, cut-side down.

Kani (King Crab)
Thinly slice shelled king crab legs and place on the rice.

Ikura (Salmon Roe)
These are shaped differently. After the sushi rice has been formed, cut a strip of nori about ½ inch higher than the sushi and long enough to go around the rice. Wrap the nori around the block of rice with the upper side open. Spoon the salmon roe into the center, and garnish with lemon wedges or thin slices of cucumber.
NOTE: Any loose filling, such as miniature scallops or other kinds of roe, can be wrapped in this fashion, with the nori forming a wall to hold the filling inside.

≡ *Makisushi*

To make makisushi, you need a bamboo sushi mat to roll the sushi.

nori sheets	wasabi (page 73)
sushi rice (page 739)	fillings (recipes follow)

1. Place a sheet of nori on the mat and spread it with a layer of sushi rice, leaving a 1-inch border along the long side. Moisten your hand in the vinegar and water to prevent the rice from sticking.

2. Brush a stripe of wasabi lengthwise across the center of the rice. Moisten the exposed nori border with the vinegar and water. With the aid of the mat, tightly roll the sushi toward the nori border. Overlap the edges and press firmly.

3. Unwrap and cut the makisushi into 1-inch sections. Arrange them, cut-side up, on a serving platter. Serve with mounds of pickled ginger and dishes of soy sauce.

Tekkamaki (Tuna Roll)
Cut fresh tuna into ½-inch-thick sticks and line them on top of the wasabi before rolling.
NOTE: This is arguably the most popular form of sushi and the one that meets with the least resistance.

Kappamaki (Cucumber Roll)
Make the same way as tekkamaki, substituting several long, thin strips of cucumber for the fish.

Oshinkomaki (Pickle Roll)
Substitute long, thin strips of pickled daikon for the tuna.

═ Glossary ═
of Ingredients

The hundreds of recipes in this book come from many countries and include ingredients from many cultures. What is a familiar food to one can seem exotic and strange to another. Some reviewers have raised questions about ingredients that I consider common knowledge and helped me realize that knowledge is common only within the same experience. Therefore, I am providing a glossary of ingredients, some common, some not, to help you in preparing these recipes.

In many instances the right ingredient is critical to the outcome of a particular recipe; in others substitutions are more than acceptable. Sometimes a substitution may be the basis of a new and possibly even better recipe. How do you know whether and what to substitute? If there is a known substitution I have tried to give such information. If none is listed, assume that the recipe needs the specific ingredient and choose another recipe rather than try to make a substitution.

Because many of the recipes are of Asian origin, they may require a trip to an Asian market. However, many foreign ingredients can be found in supermarkets across the country. Often these ingredients have a lengthy shelf life, so you need not be concerned about leftovers.

Anise, Star
A soft brown color, the stars have eight points and a strong anise flavor. Star anise is sold dry in Asian groceries and in the gourmet foods section of many supermarkets. Keeps indefinitely in a tightly covered container.

Bamboo Shoots

Sold canned in either thin slices or large chunks in most supermarkets. Asian markets sometimes sell them fresh, but canned shoots are suitable for these recipes. For dim sum, the size is not important since they will be chopped. Bamboo shoots keep indefinitely unopened. Once opened, store in the refrigerator covered with water for 2 to 4 days. They become mushy if frozen.

Banh Trang

These round or triangular sheets of rice paper are usually made with a basketwork pattern. To use the sheets, dip them into warm water for a moment, lift, and place on a counter. They quickly soften and become pliable. Wrap the stuffing in the wrapper and set aside. Deep fry until golden. In Vietnam and Thailand, the filled food packets are often put into a skillet of cold oil to cover and cooked for about 30 minutes or until hot, bubbling, and golden brown. Banh trang are found in Asian markets and some specialty food stores. They keep indefinitely.

Beans, Black, Salted, Fermented

Black beans are sold in small plastic bags in Asian markets. They can have any or all of the names listed above. Tightly covered, they keep indefinitely.

Bean Curd

Bean curd, or tofu, comes in blocks that usually weigh about 1 pound or more. Bean curd is sold soft, medium, and firm. For most of the recipes, medium is suitable. If another density is required, it is stated in the recipe. Bean curd is sold in most supermarkets as well as Asian markets and health food stores. It comes packed in water. If you keep it covered with fresh water and change the water every other day, it will keep about 1 week.

Bean Paste, Sweet or Hot

Bean paste is sold hot (sometimes called Szechuan) or sweet. It comes in small cans or jars. Once opened, store it in a covered container in the refrigerator. It will keep for 6 months or longer.

Butter

The recipes have been tested with unsalted butter. However, using salted butter is not a problem since you always add salt to taste. If a recipe specifies the quantity of salt, use about one-third less and then taste for seasoning.

Cabbage, Asian

Asians have several green vegetables that they use as cabbage. None of them look much like the green or red cabbage common to Western cooks. Bok choy has a thick white green stalk with a thick floppy green leaf. Both the stalk and the leaves can be used. Bok choy is seldom used in hors d'oeuvre, although you can line a steamer basket with the leaves. Sheo choy, or celery cabbage, is more readily available and is found in many supermarkets. It has a long stalk with pale green leaves and is used shredded or chopped in egg rolls for hors d'oeuvre. If it is not available, napa or bok choy can be substituted. All types keep about 1 week refrigerated in a plastic bag.

Chestnuts, Water

These small round roots are used as much for texture as for taste. They are sold fresh or canned. For these recipes, canned are suitable. Fresh water chestnuts are available in Asian markets, but the canned are found in most grocery stores. The fresh keep about 1 week, refrigerated. Peel before using. Once opened, canned water chestnuts will keep 1 week, covered with water and refrigerated. Can be frozen.

Chili Oil, Hot Oil

This hot oil is usually sold in small bottles with a shaker top. You can prepare your own by heating 1 cup of peanut oil to 370°F and adding 6 tablespoons of cayenne pepper. Sold in many supermarkets and all Asian markets. Keeps indefinitely.

Chili Paste with Garlic

This fiery hot pepper relish is used sparingly in some Asian recipes and should perhaps be served with a warning. It is found in Asian markets and some specialty markets. Once opened, it can be kept in the pantry in a tightly sealed container indefinitely. Sambal oelek is an acceptable substitute.

Cloud Ears/Fungus

Asian cookery uses many forms of fungus in cooking; cloud ears are just one variety. They are also called wood ears, silver ears, dried fungus, tree fungus, and brown fungus. Cloud ears are sold dried, in plastic bags, and vary in size from tiny bits to about 1½ inches. To use, soak them in hot water until soft, about 30 minutes. They increase dramatically after soaking. A teaspoon of dried tiny cloud ears can expand to ¼ cup. Sold in Asian markets, there is no substitute. They keep indefinitely.

Cocktail Sauce

The red mixture used for dipping shrimp or masking the flavor of raw oysters or clams holds a warm place in the cockles of the cocktail party goer's heart. To many, shrimp without the red sauce is not shrimp. It would appear that the more commercial the brand, the greater the appeal. Perhaps it brings back memories of one's first "adult party." Also, for many people "shrimp cocktail" has long signified luxury and fine dining as much as "pheasant under glass." Nowadays many people do manage to eat shrimp with other dips, but "the red sauce" is still needed. Generally I recommend any of the standard brands on the market. If you ever need to prepare it yourself, mix the contents of a 12-ounce jar of chili sauce with lemon juice, horseradish, dry mustard, Worcestershire, and Tabasco to taste. My preference is 2 teaspoons lemon juice, 1 tablespoon horseradish, ½ teaspoon dry mustard, 2 teaspoons Worcestershire sauce, and ¼ teaspoon Tabasco sauce. Let stand for 2 to 3 hours before serving. Pour it back into the chili sauce bottle and keep refrigerated for up to 6 months.

Coconut

Some of the recipes call for grated coconut. Of course, you can purchase fresh coconuts and grate the meat yourself, but such labor is not necessary. Most supermarkets now sell grated, unsweetened coconut. It is important to use unsweetened coconut. Sweetened coconut would drastically change the dish. Grated coconut will keep for several months in a tightly sealed container and can be frozen.

Coconut Milk

Coconut milk or cream is sold in some supermarkets. Be sure to purchase the unsweetened kind. The cans keep indefinitely. Once opened, they will keep in the refrigerator for several days and can be frozen.

Corn

A number of recipes call for corn kernels. I have not found a major difference in flavor using fresh corn, canned corn, or frozen corn. Generally I use an unsalted canned corn packed in a small amount of water. If fresh is preferred, I have tried to indicate that in the recipe.

Creole Mustard

Some fancy food stores outside of Louisiana carry this flavorful and spicy specialty of New Orleans. If you cannot locate a brand, create your own by adding 1 tablespoon of creole seasoning (recipe follows) to each cup of Dijon or brown mustard.

Creole Seasoning
Commercial creole seasonings are available in many markets. However, they are not stocked in every region of the country.

To prepare your own creole seasoning, mix the following ingredients: ¼ cup salt; 1 tablespoon each granulated garlic, pepper, and paprika; ¾ teaspoon granulated onion; and ¼ teaspoon each cayenne pepper, dried thyme, and dried oregano. The mixture will keep 6 months in a tightly sealed container.

Curry Paste
There is a difference between curry powder and curry paste. The paste generally has a more intense, but not necessarily hotter, taste than the powder. The paste usually comes in small cans, but is sometimes sold in small foil packages. The packages are more convenient as they can be stored in the pantry indefinitely. Once a can has been opened, the unused portion should be put into a clean small jar and kept tightly sealed in the refrigerator. It will last about 6 months. Curry powder can be used as a substitute.

Curry Powder
Curry powders are found in most supermarkets. They vary in flavor, intensity, and heat from packager to packager. Buy the smallest container possible of different brands to select the one that pleases you most, or have several on hand to vary the flavor of your curried dishes. It is wisest to buy curry in small quantities and replace it often since, like most dried spices, it loses flavor fairly quickly. Plan to replace it every 6 months. Keep in a tightly covered container in a cool dark place.

Eggs
The recipes have been tested with large eggs. However, on occasion I have prepared the recipes with medium or extra-large eggs and not found a major difference. In those few instances where the size of the egg is critical, I have specified the size.

Five-Spice Powder
A mixture of peppercorns, star anise, fennel seeds, cinnamon, and powdered cloves. Some brands list more than 5 spices and label it as spice powder. I have not found a major difference in flavor. It is available in small packages in Asian markets. Once opened, store in a tightly covered container. It loses its potency within 6 months. Allspice can be used as a poor substitute.

Garam Masala

A blend of seasonings ground together and used in Indian dishes. Available in some Indian markets. Keeps indefinitely in a tightly closed container.

To make your own garam masala, blend the following spices: 1 tablespoon each whole cumin seeds, whole coriander seeds, and whole cardamom seeds; ½ cinnamon stick; 1½ tablespoons black peppercorns; and ½ teaspoon whole cloves. In a nonstick skillet toast the spices until fragrant and lightly colored, about 3 minutes. Cool, then grind in a mortar and pestle or spice mill. Transfer to a jar with an airtight lid. Store up to 3 months. (Yields ¼ cup.)

Gingerroot

Fresh gingerroot is mandatory for most Chinese and many of the Asian recipes. To use, pare the skin and mince or slice the gingerroot. If fresh is not available, well-rinsed, preserved ginger can be used. It can be found in most supermarkets as well as Asian markets and keeps several weeks in the pantry or refrigerator. You can store fresh gingerroot in several ways. You can peel it, put it into a container, and cover it with sherry. Use the sherry when wine is called for in Asian dishes. Or, freeze the ginger and grate it as needed. One other method is to put the ginger into a container of damp sand. The theory is that it will continue to sprout new growths. Pull it out of the sand, rinse, cut off as much as you need, and replant. I buy a small quantity and discard if the root shrivels.

Herbs

Fresh herbs are used in all recipes unless dried is specified. You can almost always substitute one for another, using 3 times as much fresh as dried. Certain herbs, however, change their flavor completely when dried and bear little or no relation to the fresh herb.

Basil Fresh basil is almost as popular as parsley. Its distinctive flavor has little resemblance to dried basil. Fresh basil is available in many areas year round. It is easily grown, and with a sunny window and a little care, the least efficient gardener can produce a thriving plant. If you cannot get fresh basil for a recipe that requires it, make something else.

Coriander Also called Chinese parsley or cilantro (Spanish term), this herb has become a favorite in the last several years. The strong, musky flavor of fresh coriander is irreplaceable. Some writers suggest flat-leaf parsley as a substitute; however, although it looks similar, the flavor is not. Fortunately, popularity has increased availability. The dried herb is the ground root or seed and although the aroma is similar, the flavor is not the same. Unless dried is specified, fresh is necessary.

Hoisin Sauce

A thick, dark brown paste with a pungent sweet flavor, hoisin sauce is made from mashed soy beans, salt, sugar, garlic, and sometimes pumpkin. It is used as a marinade for roasted meats and as a dipping sauce alone or combined with other ingredients. Sold in cans or jars, it is available in the specialty foods section of some supermarkets and in Asian markets. It keeps indefinitely in a tightly covered container.

Horseradish

Horseradish to one cook means only freshly grated, while another automatically reaches for a bottle of prepared. I have found that the fresh offers a bit more zest, but is not so different that the quantity must be adjusted. Therefore, when I write horseradish, the cook can decide whether to use fresh or prepared.

Ketjap Manis (Indonesian Sweet Soy Sauce)

The name of American ketchup originates from the Malaysian ketjap. The original version was made from fermented fish brine. Ketjap manis is an Indonesian sweet soy sauce with spices and is used in sauces. Can be found in some specialty stores and in Asian markets. Keeps indefinitely.

Mascarpone

The Italian version of cream cheese, mascarpone has an extraordinary richness and flavor. It is really more like very thick heavy cream than cheese. It is found in cheese shops and other specialty stores. Once opened, it will keep a week or longer in the refrigerator. Check the expiration date. If it is not available, cream cheese softened and then thinned with heavy cream until almost thin enough to pour is an acceptable substitute.

Mushrooms, Dried, Asian

These vary in quality and cost. The best are thick, bulbous, relatively tightly shaped caps with a striated surface. Some mushrooms are very costly, but it is not necessary to buy the most expensive ones. Soak the mushrooms in warm water for 10 to 30 minutes until softened. You may use the strained soaking water to flavor soups or to replace the liquid in some recipes. Cut out and discard the stems. Available in many supermarkets and all Asian markets. Dried mushrooms keep indefinitely in a cool dry place. Some of the recipes call for other forms of fungus such as cloud ears (see entry).

Mushrooms, Dried, Western
There are many European and American dried mushrooms, but they are not suitable substitutes for the Asian mushrooms specified in this book.

Mustard, Chinese
There is no mystery to Chinese mustard. It is dry mustard powder sold in every market, mixed with a liquid. See page 73 for the recipe.

Nam Pla (Thai Fish Sauce)
A fish sauce made from salted fish and used in lieu of salt in many Thai dishes. It is available in some specialty food shops as well as Asian groceries. Keeps indefinitely in the pantry. You can substitute nuoc mam from Vietnam.

Nuoc Mam (Vietnamese Fish Sauce)
This is the equivalent of salt to Western cooking and soy sauce to Japanese or Chinese cookery. It is prepared from fresh anchovies and salt layered in wooden barrels and allowed to ferment for several months. The fish sauce of Vietnam is preferred; Philippine or Chinese fish sauce is not an acceptable substitute. Nam pla from Thailand may be substituted. Keeps indefinitely in the pantry.

Noodles
Although there is some question about whether the Asians invented noodles, there is none about the extraordinary variety they use in their cuisine. They make noodles from bean threads, rice, and flour. The particular recipes specify which noodles to buy. Noodle paste is also turned into sheets to be used for wontons or egg rolls (egg noodle dough) or spring rolls. Other wrappers are rice sheets or paper called *banh trang* (see entry). Follow the recipes to learn how to use these products, and then feel free to interchange the noodles and wrappers for different effects.

Egg noodles, wonton wrappers, egg roll wrappers, and some rice noodles are sold in many supermarkets. Asian markets carry these noodle products as well as banh trang. The fresh noodles keep several days in the refrigerator. Dried noodles and banh trang keep indefinitely in the pantry. The Japanese also use noodles. The three forms used here are a long, flat dried buckwheat noodle called *soba*, a wheat and water noodle that looks something like linguine called *udon* (these can be interchanged with soba), and *gyoza* wrappers. The *gyoza* are small round egg noodle wrappers suggested for certain dim sum. Wonton wrappers cut into circles are an acceptable substitute. They are sold in Asian markets.

Olive Oil

In recent years the prevalence of information on various olive oils has turned an everyday commodity into a fad of cult status. In the past the good cook bought a good quality olive oil for general use and an extra-virgin oil for salads. Today, if one believes the hype, you not only need several different brands, but you must also spend a fortune on each one. That, of course, is not true. The well-stocked kitchen needs a good all-purpose pure olive oil for cooking and an extra-virgin olive oil for drizzling over salads or marinated vegetables. Select the oils that suit you. Some are so fruity that they overpower the very foods they are supposed to enhance.

Oyster Sauce

This rich-tasting, thick brown sauce is used as a flavoring. It is sold in bottles and is found in many supermarkets as well as Asian markets. Keeps indefinitely in the refrigerator.

Sambal Oelek

A fiery hot pepper relish from Indonesia that should be used sparingly. It is only fair to warn guests when serving this unless they know about its potency. It is sold in jars in Asian markets and keeps indefinitely on the shelf. Chili paste with garlic is an acceptable substitute.

Sesame Oil

Asian and Middle Eastern countries both have sesame oils, but they are very different. The Asian version extracted from roasted sesame seeds has a full-flavored nutty aroma and taste. The Middle Eastern and the cold-pressed sesame oils found in health food stores are bland cooking oils that can be substituted for any other bland oil. They are not recommended for any of the recipes in this book.

The Asian sesame oil is an exciting ingredient used in many of the recipes in this book. It is usually added toward the end of the recipe, not as a cooking oil. It smokes at a low temperature, which can result in an overpowering taste. It can be found in the foreign foods section of many supermarkets and, of course, in most Asian markets. There is no major difference in the oils from the various Asian countries and, unlike soy sauce, Japanese and Chinese sesame oils are interchangeable. Stored in a cool, dark place, it will keep indefinitely.

Sesame Paste (Middle Eastern and Asian)

There is a major difference between sesame paste from the Middle East, called tahini, and sesame paste from Asia. The Asian variety is made from toasted sesame seeds and is a dark golden color similar to that of peanut butter. It has a fragrant toasted-nut aroma and flavor. The Middle Eastern tahini is relatively bland. It is important not to substitute one for the other. In this book Middle Eastern sesame paste is referred to as tahini and Asian sesame paste as sesame paste. Both versions keep indefinitely stored in the refrigerator in tightly covered containers. Be sure to mix the paste and oil together before using.

Shrimp

Certainly one of the most universally appealing hors d'oeuvre is shrimp. They come in all sizes, from as large as a few to a pound to literally hundreds per pound. The more shrimp to a pound, the less expensive. Unfortunately, few cooks have access to all sizes of shrimp. (If you live near an Asian community, you may find a better selection there.) And, unless you live in a Gulf coastal community, the shrimp you buy will have been frozen. If the heads have been cut off, you can be sure the shrimp were frozen and then thawed. Frozen shrimp are sold in boxes of 4 or 5 pounds, depending on the country of origin. Generally speaking, the quality is about the same. The one difference I have found is that the tiger shrimp from Burma (Manyan) have a sturdier shell, which means less meat for weight.

For the recipes in this book, use 21 to 25's (large) or 26 to 30's (medium) when whole shrimp are needed. Larger sizes are too big to be eaten politely in two bites and not worth the extra expense. Smaller shrimp are a bit stingy. However, when the shrimp are to be chopped or ground, using the much less expensive, tinier shrimp (60 or more to a pound) makes sense—provided you can get them peeled. If you had to peel very tiny shrimp, the labor cost would be greater than any savings on the shrimp.

Soy Sauce

Soy sauces vary enormously in flavor from one manufacturer to another. The recipes call for Chinese light, or thin, soy sauce unless specified otherwise. Some recipes use dark or thick soy. Japanese soy sauce has a very different flavor from Chinese. Tamari is an aged Japanese soy sauce. Neither is recommended unless specified. Domestic soy sauce has a completely different flavor and is not suitable. So-called lite soy or low-sodium soy is not recommended. If salt is a problem, it is better to select another recipe. Soy sauces of different types are found in all supermarkets. Do take the trouble to get the right soy for the dish. Soy sauce keeps indefinitely in the pantry.

Szechuan Peppercorns
Also called anise pepper, these reddish-brown berries have a more pungent flavor than black pepper. Often they are toasted in a dry skillet until fragrant before being ground into a powder. Use a mortar and pestle or a spice grinder to grind them. The whole peppercorns are available in many gourmet shops as well as Asian groceries. They will keep in a tightly sealed container for 6 months or longer.

Tahini
This bland sesame paste is made from untoasted sesame seeds. It is used commonly in Middle Eastern cookery, but is very different from the paste used in Asian cuisine (see Sesame Paste). To make your own, follow the recipe on page 103. Stir well before using and store in the refrigerator after opening. Keeps indefinitely.

Tapioca Flour
Also called tapioca starch, this flour is made from cassava like regular tapioca. It is used in some dim sum. It is sold in small bags in Asian markets and will keep indefinitely. There is no substitute for tapioca flour. However, it is usually made into a dim sum wrapper, and you can substitute wonton wrappers for the tapioca flour wrappers.

Tarama
The Greek answer to caviar. Carp roe is processed and packed in small jars. Tarama is found in Middle Eastern markets and in supermarkets in areas with a large Middle Eastern population. The jars are usually 4 or 8 ounces and are not expensive. Store in the refrigerator for up to 2 weeks before opening. After opening, pour a little olive oil over the top and keep tightly covered in the refrigerator for up to a week.

Vegetable Oil
Vegetable oils are made from a variety of products, including cottonseeds, rape seeds, soybeans, peanuts, and corn. Select any oil that has a light, almost nonexistent flavor. I find it most convenient and economical to buy the oil by the gallon and transfer it to smaller containers for everyday use. This provides a steady supply and the cost savings is considerable. The oil will last at least 6 months in a cool, dry place.

Vinegar
There are literally dozens of different vinegars on the market. You may often change a recipe, or enhance it by selecting a flavored vinegar, but make sure that it is suitable for the recipe.

Red Wine Vinegar Also called red vinegar. You may use any red wine vinegar. Balsamic or sherry vinegar can also be substituted in most instances.

Rice Vinegar Used in Asian recipes for sushi rice and many dipping sauces. It is available in Asian markets and many supermarkets. You can substitute distilled white vinegar.

White Vinegar Refers to distilled white vinegar.

White Wine Vinegar Many white wine vinegars are flavored with herbs, but for most recipes they should be unflavored, unless specified.

Wheat Starch
A wheat flour with the gluten removed, wheat starch is used in dim sum pastry. There is no substitute; if it is not available, use a different wrapper for the dim sum. Available in Asian markets. Keeps indefinitely.

Wine
Some years ago, Craig Claiborne stated the two rules for cooking with wine. They are as valid today as when he wrote them. First: If the recipe does not say sweet, use dry. Dry white, dry red, dry sherry, and you have covered most of your cooking bases. The second rule: If you will not drink it, do not use it. In other words, if it is not good enough to drink, it is not suitable in cooking, especially in any recipe where it might be reduced and the flavor strengthened.

≡ Index ≡

755